D0347780

Guide to Rural

SCOTLAND

By David Gerrard

© Travel Publishing Ltd

Published by:
Travel Publishing Ltd
Airport Business Centre, 10 Thornbury Road,
Estover, Plymouth PL6 7PP

ISBN13   9781904434689
© Travel Publishing Ltd
Country Living is a registered trademark of The National
Magazine Company Limited.

First Published: 2003
Second Edition: 2005
Third Edition: 2009

COUNTRY LIVING GUIDES:

East Anglia	Scotland
Heart of England	The South of England
Ireland	The South East of England
The North East of England	The West Country
The North West of England	Wales

PLEASE NOTE:

All advertisements in this publication have been accepted in good faith by Travel Publishing and they have not necessarily been endorsed by *Country Living* Magazine.

All information is included by the publishers in good faith and is believed to be correct at the time of going to press. No responsibility can be accepted for errors.

Editor:	David Gerrard
Printing by:	Latimer Trend, Plymouth
Location Maps:	© Maps in Minutes ™ (2009) © Collins Bartholomews 2009 All rights reserved.
Walks:	Walks have been reproduced with kind permission of the internet walking site: www.walkingworld.com
Walk Maps:	Reproduced from Ordnance Survey mapping on behalf of the Controller of Her Majesty's Stationery Office, © Crown Copyright. Licence Number MC 100035812
Cover Design:	Lines & Words, Aldermaston
Cover Photo:	Dunvegan Castle, Isle of Skye © www.alamy.com
Text Photos:	Text photos have been kindly supplied by the Pictures of Britain photo library © www.picturesofbritain.co.uk and © Bob Brooks, Weston-super-Mare

Foreword

Scotland has some of Britain's most spectacular scenery. In the Highlands, there are mountains, steep-sided glens and deep lochs while further south the scenery is gentler with flowing rivers and rolling farmland. It is also a country steeped in history and culture - with castles, cathedrals and universities throughout. So whether you want to spend time walking in the wilderness or exploring some of the most romantic ruins in the country, Scotland will not disappoint.

Each month *Country Living Magazine* celebrates the richness and diversity of our countryside with features on rural Britain and Ireland and the traditions that have their roots there. So it is with great pleasure that I introduce you to the latest in our series of *Rural Guides*.

This book will help you explore Scotland and all that it has to offer with its directory of places to stay, eat and drink, its fascinating insights into local history and heritage, and its comprehensive range of Scottish producers of food, arts and crafts. So if you're heading north across the border for the first time or are already a frequent visitor to Scotland then I hope this book will inform and entertain you. Above all, I hope that it will help you enjoy your trip and all that Scotland has to offer.

Susy Smith

Susy Smith
Editor, Country Living magazine

PS To subscribe to *Country Living Magazine* each month, call 01858 438844

Introduction

This is the third edition of *The Country Living Guide to Rural Scotland* and we are sure that it will be as popular as its predecessors. David Gerrard, a very experienced travel writer has completely updated the contents of the guide and ensured that it is packed with vivid descriptions, historical stories, amusing anecdotes and interesting facts on hundreds of places in this wild and often wonderful country. In the introduction to each village or town we have also summarized and categorized the main attractions to be found there, which makes it easy for readers to plan their visit.

The advertising panels within each chapter provide further information on places to see, stay, eat, drink and shop. We have also selected a number of walks from walkingworld.com (full details of this website may be found to the rear of the guide) which we highly recommend if you wish to appreciate fully the beauty and charm of the varied rural landscapes and coastline of Scotland.

The guide however is not simply an 'armchair tour'. Its prime aim is to encourage the reader to visit the places described and discover much more about the wonderful towns, villages and countryside of Scotland in person. In this respect we would like to thank all the Tourist Information Centres who helped us to provide you with up-to-date information. Whether you decide to explore this country by wheeled transport or on foot we are sure you will find it a very uplifting experience!

We are always interested in receiving comments on places covered (or not covered) in our guides so please do not hesitate to use the reader reaction forms provided at the rear of this guide to give us your considered comments. This will help us refine and improve the content of the next edition. We also welcome any general comments which will help improve the overall presentation of the guides themselves.

For more information on the full range of travel guides published by Travel Publishing please refer to the order form at the rear of this guide or log on to our website (see below).

Travel Publishing

Did you know that you can also search our website for details of thousands of places to see, stay, eat or drink throughout Britain and Ireland? Our site has become increasingly popular and now receives monthly over 160,000 visits. Try it!

website: www.travelpublishing.co.uk

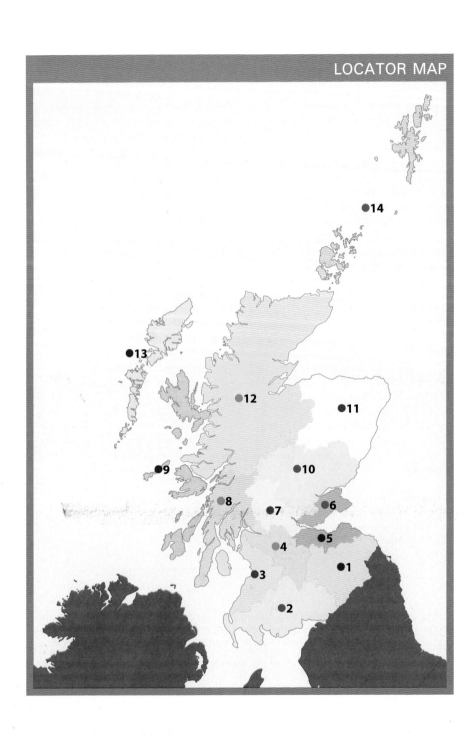

Contents

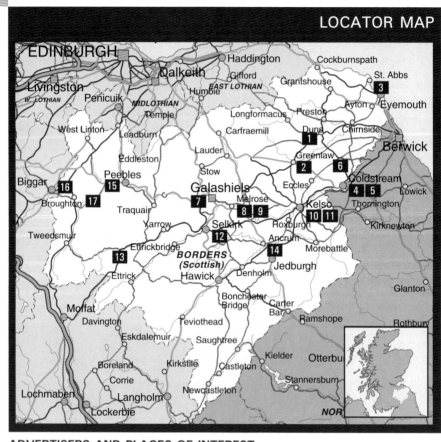

ADVERTISERS AND PLACES OF INTEREST

🏠 historic building   🏛 museum and heritage   🏚 historic site   🏞 scenic attraction   🌿 flora and fauna

1 | The Borders

Of all the regions in Scotland, the Borders has the bloodiest history. It was here, in the 15th and 16th centuries, that the constant bickering between Scotland and England boiled over into bloodshed and outright war. This was the land of the reivers, or moss troopers - men from both countries who regularly crossed the border and raped, pillaged, burnt and rustled their way into the history books. People nowadays tend to romanticise them, but in fact most were merciless thugs, and no one was safe from their activities. They even gave the word blackmail to the English language. An old legend states that when a male born in the Borders was baptised, his right hand was excluded from the ceremony so that he could use it to kill and maim.

But it was also the land of romance, of Border ballads and tales of high chivalry. The literature of Sir Walter Scott, a Borders man, is steeped in them. It was he who, almost single-handedly, invented Scotland's modern image, which depends not on the softer scenery of the Borders, but on lofty

mountains, clan chiefs, skirling bagpipes and kilts. In fact, there are, strictly speaking, no clans in the Scottish Borders. Instead there are families, such as the Armstrongs, the Kerrs, the Maxwells and the Homes.

The Borders are sometimes dismissed by people who consider them to be 'not the real Scotland'. And yet they have more historical associations than anywhere else in Scotland. It was here, and not the Highlands, that the Scottish nation as we know it today was forged. The area stretches from the North Sea in the east, to the borders of Dumfriesshire in the west, and contains four former counties – Peeblesshire, Selkirkshire, Roxburghshire and Berwickshire. The scenery is gentler than the Highlands, and the hills are rounded and green, with fertile valleys, quiet villages and cosy market towns to explore. That flat area of Berwickshire known as the Merse, roughly between the Lammermuir Hills and the English border, is one of the most intensely farmed areas in Britain.

There are castles and old houses aplenty, from Floors Castle just outside Kelso, home of the Duke of Roxburgh, to 10th-century Traquair House in Peeblesshire, said to be the oldest continually inhabited house in Scotland. Mellerstain too, is worth visiting, as are Paxton, Manderston, Thirlestane and Abbotsford.

But perhaps the area's most beautiful and haunting buildings are its ruined abbeys. Again and again English soldiers attacked

St Abbs Head

them, and again and again, as the Scots crossed the border bent on revenge, the monks repeatedly got on with rebuilding and repairing them. Today, the ruins at Melrose, Kelso, Dryburgh and Jedburgh are carefully tended by Historic Scotland.

The area's great icon is the River Tweed, which, for part of its length, forms the boundary between Scotland and England. Just east of Kelso, the border turns south, and the river is wholly Scottish. Its fame rests on salmon, though not as many are caught nowadays as there used to be. But it is still a river that in some ways defines the region, and most of its larger towns and villages, from Peebles to Coldstream, are to be found on its banks.

River Tweed, nr Innerleithen

The Borders is also an area of woodland and forests, with plenty of woodland walks. The recently created Tweed Valley Forest Park, between Peebles and Selkirk, is one of the best. At Glentress Forest, a few miles east of Peebles, you can hire mountain bikes at the Hub car park. This is one of the most visited woodland areas in Scotland, and attracts more than 250,000 visitors a year. But they are also working forests, managed by the Forestry Commission, and form an integral part of the area's economy.

Duns

- Duns Law
- Covenanter's Stone
- Duns Castle
- John Duns Scotus
- Duns Castle Nature Reserve
- Jim Clark Memorial Trophy Room
- Manderston House
- Seigneur de la Beauté

Berwickshire is an unusual county, in that the town from which it takes its name has been part of England since 1482. Therefore Greenlaw, and then, in 1853, Duns, was chosen as the county town. It is a quiet, restful place with a wide and gracious market square. Up until the 18th century, it was known as Dunse. Its motto, Duns Dings A, means Duns overcomes everything.

On its outskirts is the 713-feet-high **Duns Law** from whose summit there are magnificent views of the surrounding countryside. The Cheviot Hills to the south and the Lammermuir Hills to the north can be seen on a clear day, as can the North Sea, 12 miles away. In 1639, a Covenanting army of 12,000 men, which opposed the imposition of bishops on the Scottish church by Charles I, set up camp here under General Leslie, and a **Covenanter's Stone** commemorates this event. There are also the remains of an Iron Age fort, plus some defensive works built by the Covenanting army.

General Leslie was quartered in **Duns Castle**, built round the core of a 14th-century pele tower owned by the Earl of Moray, who had been given the surrounding lands by Robert the Bruce. In 1696, it was bought by the Hay family, who enlarged it between 1818 and 1822, creating the Gothic Revival building we see today. The family has lived here ever since. Though not open to the public, it is a venue for weddings and corporate hospitality.

NUMBER 18

18 Market Square, Duns, Borders TD11 3BY
Tel: 01361 884800
e-mail: shirlio37@yahoo.co.uk

Shirley Redpath opened her gift and coffee shop number 18 in 2006 and it has speedily established itself as a meeting point and as a place to find that inspired gift for a friend or indeed something for yourself.

In fact so popular has it become that she has now moved the coffee side just across the street to a bigger premises at 17 Market Square where she and her business partner Moira can now serve you delightful meals and sharing platters accompanied by a glass or perhaps two of wine.

Number 18 has a large range of stylish jewellery, beautful scarves and fashion accessories. From candles and bags to cufflinks and ties - pop in for a browse and you are sure to find the perfect gift or treat.

MANSEFIELD BED AND BREAKFAST

Mansefield, Greenlaw, Duns, Berwickshire TD10 6YF
Tel/Fax: 01361 810260
e-mail: timc@tesco.net
website: www.aboutscotland.com/duns/mansefield.html

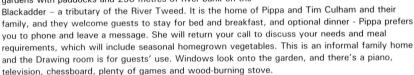

Mansefield is a superb Scottish Georgian Manse set in its own gardens with paddocks and 250 metres of river-bank on the Blackadder – a tributary of the River Tweed. It is the home of Pippa and Tim Culham and their family, and they welcome guests to stay for bed and breakfast, and optional dinner - Pippa prefers you to phone and leave a message. She will return your call to discuss your needs and meal requirements, which will include seasonal homegrown vegetables. This is an informal family home and the Drawing room is for guests' use. Windows look onto the garden, and there's a piano, television, chessboard, plenty of games and wood-burning stove.

On the western edge of Duns Law is a cairn, which marks the original site of the town, now called The Bruntons, or burnt towns. It was here that **John Duns Scotus**, known as Doctor Subtilis, or the subtle doctor, was supposed to have been born in about 1266 (though some people put his place of birth as Duns in Ireland). He was a Franciscan monk who became one of the greatest theologians and philosophers of his time. His followers were known as Scotists, and his influence is still felt within the Catholic Church to this day. However, his opponents had another, less flattering, name for them - Dunses - from which we get the word dunce. He died at Cologne on November 8th 1308, and on his tomb are the words 'Scotland bore me, England adopted me, Cologne holds'. In 1991 Pope John Paul II pronounced him Blessed, the first step on the ladder to sainthood (see also North Uist). In Duns Public Park there is a bronze statue of him, and in the grounds of Duns Castle the modern Franciscan Order erected a cairn to his memory in 1966.

Also in the grounds of Duns Castle is the quaintly named Hen Poo, a lake that is the centrepiece of the **Duns Castle Nature Reserve**, owned and run by the Scottish Wildlife Trust. There is a bird hide on the northern shore, and from here you can see mallard ducks, tufted ducks, swans., and coots. Close by, the Mill Dam is also home to many bird species.

In the town itself, there is a memorial to a famous man who lived in more recent times. Jim Clark, the racing driver, was born in Fife in 1936, but from the age of six lived on Eddington Mains, a farm near Duns. He won 25 of his 72 Grand Prix, and his win at the 1965 Indianapolis Grand Prix astonished the Americans, who considered that no one but an American could cross the finishing line first. He was world champion in 1963 and 1965. Jim Clark was killed at Hockenheim in Germany in 1968, aged 32, when a rear tyre burst during a Formula 2 race. He is buried in Chirnside Parish Church cemetery, about five miles east of Duns. In Duns itself, the **Jim Clark Memorial Trophy Room** in Newtown Street is dedicated to his memory, and attracts motor racing enthusiasts from all over the world who make the pilgrimage to view the trophies (including the two world championship trophies he won) and other mementoes on display.

On the west side of Market Square is the 19th-century Tolbooth House, situated on the site of the town house of Sir James Cockburn, who owned most of the land surrounding Duns in the 17th century. The local council have recently laid out a town trail, guiding visitors to places of interest. A leaflet is available, linked to plaques at many places within the town.

Manderston House lies a mile and a half east of the town in 56 acres of formal gardens and is open to the public. It was built between 1903 and 1905, and was the last great stately home built in Britain. Designed by architect John Kinross, it incorporates a silver staircase that is said to be the only one in the world, and was built for Sir James Miller and his wife, the Hon.. Eveline Curzon, a member of one of the oldest families in the country. Nowadays, Manderston is the home of the Palmer family, of the famous Huntly and Palmer biscuit empire, which explains why it houses a large collection of biscuit tins.

East of Duns, at Broomhouse, is the grave of the **Seigneur de la Beauté**, a handsome Frenchman who was warden of the Merse and Teviotdale. He was murdered in the 16th century by the powerful David Home of Wedderburn who considered that James V should have made him warden instead. The seigneur's head was hacked from his body and the rest of him was buried where he fell. The head was subsequently paraded round Duns by David Home.

Around Duns

COCKBURNSPATH
13 miles N of Duns just off the A1

🏰 Cockburnspath Tower   🏰 Mercat Cross

🌿 Pease Dean

Ruined **Cockburnspath Tower**, dating from the 15th and 16th centuries, has been owned in succession by the Dunbars, the Homes, the Sinclairs and the Douglases. The **Mercat Cross**, at the heart of the village, was erected in 1503 to celebrate the marriage of James IV to Margaret Tudor, the daughter of Henry VII of England. The village sits close to **Pease Dean**, a Scottish Wildlife Trust Reserve, where you can see butterflies, lichens and rare mosses. Pease Bridge was built in 1783 and at the time was the highest stone bridge in Europe.

ABBEY ST BATHANS
7 miles N of Duns on a minor road off the B6355

🚶 Southern Upland Way   🏛 Edins Hall Broch

The pretty village of Abbey St Bathans lies in the steep-sided valley of the Whiteadder Water, deep within the Lammermuir Hills, five miles north of Duns. It is truly a hidden gem, and sits on the **Southern Upland Way**, the coast-to-coast footpath that transverses Southern Scotland from Portpatrick in the west to Cockburnspath in the east. Its name is misleading, as there was never an abbey here. However, in 1170, Ada, Countess of Dunbar, founded the priory of St Mary in the village, and parts of the priory church have been incorporated into the present Parish Church. The village was chosen because, in about 500AD, St Bathan, a follower of St Columba, established a Celtic monastery here.

The tombstone of a former prioress, which touchingly shows her pet dog, is preserved within the present church. To the south, at Cockburn Law, are the ruins of the Iron Age **Edins Hall Broch**, one of the few brochs (a round, fortified stone tower) to be found in southern Scotland. It is named after Etin, a legendary giant with three heads who is said to have terrorised the area in olden times.

COLDINGHAM

13 miles NE of Duns on the A1107

🏛 Coldingham Priory 🏛 Fast Castle

The village of Coldingham, a mile from the coast, is visited mainly for the remains of **Coldingham Priory**. It was founded in 1098 by King Edgar, son of Malcolm Canmore, and he gifted it to the monks of Durham. It was blown up by Cromwell in 1648, with repairs being carried out in about 1670, though only the tower and a couple of walls were left standing. Between 1854 and 1855, the remains were restored, and today they are incorporated into the village's parish church.

Four miles northwest of the village, on the coast, are the ruins of **Fast Castle**, a former Hume stronghold. In 1410, it was held by the English, but was recovered again in 1548. The ruins are perched 70 feet above the sea on a cliff top and can be reached via a minor road, though the last few hundred yards must be done on foot. Great care needs to be taken when visiting the ruins.

ST ABB'S

12 miles NE of Duns, on the B6438

📷 St Abb's Head

The attractive fishing and holiday village of St Abb's is named after St Ebba and has a small, picturesque harbour. The village also serves as a centre for underwater diving because of the exceptionally clear waters.

The whole coastline here is rugged and spectacular, one of the most magnificent parts being **St Abb's Head** (National Trust for Scotland - see panel below), a nature reserve located to the north of the village with a large colony of seabirds. The cliffs are more than 300 feet high, and are riddled with caves once frequented by smugglers. A monastery for monks and nuns was established on the cliff tops in the 7th century, and this is where St Ebba became a nun. An old legend recounts that, once St Ebba had become too old and infirm to have control over the nuns, they spent all their time eating, drinking and gossiping, instead of living a life of austerity

St Abbs Head National Nature Reserve

Ranger's Cottage, Northfield, St Abbs, Eyemouth, Borders TD14 5QF
Tel: 018907 71443   Fax: 018907 71606
website: www.nts.org.uk

Formed by an extinct volcano, **The Head** is the best known landmark along the magnificent Berwickshire coast. Home to thousands of nesting seabirds in summer, the Head also has a wealth of other wildlife and fine views along the coast. In recognition of its importance to both wildlife and people, the Head was declared a National Nature Reserve in 1983. The offshore waters lie within a Special Area of Conservation and form part of Scotland's only Voluntary Marine Nature Reserve. New remote camera link to Nature Reserve Centre allows visitors to observe seabirds during nesting season (recorded footage out of season). Exhibition, toilets.

🏛 historic building 📷 museum and heritage 🏛 historic site 📷 scenic attraction 🌱 flora and fauna

and prayer. The whole area is now managed by the National Trust for Scotland and is a National Nature Reserve. Offshore, there is one of the best diving sites in the country.

CHIRNSIDE
5 miles E of Duns on the B6355

🏛 Parish Church   🦢 Jim Clark   🦢 David Hume

Chirnside sits on the south side of a low hill with wonderful views over the surrounding countryside, and close to where the Blackadder Water and the Whiteadder Water meet. During World War I, the peace of the village was shattered when a Zeppelin bombed it by accident. The **Parish Church** was founded by King Edgar of Scotland in the 12th century, and is partly Norman, with an impressive Norman doorway at its west end. The substantial church tower was built in memory of Lady Tweedsmuir. Within the cemetery is the grave of Jim Clark the racing driver (see also Duns). The **Jim Clark Memorial Clock**, with a silhouette of a Lotus racing car on it, stands in the middle of the village.

David Hume, the 18th-century philosopher and historian, though born in Edinburgh, was educated at Chirnside School until he was 12 years old.

EDROM
3 miles E of Duns on a minor road off the A6105

🏛 Parish Church

The small village of Edrom has a fine **Parish Church** originally dedicated to St Mary. It was built in 1732 on the site of a much earlier Norman church, and the present south aisle rests on foundations from that period. Attached to it is the Blackadder Aisle, built for Archbishop Blackadder of Glasgow in 1499. It contains a tomb and effigy dating from 1553. A burial vault in the graveyard incorporates a Norman arch, which was originally attached to the original Norman church.

HUTTON
10 miles E of Duns on a minor road off the B6460

🏛 Hutton Castle   🏛 Parish Church

Close to the village, overlooking the River Whiteadder, stands **Hutton Castle**, one time home of Sir William Burrell, shipping magnate and art collector, who donated the Burrell Collection to the city of Glasgow in 1944. Three of the rooms at the Castle are reproduced in the Collection.

Hutton Parish Church dates from 1835, and has an old bell dated 1661.

AYTON
10 miles E of Duns on the B6355

🏛 Ayton Castle

Ayton, a mile or so from the A1, is a pleasant village set beside the River Eye. Close by is **Ayton Castle**, which was bought in 1834 by William Mitchell Innes, the governor of the Bank of Scotland. He commissioned James Gillespie Graham, a leading Gothic Revival architect, to design the present day castle, which was built between 1841 and 1846. It is reckoned to be one of the best examples in the country of the style of architecture called Scottish Baronial, and is surrounded by a 6000-acre estate. It is open from May to September by appointment, and houses fine paintings, furniture and porcelain.

EYEMOUTH
12 miles E of Duns on the A1107

📷 World of Boats   🦢 Herring Queen Festival
📷 Eyemouth Museum

Scotland's second largest inshore fishing port,

picturesque Eyemouth, is nevertheless quite a small place. It stands at the mouth of the River Eye, five miles north of the Scotland/England border. The monks of Coldingham Priory founded it as a small fishing port sometime in the 13th century.

At one time Eyemouth was a smuggling centre, and some of the harbourside houses still have old cellars and tunnels where contraband was stored. The centre of the trade was at Gunsgreen House, to the south of the harbour. It dates from 1755 and was designed by James and John Adam.

The **World of Boats** is a collection of more than 400 historic boats from all over the world, from Alaska to Vietnam; the owner will show you around by appointment. Every year in July, the **Herring Queen Festival** takes place, when the gaily bedecked fishing fleet escorts the Herring Queen into Eyemouth Harbour.

Eyemouth Museum, housed in the Auld Kirk built in 1812, records the history of the town and its fishing industry. Perhaps the most poignant exhibit is a 15 feet long by four feet wide tapestry sewn in 1981 that commemorates Black Friday - October 14 1881. On that day, a great storm wrecked the whole of the town's fishing fleet, and 189 fishermen, 129 from Eyemouth alone, perished in sight of the shore.

FOULDEN

9 miles E of Duns on the A6105

🏛 Foulden Parish Church 🏛 Tithe Barn

Foulden Parish Church, at the far end of the village, dates from 1786, and was built on the foundations of a medieval church. In 1587, commissioners appointed by Elizabeth I of England and James VI of Scotland met at Foulden to discuss the execution of James VI's mother, Mary Queen of Scots. Nearby is an old

two-storey **Tithe Barn** (Historic Scotland), dating from medieval times, though it was restored in the 18th and 19th centuries. Tithe means a tenth, and each farmer in the parish was supposed to donate a tenth of his crops to the church, which were stored in the barn. The barn can only be viewed from the outside.

PAXTON

12 miles E of Duns just off the B6460 and close to the Tweed

🏛 Paxton House 🏛 Union Suspension Bridge

Near the village stands the impressive **Paxton House**, built in 1758 by Patrick Home, later the 13th Laird of Wedderburn. When he was 19, he went to Leipzig in Germany, and from there to Berlin where he was admitted to the court of Frederick the Great of Prussia. Here, he fell in love with Sophie de Brandt, the illegitimate daughter of Frederick and Lady-in-Waiting to Elizabeth Christina, Frederick's wife.

He returned home, and in anticipation of his marriage to Sophie, built Paxton House. Alas, the marriage never took place, though a pair of kid gloves given to Patrick by Sophie are on display.

The house was designed by John and James Adam, with plasterwork by their brother Robert, and it is reckoned to be the best Palladian mansion in Britain. It houses the finest collection of Chippendale furniture in Scotland, and the art gallery (added to the house in 1811) is the largest private gallery in the country. It now houses paintings from the National Galleries of Scotland.

The house stands in 80 acres of grounds designed by Robert Robinson in the 18th century, and has nature trails, woodland walks and a Paxton Ted teddy bear trail. From the award-winning red squirrel hide you can catch glimpses of what is rapidly becoming one of

Scotland's rarest mammals. There is also a tearoom and a shop, and in the Victorian boathouse on the banks of the Tweed is a museum dedicated to salmon net fishing. Well behaved dogs are welcome if kept on a lead.

Close by is the **Union Suspension Bridge** across the Tweed, connecting Scotland and England. It was built in 1820 by Sir Samuel Browne, who also invented the wrought-iron chain links used in its construction. It is 480 feet long and was Britain's first major suspension bridge to carry vehicular traffic as well as pedestrians.

LADYKIRK
7 miles SE of Duns on a minor road off the B6470 and close to the Tweed

🏛 St Mary's Church

The **Parish Church of St Mary** dates from 1500, with a tower added in 1743. It was built entirely of stone to prevent it being burnt down by the English. It is supposed to owe its origins to James IV who had it built in thanksgiving for his rescue from drowning while trying to cross the Tweed. At the same time he changed the name of the village from Upsettington to Ladykirk.

COLDSTREAM
12 miles S of Duns on the A697

🏛 Coldstream Bridge   🏛 Old Toll House

🏛 Coldstream Museum   🌿 The Hirsel

🏛 Castlelaw

The town sits on the north bank of the Tweed at a point where the river forms the border between Scotland and England. **Coldstream Bridge**, joining the two countries, was built in 1766 to a design by John Smeaton, and replaced a ford that had been a natural crossing point for centuries. On the bridge is a

---

DEAKINS TEAROOM

68a High Street, Coldstream, Berwickshire TD12 4DH
Tel: 01890 883881
e-mail: deakins.tearoom@tiscali.co.uk
website: www.deakinsofcoldstream.co.uk

Established in 2006, **Deakins Tearoom** is a traditional tea room with a modern twist. It is owned and run by Gary and Angela Deakin whose declared aim is to provide good quality, home-cooked food at a reasonable price. They pride themselves on the fact that almost everything they serve is home-made on the premises - everything from sandwich fillings, the coleslaw, cakes, tray bakes and daily specials. Their meat, bread, milk, eggs and vegetables are all supplied by local businesses.

The day starts with a good selection of breakfasts which are served until 11.30am. Lunchtime choices include a scrumptious bacon & Brie bonanza served on ciabatta, hot smoked salmon or chilli beef. Children have their own menu.

In the evening, the tearoom can be transformed into the perfect setting for a pre-wedding get together with your family and friends. The Deakins can offer menus to cater for every taste, from traditional Scottish Fayre to your favourite home cooked meal.

They also stock a range of retail goods including Tiptree jams, Border biscuits, Tracklements and Oleifera.

📖 stories and anecdotes   🦢 famous people   🎨 art and craft   ✏ entertainment and sport   🚶 walks

CALICO HOUSE

44 High Street, Coldstream, Berwickshire TD12 4AS
Bed & Breakfast Tel: 01890 885870 Fax: 01890 883025
Interior Design Tel: 0845 8733100
e-mail: contact@calicohouse.net
website: www.bedandbreakfast-luxury.co.uk
or www.calicohouse.net

Ideally situated close to Kelso and Berwick upon Tweed and within easy travelling distance of Edinburgh, **Calico House** provides the finest accommodation either on a B&B or self-catering basis.

The rooms at Calico House provide the highest standard in bed and breakfast accommodation. The rooms are en-suite and tea and coffee facilities are provided. The bedrooms are quiet and regular up-grades provide a fresh and pleasing feel to each room. Calico House is also a successful Interior Design business and the rooms reflect the nature of this business. Great care is taken to ensure that your stay is an enjoyable experience. Breakfast is provided in the Calico House Coffee shop or, weather permitting, in the outside courtyard garden.

The Blue Room - The outlook from the rear windows in the Blue Room is exceptional, looking out over the top of the slated roofs of Coldstream towards Cheviot, the highest point in the wonderful Cheviot Hills. The accommodation comprises twin beds, en-suite with walk-in shower, television and tea/coffee facilities.

The Green Room - The Green Room offers double bed accommodation with en-suite facilities. The view from the window is over the garden courtyard and, like the Blue Room being at the rear of the building it is quiet. The accommodation comprises double bed, en-suite with walk-in shower, television and tea/coffee facilities.

The Calico House Suite - When you require the very best in bed and breakfast accommodation the Calico House Suite offers the finest. The suite is ideal for couples looking for that extra luxurious place to stay. The Calico House Suite offers a large bedroom area with lounge space and a very spacious en-suite bathroom with bath and separate walk-in shower. The bed is extra large and the room is furnished to an extremely high standard in the French style. In addition the Calico House Suite has an exclusive breakfasting room.

The Calico House Apartment - Ideal for families or small groups looking for the independence of self-catering facilities in quiet and comfortable surroundings. The Apartment offers 4 spacious bedrooms, 2 bathrooms, livingroom, diningroom, fully fitted kitchen and plenty of storage space. This is the ideal venue from which to base a Borders holiday break, whether it be walking, sight seeing, cycling, golfing, fishing or just taking it easy, the Calico House Apartment will provide you with a true home from home.

The Calico House Coffee Shop is open 10.00 – 5.00 Monday to Saturday and all guests can enjoy tea, real coffee, cake or lunch throughout the day.

The motto of the town of Coldstream is "Nulli Secundus" latin for "second to none" - we want your experience at Calico House to reflect this.

Old Toll House, Coldstream

plaque that commemorates the fact that Robert Burns entered England by this route in 1787. In the 19th century, Coldstream rivalled Gretna Green as a place for runaway marriages. At the Scottish end of the bridge is the **Old Toll House**, where, in a 13 year period during the 19th century, 1466 marriages were conducted.

General Monk founded the **Coldstream Guards** in 1659, and in the following year led them on the long journey south to London where they were instrumental in effecting the Restoration of Charles II. The regiment is the only one in Britain to take its name from a town. Within Henderson Park is a memorial stone that commemorates the regiment's foundation, and the **Coldstream Museum** in Market Square houses extensive displays on its history. The museum also has a children's section and a courtyard with fountain and picnic area.

A mile north of the town is **The Hirsel**, home of the Earls of Home since 1611. The 14th Earl renounced his peerage to become the British Prime Minister, 1963-4, as Sir Alec Douglas Home. Though the house is not open to the public, the grounds can be explored. There is also a small museum, a crafts centre, a gem display and a tearoom.

Three miles north of the town, just off the A697, are the ruins of **Castlelaw**, built on a small hill. The former castle on the site was home to the Drienchester, or Darnchester family, but was pulled down in the 1500s to make way for the present building, which itself was partially dismantled in 1818. From the hill there are some good views of the surrounding countryside.

ECCLES
7 miles SW of Duns on the B6461

🏛 Eccles Parish Church

In the mid 1100s, a Cistercian nunnery was founded here by the Earl of Dunbar. Remnants of it have been built into the wall surrounding the graveyard of the present **Eccles Parish Church**, built in 1774. The

Hirsel Country Park, nr Coldstream

BUTTERLAW FARM STEADING

Boutique-Style Bed and Breakfast

nr Coldstream, Berwickshire TD12 4HQ
Tel/Fax: 01890 860699
e-mail: thesteading@butterlaw.co.uk
website: www.butterlaw.co.uk

Located near Coldstream, only 15 minutes from Kelso and the heart of the Scottish borders and 20 minutes west of Berwick and the Northumbrian coast, Butterlaw Farm Steading is a peaceful and tranquil rural setting to relax and explore the local area.

The steading, dating back over 150 years has recently been converted, the design of each room reflects owners Doreen and Michael Vee's passion for quality and attention to detail which enhances the very comfortable atmosphere.

Butterlaw is a unique luxury boutique Bed and Breakfast – with a "stylish and contemporary classic interior", designed and furnished by Michael, a leading interior designer.

There are three double / twin letting rooms each with en-suite facilities. All the bedrooms have been designed with comfort in mind along with a range of finishing touches to enrich your stay. Designer fabrics from Osborne & Little, Ralph Lauren, Zoffany, Nobilis Fontan, Mulberry and Hermes create the style, while contemporary furnishing, LCD TV's, DVD players, feature lighting and interesting design details create the ambience.

At the end of the day, relax in the Drawing Room with its log-fire, the perfect place to unwind and enjoy a complimentary night cap prior to retiring. The bookcase is filled with a comprehensive selection of books, maps, games and various novels, magazines and papers to read at your leisure. The terrace and patio is accessed from the Drawing Room where breakfast is enjoyed in the warmer summer months, or canapés and drinks in the evening.

Should your visit be for a three night break or only for one night, business or pleasure a very warm and friendly welcome is always extended...

nunnery was badly damaged during English raids in the 1540s.

FOGO

3 miles S of Duns off the B6460

🏛 Fogo Church

Fogo literally means the foggage pit, foggage being the grass, or moss, that grows in a field after the hay has been cut. **Fogo Church** dates from the 17th and 18th centuries, though parts of it - especially the lower courses of its masonry - date from the 13th century or earlier. The church bell dates from 1644, and within the vestry is one of the oldest gravestones in Berwickshire, dating from the 1300s. The church's communion cups are the oldest still in use, and date from 1662. On the outside wall of the church are stairs leading to private lofts, where the gentry once worshipped. The picturesque lych gate is now a war memorial, and in the kirkyard are the graves of 16 airmen from World War II.

GREENLAW

7 miles SW of Duns on the A697

🏛 Hume Castle

Greenlaw was the county town of Berwickshire from 1696 to 1853, when Duns replaced it. It formerly stood near the green law, or hill, a little to the southwest, and was given its burgh charter in 1596. The picturesque Market Cross dates from 1696, and the Parish Church also dates from the 17th century, with a later tower that was once used as a jail. There are many fine buildings within the town, including a town hall built in 1829. Three miles south are

the impressive ruins of **Hume Castle**, ancient seat of the Hume family. The original castle was built in the 13th century, dismantled in 1515 and rebuilt in 1519. Over the years it was captured by the English and retaken by the Scots many times over. Eventually, it was captured by Cromwell in 1651 and demolished. What you see now is a folly built in 1770 by the Earl of Marchmont. It stands 600 feet above sea level, and makes an excellent viewpoint.

LAUDER

17 miles W of Duns on the A68

🏛 Thirlstane Castle   ⚜ Duke of Lauderdale

🏛 Lauder Parish Church

The Royal and Ancient Burgh of Lauder is situated on the main A68 road running south from Edinburgh to the English Border, close to the Lammermuir Hills. The centre of the town is a prime example of the street layout of a medieval burgh with its Tolbooth (town hall) the focal point of the settlement.

To the east of the town is **Thirlestane Castle**, which is open to the public. It's a flamboyant place, with turrets, pinnacles and

Thirlestane Castle, Lauder

towers, giving it the appearance of a French château. It was originally built in the 13th century, but was extended and refurbished in the 16th century for the Maitland family. The most famous member of that family was John Maitland, second Earl and later first (and only) **Duke of Lauderdale**, who lived between 1616 and 1682. He was a close friend of Charles II and a member of the famous but unpopular Cabal Cabinet. The word cabal comes from the initials of the five men who comprised it, Maitland's being L for Lauderdale. So powerful was he that he was soon regarded as the uncrowned king of Scotland. His ghost is said to haunt the castle.

Lauder Parish Church was built in 1673 to the designs of Sir William Bruce, and is in the form of a Greek cross. The medieval church stood in the grounds of Thirlestane Castle, and legend states that the Duke had it removed in the 17th century to improve his view. He instructed a bowman to fire an arrow westwards from the castle steps. Wherever the arrow landed the Duke would build a new church. That is why the church now stands within the town of Lauder itself.

Galashiels

⚲ Lochcarron of Scotland Cashmere and Wool Centre	
🏛 Mercat Cross	🏛 Old Gala House
⚘ Bank Street Gardens	⚘ Braw Lads Gathering
🏛 Abbotsford	⚘ Sir Walter Scott

Galashiels (known locally as Gala) sits beside the Gala Water, and is a manufacturing town at one time noted for its tweed and woollen mills. As a reflection of this, the motto of the Galashiels Manufacturer's Corporation was "We dye to live and live to die".

The **Lochcarron of Scotland Cashmere**

and Wool Centre is located within the Waverley Mill in Huddersfield Street, and offers tours that explain the processes involved in the manufacture of woollens and tweeds.

On the coat of arms of the old burgh appears the words soor plooms (sour plums), which refers to an incident in 1337, when some English troops were killed after crossing the border and found stealing plums in the town. In 1503, the betrothal of James IV to Margaret Tudor, Henry VII's daughter, took place at the town's old **Mercat Cross**. Its successor dates from 1695.

Old Gala House dates from the 15th century with later additions, and at one time was the town house of the Pringles, Lairds of Gala. It is now a museum and art gallery. Its gardens have recently been re-established, with a pond, spring bulbs and rhododendrons. Exhibitions of local art are sometimes held in the house.

In Bank Street are the **Bank Street Gardens**, laid out shortly after World War II. In front of the town's war memorial (described by H V Morton as 'the most perfect town memorial in the British Isles') is a reminder of the area's bloody past - a bronze statue of a border reiver, armed and on horseback.

Every year in July, the **Braw Lads Gathering** celebrates the town's long history, with the main event being a spectacular mounted procession.

Two miles south of the town, on the banks of the Tweed, is **Abbotsford**, the home of **Sir Walter Scott**, writer and lawyer. Scott had it built between 1817 and 1822, and he lived in it until he died in 1832. Behind it is the River Tweed, as it was here that the monks of Melrose Abbey made a ford across the river, Scott decided to call his house Abbotsford. It

PIPERS CAFÉ COFFEE SHOP

Edinburgh Road, Galashiels, Selkirkshire TD1 2EY
Tel: 01896 757525 e-mail: pipercafe@btinternet.com

Pipers Café Coffee Shop takes its name from the owners being involved with the local pipeband. The cafe serves a choice of meals from toast to a large hearty breakfast; also lunches, toasties, panninis, baked potatoes, hot and cold filled rolls and sandwiches. A daily home-made soup is available every day and on Fridays there are homemade soup and pudding deals along with daily specials. All cakes and baking are made on the premises and are of a delicious high quality standard including daily baked scones. The cafe is located on the outskirts of Galashiels on the road to Edinburgh on the A7. There is plenty parking.

is built in the Scottish Baronial style and is crammed with mementoes and objects that reflect the great man's passion for Scottish history. There's a tumbler on which Burns had etched some verses, a lock of Charles Edward Stuart's hair, and a piece of oatcake found in the pocket of a Highlander killed at Culloden. There is more than a hint of Gothic about the interior, especially the panelled hallway, which contains a carriage clock - still keeping good time - once owned by Marie Antoinette.

The main focus of the house is Scott's austere study, where many of his books were written. A gallery runs round the room, and in one corner is a door with a stairway behind it. Early each morning, Scott descended these stairs from his dressing room to write for a few hours before heading for the courthouse in Selkirk.

Perhaps the most poignant room in the house is the dining room. Having returned from a trip abroad in September 1832, Scott knew that his end was near, and called for his bed to be set up at the window so that he could look out towards his beloved Tweed. He died on September 21. He had never got over the death of his wife Charlotte in 1826, and at about the same time a publishing firm in which he was a partner went bankrupt. He

decided to write his way out of debt, even though he still had his duties at Selkirk Sheriff Court to attend to. It eventually ruined his health, and he now lies beside his wife among the ruins of Dryburgh Abbey. His descendants still live at Abbotsford.

The Southern Upland Way passes through Galashiels, and you can also join the 89-mile-long Tweed Cycle Way, which passes close by. It starts at Biggar in Lanarkshire and ends up in Berwick-upon-Tweed.

Around Galashiels

CLOVENFORDS
3 miles W of Galashiels on the A72

🐟 School of Casting, Salmon and Trout Fishing

Clovenfords sits about a mile north of the Tweed, and is home to the **School of Casting, Salmon and Trout Fishing**. It offers weekly courses throughout the season.

In the 19th century, the village became famous for something you do not normally associate with Scotland - a vineyard. Grape growing was introduced into the village by William Thomson, who grew the fruit under glass at his Tweed Vineyards. Soon the grapes became famous throughout Britain and

🎬 stories and anecdotes   🐟 famous people   🎨 art and craft   ✏ entertainment and sport   🚶 walks

Western Europe, and no less a person than the Emperor of France presented him with a gold medal for their quality. He died in 1895.

STOW
5 miles N of Galashiels on the A7

| 🏛 St Mary of Wedale Parish Church |
| 🏛 Our Lady's Well 🏛 Pack Bridge |

Stow (sometimes called Stow-of-Wedale) is a delightful village on the Gala Water. The imposing **St Mary of Wedale Parish Church** has a spire more than140 feet high. To the west of the village are the lonely Moorfoot Hills, and to the east is some further moorland that separates it from Lauderdale. The B6362 leaves Stow and climbs up onto the moorland, reaching a height of 1100 feet before descending through Lauder Common into the small town of Lauder.

Just south of the village is **Our Lady's Well**, which was rebuilt in 2000 by a local man. The **Pack Bridge** across the Gala Water dates from 1655, and was the first bridge ever built across the river.

GORDON
11 miles NE of Galashiels on the A6089

| 🏛 Greenknowe Tower |

This pleasant village is the cradle of the Gordon clan, which moved north into Aberdeenshire in the 13th century when Robert the Bruce granted them the lands of Strathbogie, which had been forfeited by the Earl of Atholl.

To the north of the village are the well-preserved ruins of **Greenknowe Tower** (Historic Scotland), built in 1581 by James Seton of Touch and his wife Janet Edmonstone. It is a typical L-shaped tower house, built originally as a fortified home. The Pringles, one of the great Borders families, later acquired it.

MELLERSTAIN
10 miles E of Galashiels, on an unclassified road between the A6089 and the B6397

| 🏛 Mellerstain |

Mellerstain is a grand mansion originally designed by William Adam in the 1720s, and completed by his son Robert in 1778. It is one of the grandest Georgian houses in Britain, and holds a collection of fine furniture, as well as paintings by Van Dyck, Naismith, Gainsborough and Ramsey. The Italian terraces were laid out in 1910 by Sir Reginald Blomfield, and give excellent views out over a small artificial loch towards the Cheviots.

MELROSE
3 miles SE of Galashiels just off the A6091

| 🏛 Eildon Hills   🏛 King Arthur   🏛 Melrose Abbey |
| 🏛 Sir James Douglas   🏛 Old Melrose |
| 🏛 St Cuthbert   🏛 St Cuthbert's Way |
| 🏛 Priorwood Gardens   🏛 Harmony Garden |
| 🏛 100 Aker Wood Visitor Centre |
| 🏛 Trimontium Roman Fort |
| 🏛 Three Hills Roman Heritage Centre |

Melrose sits in the shadow of the triple peaks of the **Eildon Hills**, which have a waymarked path leading to their summits. Legend states that **King Arthur** and his knights lie buried beneath one of them, and indeed there is an old folk tale that tells of a man called Canonbie Dick who actually found the cave, thanks to a mysterious stranger, and saw the knights slumbering. A great wind rose up and blew Dick out of the cave, and no one has ever been able to find it since.

Another legend says that the entrance to the

Fairy Kingdom lies among the Eildon Hills, and that Thomas the Rhymer (see Earlston) used it to visit his lover, the Fairy Queen, for years at a time.

At the summit of Eildon Hill North are the remains of the largest hill fort in Scotland, which dates to the 10th century BC. When the Romans came, they built a watch tower within it.

Melrose, which is on the Southern Upland Way, is mainly visited nowadays to view the ruins of **Melrose Abbey** (Historic Scotland), surely the loveliest of all the Borders abbeys. It was founded in 1136 by David I for the Cistercian Order, and rose to become one of the most important in Scotland. The ruins that the visitor sees today date mainly from the late 14th and early 15th centuries, thanks to the English army of Richard II, which destroyed the earlier buildings. It was here that the heart of Robert the Bruce, Scotland's great hero during the Wars of Independence, was buried. On his death bed in 1329, the king had told **Sir James Douglas** (known as the Good Sir James to the Scots, and the Black Douglas to the English) to place his heart in a casket after his death and take it to the Holy Land. But in 1330, on his way to the Holy Land, Sir James was killed fighting the Moors at Teba in Spain. His friends didn't want him buried on foreign soil, so they boiled his body in vinegar so that his flesh would fall from his bones. The flesh

Harmony Garden

St Mary's Road, Melrose, Borders TD6 9LJ
website: www.nts.org.uk

A delightfully tranquil walled garden comprising lawns, herbaceous and mixed borders, vegetable and fruit areas, and a rich display of spring bulbs. The garden is set around an early 19th century house (not open to the public), built by Melrose joiner Robert Waugh, who named it 'Harmony' after the Jamaican pimento plantation where he had made his fortune, Harmony Garden has excellent views of Melrose Abbey and the Eildon Hills and is situated near Priorwood Garden (see below).

Priorwood Garden & Dried Flower Shop

Melrose, Borders, TD6 9PX
Tel : 01896 822493 Fax: 01896 823181
Shop: Tel: 01896 822965
e-mail priorwooddriedflowers@nts.org.uk website: www.nts.org.uk

A specialist garden where most of the plants grown are suitable for drying. The colourful and imaginative selection ensures variety for the dried flower arrangements made here. Visitors can enjoy a stroll through the orchard which includes historic varieties of apples that are organically grown. Enjoy the different blossoms in spring, a picnic here in the summer, and catch a glimpse of the impressive ruins of Melrose Abbey which overlook the garden. Priorwood Garden is a short walk from Harmony.

🎭 stories and anecdotes 🦜 famous people 🎨 art and craft ✏️ entertainment and sport 🥾 walks

was buried in Spain and his bones, along with the casket, were brought back to Scotland. In the late 1990s, during some restoration work on the abbey, the lead casket containing the heart was rediscovered and subsequently reburied within the abbey grounds. A plaque in the grounds now marks its resting place.

On a bend in the Tweed, two miles east of the town, is the site of **Old Melrose** (then called Mailros, meaning bare moor). Here, in about 650AD, Celtic monks from Iona established a monastery. Nearby, in about 635AD, a young shepherd was born. In 651AD, following a vision in which he saw the soul of St Aidan of Lindisfarne ascending to heaven, he entered the monastery to train as a monk. He eventually became Bishop of Lindisfarne, and died in 687AD. He is now known as **St Cuthbert** and is buried in Durham Cathedral. A 62 mile walking route called **St Cuthbert's Way** links Melrose and Lindisfarne.

Close to the abbey ruins is **Priorwood Gardens** (National Trust for Scotland - see panel on page 19). It specialises in plants that are suitable for drying and arranging, and classes are organised to teach the techniques involved. There is also a shop.

Harmony Garden (see panel on page 19), also run by the Trust, is close by. It is set around a 19th-century house, which is not open to the public, and has excellent views of the Eildon Hills. There are herbaceous borders, well tended lawns, and vegetable and fruit areas. It is renowned for its sense of peace and tranquillity. The house and small estate was built by Robert Waugh, a Melrose joiner, in the early 1800s after making his fortune from a Jamaica plantation called Harmony. The estate was sold to the Pitman family in 1820, and was bequeathed to the

NTS in 1996 by Mrs Christian Pitman.

The **100 Aker Wood Visitor Centre** is on the old Melrose to Newstead road, and has woodland walks, a children's play area, a coffee shop and car park.

A mile east of Melrose is Newstead, where there are the remains of **Trimontium Roman Fort**, covering 15 acres, and named after the three peaks of the Eildons. It was occupied between the late first century well into the second, and was the most important Roman settlement of the northern frontier. At its height, it housed 1500 Roman soldiers and supported a large town that covered a further 200 acres. The **Three Hills Roman Heritage Centre**, in the Ormiston Institute in Melrose's Market Square, has displays on what life was like within a Roman settlement, and has artefacts that were found there. On Thursday afternoons (and Tuesday afternoons in July and August) a guided five mile, four hour walk to the fort leaves from the Centre.

The Scottish Borders is a rugby playing area, and at Melrose that version of the game known as rugby sevens was invented.

EARLSTON
8 miles E of Galashiels on the A68

🔍 Black Hill	🐎 Thomas Learmont of Earlston
🏛 Rhymer's Tower	

The small town of Earlston is dominated by **Black Hill**, which gives a good view of the surrounding countryside. One of Scotland's earliest poets, **Thomas Learmont of Earlston,** was born here in about 1220. Also known as Thomas the Rhymer, Thomas of Erceldoune or True Thomas, he attained an almost supernatural status, as he was also a seer who could predict the future. Some ruins in the town are supposed to be of his home, **Rhymer's Tower**.

It didn't take much in those days for a man to gain a reputation for having mythical and prophetic powers, and no doubt Thomas's many trips abroad accounted for the stories of him going off to live with the Fairy Queen under the Eildon Hills for years at a time. His prophecies included Alexander III's death in 1285, the victory of Bruce over the English at Bannockburn in 1314, and Scotland's defeat by the English at Flodden in 1513.

SMAILHOLM

10 miles E of Galashiels on the B6397

- Smailholm Tower

Smailholm Tower (Historic Scotland) seems to grow out of a low, rocky outcrop, and is a four square, 60-feet-high tower, which was once surrounded by a wall. It was originally a Pringle stronghold, but was sold to the Scott family in 1645. Within it you can see a collection of costumed figures and tapestries connected with Scott's Minstrelsy of the Scottish Borders. Scott, as a child, spent a lot of time with his grandparents at the nearby farm of Sandyknowe and knew the tower well.

KELSO

16 miles E of Galashiels on the A698

- Market Square
- Town House
- Kelso Abbey
- War Memorial Garden
- Kelso Civic Week
- Royal Burgh of Roxburgh
- Roxburgh Castle
- Floors Castle
- Millennium Viewpoint
- Border Union Show
- Rennie's Bridge
- Kelso Race Course

Kelso is a gracious town with a large, cobbled **Market Square** (said to be the largest in Scotland) that would not look out of place in France or Belgium. Surrounding it are imposing 18th- and 19th-century buildings

---

JAY AND JAY

46a Horsemarket, Kelso, Scottish Borders TD5 7AE
Tel: 01573 224897
e-mail: jay.and.jay@hotmail.co.uk
website: www.jayandjay.net

Located in the picturesque town of Kelso in the Scottish Borders, **Jay and Jay** is a small shop selling stylish ladies wear. Choosing a name for the shop was really easy because the owners are Jan Rutherford and Jennifer McGillivray - the two Js! Jay and Jay has been around since 2005 but Jan and Jenny worked together for many years before that.

The clothes they stock are casual but smart and include jeans, smart trousers, knitwear, tops, shirts and jackets. Designer names include Kasbah whose unusual shapes are fun to wear and a little exotic; Junge, a Danish company whose jackets offer a comfortable fit and a luxurious feel; Oui Moments, who offer the very latest in style for today's image-conscious woman; and Sea Salt from Cornwall who use organic cotton in their fun range of casual wear; and Robell who specialise in trousers which they do really well.

Jay and Jay also stocks several ranges of jewellery, including Creative Dezigns which is a collection of jewellery made in Africa. Theirdesigns are quite bold but suit most outfits. You'll also find other makes of jewellery such as Belong, Olsen and Kasbah.

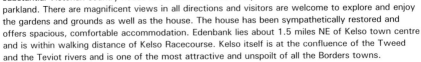

EDENBANK HOUSE

Edenbank, Kelso, Roxburghshire TD5 7SX
Tel: 01573 226734
e-mail: christina.moffatt@btopenworld.com
website: www.edenbank.co.uk

Enjoy a warm welcome and relax in comfort at **Edenbank** - a substantial Victorian country-house set in 100 acres of lovely parkland. There are magnificent views in all directions and visitors are welcome to explore and enjoy the gardens and grounds as well as the house. The house has been sympathetically restored and offers spacious, comfortable accommodation. Edenbank lies about 1.5 miles NE of Kelso town centre and is within walking distance of Kelso Racecourse. Kelso itself is at the confluence of the Tweed and the Teviot rivers and is one of the most attractive and unspoilt of all the Borders towns.

with the supremely elegant **Town House** of 1816, which now houses the tourism information centre, as its centrepiece. The centre can provide you with a town trail that will guide you to the town's architectural gems.

Kelso Abbey (Historic Scotland) was founded in 1128, after David I, who had established an abbey at Selkirk and brought over 13 monks from France, decided that Kelso was a much better place for it, as the strategically positioned Roxburgh Castle was already there to offer it protection. It was the biggest of the Borders abbeys, but during a siege by the English under the Earl of Hertford in 1545, it was almost totally destroyed. Now all that remains of the church

are the transepts, part of the tower, two nave bays and part of the west end. But the ruins are still dramatic and imposing, and are well worth a visit.

The **War Memorial Garden** in Bridge Street was part of the former abbey grounds. It has helped Kelso to win the Beautiful Scotland and Britain in Bloom competitions on several occasions. The garden was gifted to the town by the Duke of Roxburgh in 1921.

In July every year, the **Kelso Civic Week** takes place, with many events that echo similar ceremonies in other Borders towns. On the banks of the Teviot, three miles southwest of the town, once stood the proud **Royal Burgh of Roxburgh**. This was probably founded about 1113 and was a thriving walled town in medieval times with no less than four churches. Nothing now survives above ground, thanks to the repeated attentions of succeeding English armies. It was one of Scotland's original four burghs.

Where the Teviot and the Tweed meet rises a high defensive mound, the site, up until 1550, of **Roxburgh**

Kelso Market Square

🏛 historic building   🏚 museum and heritage   🏛 historic site   🝆 scenic attraction   🌱 flora and fauna

Castle. It was during a siege of the castle in 1460 that James II was killed outright when a cannon accidentally blew up in his face. The place has been suggested as yet another possible site for King Arthur's magnificent capital of Camelot.

To the west of Kelso, within parkland overlooking the Tweed, stands the magnificent **Floors Castle**, Scotland's largest inhabited castle and the ancestral home of the Duke and Duchess of Roxburghe. The original building, designed by William Adam and started in 1721, was a rather austere Georgian mansion. It was the present duke's great-great-grandfather James, the 6th Duke, who, in 1849, commissioned the fashionable architect William Playfair to embellish the plain Adam features of the building. Playfair let his imagination run riot and transformed the castle, adding a dazzling array of spires and domes. The interior houses an outstanding collection of 17th- and 18th-century French furniture, magnificent tapestries, Chinese and European porcelain and many other fine works of art. Many of the treasures in the castle today were collected by Duchess May, American wife of the 8th Duke. The castle has been seen on cinema screens worldwide in the film *Greystoke,* as the home of Tarzan, the Earl of Greystoke. The extensive parkland and gardens overlooking the Tweed provide a variety of wooded walks, and the walled garden contains splendid herbaceous borders. Queen Victoria visited the duke in 1876 and the summerhouse that was specially built for her can be seen in the outer walled garden.

The **Millenium Viewpoint**, on the other side of the Tweed and close to Maxwellheugh, was constructed in the year 2000, and is a vantage point for great views of the town and surrounding area.

Springfield Park is the venue, late in July each year, of the **Border Union Show**, which features not only agriculture but fairground amusements, trade stands and sometimes parachutists.

Rennie's Bridge is a handsome, five-arched bridge spanning the Tweed - the first in the country to feature elliptical aches rather than round or pointed. It was designed by the Scottish civil engineer John Rennie and was built in 1803 to replace an older bridge destroyed by floods. Rennie based his design for Waterloo Bridge in London on it. The broad expanse of grass beside the river is known as The Cobby.

The bridge was the scene of a riot in 1854, when people objected to paying tolls to cross it, as all the building costs had been met. So bad was it that the Riot Act was read. However, it took another three years before the tolls were withdrawn.

Horse racing in Kelso began in 1822, and **Kelso Race Course** (known as the Friendly Course) hosts horse racing all year.

EDNAM
21 miles E of Galashiels on the B6461

🐿 James Thomson   🐿 Henry Francis Lyte

The village stands on the Eden, a tributary of the Tweed, and was the birthplace of two famous men. The first was **James Thomson**, born in September 1700, who wrote the words to *Rule Britannia*. It was written about 1740 for a masque called *Alfred,* and was soon adopted as a patriotic song. The other was **Henry Francis Lyte**, born in June 1793, who wrote *Abide with Me*. A memorial to Thomson has been erected at Ferniehill, to the south of the village, and the bridge over the river has a plaque commemorating Lyte, who died in Nice in France in 1847.

MAXTON

8 miles SE of Galashiels on the A699

> 🏛 Maxton Parish Church 🏚 Maxton Cross

Maxton Parish Church was rebuilt in 1812, though it contains fragments of an earlier, medieval building. **Maxton Cross**, on the tiny village green, partially dates from the 14th century, though the main part was replaced in 1881.

DRYBURGH

7 miles SE of Galashiels off the B6356

> 🏛 Dryburgh Abbey 🌿 Field Marshal Earl Haig
>
> 🌿 St Modan 🏚 William Wallace Statue
>
> 🍃 Scott's View

The ruins of **Dryburgh Abbey** (Historic Scotland) must be the most romantically situated in all of Scotland, sitting as it does on a loop of the Tweed, which surrounds it on three sides. Nothing much remains of the great abbey church, except for the west door and parts of the north and south transepts. However, the substantial ruins of the other abbey buildings (including a fine chapter house) can still be explored. Within the north transept is buried Sir Walter Scott and his wife Charlotte, as well as **Field Marshall Earl Haig of Bemersyde**. He was Commander-in-Chief of the British Expeditionary forces in France and Flanders during World War I.

The Premonstratensian abbey was founded in 1150 by Hugh de Moreville, Constable of Scotland. The site had already been a sacred one, as it was here that **St Modan**, a Celtic monk, set up a monastery in about 60AD. In 1322, during the Wars of Independence, Edward II's army, after a successful invasion of Scotland, set fire to the place. This was the first of many sackings, including the one of 1544, when 700 English soldiers reduced

it to ruins. It was abandoned soon after.

It now forms part of the 55-mile-long Abbeys Cycle Route, taking in the other three great Borders abbeys of Melrose, Kelso and Jedburgh. A short walk from the abbey is the 31 feet high (including pedestal) **William Wallace Statue**. He spent a lot of time in the Borders hiding from the English in Ettrick Forest. The Earl of Buchan commissioned the statue in 1814.

North of Dryburgh is **Scott's View**, which gives an amazing panorama of the Eildon Hills. Sir Walter Scott used to ride up here to get inspiration, and when his funeral cortege was making its way to Dryburgh, the hearse stopped here for a short while. It is best accessed from the A68, where it is signposted from the Leaderfoot Viaduct that spans the Tweed.

ST BOSWELLS

7 miles SE of Galashiels on the A68

> 🌿 St Boisil 🌱 Mertoun House Gardens

This village is named after **St Boisil**, who was an abbot of the Celtic monastery at Old Melrose in the 7th century. The centrepiece of the village is its green, which hosts a fair on July 18 (St Boisil's Day) each year. In past times, this fair was one of the largest in the country, and attracted people - especially gypsies - from all over the Borders and beyond. At one time more than 1000 horses were offered for sale at the fair.

A mile or so to the east are **Mertoun House Gardens**. Though the house is not open to the public, the 26-acre gardens can be visited between April and September. Mertoun Kirk, in the grounds of the house, is open on alternate Sundays for church services. The original kirk was built in 1241, though the present building dates from 1658.

🏛 historic building 🖼 museum and heritage 🏚 historic site 🍃 scenic attraction 🌱 flora and fauna

THE GARDEN HOUSE

Whitmuir, Selkirk, Borders TD7 4PZ
Tel: 01750 721728
e-mail: whitmuir@btconnect.com
website: www.whitmuirfarm.co.uk

Robert and Hilary Dunlop's forebears have been farming the 400 acres of Whitmuir Farm since 1760. Today, the farm has cattle, sheep, crops and woodland, as well as its own loch which is just 5 minutes walk from the house. Known as Whitmuir Loch, it is an SSSI noted for its rich variety of flora and fauna. Fishing for pike and perch is permitted and the loch makes a wonderful giant swimming pool on warm summer days. It is also the perfect spot for a picnic.

The Garden House is a comfortable, warm and modern building of 1995, set in a south facing walled garden with a large terraced area, garden furniture and barbecue. The accommodation comprises 5 attractively furnished and decorated bedrooms, 4 with en suite bath and shower, the fifth with a private shower. One of the rooms is on the ground floor with a door to the garden. All rooms are equipped with colour TV, radio and hospitality tray. Extra beds are available for children. Evening meals and packed lunches freshle prepared from home-grown and local produce are available on request. The house is open all year. Pets are welcome.

SELKIRK
5 miles S of Galashiels on the A7

- 🐦 Sir Walter Scott 🐦 Mungo Park
- 🏛 Halliwell's House 🎨 Selkirk Glass Visitor Centre
- 🎨 Robert D Clapperton Photographic
- 🎭 Common Riding Ceremony 🏛 Bowhill
- 🎭 Bowhill Little Theatre 🏛 Newark Castle
- 🏛 Battle of Philiphaugh 🐦 Michael Scott

Once the county town of Selkirkshire, Selkirk is now a quiet royal burgh on the edge of the Ettrick Forest. It was the site of the first abbey in the Borders, which was founded in 1113 by David I. However, 15 years later, before one stone was laid, David moved the monks to Kelso, where the abbey was finally built.

In Selkirk's High Street, outside the Old Courthouse where he presided, there is a statute of **Sir Walter Scott,** who was sheriff-depute here from 1804 until his death in 1832. Within the courtroom is an audiovisual display telling of his associations with the area. Another statue in the High Street commemorates **Mungo Park**, the explorer and surgeon who was born in Yarrow, seven miles to the east, in 1771. The oldest building in the town is **Halliwell's House and Robson Gallery**, just off the market square, where there is a small museum on the ground floor and an art gallery on the upper floor.

Robert D Clapperton Photographic in Scotts Place is a working museum and photographic archive. It traded for three generations under the family name of the founder Robert Clapperton, all using the original daylight Studio. They left a unique archive of photographic images of the life and times in which they worked and the Studio where they worked.

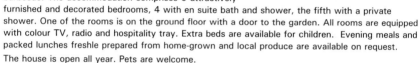

🎦 stories and anecdotes 🐦 famous people 🎨 art and craft 🎭 entertainment and sport 🏃 walks

St Boswells, River Tweed and Dryburgh Abbey

Distance: *5.0 miles (8.0 kilometres)*
Typical time: *180 mins*
Height gain: *33 metres*
Map: *Explorer 338 and 339*
Walk: *www.walkingworld.com ID:2917*
Contributor: *Mark and Tracey Douglas*

ACCESS INFORMATION:

The walk starts in St Boswells at the bus station. St Boswells is accessible by bus from most border towns and Edinburgh. There is a small carpark at the bus station and in front of the adjacent village hall. On street parking is available within the vicinity. There are no parking charges.

DESCRIPTION:

A beautiful walk along the banks of the River Tweed. The walk starts in the small charming village of St Boswells, and after an initial section on St Cuthbert's Way the walk joins the banks of the River Tweed. The middle part of the walk takes in the hamlet of Dryburgh. Here you will pass the ruins of the 12th Century Dryburgh Abbey, which is open to visitors all year round and is the last resting place of Sir Walter Scott.

A short detour from Dryburgh will take you the Wallace Monument; a large statue in memory of the 12th Century Scottish Warrior which offers commanding views over the surrounding countryside and the Eildon Hills. The final section of the walk rejoins St Cuthberts way along the banks of the Tweed back into St Boswells.

Wildlife is in abundance and you may also see the odd salmon rising particularly in the Autumn months at the salmon ladder at Mertoun Mill as they make the journey upstream to their spawning grounds.

ADDITIONAL INFORMATION

Dryburgh Abbey was founded in the 12th century by King David I and run by the monks of the Premonstratensian Order. With its location on the Scottish Frontier, the Abbey, like all the other Border Abbeys, was prone to attack and was destroyed in 1322, 1385 and finally in 1544. Now in the ownership of Historic Scotland, the Abbey is open to the public all year round.the poet sits on top of the domed roof.

FACILITIES

There are toilets in St Boswells and outside Dryburgh Abbey.The Buccleuch Hotel in St Boswells in open to non residents and serves food all day. There are a couple of small convenience shops in St Boswells.

FEATURES:

River, toilets, wildlife, birds, great views, gift shop, food shop, mostly flat, public transport, ancient monument

WALK DIRECTIONS:

1 | From the bus station, turn right along the main street passing in front of the small row of shops. Just past the last shop (The Village Store) turn left up the lane (The Wynd) and continue up passing the Air Cadet Hut until you meet a small track. Carry on and after about 50m take a right at the path junction. Go along this track ignoring the turn off to the right and within 200m the track will fork. Take the right fork up the flight of wooden steps and continue along this track for about 150m until you meet a tarmac road. Continue straight ahead on this road for about 150m until you reach the top of the Golf Course brae.

2 | Turn left down the golf course brae, continue past the clubhouse and once you reach the course turn right. Keeping the fence to your right you will shortly join a footpath. Continue along the path which is part of St Cuthberts Way, keeping the fence to your right and the golf course to your left - be aware of golf being played! After about 1km you

will reach the end of the golf course. Carry on along the path and you will shortly have the River Tweed on your left. Continue along the path passing the Cauld and Salmon Ladder until you reach Mertoun Bridge.

3 | Climb the wooden staircase onto Mertoun Bridge be careful of traffic as you step out onto the road. Turn left and cross the bridge. Take great care crossing the bridge, face oncoming traffic. On reaching the end of the bridge turn left on to a track and head for the cottages at Mertoun Mill. Pass in front of the cottages and the old mill buildings and you will reach a set of steps.

4 | Climb the steps, cross over the stile at the top and turn left along the field keeping the fence to your left, at the end of the field go through a gate and carry on down the track which will eventually take you down to the banks of the River Tweed. Carry on upstream,(you will observe the Golf Course on the opposite bank) for about 1km , cross a stile and carry on along the grass track keeping on straight ahead until you meet a small ladder stile.

5 | Cross the ladder stile and turn right along the road. Within 200m you will pass the entrance to Dryburgh Abbey. (You will have passed a toilet block on your right). Carry on straight ahead passing the parking area, the road will curve to the left and within 100m you will arrive at the entrance gate to Dryburgh Abbey Hotel.

6 | If you wish to visit the monument, turn right and follow the road up the gentle hill for about 250m. Once you pass the final house on the left 'Newmains' turn left up the track which is signposted for the Wallace Statue. Carry on along this track for 500m before turning right up to the Monument. You will enjoy commanding

views of the surrounding countryside and the Eildon Hills. (If you don't wish to visit the Wallace Monument, carry on direct to Waymark 8 by carrying on straight ahead down the road signposted as a dead-end towards the Tweed.)

7 | Retrace your steps to take you back to Waymark 6 by turning right before the gates of Dryburgh Abbey Hotel. Carry on down this road for 300m to the suspension bridge which will shortly come into view.

8 | You may wish to make a short visit to the Temple of the Muses which you will observe on the small hill on your right next to the bridge. Cross the suspension bridge and then turn immediately left down the track - you are now re-joining St Cuthberts Way. Follow this track for 1.5km following the signs for St Cuthberts Way and keeping the River Tweed on your left until you arrive at a footbridge crossing a small stream.

9 | Cross the small bridge and follow the track right up the hill. Ignore the paths which turn off to the left and keep on until you reach a tarmac road, turn right along this road and then first left which will take you back into St Boswells before turning left to the Bus Station.

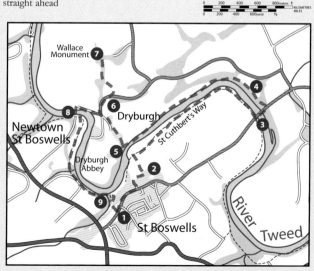

The present proprietors, the fourth generation, demonstrate features of the studio, which has been set up as a working museum and photographic archive,

At the **Selkirk Glass Visitor Centre** at Dunsdalehaugh, you can see glass paperweights being made.

In common with many Borders towns, Selkirk has its **Common Riding Ceremony**, held annually in June, when more than 500 riders regularly set out to patrol the marches, or boundaries, of the town lands. But the ceremony also commemorates the darkest day in the town's history. In 1513, Selkirk sent 80 of its bravest men to fight alongside James IV at Flodden, taking with them the town flag. The battle was a disaster for Scotland, with the flower of Scottish manhood, including the king himself, being killed. Only one Selkirk man, named Fletcher, returned, without the Selkirk flag but bearing a bloodstained English one, which can be seen in Halliwell's House. A memorial to the fallen can be found outside the Victoria Halls in the High Street.

The Scottish Borders Archive and Local History Centre is within St Mary's Mill, and offers research facilities on local history, geography and genealogy, including the records of the old counties of Berwickshire, Selkirkshire, Roxburghshire and Peeblesshire.

Three miles west of the town is **Bowhill**, the Borders home of the Duke of Queensberry and Buccleuch. It is a fine early 19th-century mansion, and in its grounds is **Bowhill Little Theatre**, which presents many professional plays. A James Hogg Exhibition is housed in a building off the courtyard. There is also a visitor centre, rural walks, a restored Victorian kitchen and a display of fire engines.

The ruins of **Newark Castle** are also within its grounds, dating from about 1450. In 1645 the **Battle of Philiphaugh** took place nearby, when Leslie's Covenanting army met and defeated a royal army commanded by Montrose. Leslie's prisoners were taken to Newark Castle and it was there, on September 13 1645, that several hundred soldiers and camp followers of Montrose's army were savagely butchered. In 1810, when excavations were taking place beside the castle, bones were uncovered in a field known as Slain Men's Lea. The tower can only be viewed from the outside.

Aikwood Tower, (not open to the public), home of Sir David Steel, was once the home of **Michael Scott** the legendary wizard. Scott lived from about 1175 to 1230, and was one of the cleverest men of his age. He was credited with dividing the Eildon Hills into three, though the Roman name for the hills (Trimontium) shows that they always had three peaks. He was educated at Durham Cathedral School and later Oxford, Paris and Bologna, where he studied mathematics, law and theology. In his day he was known as the 'wonder of the world'. His reputation spread all over Europe as a man who had learned everything there was to know in the Christian world.

He is also said to have dabbled in alchemy, and some of the legends attached to him and his so-called wizardry (such as his 'demon horse' and 'demon ship') were no doubt borrowed from the story of Merlin the Magician. He probably died in Italy (some say after being hit by a piece of masonry that had fallen from a church) and was buried there. The tower was granted to Master Michael Scott, a descendant of the wizard, by the infant James V in 1517. Previously, it had been held by the crown.

The Ettrick Water, a tributary of the Tweed, flows to the west of the town, and it is joined a couple of miles out of town by the Yarrow Water. The Vale of Yarrow is very scenic, with the hamlet of Yarrow itself being very picturesque. Scott's great-grandfather was once minister of Yarrow Parish Church. It was built about 1640 to replace the medieval St Mary's Church, which stood above St Mary's Loch.

ST MARY'S LOCH

Loch of the Lowes   Isabella Shiels

James Hogg

The loch is in a truly beautiful setting of rounded, green hills. Both Scott and William Wordsworth have sung its praises, but no words can adequately describe this delightful sheet of water. A narrow spit of land separates it from the smaller **Loch of the Lowes**, with Tibbie Shiel's Inn, now an angling hostelry, situated between them. It was opened in 1824, and is named after **Isabella Shiels**, the woman who ran it until 1878. Her visitor's book is still in existence, and records such names as R L Stevenson, Gladstone and Thomas Carlyle. It is a favourite stopping point on the Southern Upland Way, which passes close by.

James Hogg, nicknamed The Ettrick Shepherd, was also a frequent visitor. He was born at Altrive Lake (not a lake, but a farm) nearby in 1770, and wrote *Confessions of a Justified Sinner*, one of the great books of the 19th century.

TIBBIE SHIELS INN

St Mary's Loch, Selkirkshire TD7 5LH
Tel: 01750 42231
e-mail: alistirmoody@hotmail.co.uk
website: www.tibbieshiels.com

Commanding a spectacular view of St Mary's Loch, the **Tibbie Shiels Inn** takes its name from its first landlady, Isobel (Tibbie) Shiel, who presided over the hostelry from the mid-1820s until 1878. A contemporary description of the inn records that it was thatched and consisted of two downstairs rooms, one of them the kitchen, and an attic reached by a steep wooden stair. It was in this attic that many of the inn's famous visitors slept, amongst them Sir Walter Scott and James Hogg, the distinguished poet and novelist. But most of Tibbie's patrons were anglers who come to fish in the loch and its streams.

Today, the inn still attracts anglers along with those who come to enjoy the sailing, cycling, hang gliding and walking available here - the inn is on the coast to coast Southern Upland Way. Mine host, Alistir Moody, also enjoys music and a good party "so there will be some of that too" he says. He is also building a separate restaurant overlooking the loch as well as a bunk house to sleep up to 12 guests. The current accommodation comprises 5 guest bedrooms, all very comfortable and attractively furnished and decorated.

Memorial Gardens, Hawick

Hawick

- 🏞 Hawick Common Riding 🏛 Drumlanrig's Tower
- 🌿 Wilton Lodge Park 🎭 Andrew James Guthrie
- 🏛 Hawick Museum & Scott Art Gallery

Hawick is the largest town in the Borders, and is famous for the quality of its knitwear, with names like Pringle and Lyle and Scott being known worldwide.

The **Hawick Common Riding** takes place in June each year, and commemorates yet another skirmish between the English and the Scots. This occurred in 1514, when some Hawick men beat off English soldiers camped near the town at Hornshole and captured their banner. A disagreement of a different kind took place in the mid 1990s, when two women riders tried to join what had traditionally been an all-male occasion. Their participation provoked hostile opposition, even from some women. It took a court case to establish that women had the right to join in, though even today some people still tolerate their presence rather than welcome it.

St Mary's Parish Church was built in 1763, and replaced an earlier, 13th-century church.

The town's oldest building is the 16th-century **Drumlanrig's Tower**. In 1570, it survived a raid by English troops that destroyed the rest of Hawick, and was once a typical moated L-shaped Borders tower house before the area between the two 'legs' was filled in to convert it into an elegant town house. At one time it belonged to the Douglases of Drumlanrig in Dumfriesshire, and it was here that Anna, Duchess of Buccleuch, and wife of the executed Duke of Monmouth, once stayed. The basement was later used as a prison, and finally a wine cellar when it became a hotel. Now the tower has been restored and houses the town's visitor information centre and an exhibition explaining the history of the Borders.

The award-winning **Wilton Lodge Park** sits by the banks of the Teviot, and has 107 acres of riverside walks, gardens, a tropical glasshouse, recreational facilities and a café. Within it is the **Hawick Museum and Scott Art Gallery**, which explains the history of the town and its industries. The gallery has a collection of 19th- and 20th-century Scottish paintings, and regularly hosts exhibitions of works by local and national artists. Many of the mills in the town, such as Peter Scott and Company in Buccleuch Street and Wrights of Trowmill outside the town, have visitor centres and guided tours. The Hawick Cashmere Company, based in Trinity Mills in Duke Street, has a viewing gallery and shop. And if Duns has its Jim Clark Memorial

Trophy Room, Hawick has its Jimmy Guthrie Statue. **Andrew James Guthrie** was a local TT rider who won six Tourist Trophy races on the Isle of Man. He was killed in 1937 while competing in the German Grand Prix at Chemnitz.

Around Hawick

MINTO
5 miles NE of Hawick off the B6405

🏛 Parish Church 🏛 Fatlips Castle

🏛 Barnhills Tower

Minto was founded in the late 1700s as a planned village by the 2nd Earl of Minto. It was laid out by the architect William Playfair. The **Parish Church** was completed in 1831, and replaced an earlier building dating from the 13th century.

On top of Minto Crags sits the curiously named **Fatlips Castle**, built in the 16th century for the Turnbull family. It was restored in 1857 and used as a shooting lodge and private museum, though it is now a ruin.

To the east of Fatlips are the ruins of **Barnhills Tower**, another Turnbull stronghold.

Fatlips Castle, Minto

It was built in the 16th century, but now only a few decayed walls are left standing.

DENHOLM
4 miles NE of Hawick on the A698

🧍 John Leyden 🧍 Sir James Murray

In 1775, this pleasant village, with its village green, was the birthplace of **John Leyden**, poet, doctor, linguist and friend of Sir Walter Scott. He was educated at the local school, and, so gifted that he entered Edinburgh University when only 15 years old. The John Leyden Memorial, which stands on the green, commemorates the great man, who died in 1811 on the island of Java. He was the son of a local farmer, and in 1806 had settled in Calcutta, where he became assay master to the local mint. While thre he wrote about the local languages.

Also born in the village was **Sir James Murray** (1837-1915), who undertook the tremendous task of editing the *New English Dictionary on Historical Principles*, forerunner of the *Oxford English Dictionary*.

JEDBURGH
14 miles NE of Hawick on the A68

🎗 Fastern Even Handba' 🏛 Jedburgh Abbey

🌿 Cloister Garden 🏛 Jedburgh Castle Jail

🏛 Mary Queen of Scots House

🌿 Monteviot House Gardens

🌿 Teviot Water Gardens 🏛 Redeswire Raid

🌿 Jedforest Deer & Farm Park 🐾 Carter Bar

The route of the present day A68 was at one time the main route from Edinburgh to England, so Jedburgh saw many armies passing along its streets when Scotland and England were constantly at war with each other. The locals once called the town Jethart, and it is still remembered in the expression

Jethart justice, meaning hang first and try later, a throwback to the bad old days of the reivers.

Every year at Candlemas (February 2) the **Fastern Even Handba'** game is played in the town, when the 'Uppies' play the 'Doonies' and chase beribboned balls through the streets of the town. Though the present game dates from the 18th century, it is thought that it had its origins in the 16th century, when the severed heads of English reivers were used instead of balls.

Jedburgh is an attractive small town with gaily-painted houses, especially in the Market Place and the Canongate, and it regularly wins awards in Beautiful Scotland in Bloom competitions. **Jedburgh Abbey** (Historic Scotland), on the banks of the Jed Water, was founded in 1138 by David I for the Augustinians. It was destroyed nine times by the invading English. Each time, save for the last one, the monks painstakingly rebuilt it. It is the most complete of all the Borders abbeys. A visitor centre explains its story, with one of its more intriguing exhibits being the Jedburgh Comb, found during excavations. The **Cloister Garden** was planted in 1986, and shows what a typical monastic garden would have looked like in the early 1500s.

Not far from the abbey is **Mary Queen of Scots House**. Here, in October 1566, Mary

Stuart stayed for four weeks when presiding at local courts in the Borders. While she was there, she made an arduous journey to Hermitage Castle to visit her lover, the Earl of Bothwell, which nearly killed her. When Elizabeth I held her in captivity, she declared that she would have preferred to have died in Jedburgh than England. Now the house is a museum and visitors centre with displays on the tragic queen's life.

Jedburgh Castle Jail, in Castlegate, was a 19th century reform prison, which now houses a display about the history of the town. Four miles northeast of Jedburgh are the **Monteviot House Gardens**, which have a pinetum, a herb garden and a riverside garden linked by bridges.

Five miles northeast of Jedburgh, off the A698, are the **Teviot Water Gardens**, planted on three levels above the River Tweed. There are three riverside walks, a bird hide and a café.

Jedforest Deer and Farm Park is five

Monteviot House Gardens, Jedburgh

miles south of Jedburgh on the Mervinslaw Estate, just off the A68. It is a modern working farm with a deer herd and rare breeds. There are also birds of prey demonstrations using eagles, owls and hawks, and plenty of ranger-led activities.

Four miles beyond the Farm Park, the A68 reaches the English border at **Carter Bar**, which is 1370 feet above sea level in the Cheviots. From here there is a wonderful view northwards, and it almost seems that the whole of southern Scotland is spread out before you. In the 18th century, herds of sheep and cattle were driven over this route towards the markets in the south.

The last Borders skirmish, known as the **Redeswire Raid**, took place here in 1575. It took the arrival of a contingent of Jedburgh men to turn what was going to be a Scots defeat into a victory.

ANCRUM
10 miles NE of Hawick on the B6400

🏛 Battle of Ancrum Moor	🏛 Ancrum Parish Church
🏛 Waterloo Monument	
🌿 Harestanes Countryside Visitor Centre	

Ancrum is a typical Borders village, to the north of which was fought the **Battle of Ancrum Moor** in 1545. It was part of what was known as the Rough Wooing, when Henry VIII tried to force the Scots into allowing the young Mary, Queen of Scots, to marry his son Edward. Three thousand English and Scottish horsemen under Lord Eure were ambushed by a hastily assembled army of Borderers. During the battle, the Scots horsemen changed sides when they saw that the Borderers were gaining the upper hand, resulting in a total rout.

Ancrum Parish Church was built in 1890,

MAINHILL GALLERY

Ancrum, Jedburgh, Roxburghshire TD8 6XA
Tel: 01835 830545
e-mail: mainhillgallery@aol.com
website: www.mainhill-gallery.co.uk

Originally located at Mainhill near St Boswells, the **Mainhill Gallery** was founded in 1983 by Di and Bill Bruce who were farmers for some 20 years before deciding on a change of direction. Their first exhibition, 'The Wilkie Tradition' was a great success and paved the way for a well-merited reputation for exhibiting fine Scottish art.

They moved to Ancrum in 1989 and they began to deal in more modern work, including sculpture and ceramics.

There are now eight contemporary artists on the gallery's books. They include the talented painters Kate Boxer and Caroline Hunter who both seem set for distinguished careers.

The gallery presents some 5 shows a year and also attends major art fairs in the UK. "It's quiet in the Borders" says Di Bruce. But that's not a worry for the Bruces.

Such is the quality of the work on show, discriminating lovers of art will always beat a path to this outstanding gallery.

🏛 stories and anecdotes   🦅 famous people   🎨 art and craft   ✏ entertainment and sport   🥾 walks

though the ruins of the earlier 18th-century church still survive in the graveyard. It is thought that the original Ancrum church was built in the 12th century.

Two miles east of the village, on Peniel Haugh, is the 150-feet-high **Waterloo Monument**, erected by the Marquis of Lothian between 1817 and 1824 to commemorate the Battle of Waterloo. Though there are stairs within the tower, it is not open to the public. The best way to reach it is to walk from the **Harestanes Countryside Visitor Centre**, which is nearby. The Centre has countryside walks, activities and displays, all with a countryside theme, as well as a car park, gift shop and tearoom.

MOREBATTLE
18 miles NE of Hawick on the B6401

🏰 Linton Church 👺 Linton Worm

🏰 Cessford Castle

This little village sits on the St Cuthbert's Way, close to the Kale Water. Its name comes from the botl, or dwelling, beside the mere, which was a small loch. In the 19th century, the loch was drained to provide more agricultural land. The surrounding area was once a hiding place for Covenanters fleeing the persecution of Charles II's troops in the 17th century.

To the north of the village is **Linton Church**, which has Norman details, a fine Norman font and a belfry dated 1697. One Norman survival is the tympanum above the door, which commemorates the killing of the **Linton Worm** by John Somerville in the 13th century. The Linton Worm was 12 feet long, and lived in a cave below

the church. It terrorised the district, and the local people were powerless against it. John noticed that when it saw anything it wanted to eat, it opened its mouth wide. So he made a special spear that had inflammable materials instead of a point, and when he approached the worm on horseback with the spear blazing, it duly opened its mouth to devour him. John stuck the spear down the worm's throat, and the worm was killed. For this act the king granted him the lands of Linton.

The church sits on a low mound of fine sand, which is almost certainly a natural feature. However, a local legend tells a different story. It seems that a young man was once condemned to death for murdering a priest. His two sisters pleaded for his life, saying they would carry out a specific task to atone for his crime. They would sieve tons of sand, removing all large grains, and from the small grains build a mound on which a church building could stand. The church authorities agreed to this, and the women set to work. Eventually, after many years, a mound of sand was created, and a church was indeed built on it.

The ruins of the L-shaped **Cessford Castle**, which surrendered to the English in

Cessford Castle Ruins, Morebattle

1545, lie two miles to the southwest. It was built by the Kerrs in about 1450, and was once one of the most important castles in the Borders.

KIRK YETHOLM
22 miles NE of Hawick on the B6352

🚶 Pennine Way   ⛪ Yetholm Parish Church

This village in the Bowmont Valley is at the northern end of the **Pennine Way**, with St Cuthbert's Way passing close by as well. It got its name from the Scottish word yett, meaning a gate, as it was one of the gateways into England. It, and to a lesser extent its twin village of Town Yetholm, were famous at one time as being where the kings and queens of the Scottish gypsies lived. The most famous queen was Esther Faa Blyth, who ruled in the 19th century. In 1898, Charles Faa Blyth, her son, was crowned king at Yetholm. Though the title had lost much of its meaning by this time, the coronation was attended by an estimated 10,000 people. A small cottage is still pointed out as his 'palace'.

St Cuthbert's Way passes through the village, and the Pennine Way, which snakes over the Pennines in England, ends at **Yetholm Parish Church**, an elegant building with a small tower. It was built in 1836 and has a Burgerhuys bell cast in 1643.

NEWCASTLETON
20 miles S of Hawick, on the B6357

🏛 Liddesdale Heritage Centre Museum

🎵 Newcastleton Traditional Music Festival

🚶 Dykescroft Information Centre

🚶 Newcastleton Historic Forest Walk

⛪ Hermitage Castle

Newcastleton, in Liddesdale, is a planned village, founded by the third Duke of Buccleuch in 1793 as a handloom-weaving centre. The **Liddesdale Heritage Centre Museum** is in the old Townfoot Kirk in South Hermitage Street, and has attractive displays about the history of the area and its people.

This is the heartland of the great Borders families of Kerr, Armstrong and Elliot, and was always a place of unrest before Scotland and England were united. The border with England follows the Liddel Water then, about three miles south of Newcastleton, strikes east along the Kershope Burn for a mile before turning northeast. At Kershopefoot, where the Kershope Burn meets the Liddel Water, the Wardens of the Western Marches of both Scotland and England met regularly to settle arguments and seek redress for crimes committed by both sides. A jury of 12 men settled the disputes, with the Scots choosing the six English, and the English choosing the six Scots. However, even these meetings were known to result in violence, and many a Scottish or English warden and his entourage were chased far into their own territory if redress was not forthcoming.

Every year, in July, the village holds the **Newcastleton Traditional Music Festival**, one of the oldest such festivals in Scotland. It was founded in 1970, and has concerts, ceilidhs and competitions. There are many informal music sessions held throughout the village. On the last day of the festival the Grand Winners Concert is held.

A mile from the village, off the Canonbie road, is the Millholm Cross, It has the initials AA and MA carved on it. The AA is thought to be Alexander Armstrong, a reiver from nearby Mangerton Tower.

The **Dykescroft Information Centre and Newcastleton Historic Forest Walk** lie to the south of the village, off a minor road. It is closed in February and March each year. One walk ends at Priest Hill, where there is a 200-year-old hill fort. Within the forest can be seen one of the 7stanes, seven mountain biking centres spanning the south of Scotland, from the heart of the Scottish Borders to Dumfries and Galloway. 'Stane' is the Scots word for stone, and at each of the 7stanes locations, you'll find a stone sculpture reflecting a local myth or legend. The sculpture at Newcastleton resembles the tail fin of an aircraft and faces north to south. On the north side, representing Scotland, *Auld Lang Syne* is inscribed and on the south side, representing England, the words of *Jerusalem*.

The highlight of this particular stane is that it stands right on the border between Scotland and England. The hole in the middle allows people to stand on either side of the border and shake hands through the stane.

Five miles north of Newcastleton is the massive bulk of **Hermitage Castle** (Historic Scotland). It dates from the 1300s and its imposing walls and stout defences reflect the bloody warfare that was common in this area before the union of Scotland and England. It belonged to the de Soulis family, who built the original castle of wood in the mid 13th century. However, in 1320, William de Soulis was found guilty of plotting against Robert the Bruce, and his lands and property were confiscated by the crown. The castle later became a Douglas stronghold.

While staying in Jedburgh, Mary Stuart covered the 50 miles between there and Hermitage and back again in one day to visit the Earl of Bothwell, whom she later married. During her journey she lost a watch, which was recovered in the 19th century.

A few miles north of the village is Castleton, the site of a lost village. All that remains of the medieval St Martin's Church is the kirkyard, and a series of earthworks marks where a castle belonging to the Soulis family once stood. The village also had a green, and this is marked by a commemorative stone.

Peebles

🖉 Beltane Week	🖼 Tweeddale Museum & Gallery		
🏛 Cross Kirk	🏛 Peebles Parish Church		
🖉 Eastgate Theatre	🌱 Glentress Forest		

An attractive former county town, Peebles sits on the banks of the River Tweed. Though it looks peaceful enough nowadays, its history is anything but. It was burnt to the ground by the English in 1545, occupied by Cromwell in 1649, and again by Charles Edward Stuart in 1745.

In June each year, the Town holds its **Beltane Week**, with the crowning of the Beltane Queen. The ceremony's origins go right back to pagan times, though the present Beltane Week celebrations date only from the 19th century, when they were revived. The Chambers Institute was founded in 1859 by local man William Chambers who, with his brother Robert, went on to found the great Chambers publishing house in Edinburgh. Within the Institute is the **Tweeddale Museum and Gallery**, where the history of the town is explained. Here you can also see the extraordinary classical frieze commissioned by William Chambers, which is based on parts of the Parthenon Frieze in the British Museum and on the Alexander Frieze commissioned in 1812 by Napoleon Bonaparte.

The ruins of the **Cross Kirk** (Historic Scotland), founded in 1261 as the church of a Trinitarian Friary, are to the west of the town. The Trinitarians were a monastic order

JOANNA THOMSON JEWELLERY

Mailingsland Cottages, Peebles EH45 8PH
Tel/Fax: 01721 722936
e-mail: joannathomson@btconnect.com
website: www.jewellery-scotland.com

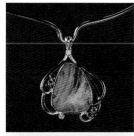

When you wear a piece of **Joanna Thomson Jewellery** you can be sure that people will remark on it. Each item is made in her unmistakable style that is a unique blend of the romance of Art Nouveau, the roots of her Celtic heritage and the wonderful richness of the natural world. Joanna has been designing and creating hand-crafted jewellery in Scotland for more than 33 years and she now works from the studio attached to her home in the rolling hills of the Borders.

Joanna has used silver, different colours of gold, mixtures of gemstones and built up collections of pendants, earrings, brooches and rings; but this is just the starting point - the options are varied and potentially endless! For instance, if you see a ring design you like, you can have it in silver or gold, 9ct or 18ct, yellow or white, maybe both. You could have a diamond, a ruby and moonstone or a garnet or perhaps an aquamarine, or maybe a mixture of stones...

So, if you are looking for a gift for a loved one, or treating yourself, you can be sure of finding just the right thing amongst Joanna's extensive range.

founded in 1198 by St John of Math, a Frenchman, to redeem captives taken by the Saracens in the Holy Land during the Crusades. The tower of the former St Andrews Church still survives just off Neidpath Road. The present **Peebles Parish Church** is an imposing Victorian building at the west end of the High Street, a short distance from the quaintly named Cuddy Bridge over the Eddleston Water, a tributary of the Tweed. One of the hidden places of the town is to be found beyond an archway leading from the high street - the Quadrangle. Surrounding the town's war memorial are well laid out, colourful gardens.

Eastgate Theatre and Arts Centre is housed in a 19th-century church. It has a programme of drama and exhibitions throughout the year, and there is a small café.

Peebles also has the distinction of being ranked as the Top Independent Retailing Town in Scotland, and second in the UK, for its range of independent shops, in marked contrast to the ubiquitous 'cloned towns' predominant in other areas.

One mile east of Peebles off the A72 is **Glentress Forest**. It is now the most visited tourist attraction in the Scottish Borders, and is said to have the country's best mountain biking course.

Around Peebles

NEIDPATH CASTLE
1 mile W of Peebles on the A72

🏠 Neidpath Castle

Neidpath Castle stands on the banks of the Tweed. The previous castle that stood here was built by the Fraser family in the 14th century. It subsequently passed to the Hays when the daughter of Sir Simon Hay married

Gilbert de Hay of Yester. It was probably Gilbert who built the present castle.

In 1685, William Douglas, the first Duke of Queensberry, bought it and it remained a Douglas property until 1810, when it passed to the Earl of Wemyss. Sir Walter Scott visited it frequently when his friend, Adam Ferguson, rented it at the end of the 18th century.

Robert Smail's Printing Works, Innerleithen

It is the epitome of a Scottish tower house, and originally consisted of three great vaulted halls, one above the other (though the top vault was subsequently removed and replaced by a timber roof), reached by winding stone staircases. There is a genuine dungeon below what was the guardroom, prisoners were sometimes lowered into and in many cases forgotten about. Mary Stuart and James VI both visited the castle, reflecting the importance of the Hay family in the 16th century. The castle is privately owned, and is open to the public. Batik wall hangings depict the tragic life of Mary Stuart.

KAILZIE GARDENS
3 miles E of Peebles on the B7062

🌿 Kailzie Gardens

Extending to 14 acres, **Kailzie Gardens** sit on the banks of the Tweed, surrounded by hills. The main part is contained in an old walled garden, plus, there is a 15-acre wild garden and woodland walks among rhododendrons and azaleas. There is also a restaurant, gift shop and 18-hole putting green.

INNERLEITHEN
6 miles E of Peebles on the A72

🏛 St Ronan's Well Interpretive Centre

🏛 Robert Smail's Printing Works

Innerleithen is a small town that was the original for Sir Walter Scott's St Ronan's Well. It used to be a spa town, and the **St Ronan's Well Interpretive Centre** at Well's Brae explains the history of the wells, whose waters were full of sulphur and other minerals. You can sample the water if you're brave enough. In the High Street is **Robert Smail's Printing Works** (National Trust for Scotland). This was a genuine print works that still retained many of its original features and fittings when taken over by the Trust in 1987. Now you can see how things were printed more than a century ago, and even have a go at type-setting yourself.

TRAQUAIR
6 miles SE of Peebles on the B709

🏛 Traquair House 🏛 Bear Gates 🌿 Traquair Fair

Traquair is a small village visited mostly for the magnificent **Traquair House**. It is reputed to be the oldest continuously

River Tweed, nr Innerleithen

produces a fine range of ales that can be bought in the estate shop. It is said that when Charles Edward Stuart visited, he too enjoyed a glass or two of Traquair Ale.

The **Traquair Fair** is held at the beginning of August each year, with music, dance, theatre, puppetry and children's entertainment.

inhabited house in Scotland and has its origins in a royal hunting lodge built on the banks of the Tweed in about 950AD. In its time, 27 kings and queens have visited the place, including Alexander I in the 11th century, Edward I of England (known as the Hammer of the Scots) in the 13th, and Mary Stuart in the 16th. One laird of Traquair fell with his king at Flodden, and in the 18th century the then laird, the fifth Earl of Traquair, supported the Jacobite cause.

Charles Edward Stuart visited in 1745, and when he left, the laird closed the **Bear Gates** at the end of the long drive, vowing that they would never be opened until a Stuart ascended the British throne once more. They have remained closed ever since. Within the house itself are secret passages and priests' holes, as the owners reverted to Roman Catholicism in the early 17th century. It is still the family home of the Maxwell Stuart family.

In 1965, the then laird renovated the brewhouse, which lies beneath the private chapel, and the Traquair House Brewery now

DRUMELZIER
8 miles SW of Peebles, on the B712

It is reputed that one of King Arthur's knights lies buried where the Drumelzier Burn joins the Tweed, just north of the village. At Drumelzier Haugh is an old standing stone known as Merlin's Stone, and on Tinnis Hill there is a stone circle. At one time Drumelzier Castle, owned by the Tweedie family, stood close to the village, but now little remains above ground. In the graveyard of Drumelzier Parish Church is an old burial vault of the Tweedies.

LYNE
4 miles W of Peebles on the A72

🏠 Lyne Church

Lyne Church, perched picturesquely on a hillside above the road, is said to be the smallest parish church in Scotland. A chapel has stood here since the 12th century at least, but the present church was built about 1645. It contains a pulpit and two pews reputed to be of Dutch workmanship.

STOBO
5 miles W of Peebles on the B712

🏛 Stobo Church

🌿 Dawyck Botanic Garden & Arboretum

Stobo Kirk, one of the oldest and most beautiful in the area, has a Norman tower, nave and chancel, with some later features and additions. **Stobo Castle** is set in some lovely grounds and is now one of Scotland's most luxurious health farms and spa. Two miles south, along the B712, is the **Dawyck Botanic Garden and Arboretum** (see panel opposite), an outpost of the National Botanic Gardens in Edinburgh. It sits on the Scrape Burn, another tributary of the Tweed, and houses a unique collection of conifers,

rhododendrons and other tree species within its 50 acres.

The original garden was laid out in the late 1600s by Sir James Naesmyth, who imported trees and shrubs from North America. In 1832, the garden was landscaped by Italian gardeners who built bridges, terraces and steps.

BROUGHTON
10 miles W of Peebles, on the A701

🐿 John Buchan   🏛 John Buchan Centre

Broughton is forever associated with the author and Governor-General of Canada, **John Buchan**, whose most famous work is undoubtedly *The Thirty Nine Steps*. Though born in Perth, his maternal grandparents

---

SKIRLING HOUSE

Skirling, by Biggar,
Lanarkshire ML12 6HD
Tel: 01899 800274
Fax: 01899 860255
e-mail: enquiries@skirlinghouse.com
website: www.skirlinghouse.com

Standing beside the village green, at the heart of a peaceful Borders village, **Skirling House** was designed in 1908 by the Arts and Crafts architect Ramsay Traquair for Lord Carmichael. It became his country retreat and contained the family's art collection which included a magnificent 16th century Florentine carved ceiling in the Drawing Room. Owners Bob and Isobel Hunter have been welcoming guests here since 1994 and have won many coveted awards including being graded 5 Star by the Scottish Tourist Board. The house has 5 individually decorated bedrooms - 3 doubles, 1 twin and one that can be either. All are en suite and equipped with TV, DVD and CD players as well as a selection of books.

Breakfast is very special at Skirling House - mini-muffins, French toast with caramelised apples and black pudding, Texas sausage biscuit, freshly squeezed orange juice, fruit compôte and stewed fruits are all freshly prepared. Bob and Isobel prepare to order any combination of cooked breakfast for guests, including kippers and there is always a blackboard special. The eggs for breakfast are provided by the Hunters' own chickens - part of their animal collection that includes 3 black Labradors, 3 cats and several white doves.

🏛 historic building   🏛 museum and heritage   🏛 historic site   🐿 scenic attraction   🌿 flora and fauna

Dawyck Botanic Garden

Stobo, Peebleshire EH45 9JU
Tel: 01721 760254
website: www.rbge.org.uk

In the depths of the Scottish Boarders, Dawyck Botanic Garden has a stunning collection of trees and shrubs. Benefiting from a cooler continental climate, and with over 300 years of tree planting, Dawyck is truly one of the world's finest arboreta. Exotic conifers dating back to 1680, along with the unique Dawyck Beech and some of the tallest trees in Britain, make Dawyck a jewel in the crown of the Scottish Borders.

Carpets of bulbs mark the arrival of spring especially on the banks of the Scrape Burn which turn white with drifts of snowdrops. Magnificent colour in early summer is provided by the Garden's collections of rhododendrons particularly those in the Azalea Terrace. Dawyck's famous collection of trees and shrubs ensures that autumn is a memorable time of year, with flaming leaves and luscious berries.

Special trails highlight just a few of the special collections at Dawyck. Follow the intrepid adventures of David Douglas or discover more about our native natural heritage with the Scottish Rare Plant Trail. Find out about fungi, mosses and lichens in the world's first-ever reserve for non-flowering plants.

Providing light refreshments, including delicious home baking, the Conservatory has gifts and souvenirs as well as a good selection of plants for the discerning gardener.

farmed nearby, and his father, a Free Church minister, married his mother in the village. The old free kirk is now the **John Buchan Centre**, with displays about his life and writings. The village is also home to the famous Broughton Ales.

WEST LINTON
14 miles NW of Peebles, just off the A702

🏛 St Andrew's Parish Church ⛲ Lady Gifford's Well

🌿 Whipman Ceremonies

West Linton is a delightful village, and one of the hidden gems of Peeblesshire. The picturesque **St Andrew's Parish Church** of 1781 stands in the middle of the village, and the surrounding gravestones testify to the craftsmanship of the many stone carvers who used to live in the area. The local **Whipman Ceremonies** take place in June each year. They originated in 1803, when some local agricultural workers decided to form a benevolent society known as the Whipmen of Linton. Now the week-long festivities include honouring the Whipman (meaning a carter) and his Lass. In the centre of the village stands **Lady Gifford's Well**, with a stone carving of 1666 on one of its sides.

One of the many streets is quaintly called Teapot Lane, as a tap once stood here where the women of the village drew water into teapots to make tea.

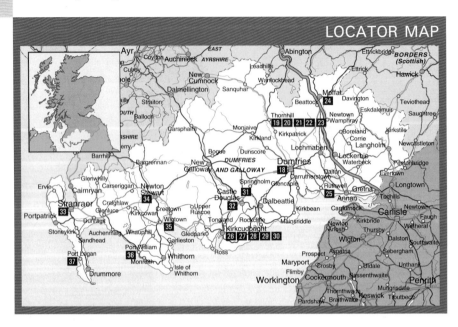

LOCATOR MAP

ADVERTISERS AND PLACES OF INTEREST

🏢 historic building 🏛 museum and heritage 🏚 historic site ⚘ scenic attraction 🐾 flora and fauna

2| Dumfries & Galloway

People scurrying north along the M74 rarely turn off at Gretna and head for Dumfries and Galloway. This is a pity, as it is a wonderful area that can match anything in Scotland for beautiful scenery, grandeur and history. There are more than 200 miles of coastline with small coves, neat fishing ports, towering cliffs and wonderful sandy beaches. There also are beautiful villages, old abbeys and castles, vibrant towns and country roads that meander through soft, verdant scenery or climb up into bleak moorland landscapes that were made for walking. In the fields you will see herds of the region's own indigenous cattle - the Belted Galloways, so called because they have a wide white band running round their bodies.

Dumfries is the largest town in the area, and is a lovely place, full of old red sandstone buildings and great shopping facilities. It is where Scotland's national poet, Robert Burns, is buried, and any trip to Scotland should include a visit to St Michael's Kirkyard to see his mausoleum. Kirkcudbright, because of the quality of light found there, has had an artists' colony since Victorian times, and is a gracious place full of Regency and Georgian buildings. Wigtown is Scotland's official book town, and Stranraer, with its ferries, is a gateway to Northern Ireland. Then there's Lockerbie, forever associated with the air disaster of 1988.

The area contains three former counties - Dumfriesshire, Kirkcudbrightshire and Wigtownshire, and each one has its own particular charm. You can explore beautiful Nithsdale in Dumfriesshire, for instance, and visit Drumlanrig Castle, one of the homes of the Duke of Queensberry and Buccleuch. Kirkcudbrightshire was the birthplace of John Paul Jones, founder of the American navy, and Wigtownshire was where Christianity was introduced into Scotland.

Surrounding the fertile fields and picturesque towns of coastal Galloway are the high hills and bleak moorland that cut off Dumfries and Galloway from the rest of Scotland. Because of this, the area was almost independent of Scottish kings in medieval times, and was ruled by a succession of families, from the ancient Lords of Galloway to the mighty Douglases. All have left their mark in

Glenwhan Gardens, Stranraer

Galloway Forest Park

sweetheart to the English language; at Glenluce - a word that means valley of light - are the wonderful ruins of Glenluce Abbey; and south of Kirkcudbright is Dundrennan, where Mary Stuart - better known as Mary, Queen of Scots - spent her last night on Scottish soil. The castles are equally as impressive. Drumlanrig, Threave, Cardoness, Caerlaverock; the names trip off the tongue, and go to the very heart of Scotland's history.

From the middle of August to the end of October each year, the area holds its Gaelforce Festival, bringing together musical events, literary festivals, traditional Scottish entertainment, concerts, drama and art.

This part of Scotland has a mild climate, and at one time the coastline was nicknamed the

stone, such as Devorgilla's Bridge in Dumfries, and the mighty Threave Castle, built on an island in the River Dee.

Then there are the abbeys, for, like the Borders, this was an area much favoured by medieval monks. At New Abbey are the ruins of a monastery that gave the word

Scottish Riviera. First-time visitors are always surprised to see palm trees flourishing in cottage gardens near the coast, or in the grand, formal gardens such as Logan Botanic Garden or Castle Kennedy Garden in Wigtownshire. But then, Dumfries and Galloway has always been full of surprises.

Dumfries

- 🏛 Burns Mausoleum 🏛 Burns' House
- 🏛 Globe Inn 🏛 Robert Burns Centre
- 🏛 Midsteeple 🏛 Theatre Royal
- 🎨 Organised Chaos 🏛 Devorgilla's Bridge
- 🏛 Old Bridge House 🏛 Dumfries Museum
- 🏛 Lincluden College 🐎 Archibald the Grim
- 🏛 Crichton Memorial Church

The Royal Burgh of Dumfries certainly lives up to its nickname of the Queen of the South. It has a lovely location on the banks of the River Nith, and was once voted the town with the best quality of life in Britain.

The town is forever associated with Scotland's national poet, Robert Burns. Though born in Ayrshire, he died in Dumfries, and lies in the **Burns Mausoleum** within the kirkyard that surrounds St Michael's Parish Church, built in the 1740s. Also buried there are his wife, Jean Armour, and five of their family. Burns had a family pew in St Michael's (marked by a plaque), and long after his death his wife was a regular attender. The mausoleum was built in 1815, in Grecian style, and in that year Burns' remains were transferred there. Also in the kirkyard are the graves of many of his friends.

Not far away is Burns Street (formerly Mill Vennel), where **Burns' House** is situated. He lived here from 1793 until his death in 1796 at the early age of 37. It is open to the public, and though not a grand house, it was nonetheless a substantial building for its day, showing that by the end of his life Burns had achieved some form of financial stability due to his work as an exciseman. On display are letters and manuscripts, the pistol he carried with him on his rounds and the chair in which he sat when he wrote his last poems.

The **Globe Inn** was the poet's howff, or favoured drinking place, and can still be visited. It was established in 1610, and can be found down a narrow passage off the main street.

On the west bank of the Nith is the **Robert Burns Centre** (free) which tells the full story of the poet and his connections with the town. There is a fascinating scale model of Dumfries in the 1790s and a haunting audio-visual presentation (for which there is a small charge), as well as a bookshop and a cafe-gallery with a lively exhibition programme.

Another writer associated with Dumfries is J M Barrie. Though not born here, he attended Dumfries Academy, a handsome building in Academy Street. While at the school, he stayed in a house in George Street and later admitted that the games of pirates he and his friends played in the garden sloping down to the Nith gave him the idea for Peter Pan and Captain Hook.

Dumfries is an ancient town, with a royal charter from William I dated 1186. It was here, in 1306, that Robert the Bruce murdered the Red Comyn, a rival contender for the throne of Scotland. The deed took place before the high altar of Greyfriar's Monastery, a deed for which Bruce was excommunicated by the Pope. However, this didn't seem to worry the man, as he immediately had himself crowned king of Scotland at Scone in Perthshire in the presence of Scottish bishops, who continued to give him communion. Nothing now remains of the monastery, though the present Greyfriar's Kirk, a flamboyant building in red sandstone, is close to where it once stood.

In the High Street stands the **Midsteeple**, built of red sandstone in 1707. It was formerly the town hall and jail, and on its south face is a carving of an ell, an old Scots cloth measurement of about 37 inches. There

MOGERLEYS BUTCHERS

49 Friars Vennel, Dumfries DG1 2RQ
Tel: 01387 253590
e-mail: mogerleys@btconnect.com
website: www.mogerleys.com

"One of the best butchers on the planet" was the verdict of The Herald Magazine after a visit to **Mogerleys Butchers** in the heart of old Dumfries. Believed to be one of the oldest butchers in Scotland, Mogerleys is also quite venerable having been established in 1876. Its present owner, Gordon J Little, has been here since 1988 taking over from his father. His shop is immaculate and there's a slight hint of spice in the air. The counters are packed with enticing displays that include award-winning Scottish pork sausages and speciality sausages, black puddings, various pies in all shapes and sizes, haggis of course, all kinds of meat cuts, enormous goose eggs and the curious "savoury duck". Of course, it's not duck at all but a peppery spicy pork loaf baked in the of what looks like a small Cruise missile.

A visit to Mogerleys is worth the trip to Dumfries by itself but if you can't get to this wonderful shop, a mail order service is available. The shop itself is open from 6am to 5pm, Monday to Saturday.

---

is also a table of distances from Dumfries to various important Scottish towns. One of the towns however, is in England - Huntingdon. Three successive Scottish kings in medieval times held the earldom of Huntingdon, and it was one of the places where Scottish drovers took cattle to market in the 17th and 18th centuries.

In Shakespeare Street, rather appropriately, you will find the famous **Theatre Royal**, the oldest working theatre in Scotland, dating from 1792. Burns regularly attended performances here.

Dumfries proper sits on the east bank of the Nith. On the west, up until it was amalgamated into Dumfries in 1929, was the separate burgh of Maxwelltown, which was in Kirkcudbrightshire. Joining the two towns is **Devorgilla's Bridge**. Though the present

bridge dates from 1431, the original structure was built by Devorgilla, Lady of Galloway, in the 13th century. Her husband was John Balliol, who founded Balliol College in Oxford.

At the Maxwellton end of the bridge is the **Old Bridge House Museum**, with exhibits and displays illustrating everyday life in the town. The museum building dates from 1660, and is built into the structure of the bridge. Also on the Maxwellton side of the river is **Dumfries Museum**, housed in an 18th-century windmill, and with a Camera Obscura that gives fascinating views of the town.

On the northern outskirts of the town, but now surrounded by modern housing, are the beautiful red sandstone remains of **Lincluden College** (Historic Scotland). Built originally in 1164 as a Benedictine nunnery by Uchtred, Lord of Galloway, it was suppressed in the late 14th century by **Archibald the Grim**, third Earl of Douglas, and replaced by a collegiate church. The present ruins date from that time. One of its main features is the elaborate canopied tomb of Princess Margaret, daughter of Robert III and widow of the Earl of Douglas. Adjoining the site is the Norman Lincluden Motte, which was later terraced and incorporated into a garden. The adjoining tower house was built in the late 1500s, after the Reformation, by the commendator of the college, William Stewart.

To the east of the town at Heathhall is the Dumfries and Galloway Aviation Museum, run by a group of amateur enthusiasts. It has three floors of displays in what was the control tower of the old airfield of RAF Tinwald Downs. It holds a fascinating collection of military aircraft, both propeller and jet driven, as well as engines, memorabilia and photographs.

Within what was Crichton Royal Hospital in Bankend Road, is the cathedralesque **Crichton Memorial Church**, designed by Sydney Mitchell and built between 1890-1897 as part of a mental hospital. For those interested in genealogy, the Dumfries and Galloway Family History Research Centre in Glasgow Street must be visited. There are archives, fiches and books about local history and families, though there is a modest fee for the use of the facilities.

Around Dumfries

HOLYWOOD
2 miles north of Dumfries off the A76

🏛 Holywood Parish Church

The present **Holywood Parish Church** of 1779 (with a tower dating to 1821) was partly built from the stones of a great medieval abbey that once stood here, of which nothing now remains above ground. To the west, on the other side of the A76, is a stone circle known as the Twelve Apostles, though one massive stone is now missing.

DALSWINTON
6 miles N of Dumfries on a minor road off the A76

The hamlet of Dalswinton is no more than two rows of cottages on either side of the road. But it is an attractive place, built as an estate village. When Robert Burns was living locally at Ellisland Farm, Patrick Millar owned Dalswinton House, in the grounds of which (not open to the public) is Dalswinton Loch. Patrick encouraged William Symington, originally from Leadhills, to experiment with his steam-driven boat on the waters of the loch in the late 18th century, and it is thought that Burns may have been a passenger on one of the sailings.

Devorgilla's Bridge, Dumfries

ELLISLAND

6 miles N of Dumfries on the A76

🖉 Robert Burns   🏛 Ellisland Farm

Robert Burns brought his family south from Mauchline to Ellisland in June 1788. However, there was no farmhouse at the time, and he had to have one built, meaning that he couldn't move in properly until the following year. He leased the 170-acre **Ellisland Farm** from Patrick Millar of Dalswinton, but found the soil to be infertile and stony. So much so that, by 1791, he gave up the unequal struggle to make a living from it, and moved with his family to Dumfries.

The farm sits in a beautiful spot beside the Nith, and it was this romantic location that made Burns choose it in the first place. Here he wrote some of his best poetry, including *Auld Lang Syne* and his masterpiece of the comic/macabre, *Tam o' Shanter*. Burns used to recount that Tam o' Shanter was conceived while walking the banks of the Nith, and he laughed out loud as he thought up his hero's adventures with the witches. Now the farmhouse houses a lively museum dedicated to his memory. To the north is Hermitage Cottage, which Burns used as a place to muse and write poetry.

AE

8 miles N of Dumfries on a minor road off the A701

The small village of Ae is famous for having the shortest name of any town or village in Britain, and for having the only place name with no consonant in it. It takes its name from the Water of Ae, and was founded in 1947 to house forestry workers. It is set in a great conifer forest, which has some good walks and footpaths as well as mountain biking trails.

CLOSEBURN

11 miles N of Dumfries on the A76

🏛 Parish Church

Closeburn sits in one of the most beautiful parts of Dumfriesshire - Nithsdale. To the north of the village the wooded dale closes in on either side, with the River Nith tumbling through it. To the south, it gradually opens out into a wide, fertile strath, dotted with green fields and old, whitewashed farms. The **Parish Church** stands some distance away from the village, and is an attractive Victorian building with a slim tower. Fragments of the older church, which date from 1741, can be seen in the kirkyard. Closeburn Castle (private) has been continuously inhabited since the 14th century, when it was built by the Kirkpatricks, who were closely associated with Robert I.

A small road winds up eastwards from just south of Closeburn into the moorland above the village. It makes an interesting drive, and takes you past the small but picturesque Loch Ettrick.

THORNHILL

13 miles N of Dumfries on the A76

🏛 Boatford Cross   🏛 Morton Castle

This lovely village, with its wide main street and pollarded trees, has a French feel to it, and was laid out in 1714 by the Duke of Queensberry. At the crossroads in the middle of the village is a monument surmounted by a winged horse, a symbol of the Queensberry family. In a field to the west of the village, and close to the bridge over the Nith, is the 15th-century **Boatford Cross**, associated with the ferry and ford that preceded the bridge.

Three miles north of the village, and to the west of the A702, are the remains of 15th-century **Morton Castle**, situated romantically on a tongue of land jutting out into Morton

ZITAN

Townhead Street, Thornhill,
Dumfries & Galloway DG3 5NW
Tel: 01848 330758
e-mail: zitan@tiscali.co.uk
website: www.zitan.co.uk

Sue Collins-Taylor lived in Hong Kong for nineteen years, friends increasingly asked her to bring back a variety of items from her visits there and so **Zitan** was born. Sue's *"aim is to bring antique Chinese furniture, curios and other items of beauty and quality from China at an affordable price."*

At Zitan, in South Scotland, there is a large and varied selection of antique Chinese furniture and other Chinese pieces; some of the furniture is highly decorative and very flamboyant, designed to dominate a room. Other pieces are plainer and understated adding a subtle hint of Chinese style to your interior design scheme. Whatever your design style, at Zitan, there is furniture and other pieces to suit you. In no time you will come to appreciate the wonderful skills of the people who produced these beautiful exquisite goods. Additionally you will find that these lovely Chinese pieces will readily mix with furniture both modern and antique from all corners of the world.

Zitan has recently moved from a small shop to an old church in Thornhill, which has given much more space to the displays enabling a more leisurely walk-round the "Aladdin's Cave" of delightful original and unique items. The Zitan shop is overflowing with the rich colours and sumptuous brocades, delicate carvings, and lustrous woods that are so typical of the wonders of China. Great care and consideration is given to the wonderful displays which add a touch of elegance.

The stock-holding at Zitan is extensive, incorporating antique and modern ranges of large and small cabinets, through to buckets and boxes, abacus, ladder, washstand, camphorwood chests, chairs, lamps, lanterns, panels, carvings, tables, mirrors and stands. The list is endless as to what can be bought in her store, none of which you will find in any High Street store. For those who have something special in mind as a present, Sue makes the trip twice each year, to Hong Kong, to restock her shop and is more than willing to seek out an item for a customer while she is there. Sue loved her experience of living in Hong Kong and now can incorporate her love of the country into her business as she still has close connections with the country on a regular basis. Zitan is a little gem in the rural village of Thornhill and well worth a visit.

THORNHILL STORES

124a Drumlanrig Street, Thornhill,
Dumfriesshire DG3 5LS
Tel: 01845 332214 / 330262

Located in the thriving town of Thornhill is where you will find a delightful Butchers and Deilcatessen. The core business at **Thornhill Stores** is that of a traditional Butcher selling quality meat and poultry sourced in Scotland. A member of the Scotch Butchers Club, it boasts beef from Speyside and the Clyde Valley, Ayrshire pork and bacon and Galloway lamb complimented by a variety of sausages and oven-ready meals which are available on the premises.

In keeping with current trends, Thai, Indian and Chinese sauces and condiments, pasta and cook-in sauces are stocked together with chutneys, jams, marmalades and locally produced honey. To the rear of the butchery is a well-stocked delicatessen offering a wide selection of cooked meats, Scottish and Continental cheeses, pates, olives, pies, salads, Selkirk Bannocks and a range of oatcakes. You will also find oak and peat-smoked salmon, kippers and marinated herrings from Achiltibuie in the Summer Isles.

The business, in its 21st year, is owned and managed by husband and wife team, Jack and Barbara, and a staff of three who provide a helpful and knowledgeable service. Our aim, says Jack, is for people to visit us as customers and go away as friends. The Stores are open from 8.30am to 12.45pm, and 2pm to 5.30pm, Monday to Friday; on Saturday the shop closes at 5pm, closed on Sunday.

🏛 historic building 🏚 museum and heritage 🏛 historic site 🍃 scenic attraction 🌱 flora and fauna

THOMAS TOSH (TT)

19 East Morton Street, Thornhill,
Dumfries & Galloway DG3 5LZ
Tel: 01848 331553
Fax: 01848 331552
e-mail: info@thomastosh.com
website: www.thomastosh.com

Art gallery, café, antiques room,
gift and book shop all combine to
*make **Thomas Tosh** a unique*
place for you to visit.

The gallery exhibits artists from within Dumfries & Galloway and outside the region. New exhibitions are launched regularly throughout the year. So there will always be something interesting and entertaining to see. Thomas Tosh's website (www.thomastosh.com) has details of forthcoming shows and events, and an extensive archive of previous exhibitions. And entrance to the gallery is always free.

In the café, they have selected great Fairtrade tea and coffee, and all the cakes and food dishes are hand made on the premises. They try to use seasonal organic fruit and veg in the daily lunch menus and are supplied by the local and renowned Loch Arthur Creamery. The selection of dishes changes daily and includes lots of choice for vegetarians.

If you are looking for a present - or even a treat for yourself - Thomas Tosh has something for every occasion. They seek out new suppliers in Dumfries & Galloway and from around the globe to bring you all sorts of fresh ideas. They stock beautiful home fragrances and candles, glass and ceramic ware, and their toiletries section caters for everyone from babies upwards.

Or you could choose something from their bookshelves where you'll find gift books and guides on local walks, history, culture and wildlife in Dumfries & Galloway alongside children's books and general interest titles. They also have a wide range of cards created by local artists.

The Old Parish Hall building that houses Thomas Tosh is the perfect setting for the carefully chosen selection of antiques. Chairs, wardrobes and tables are just some of the pieces available. They also offer a range of fabulous modern furniture made exclusively for Thomas Tosh by local craftspeople.

GILLBANK HOUSE B&B

8 East Morton Street, Thornhill, Dumfriesshire DG3 5LZ
Tel: 01 848 330 597
e-mail: hanne@gillbank.co.uk website: www.gillbank.co.uk

Gillbank House B&B is a traditional Victorian House on a quiet street in the centre of the picturesque town of Thornhill in Dumfries & Galloway – 'SCOTLANDS BEST KEPT SECRET'. Drumlanrig Castle, home of The Duke of Buccleuch and Queensberry is only 3.5 miles away and Andy Goldworthys art working can be seen in the surrounding countryside, ie The Striding Arches.

Gillbank House offers a homely atmosphere with excellent service and boasts an AA 5 Diamond rating. The 6 comfortable and spacious bedrooms are all en-suite with 2 of the rooms on the ground floor next to the private car park. Motorbikes and cyclists are most welcome and we have secure bicycle storage available.

Surrounded by beautiful Scottish countryside, the rural location is the ideal place for walking, cycling, golf, fishing or simply relaxing. We recommend Thornhill Inn for a freshly prepared and great tasting evening meal, located less than 100 yards from Gillbank House (see below).

THORNHILL INN

103-106 Drumlanrig Street, Thornhill, Dumfriesshire DG3 5LU
Tel: 01848 330326 Fax: 01848 331713
e-mail: info@thornhillinn.co.uk website: www.thornhillinn.co.uk

Located in the centre of great walking, fishing, shooting, golfing, cycling and sight seeing activities. **Thornhill Inn**, an old coaching Inn, is the ideal base for an active or sedate break - the welcoming ambience of this comfortable Inn with a reputation for warm hospitality and good food enables you to do just that and concentrate on enjoying the spectacular scenery in the Nith valley. The south west of Scotlands 'BEST KEPT SECRET'.

All 11 bedrooms are well appointed with en-suite facilities and Sky TV. The Inn boasts a cosy bar with log fire and a restaurant with great homemade food. The pub has the full Sky Sports package shown on 2 big flat screens for all the big live games.

If you prefer a traditional B&B/Guesthouse then we can recommend Gillbank House located 100 yards from the Inn (see above).

Thornhill Inn and Gillbank House are owned and operated by the Gronberg Family. Both establishments are easily accessible from Dumfries bypass A75 or the M74 junction 14 from Elvanfoot on the A702 through the scenic Dalween Pass. When Booking, please quote 'TCLG'

Loch. A castle of some kind has stood here since the 12th century, though the present castle was built by the Douglases, who were the Earls of Morton. In 1588, the castle was sacked by the troops of James VI, who were conducting a campaign against the Maxwells.

Against the wall of a building in East Morton Street is the bust of Joseph Laing Waugh, Thornhill's own novelist and poet, who set some of his books, written in lowland Scots, in and around the village.

DRUMLANRIG CASTLE

16 miles N of Dumfries on a minor road off the A76

🏛 Tibbers Castle 🌿 Drumlanrig Sycamore

Drumlanrig Castle is set in a 120,000-acre estate, and is the Dumfriesshire home of the

---

🏛 historic building 🏛 museum and heritage 🏛 historic site 🏵 scenic attraction 🌿 flora and fauna

Duke of Queensberry and Buccleuch. It was built by William Douglas, 1st Duke of Queensberry, and completed in 1691. It stands on the site of an earlier Douglas castle, and contains many fine paintings, including works by Gainsborough, Rembrandt and Hans Holbein. Its name comes from the word drum, meaning a low hill, on a lang, or long, rig, or ridge. Therefore it is the low hill on the long ridge.

In the summer of 2003, the castle was the scene of a daring burglary when a painting by Leonardo da Vinci worth millions of pounds was stolen from it in broad daylight. Within the estate is a country park and gardens, the ruins of **Tibbers Castle**, and some of the outbuildings have been converted into craft workshops. The **Drumlanrig Sycamore** is one of the largest sycamores in the country, and here, there is also the first Douglas fir ever planted in the United Kingdom.

DURISDEER

19 miles N of Dumfries on a minor road off the A702

Parish Church · Durisdeer Marbles

The tiny hamlet of Durisdeer sits at the end of a narrow road leading off the A702, and not many people know about it. It consists of a handful of cottages and a **Parish Church** built in 1699; the church is unusual in that it has, attached to it, the former parish school. It is also surprisingly large for such a small hamlet, but this is due to the fact that it is the church for the Queensberry estate. But it also hides a secret that makes it special - the wonderful **Durisdeer Marbles**. They are, in fact, an elaborate funerary monument constructed in 1713 to the 2nd Duke of Queensberry and his wife, who lie buried in the crypt beneath. They were carved in marble by the Flemish sculptor Jan Nost, and are said to be the best of their kind in the country.

PENPONT

13 miles N of Dumfries on the A702

Parish Church · Joseph Thompson · Andy Goldsworthy

This small, attractive village is well worth a visit in the summer months to see the colourful gardens that surround some of the old picturesque cottages. The cathedralesque **Parish Church** is Victorian, and seems far too large for such a small place.

Penpont was, in 1858, the birthplace of **Joseph Thomson** the African explorer, after whom Thomson's gazelle is named. He studied at Edinburgh University before joining an expedition to Africa in 1878, thus starting a long association with the continent. He died at the young age of 37 in 1895, his body wasted by the many diseases he had contracted.

On a slight rise in a field just off the road to Moniaive is a piece of sculpture shaped like an egg. This is the work of **Andy Goldsworthy**, the famous sculptor, who was born in Cheshire but now lives in the village.

KEIR

12 miles N of Dumfries on a minor road off the A702

Kirkpatrick MacMillan

Keir is no more than a hamlet with a small Parish Church dating mainly from 1814. It was near here that **Kirkpatrick MacMillan**, inventor of the modern bicycle, was born in 1813, and while his brothers all went on to become successful in their careers, Kirkpatrick was content to stay at home and ply the trade of a blacksmith.

Hobbyhorses, which relied on riders pushing themselves forward with their feet, had been around since the early part of the

19th century, but Kirkpatrick MacMillan's bicycle was the first to incorporate revolving pedals. On June 6 1842, he set out on a 70-mile ride to Glasgow on his bicycle, and was greeted by crowds when he arrived there. However, while passing through the Gorbals, he knocked down a young girl, and even though she wasn't badly injured, he was fined five shillings by a Glasgow magistrate, the first recorded case of a cyclist being fined for a traffic offence. However, rumour has it that the magistrate offered to pay the fine out of his own pocket if Kirkpatrick would allow him to have a ride on the bicycle.

TYNRON

15 miles N of Dumfries on a minor road off the A702

🏛 Parish Church

This small, pretty conservation village has only one building dated later than 1900. The **Parish Church**, which looks as if it is far too big for such a small place, was built in 1837, and was one of the last in Scotland to be lit by oil lamps. Early in the 20th century, a distillery that had a contract to supply the Palace of Westminster was situated in the village.

DUNSCORE

8 miles NW of Dumfries on the B729

🕊 Jane Haining 🎬 The Buchanites 🌳 Glenkiln

Dunscore (pronounced Dunsker) is a small, attractive village with a neat, whitewashed Parish Church dating from 1823. When Robert Burns and his family stayed at Ellisland Farm, four miles to the east, they used to worship in its predecessor.

Not far from Dunscore is Lochenhead Farm, birthplace in 1897 of **Jane Haining**, the only British person to have died at

Auschwitz during World War II. While still young, she joined the Church of Scotland's Jewish Mission Service, and was eventually appointed matron of the Jewish Mission in Budapest in 1932. In 1944, she was arrested, purportedly because she had been listening to BBC broadcasts, but actually because she had been working among the Jews. She was taken to Auschwitz, and died there on July 17 1944. Her death certificate gave the cause of death as cachexia, a wasting illness sometimes associated with cancer, but there is no doubt she was gassed.

The isolated farm of Craigenputtock, where Thomas Carlyle lived while writing *Sartor Resartus*, lies off an unmarked road five miles to the west. It was here that an unusual - not to say hilarious - event took place concerning a small religious sect known as **The Buchanites**, founded by Mother Buchan in Irvine, Ayrshire, in the 18th century. She attracted a wide following, claiming she could bestow immortality on a person by breathing on them, and that she herself was immortal.

Elspeth Buchan also claimed that her followers would ascend to heaven in bodily form, without the inconvenience of death. The cult was eventually hounded from Irvine by the town magistrates, and headed south towards Dumfries. In a large field near Craigenputtock, Elspeth decided that it was time her followers went to heaven, so she had a wooden platform set up in a field at Craigenputtock. She and her followers assembled on it, their heads shaved apart from a small tuft that the angels would grasp to lift them up into God's kingdom. However, in the middle of the service the platform collapsed, throwing her and her followers to the ground. The sect eventually broke up when Elspeth had the nerve to die a natural death.

Out of doors at **Glenkiln**, beside Glenkiln Reservoir four miles (as the crow flies) south west of Dunscore, is a collection of sculptures by Henry Moore and Rodin.

MONIAIVE
16 miles NW of Dumfries on the A 702

> 🎨 James Paterson 🦢 Bonnie Annie Laurie
>
> 🖉 Scottish Comic Festival 🎨 Moniaive Folk Festival

Moniaive, caught in a fold of the hills at the head of Glencairn, through which the Cairn Water flows to join the Nith, must surely be one of the prettiest villages in Dumfriesshire. It is actually two villages, Moniaive itself and Dunreggan, on the northeast side of the river. Within the village is the Renwick Monument, which commemorates a Covenanting martyr who died in 1688.

James Paterson was a painter who was a member of the group known as the Glasgow Boys. In 1882, he settled in the village with his wife, and lived there until 1906, when he moved to Edinburgh. Several of his paintings show scenes in and around the village.

Three miles east is the great mansion of Maxwelton House (not open to the public), formerly known as Glencairn Castle. It was here that Anna Laurie (her real name), of **Bonnie Annie Laurie** fame, was born in 1682. The song was written by William Douglas of Fingland, though he later jilted her and joined the Jacobite army. Anna herself went on to marry Alexander Fergusson, 14th Laird of Craigdarroch.

Every September the village hosts the **Scottish Comic Festival**, with displays and exhibitions, as well as talks by cartoonists and comic illustrators. There is also the **Moniaive Folk Festival** in May each year.

WANLOCKHEAD
25 miles N of Dumfries on the B797

> 🚶 Mennock Pass 🏛 Museum of Lead Mining
>
> 🏚 Lochnell Mine 🏛 Miners' Library
>
> 🏚 Straitsteps Cottages
>
> 🖉 Gold Panning Championships

People are usually surprised to discover that Scotland's highest village isn't in the Highlands, but in the Lowlands. Wanlockhead, in the Lowther Hills, is 1531 feet above sea level, and is a former lead mining village that is right on the Southern Upland Way. It is best approached from the A76, passing through one of the most beautiful and majestic glens in southern Scotland - the **Mennock Pass**. As you drive up, keep your eyes open for a small cross laid flat into the grass on the north side of the road. It commemorates Kate Anderson, a nurse who was killed here in 1925 when she was returning to Sanquhar after attending a patient. She fell off her bicycle in a snowstorm and broke her neck.

In the middle of Wanlockhead, in what was the village smithy, you'll find the **Museum of Lead Mining**, which explains all about the industry, and gives you the opportunity to go down the **Lochnell Mine**, a former working mine. The **Miners' Library** is situated on a rise above the museum, and was founded in 1756 by 35 men. At the height of its popularity it had 3000 books on its shelves. Within the village you'll also find the Beam Engine, which has recently been restored. It used to pump water from one of the mines using, curiously enough, water to power it. Also in the village are the **Straitsteps Cottages** where you can experience what it was like to live as a miner in the 18th and 19th centuries. One cottage depicts a cottage interior around 1740 and the second around 1890. The artefacts on show, illustrate how the people of Wanlockhead lived, worked and played, and the tour guide explains how the miners' families lived during these two time-periods.

The Leadhills and Wanlockhead Light Railway is Britain's highest adhesion railway, reaching 1498 feet above sea level. It was originally built to take refined lead to Scotland's central belt, but finally closed in 1938. Now a length of two-feet gauge track has been re-opened between Wanlockhead and its twin village of Leadhills, and trips are available at weekends during the summer.

Lead is not the only metal associated with Wanlockhead. This whole area was once known as God's Treasure House in Scotland, because of the gold found here. In fact, the Scottish crown was refashioned for James V in the 16th century from local gold. The largest nugget of gold ever discovered in the UK was found close to Wanlockhead. It weighed all of two pounds, and was the size of a cricket ball. Gold panning is still a popular activity in the local streams, and the **UK National Gold Panning Championships** are held here every May.

SANQUHAR

28 miles N of Dumfries on the A76

St Bride's Church   Sanquhar Tolbooth
Sanquhar Post Office   Sanquhar Historic Walk
Sanquhar Castle   Richard Cameron

Sanquhar (pronounced San-kar) is a small town in Upper Nithsdale that was created a royal burgh in 1598. The name comes from the language of the ancient Britons, and means Old Fort. The site of this fort was on a small hill to the north of the town, close to **St Bride's Church**, which was built in 1824 on the site of a much older church. Within the church is a small collection of stone carvings, including one of St Nicholas and a medieval cross.

The **Sanquhar Tolbooth** was built to the designs of William Adam in 1735 as a town hall, schoolroom and jail, and now houses a small museum. It was in a house opposite the Tolbooth that William Boyd, 4th Earl of Kilmarnock, lodged while on his way south to be tried and executed for his part in the Jacobite uprising. There is a plaque on the wall commemorating his stay. In Main Street is **Sanquhar Post Office**, dating from 1712, the oldest continuously used post office in the world. The Southern Upland Way passes through the burgh, and the **Sanquhar Historic Walk** takes you round many of the town's attractions and historic sites.

To the south of Sanquhar are the ruins of **Sanquhar Castle**, originally an old Crichton stronghold. It fell into the hands of the Douglases, and it was here that William Douglas, who wrote the original version of the song *Annie Laurie*, was born in 1672. The castle was founded in the

Sanquhar Castle

11th century, though what you see now dates from much later.

In the 17th century, Sanquhar was a Covenanting stronghold. Charles II had imposed bishops on the Church of Scotland, and the Covenanters took up arms to keep the church Presbyterian. These times were known as the Killing Times, and many people were executed for following the dictates of their conscience. One of the most militant Covenanters was **Richard Cameron**, who rode into Sanquhar in 1680 and attached what became known as the Sanquhar Declaration to the Market Cross. This disowned the king, which was effectively treason. Cameron was subsequently killed at the Battle of Airds Moss in the same year.

The Riding of the Marches is an ancient ceremony, and takes place every August. The burgh boundaries are ridden by horse riders to ensure that adjoining landowners have not encroached onto burgh or common land - a regular occurrence in the past.

One of the more unusual cottage industries in Sanquhar during the 18th and 19th centuries was the hand-knitting of gloves. The intricate patterns soon made them popular throughout the country. Up until the 1950s, these patterns had never been published. Now it is possible once more to buy both hand- and machine-knitted gloves and garments made from the distinctive patterns.

A series of plaques on various buildings takes you on a historic walk round the town - a leaflet is available in the local tourist office.

ELIOCK HOUSE
26 miles N of Dumfries on a side road running parallel to the A76

🐉 James Crichton

Set deep in the heart of Nithsdale, off a minor road, Eliock House (private) was the birthplace in 1560 of **James Crichton**, better known as the Admirable Crichton. He was the son of the then Lord Advocate of Scotland, and was educated at St Andrews University. He travelled extensively in Europe, where he followed careers in soldiering and lecturing at universities. Though a young man, he could speak 12 languages fluently, and was one of the best swordsmen of his day. However, this didn't prevent him from being killed in Mantua in Italy in 1582 while a lecturer at the university there.

The story goes that he was returning from a party one evening when he was set upon by a gang of robbers, and defeated each one in a sword fight. He then realised that one of the robbers was a pupil at the university, Vincentio di Gonzaga, son of the Duke of Mantua, ruler of the city. Realising what he had done, he handed Vincentio his sword and asked forgiveness. Vincentio, however, was a nasty piece of work. He took the sword and stabbed the defenceless James through the heart, killing him outright.

KIRKCONNEL (UPPER NITHSDALE)
31 miles N of Dumfries on the A76

🏛 St Connel's Church 🎨 Alexander Anderson

This former mining village in upper Nithsdale is not to be confused with Kirkconnell House near New Abbey or Kirkconnel graveyard in Annandale. **St Connel's Church** dates from 1729, and is a fine looking building to the west of the village.

High on the hills above the village are the scant remains of an even earlier church, which may date from before the 11th century. Near the present parish church is a monument to **Alexander Anderson**, a local poet who wrote under the name of The Surfaceman. Though

🎭 stories and anecdotes 🐉 famous people 🎨 art and craft 🎟 entertainment and sport 🥾 walks born in lowly circumstances, he rose to become chief librarian at Edinburgh University and subsequently the secretary of the Edinburgh Philosophical Union.

The Kirkconnel Miners Memorial commemorates the men who lost their lives in the Upper Nithsdale mining industry between 1872 and 1968.

MOFFAT
20 miles NE of Dumfries on the A701

- 🐦 Lord Dowding 🐦 John Loudon McAdam
- 🦋 DE Stevenson 🏛 Moffat Museum
- 🏛 Black Bull Inn 🏛 Star Hotel 🏛 Moffat House
- 🌿 Craiglochan Gardens

Sheep farming has always been important in Annandale, and this is illustrated by the ram that surmounts the Colvin Fountain in the middle of Moffat's broad High Street. The town is situated in a fertile bowl surrounded by low green hills, and at one time was a spa, thanks to a mineral spring discovered on its outskirts in the 17th century. By 1827, the sulphurous water was being pumped into the town, and by Victorian times it had become a fashionable place to visit and take the waters.

Moffat was the birthplace, in 1882, of **Air Chief Marshal Lord Dowding**, architect of the Battle of Britain. A statue of him can be found in Station Park. Though he wasn't born in the town, **John Loudon McAdam**, the great road builder, is buried in the old kirkyard at the south end of the High Street. He lived at Dumcrieff House, outside the town, and died in 1836. Though born in Edinburgh, Dorothy Emily Stevenson, better known as the novelist **DE Stevenson**, lived in Moffat,

---

HARTFELL HOUSE AND THE LIMETREE RESTAURANT

Hartfell Crescent, Moffat, Dumfriesshire DG10 9AL
Tel: 01683 220153
e-mail: enquiries@hartfellhouse.co.uk
website: www.hartfellhouse.co.uk

Located in a peaceful rural setting on the edge of the charming town of Moffat, **Hartfell House** is the perfect choice for bed and breakfast accommodation. It overlooks the surrounding hills, yet is only a few minutes walk from the attractive town centre. The house is a stunning example of Victorian architecture and retains some beautiful original features including ornate cornices and woodwork. The guest lounge boasts spectacular views of the Moffat hills.

The house has 7 spacious, tastefully decorated bedrooms on three floors. Each room has en suite shower facilities and is equipped with digital freeview TV, radio alarm and hair dryer. The hospitality tray offers a range of Fairtrade tea and coffee, including decaffeinated and herbal options, as well as Scottish Border biscuits. Most of the beds have memory foam mattresses which, together with the luxurious towels and complimentary Scottish Fine Soap toiletries, ensure your stay is as relaxing as possible. A full Scottish breakfast is cooked to order using the finest local ingredients, and a continental buffet is also provided. In the evening, the dining room is transformed into the Limetree Restaurant which has been awarded an AA Rosette and is very popular with Moffat residents.

🏛 historic building 🏛 museum and heritage 🏛 historic site 🌿 scenic attraction 🌿 flora and fauna

and died there in 1973. She is buried in the local cemetery. The small **Moffat Museum** at The Neuk, Church Gate, charts the history of the town and the people associated with it, including Dowding, McAdam and Stevenson.

The **Black Bull Inn** is one of the oldest in Dumfriesshire, and dates from 1568. Burns was a regular visitor, and Graham of Claverhouse used it as his headquarters while hunting Covenanters in the district. Another hostelry in Moffat that has a claim to fame, albeit a more unusual one, is the **Star Hotel** in the High Street. It is only 20 feet wide, making it the narrowest hotel in Britain. On the other side of the road is the former **Moffat House**, designed by John Adam for the Earl of Hopetoun and dating from the 1750s. It, too, is now a hotel.

Two miles east of the town, on the A708, are **Craiglochan Gardens**, which are open during the summer months. They extend to

Grey Mare's Tail Waterfall

four acres, and there is a small nursery.

GREY MARE'S TAIL
28 miles NE of Dumfries just off the A708

The A708 winds northeast from the town, and takes you past St Mary's Loch as you head for Selkirk. About eight miles along the road is a waterfall called The Grey Mare's Tail (National Trust for Scotland), fed by the waters of tiny Loch Skeen, high up in the hills. The surrounding area has changed little since the 17th century, when it was a hiding place for Covenanters. It is now a 2150-acre nature reserve, and is rich in fauna and flora, including a herd of wild goats. During the summer months there is a programme of guided walks starting from the visitor centre.

TWEEDSWELL
26 miles NE of Dumfries, well off the A701

🏃 Hartfell

Tweedswell is the source of the Tweed, and sits 1250 feet above sea level. It is worth noting that within an area of no more than a few square miles, three rivers rise. The Tweed flows east, the Annan flows south, and the Clyde flows north.

Nearby is a great hollowed-out area among the hills known as the Devil's Beef Tub. Border reivers once used to hide their stolen cattle here. To the east towers the 2651-feet-high **Hartfell**, supposedly the seat of Merlin the Magician in Arthurian days.

ESKDALEMUIR
23 miles NE of Dumfries on the B709

🎨 Eskdalemuir Geomagnetic Observatory

Eskdalemuir, high in the hills, holds one of Dumfriesshire's hidden gems. The Samye Ling Centre, founded in 1967 by two refugee Tibetan abbots, is the largest Tibetan Buddhist monastery in Western Europe. Not only is it a monastery, but also a place where Tibetan culture, customs and art is preserved. To see its colourful Eastern buildings, its flags flying and its prayer wheels revolving in what is a typical Scottish moorland setting, comes as a great surprise.

Close by is **Eskdalemuir Geomagnetic Observatory**, opened in 1908. It was built here for an unusual reason. The observatory was originally at Kew in London, but the sensitive geomagnetic instruments used to measure the earth's magnetic field were affected by the overhead electricity lines that powered the trams. It was at Eskdalemuir in June 1953 that the highest short-term rainfall for Scotland was recorded - 3.15 inches in half an hour. This represents about 15% of Scotland's average annual rainfall.

LANGHOLM
24 miles NE of Dumfries on the A7

- Hugh McDiarmid
- James Robertson Justice
- Armstrong Clan Museum
- Langholm Castle
- Common Riding Ceremony

Though within Dumfriesshire, the 'muckle toon' of Langholm, in Eskdale, is more of a Borders town than a Dumfries and Galloway one. It was here, in 1892, that Christopher Murray Grieve the poet - better known as **Hugh McDiarmid** - was born, though it took many years for the people of the town to formally acknowledge his undoubted contribution to Scottish literature. Also born in the town, but not a native, was **James Robertson Justice**, the actor and stalwart of 1950s and 60s British cinema. His mother was passing through and was forced to stop at the Crown Hotel, where he was delivered.

This is Armstrong country, and when Neil

Armstrong, the first man to set foot on the moon, came to Langholm in 1972, he was given the freedom of the burgh. The **Armstrong Clan Museum** at Lodge Walk in Castleholm traces the history of one of the greatest Borders family. **Langholm Castle**, now a ruin (though there has been some restoration work done on it) dates from the 16th century, and stands at the confluence of the River Esk and the Ewes Water. It can be accessed from the car park beside the museum. On the last Friday in July the annual **Common Riding Ceremony** is held in the town.

On a hillside to the east of the town is the Malcolm Monument, in memory of Sir John Malcolm, who died in 1833. He was born at Burnfoot, a farm near Langholm, in 1769, and became a major-general who distinguished himself in India.

WESTERKIRK
29 miles NE of Dumfries on the B709

- Thomas Telford
- Bentpath Library

The parish of Westerkirk lies a few miles northwest of Langholm, and it was here that **Thomas Telford**, the great civil engineer, was born in 1757. The son of a shepherd, he left school at 14 and was apprenticed to a stone mason in Langholm. However, he was destined for greater things, and rose to be the greatest civil engineer of his generation, building the Ellesmere Canal, the Caledonian Canal and the Menai Straits Bridge in Wales. Within the parish is the unique **Bentpath Library**, founded in 1793 for the use of the antimony miners who used to work in the nearby Meggat Valley. It is still in use today, though only the people of the local parishes may borrow from its stock of 8000 books. On his death in 1834, Thomas Telford bequeathed money to it.

LOCKERBIE
10 miles NE of Dumfries off the M74

🌱 Remembrance Garden 🏛 Battle of Dryfe Sands

🏛 Burnswark

This quiet market town in Annandale is remembered for one thing - the Lockerbie Disaster of 1988. On the evening of December 21, Pan Am flight 103 exploded in mid-air after a terrorist bomb was detonated within its hold. The cockpit crashed into a field at Tundergarth, two-and-a-half miles east of the town, and its fuselage crashed into the town itself, killing all the passengers and crew, as well as 11 people on the ground. The **Remembrance Garden** is situated within the town cemetery to the west of the motorway on the A709. It is a peaceful spot, though there is still an air of raw emotion about the place, and no one visits without developing a lump in the throat.

On December 6 1593, the **Battle of Dryfe Sands** took place on the banks of the Dryfe Water north of the town. The two great families in the area - the Maxwells and the Johnstones - continually fought over who should be the dominant family on the western border. Eventually, the Maxwells brought things to a head by marching into Johnstone territory with 2000 men. The Johnstones could only muster 400, and a Maxwell victory seemed to be a foregone conclusion. However, when they met in battle at Dryfe Sands, the Johnstones won the day, killing over 700 Maxwells.

To the south of the town is **Burnswark**, where 2nd century Roman forts are built on the site of an Iron Age fort.

HIGHTAE
8 miles E of Dumfries on a minor road off the B7020

Rammerscales House (private) is an 18th-century manor house with fine views from its grounds. There is a walled garden and a woodland walk. It is open in August each year.

LOCHMABEN
8 miles NE of Dumfries on the A709

🏰 Lochmaben Castle 🦜 William Paterson

Lochmaben is a small royal burgh in Annandale. In the vicinity are many small lochs in which can be found the vendace, a rare species of fish with a stream-lined body and protruding lower jaw.

Near the Castle Loch stand the scant remains of **Lochmaben Castle** (Historic Scotland), which originally covered 16 acres. It

Rammerscales House, Hightae

Lochmaben Castle

can only be viewed from the outside. An earlier 12th-century castle (now no more than a small earthwork on the local golf course) was the home of the Bruce family, Lords of Annandale, and is said to be the birthplace of Robert the Bruce (later Robert I), though Turnberry in Ayrshire lays a similar, and perhaps more likely, claim.

About three miles to the southwest is Skipmyre, where **William Paterson** was born. He was the driving force behind the ill-fated Darien Scheme of 1698, which sought to establish a Scottish colony in modern day Panama. Many Scots who went to Central America perished there, and it almost bankrupted the country. He was more successful in another venture - he proposed the creation of the Bank of England in 1690 and in the face of political hostility succeeded in 1694.

TORTHORWALD
4 miles E of Dumfries on the A709

🏛 Cruck Cottage   🏛 Torthorwald Castle

Within the village, on a narrow road off the A709, is **Cruck Cottage**, an early 18th-century example of a thatched cottage made in the traditional way, with 'crucks', or thick, curved wooden supports. They were placed some yards apart within holes in the ground so that they leaned towards each other, forming the shape of an A.

The ruined 14th-century **Torthorwald Castle** was once a stronghold of the Carlyle and Kirkpatrick families. In 1544, Lord Carlyle destroyed the castle during a dispute with his sister-in-law.

CAERLAVEROCK
7 miles S of Dumfries on the B725

🏛 Caerlaverock Castle

🐦 Caerlaverock Wildfowl & Wetlands Trust

🏃 Solway Coast Heritage Trail

Think of an old, romantic, turreted medieval castle surrounded by a water-filled moat, and you could be thinking of **Caerlaverock Castle** (Historic Scotland). An earlier castle was built by the Maxwells as their main seat to the southeast of the present castle, but this was soon abandoned in favour of the present site. It dates from the 13th century, and was attacked by Edward I in 1300 during the Wars of Independence. It is triangular in shape, with a turret at two corners and a double turret at the other, where the entrance is located. It was attacked by Covenanters in 1640 and dismantled, though in the early 1600s the then Earl of Nithsdale had some fine courtyard buildings constructed within the walls in the Renaissance style.

Caerlaverock Wildfowl and Wetlands Trust is about three miles west of the castle, and is situated in a 1400-acre nature reserve. Here, a wide variety of wildlife can be observed, including swans and barnacle geese. If you're lucky, you may also come across the extremely rare natterjack toad. There are three observation towers, 20 hides and a wild swan observatory linked by nature trails and screen approaches. There are also picnic areas, a gift shop, refreshments and binocular hire. Some facilities are wheelchair friendly.

The place is on the well-signposted **Solway Coast Heritage Trail**, which stretches from Gretna in the east to Stranraer in the west.

ANNAN

14 miles E of Dumfries, on the A75

🏛 Town Hall 🦜 Edward Irving
🦜 Hugh Clapperton 🏛 Parish Church
🏛 Historic Resources Centre
🎣 Haaf-net fishing 🎬 Solway Viaduct

The picturesque old Royal Burgh of Annan, even though it is a mile from the coast, was once a thriving seaport, and had a boat-building yard. Even today, there is a small, silted up quay on the River Annan. The Burns Cairn stands nearby commemorating the fact that Robert Burns visited here as an excise man.

The predominant stone in the town is red sandstone, epitomised by the handsome **Town Hall** of 1878, which dominates the High Street.

Edward Irving, the founder of the Catholic Apostolic Church, which thrived on elaborate ceremony and a complicated hierarchy of ministers and priests, was born here in 1792. He started his career as a clergyman in the Church of Scotland church in Regent Square, London, and earned a great reputation as a preacher and what we would now call a Pentecostal scholar, for which he was ejected from the Church of Scotland in 1833.

Four years earlier, **Hugh Clapperton** the explorer had been born in the town. At the age of 13, he became a cabin boy on a ship sailing between Liverpool and North America, and later went to the Mediterranean after being press-ganged into the Royal Navy. He died in Nigeria in 1827 while searching for the source of the Niger. His notebooks and diaries have been published under the title *Difficult and Dangerous Roads*. Another Annan man was Thomas Blacklock, born in 1721. He was the first blind man to be ordained a minister in the Church of Scotland. **Annan Parish Church** in the High Street, with its stumpy spire, dates from 1786. The place has associations with the Bruce family, who were Lords of Annandale. In Bank Street is the **Historic Resources Centre**, a small museum that puts on a programme of displays and exhibitions.

Haaf-net Fishing is a means of catching fish that stretches back to Viking times, and it is still carried out at the mouth of the River Annan from April to August each year. The fishermen stand chest deep in the water wielding large haaf nets, which are attached to long wooden frames. In 1538, James V granted the haaf net fishermen of Annan a royal charter. In 1992, the rights of the fishermen were challenged in court by the owners of a time-share development further up the river, but the judge decided that the charter still held good today.

South of the town, at one time, was the **Solway Viaduct**, a railway bridge that connected Dumfriesshire to Cumbria across the Solway Firth. It was opened for passenger trains in 1870, and at the time was the longest railway bridge across water in Britain. In 1881, parts of the bridge were damaged when great ice flows smashed into its stanchions. The then keeper of the bridge, John Welch, plus two colleagues, remained in their cabin on the bridge as the lumps of ice, some as big as 27 yards square, careered into the bridge's supports. At 3.30 in the morning, when disaster seemed imminent, they were ordered to leave. Two lengths of the bridge, one 50 feet long, and one 300 feet long, collapsed into the firth, and 37 girders and 45 pillars were smashed beyond repair. However, unlike the Tay Bridge disaster, there was no loss of life. Finally, in 1934, the bridge was dismantled, and all that is left to see nowadays are the approaches on both shores, and a stump in the middle of the water.

RUTHWELL
10 miles SE of Dumfries off the B724

🏛 Ruthwell Cross   🏛 Savings Bank Museum

Within the Parish Church of 1800 is the famous 18-feet-high **Ruthwell Cross**. It dates from about 800AD when this part of Scotland was within the Anglian kingdom of Northumbria. The carvings show scenes from the Gospels, twining vines and verses from an old poem called *The Dream of the Rood*, at one time thought to have been written by Caedmon of Whitby.

In 1810, the Rev Henry Duncan founded the world's first savings bank in the village. The original Ruthwell Parish Bank is now home to the **Savings Bank Museum** (see panel below). The 18th-century building houses a collection of early home savings boxes, coins and bank notes from many parts of the world.

POWFOOT
13 miles SE of Dumfries on a minor road off the B724

Today Powfoot is a quiet village on the Solway coast. But in the late 19th and early 20th century plans were laid to make it a grand holiday resort with hotels, formal gardens, woodland walks, a promenade, a pier, golf courses and bowling greens. The whole scheme eventually collapsed, though some of the attractions were actually built. Now the village is famous for its red brick housing and terraces, which look incongruous on the shores of the Solway, but wouldn't look out of place in Lancashire.

Savings Bank Museum

Ruthwell, Dumfries DG1 4NN
Tel: 01387 870640
e-mail: info@savingsbankmuseum.co.uk
website: www.savingsbankmuseum.co.uk

Dr Henry Duncan was an accomplished artist and some of his work is displayed in the museum, but he is best remembered as the man who identified the first fossil footprints in Britain. Minister of the Ruthwell parish church for 50 years, he opened the world's first commercial savings bank in 1810. The museum also houses a large collection of early home savings boxes, coins and bank notes from many parts of the world. Open 10am-1pm and 2pm-5pm, Tuesday to Saturday 1st October to Easter and every day Easter to 30th September. Admission free.

🏛 historic building 🏛 museum and heritage 🏛 historic site 🜨 scenic attraction 🌿 flora and fauna

EASTRIGGS

18 miles E of Dumfries on the A75

🏛 Eastriggs Heritage Project

A huge government works manufacturing explosives and gunpowder once stretched from Longtown in the east to Annan in the west, a total of nine miles. The **Eastriggs Heritage Project**, in St John's Church on Dunedin Road, traces the lives of the 30,000 workers who manufactured what Sir Arthur Conan Doyle called The Devil's Porridge. At its height, the whole complex employed more than 30,000 people from all over the United Kingdom.

GRETNA GREEN

23 miles E of Dumfries off the M74

🏚 Old Toll House   🏚 Old Blacksmith's Shop

This small village, just across the border from England, is the romance capital of Britain. In the 18th century, it was the first stopping place in Scotland for coaches travelling north, so was the ideal place for English runaways to get married.

In 1754, irregular marriages in England were made illegal, and the legal age at which people could get married without parental consent was set at 21. However, this didn't apply in Scotland, and soon a roaring trade in runaway marriages got underway in the village. The actual border between Scotland and England is the River Sark, and one of the places where marriages took place was the **Old Toll House** (now bypassed by the M74) on the Scottish side of the river. Another place was Gretna Hall. Dating from 1710, this is now a hotel.

But perhaps the most famous was the **Old Blacksmith's Shop**, built in about 1712. A wedding ceremony in front of the anvil became the popular means of tying the knot, and the

Anvil Priests, as they became known, charged anything from a dram of whisky to a guinea to conduct what was a perfectly legal ceremony. By 1856, the number of weddings had dropped, due to what was called the Lord Brougham Act, which required that at least one of the parties to the marriage had to have been resident in Scotland for the previous 21 days. This act was only repealed in 1979.

However, couples still come from all over the world to get married before the anvil in Gretna Green, though the ceremony is no more than a confirmation of vows taken earlier in the registry office. The Old Blacksmith's Shop is still open, and houses an exhibition on the irregular marriage trade.

Gretna Green was within the Debatable Lands, a stretch of land that, as its name implies, was claimed by both Scotland and England. It was therefore a lawless area in the 15th and 16th centuries, as no country's laws were recognised, and no one could adequately police it.

About a mile to the southwest is the Lochmaben Stone, a huge rock where representatives from the two countries met to air grievances and seek justice. It is also sometimes known as the Clochmaben Stone, Maben being a shadowy figure associated with King Arthur.

In the nearby village of Gretna is the Gretna Gateway Outlet Village, a complex of shops selling designer label fashions.

ECCLEFECHAN

14 miles E of Dumfries on the B7076

🏚 Carlyle's Birthplace

This small village's rather curious name means the church of St Fechan or Fechin, a 7th-century Irish saint. Within it you will find **Carlyle's Birthplace** (National Trust for

Scotland), where Thomas Carlyle, the celebrated historian, essayist and sage, was born in 1795. Called The Arched House, it was built on the main street by Thomas's father and uncle, who were both master masons. The three rooms of the museum contain many of Carlyle's possessions and provide a fascinating insight into 19th-century life in a small Scottish town. The birthplace has been open to the public since 1883, and

Thomas Carlyle's Birthplace Museum

has changed very little in that time, so gives an authentic insight into a Victorian household.

DALTON
9 miles E of Dumfries on the B7020

🏺 Dalton Pottery

This little village has picturesque cottages dating from the mid 1700s. The parish church dates from the late 19th century, though the remains of an earlier church, with some medieval fragments, stands in the kirkyard. Half a mile west, on a minor road, is **Dalton Pottery**, which sells a range of porcelain giftware. Young and old alike can also have fun decorating pots and tiles using ceramic felt-tipped pens, which are fired in a small kiln and ready to take away the same day. You can also throw a pot on a wheel, though you have to return to collect it some time later.

KIRKCONNEL (KIRTLEBRIDGE)
17 mile E of Dumfries off the M74

🎭 Fair Helen of Kirkconnel Lee

In the kirkyard of the ruined Kirkconnel Church are said to be the graves of **Fair Helen of Kirkconnel Lee** and her lover Adam Fleming. Their story is a romantic one, and has been celebrated in a famous ballad.

Helen Irving was loved by two men, Adam Fleming and a man named Bell (whose first name isn't known) of nearby Bonshawe Tower. Helen found herself drawn towards Adam, and Bell was consumed with jealousy. He therefore decided to kill his rival. He waylaid the couple close to the kirkyard, and pulled out a pistol. As he fired, Helen threw herself in front of her lover, and was shot dead. There are two versions of the story after this. One says that Adam killed Bell where he stood, and another says he pursued him to Madrid, where he killed him. Either way, he was inconsolable, and joined the army. But he could never forget Helen, and one day he returned to Kirkconnel, lay on her tombstone, and died of a broken heart. He was buried beside her. It's a poignant tale, but there is no proof that the events actually took place.

KIRKPATRICK FLEMING
20 miles E of Dumfries off the M74

🏛 Robert the Bruce's Cave

This pleasant little village is visited mainly to see **Robert the Bruce's Cave**, where the great man is supposed to have seen the industrious spider, though similar claims are made for other caves in both Scotland and

Ireland. It is known that Sir William Irving hid Robert the Bruce here for three months while he was being hunted by the English.

CANONBIE
26 miles E of Dumfries on the B6357

🏛 Gilnockie Castle 🐎 Johnnie Armstrong

🏛 Gilnockie Tower

Canonbie means the town of the canons, because a priory once stood here. The English destroyed it in 1542, and some of the stones may have been used in the building of Hollows Bridge across the River Esk, Scotland's second fastest flowing river. This is the heart of the Debatable Lands, and was a safe haven for reivers. Beyond the bridge, and marked by a stone and plaque, is the site of **Gilnockie Castle**, home of **Johnnie Armstrong**, one of the greatest reivers of them all. So much of a threat was he to the relationship between Scotland and England that James V hanged him in 1530. The story goes that Johnnie and his men were invited to a great gathering at Carlanrig in Teviotdale where they would meet the king, who promised them safe passage. Taking him at his word, Johnnie and a band of men set out. However, when they got there, James had them all strung up on the spot. Perhaps the most amazing aspect of this tale is that the king was no world-weary warrior, but an 18-year-old lad at the time.

Gilnockie Tower, which dates from the 16th century, was a roofless ruin until 1980, but now it houses a small museum and Clan Armstrong library.

The Scots Dyke, two miles south of the village, was erected in the 16th century in an attempt to delineate the boundary between Scotland and England. It consists of a dyke, or low, earthen wall, and an accompanying ditch.

NEW ABBEY
6 miles S of Dumfries on the A710

🏛 Sweetheart Abbey 🎭 Lady Devorgilla

🏛 New Abbey Corn Mill

🏛 Shambellie House Museum of Costume

This attractive little village sits in the shadow of The Criffel, an 1866-feet-high hill that can be seen from miles around. Within the village you'll find the beautiful red sandstone ruins of **Sweetheart Abbey** (Historic Scotland), which date from the 13th and 14th centuries. It was founded for the Cistercians in 1273 by Devorgilla, Lady of Galloway, in her own right. The story of **Lady Devorgilla** has been told many times, but it remains as touching as ever. In 1230, Devorgilla, daughter of Alan, last of the Kings of Galloway, married John Balliol, a marriage that by all accounts was supremely happy. There were a few setbacks, however. John Balliol managed to offend the powerful Prince-Bishop of Durham and as part of his penance was obliged to finance a hostel for students at Oxford, a modest establishment that his wife later expanded into Balliol College.

John died in 1268 and Devorgilla, grief-stricken, had his heart embalmed, and for the 21 years of her widowhood carried it with her in a casket of silver and ivory. In his memory she founded several religious houses, amongst them Dulce Cor, Sweet Heart, at New Abbey and it was here, in 1289, that she was buried beneath the High Altar together with her husband's heart. Sweetheart Abbey today is one of the finest sights in the country, a romantic ruin of rose-red stone that seems to glow in the setting sun. In its graveyard lies William Paterson, founder of the Bank of England and chief proponent of the Darien Scheme in 1698 (see also Lochmaben).

At the other end of the village is the **New Abbey Corn Mill** (Historic Scotland), dating from the late 18th century. It is in full working order, and there are regular demonstrations on how a water powered mill works. The original mill on the site is thought to have belonged to the monks of Sweetheart Abbey, and the millpond behind the mill is thought to have been constructed by them.

Shambellie House is a large mansion designed by David Bryce on the outskirts of New Abbey, which houses the **Shambellie House Museum of Costume**, part of the National Museums of Scotland. The house and its collection were given to the National Museums in 1977 by the then owner, Charles Stewart, and most of the costumes, which range from Victorian to the 1930s, are now displayed in appropriate settings.

KIRKBEAN
6 miles SW of Dumfries, on the A710

🏠 Arbigland 🐟 John Paul Jones

🐟 Dr James Craik

About two miles south of the village is the estate of **Arbigland**, birthplace in 1747 of the founder of the American navy, **John Paul Jones**. Paul was the son of an Arbigland gardener, and went to sea when he was about 13 years old. The cottage in which he was born is now a small museum.

Kirkbean Parish Church was built in 1776, and inside is a font presented by the American Navy in 1945. To continue the American theme, **Dr James Craik**, Physician General of the United States Army during the American Revolution, was also born on the estate. However, James was not born in the same humble circumstances as John Paul Jones. His father Robert was a Member of Parliament, and owned the estate.

BEESWING
9 miles W of Dumfries, on the A711

This small village was laid out in the 19th century. The only remarkable thing about it is its name. It must be the only village in Scotland that is named after a horse. Beeswing was one of the most famous horses in the mid 1800s. Her finest performance was in the Doncaster Cup, which she won in 1840. A local man won so much money on the race that he opened an inn called The Beeswing, and the village grew up around it.

CROCKETFORD
9 miles W of Dumfries, on the A75

🎞 Elspeth Buchan

It was at Crocketford that the sorry tale of **Elspeth Buchan**, who founded a religious sect called the Buchanites, came to a macabre end. Part of the sect's beliefs was that Elspeth was immortal, and that she could bestow immortality on others by breathing on them. After having been driven out of Irvine, she and her followers headed south towards Dumfriesshire and settled there. Alas, Elspeth disappointed her followers by dying a natural death, and the sect broke up.

But one man, who lived in Crocketford, still believed in her immortality, and that she would rise from the dead. He therefore acquired her body and kept it in a cupboard at the top of the stairs in his cottage, where it gradually mummified. Eventually, he built an extension to the cottage, on the other side of the wall from the fireplace, and kept the corpse there. He even had a small opening cut through the wall so that he could examine the corpse every day to see if it had come alive again. Of course it didn't, but this never shook his belief in her resurrection, and the body remained in the cottage with him until his own death.

Kirkcudbright

- 🐿 Billy Marshall 🏛 Greyfriar's Kirk
- 🏛 MacLellan's Castle 🎨 Harbour Cottage Gallery
- 🏛 Broughton House 🌱 Japanese Gardens
- 📷 Tolbooth 📷 Stewartry Museum
- 🐿 Dorothy L Sayers 🐿 Ronald Searle

Kirkcudbright (pronounced Kirk-coo-bray) is one of the loveliest small towns in Scotland, Its name simply means the kirk of St Cuthbert, as the original church built here was dedicated to that saint. It was an established town by the 11th century, and has been a royal burgh since at least 1455. It sits close to the mouth of the Dee, and is still a working port with a small fishing fleet.

Kirkcudbright was once the county town of Kirkcudbrightshire, also known as the Stewartry of Kirkcudbright. It is a place of brightly painted Georgian, Regency and Victorian houses, making it a colourful and interesting place to explore. This part of Galloway has a very mild climate, thanks to the Gulf Stream washing its shores, and this, as well as the quality of light to be found here, encouraged the founding of an artists' colony. On a summer's morning, the edge between light and shadow can be as sharp as a knife, whereas during the day it becomes diffused and soft, and artists have been reaching for their paints and palettes for years to try and capture these two qualities. Even today, straw-hatted artists can be seen at the harbourside, trying to capture the scene.

It is said that St Cuthbert himself founded the first church here, which was located within the cemetery to the east of the town. Down through the years, gravediggers have often turned up carved stones that belonged

🎭 stories and anecdotes 🐿 famous people 🎨 art and craft 🎪 entertainment and sport 🏃 walks

---

NUMBER ONE B&B

1 Castle Gardens, Kirkcudbright DG6 4JE
Tel: 01557 330540   Fax: 01557 331332
e-mail: enquiries@number1bedandbreakfast.co.uk
website: www.number1bedandbreakfast.co.uk

Number One Bed and Breakfast is a beautifully appointed and recently refurbished family home which is a classical grade B listed building in the heart of the historic and vibrant town of Kirkcudbright. Conveniently located adjacent to the impressive remains of McClellan's Castle in the most historic part of this artist town. Number One is a member of Visit Scotland's Quality Assurance scheme and is proud to be rated a 4 star establishment. Take advantage of your hosts, Anne's, local knowledge, she will make sure your stay encompasses all the wonderful scenic routes in the locality, lovely short walks or for the more adventurous, superb long scenic walks. Parking is available for guests.

---

to it. Within the graveyard is Billy Marshall's Grave. **Billy Marshall** was known as the King of Galloway Tinkers, and the gravestone states that he died in 1792 aged 120 years. Don't be surprised to see coins lying on top of the gravestone. It's supposed to be an old gypsy custom, whereby a passing gypsy or tinker without money could use the coins to buy food. The money nowadays is usually left by tourists, with the main beneficiaries being local children.

The present Parish Church is a grand affair in red sandstone near the centre of the town, and dates from 1838. Parts of a much older

---

BAYTREE HOUSE B&B AND S-C GARDEN STUDIO APARTMENT

Baytree House, 110 High Street, Kirkcudbright DG6 4JQ

Tel: 01557 330824 e-mail: info@baytreekirkcudbright.co.uk web: www.baytreekirkcudbright.co.uk

The pretty harbour town of Kirkcudbright (pronounced 'Kirk-coo-bree') is nestled on the banks of the River Dee estuary as it flows into the Irish Sea. With so many things to do in the area, a pleasant and convenient place to stay is the elegant Baytree House or its self-catering and self-contained Garden Studio.

Baytree House is a beautiful four-star Georgian property conveniently located in the historic High Street. As the High Street is no longer the town's main thoroughfare it is relatively peaceful

compared to St. Cuthbert's and St Mary's Streets. All rooms are spacious and comfortable with views down Castle Street towards MacLellan's Castle and the harbour. Each has ensuite bath and/or shower and is generously equipped. A wide choice of delicious breakfasts is served in the sunny dining room overlooking the pretty garden. The grand and elegant drawing room is wonderfully luxurious, especially during colder months with its roaring open fire.

The self-catering Garden Studio is a pretty hide-away located to the rear of Baytree House with its own private entrance down Palmer's Close. It offers comfortable and secluded self-catering accommodation for two people and consists of a converted 18th century stable building containing a living and sleeping area with ensuite shower room and kitchenette, conservatory and a private garden.

Four Star Rating - Majore Credit Cards Accepted - Free Wi-Fi Access/Laptop loan

Cycle/Bike/Fishing/Golf Storage - Children Welcome - Pets Welcome

---

🏛 historic building 🏠 museum and heritage 🏛 historic site 🔱 scenic attraction 🐦 flora and fauna

SCOTTISH SHOWCASE GALLERY

Riverside Mills, Beaconsfield Place, Kirkcudbright DG6 4DP
Tel: 01557 339 400
e-mail: info@showcasegallery.co.uk   website: www.showcasegallery.co.uk

Situated by the arched bridge, alongside the harbour in this scenic artist's town, is the **Scottish Showcase Gallery**. Riverside Mills is an old storage mill, now refurbished and transformed into a light and spacious gallery on two floors to display all the art to its best advantage. Covering 3,000 sq.ft., the ground floor gallery displays limited edition prints and sells gifts and art materials, whilst the upper floor displays a wide range of original art and craftwork.

The gallery artists are chosen for the quality of their art and, in this sense, it is truly a showcase for the very best of Scottish art, craftwork and printmaking. Though some work is sourced regionally, the majority of the works are from artists based all over Scotland and the Isles. There is no other gallery in Scotland that offers such a diverse and wide-ranging selection of such excellent and interesting works.

Every month we feature an exhibition, either a solo show or a joint show of several artist's work which is specifically themed, for example Highland Art, West Coast Art, Colourists and other such essentially Scottish themes. For more information or an invitation to these exhibition Preview Nights, please visit our website www.showcasegallery.co.uk

The gallery is open from late March until the end of December, 7 days a week, Monday to Saturday from 10am-5pm and on Sundays from 12 noon until 4pm.

church are to be found near the harbour. **Greyfriar's Kirk** is all that is left of a 16th-century Franciscan monastery that stood here, though it has been largely rebuilt over the years. Within it is the grand tomb of Sir Thomas MacLellan of Bombie and his wife Grizzell Maxwell, which was erected in 1597. But the tomb isn't all it seems. The couple's son, in an effort to save money, used effigies from an earlier tomb within what is essentially a Renaissance canopy. The friary is thought to have been founded in 1224 by Alan, Lord of Galloway and father of Devorgilla, who founded Sweetheart Abbey.

Nearby, in Castle Street, are the substantial ruins of **MacLellan's Castle** (Historic Scotland), built by the same Sir Thomas who lies in the Greyfriar's Kirk. It isn't really a castle, but a grand town house. Sir Thomas, who was obviously his son's role model where thrift was concerned, used the stones from the friary as building material. Sir Thomas was a local magnate and favourite of the king who became provost of Kirkcudbright. Look out for the small room behind the fireplace in the Great Hall. Sir Thomas used to hide himself there and listen to what was being said about him in the Great Hall through a small opening in the wall called the Laird's Lug.

Walk up the side of the castle into Castle Bank, passing the whitewashed **Harbour Cottage Gallery**, where there are regular exhibitions of work by local artists, and you arrive at the High Street. This must be one of

FLUDHA GUEST HOUSE

Tongland Rd, Kirkcudbright,
Dumfries & Galloway DG6 4UU
Tel: 01557 331443
e-mail: stay@fludha.com
website: www.fludha.com

"Fludha" stands in a raised and commanding position, looking down over a bend in the river Dee, with eye catching southerly views towards Kirkcudbright with McLellan Castle the main focal point. Located towards the edge of town, with riverside walks and a private drive through 2 acres of grounds makes Fludha feel like a very special place.

Totally renovated by Stephen and Christine Laycock, "Fludha" is the first guest house, B&B or hotel in Dumfries & Galloway to be awarded 5 stars by the Scottish Tourist Board. Fludha has 6 double rooms comprising two twin rooms (one suitable for wheelchair access), 3 double rooms (all with king sized beds) and a king sized suite. All have beautiful en-suite facilities. Evening meals, licensed, free (private) parking, free WiFi and a no children policy.

As well as award winning accommodation Fludha also provides award winning breakfast. After a day "out and about" in Galloway's glorious countryside why not dine in Fludha's elegant surroundings in the evening? Christine's home cooked multiple choice menu will delight even the most discerning of food lovers. All of which is absolutely perfect when accompanied by a glass or two of wine from the quality wine list. With great views south and west over the river from the dining room there is no better place to sit and watch the sun go down.

the most charming and colourful streets in Scotland. The elegant Georgian and Regency houses - some of them quite substantial - are painted in bright, uncompromising colours, such as yellow, green and pink. Auchingool House is the oldest, having been built in 1617 for the McCullochs of Auchengool. **Broughton House**, dating from the 18th century, is now owned by the National Trust for Scotland, and was the home of A E Hornel the artist. He was one of the Glasgow Boys, and died in 1933. The house is very much as it was when he lived there. Behind the house are the marvellous **Japanese Gardens**, influenced by trips that Hornel made to the Far East.

Further along the street is Greengates Close (private), which was the home of Jessie M King, another artist. A few yards further on, the High Street takes a dog leg to the east, and

here stands the early 17th-century **Tolbooth**, which has been refurbished and now houses a museum and art gallery telling the story of the artists' colony. The Queen opened it in 1993. This was the former town house and jail, and John Paul Jones, founder of the American navy, was imprisoned here at one time for murder. He got his revenge in later years when he returned to the town aboard an American ship and shelled the nearby St Mary's Isle, where the seat of the Earl of Selkirk was located and a medieval priory of nuns once stood.

This 'isle' is, in fact, a peninsula, and to confuse matters even further, one of the smaller bays in Kirkcudbright Bay (itself an inlet of the Solway Firth) is called Manxman's Lake, one of the few instances in Scotland of a natural stretch of water being called a lake rather than a loch. A walk up St Mary's Wynd beside the Tolbooth and past the modern school takes you to Castledykes, where once stood a royal castle. Edward I stayed here, as did Henry VI and Queen Margaret after their defeat at the Battle of Towton in 1461 during the Wars of the Roses. James IV used it as a staging post on his many pilgrimages to Whithorn. In St Mary's Street is the **Stewartry Museum**, which has many artefacts and displays on the history of the Stewartry of Kirkcudbright. On the opposite side of the street is the Town Hall, where themed painting exhibitions are held every year.

The town also has its literary associations. **Dorothy L Sayers** set her Lord Peter Wimsey whodunit *Five Red Herrings* among the artists' colony. It's not one of her best, as it over-relies on a detailed knowledge of train times between Kirkcudbrightshire and Ayrshire, and of the paints found on an artist's palette. **Ronald Searle** also knew the town, and he based his St Trinians innocents on St Trinian's School in Edinburgh, attended by the daughters of Kirkcudbright artist W. Miles Johnston.

Kirkcudbright was where the village scenes in the cult movie The Wicker Man were filmed, and indeed many locations in Dumfries and Galloway - and even Ayrshire - stood in for the fictional Summerisles, where the action is supposed to have taken place.

Around Kirkcudbright

TONGLAND
2 miles N of Kirkcudbright on the A711

🏛 Tongland Abbey

The small village of Tongland was once the site of the great **Tongland Abbey**, founded in 1218 by Fergus, Lord of Galloway, and the

scant remains - no more than a medieval archway in a piece of preserved wall - can still be seen in the kirkyard. The abbey's most famous inmate was Abbot John Damien, known as the Frenzied Friar of Tongland, who achieved fame by jumping off the ramparts of Stirling Castle in an attempt to fly like a bird.

Tours are available of Tongland Power Station, the largest generating station in the great Galloway hydroelectric scheme built in the 1930s. Close by is Tongland Bridge, a graceful structure across the Dee designed by Thomas Telford and built in 1805.

LOCH KEN
9 miles N of Kirkcudbright between the A713 and the A762

Loch Ken is a narrow stretch of water almost nine miles long, and nowhere wider than a mile. It was created in the 1930s as the result of the great Galloway hydroelectric scheme, with the turbines being housed in the power station at Tongland, further down the Dee. Other schemes were constructed at Clatteringshaws and Loch Doon.

Loch Ken is a favourite spot for bird watching and sports such as sailing, fishing and water skiing, and round the shores are small nature reserves. Details about using the loch are available from the Loch Ken Marina, off the A713 on the eastern shore. At the Marina you will also find the Loch Ken Water Ski School.

NEW GALLOWAY
17 miles N of Kirkcudbright on the A762

🏛 Scottish Alternative Games 🏛 Kenmure Castle

Though New Galloway is a small village with a population of about 300, it is still a proud royal burgh - the smallest in Scotland, but still

Galloway Forest Park

drama of lonely moorland with fertile, wooded valleys. To the west of New Galloway stretches Galloway Forest Park, the largest forest park in Britain, covering 300 square miles of forested hills, wild and rugged moorland and numerous lochs. It's a vast and beautiful area criss-crossed by waymarked Forestry Commission trails and longer routes, such as the Southern Upland Way. It's also home to a rich variety of fauna, such as feral goats, red deer, falcons and even golden eagles.

A mile to the south, near Loch Ken, are the ruins of **Kenmure Castle**, which belonged to the Gordon family. To say that the building is unlucky would be an understatement, as it has been burnt down three times and rebuilt twice. After the last burning in the 1880s, it was left as a shell.

boasting its own town hall. This picturesque place is a planned burgh, having been laid out in the early 1600s by Viscount Kenmure.

Each year in early August, New Galloway plays host to the **Scottish Alternative Games**. It's a refreshing antidote to all the traditional games held in Scotland, where tossing the caber, throwing the hammer, shot putting and Highland dancing take place. Instead there are sports such as gird and cleek (hoop and stick) racing, hurlin' (throwing) the curlin' stane, snail racing, flingin' the herd's bunnet (throwing the herdsman's bonnet) and tossin' the sheaf.

This part of Kirkcudbrightshire is known as the Glenkens, an area combining the high

BALMACLELLAN
18 miles N of Kirkcudbright off the A712

🕊 Robert Paterson

🥾 Balmaclellan Clog & Shoe Workshop

This attractive little village was the home of **Robert Paterson**, a stonemason who was the model for Old Mortality in Scott's book of the same name. He travelled Scotland cleaning up the monuments and gravestones of the Covenanters, a group of men and women who fought Charles II's attempts to impose bishops on the Church of Scotland. Eventually he left home for good to concentrate on this work, leaving behind a no doubt angry wife and five children. Up to his death in 1800, he continued to travel the country, usually on an old grey pony. A statue of him and his horse sits inside the kirkyard of the whitewashed parish church

Just outside the village you will find **The Balmaclellan Clog and Shoe Workshop**, where 20 styles of footwear are made by hand. Visitors can look round the workshop and see shoes and clogs being made.

ST JOHN'S TOWN OF DALRY
19 miles N of Kirkcudbright on the A713

🏛 Gordon Aisle   🏛 Earlston Castle

St John's Town of Dalry, sometimes known simply as Dalry, lies on the Southern Uplands Way, and is a picturesque Glenkens village with many old cottages. It got its name from the Knights Hospitaller of the Order of St John of Jerusalem, an order of military monks that owned the surrounding lands in medieval times.

Within the village is a curious chair-shaped stone known as St John's Stone. Local tradition says that John the Baptist rested in it. In the kirkyard is the **Gordon Aisle**, part of the medieval church that stood here before the present church of 1832. When a reservoir was created at lonely Lochinvar near Dalry in 1968, the waters of the loch were raised, covering the scant ruins of a castle owned by the Gordons. This was the home of the famous Young Lochinvar, written about by Scott in his famous lines from *Marmion*:

"O, young Lochinvar is come out of the west,
Through all the wide border his steed was the best..."

A cairn by the loch side, which is reached by a narrow track, records the existence of the castle. It was built using stones from the castle ruins.

Earlston Castle, overlooking Earlston Loch to the north of the village, was also a Gordon stronghold. It was the birthplace of Catherine Gordon, later Mrs Catherine Stewart, who befriended Burns and encouraged him to write poetry when she lived in Stair Castle in Ayrshire. She was buried, along with two daughters, in Stair kirkyard in Ayrshire.

CARSPHAIRN
27 miles N of Kirkcudbright on the A713

🏛 Carsphairn Heritage Centre

Close to this quiet village there used to be lead mines. John Loudon MacAdam, the roads pioneer, whose father came from near the village, experimented on his revolutionary road surfaces on what is now the A713 north of the village. The **Carsphairn Heritage Centre** has displays and exhibits on the history of the village.

CASTLE DOUGLAS
9 miles NE of Kirkcudbright off the A75

🎨 Castle Douglas Art Gallery

🦅 Ken Dee Marches Nature Reserve

Castle Douglas is Scotland's food town, and offers real Scottish produce, such as meat, fish, vegetables, baking and drinks in its many small, specialist shops. It is a pleasant town based round what was a small village known as Carlingwark. It was founded in the 18th century by William Douglas, a local merchant who earned his money trading with Virginia and the West Indies. He wanted to establish a thriving manufacturing town based on the woollen industry, and though he was only partly

CROYS HOUSE

Bridge of Urr, Castle Douglas,
Dumfries & Galloway DG7 3EX
Tel: 01556 650237
e-mail: alan.withall@aol.com website: www.croys-lodge.co.uk

Croys is part Georgian built in 1744 with Victorian additions added in 1870 and is run as a small B&B accommodation by Pat and Alan Withall. The property is bounded on the southern side by the river Urr which was fished in days gone by but hasn't been touched for 9 years. and is rich in salmon trout and sea trout in the season. Croys is set in 35 acres of gardens, parkland and pasture, which is the home of rare breeds of sheep, cattle and horses. Free range Tamworth pigs are also kept for the beautiful bacon, sausages and pork - used wherever possible for breakfasts and evening meals.

Accommodation includes one double king size with en suite bathroom; a second double bedroom with a four poster bed has an adjoining twin room with French beds - ideal for two children. These rooms have their own private bathrooms. The halls and dining room have large open log fires which provides something extra during the winter time. Guests have their own sumptuous drawing room where they can enjoy the peace and quiet of Croys to the full. TVs are available in the bedrooms.

There is an original walled garden which has been restored to its former glory and provides the source of fresh fruit and vegetables used in the preparation of food for the house.

In addition to Croys House, Croys Lodge also stands on the estate and provides a very comfortable self catering lodge house that sleeps six. See website for further details.

---

successful, he did lay the foundations for a charming town where some of his original 18th-century buildings can still be seen.

On the edge of the town is Carlingwark Loch, where crannogs (dwellings built on artificial islands) have been discovered. It was joined to the River Dee in 1765 by Carlingwark Lane, a narrow canal. Marl, a limey clay used as manure, was dug from the bed of the loch and taken down river to Kirkcudbright on barges.

In Market Street is the **Castle Douglas Art Gallery**, gifted to the town in 1938 by the artist Ethel Bristowe. It hosts a continuing programme of painting, sculpture and craft exhibitions.

Northwest of the town, the **Ken Dee Marches Nature Reserve** follows the woodland and marshes along the River Dee and Loch Ken.

THREAVE CASTLE
8 miles N of Kirkcudbright, close to the A75

🏛 Threave Castle

On an island in the River Dee stand the magnificent ruins of **Threave Castle** (Historic Scotland), reached by a small ferry that answers the call of a bell on a jetty on the riverbank. The castle was built by Archibald Douglas, 3rd Earl of Douglas - known as Archibald the Grim - soon after he became Lord of Galloway in 1369. It was Archibald's father, the Good Sir James, who died while on his way to the Holy Land with the heart of Robert the Bruce (see also Melrose, Cardross and Dunfermline). When Archibald the Grim died at Threave in 1400, he was the most powerful man in southern Scotland, and almost independent of the king, Robert III. It

---

🏛 historic building 🏛 museum and heritage 🏛 historic site ⚜ scenic attraction 🌿 flora and fauna

Threave Estate and Gardens

Castle Douglas, Dumfries & Galloway, DG7 1RX
Tel: 01556 502575 Fax: 01556 502683
Ranger/natural ist: tel (01556) 503702
e-mail threave@nts.org.uk website: www.nts.org.uk

Threave Garden is delightful in all seasons. At 26 ha (64 a), it is best known for its spectacular springtime daffodils (nearly 200 varieties), but herbaceous beds are colourful in summer and trees and heather garden are striking in autumn. The Victorian house is home to the Trust's School of Practical Gardening. The principal rooms in **Threave House** opened to the public for the first time in 2002 and have attracted great interest ever since. The interiors have been restored to their appearance in the 1930s, and from the house visitors can enjoy impressive vistas of the Galloway countryside. Guided walks. Maxwelton Collection of local bygones in the Visitor Centre on show. Plant Centre.

Threave Estate is a wildfowl refuge and is designated a Special Protection Area for its breeding waders and wintering wildfowl. The important wetlands are designated an Area of Special Scientific Interest. Threave provides a good example of integrated management of the land, taking account of agriculture, forestry and nature conservation. Marked walks include a 2.5 km estate trail through this variety of landscapes, and hides provide good cover to observe bird activity. A Countryside Centre in the old stables highlights nature conservation, forestry and agriculture at Threave.

was Archibald's son, also called Archibald, who married Princess Margaret, daughter of Robert III. When James II laid siege to the castle in 1455 to curtail the power of the Douglases, it took two months before the occupants finally surrendered.

THREAVE GARDENS

7 miles NE of Kirkcudbright, on the A75

🌱 Threave Gardens & Estate

Threave Gardens and Estate (National Trust for Scotland - see panel above)

surround a house built in 1872 by William Gordon, a Liverpool businessman. In 1948, the estate was given to the National Trust for Scotland by William's grandson. The gardens were created from scratch, and now house the Trust's School of Practical Gardening. The house itself is open to the public, with its interiors restored to how they would have looked in the 1930s when the place was owned by the Gordon family. The Maxwell Collection of local bygones is on display within the visitor centre.

🎭 stories and anecdotes 🦢 famous people 🎨 art and craft 🎭 entertainment and sport 🚶 walks

KIPPFORD

10 miles NE of Kirkcudbright off the A710

The tides in the Solway Firth are among the fastest in Britain, but this hasn't prevented the picturesque village of Kippford from becoming a great yachting centre. It was once a thriving port and fishing village, and it even had its own shipyard. Like its neighbour Rockcliffe, five miles away, it was also once a smuggling village.

PALNACKIE

10 miles NE of Kirkcudbright on the A711

- World Flounder Tramping Championships
- North Glen Gallery   Orchardtown Tower

This small, attractive village on the west bank of the Water of Urr is a mile from the sea, though at one time it was a thriving port. However, the meanderings of the river meant that ships were usually towed upstream by teams of horses. Each year, in summer, it hosts one of the most unusual competitions in Great Britain - the annual **World Flounder Tramping Championships**, held at the end of July. People come from all over the world to compete, making it a truly international event. The object is to walk out barefoot onto the mud flats south of the village at low tide, feeling for the flounders hiding beneath the mud with your toes as you go. The person who collects the largest weight of flounders wins the championship. It may seem a light-hearted and eccentric competition, but it has a firm basis in local history, as this was once a recognised way of catching fish.

The **North Glen Gallery** features glassblowing and interior and exterior design. It is also a good place to get advice on local walks and wildlife.

A mile southwest of the town is

Orchardton Tower, the only round tower house in Scotland; it dates from the middle of the 15th century, and was built by a John Cairns. In the 17th century it passed to the Maxwells, one of whose members, Sir Robert Maxwell, was on the losing side at the Battle of Culloden. He was wounded, captured and taken to Carlisle for execution. However, among his papers was his commission in the French Army. As a result he was treated as a prisoner of war and later sent to France. He eventually returned to Orchardton, and his story became the inspiration for Sir Walter Scott's novel *Guy Mannering,* or *The Astrologer.*

DALBEATTIE

11 miles NE of Kirkcudbright on the A711

- Dalbeattie Museum   Dalbeattie Granite Garden
- Buittle Castle & Bailey   Old Buittle Tower
- Lt William Murdoch   Motte of Urr
- Robert The Bruce   Scree Hill

This small town stands just east of the Water of Urr, which at one time was navigable as far up-river as here. Ships of up to 60 tons could make the six-mile trip from the open sea beyond Rough Island, pulled by teams of horses. Now the Pool of Dalbeattie (the name given to the port area) is derelict, and the river has silted up.

Dalbeattie was a planned town, founded in the 1790s as a textile centre by two landowners - George Maxwell and Alexander Copland- who sold feus, or tenancies, to various people so that they could build houses. Close by there were easily worked deposits of granite, which also provided employment. The granite was of high quality, and was used in the building of Sydney Harbour Bridge, Liverpool Docks and the Thames Embankment.

In Southwick Road you'll find the

Dalbeattie Museum, which has displays and exhibits about the history of the town. It has a particularly fine collection of Victoriana. Within Colliston Park is the **Dalbeattie Granite Garden**, designed by Solway Heritage to celebrate the beauty of the stone and the workers and craftsmen who mined it.

On the west bank of the Urr, about a mile from the town, is all that remains of **Buittle Castle and Bailey**, home to John Balliol, son of Devorgilla.

Robert I established a burgh here in 1325, and a recent archaeological dig has revealed that the castle's large bailey (an enclosed space next to the castle) may have housed it. A later tower house, the **Old Buittle Tower**, stands close by. It has occasional displays of arms and armour.

On the wall of the former town hall is the Murdoch Memorial to **Lt William Murdoch**, who was the First Officer aboard the Titanic when it sank in 1912. Over the years he has been unfairly accused of being, among other things, a coward who shot passengers attempting to leave the ship. He was also accused of not allowing third-class passengers near the lifeboats and of accepting bribes from first-class passengers to let them board lifeboats to which they were not entitled.

The recent film also treated him unfairly, though the witness statements presented at the later official Board of Trade Enquiry cleared him of all these charges. In 1996 his name was finally and officially cleared of any wrongdoing.

Three miles north of Dalbeattie is the **Motte of Urr**, a 12th-century motte-hill and bailey that is the largest non-industrial man-made hill in Scotland. At its summit, there was once a large, wooden castle, supposedly built by William de Berkeley. It stands close to the Water of Urr, and at one time the river flowed

by on either side, creating an island that was easily defendable. Tradition says that **Robert the Bruce** fought an English knight called Sir Walter Selby at the Motte of Urr. The wife of a man called Sprotte, who at that time lived within the motte, saw the fight, and observed that Selby was gaining the upper hand. So she rushed out and jumped on him, bringing him to his knees in front of the Scottish king.

However, Bruce chose to spare Selby, and both men retired to the woman's house. She produced one bowl of porridge and placed it before Robert, saying that she would not feed an Englishman. However, Robert told her to go outside and run as fast as she could. He would grant her and her husband all the land she could cover. The woman did so, and Robert and Walter finished off the porridge between them. Robert kept his promise, and the Sprottes were granted 20 acres of land. They owned the land for more than 500 years, with the condition that if a Scottish king were to pass by, they were to give him a bowl of porridge.

Five miles southwest of Dalbeattie is **Scree Hill**, with marked walks through forest and woodland to its top, from where there are excellent views.

ROCKCLIFFE
10 miles E of Kirkcudbright on a minor road off the A710

🪶 Rough Island   🏛 Mote of Mark   🚶 Jubilee Path

Rockcliffe was at one time a great smuggling centre, but is now a quiet resort sitting on the Rough Firth, one of the smallest firths in Scotland. Off the coast is **Rough Island** (National Trust for Scotland), a bird sanctuary. It can be accessed at low tide. Close to the village is the great **Mote of**

Mark (National Trust for Scotland), the site of a 5th-century fort. Mark was the king featured in the story of Tristan and Isolde, though there is no proof that the fort was ever his. It is more likely to have been built by a powerful Dark Ages chief.

There are a number of footpaths connecting Rockcliffe with Kippford, the two-mile-long **Jubilee Path** (National Trust for Scotland) being the main one. There is a programme of ranger-guided walks along it in the summer months. Castlehill Point, a mile south of the village on a clifftop, can be reached by a pathway. It has the remains of an old fort.

DUNDRENNAN
4 miles SE of Kirkcudbright on the A711

🏛 Dundrennan Abbey

This quiet village is now visited mainly because of the ruins of the once substantial **Dundrennan Abbey** (Historic Scotland). It was founded in 1142 by David I and Fergus, Lord of Galloway, for the Cistercian monks of Rievaulx in Yorkshire, and was where Mary Stuart spent her last night on Scottish soil in 1568 before sailing for England and her eventual execution. Little of the grand abbey church now remains, though the chapter house and some of the other buildings are well worth seeing, as are some interesting grave slabs.

TWYNHOLM
3 miles NW of Kirkcudbright on the A75

🏛 David Coulthard Museum

Twynholm is the home village of David Coulthard the racing driver, and within the **David Coulthard Museum** in Burnbrae you can learn about the man's life. There is also a gift shop and tearoom.

GATEHOUSE OF FLEET
6 miles NW of Kirkcudbright off the A75

🌿 Cally Gardens   🏛 Mill on the Fleet

🏛 Cardoness Castle   🏛 Anworth Parish Church

This neat little town was the original for the Kippletringan of Scott's *Guy Mannering*. It sits on the Water of Fleet, about a mile from Fleet Bay, and was at one time a port, thanks to the canalisation of the river in 1823 by a local landowner, Alexander Murray of Cally House. The port area was known as Port MacAdam, though the site has now been grassed over. Cally House is now a hotel, though next to it are the **Cally Gardens**, laid out within a two-and-a-half-acre walled garden.

Gatehouse of Fleet was established in the 1760s as a cotton-weaving centre by James Murray of Broughton, and today it remains more or less the way he planned it. He wished to create a great industrial town, though nowadays it is hard to imagine 'dark satanic mills' in such an idyllic setting. Within one of the former cotton mills is a museum, the **Mill on the Fleet**, which tells the story of the town's former weaving industry.

It was supposedly in Gatehouse of Fleet, in the Murray Arms, that Burns set down the words to *Scots Wha Hae*. About a mile west of the town stands the substantial ruins of 15th-century **Cardoness Castle** (Historic Scotland), former home of the McCullochs of Galloway. It stands on a rocky platform above the road, and is open to the public.

The small hamlet of Anworth is just off the A75 to the west of the town. The ruins of the ancient **Anworth Parish Church** can be seen, set in a small kirkyard. The Rev Samuael Rutherford was the minister here in the 17th century. He is best remembered for being exiled from his parish to Aberdeen because of his opposition to a Church of Scotland with

Cairn Holy

bishops. After he was admitted back into the church, he became a professor of theology at St Andrews University.

CAIRN HOLY
11 miles W of Kirkcudbright off the A75

🏛 Cairn Holy 🏛 Carsluith Castle

Cairn Holy (Historic Scotland) comprises two chambered cairns dating from between 2000 and 3000BC. The most remarkable thing about their construction is how our ancestors managed to raise such huge stones. The place is supposed to mark the grave of an ancient, mythical king of Scotland called Caldus. About a mile north of the cairns are the ruins of **Carsluith Castle**, dating from the 16th century. The castle was built by the Browns of Carsluith.

CREETOWN
14 miles NW of Kirkcudbright on the A75

💎 Creetown Gem Rock Museum

🏛 Creetown Exhibition Centre

🎵 Creetown Country Music Weekend

Set at the mouth of the River Cree, the neat village of Creetown was once a centre for the mining of granite. Now it is visited chiefly because of the **Creetown Gem Rock Museum**, housed in a former school. It was established in 1971, and since then has amassed a remarkable collection of gemstones and minerals from all over the world. One of the finest privately-owned collections of gemstones, crystals, minerals and fossils in Britain, its showroom galleries extend over 3000 sq ft and contain almost every known gemstone and mineral from around the world, including huge specimens from the quartz and fluorite crystal groups, exquisite geodes lined with amethyst, agates with spectacular colour bands, opals and even diamonds. There is also a fossilised dinosaur egg and meteorites from outer space.

The **Creetown Exhibition Centre** in St John's Street has exhibits on local history and wildlife, as well as occasional exhibitions by local artists. Over a weekend in September each year, the **Creetown Country Music Weekend** takes place, featuring the best in country music. There is also a street fair, parades and children's activities.

🎬 stories and anecdotes 🐦 famous people 💎 art and craft 🎵 entertainment and sport 🥾 walks

WILLIAM FRASER FAMILY BUTCHER

69 Hanover Street, Stranraer,
Dumfries & Galloway DG9 7RX
Tel: 01776 703469
e-mail: webmaster@gamefowl.co.uk

William Fraser Family Butcher was established way back in 1887 and is now owned and run by William Hall who has himself notched up some 25 years as a butcher. He lives on a small farm just outside the village of Kirkcolm near Stranraer together with his wife and 3 children. "I love my job" he says "and am always willing to learn, teach others, to hear new ideas and be open to new products on the market".

William and his staff make all the products they sell on the premises, and they are all based on the finest of meat. They sell their sausages, black puddings and haggis throughout the UK and Ireland, and also export around the world. In all, about three quarters of a tonne of sausages and burgers are sold *every week*! There are about 10 different varieties of sausages, burgers and haggis, as well as white pudding, fruit pudding and a large selection of cooked pies, ready meals and stir fries. All the beef is sourced at the local market and only the top grades are purchased, including many prize-winning sources. In season, the shop also stocks a wide range of game. Everything is keenly priced and the service is genuinely friendly.

William's shop still occupies the original traditional brick building in which the business started in 1887. It has one of the best window displays of its products you will see in Scotland and the inside walls are adorned with pictures of the past and original owners. "It hasn't changed much over the years" says William, "apart from the colour of the paint".

William took over the business in November 2008 when his father retired. His plans for the future include building new and larger premises to meet the demands of the 21st century and will also be venturing into producing ready meals. He also intends to build a slaughterhouse on his own farm to cut down on expenses and to meet the demand for local produce with full traceability.

Stranraer

- 🏰 Castle of St John 🏰 Old Town Hall
- 🐦 Sir John Ross 🌱 Castle Kennedy Gardens
- 🌱 Glenwhan Gardens

Sitting at the head of Loch Ryan, and on the edge of the Rhinns of Galloway, that hammer-shaped peninsula that juts out into the Irish Sea, Stranraer is a royal burgh and was at one time the only Scottish port serving Northern Ireland. A town of narrow streets and ancient alleyways, Stranraer was granted its royal burgh charter in 1617.

In the centre of the town is the **Castle of St John**, a tower house built by the Adair family in the 16th century. Claverhouse used it as a base while hunting down Covenanters in the area, and it was later used as the town jail. It is now a museum and interpretation centre. There is another museum in the **Old Town Hall**, which explains the history of the town and the county of Wigtownshire.

North West Castle is now a hotel, but at one time it was the home of **Sir John Ross** (1777-

1856), who explored the legendary North West Passage north of Canada connecting the Atlantic and the northern Pacific. He was born near Kirkcolm, son of a minister, and joined the navy at the age of nine, reaching the rank of commander by the time he was 35 years old. On one of his expeditions he discovered the Boothia Peninsula, mainland America's northernmost point. He later served as British consul in Stockholm.

On the sea front is the Princess Victoria Monument, which commemorates the sinking of the car ferry Princess Victoria on January 31 1953. It had left Stranraer bound for Larne with 127 passengers and 49 crew, and on leaving the shelter of Loch Ryan encountered a horrific gale. Though lifeboats were launched, it eventually sank with the loss of 134 lives.

Three miles east of Stranraer are the magnificent **Castle Kennedy Gardens**. They cover 75 acres between two small lochs, and are laid out around the ivy-clad ruins of Castle Kennedy, destroyed by fire in 1710. The 2nd Earl of Stair began creating the gardens in 1733, and being a field marshal under the Duke of Marlborough, he used soldiers to construct some of it. Also within the gardens is the relatively modern Lochinch Castle, the present home of the Earl and Countess of Stair. It is not open to the public.

South of the

Glenwhan Gardens, Stranraer

A75 is Soulseat Loch, where there is good fishing. A narrow peninsula with a few bumps and indentations on it juts out into the water - the site of Soulseat Abbey, of which not a stone now remains above ground. It was founded for the Premonstratensian Order of canons by Fergus, Lord of Galloway, in 1148, and dedicated to St Mary and St John the Baptist.

Three miles beyond Castle Kennedy on the A75, is the village of Dunragit, where you'll find **Glenwhan Gardens**, overlooking beautiful Luce Bay. They were started from scratch in 1979 and now cover 12 acres.

Around Stranraer

CAIRNRYAN
5 miles N of Stranraer on the A77

Cairnryan is strung out along the coast of Loch Ryan. Between the main road and the coast is a complex of car parks, piers, jetties and offices, as this small village is the Scottish terminus of the ferries to Northern Ireland. It was developed as a port during World War II, and had a breaker's yard. It was here that the famous aircraft carrier *HMS Ark Royal* was scrapped.

The Atlantic U-boat fleet surrendered in Loch Ryan in 1945, and were berthed at Cairnryan before being taken out into the Atlantic and sunk.

GLENTROOL
20 miles NE of Stranraer on a minor road that leaves the A714 at Bargrennan

🐦 Glentrool Visitor Centre

It was here, close to the lovely but lonely waters of Loch Trool, that Robert I defeated an English army in 1307, a year after his

coronation. His soldiers had hidden themselves in the hills above the loch and, when the English troops went past, they rolled great boulders down on them before attacking. It was a turning point in the Wars of Independence, as up until then Robert had had little success. Bruce's Stone above the loch commemorates the event. It is said that Bruce rested here after the battle was over. The **Glentrool Visitor Centre**, three miles away, offers information about the surrounding forest walks, and has a small tearoom and gift shop.

GLENLUCE
8 miles E of Stranraer off the A75

🎏 Alexander Agnew   🏛 Glenluce Abbey

The attractive little village of Glenluce has been bypassed by the A75, one of the main routes from southern Scotland and northern England to the Irish ferries at Stranraer and Cairnryan. At one time it was the home of **Alexander Agnew**, nicknamed the "Devil of Luce". He was a beggar who, in the mid 1600s, asked for alms from a weaver named Campbell in the village, but was refused. He thereupon cursed the family and its dwelling, and strange things began to happen. Stones were thrown at their doors and windows when there was no one about, and clothes were ripped from the children's beds as they slept. If this wasn't bad enough, Agnews was heard to say that there was no God but salt, meal and water - a clear case of atheism. He was eventually hanged for blasphemy at Dumfries.

A mile to the northwest are the ruins of **Glenluce Abbey** (Historic Scotland), founded in 1190 by Roland, Lord of Galloway, for Cistercian monks from Dundrennan Abbey. Its best preserved feature is its chapter house. The end came in 1560, with the advent of the Reformation.

However, the monks were allowed to live on within the abbey, the last one dying in 1602. Mary Stuart once visited, as did James 1V and Robert the Bruce.

Castle of Park is an imposing tower house built in about 1590 by Thomas Hay, son of the last abbot of Glenluce. A stone over the door commemorates the event. It is now owned by the Landmark Trust, and used as rented holiday accommodation.

Immediately after the Reformation, the then Earl of Cassillis, head of the great Kennedy family, claimed the property and lands of Glenluce. He persuaded one of the monks to forge the abbot's signature on a document granting him the lands, then had the monk

murdered. He then executed the men who had done the foul deed on his behalf in the name of justice.

NEWTON STEWART

22 miles E of Stranraer on the A75

- 🏛 Newton Stewart Museum
- 🌿 Wood of Cree Nature Reserve
- 🏛 Sophie's Puppenstube & Dolls House Museum

The burgh of Newton Stewart sits on the River Cree, close to where it enters Wigtown Bay. It is a pleasant, clean town, founded in the 17th century by William Stewart, son of the Earl of Galloway. A ford once stood where the present bridge crosses the Cree, and

THE RIVERBANK RESTAURANT - GIFT SHOP

Goods Lane, Newton Stewart,
Dumfries & Galloway DG8 6EH
Tel: 01671 403330
e-mail: kennydawson10@yahoo.co.uk

Overlooking the River Cree, Cairnsmore and the Galloway Forest.

In the restaurant you will find a good selection of main dishes including, Riverbank Haddock, homemade lasagne or the Riverbank " Ultimate" Combo - a tasty chicken combination, or the Chef's Daily Special. Also available:- All day breakfast, home made soup, sandwiches, toasties, panini hot melts, salads and traditional oven-baked potatoes. A special childrens menu is also included. There is a selection of home made sweets and cakes, including home made scones, and a wide choice of teas and coffee's.

The restaurant is licensed, and opens 10.00am to 4.00pm in summer and 10.00am to 3.30pm November to March - Monday to Saturday inclusive. The owners aim to provide a high leve of service for all customers. Staff are trained in house, and a policy of continuous quality control is maintained.

A look in the book and gift shop is well worth including in your visit to the restaurant. The range of gifts include:- clocks, leather goods, ceramics, jewellery, decorative stationery, hand made soap and bath salts, locally made crafts and greeting cards by local artists. The books include a general stock of new and second hand books with an emphasis on Scottish arts and crafts, and countryside plus a good childrens selection. There are also books and pamphlets by local writers and historians. Ordnance survey maps, current road maps and guides are also available. Browsers are welcome.

Larg Hill and Bruntis Loch

Distance: *4.0 miles (6.4 kilometres)*
Typical time: *120 mins*
Height gain: *25 metres*
Map: *Explorer 319*
Walk: *www.walkingworld.com ID:2365*
Contributor: *Tony Brotherton*

ACCESS INFORMATION:

Turn off the A75 at Palnure, three miles east of Newton Stewart, then follow signs for Galloway Forest Park and park in the Kirroughtree Visitor Centre car park. Bus Service 500 runs Monday to Saturday along the A75 between Stranraer and Newton Stewart to the west and Gatehouse of Fleet, Castle Douglas and Dumfries to the east; alight at Palnure and walk the mile or so via Stronord to the visitor centre's car parks.

DESCRIPTION:

When the Scots find a name they like, they tend to use it liberally. Thus in Galloway, there are no

fewer than three mountains which include the name 'Cairnsmore'. Similarly, there are several hills named 'Larg', two of which are within sight of each other; confusingly, one Larg 'Hill' is actually a mountain of over 2,000ft! Set within the Galloway Forest Park, this pleasant walk follows Forestry Commission Scotland's trail around the 'other' Larg Hill, a more modest 561ft (171m). The route starts from Kirroughtree Visitor Centre and is mainly level or of easy gradients and along good paths, tracks and forest roads. It skirts lovely Bruntis Loch and follows the course of a tumbling burn back to the visitor centre. There are occasional views across open countryside and of mountains and the Solway Firth.

FACILITIES

The visitors' centre is open daily from Easter to the end of October, from 10.30 am until 5.30 pm.

FEATURES:

Hills or fells, mountains, lake/loch, sea, toilets, play area, wildlife, birds, flowers, great views, butterflies, café, gift shop, food shop, good for kids, mostly flat, public transport, nature trail, teashop, waterfall, woodland

WALK DIRECTIONS

1 | From car park, walk towards visitor centre but follow 'forest walks' sign to pass behind white Daltamie House and locate start of various forest trails indicated by three posts. We are to follow 'blue' trail today. Take rising woodland path and presently an isolated building will appear on left.

2 | Further on, path momentarily runs alongside Old Military Road before veering right and left into woodland, then joining road.

3 | Now walk right along road. Ignore rising forest road off to right, marked 'no unauthorised vehicles', then take this next turn right.

4 | Where track comes in from right, bear left past blue-banded post.

5 | Continue along woodland track to bench-seat and a view across country to Newton Stewart. Further along track is a view towards larger Larg Hill and other mountains of the Minnigaff Group.

6 | Carry on and go right as per arrow, onto forest road. Hereabouts is your glimpse of sea.

7 | Continue along road, passing by turn-off signed to Auchlannochy. Further on, look for a turn-off left. Follow descending path through trees and at crossing forest road, where to go right leads to Little Bruntis Loch, we turn left. Through trees, Cairnsmore of Fleet (2,231ft - 711m) may be seen here.

8 | Route follows road until a turn-off right. (Tracks, paths etc for this and following three points are not marked on map, so just keep following blue-banded marker-posts).

9 | Path leads along to a road, where you again turn right. Along the road, Bruntis Loch may be glimpsed through trees to left; turn down path to reach its shore. Tired? Rest awhile on a handy perch, courtesy of John Crosbie; several more such seats are secreted throughout Galloway Forest Park, part of its commissioned art programme. Further opportunity to rest is provided by a picnic table-seat at the southern end of Bruntis Loch.

10 | To continue, drop down on path and turn left (repeat, left) along track, soon to follow this delightful burn.

11 | Branch right at a marker-post and rejoin Brunton Burn by this waterfall.

12 | Finally, return to start via 'all walkers path to car parks' command and reward yourself with refreshments and array of cakes at visitor centre and gift shop!:

it was used by pilgrims to Whithorn and St Ninian's shrine. **Newton Stewart Museum** is within a former church in York Road, and has displays and exhibits about the history of the town and immediate area. In Queen Street you'll find an unusual but internationally known little museum called **Sophie's Puppenstube and Dolls House Museum**, which has 50 beautifully made doll's houses and room settings. The scale is 1:12, and all the exhibits are behind glass. There is also a collection of more than 200 exquisitely dressed dolls.

The **Wood of Cree Nature Reserve** is owned and managed by the Royal Society for the Protection of Birds, and lies four miles north of the town on a minor road running parallel to the A714. It has the largest ancient woodland in Southern Scotland, and here you can see many birds including redstarts, pied flycatchers and wood warblers. There is a picnic area and nature trails.

Six miles west of Newton Stewart is the picturesque village of Kirkcowan, which has a church dating from 1834 with external stairs to the gallery.

WIGTOWN
23 miles E of Stranraer on the A714

🏛 Martyrs Graves   ⚗ Bladnoch Distillery

🏛 Torhouse Stone Circle

This small royal burgh has achieved fame as being Scotland's Book Town, and has many bookshops and publishing houses. The focus for book activity, apart from the shops, are the County Buildings of 1863, During the two book fairs held here every year - one in May and one in September - many of the readings, talks and events take place within the County Buildings.

In the kirkyard of Wigtown Parish Church are the remains of the medieval church, dedicated to St Machuto, who is known in France as St Malo, and who gave his name to

HILLCREST HOUSE

Maidland Place, Wigtown,
Dumfries & Galloway DG8 9EU
Tel: 01988 402018
e-mail: info@hillcrest-wigtown.co.uk
website: www.hillcrest-wigtown.co.uk

At the Hotels of the Year Awards, 2008, the judges commented that: "**Hillcrest House** is today operated by Deborah and Andrew Firth who have over the last 2 years developed their own style of hospitality. Expect the informal and even a touch of Bohemian; also confidently expect terrific eating based to a remarkable degree on local to very local produce. It's not a posh place but is rather full of character." The house was built in 1875 and retains much of its original Victorian character and charm, with open views over Wigtown Bay Nature Reserve - Britain`s largest local nature reserve, and it's only a leisurely stroll to both the harbour and the town centre with its many bookshops.

The accommodation at Hillcrest comprises 6 spacious, airy, comfortably furnished and individually decorated rooms. All have thermostatically controlled heating, colour TV, complimentary Fairtrade hot drinks and biscuits, radio/CD player, bathrobes and hairdryer.

Breakfast at Hillcrest is definitely something to look forward to. You can have anything from porridge, the full Scottish, to a poached egg on toast or anything in between. Finish with toast and locally made jam or marmalade. Evening meals are available by arrangement.

---

the French port. Also in the kirkyard are the **Martyrs Graves**. In 1685, during the time of the Covenanters, two women - one aged 18 and one aged 63 - were tied to stakes at the mouth of the River Bladnoch for adhering to the Covenant and renouncing Charles as the head of the church. Rather than give up their principles, they drowned as the tide rose over their heads. The spot where the martyrdom took place is marked by the small Martyrs Monument on what are now salt marshes. On a small hill behind the town is another Covenanters Monument, this time a slender column.

One mile west of the town is **Bladnoch Distillery**, Scotland's most southerly whisky distillery. There is a visitor centre and shop, and guided tours are available showing the distilling process.

Four miles west of the town, reached by the B733, is the Bronze Age **Torhouse Stone Circle**, built around 1500 to 2000BC. It consists of 19 boulders forming a circle, with three other boulders in a line within. It is of a type more commonly found in Aberdeenshire and northeast Scotland.

CHAPEL FINIAN
16 miles SE of Stranraer on the A747

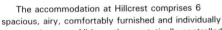
Old Place of Mochrum

Beside the road that runs along the western shore of The Machars, the name given to that great peninsula that sticks out into the Irish Sea between Luce and Wigtown Bays, you'll find the foundations of a small church. The most interesting thing about them is their

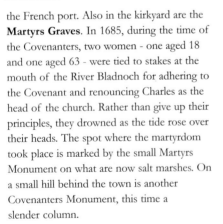

great age, as they probably date from the 10th century. Later on the chapel was probably used as a stopping off point for people making a pilgrimage to St Ninian's Shrine at Whithorn, 12 miles to the southeast. The chapel was dedicated to St Finian of Moville who lived during the 6th century and founded a great monastic school in Northern Ireland where St Columba studied.

Old Place of Mocrum, Chapel Finian

Four miles inland from the chapel, and reached by a minor road off the A7005, is the **Old Place of Mochrum**, on the northern edge of lonely Mochrum Loch. It was originally built in the 16th century by the Dunbar family, and was restored by the Marquis of Bute between 1876 and 1911. The gardens are particularly fine.

MONREITH
23 miles SE of Stranraer on the A746

🐾 Animal World & Gavin Maxwell Museum

This small village lies on Monreith Bay. The ruins of the old church of Kirkmaiden-in-Fernis can still be seen, the chancel now a burial place for the Maxwells of Monreith.

The **Animal World & Gavin Maxwell Museum** has displays about local wildlife. It is named after Gavin Maxwell, author of *Ring of Bright Water*, who was born at nearby Elrig, which features in his book *The House of Elrig*.

WHITHORN
26 miles SE of Stranraer on the A746

🐦 St Ninian 🏛 Whithorn Priory 🏚 Priory Museum
🏚 Whithorn Visitors Centre 🏚 St Ninian's Cave
🐾 Woodfall Gardens 🐾 Galloway House Gardens
🏛 Cruggleton Church 🏛 St Ninian's Chapel

This tiny royal burgh (no bigger than a village) is often called the Cradle of Scottish Christianity. A century before Columba came

---

MONREITH ARMS HOTEL

3 The Square, Port William, Newton Stewart, Dumfries & Galloway DG8 9SE
Tel: 01988 700232
e-mail: monreitharmshotel@supanet.com
website: www.monreitharms.co.uk

A former coaching inn, the **Monreith Arms Hotel** has been the focal point of Port William for the past 300 years. The hotel has two bars - a public bar, very popular with the locals, and a lounge bar where you can have a quiet drink or a bar meal. Food is available from noon until 2pm, and from 6pm to 9pm (8.30pm in quieter periods). The accommodation comprises 10 newly refurbished bedrooms, each with its own private facilities. There are also 2 special suites with a seating area and luxurious bathroom with Jacuzzi bath.

🎭 stories and anecdotes 🐦 famous people 🎨 art and craft 🎭 entertainment and sport 🐾 walks

to Iona, a monk called **St Ninian** set up a monastery here. He is a shadowy figure who may have been born in either Galloway or Cumbria, the son of a tribal chief. He almost certainly visited Rome, and stayed with St Martin of Tours, whom he greatly admired. Some sources say he died in 432AD.

The monastery would have been a typical Celtic foundation, with a high circular bank, or rath, enclosing an area of monks' cells, workshops and chapels. This monastery was different in one respect, however. The main church was made of stone, not the more common wood, and was painted white. For this reason it was called Candida Casa, or White House. When this part of Scotland was later absorbed into the kingdom of Northumbria, the name was translated into Anglo Saxon as Hwit Aerne, from which Whithorn is derived.

The place was subsequently an important ecclesiastical and trading centre. In the 12th century Fergus, Lord of Galloway, founded **Whithorn Priory** (Historic Scotland), and its church became the cathedral for the diocese of Galloway. All that is left of the priory church is its nave and crypt. To the east of the crypt may be seen some scant foundations that may be all that is left of Ninian's original whitewashed church. The cathedral, with its relics of St Ninian, eventually became a place of pilgrimage, and many Scottish monarchs, especially James IV, made the journey to pray there.

The town's main street, George Street, is wide and spacious, with many small Georgian, Regency and Victorian houses. The Pend, dating from about 1500, is an archway leading to the priory ruins, and above it are the royal arms of Scotland. Close to the priory is the **Priory Museum**

(Historic Scotland), with a collection of stones on which are carved early Christian symbols. One of them, the Latinus Stone, dates from the 5th century, and may be the earliest carved Christian stone in Scotland. Some years ago, excavations were undertaken at Whithorn, and at the **Whithorn Visitors Centre**, owned by the Whithorn Trust, you can learn about the excavations and what was found there.

St Ninian's Cave is on the shore three miles southwest of the town. It has incised crosses on its walls, and a legend states that St Ninian himself came to this cave to seek solitude and to pray. At Glasserton, two miles west of Whithorn, are the **Woodfall Gardens**, covering three acres within an old walled garden. They were laid out in the 18th century by Keith Stewart, second son of the Earl of Galloway. He was an admiral in the British navy when he was given the 2000 acres of the barony of Glassertion in 1767. And at Garlieston, four miles north of the town, are the **Galloway House Gardens**, laid out informally at the ruined Cruggleton Castle, and with walks leading down to the shores of Cruggleton Bay. The medieval **Cruggleton Church** sits by itself in a field, and was built as a chapel for the castle. It was restored in the 19th century by the Marquis of Bute; a key for it is available at nearby Cruggleton farm.

Three miles to the southeast is the tiny fishing village of Isle of Whithorn. On a headland are the 13th-century ruins of the tiny **St Ninian's Chapel**. Though it sits on the mainland, the small area surrounding it may at one time have been an island, giving the village its name. It was probably built for pilgrims to Whithorn Priory who came by sea.

KIRKMADRINE

8 miles S of Stranraer on a minor road off the A716

🏛 Kirkmadrine Stones

In the porch of what was the tiny parish church of Toskerton are the **Kirkmadrine Stones**, thought to be the oldest inscribed stones in Scotland after those at Whithorn. They were discovered when the church was being rebuilt and converted into a burial chamber by a local family, the McTaggarts of Ardwell. Parts of the former medieval church have been incorporated into the burial chamber, though it is thought that there has been a church on this site since the 6th century.

ARDWELL

10 miles S of Stranraer on the A716

🌱 Ardwell Gardens

Ardwell Gardens are grouped round the 18th-century Ardwell House. They feature azaleas, camellias and rhododendrons, and are a testimony to the mildness of the climate in these parts. They include a woodland and a formal garden, as well as good views out over Luce Bay from the pond.

PORT LOGAN

12 miles S of Stranraer on the B7065

🌱 Logan Fish Pond   🌱 Logan Botanic Garden

Port Logan is a small fishing village situated on Port Logan Bay. Close by is the **Logan**

Logan Fish Pond

Port Logan, Stranraer DG9 9NF
Tel: 01776 860300
website: www.loganfishpond.co.uk

The first time visitor to **Logan Fish Pond** is often amazed and surprised by what they see. Not until they enter through the original Fish Keepers Cottage and have their first glimpse of the pond below do they have any idea of what this unique and historic attraction holds.

In 1788 Andrew McDouall Laird of Logan decided to create a Fish Larder for storing live sea fish by adapting a natural rock formation in the form of a blow hole, formed during the last ice-age. The work took 12 years and was finished in 1800. Many visitors return year after year and indeed some have been doing so for fifty or sixty years, feeding the fish today as they remember doing so as children.

In the springtime, the area around the Pond is a carpet of daffodils, primroses and bluebells and later in the year these are replaced with an abundance of wild flowers, including thrift and sea campion.

On the rocks next to the Fish Pond is a restored Victorian Bathing Hut which adjoins a Bathing Pool. Recent additions to the original pond include Touch Pools, Cave Aquarium and Gift Shop. Open 1st February to 30th September 10am to 5pm and 1st October to early November 10am to 4pm. Some disabled access.

🎭 stories and anecdotes 🦜 famous people 🎨 art and craft 🎭 entertainment and sport 🚶 walks

Fish Pond (see panel on page 91), a remarkable tidal pond famous for its tame sea fish, which can be fed by hand. It was constructed in about 1800 as a source of fresh fish for the tables of nearby Logan House.

If anywhere illustrates the mildness of the climate in this part of Scotland, it is **Logan Botanic Garden**, part of the National Botanic Gardens of Scotland. Here, growing quite freely, are exotic plants and trees such as the tree fern (which can normally only survive in glasshouses in Britain), the eucalyptus, palm trees, magnolias and passionflowers. In fact, more than 40% of all the plants and trees at Logan come from the southern hemisphere. Within the garden is the Discovery Centre, which gives an insight into the plants that grow here.

The village achieved national fame when the TV series *Two Thousand Acres of Sky*, supposedly set on a Hebridean island, was filmed in and around Port Logan.

KIRKMAIDEN
15 miles S of Stranraer on the B7065

🏠 Kirkmaiden Information Centre

Kirkmaiden is Scotland's most southerly parish. Four miles south of the village is the Mull of Galloway, Scotland's most southerly point. It comes as a surprise to some people when they learn that places like Durham in England are further north. The lighthouse was built in 1828 to the designs of Robert Stevenson, and sits on the massive cliffs, 270 feet above the sea. In Drummore, half a mile to the east of the village, is the **Kirkmaiden**

Coast near Portpatrick

The Harbour, Portpatrick

round a little harbour that is always busy and, with its old cottages and craft shops, has become a small holiday resort.

On a headland to the south of the village are the ruins of **Dunskey Castle**, built in the early 16th century by the Adair family. The recently re-established **Dunskey Garden and Woodland**

Information Centre, which has displays and exhibitions about the area.

PORTPATRICK
6 miles SW of Stranraer on the A77

🏚 Dunskey Castle 🏚 Portpatrick Parish Church

🐦 Dunskey Garden & Woodland Walk

This lovely little village is at the western end of the Southern Upland Way. At one time it was the main Scottish port for Northern Ireland, but was in such an exposed position that Stranraer eventually took over. It sits

Walk is well worth visiting. Every Wednesday afternoon in summer, there are guided tours conducted by the gardener. Within the village is the ruined **Portpatrick Parish Church**. It was built in the 17th century, and unusually, has a round tower.

Built as a hunting lodge in 1869 by Lady Hunter Blair, Knockinaam Lodge stands to the south of the village. It is now a hotel, but it was here, during the closing stages of World War II, that Churchill and Eisenhower planned the Allied strategy.

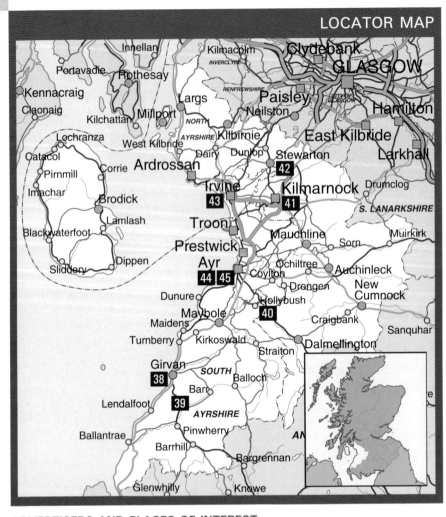

LOCATOR MAP

ADVERTISERS AND PLACES OF INTEREST

Accommodation, Food and Drink

Arts and Crafts

Place of Interest

Specialist Food and Drink Shops

🏛 historic building 🏚 museum and heritage 🏛 historic site ◔ scenic attraction ❧ flora and fauna

3 | Ayrshire & Arran

Ayrshire was at one time Scotland's largest Lowland county. Facing the Firth of Clyde, it is ringed by moorland and hills, which slope down to a rich agricultural patchwork of small fields, country lanes, woodland and picturesque villages. The poet Keats, when he made his pilgrimage in 1818 to the birthplace of Robert Burns in Alloway, compared its scenery to that of Devon. Indeed, in places you almost feel you are in an English rural landscape.

The county was formerly divided into three parts. Carrick is the most southerly, and owes a lot to neighbouring Galloway. It is separated from Kyle, a rich dairying area where the native Ayrshire cattle can be seen dotting the fields, by the River Doon. To the north, beyond the River Irvine, is Cunninghame, which at one time was the most industrialised of the three, though it managed this without losing too much of its rural aspect.

Kyle itself was divided by the River Ayr into Kyle Regal and Kyle Stewart, reflecting the fact that one section was ruled directly by the king, while the other was ruled by high stewards of Scotland, who eventually went on to be kings in their own right.

Ayrshire and Robert Burns, known to all Scottish people as Rabbie (never, ever Robbie!) are inextricably linked. He was born in Alloway, which nowadays is a prosperous suburb of Ayr, and spent the first 29 years of his life in the county before moving south to Dumfriesshire. We know a lot about the man, and all the places in Ayrshire where he lived, drank, courted and caroused are well signposted. A full week could easily be spent meandering along the main roads and narrow lanes of the county, visiting such towns and villages as Tarbolton, Mauchline, Ayr, Kilmarnock, Irvine, Failford and Kirkoswald. Every year in May, the Burns an' a' That Festival takes place throughout Ayrshire to celebrate his life and work. Venues include pubs, concert halls, theatres, museums and churches. The most spectacular concert is held out of doors at Culzean Castle.

There are three main towns in the county - Ayr, Kilmarnock and Irvine. Irvine is the largest, though it was not always so. In the 1960s, it was designated a

Culzean Castle

new town, and took an overspill population from Glasgow. Industrial estates were built, factories were opened and new housing established. However, its central core is still worth exploring. Kilmarnock is traditionally the industrial centre, though it is an ancient town, and Ayr was the administrative and commercial capital

Holy Island from Dippin Head, Isle of Arran

before Ayrshire ceased to exist as a local government unit in the 1970s.

Up until the 1960s, when more exotic places took over, the Ayrshire coast was Glasgow's holiday playground. Known as the Costa del Clyde, it attracted thousands of people each year who flocked to such holiday resorts as Troon, Largs, Prestwick, Girvan and Ayr itself. Those halcyon days are gone, though it is still a popular place for day trips and for people to retire to, giving it a new nickname - the Costa Geriatrica. The coastline is also famous for golf. The first British Open Golf Championship was held at Prestwick in 1860, and both Troon and Turnberry have regularly hosted the tournament in modern times.

Ayrshire is also a county of castles, from the spectacular Culzean (pronounced Cull-ane) perched on a cliff top above the sea, to Kelburn near Largs or Dean Castle in Kilmarnock, with its collection of rare musical instruments.

The Ayrshire coalfield used to employ thousands of people, though nowadays not a single deep mine remains. But even at its height, the industry never did as much damage to the environment as in, say, South Yorkshire or the Welsh valleys. Now you would never suspect that the industry ever existed at all, and a day just motoring round the quiet lanes is a relaxing experience in itself.

Twenty miles offshore is the island of Arran, at one time within the county of Bute, but now more associated with Ayrshire. It has been called "Scotland in Miniature", and is a wonderful blend of wild scenery, pastoral views and rocky coastlines. Its history stretches right back into the mists of time, as the many standing stones and ancient burial cairns testify. It is properly part of the Highlands, and Gaelic used to be the predominant language. A ferry connects it to Ardrossan on the Ayrshire coast.

Also within Bute were two other islands - Great and Little Cumbrae. Little Cumbrae is largely uninhabited, apart from one or two houses, but on Great Cumbrae is the town of Millport, a gem of a holiday resort. Within Millport is another gem - Cumbrae Cathedral, the smallest cathedral in Britain. A short ferry crossing from Largs takes you to the island.

Maybole

🏛 Parish Church 🏛 Town Hall 🏛 Maybole Castle
🗺 Electric Brae

This small, quiet town is the capital of Carrick, and sits on a hillside about four miles inland from the coast. It was here that Burns's parents, William Burnes (he later changed the name to Burns) and Agnes Broun met in 1756.

In 1562, a famous meeting took place in Maybole between John Knox, the Scottish reformer, and Abbot Quentin Kennedy of nearby Crossraguel Abbey. The purpose of the meeting was to debate the significance and doctrine of the mass, and it attracted a huge crowd of people, even though it was held in a small room of the house where the provost of the town's collegiate church lived. Forty people from each side were allowed in to hear the debate, which lasted for three days. It only broke up - with no conclusion reached - when the town ran out of food to feed the thronging masses round the door.

The ruins of Maybole Collegiate Church (Historic Scotland) can still be viewed, though they are not open to the public. The church, dedicated to St Mary, was founded by Sir John Kennedy of Dunure in 1371 for the saying of daily prayers for himself, his wife Mary and their children. The clergy consisted of one clerk and three chaplains who said the prayers. The present ruins date from a rebuilding in the 15th

century, when it became a full collegiate church with a provost and a 'college' of priests. The present **Parish Church** dates from 1808, and has an unusual stepped spire.

At one time Maybole had no less than 28 lairds' town houses, each one referred to as a castle. Now there are only two left, one at each end of the main street. The 'upper' one is now part of the **Town Hall**, and was the 17th-century town house of the lairds of Blairquhan Castle, about five miles to the east. The other is still referred to as **Maybole Castle** though it too was a town house, this time for the Earls of Cassillis. The largest and finest of the 28 town houses, it dates from the mid 1500s and was built in traditional Scottish Baronial style with a square tower and round turrets.

A few miles west of Maybole on the A719 road between Ayr and Turnberry, near the farm of Drumshang, is the curiously named **Electric Brae**. Stop your car on the convenient layby at the side of the road, put it out of gear, let off the brake, and be amazed as it rolls uphill. Better still, lay a football on the layby's surface, and watch it roll uphill as well. The phenomenon has

Maybole Castle

🎬 stories and anecdotes 🦢 famous people 🎨 art and craft ✏ entertainment and sport 🚶 walks

nothing to do with electricity, ley lines, earth magic, the unseen world of the earth's energy system or the same power displayed by poltergeists when they move objects, but everything to do with an optical illusion. The surrounding land makes you think that the road rises towards the west when in fact it descends.

Around Maybole

KIRKMICHAEL
3 miles E of Maybole on the B7045

🏛 Parish Church   🏛 International Guitar Festival

Like its neighbour Crosshill, Kirkmichael is a former weaving village. However, its roots lie deep in Scottish history. The **Parish Church** dates from 1790, and the picturesque lych-gate from about 1700. Within the kirkyard is the grave of a Covenanter called Gilbert MacAdam, shot in 1686 by Archibald Kennedy.

Every May, Kirkmichael is the scene of the **International Guitar Festival**, which draws musicians from all over the world. It covers everything from jazz to pop and country to classical. Huge marquees are erected, and local

pubs host impromptu jamming sessions and folk concerts. It was founded by the internationally renowned jazz guitarist Martin Taylor, who lives locally.

DALMELLINGTON
11 miles E of Maybole on the A713

🏛 Dunaskin Open Air Museum

🏛 Dalmellington Iron Works   🏛 Brickworks

🏛 Scottish Industrial Railway Centre

🏛 Cathcartson Centre   🏛 Loch Doon Castle

This former mining village sits on the banks of the Doon. Over the past few years, it has exploited its rich heritage, and created some visitor centres and museums that explain the village's industrial past. The **Dunaskin Open Air Museum** covers 110 acres and has many facets, each of which is well worth exploring. The **Dalmellington Iron Works** were first opened in the 1840s, and are now the largest restored Victorian Ironworks in Europe. Other attractions include the **Brickworks** and the **Scottish Industrial Railway Centre**, where steam trains run on a restored track. The **Cathcartson Centre** in the village is housed in weaving cottages dating from the 18th century and shows how weavers lived long ago.

Dalmellington is the starting point for the new Scottish Coal Cycle Route, which runs from Dalmellington to Coalburn, 40 miles away in Lanarkshire. It is part of the National Cycle Network.

A couple of miles beyond Dalmellington is a minor road that takes you to lovely Loch Doon, surrounded by lonely

Loch Doon Castle, Dalmellington

hills and moorland, and the source of the river that Burns wrote about. It was here, during World War I, that a School of Aerial Gunnery was proposed. Millions of pounds were wasted on it before the plans were finally abandoned. When a hydroelectric scheme was built in the 1930s, the water level of the loch was raised. **Loch Doon Castle**, which stood on an island in the loch, was dismantled stone by stone and reassembled on the shore, where it can still be seen.

In the late 1970s, it was announced that 32 deep tunnels would be bored in the hills surrounding the loch to store most of Britain's radioactive waste. After many protests by local people, the idea was abandoned.

CROSSHILL
3 miles SE of Maybole, on the B7023

Crosshill is a former handloom-weaving village established in about 1808 with many small, attractive cottages. Many of the weavers were Irish, attracted to the place by the prospect of work. There are no outstanding buildings, nor does it have much history or legend attached to it. But it is a conservation village with a quiet charm, and well worth visiting because of this alone. Some of the original cottages built by the Irish immigrants in the early 1800s can still be seen in Dalhowan Street.

STRAITON
6 miles SE of Maybole on the B741

🐟 Nick o' the Balloch	🏛 Blairquhan
🏛 Hunter Blair Monument	

A narrow road runs south from this lovely village called the **Nick o' the Balloch**. It doesn't go through the Carrick of gentle fields or verdant valleys, but over the wild hills and moorland that make the edges of

this area so beautiful, and finally drops down into Glentrool.

Straiton itself sits beside the water of Girvan, and has picturesque little cottages facing each other across a main street, some with roses growing round the door. It was a planned village, laid out in 1760 by the Earl of Cassillis on the site of a small hamlet. The local pub, The Black Bull, dates from 1766, while parts of St Cuthbert's Parish Church date back to 1510.

Close to the village is **Blairquhan** (pronounced Blair-whan), a Tudor-Gothic mansion built between 1821 and 1824 to the designs of the famous Scottish architect William Burn. It stands on the site of an earlier tower house dating from 1346 that was once a McWhirter stronghold before passing to the Kennedys. It is now owned by the Hunter Blair family, and is open to the public in summer. It has a fine collection of paintings by the Scottish Colourists. On a hill above the village stands the **Hunter Blair Monument**, built in 1856 to commemorate James Hunter Blair, killed at the Battle of Inkerman.

Many of the scenes in the film *The Match* (also called *The Big Game*) were shot in Straiton, which became the fictional Highland village Inverdoune.

OLD DAILLY
9 miles S of Maybole on the B734

🏛 Old Dailly Parish Church	🖋 William Bell Scott
🌿 Bargany House	🏛 New Dailly Parish Church
🏛 Dalquharran Castle	

Old Dailly was originally called Dalmakerran, and was once an important village, with many cottages, a manse for the minister and a mill. Now it is a row of council houses close to the ruins of 14th-century **Old Dailly Parish Church**. Within the kirkyard are two hefty

stones called the Charter Stones, which men used to try to lift during trials of strength.

Buried in the kirkyard is the pre-Raphaelite artist **William Bell Scott**, who was staying at nearby Penkill Castle (private) when he died. Many members of the pre-Raphaelite Brotherhood visited the place, including Dante Gabriel Rossetti. Close by is the 17th-century fortified mansion **Bargany House**, once a Kennedy stronghold. The house is private, but the marvellous gardens are open to the public for a few weeks in late spring/early summer.

Three miles to the east is the mining village of New Dailly with its T-shaped **New Dailly Parish Church** of 1766. Close by, on the opposite side of the Girvan Water, are the substantial ruins of **Dalquharran Castle**. It was designed by Robert Adam and built between 1780 and 1791 for Kennedy of Dunure. The castle is currently being renovated with plans to turn it and its estate into a luxury hotel and golf resort, with Jack Nicklaus designing the golf course. The ruins of the 15th-century Old Dalquharran Castle are close by.

BARR

11 miles S of Maybole on the B734

🏠 Laird of Changue

Tucked in a fold of the Carrick hills, Barr is an idyllic village that was once the site of the wonderfully named Kirkdandie Fair. It was the largest annual fair in southern Scotland during the late 18th and early 19th century, and was held on a strip of land where Kirkdandie (or Kirkdominae) Church once stood. Its main claim to fame was the fighting that took place there every year, and it soon became known as the Donnybrook of Scotland. People even came over from Ireland to participate in the great pitched

battles. So famous did it become that a ballad was written about it, describing at least 63 tents, the sound of pipes and people socialising, dancing, drinking and eating.

Above Barr is the estate of Changue (pronounced Shang), to which an old legend is attached. The cruel and wicked **Laird of Changue** was a smuggler and distiller of illicit whisky who enjoyed the fruits of his own still a bit to much, and was therefore always penniless. One day, while walking through his estates, Satan appeared and offered him a deal. If he handed over his soul when he died, he would become rich. The laird, who was a young man, agreed, and duly prospered. But as he grew older he began to regret his rashness, and when Satan at last appeared before him to claim his soul - at the same spot where he had appeared all those years before - the laird refused to keep his side of the bargain.

Instead he challenged the Devil to fight for it. Drawing a large circle on the ground round both of them, he said that the first person to be forced out of it would be the loser. After a bitter struggle, the laird cut off the end of Satan's tail with his sword, and he jumped out of the circle in pain. The laird had won. Up until the end of the 19th century, a great bare circle on some grassland was shown as the place where all this took place. It's a wonderful story, but no one has ever managed to put a name or date to this mysterious laird. And it has often been pointed out that if Satan had bided his time, he would have had the soul of the laird in the usual way, so wicked was he.

COLMONELL

19 Miles S of Maybole on the B734

🏠 Kirkhill Castle

The River Stinchar is the southernmost of Ayrshire's major rivers, and flows through a

lovely glen bordered on both sides by high moorland and hills. In this valley, four miles from the sea, sits Colmonell. It's an attractive village of small cottages, with the romantic ruins of the old Kennedy stronghold of **Kirkhill Castle** standing next to the village hall. Knockdolian Hill, two miles west, was at one time called the false Ailsa Craig because of its resemblance to the volcanic island out in the Firth of Clyde.

BALLANTRAE
22 miles S of Maybole on the A77

🏠 Bargany Aisle 🏠 Ardstinchar Castle
🏠 Glenapp Castle

When on a walking tour of Carrick in 1876, R L Stevenson spent a night in Ballantrae, a small fishing village. However, dour villagers took exception to his way of dressing, and almost ran him out of town. He got his revenge by writing *The Master of Ballantrae*, which confused everyone by having no connection with the place whatsoever.

In the churchyard is the **Bargany Aisle**, containing the ornate tomb of Gilbert Kennedy, laird of Bargany and Ardstinchar, who was killed by the Earl of Cassillis (also a Kennedy) in 1601. A bitter feud between the Cassillis and Bargany branches of the Kennedy family had been going on right through the 16th century, with no quarter given or taken. Matters came to a head when the two branches met near Ayr, and Bargany was killed. The power of the Bargany branch was broken forever, and the feud fizzled out. The ruins of **Ardstinchar Castle**, Bargany's main stronghold, can still be seen beside the river. It was built in 1421, and in August 1566, Mary Stuart stayed there.

Glenapp Castle, a few miles south of the

village just off the A77, was designed in 1870 by the noted Victorian architect David Bryce for James Hunter, the Deputy Lord Lieutenant of Ayrshire. It is now a luxury hotel surrounded by 30 acres of grounds and gardens.

LENDALFOOT
18 miles S of Maybole on the A77

🏠 Sir John Carleton 🏠 Sawney Bean

Carleton Castle, now in ruins, was the home of **Sir John Carleton,** who, legend states, had a neat way of earning a living. He married ladies of wealth, then enticed them to Gamesloup, a nearby rocky eminence, where he pushed them to their deaths so inheriting their money. Sir John went through seven or eight wives before meeting the daughter of Kennedy of Culzean. After marrying her, he took her to Gamesloup, but instead of him pushing her over, she pushed him over, and lived happily ever after on his accumulated wealth. It is said that you can still occasionally hear the screams of the women as they were pushed to their death.

But if it's a gruesome tale you're after, then you should head for Sawney Bean's Cave, a few miles south of the village, on the shoreline north of Bennane Head, and easily reached by a footpath from a layby on the A77. Here, in the 16th century, lived a family of cannibals led by **Sawney Bean** (Sawny being Scots for Sandy), which waylaid strangers, robbed them, and ate their flesh. They evaded capture for many years until a troop of men sent by James VI trapped them in their cave. They were taken to Edinburgh and executed. It's a wonderful story, but no documentary proof has ever been unearthed to prove that it really happened.

KIRKOSWALD
4 miles SW of Maybole on the A77

🏛 Kirkoswald Parish Church 🏛 Church of St Oswald

🏛 Souter Johnnie's Cottage

It was to Kirkoswald, in 1775, that Burns came for one term to learn surveying. Though his poem *Tam o' Shanter* is set in Alloway, all the characters in it have their origins in the parish of Kirkoswald, which was where his maternal grandparents came from.

Kirkoswald Parish Church dates from 1777, and was designed by Robert Adam while he was working on Culzean Castle. Dwight D Eisenhower worshipped here twice, one of the occasions being when he was president of the United States. Another visitor is not so well known, though the airline he helped to found is. The late Randolph Fields, together with Richard Branson, founded Virgin Airlines. Randolph loved this part of Ayrshire, and when he died in 1997, he left some money for the restoration of the church. A year later his widow presented the church with a small table, on which is a plaque commemorating his donation.

The old parish **Church of St Oswald** stands at the heart of the village. It is a ruin now, but it was here, in 1562, that Abbot Quentin Kennedy of Crossraguel Abbey preached forcefully against the Reformation and in favour of the sacrifice of the mass. He challenged anyone to debate the matter with him, and John Knox, who was in the area, agreed to take him on. They met in nearby Maybole, where the two of them debated over three days without resolving the issue. In its kirkyard are the graves of many people associated with Burns, including David Graham of Shanter Farm near Maidens, the real life Tam o' Shanter.

The church also contains one interesting relic - Robert the Bruce's Baptismal Font. Both Lochmaben in Dumfriesshire and Turnberry Castle, within the parish of Kirkoswald, claim to have been the birthplace of Robert the Bruce. Turnberry is the more likely, as it was the ancestral home of the Countess of Carrick, Bruce's mother, and it is known that she was living there at about the time of his birth. The story goes that the baby was premature, and was rushed to Crossraguel Abbey for baptism in case he died. When Crossraguel was abandoned after the Reformation, the people of Kirkoswald rescued the font and put it in their own church.

Within the village you'll also find **Souter Johnnie's Cottage** (National Trust for Scotland). John Davidson was a souter, or cobbler, and featured in *Tam o' Shanter*. Now his thatched cottage has been turned into a small museum. One room at the back of the cottage is given over to the souter's workshop, complete with fire and all the tools needed for shoemaking. At the other end of the cottage is a room re-creating aspects of the parlour, with a large dresser and fire, and a bedroom complete with box beds along one wall.

CROSSRAGUEL ABBEY
2 miles SW of Maybole, on the A77

🏛 Crossraguel Abbey 🏛 Baltersan Castle

The romantic ruins of **Crossraguel Abbey** (Historic Scotland) sit complacently beside the main Ayr-Stranraer road. They are very well preserved, and give a wonderful idea of the layout of a medieval abbey. Some of the architecture and stone carving, such as that in the chapter house, is well worth seeking out. Duncan, Earl of Carrick, founded it in 1244 for Clunaic monks from Paisley Abbey, though most of what you see nowadays dates

Crossraguel Abbey

son of the Lord of Annandale, and she persuaded him to marry her. The result of the marriage was Robert the Bruce, who himself became Earl of Carrick on his mother's death. Because Robert ascended the throne of Scotland as Robert I, the earldom became a royal one, and the present Earl of Carrick is Prince Charles.

Built onto the scant ruins of the castle is

from after the 13th century. The name is supposed to come from an old cross that stood here before the abbey was built, and it may mean the regal, or royal cross, or the cross of Riaghail, possibly a local chief.

To the north are the ruins of **Baltersan Castle**, an old fortified 16th-century tower house built either for John Kennedy of Pennyglen and his wife Margaret Cathcart, or as the residence of Quentin Kennedy, the Abbot of Crossraguel from 1548 until 1564.

TURNBERRY
7 miles SW of Maybole on the A719

🏚 Turnberry Castle 🏚 Turnberry Lighthouse

Very little now survives of the 12th-century **Turnberry Castle,** where Robert the Bruce is supposed to have been born. The story of how his parents met is an unusual one. Marjorie, Countess of Carrick, the young widow of Adam de Kilconquhar, saw a knight passing by her castle at Turnberry. She immediately became infatuated with him, and had him kidnapped and brought into her presence. He turned out to be Robert de Brus,

Turnberry Lighthouse, surrounded on three sides by the championship golf course. The elegant five star Turnberry Hotel is situated southeast of the castle, just off the main road, and is one of the premier hotels in Scotland. It even has its own small runway for aircraft, and at one time had its own railway line from Ayr to bring guests to the hotel. During World Wars I and II, all this area was an airfield, and the runways can still be seen. There is a War Memorial on the golf course dedicated to the men of the airfield who died in World War I. It is in the shape of a double Celtic cross, and was erected by the people of Kirkoswald parish in 1923. In 1990, the monument was altered so that the names of the airmen killed during World War II could be added.

GIRVAN
10 miles SW of Maybole on the A77

🐦 Ailsa Craig 🏚 Auld Stumpy

🌿 Knockcushan Gardens 🎨 McKechnie Institute

This pleasant little town is the main holiday resort in Carrick. It is also a thriving fishing port, with many boats in the harbour at the

THISTLENEUK BED & BREAKFAST

19 Louisa Drive, Girvan,
South Ayrshire KA26 9AH
Tel: 01465 713044
e-mail: anderson.thistleneuk@talktalk.net

Located just one hundred yards from the sea front and a sandy beach, **Thistleneuk Bed & Breakfast** offers comfortable accommodation in a relaxing atmosphere. Owner Morag Anderson arrived here in 2005 and extends a warm welcome to all her guests. The house has 6 attractively furnished and decorated guest bedrooms, all with en suite facilities and TV. Three of the rooms enjoy sea views. There's plenty to see and do in the area with trout or deep sea fishing, and horse riding available locally, as well as coastal walks and cycle routes.

PEINN MOR POTTERY

The Old School, Pinmore, By Girvan,
Ayrshire, Scotland KA26 0TR
Tel: 01465 841662
e-mail: info@peinnmor.co.uk
website: www.peinnmor.co.uk

Peinn Mor Pottery and Gallery is the home and studios of potters, Keith and Beryl Dawdry, at the former village school in Pinmore.

Keith works on the wheel to throw distinctive functional and decorative items. Beryl makes unique figurative pieces and striking handbuilt vessels. They use coloured slips and glazes throughout the making process to produce wonderful surfaces.

The Gallery displays an ever-changing selection of their work along with ceramics by their son and daughter in law, Simon and Clare. Peinn Mor Pottery is 4 miles south of Girvan, clearly signposted just off the A 714. The Gallery is open all year, Wednesdays to Sundays, 11am – 5pm. Outwith these times, by appointment. Please phone ahead if coming far. Plenty of off road parking.

© Andy Aitchison / Ashden Awards

mouth of the Water of Girvan. Though there is a long, sandy beach, a boating pond and a small funfair in summer, the town is a quiet place overlooked by the bulk of Byne Hill to the south. From the top there is a fine view of the Firth of Clyde, and on a clear day the coast of Northern Ireland can be seen. The small Crauford Monument above Ardmillan House, on the western side, commemorates Major A C B Crauford, who took part in the capture of the Cape of Good Hope in 1795.

Out in the Firth of Clyde, the bulk of **Ailsa Craig** rises sheer from the water. It is the plug of an ancient volcano, and is now a bird sanctuary. Trips round it are available from Girvan harbour.

Within the town, in Knockcushan Street, is a small, curious building with a short spire that has been given the nickname **Auld Stumpy**. It was built in the early 1800s as the town jail with cells on the first, second and third floors of the building, with a clock tower above.

Exhibits in the tower include a 16th-century wrought iron cannon and police memorabilia.

Behind Knockcushan House, near the harbour, are **Knockcushan Gardens**, the site of a court held by Robert the Bruce in 1328. There is a memorial commemorating this event as well as an aviary.

At the **McKechnie Institute** in Dalrymple Street art exhibitions are sometimes held.

CULZEAN CASTLE
4 miles W of Maybole off the A719

🏰 Culzean Castle   🌳 Culzean Country Park

🏛 Eisenhower Presentation

Culzean Castle (National Trust for Scotland), perched on a cliff above the Firth of Clyde, is possibly the most spectacularly sited castle in Scotland. It was designed by Robert Adam in 1777 and built round an old keep for the 10th Earl of Cassillis. It has some wonderful features, such as the Oval Staircase and the Circular Saloon with its views out over the Firth. Surrounding the castle is **Culzean Country Park** whose attractions include a walled garden, the swan pond, the deer park and the fountain court.

In gratitude for his part in World War II, the National Trust for Scotland presented General Eisenhower with the life tenure of a flat in Culzean. Eisenhower accepted, and spent a few golfing holidays here. The **Eisenhower Presentation**, within the castle, explains his connections with the area, and has exhibits about D-Day.

On the shoreline are the Gasworks, which produced coal

Culzean Castle

Croy to Maidens via Culzean Country Park

Distance: *3.4 miles (5.4 kilometres)*
Typical time: *120 mins*
Height gain: *0 metres*
Map: *Explorer 326 Ayr & Troon*
Walk: *www.walkingworld.com ID:799*
Contributor: *Joice and Dougie Howat*

Take the A719 south from Ayr. Soon after Croy Brae take the road to the right to Croy Beach. There is a choice of parking either at the top or bottom of the hill. Ideally this is a one-way walk, so drop your passengers at the top of this road and they can walk to the lower car park, while a second car is taken to the finish location at Maidens. To drive to the finishing car park, continue south on the A719. Turn right at the T-junction (towards Culzean Country Park). Continue past the park entrance to Maidens. At a sharp 90-degree bend in the road to the left, take the small road to the right. The car parking is along this road.

The walk can easily be altered to become a circular walk should this be preferred. Once you reach the swan pond in Culzean Country Park (Waymark 9) take any of the paths signposted towards the Home Farm, then return along the coast.

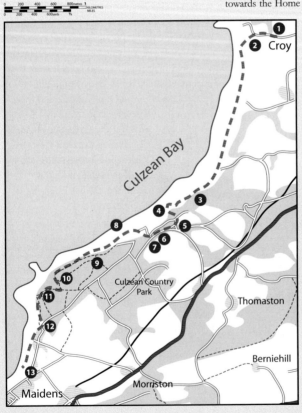

ADDITIONAL INFORMATION:

This walk is good for kids and other features include woodland and a country house. It is worth stopping in the lay-by at Croy Brae. The road here is an optical illusion. Going south the road looks as though it is downhill, when in fact it is uphill. Take your foot off the break and see the car freewheel the wrong way!

DESCRIPTION:

A coastal walk which takes in part of the rugged headland by Culzean Castle (a National Trust for Scotland property). Starting outside the park boundaries at Croy Shore, the walk takes you along the coast to reach the castle. This can be seen from a long distance away, sitting high up on the headland with its impressive vantage point. Having passed through the ornamental gardens of the castle, the walk continues back down onto the shore. As some of the bays are very rocky (and under water at high tide), the walk turns inland to take in the cliff walk within the park boundaries. This path has magnificent views to the west and south - on a good day both the Mull of Kintyre and Northern Ireland can be seen from the section of path (not to mention the nearer island of Arran).

FEATURES:

Sea, pub, toilets, museum, play area, castle, National Trust/NTS, wildlife, birds, flowers, great views

WALK DIRECTIONS:

1 | Leave the top car park and follow the road down to the lower car park. Wait here for the drivers to join you.

2 | Turn left onto the beach at the shore car park. Walk along the beach until you reach some small cottages which are right on the shore at Seganwell.

3 | There are steps here which lead upto the Culzean Home Farm with restaurant, shop and toilets. However, the coastal walk continues in woodland parallel to the shore.

4 | At the next bay take the path away from the shore, past the Gas House and Gas Keeper's Cottage. There are interesting exhibits here, showing how the gas was made in the past to light the castle. The coast becomes very rocky here so it is worth entering Culzean Park; the entry is free from the coast. Follow the path up through the trees towards the castle. At the top of the steps, this is the view back towards Croy and the start of the walk. Follow the path to the right towards the castle.

4 | Branch left towards the castle's forecourt. There are toilets and a shop in the old stables. The castle is also worth a visit, but it takes some time and there is a charge to the Scottish National Trust. Take the gate to the left of the castle and follow the path along the side.

6 | Descend the steps to the gardens and Fountain Court. The Orangery always has interesting flowers, protected from the frost. Continue through the gardens in a southerly direction.

7 | Continue south through a gap in the wall, into a grassy field. There are many routes through the park. All will take you towards Maidens if you chose southerly directions. Cut across the field directly towards the sea, to reach some wooden steps. Follow the wooden steps down past the cannons, to the boathouse beach and past the Dolphin House.

8 | Turn left and continue along the coast in a southerly direction. Take care as you will need to pick your way over some rocks at the end of this bay. Continue along the next bay to reach another set of wooden steps. Take the steps and wooden walkway through the marshy area, back to a T-junction on a well-trodden path. Turn right and follow the path.

9 | Turn right again at the 'Cliff Walk' sign. This path is high above the sea, with magnificent views. The path eventually turns inland and descends to the Swan Pond.

10 | Turn to the right at the side of the pond, but only walk a few metres, to reach a junction with a smaller path off to the right. Now leave the main path for a smaller one signposted 'Port Carrick, Barwhin Hill'. Alternatively, continue on the main path to toilets and a children's play area.

11 | Take the fork to the left which leads down to the beach, out of the park to Maidens Shore.

12 | Follow the path down to reach the shore. Turn left and continue along the beach to reach Maidens car park.

13 | The end of the walk and hopefully where you have a car dropped off to take you back. Nearby is the Wildings Hotel, should its services be required.

gas to heat and light the castle. The caves beneath the castle were at one time used by smugglers. A recent archaeological dig unearthed human bones dating from the Bronze Age, showing that the caves have been occupied for thousands of years. However, access to them is barred, as they can be dangerous.

DUNURE
5 miles NW of Maybole off the A 719

🏛 Dunure Castle 🎭 Roasting of the Abbot

This pretty little fishing village would not look out of place in Cornwall. Arriving by car, you drop down towards it, getting excellent views of the cottages and pub, all grouped round a small harbour.

To the south of the village are the ruins of **Dunure Castle**, perched on the coastline. This is the original castle of the Kennedys, and dates mostly from the 14th century. It was here that the famous **Roasting of the Abbot** took place in 1570. The Kennedys were at the height of their powers, and Gilbert Kennedy, 4th Earl of Cassillis, owned most of the land in Carrick. He was, as his contemporaries observed, 'ane very greedy man', and coveted the lands of Crossraguel Abbey, which, at the Reformation, had been placed in the hands of Allan Stewart, as commendator, or lay abbot, of the abbey. Gilbert invited Allan to Dunure Castle for a huge feast, and when Allan accepted, had him incarcerated in the Black Vault. He then stripped him and placed him on a spit over a great open fire, turning him occasionally like a side of beef. Eventually, Allan signed away the lands, and was released. He immediately protested to the Privy Council and the Regent (James VI was still a child at the time), ordered Kennedy to pay for the lands.

Such was Kennedy's power that he ignored the order.

Ayr

🏛 Town Hall	🏛 Auld Parish Kirk		
🏛 Tam o' Shanter Inn	🏛 Auld Brig o'Ayr		
🏛 Loudoun Hall	🏛 Lady Cathcart's House		
🏛 Newton Tower	🌿 Belleisle Estate & Gardens		
🖼 Rozelle House Galleries	🏛 Greenan Castle		
🎠 Ayr Racecourse			

Ayr is the major holiday resort on the Ayrshire coast. It stands at the mouth of the River Ayr, on the south bank, and was formerly the county town of Ayrshire. Always an important place, it was granted its royal charter in the early 1200s, and is the old capital of the Kyle district. Its most distinctive feature is the tall, elegant steeple of the **Town Hall**, built

St John's Tower, Ayr

between 1827 and 1832 to the designs of Thomas Hamilton. Seen from the north, it blends beautifully with the a cluster of fine Georgian buildings beside the river.

After the Battle of Bannockburn, Bruce held his first parliament here, in the ancient kirk of St John the Baptist, to decide on the royal succession after he died. The kirk is no longer there except for the tower, now called St John's Tower, which stands among Edwardian villas near the shore. Oliver Cromwell dismantled the church and used the stone to build Ayr Citadel, which has now gone as well, save for a few feet of wall near the river and an arch in a side street. To compensate, he gave the burgh £600 to build a new church, which is now known as the **Auld Parish Kirk**, situated on the banks of the river where a friary once stood. It dates from the mid 1600s, and is a mellow old T-plan building surrounded by tottering gravestones. Within the lych gate can be seen a couple of mortsafes, which were placed over fresh graves to prevent grave robbing in the early 1800s.

Ayr was the starting off point for Tam o' Shanter's drunken and macabre ride home after spending the evening at an inn, as portrayed in Burns's poem of the same name. In the High Street is the thatched **Tam o' Shanter Inn**, where the inebriated cobbler was supposed to have started his journey. At one time the pub was a small museum, but now it has reverted to its original purpose, and you can enjoy a drink within its walls, which are adorned with quotations from the great poet. A few yards from the pub stands the William Wallace Tower, which commemorates the Scottish patriot who was imprisoned in the town in 1297 for setting fire to a barn with 500 English soldiers inside.

Robert Burns and Ayr are inseparable. He was born in a village to the south of the town, which has now become a well-heeled suburb, and his influences are everywhere. Off the High Street is the **Auld Brig o' Ayr**, which dates from the 14th century, and down river is the New Bridge, dating from 1878. In a poem called *The Twa Brigs*, Burns forecast that the Auld Brig would outlast the new one. He was right - the New Bridge of Burns's time was swept away in a flood, to be replaced by the present New Bridge, while the Auld Brig still survives.

The second oldest building in the town is **Loudoun Hall**, in the Boat Vennel close to the New Bridge. It was built about 1513 as a fine town house for the Campbells of Loudoun, hereditary sheriffs of Ayr. It was due for demolition just after the war, but was saved when its importance was realised. South of Loudoun Hall, in the Sandgate, is **Lady Cathcart's House**, a tenement building that dates from the 17th century. Within it, in 1756, John Loudon McAdam, the roads engineer, is believed to have been born.

The bridges of Ayr take you to Newton upon Ayr on the north bank of the river, which was once a separate burgh with a charter dated from 1446, but now part of the town. Part of its old Tolbooth survives as **Newton Tower**, now on an island in the middle of the street.

The **Belleisle Estate and Gardens** are to the south of the town, with parkland, deer park, aviary and pets corner. Nearby is **Rozelle House Galleries and Gardens**. There are art exhibitions within the mansion house, plus a tearoom and craft shop.

Also south of the town, perched precariously on a cliff top and always seeming to be in imminent danger of collapsing into the sea, is **Greenan Castle**, a 17th-century tower house. It was built in 1603 for John Kennedy of Baltersan and his third wife Florence MacDowell, who owned the lands of Greenan. It is typical of many such tower houses in Ayrshire, but some experts believe it has one unique claim to fame - it may mark the real spot where King Arthur's Camelot once stood.

Ayr Racecourse is Scotland's leading racecourse, and is the venue for the Scottish Grand National in April and the Scottish Derby in July.

Around Ayr

PRESTWICK
2 miles N of Ayr town centre, on the A79

🏛 Elvis Presley	🏛 Parish Church of St Nicholas
🏛 Bruce's Well	

Prestwick is one of the oldest towns in Scotland, having been granted its original burgh charter in the 12th century. It was also one of the most popular holiday resorts for Glaswegians until Spain and Florida took over, and has a long, sandy beach.

To the north of the town is Prestwick International Airport, at one time the main transatlantic airport for Glasgow. It is still a busy place, being a favourite starting point for those holidays in warmer climes that eventually saw off Prestwick as a holiday resort. On March 2 1960, the airport had possibly its most famous visitor - **Elvis Presley**. Having been discharged from the American army, his plane touched down at the airport for refuelling when he was returning home from Germany. He stayed at the American air force base (now gone) for just under an hour, and then re-boarded his

flight. It was the only time that The King ever set foot in Britain. A plaque in the airport commemorates his visit, and people still turn up from all over Europe to pay their respects. In later life, someone asked Elvis what country he would like to visit, and he replied that he would like to go back to Scotland, possibly also because he had Scottish ancestors.

The name Prestwick means priest's burgh, and the ruins of the ancient **Parish Church of St Nicholas** are near the coastline. There was a lazar house at Kingcase, where Robert the Bruce went to seek a cure for his leprosy. **Bruce's Well** can still be seen there.

The very first British Open Golf Championship was held at Prestwick in 1860 (with eight competitors) and for 12 years after. A cairn near the golf course, unveiled in 1977 by Henry Cotton, commemorates the event.

MONKTON
4 miles N of Ayr on the A79

🏛 St Cuthbert's Church	🏛 Muckle Stane
🏛 James MacRae	

Traffic between Glasgow and Ayr used to thunder through Monkton, but now it is more or less bypassed. It sits on the edge of Prestwick Airport, and at one time the main road cut right across the main runway. This meant that traffic was held up every time an aircraft took off or landed - a magnificent sight, but inconvenient for cars and buses.

The ruins of 13th-century **St Cuthbert's Church** stand at the heart of the village. At one time the Rev Thomas Burns, Robert Burns's nephew, was minister here. A church has certainly stood here since 1227, when it is mentioned in a charter of Walter, Bishop of Glasgow, as belonging to Paisley Abbey. In 1834, Monkton parish was united with

Prestwick, and a new church was built to serve both communities.

William Wallace, it is said, once fell asleep in the church, and had a dream in which an old man presented him with a sword and a young woman presented him with a wand. He took it to mean that he must continue his struggle for Scotland's freedom.

The **Muckle Stane** is an 'erratic' (a boulder brought by an ice flow towards the end of the last Ice Age), and previously stood in a field outside the village. In 1998, it was relocated within the village.

To the north of the village is a curious monument known as MacRae's Monument, which looks like the truncated top part of a church tower and spire. It commemorates **James MacRae,** Governor of Madras in the early 18th century. He was born in Ochiltree in humble circumstances, his father having died before he was born. He was then brought up by a carpenter called Hugh McGuire. When MacRae returned from India in 1731 a rich man, he bought the Orangefield estate (a site now occupied by part of Prestwick Airport). He also found his old benefactor living in poverty. He bought him the estate of Drumdow at Stair, east of Monkton, and introduced his daughters into polite society, each of them making good marriages. One of them became the Countess of Glencairn. MacRae was buried in the churchyard at Monkton, though no stone now marks his grave. A curious tale tells of a gravedigger who once inadvertently dug up MacRae's coffin in the 19th century and stripped it of its lead. However, the silver plaque on the coffin lid he gave to the authorities in Ayr.

The estate of Ladykirk is to be found a few miles east of Monkton. It was here, in Ladykirk Chapel (which has all but vanished),

that Robert II (the first Stewart king) married his first wife, Elizabeth Mure of Rowallan, in 1347. It was a marriage that some people considered unlawful, as the couple were related. But later in the year Pope Clement VI declared it a lawful marriage. From it came Robert III, Robert II's successor.

TROON
6 miles N of Ayr, on the A759

This seaside resort is synonymous with golf since the British Open has been held here many times. It is a young town, having been laid out in the early 1800s by the 4th Duke of Portland who wished to create a harbour from which to export the coal mined in his Ayrshire coalfields. It formed the western terminus of Scotland's earliest rail line, the Troon/ Kilmarnock Railway, which was opened in 1812. In 1816, the Duke introduced a steam locomotive onto the line, and it started pulling passenger trains. The town is now the Scottish terminal for the Scotland/Ireland P&O express ferry service.

On the shoreline is the Ballast Bank, created over the years by ships that discharged their ballast before taking on coal for Ireland. Behind Troon a narrow road climbs up into the Dundonald Hills, from where there is a magnificent view of the Firth of Clyde.

SYMINGTON
6 miles N of Ayr off the A77

🏚 Symington Parish Church   🏛 Barnweil Monument

Symington is a pleasant village of old cottages, though a large estate of council housing on its northern edge has somewhat marred its picturesqueness. It is named after its Norman founder, Simon Lockhart, and at its heart is **Symington Parish Church**, Ayrshire's oldest church still in use. This Norman building, formerly dedicated to the Holy Trinity, was originally built about 1150, and has in its east wall a trio of delightful Norman windows. It has its original piscina in the south wall, and an ancient timbered roof.

On a hillside to the west of the village, at a spot called Barnweil, is the Victorian **Barnweil Monument**, looking for all the world like a church tower without a church. This marks the spot where Wallace watched the 'barns o' Ayr burn weel' after he set fire to them. Next to it are the scant remains of Barnweil Church, where John Knox once preached. The parish of Barnweil was suppressed in 1673, and the church, which may have been one of the oldest in Ayrshire, gradually fell into ruin.

DUNDONALD
8 miles N of Ayr on the B730

Dundonald Castle

🏚 Dundonald Castle

Dundonald Castle (Historic Scotland) is one of Scotland's royal castles, and sits on a high hill overlooking the village. The hill has been occupied for at least 3000 years, and has been the site of at least three medieval castles. What you see nowadays are the remains of the third castle, built in the 14th century by Robert II, grandson of Robert the Bruce and the first Stewart king of Scotland, to mark his accession to the throne in 1371. It was here, in his favourite residence, that Robert died in 1390. When Boswell and Dr Johnson visited the castle in 1773 during their Scottish journey, Johnson was much amused by the humble home of 'Good King Bob', though in the 14th century the castle was much larger than it is now, having

stables, a brew house and a blacksmith's workshop. Over the years, the castle has been owned by many families, including the Wallaces and the Cochranes, who later became Earls of Dundonald.

At the top, now reached by a metal staircase, are what would have been the royal apartments, and it is here that Robert II no doubt died. There are fine views northwards and eastwards over central Ayrshire.

TARBOLTON
7 miles NE of Ayr on the B744

🏚 Bachelors' Club   🏚 Tarbolton Parish Church

When Burns stayed at nearby Lochlee Farm (private) both he and his brother Gilbert looked to Tarbolton for leisure activities. In 1780, they founded a debating society, which met in a thatched house in Sandgate Street in the village. This 17th century house is now the **Bachelors' Club** (National Trust for Scotland). Burns was initiated into Freemasonry in 1781 in the upper room, which was also used for dancing classes, and was conveniently linked by an outside stair to the adjacent inn. Round the fireplace in the upper room you'll see a helical pattern drawn in chalk - an old Ayrshire custom to prevent the Devil from entering the house by way of the chimney.

The farm of Lochlee (also known as Lochlea) sat beside a now drained loch to the west of the village, and had poor soil. When Burns's father died in 1784, the family moved to Mossgiel near Mauchline. In 1779, Burns wrote *The Tarbolton Lassies*, which praises the young women of the village.

Tarbolton Parish Church is an elegant, imposing building of 1821 standing on a low hill.

MAUCHLINE
10 miles NE of Ayr on the A76

- Jean Armour
- Burns House Museum
- Robert Burns
- William Fisher
- Poosie Nancy's Inn
- Burns Memorial
- Abbot Hunter's Tower
- Ballochmyle Viaduct

When Burns's father died at Lochlee near Tarbolton, the Burns family moved to Mossgiel Farm near the village of Mauchline. The farmhouse that Burns knew is no more, but its successor still stands to the north of the village, with its farmhouse looking considerably more prosperous than the one Burns knew. It was in Mauchline that he met **Jean Armour**, his future wife, and it was here that they first settled down. Jean lived in a house (now gone) in the Cowgate, daughter to

a prosperous stone mason who, not surprisingly, originally disapproved of Jean seeing a penniless failed farmer who had a deserved reputation as a womaniser and who wrote verse. So much so that Jean's mother packed Jean off to her uncle in Paisley, even though the couple had signed a marriage pact that was legal under Scots law of the time. Not only that - she was pregnant.

But eventually the Armours bowed to the inevitable, and Jean and Robert set up home in Castle Street (which at that time was the main street of the village and was called Back Causeway). Their home now houses the **Burns House Museum**. The red sandstone building actually had four families living in it in the 18th century, but it has now been converted so that various displays and exhibitions can be accommodated. Robert and Jean's apartment has been furnished in much the same way as it would have been in 1788 when they moved in. Across from it, but now a private house, was Nance Tinnock's Inn, Burns's favourite drinking place.

Robert Burns lived in Mauchline from 1784 until 1788, when he and his family moved to Dumfriesshire. The four years were the most productive in his life, and to his time in Mauchline we owe *To a Mountain Daisy, To a Mouse, Holy Willie's Prayer* and *The Holy Fair*. But these were also troubled times for him. As he struggled to eke a living from the poor soil of Mossgiel, he even contemplated emigrating to Jamaica. However, the success of his first book of verse, now called the Kilmarnock Edition, made him change his mind. It also, to some extent, softened the Armours' opinion of him.

The Parish Church you see today is not the one that Burns knew. The old Norman church of St Michael was pulled down and rebuilt in 1826, though the kirkyard still has many graves connected with the poet (including the graves of four of his children). A chart on the church wall explains where each one is. Another one to look out for is that of **William Fisher**. William was an elder in Mauchline Kirk, and the butt of Burns's satirical poem *Holy Willie's Prayer*, in which he attacks the cant and hypocrisy of the church. Willie asks God's forgiveness for his own, understandable sins, while asking that he severely punish the sins of others. Opposite the church is **Poosie Nansy's Inn**. Though not a great frequenter of this inn, the poet still drank there occasionally, and Burns enthusiasts can drink there today.

To the north of the village is the **Burns Memorial**, built in 1897. It is a tall, red sandstone tower with a small museum inside. From the top, you get good views of the rich agricultural lands of Ayrshire. Beside the memorial, and forming part of it, are some pleasant alms cottages for old people.

Gavin Hamilton was Burns's friend and landlord. His house can still be seen, attached to the 15th-century **Abbot Hunter's Tower**. The tower looks like a small castle, but was in fact the monastic headquarters, or grange, of the Ayrshire estates owned by Melrose Abbey.

The **Ballochmyle Viaduct**, to the south of the village, carries the Glasgow to Dumfries line across the River Ayr, and is considered to be one of the finest railway bridges in the world. Work started on it in 1843, and it is still Britain's highest stone and brick railway bridge, being 163 feet above the river. It has three smaller arches at either end, and one long, graceful arch in the middle that spans 181 feet. One of the main scenes from the film *Mission Impossible* was filmed there with Tom Cruise, though in the film it was supposed to be on the London to Paris line.

During World War I, a pilot is said to have flown under the main arch.

Burns used to wander through the Ballochmyle estates, which sit on the banks of the River Ayr. One day, in about 1786, when he was strolling along the banks, he saw Miss Wilhelmina Alexander, Claud's sister. He was so taken by her that he wrote *The Lass o' Ballochmyle*, one of his most famous works, in her honour. He sent it to her, but so angry was she that she never replied. However, the anger was more to do with the fact that she was in her 40s at the time, and thought that Burns was having a joke at her expense. In later years, however, she cherished the poem.

FAILFORD
7 miles E of Ayr on the B743

🏛 King Cole's Grave   ⚄ River Ayr Way

Near this little village, in 1786, Burns took his farewell of Highland Mary, who would die soon after in Greenock. Burns, disillusioned by his treatment at the hands of Jean Armour's parents, had asked her to accompany him to Jamaica. They exchanged Bibles, which was seen as a marriage contract, and Mary set off home to Dunoon to prepare for the voyage. However, en route she died in Greenock. The Failford Monument, on a slight rise, commemorates the meeting.

A mile east of Failford, in a field, are the remains of a tumulus known as **King Cole's Grave**. Legend tells us that Old King Cole of nursery rhyme fame was a real person - a British king called Coel or Coilus, who ruled in Ayrshire. In the Dark Ages, he fought a great battle against the Scots under their king, Fergus. Cole's army was routed, and he fled the battlefield. Eventually he was captured and killed. His supporters later cremated his body and buried it with some pomp at the spot where he died. The Kyle area of Ayrshire is supposed to be named after him.

The tumulus was opened in 1837, and some cremated bones were discovered in two small urns. Up until recently, the nearby stream was referred to locally as the Bloody Burn, and one field beside the stream was known as Deadmen's Holm, as that is where those killed in the battle were supposedly buried. Tales were often told of bits of human bone and armour being turned up by men ploughing the field.

In the Failford Inn you'll find the guide centre for the recently opened 44-mile **River Ayr Way**. This is a long-distance footpath that follows the course of the River Ayr from its source at Glenbuck to the sea and passes through some of Ayrshire's most stunning scenery and sites of interest

OCHILTREE

11 miles E of Ayr on the A70

> 🐦 George Douglas Brown

Ochiltree was the birthplace of yet another Ayrshire writer, **George Douglas Brown**, who was born here in 1869, the illegitimate son of a local farmer and a serving girl. He went on to write *The House with the Green Shutters*, a hard, unrelenting book about life in Scotland in the late 1800s. He wanted to banish the 'kailyard school' of writing, which saw Scotland's countryside as being comfortable and innocent, full of couthy, happy people of unquestionable worth. He set his book in the fictional town of Barbie, which is a thinly disguised Ochiltree, and not many characters in the book have redeeming features. One of the village's cottages (not open to the public) now has green shutters, and is itself known as the House with the Green Shutters.

AUCHINLECK

13 miles E of Ayr off the A76

> 🐦 James Boswell   🏰 Auchinleck House
> 🏛 Auchinleck Kirk

Burns is not the only famous literary person associated with Ayrshire. Though born in Edinburgh, **James Boswell** was the son of a Court of Session judge who lived in **Auchinleck House**, perhaps the finest example of an 18th-century country villa to survive in Scotland. The judge had the house built in about 1760 as his country seat, and Boswell brought the great Dr Johnson there to meet him when the pair were touring Scotland. They didn't hit it off.

Auchinleck House is now owned by the Landmark Trust and the ground floor of the house, including the Museum Room, is open for visits by appointment on Wednesday afternoons during the season. The grounds are open throughout the spring and summer.

Boswell died in 1795, and lies in a small mausoleum attached to the old **Auchinleck Kirk**, which is no longer used for worship. It now houses a museum dedicated to the writer and biographer.

SORN

14 miles E of Ayr on the B743

> 🏰 Sorn Parish Church   🏰 Sorn Castle
> 🐦 Prophet Peden

Sorn is one of the most picturesque villages in the county and has won national and international awards for its tidiness and well-kept gardens. It sits beside the River Ayr, which is spnned by an 18th-century bridge, and has many delightful cottages. **Sorn Parish Church** dates from 1658, and the lofts, or galleries, are reached by stairs on the outside of the walls. **Sorn Castle** dates from the 14th century, with later additions. It was built by a branch of the Hamilton family, and James VI once visited on horseback in the depths of winter to attend the wedding of Isobel Hamilton, the daughter of his Treasurer, Lord Seton. James VI's journey to Sorn so sickened him that he later said that if he were to play a trick on the devil, he would send him from Glasgow to Sorn on a cold winter's day. The castle is open to the public from mid-July to early August each year.

Alexander Peden was born at Auchincloich near Sorn in 1626. Known as **Prophet Peden**, he was a Covenanter who held secret conventicles, or prayer meetings, at lonely spots all over central Ayrshire. The whole area abounds with places that have been named after him, such as Peden's Pulpit and Peden's Table. There is even a field called Preaching Peden.

CUMNOCK
15 miles E of Ayr off the A76

🏛 Cumnock Old Parish Church

🏛 James Keir Hardie

Cumnock is a small industrial town that was granted its burgh charter in 1509. In the middle of its square stands **Cumnock Old Parish Church**, built in the mid 1800s. It's a four-square building that seems to sprout transepts, apses and porches in all directions.

Two miles west of the town, at Lugar, is Bello Mill (private), birthplace in 1754 of William Murdoch, discoverer of gas lighting and, believe it or not, the man who invented the wooden top hat. He conducted his gas experiments in a cave on the banks of the Lugar Water upstream from Bello.

Dumfries House (private), one mile west of Cumnock, was designed for the 4th Earl of Dumfries in the mid 1700s by John and

Robert Adam. It is said that James Armour, Robert Burns's father-in-law, was one of the masons who worked on the building of the house.

At the north end of the town, is the house that **James Keir Hardie**, the founder of the Scottish Labour Party, built for himself. Though born in Lanarkshire, he considered himself to be a Cumnock man. He was first of all MP for West Ham in London, and later for Merthyr Tydfil in Wales. His bust can be found outside the Town Hall.

MUIRKIRK
23 miles E of Ayr on the A70

🏛 Battle of Airds Moss

This former mining and iron-working town is surrounded by bleak but lovely moorland. To the west is the site of the **Battle of Airds Moss**, fought in 1680 and marked by a memorial. A Covenanting army was heavily defeated by government troops. Just south of the town, and along an unmarked road, is a small monument to John Loudon McAdam, the road builder, who owned a tar works in the vicinity.

NEW CUMNOCK
18 miles E of Ayr on the A76

The parish of New Cumnock was carved from the much older parish of Cumnock in 1650, with a church being built on the site of Cumnock Castle, once owned by the Dunbars. The ruins of the church can still be seen.

It was near here that the Knockshinnoch Mining Disaster took place in 1950. A slurry of mud and peat filled some workings that were close to the surface, trapping 129 miners underground. The rescuers showed great bravery and 116 men were eventually brought out alive. A feature film, *The Brave Don't Cry*, was made about the disaster in 1952.

To the south of the village is Glen Afton, through which flows the Afton Water. A cairn marks the spot where Burns was inspired to write *Flow Gently Sweet Afton*.

DALRYMPLE
5 miles SE of Ayr on the B7034

🎦 *Brigadoon*

In this quiet little village of weavers' cottages Burns first received an education. While staying at Mount Oliphant, he and his brother Gilbert attended the Parish School on alternate weeks. The village sits beside the River Doon, and has a small Parish Church built in 1849.

Some people say it was the inspiration for the musical **Brigadoon**, about a mysterious Scottish village that only appears every 100 years. Alan Jay Lerner, who wrote the words, was looking for a way of turning a German fairy tale about a magical village called *Germelshausen* into a musical. One day, while in Scotland, he suddenly happened upon Dalrymple, which sits in a small glen, hidden until you're almost upon it. He immediately thought of locating his musical in Scotland, and called it Brigadoon because there really is a bridge over the River Doon in the village. He also called one of the characters Charlie Dalrymple.

Two miles south, and straight out of a fairy tale as well, is Cassillis Castle (private), the home of the Marquis of Ailsa, head of Clan Kennedy. It is a wonderful concoction of pepper pot turrets and towers built originally in the 15th century, but added to throughout the years. It is here that the hanging of Johnny

---

ALT-NA-CRAIG

Skeldon, Hollybush, By Ayr, Scotland KA6 7EB
Tel/Fax: 01292 560555
e-mail: jmsmillie@altnacraig.co.uk
website: www.altnacraig.co.uk

Situated in the heart of Burns Country and overlooking picturesque River Doon, **Alt-na-Craig** is a friendly family home with the accent on customer care. Ideally positioned next to the Old Skeldon Woollen Mills, it is a spacious modern villa in a quiet rural area between two country villages offering a choice of eating-places.

A warm welcome awaits you at the 4 star guesthouse hosted by Mandy. Luxury accommodation with spacious and tastefully decorated rooms including two en-suites - upstairs is a large en-suite and the downstairs en-suite caters for elderly and disabled guests - both recently upgraded with hairdryer, alarm clock,

hospitality tray with tea & coffee and televisions too. Drying facilities are offered as many fishermen stay here and a freezer for their many catches.

Mandy is a trained chef and offers evening meals all home produced and delicious homemade shortbread for you to try (by arrangement) – or if you prefer to go out The Hollybush Inn is only 2 minutes by car from here. There is a private driveway for guests to park their car in front of the house. As well as a large garden looking out to countryside and also play area for children Close to many Ayrshire Golf Courses and to Prestwick Airport.

🎦 stories and anecdotes 🦅 famous people 🎨 art and craft 🍂 entertainment and sport 🚶 walks

Bridge across river, Alloway

for his time, thanks to his far-sighted father. He knew his Classics, he could speak French and some Latin, he could read music, he took dancing lessons, and he could play both the fiddle and, surprisingly, the guitar. When he went to Edinburgh in later life, he was possibly better educated than some of the gentry who patronised him. Two of his sons, James Glencairn Burns and W Nicol Burns, attained the ranks of Lieutenant Colonel and Colonel respectively in the British Army.

Faa and his men from the Dule Tree is supposed to have taken place.

At one time, Alloway was a small country village. Now it forms part of Ayr, and is full of large, impressive houses that illustrate the relative affluence of this part of Ayrshire.

ALLOWAY
2 miles S of Ayr town centre on the B7024

- Robert Burns
- Burns Cottage
- Burns Museum
- Alloway Kirk
- Burns Monument
- Brig o'Doon
- Burns National Heritage Park

Alloway is one of the iconic places on any **Robert Burns** journey of exploration. It was here, in 1759, that Scotland's national poet was born in a cottage that his father built with his own hands. Burns was not the uneducated 'ploughman poet' from the peasant classes that his more romantic admirers would have us believe. His father was a tenant farmer, and although not well off, still managed to employ workmen and serving girls on his farm. Today, **Burns Cottage** is a place of pilgrimage with people coming from all over the world to pay their respects. Within the grounds of the cottage is the **Burns Museum**, which contains many of his manuscripts, letters and possessions.

Burns himself was a highly educated man

Alloway Kirk is where Robert's father, William Burns, is buried, and it was the main setting for the poem *Tam o' Shanter*. It dates from the early 16th century, but even in Burns's day it was a ruin. Across the road, within some beautiful gardens, is the Grecian **Burns Monument**, built in the 1820s. Inside is a small museum.

Spanning the Doon is the graceful **Brig o' Doon**, a single arched bridge dating from the 15th century or possibly earlier. It was across the Brig o' Doon that Tam o' Shanter was chased by the witches he disturbed in Alloway Kirk. However, he managed to gain the keystone of the bridge and escaped unharmed, as witches cannot cross running water, even though his horse lost its tail. In Burns's day, the bridge lay on the main road south into Carrick, but a newer, wider construction now carries traffic south.

Across the road from Alloway Kirk is the **Burns National Heritage Park**, a visitor centre with two audiovisual shows within its large auditorium. One illustrates Burns's life and times, while the other, the Tam o' Shanter Experience, re-creates what happened to Tam o' Shanter after he left the inn and made his fateful ride south from Ayr.

East of Alloway is Mount Oliphant Farm (private) to which Burns and his family moved when he was seven years old.

ST QUIVOX

2 miles NE of Ayr just off the A77

🏛 Parish Church 🏛 Oswald Hall

The tiny **Parish Church** is a small gem of a building. Though altered beyond recognition over the years, its basic fabric is still medieval. The church takes its name from a shadowy Celtic saint called variously St Kevock, St Kennocha, St Kenochis, St Cavocks and St Evox. It was restored by Lord Cathcart of Auchincruive - and no doubt altered to suit Protestant services - in 1595.

To the east is **Oswald Hall**, designed by Robert Adam for James Oswald in 1767. It is now a conference centre. The surrounding Auchincruive estate is one of the campuses of the Scottish Agricultural College.

Kilmarnock

🏛 Laigh Kirk 🏛 Old High Kirk 🐦 John Nesbit

🎨 Burns Statue 🐦 Johnnie Walker

🏛 Dick Institute 🏛 Dean Castle

🐦 Dean Castle Country Park

🎬 Countess of Kilmarnock 🐦 Howard Park

🏛 Old Sheriff Court 🐦 Gatehead Viaduct

Though it is now largely an industrial town,

Kilmarnock was granted its burgh charter in 1592, so its roots go deep into Scottish history. Legend says it grew up round a church founded by St Marnock, a Celtic saint, in the 7th century. The present **Laigh Kirk** (now called The Laigh West High Kirk) in Bank Street dates from 1802. It has a 17th-century steeple (a date stone on it says 1410, but this may refer to an earlier building), and is supposed to stand on the site of the earlier church. In 1801, during a service, 29 people were trampled to death when plasterwork started falling off the ceiling of the previous kirk, causing a mad rush for the doors. When the church was rebuilt, it was given 13 exits in case that ever happened again. The town's other old church is the **Old High Kirk**, which dates from the early 1730s.

Kilmarnock has many Burns associations - the first edition of his poems was published in the town, at Star Inn Close (now gone) in 1786. Today, a copy of that first edition is worth many thousands of pounds. A stone marking the spot can be found in the small shopping mall. Also in the mall is a stone marking the spot where Covenanting martyr **John Nesbit** was executed in 1683. His grave can be seen in the kirkyard of the Laigh and West High Kirk.

Burns Statue, unveiled in the mid 1990s by the Princess Royal, stands at Kilmarnock Cross. It is the work of Sandy Stoddard, whose other works include the statue of David Hume on Edinburgh's Royal Mile and the sculptured friezes in the Queen's Gallery in Buckingham Palace.

In truth, Kilmarnock's shopping centre, notably Kilmarnock Cross and King Street, is dull and unattractive, due to uninspired modern developments. But if you go down Cheapside towards Bank Street and the

LUXURY CAPITAL APARTMENTS

56d London Road, Kilmarnock, Ayrshire KA3 7AJ
Tel: 07917 325469
e-mail: danny_fraser@talktalk.net
website: www.luxurycapitalapartments.com

Located in a modern building in the Tollcross area of Edinburgh, with easy access to the many attractions of the city centre, **Luxury Capital Apartments** offer top quality self-catering accommodation equipped with first class modern facilities. All the apartments have been finished to a high standard, including an en suite master bedroom, separate luxury shower room with superb fittings such as Villroy Boch sanitary ware and Grohe showers.

At present, there are four apartments available, all featuring a two bedroom layout - a master bedroom and a twin bedroom sleeping four persons comfortably. However, some of the apartments can accommodate up to six people by utilising a high quality sofa bed. High chairs and cots are available on request. Each apartment has a fully equipped, brand new, modern kitchen with integrated appliances by Smeg. Other amenities include a 32-inch LCD digital TV, DVD player and DAB/Digital radio, free WiFi Broadband internet access, and hairdryer. There is also free, secure underground parking.

The apartments are available from a minimum of two nights with special rates available for longer lets.

---

narrow streets round the Laigh and West High Kirk, you get an idea of what the 18th century town looked like.

It was in a shop in King Street that Johnnie Walker first started bottling and selling whisky in 1820. The Johnnie Walker Bottling Plant in Hill Street is now one of the largest plants of its kind in the world. **Johnnie Walker** himself lies in the kirk yard of St Andrew's Glencairn Church (no longer used for worship) to the south of the town centre, and his statue can be found in the Strand.

One place not to be missed is the **Dick Institute**, the town's museum, art gallery and library. It is housed in a grand classical building, and has impressive collections featuring

Dean Castle, Kilmarnock

---

geology, archaeology, biology and local history. The gallery is also impressive, with paintings by Corot, Constable, Turner and Kilmarnock's own painter, Robert Colquhoun. The area around the Dick Institute is particularly attractive, with a war memorial, Victorian houses, and the richly decorated façade of the old technical college, now being converted into flats. Across from the Dick Institute is the statue of Kilmarnock's own Dick Whittington - James Shaw (known affectionately in the town as Jimmy Shaw), who became Lord Mayor of London in 1805.

To the northeast of the town centre is the town's oldest building, **Dean Castle**. It was the home of the Boyd family, who became Earls of Kilmarnock, and is in fact two castles within a curtain wall - the 14th-century Keep and the later Palace. Both are open to the public, and house wonderful collections of tapestries, musical instruments and armour. Surrounding it is **Dean Castle Country Park** with many walks and a small children's zoo.

The Boyd family rose to become the most important family in Scotland in the 1460s when Sir Robert Boyd became Regent of Scotland. In 1746, the last earl was beheaded in London for fighting alongside Charles Edward Stuart at Culloden, and all his lands and titles were forfeit.

During his trial in London, his young wife, the **Countess of Kilmarnock**, stayed at the Boyd's other residence in the town - Kilmarnock House (now gone). Daily she walked its grounds, awaiting news of her husband's fate. These grounds are now the **Howard Park**, which has a tree-lined avenue known as Lady's Walk. The Countess herself died shortly after her husband, and some people say that her ghost still haunts the park.

Kilmarnock Academy, which stands on an eminence overlooking the town centre, is said to be one of the few schools in the world that has produced two Nobel Prize winners - Sir Alexander Fleming (1945, for Medicine) and Lord Boyd Orr (1949, for Peace).

Across from the new sheriff court building near the park is the **Old Sheriff Court** of 1852, an attractive building in neoclassical style. It stands on the site of one of the termini of Scotland's first railway, the Troon/ Kilmarnock Railway, built by the Duke of Portland in 1812. Two miles west of the town is the **Gatehead Viaduct**, built in 1807 to take the railway over the River Irvine. Though it no longer carries a railway line, it is still Scotland's oldest railway bridge. The viaduct was recently renovated and is now accessible to the public.

In 1862, at Crosshouse, a mining village west of Kilmarnock, **Andrew Fisher** was born. He rose to become Prime Minister of Australia on three separate occasions.

Around Kilmarnock

KILMAURS
2 miles NW of Kilmarnock, on the A735

🏚 Tolbooth 🏚 St Maurs Glencairn Church

🏚 Glencairn Aisle 🐟 John Boyd Orr

Kilmaurs is a former weaving village, and though only a few fields separate it from Kilmarnock's suburbs, it is still a small, self-contained community with many small cottages. At its centre is the old 17th-century **Tolbooth**, still with the jougs installed which were placed round wrongdoers' necks as a punishment.

St Maurs Glencairn Church dates from 1888, and replaced an earlier medieval collegiate church founded by the Earls of Glencairn, who lived close by. **Glencairn**

Aisle, the 16th-century burial vault of the Earls of Glencairn, still stands to the rear of the church. It has an ornate monument inside to the 7th earl and his family. It dates from around 1600, and carries an inscription that reads 'nothing is surer than death, be therefore sober and watch in prayer'.

The village takes its name from St Maura, daughter of a Scottish chieftain on the island of Little Cumbrae in the Firth of Clyde. **John Boyd Orr**, first director of the United Nations Food and Agricultural Organisation and Nobel prize-winner, was born in Kilmaurs in 1880.

Kilmaurs Place (private) dates from the 17th century, and was built as a replacement for the earlier Kilmaurs Castle. It was the home of the Earls of Glencairn and later of the powerful Montgomery family.

STEWARTON
5 miles N of Kilmarnock on the A735

David Dale   Parish Church of St Columba

Stewarton is famous as being the home of bonnet making in Ayrshire. It was the birthplace, in 1739, of **David Dale**, the industrialist and social reformer who founded New Lanark, and later sold it to his son-in-law, Robert Owen. The **Parish Church of St Columba** dates originally from 1696, though it has been much altered.

FENWICK
4 miles N of Kilmarnock off the A77

Fenwick Parish Church

Fenwick (pronounced Fennick) is really two villages - High Fenwick and Laigh Fenwick. They lie on the edge of the Fenwick Moors, which separate the farmlands of Ayrshire

---

DUNLOP DAIRY

West Clerkland Farm, Dunlop Road, Stewarton, Ayrshire KA3 5LP
Tel: 01560 482494
e-mail: aneldorward@googlemail.com

From the 18th century to around the 1940s, most farms in the west of Scotland made Dunlop cheese which was as famous then as Cheddar, Cheshire or Wensleydale. In 1989 the Dorward family revived the old tradition at their Clerkland Farm by opening the **Dunlop Dairy**. Since then, they have been consistent winners of awards, including several gold awards and "Best British Modern Cheese" at the British Cheese Awards. Their hand-crafted cheeses are made with the milk from their small herd of native Ayrshire cows, their Saanen and Toggenburg goats, and their flock of Friesland sheep.

The cheeses are produced under modern hygienic conditions but using traditional methods which are natural and basic. The result is unspoiled, quality award-winning cheeses. Every batch is individual, varying as the milk changes throughout the seasons. You can buy the cheeses from specialist cheese shops, delicatessens and farmers' markets or from the Dorward's own farm shop where the whole range is available as well as free range eggs. There's also a tearoom serving delicious home baking. The shop is open daily from 9am to 5pm; the tea room from 10am to 4pm.

---

historic building   museum and heritage   historic site   scenic attraction   flora and fauna

from Glasgow and its suburbs, and were originally weaving villages. Some of the cottages still show their weaving origins, with two windows on one side of the door to allow plenty of light to enter the room containing the loom, and one window on the other. **Fenwick Parish Church**, which dates from 1643, is an attractive whitewashed building with a Greek cross plan. On one wall hangs the original jougs, where wrongdoers were chained by their necks to the wall.

Two miles southeast of the village is the quaintly named, and often photographed, hamlet of **Moscow** (pronounced Moss-cow rather than Moss-coe), which actually has a burn called the Volga flowing through it. And five miles to the north, off the B764, is Lochgoin Farm, which has a small museum commemorating the Covenanters.

Fenwick was the birthplace, in 1803, of John Fulton, a shoemaker who gained considerable fame throughout Scotland by making orreries - working models of the solar system where the planets revolve round the sun and satellites revolve round the planets, all synchronised by the use of gearing. Fulton built three such orreries, one of which is still on show in the New Kelvin Galleries in Glasgow.

DUNLOP
7 miles N of Kilmarnock on the A735

- Parish Church Hans Hamilton Tomb
- Clandeboye Hall Dunlop Cheese

Dunlop is a delightful village of small weavers' cottages. The **Parish Church** dates from 1835, though it has fragments from the earlier church incorporated into the north aisle. In the kirkyard is the ornate early 17th-century **Hans Hamilton Tomb**, contained within a small mausoleum. Hamilton was Dunlop's first

Protestant minister, and was made Viscount Clandeboye by James VI. The small **Clandeboye Hall**, beside the mausoleum, dates from the 17th century, and was the village's first school.

It was in a farm near the village that the famous **Dunlop cheese** was first manufactured in the 17th century, by a farmer's wife called Barbara Gilmour. It is made from the milk of Ayrshire cattle, and closely resembles a Cheddar. Barbara was buried in the kirkyard, where her grave can still be seen. Cheese making was recently revived in the village, and Dunlop cheese, which is harder than the original variety, is made by Dunlop Dairy (see panel opposite), which also produces a range of sheep and goat's cheeses.

GALSTON
4 miles E of Kilmarnock on the A71

- Parish Church St Sophia's RC Church
- Barr Castle Loudoun Castle Auld Yew Tree
- Loudoun Castle Theme Park
- Lady Flora Hastings Loudoun Kirk

This pleasant little town in the Irvine Valley has a splendid **Parish Church** dating from 1808. One of its ministers, Perthshire-born Robert Stirling, was the inventor of the Stirling Engine. He died in 1878.

Another church worth visiting is **St Sophia's RC Church**, modelled on the Hagia Sophia in Istanbul. **Barr Castle** is a solid, 15th-century tower house once owned by the Lockhart family. William Wallace is said to have taken refuge within the walls of a previous castle on the site in the 13th century. When the English troops surrounded it he escaped by jumping from a window onto a tree. An ancient game of handball used to be played against the castle walls by the locals. The castle is now a small museum with many exhibits relating to local history.

To the north of the town are the impressive ruins of **Loudoun Castle**, ancestral home of the Campbells of Loudoun, which burnt down in 1941. In their heyday, the Campbells entertained so lavishly that the castle was called the Windsor of Scotland. Three ghosts reputedly haunt it - a Grey Lady, a Phantom Piper and a Benevolent Monk. At one time, the great sword of William Wallace was kept within the castle, but it was sold in 1930. Beside its walls is the **Auld Yew Tree**, under which Hugh, 3rd Earl of Loudoun, prepared the draft of the Treaty of Union between Scotland and England. Today, the **Loudoun Castle Theme Park** fills the grounds of the castle.

Loudoun Castle was the birthplace of **Lady Flora Hastings**, who shook the monarchy and government to its core in 1839. Queen Victoria was 20 years old at the time, and had been on the throne for just two years. Lady Flora was a Lady of the Bedchamber who contracted a disease that so swelled her abdomen, she appeared pregnant. Gossip raged through the court, and she was shunned, even though doctors whom she consulted confirmed that she wasn't pregnant but ill, and had an enlarged liver.

Neither the government nor the Queen did anything to dispel the rumours, and people began to sympathise with the young woman. Soon it was the Queen's turn to be shunned, and she was shocked when people turned their back on her as she proceeded through London by coach. It wasn't until Lady Flora was on her deathbed in Buckingham Palace that a grudging reconciliation took place, though no apology was ever given. The Campbells were so incensed by Flora's treatment that when postage stamps were introduced bearing Victoria's image, family members stuck them onto envelopes upside down.

A mile or so away from Loudoun Castle are the ruins of the medieval **Loudoun Kirk**, at one time dedicated to St Michael. Flora now lies in the choir, which has been converted into a burial vault for the Campbells of Loudoun, and a slim monument stands in the kirkyard to her memory. The Campbells coat-of-arms can still be seen on the choir walls, above the entrance to the vault. The church seems isolated today, but this was not always so. Up until just after the World War II, a village stood here as well. However, the houses had no running water, electricity or sewage services, so were demolished, though the outlines of many gardens can still be seen.

Attached to a wall of the ruined kirk is a plaque that commemorates the Belgian paratroopers who trained at Loudoun Castle during World War II.

NEWMILNS

7 miles E of Kilmarnock on the A71

🏠 Town House 🏠 Newmilns Tower

Newmilns is a small lace-making and weaving town in the Irvine Valley, which was granted its charter in 1490, making it the oldest inland burgh in Ayrshire. The small crow-stepped **Town House**, or Tolbooth, dates from 1739, and behind the Loudoun Arms, which itself dates from the 18th century, is **Newmilns Tower**, an early 16th-century tower house built by Sir Hugh Campbell, Earl of Loudoun. Sir Hugh was perhaps the most tragic member of the Campbell of Loudon family. After being involved in the murder of a member of the powerful Kennedy family during an ongoing feud, his wife and nine children were killed when the Kennedys besieged Loudoun

Castle, a few miles away.

The Lady Flora Institute, built in 1877 as a girl's school, commemorates the tragic Lady Flora Hastings, a lady-in-waiting to Queen Victoria (see Galston above). The institute is now private housing.

During the American Civil War, the weavers of Newmilns sent a message of support to Abraham Lincoln, and he in turn sent back an American flag. This was subsequently lost, but in 1949, the American Embassy gave the town a replacement, which is now housed in the early 19th-century Parish Church in the main street.

DARVEL

8 miles E of Kilmarnock, on the A71

Situated in the lovely Irvine Valley, Darvel is a small, attractive town that was laid out in the late 18th and early 19th century. Like its neighbour Newmilns, it is a lace-making town, the skills having been brought here by the Dutch in the 17th century. It was in Lochfield, near Darvel, that Sir Alexander Fleming, the discoverer of penicillin, was born in 1881. To the east of the town rises the immense bulk of Loudoun Hill, the plug of a former volcano. A Roman fort was built here in about 60AD, and

finally abandoned 100 years later. Nothing now remains of it due to sand and gravel excavation. Both William Wallace and Robert the Bruce fought battles at Loudoun Hill against the English, in 1297 and 1307 respectively. South of the town is the quaintly named Distinkhorn, the highest hill in the area.

IRVINE

7 miles W of Kilmarnock on the A71

- Edgar Allan Poe
- Alexander MacMillan
- John Boyd Dunlop
- Dreghorn Parish Church
- Seagate Castle
- Marymass Week
- Scottish Maritime Museum
- Eglinton Country Park

Irvine is an ancient seaport and royal burgh which, in the 1960s, was designated as Britain's first seaside new town. It is a mixture of old and new, and has many unattractive industrial estates surrounding it. However, the historical core has been preserved, though a brutally modern and totally unnecessary shopping mall straddling the River Irvine dominates it. Robert Burns learned flax dressing in Irvine in 1781, and lodged in a house in the cobbled Glasgow Vennel. A

Scottish Maritime Museum

Harbourside, Irvine KA12 8QE
Tel: 01294 278283 Fax: 01294 313211
website: www.scottishmaritimemuseum.org

The museum is sited in three locations - the Scottish Maritime Museum at Irvine, Clydebuilt at Braehead and the Denny Ship Model Experiment at Dumbarton. At Irvine you will have the opportunity for a guided tour which includes a restored 1920's shipyard workers 'Tenement Flat' and a collection of

moored vessels in the harbour, some of which can be boarded. Trips are occasionally available for visitors. The museum shop stocks a wide selection of souvenirs and light meals, snacks and drinks are served at the Puffers Coffee Shop on the wharf. Check website for opening times.

stories and anecdotes   famous people   art and craft   entertainment and sport   walks

small museum has been created within both it and the heckling shop behind it.

Irvine has other, more unexpected, literary associations. In 1815, the American writer **Edgar Allan Poe**, spent a couple of months in the town, attending the local school. It is said that part of his lessons was to copy the epitaphs from the tombstones in the kirkyard of the Parish Kirk, which may have prepared him for some of the macabre tales he wrote in later life. **Alexander MacMillan**, who founded the great publishing house, was also a native of the town.

In the nearby village of Dreghorn, in 1840, yet another famous Ayrshireman was born - **John Boyd Dunlop**, who invented the pneumatic tyre. He came from a farming background, and graduated from Edinburgh University as a veterinary surgeon. He practised in Edinburgh and then Belfast. He found the roads of Ulster to be stony and rough, and eventually invented an inflatable tyre to overcome the discomfort of travelling on them. Unfortunately, unknown to him, another Scot, Robert William Thomson, had patented the idea before him, and only after a court case could he set up the Dunlop Rubber Company.

Dreghorn Parish Church, built in 1780, is unusual in that it is six-sided. It was built by Archibald, the 11th Earl of Eglinton, and used to have the nickname of the 'threepenny church', as its shape reminded people of the old threepenny bit.

The ruins of **Seagate Castle** date from the early 1500s, and it is said that Mary Stuart lodged here briefly in 1563. Every August the town holds **Marymass Week**, which supposedly commemorates her visit. However, the celebrations probably have more to do with a pre-Reformation religious festival, as the parish church was formerly dedicated to St Mary.

In the 18th century, Irvine saw the founding of perhaps the most unusual religious cult ever seen in Scotland - the Buchanites. Elspeth Buchan was the daughter of a publican, and claimed she could bestow immortality on a person by breathing on them, and that she herself was immortal. She attracted a wide following, including a gullible Irvine clergyman, but was hounded, along with her followers, from the town. She eventually died a natural death, and the cult broke up.

Down by the harbour side is the Magnum Leisure Centre, one of the biggest centres of its kind in Scotland. It has a theatre and concert hall, an indoor bowling green, an ice rink, swimming pool and fitness and coaching areas.

Near the Magnum Centre is one of the three sites of the **Scottish Maritime Museum** (see panel on page 125). It houses a large collection of ships and small craft. There's also the Linthouse Engine Works, which houses a vast collection of maritime machinery, such as engines, winding gear and so on. In the Shipworker's Tenement Flat, a typical 'room and kitchen' flat dating from the 1920s has been re-created, showing how shipyard workers lived in those days. Visitors can also board the *Spartan*, one of the last puffers in Scotland. These small cargo boats, immortalised in the *Para Handy* tales by Neil Munro, sailed the west coast of Scotland for many years.

In 1839, Irvine was the setting of the grand Eglinton Tournament, organised by the 13th Earl of Eglinton at his home, Eglinton Castle, on the outskirts of the town. Here, a great medieval tournament was to be re-created, with jousting, horse riding and other knightly pursuits for the great and the good. They

Kilwinning Abbey

St Columba in Ireland. In the 12th century, the great Tironensian **Kilwinning Abbey** was built on the site, and its ruins still dominate the town centre, though they are not as extensive as those of Ayrshire's other great abbey, Crossraguel. Kilwinning's abbey was founded by Hugh de Morville, High Constable of Scotland and a relation of Richard de Morville, one of the murderers of Thomas à Becket at Canterbury. The tower you see nowadays was built in 1815, and replaced the original medieval one that fell down the year before. Kilwinning Parish Church, which sits within the ruins of the abbey, was built in 1775.

The Ancient Society of Kilwinning Archers is one of the oldest archery organisations in the world, and each year in August holds the **Papingo Shoot**, where archers shoot upwards at a target (the papingo) held from a window of the tower. The papingo is usually a wooden pigeon, and such shoots were once common throughout Britain.

A few miles out of town, on the A737, is **Dalgarven Mill** dating from about 1620. It is now a museum dedicated to country life in Ayrshire.

attended from all over Europe, but alas, the three-day event was a wash-out due to colossal rainstorms. Little remains of the castle, but the grounds have been turned into **Eglinton Country Park**.

KILWINNING
9 miles NW of Kilmarnock on the A737

🏛 Kilwinning Abbey 🎯 Papingo Shoot

🏛 Dalgarven Mill

Though nowadays a continuation of Irvine, Kilwinning was, up until 1975, a separate burgh. Its former name was Segtoune, meaning the saint's town, as it was founded in the 7th century by St Winnin, whom some people associate with St Finnan of Moville, who taught

ARDROSSAN, SALTCOATS & STEVENSTON
11 miles W of Kilmarnock on the A78

🏛 Ardrossan Castle 🗼 Obelisk

🏛 St Peter in Chains 🚢 Horse Island

⚓ Clyde Marina 🏛 North Ayrshire Museum

These towns form a trio of holiday resorts on the Ayrshire coast. Ardrossan is the most

🎭 stories and anecdotes 🐦 famous people 🎨 art and craft 🖋 entertainment and sport 🚶 walks

industrialised and is the ferry terminal for Arran. It is a planned town, with its core being laid out in the early 19th century by the 12th Earl of Eglinton. The ruins of 15th-century **Ardrossan Castle**, once a stronghold of the Montgomeries, stand on Castle Hill overlooking the main streets. Cromwell is said to have plundered some of its masonry to build the Citadel at Ayr. The ruins and the land surrounding them were given to the town by the Earl of Eglinton as a public park. The **Obelisk** at the highest point on the hill commemorates a local doctor, Alexander McFadzean, who promoted piped water and gas supplies in the town. At the foot of the hill stands **St Peter in Chains**, designed by Jack Coia, one of Scotland's best-known architects, and built in 1938. It is reckoned to be one of the finest modern churches in Ayrshire.

Just off the coast is **Horse Island**. Though it looks peaceful enough, it has been the scene of many shipwrecks over the years, and many sailors have found themselves marooned on it after their ships struck its submerged reefs. It is now a RSPB reserve. At the **Clyde Marina** is a sculpture park featuring works by the Japanese artist Hideo Furuta, who lives and works in Scotland.

Up until the 1930s, Ardrossan Docks, was one of the main supply ports for the Hudson Bay Company, and the harbour was crammed with ships loading supplies for North America and unloading furs, fish and sometimes animals.

At Saltcoats the **North Ayrshire Museum**, housed in a former church, has an interesting local history collection. The town has a fine beach, and its name is a reminder of the times when salt was produced here from seawater. The small harbour dates from the late 17th century with later alterations, and at low tide

fossilised trees can be seen on the harbour floor. It was in Saltcoats, in 1793, that Betsy Miller, the only woman ever to have become a registered ship's captain, was born.

Stevenston is a straggling town, with a High Church that dates from 1832. It has a good beach, though it is some way from the centre of the town. Nearby, at Ardeer, the British Dynamite Company established a factory in 1873. It later became Nobel's Explosives Company, and in 1926 became part of ICI.

On the seawall of the beach is a portrait of Robert Burns, which is 25 feet high and about 16 feet wide.

DALRY
11 miles NW of Kilmarnock on the A737

🏛 Parish Church of St Margaret 🏛 Blair

This small industrial town's square is dominated by the **Parish Church of St Margaret**, dating from the 1870s. The town's name comes from the Gaelic Dal Righe, meaning the King's Field, which shows that at one time it must have had royal connections. To the southeast of the town is **Blair**, a large mansion centred on what was a typical Scottish tower house of the 12th century. The parkland that surrounds it was laid out by William Blair in the 1760s. It is the home of Clan Blair, who were supporters of both Bruce and Wallace. It was at one time the home of the daughter of the English King John, who had married William de Blare. Now the mansion can be hired as a venue for conferences and seminars.

BEITH
11 miles NW of Kilmarnock off the A737

🏛 Auld Kirk 🏛 High Church

Beith is a small attractive town, and at 500 feet is the highest town in Ayrshire. The remains

of the **Auld Kirk** date from the late 1500s, while the impressive **High Church** dates from the early 19th century. Eglinton Street is the most attractive part of the town, with small, neat two-storey buildings dating from the late 18th and 19th centuries.

KILBIRNIE

12 miles NW of Kilmarnock on the A760

🏛 Barony Parish Church 🏛 Place of Kilbirnie

Kilbirnie literally means the kil or cell of St Birinus or Birinie, a West Saxon monk who died at Dorchester in Dorset in 650AD. Within the town you'll find the **Barony Parish Church**, dating from the 15th century. Inside is some wonderfully exuberant woodwork from the 17th and 18th centuries, including the extravagant Crawford Loft and the Cunninghame Aisle. In medieval times it was dedicated to St Brendan of Clonfert in Ireland. Standing next to the golf course are the ruins of the **Place of Kilbirnie**, a former castle of the Crawford family dating from the 15th century.

WEST KILBRIDE

16 miles NW of Kilmarnock off the A78

West Kilbride is a sedate village of Glasgow commuters, perched above its twin village of Seamill, on the coast. Law Castle was built in the 15th century for Princess Mary, sister of James III, on her marriage to Thomas Boyd of Kilmarnock, who became the Earl of Arran. However, the marriage was later annulled and he had to flee to the Continent where he died in Antwerp. Mary eventually remarried - to James Hamilton, first Lord Hamilton - and the Earlship of Arran passed to their son.

At the hamlet of Portencross, out on a headland beyond Seamill, are the substantial ruins of 14th-century Portencross Castle, another Boyd stronghold. Also on the headland is Hunterston Castle (not open to the public), ancestral home of Clan Hunter, and Hunterston Nuclear Power Station.

THE CUMBRAES

19 miles NW of Kilmarnock, in the Firth of Clyde

🏛 Cathedral of the Isles ✈ Crocodile Rock

🏛 University Marine Biological Station

🏛 Museum of the Cumbraes

These two islands - Little Cumbrae and Great Cumbrae - were once in the county of Bute. Little Cumbrae is privately owned, but Great Cumbrae can be visited by a frequent ferry from Largs, the crossing taking only 10 minutes.

The only town on the island is Millport, a small, attractive holiday resort with a unique feature - the **Cathedral of the Isles**, Britain's smallest cathedral. It is sometimes referred to as Europe's smallest, but this honour is held by an even smaller cathedral in Greece. Nevertheless, it is a real gem, and was completed in 1851 as part of a theological complex funded by George Boyle who later became the 6th Earl of Glasgow. Its nave is 40 feet by 20 feet, and can only seat 100 people. It was designed by William Butterfield, who also designed Keble College, Oxford. The ceiling is painted with all the wild flowers found on the island.

Crocodile Rock is on the beach. It is, as the name suggests, a rock shaped like a crocodile's head, and has been painted with eyes and teeth so that the resemblance is even more evident. It is said that the rock got its name after a Millport town councillor, on leaving a pub where a council meeting had just finished, remarked that the rock on the foreshore resembled a crocodile.

On the eastern shore of the island, facing the mainland, is the **University Marine Biological Station**. It is an institution of both Glasgow and London Universities, and offers students research facilities, tuition in diving and in marine biology. It houses a museum, which is open to the public.

The **Museum of the Cumbraes** can be found at The Garrison, just off the seafront. There are exhibits and displays on Millport's heyday as one of the Clyde holiday resorts.

LARGS
19 miles NW of Kilmarnock on the A78

🏛 Battle of Largs	🏛 Vikingar!	🏛 Largs Museum
🏚 Skelmorlie Aisle	🐿 Sir Thomas Brisbane	
🐿 Sir William Burrell	🏚 Kelburn Castle	

Largs is the epitome of the Ayrshire seaside town. During the last fortnight in July, hordes of Glaswegians used to descend on places like this for their annual fortnight's holiday. Those days are gone, but the towns themselves have adapted, and now cater for retired people and day-trippers. In fact, the town of Largs is possibly the favourite retirement town in Scotland.

It is still a lively, attractive place, and is the mainland terminal for the Cumbrae Ferry. It was south of here that the **Battle of Largs** took place in 1263, when the Scots defeated a force led by King Haakon IV of Norway and finally threw off the Norse yoke. A tall thin monument south of the town, affectionately known as the Pencil, commemorates the event. Within the town you'll find **Vikingar!** a museum and interpretation centre that examines and explains the life and travels of the Vikings.

Largs Museum, with its local history collection, is also worth a visit, as is the

Skelmorlie Aisle (Historic Scotland). It was built in 1636, and stands in the old kirkyard in the centre of the town. It was built as a transept of the former medieval parish church. Within it is the mausoleum of Sir Robert Montgomery of Skelmorlie and his wife, Dame Margaret Douglas. It is a Renaissance-style tomb with wonderful stone carving.

Sir Thomas Brisbane was born in Largs in 1773. After a distinguished military career, he was appointed Governor of New South Wales in 1820, and gave his name to the city of Brisbane and the Brisbane River. There is also a crater on the moon named after him. He died in 1860, and lies in the Brisbane Vault next to the Skelmorlie Aisle. In the local cemetery is buried **Sir William Burrell**, shipping magnate and millionaire, who gave the Burrell Collection to the city of Glasgow in 1944.

Kelburn Castle stands to the south of the town, overlooking the Firth of Clyde, of which it has spectacular views. It is the ancestral home of the Boyles, Earls of Glasgow, and parts of it date back to the 13th century. Its grounds are now a country park, with gardens, an adventure playground, woodland walks, a pet's corner and craft workshops.

Isle of Arran

🏔 Goat Fell	🐿 Arran Brewery	🐿 Arran Aromatics
🏚 Brodick Castle	🏛 Isle of Arran Heritage Museum	
🏔 Corrie	🏔 Glen Chalmadale	🏚 Lochranza Castle
🐿 Isle of Arran Whisky Distillery	🏔 Twelve Apostles	
🏛 Auchagallon Stone Circle	🏛 King's Cave	
🏚 St Molas Church	🐿 Torrylinn Creamery	
🏔 Glenashdale Falls	🏛 Giant's Graves	

Arran (13 miles and 55 minutes from Ardrossan by ferry) is called Scotland in miniature, as it is mountainous in the north, low lying in the middle, and rises again towards the south. It is 19 miles long by about 10 miles across at its widest, and within its 165 square miles it has history and spectacular scenery aplenty. This is an island of Celtic saints, mysterious standing stones, craft workshops, cairns and old castles. It was a Gaelic speaking island up until the early 19th century, though the place names owe as much to the language of the Norsemen who settled here in the 10th and 11th centuries as they do to Gaelic. In fact, Brodick, one of the main settlements, comes from the Norse for broad bay.

The northern portion can be every bit as spectacular as the Highlands, and for those with the stamina, a climb to the summit of **Goat Fell**, at 2866 feet the island's highest peak, is a must. There are two recognised routes to the top, with both routes eventually converging, and information on each can be had at the tourist office in Brodick.

Just north of Brodick is the **Arran Brewery**, which has a visitor centre and shop. There are also viewing galleries where you can see the brewing process. And at Home Farm, also near Brodick, is **Arran Aromatics**, Scotland's leading producer of body care products and scented candles. Again, you can watch the manufacturing processes from a viewing gallery.

Beneath Goat Fell, is **Brodick Castle** (National Trust for Scotland).

This former Hamilton family stronghold occupies a wonderful location, surrounded by mature gardens. There has been a castle of sorts here since the Dark Ages, and it is known that a Norse fort also stood on the site. The present building dates from the 16th century and later, and inside there is a collection of paintings and furniture. Around 1844, the 10th Duke of Hamilton and his wife, Princess Marie of Baden, engaged on a building project that almost doubled the size of the castle.

On the northern outskirts of the village is the **Isle of Arran Heritage Museum**, which is well worth a visit as it shows the history of the island's ordinary people. North of Brodick, on the A841, is the beautiful village of **Corrie**, with its small harbour, whitewashed cottages and gardens aflame with colour in the summer months.

The road from Corrie follows the coast north, then turns northwest and goes through the bleak but extremely beautiful **Glen Chalmadale** before bringing you to Lochranza (Loch of the rowan tree river). On the shores of this small village are the

Pirnmill, Isle of Arran

The Twelve Apostles, Isle of Arran

Catacol in favour of deer. From here you get a good view across to the Mull of Kintyre, which is only four miles away.

Further on, and inland from Machrie Bay, is the wonderful **Auchagallon Stone Circle**, a Bronze Age burial cairn with a circle of 15 upright slabs surrounding it. There are several ancient monuments in the area, including the Machrie Moor Stone Circle and the Moss Farm Road Stone Circle. It is said that this part of Arran has more stone circles per square mile than anywhere else in Scotland.

The magnificent cliffs at Drumadoon stand high above a raised beach, and are spectacular. The **King's Cave** is close to the shore, and is supposed to be the cave where Robert the Bruce

imposing ruins of **Lochranza Castle** (Historic Scotland), built in the 16th century on the site of an earlier castle. It started life as a hunting lodge for the Scottish kings before passing first to the Campbells, and then the Montgomeries, Earls of Eglinton.

At the entrance to the village is the **Isle of Arran Whisky Distillery**, which has guided tours and a visitor centre. In the summer months a small car ferry runs from the Mull of Kintyre to Lochranza, the crossing taking about 35 minutes.

Beyond Lochranza is the small village of Catacol, with a row of identical whitewashed cottages known as **The Twelve Apostles**. They were built in the 19th century to accommodate islanders cleared from Glen

saw his spider, (though many other places in Scotland and Ireland make a similar claim). From the village of Blackwaterfoot, south of Machrie Bay, a road called The String cuts across the centre of the island towards Brodick. The village of Shiskine, on The String, has the lovely **St Molas Church**, with an ancient stone carving of the saint embedded in its wall. The Balmichael Visitor Centre is within a converted mill complex and has speciality shops and facilities for various outdoor activities.

South of Blackwaterfoot the road continues on towards Lagg, and if you need convincing about the mildness of the climate hereabouts, the palm trees in the gardens of the Lagg Inn should do the trick. The **Torrylinn Creamery**, which makes traditional Dunlop cheese in the original way, has a viewing gallery and shop. The tiny island of Pladda, with its lighthouse of 1790, can be seen about a mile from the coast before the road turns north once more towards Whiting Bay, another small village and holiday resort. At one time it was a fishing port, and took its name

Holy Island from Dippin Head, Isle of Arran

from the whiting that were caught in the bay. A splendid walk starts from south of the village towards **Glenashdale Falls** and the prehistoric burial cairns known as the **Giant's Graves**.

Lamlash sits on Lamlash Bay. Having the local high school, the hospital and the local government offices, it is the island's capital. In the bay rises the magnificent bulk of Holy Island, so called because the Celtic St Molas lived a life of austerity here in the 6th to 7th century. Nowadays it has regained its religious significance as it is home to a Tibetan Buddhist monastery and retreat. Near Lamlash is the factory Arran Provisions, the island's biggest employer. It makes a wide range of mustards, jams and preserves, and has a visitor centre and shop.

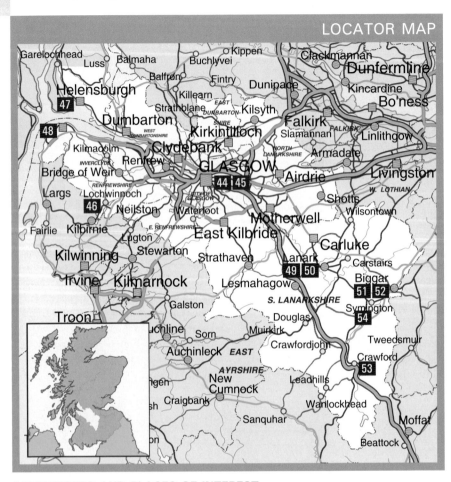

LOCATOR MAP

ADVERTISERS AND PLACES OF INTEREST

🏠 historic building 📷 museum and heritage 🏛 historic site ♣ scenic attraction 🌿 flora and fauna

4 | Glasgow & West Central Scotland

Glasgow and West Central Scotland was at one time the country's industrial hub. Heavy engineering, shipbuilding, coal mining and steelworks predominated, providing work for thousands and fortunes for the favoured few. As well as the city of Glasgow, the area takes in the former counties of Dunbartonshire, Renfrewshire and Lanarkshire, which all played their part in Scotland's rich industrial history. But while it is still Scotland's most populous area, and where the bulk of its industry and commerce is located, it is now clean and attractive, with much to do and see.

The scenery can be outstanding, from the upper reaches of the Clyde, with its quiet pastoral scenery and cosy villages surrounded by high, lonely moorland, to the hills above Greenock and of course, the bonnie banks of Loch Lomond. Then there's Glasgow itself. Once a gritty working class city with an image problem, it has burgeoned into a sophisticated, cosmopolitan city with a lively café society (at least once during a visit, do what the locals do - sit at a pavement café sipping coffee while people watch you watching them). There are art galleries and museums galore, bars, shops and shopping malls (it is the second largest shopping centre in

Britain), award-winning restaurants, glitzy hotels, concert halls and nightclubs.

It is home to Scottish Opera, The Royal Scottish National Orchestra, Scottish Ballet, and a string of theatres where you can see anything from serious drama to variety shows. It is also one of Britain's best dressed cities, and it is reckoned that there are more Armani and Versace outfits worn here than anywhere else in Britain outside London.

That area of the West End known as Kelvinside is the city's wealthiest area. It isn't just a place of trendy flats and apartments, though these abound. It also has some seriously large mansions in the streets north and south of Great Western Road. These are occupied by professional people such as TV personalities, doctors, writers and lawyers, who appreciate the leafy elegance of the area.

And in the centre of Glasgow is the Merchant City, once run down and seedy, but

Trossachs, nr Dumbarton

now home to the city's café society. New apartment blocks have recently been built and older properties have been converted into flats.

But there is still the quirky Glasgow - the city of fish and chips shops, betting shops, working men's pubs, raucous laughter and street markets, including the famous Barras, held every Saturday and Sunday in the East End. The city is ringed by enormous council estates that took the families who used to live in the teeming tenements. It may not be the image of Glasgow that some people would like to project, but they are still there, and in their own way they have as much to do with the city's character as the smart bars, restaurants, concert halls and theatres.

Glasgow has always been an easy place to get out of. Within half an hour of the city centre you can be admiring the grandeur of bens, glens and lochs, taking it easy in some wonderfully bucolic pastoral scenery, or strolling along a lonely beach that has a backdrop of magnificent hills.

Loch Lomond is renowned the world over. A train will take you straight to its bonnie banks in just under an hour, and it's a journey thousands of Glaswegians make. We're on the edge of the Highlands here, and indeed the Highland Boundary Fault, which separates the Highland from the Lowlands, passes through the loch.

The River Clyde has traditionally been a working river, its banks once ringing to the sound of shipbuilding. But there is another Clyde, one that isn't so well known. The upper reaches of the river, in rural Lanarkshire, present an altogether different picture. Within the verdant Clyde Valley, you'll find quiet orchards, green fields, woodland, small attractive villages and cosy pubs. The area around Lanark is green and pleasant, with small farms, woodland, low rounded hills and quiet country roads. And the lonely moorland where the river rises has a gaunt but compelling beauty.

The towns also have their attractions. Helensburgh, Gourock and Dumbarton (once the capital of the Kingdom of Strathclyde) sit on the shores of the Firth of Clyde. Hamilton, Paisley, Lanark, Motherwell and the new town of East Kilbride are inland towns, and each has its attractions, such as the magnificent Paisley Abbey or the impressive shopping malls (the largest in Scotland) in East Kilbride. In some towns close to Glasgow, such as Motherwell, Airdrie or Coatbridge, the excesses of industry once blighted the landscape, but these have been cleaned up, and some places, such as Summerlee at Coatbridge, have taken this industrial heritage and turned it into a tourist attraction.

This whole area was once the powerhouse of Scotland. It is not ashamed of the fact, nor should it be. Coal was mined here, steel was produced, heavy industry sent smoke pluming into the sky, ships were built, deals were struck and money made. Money is still being made in the area, but now it comes from electronics, banking, tourism, broadcasting and publishing. But the people haven't changed. They have remained hardworking and friendly, with a pride in the past and a great faith in the future.

Glasgow

- 🏛 Cathedral of St Mungo 🏛 St Mungo's Museum
- 🏛 Provand's Lordship 🏛 Glasgow Science Centre
- 🏛 The Tall Ship at Glasgow Harbour 🏛 Clydebuilt
- 🎨 Kelvingrove Art Gallery 🏛 City Chambers
- 🪨 Fossil Grove 🏛 Glasgow Museum of Transport
- 🏛 Hunterian Museum 🎨 Hunterian Art Gallery
- 🌿 Glasgow Botanic Gardens 🏛 Hutcheson's Hall
- 🎨 Gallery of Modern Art 🏛 Glasgow Police Museum
- 🎨 Centre for Contemporary Arts 🏛 Tenement House
- 🏛 Tolbooth Steeple 🏛 Templeton's Carpet Factory
- 🏛 Scottish Football Museum 🏛 Celtic Visitor Centre
- 🏛 National Piping Centre 🏛 Martyr's Public School
- 🏛 Heatherbank Museum of Social Work
- 🐦 Charles Rennie Mackintosh 🏛 Holmwood House
- 🏛 Glasgow School of Art 🏛 Scotland Street School
- 🏛 Museum of the Royal Highland Fusiliers
- 🐦 Greek Thomson 🎨 Burrell Collection
- 🏛 Pollok House

Glasgow has worked hard on its image over the past few years. Gone are the constant references to gang fights, organised crime, drunkenness, ugly industrial townscapes and bad housing. Now people talk of trendy nightspots, theatres, restaurants, pavement cafés and art galleries.

The city has changed its image more than once over the years. It was founded in the 7th century by St Kentigern, also known as St Mungo, and started life in early medieval times as a small religious community grouped round a cathedral. In the 17th and 18th centuries, it became a city of trade, dealing with the American colonies in such commodities as tobacco and cotton, which made many people very rich indeed. In the 19th century it became a city of industry, with shipyards and heavy engineering works. Now it relies mostly on tourism, the media, service industries and the arts for employment.

The area round the **Cathedral of St Mungo** (Historic Scotland) is where it all started. This was where St Kentigern, or Mungo, established a small church in the 6th century. The present cathedral was founded in the 12th century by David I, and the building shows work from this period onwards. It is the only Scottish mainland cathedral that escaped the Reformation of 1560 more or less intact. In its crypt is the Tomb of St Mungo, once a place of pilgrimage, but now visited by pilgrims of a different sort - tourists. The Blackadder Aisle is a wonderful piece of architecture added by Archbishop Robert Blackadder in about 1500.

St Mungo's Cathedral, Glasgow

🎬 stories and anecdotes 🐦 famous people 🎨 art and craft 🎟 entertainment and sport 🚶 walks

On a hill behind the cathedral is the Necropolis, Glasgow's ancient burial ground, and in front of the cathedral is the modern (and looking anything but modern) **St Mungo's Museum of Religious Life and Art**. Across from it is Glasgow's oldest house, **Provand's Lordship**, built in 1471 as a manse for the former St Nicholas Hospital.

The Clyde made Glasgow, and Glasgow made the Clyde, runs an old, but true, saying. In the 17th century, the city was seen as being wholly inland, and the river was so shallow that people could wade across it. But in 1768, a man called John Golborne began canalising and deepening it to allow large ships to sail right up into the city. **The Tall Ship at Glasgow Harbour** (see panel below) in Stobcross Road, tells the story of the river and the industries it spawned. The centrepiece is the tall ship itself, the *S V Glenlee*, built in 1896. At Braehead, on the south side of the river, and a few miles downstream, is another museum that celebrates the Clyde - the award-winning **Clydebuilt**. It is part of the Scottish Maritime Museum and tells the river's story from the 1700s up to the present day.

The Clyde Waterbus Service takes you on a boat trip along the Clyde from the city centre to Braehead, with a commentary on the history of the river as you go.

Close to the Tall Ship is the Scottish Exhibition and Conference Centre, a mammoth complex of halls and auditoriums, including what Glaswegians now refer to as the Armadillo, a metal and glass creation whose design owes more than a little to Sydney Opera House. And across the river from it is the city's newest attraction, the **Glasgow Science Centre**. Built on the site of the Glasgow Garden Festival, it is a combination of museum, laboratory and hands-on exhibition area that explores science and discovery, and has four floors featuring more than 300 exhibits. The accompanying Glasgow Tower is Scotland's tallest freestanding structure at 412 feet, and there's also an IMAX Theatre.

Glasgow has always been a city of museums and art galleries, even when it relied on industry for its employment. Like most large cities, its West End is where the well-off built their mansions, as the prevailing south-westerly

The Tall Ship at Glasgow Harbour

100 Stobcross Road, Glasgow G3 8QQ
Tel: 0141 222 2513
e-mail: info@thetallship.com
website: www.thetallship.com

Sail through 100 years of maritime history at the Tall Ship at Glasgow Harbour. Follow the remarkable restoration of the Glenlee from an abandoned hulk in Seville harbour to her fullyrigged splendour today and learn about the living conditions aboard a deep sea trading ship. Explore the cargo hold where you will see what goods she carried, the deck house where the crew lived, the poop deck and the galley. Also in the harbour is the Pier 17 restaurant, a gift shop and various exhibitions and events. Phone for details.

🏚 historic building 🏛 museum and heritage 🏛 historic site 🝤 scenic attraction 🌿 flora and fauna

Kelvingrove Art Gallery, Glasgow

winds carried the smells of the city away from them. Here you'll find the **Kelvingrove Art Gallery and Museum** which benefited from a £27.9m refurbishment before re-opening in 2006. It is housed in a grand red sandstone building that froths with detail. It has internationally important collections on archaeology, botany, zoology, geology and all the other ologies you can think of. There are Egyptian mummies, fossils, stuffed animals, dinosaur skeletons, clothing and uniforms from all over the world, as well as weapons, and a host of other material. The art collection is stunning, and is possibly the most comprehensive civic collection in Europe. The museum's magnificent organ was built at the turn of the last century by Lewis and Co Ltd, London, and organ recitals have been a feature of Kelvingrove ever since the building opened.

The **Glasgow Museum of Transport**, with trains, carriages, motorcars and a marvellous collection of model ships, sits opposite the Kelvingrove Art Gallery and Museum. Perhaps the most striking display is the one on Glasgow's underground system. The system forms a simple loop round the city centre and West End, and in the late 1970s was upgraded, with orange trains taking the place of the much-loved wood and metal ones. The Glaswegians immediately dubbed it the Clockwork Orange and the name has stuck. More properly, it is known as the Glasgow Subway, rather than underground or metro.

Also in the West End, just off Byres Road (the area's trendiest street) are the **Hunterian Museum** and the **Hunterian Art Gallery**, which form part of Glasgow University. The museum has fine collections covering geology and numismatics, while the gallery has paintings, furniture and interior design by Mackintosh and Whistler. At the top of Byres Road is the **Glasgow Botanic Gardens** with, at its centre, the Kibble Palace, a huge greenhouse with plants from all over the world. It is named after its builder John Kibble, who erected it beside his house on the banks of Loch Long. It was rebuilt here in 1873, after being dismantled and sailed up the Clyde.

Within Victoria Park, further to the west, is the **Fossil Grove** (open between April and September only), undoubtedly the city's most ancient attraction. It consists of fragments of an ancient forest over 330 million years old which was discovered in 1887. They are housed within a small building to protect them.

The heart of Glasgow nowadays is George Square, a huge open space in front of the

Victorian **City Chambers** (conducted tours available). There are statues galore, and it is a favourite place for city workers to relax in the sun. The City Chambers themselves reflect Glasgow's wealth and confidence in the Victorian era, and so opulent are the interiors that they stood in for the Vatican in the film *Heavenly Pursuits*. Round the corner you'll find **Hutcheson's Hall** (National Trust for Scotland), founded in 1641 as a hospice, though the building itself is 18th century. It was designed by David Hamilton, and has a small exhibition about the Merchant City, that area that housed the homes and offices of the rich 17th- and 18th-century merchants who traded with America. Nowadays, it is an area of expensive apartment blocks, smart bars, restaurants and pubs. Not far away, in Queen Street, is the **Gallery of Modern Art**, housed in an elegant, neo-classical building. It has four floors of work by modern artists such as Christine Borland and Toby Paterson. In Buccleuch Street near Charing Cross, is the **Tenement House** (National Trust for Scotland). Built in the late 19th century, it re-creates the genteel tenement living conditions that were common among Glasgow's lower middle classes in the early 20th century. It is open between March and October. The **Centre for Contemporary Arts** (CCA) is at 320 Sauchiehall Street, and has a changing programme of events, performances and exhibitions. There are six galleries, a small cinema, bookshop and bar/restaurant

The Mitchell Library is an imposing domed building in North Street, not far from Charing Cross. It is Britain's largest municipal library, and has collections covering Scottish and local history, genealogy, and Robert Burns.

The **Glasgow Police Museum** is in St Andrews Square (to the east of Glasgow Cross), with exhibits highlighting the Glasgow Police Force between 1800 and 1975. And at the Cross itself is the old **Glasgow Tolbooth Steeple**, dating from the 1620s. At one time it provided offices for the City Council, and had a jail incorporated into it.

Glasgow Green, a huge area of parkland in the city's east end, is Glasgow's lung. It has been common land for centuries, and it was here that Charles Edward Stuart mustered his troops during the Jacobite Uprising when he occupied the city. Now it is the city's largest park, with its centrepiece being the People's Palace and Winter Gardens, a museum and glasshouse complex that tells the city's own story. Close to it is the Doulton Fountain, at 46 feet high and 70 feet wide, the world's largest terracotta fountain. It was recently refurbished at a cost of £3.75m. On the eastern edge of Glasgow Green is one of the city's most colourful buildings - **Templeton's Carpet Factory** (now a business centre). It is based on a Venetian design, with walls that incorporate multi-coloured bricks.

Glasgow is synonymous with football, and at the redeveloped Hampden Park, on the south side of the Clyde, is the **Scottish Football Museum**. It reveals the sights, sounds and stories of the world's most popular game, and tells how it almost shaped the history of Glasgow in the late 19th and 20th centuries. You can see such things as the oldest football ticket in the world, the Scottish Cup trophy and Kenny Dalgleish's 100th Scottish cap.

At Celtic Park in the Parkhead area of the city is the **Celtic Visitor Centre**, which traces the history of Celtic Football Club, one of Glasgow's 'big two' football clubs. There are exhibits, a stadium tour and a shop selling Celtic memorabilia. Rangers Football Club is

Glasgow's other major team, with Ibrox, in Govan, to the south of the river. The Rangers Tour Experience takes you on a guided tour of the stadium, including the Trophy Room.

If you want to immerse yourself in something typically Scottish, then the **National Piping Centre** in Otago Street has a small museum dedicated to Scotland's national instrument. Within the Caledonian University on Cowcaddens Road, not far away, is the **Heatherbank Museum of Social Work**. It has displays on housing, health and childcare, and looks at how socially excluded people were cared for in the past.

Charles Rennie Mackintosh is the most famous of Glasgow's architects, and was born in 1868. He designed a number of buildings in Glasgow, and there are organised tours taking you to the best of them arranged by the Charles Rennie Mackintosh Society. His most famous building is the **Glasgow School of Art** in Renfrew Street. It is still a working college, though tours are available by appointment. On the south side of the river is the **Scotland Street School**, now a museum dedicated to education. Another school is the **Martyr's Public School** in Parson Street. It is no longer used as a school and is open to the public. The Willow Tea Rooms in Sauchiehall Street still sells traditional Scottish high teas amid Mackintosh's designs, and the Queen's Cross Church on Garscube Road is now the headquarters of the Charles Rennie Mackintosh Society. At Bellahouston Park, on the south side, is the House for an Art Lover, which interprets some of the incomplete designs Mackintosh submitted to a competition in a German magazine. The Lighthouse, Scotland's centre for architecture, design and the city, is in Mitchell Lane and has a Mackintosh interpretation centre. It is housed in a Mackintosh-designed building that was once the home of Glasgow's daily newspaper, *The Herald*. In the Hunterian Art Gallery there is also the Mackintosh House, featuring the principal rooms from Mackintosh's own house, together with a collection of designs and watercolours.

Another Glasgow architect, formerly overshadowed by Mackintosh but now more widely known, was Alexander Thomson (1817-1875), known as **Greek Thomson** because of the Greek influences in his work. He designed St Vincent Street Church, as well as **Holmwood House** (National Trust for Scotland) in Netherlee Road, in the southern suburbs.

Charles Rennie Mackintosh Church, Glasgow

GLASGOW AND WEST CENTRAL SCOTLAND

Perhaps Glasgow's most famous modern attraction is the **Burrell Collection**, housed in a purpose-built complex of galleries in Pollok Country Park, south of the river. William Burrell (see also Largs and Hutton Castle) gifted a huge collection of art and historical objects to the city of Glasgow, and now more than 8000 of them are on display. A whole day could be spent going round the collection. Also in the park is **Pollok House** (National Trust for Scotland - see panel below), a Georgian mansion that houses the Stirling Maxwell collection of decorative arts.

Glasgow is Britain's second largest shopping centre, the three main shopping streets being Argyle Street, Sauchiehall Street and Buchanan Street. There are also enormous shopping malls. The St Enoch Centre is just off Argyle Street, the Buchanan Galleries are at the corner of Buchanan Street and Sauchiehall Street, while the Braehead Shopping Centre is south of the river on the city's western fringes, near Renfrew. There's also the Forge at Parkhead, in the East End.

Within the city centre there are two exclusive retail developments. Princes Square, off Buchanan Street, is a mix of upmarket shops and cafés, while the Italian Centre is where you'll find the designer labels.

In Sauchiehall Street is the **Regimental Museum of the Royal Highland Fusiliers**. It is Scotland's second oldest infantry

Pollok House

Pollok Country Park, 2060 Pollokshaws Road, Glasgow G43 1AT
Tel: 0141 616 6410 Fax: 014) 616 6521
e-mail pollokhouse@nts.org.uk
website: www.nts.org.uk

Visit **Pollok House** and capture the flavour of one of Scotland's grandest Edwardian country houses, It is the ancestral home of the Maxwells of Pollok, who have lived on this site for 700 years. The

present house, which replaced three earlier structures, was begun in 1747. It was extended from 1890 by Sir John Stirling Maxwell Bt, KT, a founder member of The National Trust for Scotland.

The house contains much original furniture as well as some of the finest Spanish paintings in Britain. A rare survival is the magnificent suite of servants' quarters, which shows the scale of country house life around 1900. These contain the popular Edwardian Kitchen Restaurant, renowned for its lunch menu and home baking, and the shop in the Housekeeper's Room. At weekends, visitors can see a reconstruction, of the way the house might have been run at the turn of the last century. Pollok House is set amid formal and walled gardens at the heart of Pollok Country Park.

 historic building 🏛 museum and heritage �🏚 historic site 🝔 scenic attraction 🜉 flora and fauna

regiment, and was formed in the 1960s when the Highland Light Infantry amalgamated with the Royal Scottish Fusiliers.

Around Glasgow

KIRKINTILLOCH
7 miles NE of Glasgow city centre on the A803

🏛 Auld Kirk Museum 🎨 Craft Daft

The old burgh of Kirkintilloch sits beside the Forth and Clyde Canal, which has recently been re-opened after a multi-million pound refurbishment. It connects the Firth of Clyde and the Firth of Forth, with a further canal, the Union Canal, connecting it to Edinburgh. The **Auld Kirk Museum** is housed in the former parish church, which dates from 1644. In Peel Park are some Roman remains from the Antonine Wall.

Craft Daft (On a Raft) is a craft studio on a canal boat moored in the Forth and Clyde Canal at Glasgow Bridge. Here you can paint a ceramic ornament to take away immediately, or a mug or plate to collect in a day or two. You can also try glass painting, silk painting, encaustic wax, pyrography or quilling.

CUMBERNAULD
12 miles NE of Glasgow off the A80

🌿 Palacerigg Country Park

Set on a hill above the A80, Cumbernauld is one of Scotland's new towns. It was created in 1956 as a population overspill for Glasgow City and was built partly on what was an old country estate. It is now the eighth most populous settlement in Scotland, the largest in North Lanarkshire, and also larger than two of Scotland's cities, Inverness and Stirling. In 1981, it provided the setting for the hit film *Gregory's Girl*. To the southeast of the town,

Palacerigg Country Park covers 750 acres and has an animal collection that is unique in Central Scotland. In addition to some friendly farm animals, the menagerie includes rare breeds such as Eriskay ponies, North Ronaldsay and Boreray sheep, Shetland and white park cattle, Bagot and Guernsey goats, Tamworth pigs and Scots grey and Scots dumpy poultry.

KILSYTH
11 miles NE of Glasgow on the A809

🏛 Battle of Kilsyth

The **Battle of Kilsyth** was fought on August 15 1645, when the first Marquis of Montrose routed a Covenanting army led by William Bailiie of Letham. A reservoir is now located where Montrose's army camped, and a cairn marks the spot where the battle took place.

RUTHERGLEN
2 miles SE of Glasgow city centre on the A749

This royal burgh is one of the oldest in Scotland, having been granted its royal charter by David I in the 12th century. For a short while the burgh was incorporated into the city of Glasgow, something that was greatly resented by some of its citizens. Since 1997, the town has formed part of the local authority area of South Lanarkshire. A gable of its medieval Parish Church survives in the kirkyard of its more modern successor. Robbie Coltrane (Hagrid in the Harry Potter films) was born here, and for a short while Stan Laurel lived in the town and went to a local school.

NEWTON MEARNS
7 miles S of Glasgow on the A77

🌿 Greenbank House

Newton Mearns is a commuter town of smart

bungalows and substantial houses. The four-square Parish Church dates from 1755, and close by is **Greenbank House** (National Trust for Scotland) surrounded by beautiful gardens. The house is not open to the public but the walled garden and 16 acres of woodland are.

CLYDEBANK
7 miles W of Glasgow city centre on the A814

🏛 Clydebank Museum

Clydebank is a former shipbuilding town, and it was here that the *Queen Mary*, the *Queen Elizabeth* and the *Queen Elizabeth II* were built. The town suffered more damage in proportion to its size than any other British town from air raids in World War II. In early 1941, during the Clydebank Blitz, the centre of the town was flattened, other parts severely damaged and many people were killed. The **Clydebank Museum** at the Town Hall in Dumbarton Road has exhibits devoted to the Blitz, as well as to the famous Singer sewing machine factory that once stood in the town.

PAISLEY
5 miles W of Glasgow city centre on the A761

🏛 Paisley Abbey   🐿 John Witherspoon

🏛 Thomas Coats Memorial Church

🏛 Paisley Museum & Art Gallery

🏛 Sma' Shot Cottages   🐿 Paisley Arts Centre

🐿 Robert Tannahill   🌱 Gleniffer Braes Country Park

🌱 Jenny's Well Local Nature Reserve

🏛 Wallace Memorial

The large town of Paisley is centred on the great Abbey Church of Saints Mary the Virgin, James the Greater of Compostella, Mirin and Milburga. It is better known as **Paisley Abbey**. The abbey was founded in the 12th century by Walter FitzAlan, first High Steward of Scotland and progenitor of the Stewart dynasty. Within its walls are the tombs of most of the non-royal High Stewards, as well as that of Princess Marjory, daughter of Robert the Bruce. Her grandson, Robert III, is also buried here. It can legitimately claim to be the birthplace of the Stewart dynasty, because Robert II, the first Stewart king, was born at the abbey in 1316. Marjory had been seriously injured in a riding accident at Knock, a nearby hill, and she was brought to the abbey where she died soon after giving birth to her son.

The building as you see it now was built from the 12th century onwards, though the bulk dates from the 15th century. The choir was rebuilt in the early 1900s. Within the abbey is a memorial to **John Witherspoon**, a former minister of the Laigh Kirk, who signed the American Declaration of Independence. A statue of him can also be found in front of Paisley University.

Another famous Paisley church is the Baptist **Thomas Coats Memorial Church**, sometimes known as the Baptist Cathedral because of its size. It was built in 1894 in memory of Thomas Coats of the Coats and Clark thread-making firm. The same Thomas Coats gifted the Coats Observatory to the town's Philosophical Institution in 1883. It is now open to the public. Adjacent is **Paisley Museum and Art Gallery**, with displays of Paisley shawls and other memorabilia.

Paisley was the birthplace of many famous people. Tom Conti the actor was born here, as were John Byrne the artist and writer (whose most famous work is undoubtedly the TV series *Tutti Frutti*), Andrew Neill, now editor of *The Scotsman*, Gerry Rafferty the singer, and Fulton Mackay of *Porridge* fame.

At the Corner of Shuttle Street and George Place are the 18th- and 19th-century weaving cottages known as **Sma' Shot Cottages**,

Coats Observatory, Paisley

Cottage in Queen Street in 1774. He was a silk weaver who wrote the words to such beautiful songs as *Jessie the Flower o' Dunblane* and *The Braes o' Gleniffer*. The actual braes (hillsides) themselves now form part of the 1300-acre **Gleniffer Braes Country Park**, to the south of the town. There are spectacular views from the Robertson Car Park, and guide tours are available.

Jenny's Well Local Nature Reserve, on the south bank of the White Cart Water, is less than a mile from the centre of the town, and is locked between a council estate and a chemicals factory. For all that, it is a haven for wildlife with some pleasant walks. To the north of Paisley, on the other side of the M8, is Glasgow International Airport.

The village of Elderslie, a mile west of the town, is the supposed birthplace of William Wallace, and the **Wallace Memorial,** built in 1912, explains his exploits.

housing an interpretation centre that gives an insight into the living conditions of Paisley's weaving families in the past. Nearby, in New Street, is **Paisley Arts Centre**, housed in the former Laigh Kirk of 1738.

In the 18th century, the town was famed for its poets, the most famous being **Robert Tannahill**, who was born in Tannahill

LOCHWINNOCH
16 miles SW of Glasgow on the B786

🐦 Clyde Muirshiel Regional Park

🏛 Castle Semple Church

🐦 Lochwinnoch Nature Reserve

The **Clyde Muirshiel Regional Park** covers 106 square miles of magnificent countryside

---

EAST LOCHHEAD

Kilbirnie Road, Lochwinnoch, Renfrewshire PA12 4DX
Tel/Fax: 01505 842610
e-mail: admin@eastlochhead.co.uk website: www.eastlochhead.co.uk

The Andersons offer you, (and well-behaved pets), a warm welcome at **East Lochhead**. The 4-star quality self-catering cottages in a courtyard layout, have fully equipped kitchens and gas central heating throughout. Lochwinnoch is just 20 miles from Glasgow in a lovely setting between the moors of Clyde Muirshiel Regional Park and Castle Semple Loch. It provides easy access to Ayrshire's coast, golf courses, the islands of Arran, Bute and Cumbrae; Loch Lomond, the Trossachs and the varied attractions of Glasgow.

🎭 stories and anecdotes 🐦 famous people 🎨 art and craft 🎭 entertainment and sport 🚶 walks

from Greenock to Inverkip and down into Ayrshire. It is ideal for walking, cycling, fishing and observing wildlife. There is also sailing on Castle Semple Loch. Near its shores are the ruins of **Castle Semple Church**, founded in the early 16th century by John Semple. He was later killed at the Battle of Flodden in 1513, and his tomb can be seen at the east end of the church.

The **Lochwinnoch Nature Reserve** is run by the RSPB, and has nature trails through woodland, with viewing areas and a visitor centre.

KILBARCHAN
11 miles SW of Glasgow, off the A761

🏛 The Weaver's Cottage   🎵 Habbie Simpson

This is undoubtedly the most picturesque village in Renfrewshire, a huddle of charming 18th-century weaving cottages. **The Weaver's Cottage** (National Trust for Scotland) dates from 1723, and shows what a typical weaver's home (complete with working loom) was like.

In a niche on the wall of the Steeple Hall of 1755, is a statute to **Habbie Simpson**, the village's famous 17th-century piper. It is a bronze reproduction of one made in wood by Archibald Simpson in 1822.

RENFREW
5 miles W of Glasgow on the A8

🏛 Battle of Renfrew

🏛 Renfrew Community Museum

The ancient burgh of Renfrew was granted its charter in 1143, making it one of the oldest in Scotland. It was here, in 1164, that one of the lesser-known, but still important, Scottish battles took place - the **Battle of Renfrew**. It was fought between Somerled, Lord of the Isles, and the royal army of Malcolm IV led by Walter FitzAlan, founder of Paisley Abbey and

first High Steward of Scotland. This battle brought the Western Isles fully under the control of the Scottish monarchy. The story of the battle is an intriguing one. Somerled had sailed up the Clyde the previous year with 15,000 troops carried in more than 160 great warships. One version of the story says that the king had bribed Somerled's nephew to murder him, which he did, and the troops returned home. Another version - probably the true one - says that Somerled was killed during the battle along with his heir, and they were carried off to be buried in Saddell Abbey on the Mull of Kintyre.

The **Renfrew Community Museum** in the Brown Institute in Canal Street was opened in 1997 to coincide with the 600th anniversary of the town being granted royal burgh status. It has displays of local history.

BEARSDEN AND MILNGAVIE
6 miles NW of Glasgow city centre on the A809 and A81

🏛 Roman Bathhouse   🚶 West Highland Way

🎨 The Lillie Art Gallery

These two prosperous towns are firmly within Glasgow's inner commuting belt, and are full of large Victorian and Edwardian mansions as well as the more modest bungalows of the 1930s. The Antonine Wall (named after Roman Emperor Antoninus Pius) passes close by. It was built of turf in the 2nd century to keep out the warring tribesmen of the north, and stretched for 37 miles between the Clyde and the Forth. In Bearsden there are the remains of a **Roman Bathhouse.**

Mugdock Country Park sits off the A81 north of Milngavie (pronounced Mull-guy) which is the starting point for the 95-mile-long **West Highland Way**, which connects the Glasgow conurbation with Fort William.

🏛 historic building 🏛 museum and heritage 🏛 historic site 🔱 scenic attraction 🌱 flora and fauna

Trossachs, nr Dumbarton

The Lillie Art Gallery, in Station Road, Milngavie, was founded by banker and amateur artist Robert Lillie, and opened in 1962. It has a collection of 20th-century Scottish paintings, including works by the Scottish Colourists, Joan Eardley and Philip Reves.

Dumbarton

🏛 Dumbarton Castle 🏛 Denny Tank Museum

🏛 College Bow 🍃 Overtoun Estate

The town sits where the River Leven, fed by Loch Lomond, enters the Clyde, and is dominated by **Dumbarton Castle** (Historic Scotland), which sits high on a volcanic plug 240 feet above the Firth of Clyde. It is one of the oldest fortified sites in Britain, and from the 8th to the early 11th centuries was the capital of the ancient kingdom of Strathclyde. It was incorporated into Scotland in 1034, when its king, Duncan, also assumed the throne of Scotland. The name itself means the Fort of the Britons, and though the town is called Dumbarton, the former county is Dunbartonshire, with an 'n'. The castle now mainly consists of modern barracks, but there

is still plenty to see, including a 12th-century gateway, a dungeon and a museum. From the top there is a splendid view out over the Firth of Clyde. It was from Dumbarton in 1548 that Mary Queen of Scots set sail for France and her eventual marriage to Francis, the Dauphin. This was considered to be much safer than leaving from an east coast port, as Henry VIII's ships were patrolling the North Sea. The English king had wanted Mary to marry his son Henry, and when the Scottish parliament refused to ratify such an agreement, Henry tried unsuccessfully to force the marriage, a period known as the Rough Wooing.

The **Denny Tank Museum** in Castle Street forms part of the Scottish Maritime Museum. It is the oldest experimental water tank in the world, and is the length of a football pitch. It was built in 1882 as part of Denny's shipyard, whose most famous ship was undoubtedly the tea clipper the *Cutty Sark*. It was here that hull shapes were tested in water using carefully crafted models before the ships themselves were built. On display are many of the models built by Denny craftsmen.

Though Denny was famous for its ships, it also has a place in aircraft history, as it built the first helicopter capable of flight in 1909, as well as the world's first hovercraft, half a century later.

In Church Street is an old archway called the **College Bow** once part of the long-gone Collegiate Church of St Mary. On the hillside above the town is the beautiful **Overtoun Estate**, which commands wonderful views over the Firth. It was bequeathed to the people of Dumbarton by Douglas White, a London doctor, in 1939. Old Kilpatrick, to the west of the town, is supposed to be the birthplace of St Patrick, who was captured by raiders and taken to Ireland in the 4th century.

Around Dumbarton

BALLOCH
4 miles N of Dumbarton on the A811

- ⚲ Loch Lomond   ⚲ Antartex Village Visitor Centre
- ⚘ Loch Lomond & the Trossachs National Park
- ⚲ Duncryne Hill   ⚘ Balloch Castle Country Park
- ⚹ Leven Valley Heritage Trail
- 🏛 Motoring Memories Museum

This pleasant town sits at the point where the River Leven (at five miles long, Scotland's shortest river) leaves **Loch Lomond** on its way to Dumbarton and the Clyde. The loch is recognised as Scotland's largest and most beautiful sheet of water, covering more than 27 square miles. The **Loch Lomond and the Trossachs National Park** was Scotland's first national park, opened in 2002, and Lomond Shores at Balloch includes the National Park Gateway.

The loch is at its widest to the south. It gradually narrows and gets deeper as it goes north, and at some points reaches a depth of more than 600 feet, making it the third deepest loch in Scotland. Many songs have been written about this stretch of water, the most famous being the *Bonnie, Bonnie Banks o'*

Loch Lomond. The song was written by a Jacobite prisoner held in Carlisle Castle who was due to be executed. He is telling a fellow prisoner whose life had been spared that he (the condemned man) will be in Scotland before him because he will take the 'low road', the road of death, while his colleague will take the 'high road', or the road of life.

At the nearby village of Gartocharn is **Duncryne Hill** (nicknamed The Dumpling by locals), where you get a marvellous view, not just of the loch, but also of the surrounding countryside. The Highland Boundary Fault, which separates the Lowlands of Scotland from the Highlands, passes through Loch Lomond from Glen Fruin on the west, to Balmaha on the east. The **Balloch Castle Country Park**, northeast of Balloch, has lochside walks, gardens and a visitor centre. South from the town you can follow the **Leven Valley Heritage Trail**, taking you down the valley of the Leven to Dumbarton, passing such small industrial towns as Alexandria and Renton.

In Alexandria is the **Antartex Village Visitor Centre**. It incorporates a factory making sheepskin coats (with factory tours available), a mill shop and a small craft village. Close by is the Loch Lomond Factory Outlets and **Motoring Memories Museum**, housed in a magnificent building where one of Scotland's former makes of car, the Argyll, was manufactured.

Renton has a special place in the hearts of all Scottish football supporters. Not only was Renton Football Club responsible for the founding of the Scottish League, it became 'champions of the United Kingdom and the world' in 1888 when it beat West Bromwich Albion at Hampden Park.

Hamilton

- Hamilton Mausoleum
- Chatelherault
- Chatelherault Country Park
- Cadzow Castle
- Hamilton Parish Church
- County Buildings
- Low Parks Museum
- Sir Harry Lauder

Hamilton was once the county town of Lanarkshire, Scotland's most populous and industrialised county. It became a royal burgh in 1548, though it lost this status in 1669. It has strong connections to one of the most important families in Scotland, the Dukes of Hamilton, Scotland's premier dukes. Up until medieval times, the town was known as Cadzow, but gradually Hamilton took over as the family grew in importance. By the 1920s, when it was demolished, the immense Hamilton Palace, home to the dukes, was the grandest non-royal residence in Britain.

Not a stone now remains of it above ground, though the Hamilton's burial place, the grandiose **Hamilton Mausoleum**, still remains. It is a curious building with an immense dome, and is full of Masonic symbolism. It consists of a chapel above and a crypt below, and was built in the mid-19th century for Alexander, the 10th Duke (nicknamed Il Magnifico). He had his ancestors removed from the ruins (now gone completely) of the old Collegiate Church of Hamilton and re-interred in the crypt. When he himself died, he was laid to rest in the sarcophagus of an Egyptian princess, which was placed in the upper chapel. A curious tale tells of how the duke was found to be too tall to fit into the sarcophagus when he died, so his legs were broken and folded over. However, that's all it is - a tale. The duke was indeed too big for the sarcophagus, but he knew this long before he died, as he used to

lie in it. So he had stonemasons enlarge it.

The crypt is entered through the middle arch of three arches. Above each arch is a carved head, representing life, death and immortality.

The bodies were all removed from the mausoleum in 1921, and the place can now be visited. It was never used as a chapel, however, as it is reckoned to have the longest echo of any building in Britain. One thing to note is that the crypt doors lock from the inside. The reason is simple - once a month a servant was sent from the palace to dust and clean the huge coffins. To prevent ghoulish sightseers, a policeman was stationed outside and the servant locked herself in.

A two-mile long Grand Avenue once stretched from the palace all the way to **Chatelherault**, pronounced Shattly-row, a Hamilton hunting lodge east of the town. Most of the avenue is gone, but Chatelherault survives, having been refurbished in the 1980s in the largest refurbishment project of its time in Britain. It was officially re-opened in September 1987 by the Duke of Gloucester. Originally designed by William Adam in the 1730s, the lodge once also housed the Duke's hunting dogs, and was therefore known as the Dog Kennels. Now it houses a museum and interpretation centre. The lodge got its name because the Dukes of Hamilton were also the Dukes of Chatellerault near Poitou in France. The title was bestowed in 1548 by Henry II of France in recognition of the part the family played in arranging the marriage of Mary Stuart to his son Francis, the Dauphin. The spelling of the name changed over the years, and Chatellerault gradually became Chatelherault.

Surrounding the lodge is **Chatelherault Country Park**, with more than 10 miles of woodland walks. The ruins of **Cadzow Castle**, the original home of the Hamiltons, and where Mary Stuart once stayed, can be seen within the park. There are also the remains of an old Iron Age Fort and the Cadzow Oaks, which are very ancient. In a field in front of Chatelherault is a small but famous herd of White Cattle.

Hamilton Parish Church, within the town, was designed by William Adam in the early 1730s at the same time as he was designing Chatelherault. It is an elegant building in the shape of a Greek cross, with a cupola over the crossing. The pre-Norman Netherton Cross stands at the church entrance, and in the kirkyard is the Heads Monument, commemorating four Covenanters beheaded in Edinburgh after the Pentland Rising of 1666.

In Almada Street you'll find the town's most prominent landmark - the **County Buildings**. They were built in the 1960s for the then Lanarkshire County Council, and were modelled on the United Nations building in New York. It is one of the few 1960s buildings in Scotland to be listed.

Based in an old 17th-century coaching inn, once known as the Hamilton Arms, is the **Low Parks Museum**, which has displays and memorabilia on local history. It also houses a large display on Lanarkshire's own regiment - the Cameronians (Scottish Rifles). Raised as a Covenanting force in 1689, it took its name from Richard Cameron, a Covenanting minister who opposed bishops in the Church of Scotland and the king being its head. It chose to disband itself in 1968 rather than amalgamate with another regiment. Most of the Low Parks, which at one time formed some of Hamilton Palace's parkland, has been given over to a huge retail development that includes a multi-screen cinema and supermarket.

In the Bent Cemetery is the simple grave of one of Scotland's best-known entertainers, **Sir Harry Lauder**. Born in Portobello near Edinburgh in 1870, he at one time worked in the coalmines in Quarter, a village near Hamilton. He died in 1950. Nearby is the plot where the members of the Hamilton family who formerly lay in the mausoleum are now buried. The 10th Duke, who had the mausoleum built, still lies in his Egyptian sarcophagus.

Hamilton is the start of one of Scotland's 10 national tourist routes, the Clyde Valley Tourist Route. It follows the Clyde Valley all the way south to Abington on the M74.

Around Hamilton

AIRDRIE AND COATBRIDGE
7 miles N of Hamilton on the A89

🐦 John Reith   🏛 Summerlee Heritage Centre

🏃 North Calder Heritage Trail   🦋 Time Capsule

🌿 Drumpellier Country Park

The twin towns of Airdrie and Coatbridge are industrial in character. In Coatbridge, in 1889, **John Reith**, the first general manager of what was then the British Broadcasting Company was born. Single-handedly he shaped the character of the organisation.

The town is home to the **Summerlee Heritage Centre**, built on the site of the old Summerlee Ironworks, which traces the history of the area's old industries - steel making, coalmining and the manufacture of heavy plant. Tramlines have been laid out and there is a small collection of trams from all over Europe. There is also a short section of the Summerlee branch of the Monklands Canal (now closed), which ran from Glasgow to the Lanarkshire coalfields. The canal was built between 1770 and 1794, and at one time was the most profitable in Scotland. The **North Calder Heritage Trail** runs from Summerlee to Hillend Reservoir, and passes many sites connected with the past industry of the area.

The **Time Capsule** is one of the largest leisure centres in the area. In the **Drumpellier Country Park** there is a visitor centre, butterfly house, formal gardens, golf course and pets' corner.

MOTHERWELL AND WISHAW
3 miles E of Hamilton on the A721

- 🏛 Motherwell Heritage Centre
- 🌿 Strathclyde Country Park 🏛 Roman Bathhouse
- 🌿 Amazonia 🏛 Carfin Pilgrimage Centre
- 🏛 Shotts Heritage Centre

The twin towns of Motherwell and Wishaw were, up until 1975, included in the one burgh. They were steel-making towns, though the steelworks at Ravenscraig have now gone. The award-winning **Motherwell Heritage Centre** on High Road has a number of exhibitions, and hosts varied activities with a heritage theme. To the west of Motherwell, adjoining the M74, is the 1100 acres of **Strathclyde Country Park**, built on waste ground in the early 1970s. Within it there is an international-sized rowing lake where the rowing events of the 1986 Commonwealth Games were held. On its banks are the remains of a **Roman Bathhouse**. There are guided walks throughout the year, as well as nature trails and a camping and caravanning site. M&D's Theme Park is located near the north banks of the loch.

Amazonia is Scotland's only indoor rain forest attraction and houses reptiles, insects and animals connected with the Amazon rain forest.

A mile northeast of Motherwell is the small industrial village of Carfin, where you will find the Lourdes-inspired **Carfin Pilgrimage Centre and Grotto**, created in the 1920s by Fr Thomas Nimmo Taylor, the local priest, helped by out-of-work miners. There are displays and exhibits that help explain the notion of pilgrimage, not only in the Roman Catholic religion, but also in all major religions.

The **Shotts Heritage Centre** is in Benhar Road in Shotts, eight miles to the west of Motherwell and Wishaw. There are displays on the history of this former mining town. Kirk o' Shotts, built in 1820, lies to the east of the town, and can easily be seen from the M8 motorway. Its future is in jeopardy, as it is badly in need of restoration. Within its kirkyard is a gravestone marking the last resting place of William Smith, a Covenanter who fought at Rullion Green in 1666.

DALSERF
7 miles SE of Hamilton town centre off the A72

- 🏛 Dalserf Parish Church

Once a sizeable village with inns and a ferry across the Clyde, Dalserf has now shrunk to no more than a few cottages and a church. **Dalserf Parish Church**, with its whitewashed walls, looks more like a house than a place of worship, and dates from 1655, though an ancient chapel dedicated to St Serf stood here before that. The building is a rare survivor of a mid 17th-century Scottish church. Most from that period were simply built, with earth floors and a thatched roof. In the 18th and 19th centuries they were usually demolished to make way for something more imposing. Dalserf has lasted because the parish was a poor one, and couldn't afford to rebuild, preferring instead to upgrade whenever it could. In the kirkyard is a pre-Norman hogs back grave slab, which was dug up in 1897, and also a memorial to the Rev John Macmillan, sometimes called 'the last of the Covenanters'. He died in 1753.

STONEHOUSE
6 miles S of Hamilton on the A71

🐦 Patrick Hamilton   🏛 Old St Ninian's Parish Church

This former weaving village still has rows of 18th- and 19th-century weaving cottages. On one side of the main door is a large window, that allows plenty of light into the room which housed the loom, and on the other is a small window, which allowed light to enter the main living quarters.

Patrick Hamilton, Scotland's first Protestant martyr, was born in Stonehouse in about 1503. He was burned at the stake in St Andrews in 1528. The Alexander Hamilton Memorial Park was opened in 1925, the gift of a local man. It has a bandstand, which was originally made for the Great Glasgow Exhibition of 1911.

The remains of the **Old St Ninian's Parish Church** are to the north of the village, surrounded by an old kirkyard. A prehistoric burial kist was once dug up in the kirkyard, showing that the site may have had a religious significance long before Christianity came to the area.

STRATHAVEN
7 miles S of Hamilton on the A723

🏛 Strathaven Castle   📷 John Hastie Museum

🏚 Battle of Drumclog   🌺 Spectacle E'e Falls

Strathaven (pronounced Stray-ven) is a real gem of a small town, which sits at the heart of Avondale. The ruins of **Strathaven Castle** (also known as Avondale Castle) are all that is left of a once large and powerful 14th-century

stronghold. It was built by the Douglas family, then passed to the Stewarts, who became Earls of Avondale, and eventually came into the hands of the Hamiltons. A legend says that before the Reformation, a wife of one of the owners was walled up alive in the castle, and when parts of a wall fell down in the 19th century, human bones were found among the rubble. On the edge of the John Hastie Park is the **John Hastie Museum**, which has local history collections.

Close to the cemetery is the James Wilson Monument. James Wilson was born in Strathaven in 1760, his father being a weaver. He was a free thinker on the matter of religion, and was also a radical reformer, something of which the local landowners did not approve. In 1820, a band of reformers, of which he was a member, posted a bill on the streets of Glasgow that was held to be treasonable. He was arrested near Falkirk and executed in 1820.

To the west of the town, at Drumclog, the **Battle of Drumclog** was fought, at which an army of Covenanters overcame government troops in 1679. A memorial on a minor road off the A71 commemorates the event. At the small village of Sandford, two miles to the south, are the lovely 50-feet-high **Spectacle E'e Falls** on the Kype Water, a tributary of the Avon.

EAST KILBRIDE
5 miles W of Hamilton on the A726

🏛 Hunter House   🌿 Calderglen Country Park

🌿 James Hamilton Heritage Park

📷 Scottish Museum of Country Life

East Kilbride is the largest and undoubtedly the most successful of Scotland's new towns. Work started on laying it out in 1947 round an

---

🏛 historic building 📷 museum and heritage 🏚 historic site 🌺 scenic attraction 🌿 flora and fauna

old village, and now it has a population of about 70,000. It is renowned for its shopping facilities, and has four shopping malls, Princes Mall, the Plaza, the Olympia Centre and Centre West, which together make up the largest undercover shopping area in Scotland.

In the Calderwood area of the town is **Hunter House**, birthplace in the 18th century of the Hunter brothers, John and William, pioneering surgeons and anatomists who worked in both Glasgow and London. The house has a small display and museum about the two men and their lives. The Hunterian Museum in Glasgow is one of their legacies.

On the outskirts of the town is **Calderglen Country Park**, based on Torrance House (private). It has play areas, nature trails and a children's zoo. To the north of the town is the **James Hamilton Heritage Park**, with a 16-acre boating loch. Behind it is the restored Mains Castle (private), which was built by the Lindsay family in the early 15th century and subsequently sold to the Stuarts of Torrance. Up until the 1970s it was a ruin. Close by, the **Scottish Museum of Country Life** is based around Wester Kittochside Farm, which was home to the Reid family from the 16th century. In 1992, the last of the family, Margaret Reid, gifted it to the National Trust for Scotland. Run jointly by the National Museums of Scotland and the National Trust, it explains rural life in Scotland throughout the ages and has a huge collection of farm implements and machinery. The elegant farmhouse of Wester Kittochside, which dates from 1783, is also open to the public.

EAGLESHAM
9 miles W of Hamilton on the B764

🏛 Parish Church 🐦 Rudolf Hess

The conservation village of Eaglesham was planned and built by the Earl of Eglinton in the mid 1700s. It is shaped like a huge A, with the point facing the moorland to the west of the village. Between the two arms of the A is a large village green area known as the Orry, on which a cotton mill once stood. The lovely period cottages and houses in the village make a perfect picture of Scottish rural life, though the village has largely been colonised by commuters from Glasgow and Lanarkshire. The **Parish Church**, which dates from 1788, has the look of an Alpine church about it, and it is reckoned that while planning Eaglesham the 10th Earl was influenced by villages he had admired in northern Italy.

It was in a field near Eaglesham in 1941 that **Rudolph Hess**, Hitler's deputy, landed after he parachuted from an ME 110. He was found by a local farmer called David McLean, who took him home and treated him firmly but politely. Hess gave his name as Alfred Horn, but his real identity was soon established. He said he was on a secret mission to speak to the Duke of Hamilton, and a map he possessed showed that he had been trying to reach Dungavel House, one of the Duke's hunting lodges near Strathaven.

He was then taken to Maryhill Barracks in Glasgow, where he was sometimes in the custody of Corporal William Ross, who went on to become the Secretary of State for Scotland in the Wilson government. Hess was later moved to Buchanan Castle near Drymen in Stirlingshire, where he was interrogated.

BOTHWELL
2 miles NW of Hamilton off the M74

🏛 St Bride's Parish Church 🐦 Joanna Baillie
🏛 Bothwell Castle 🏚 Battle of Bothwell Bridge

In the centre of this small town is **St Bride's Parish Church**, with a chancel dating from

1398. It was built as part of a collegiate church by Archibald the Grim, 3rd Earl of Douglas, and has a roof made entirely of stone. A year after it was built, it was the scene of a royal wedding when David, son of Robert III, married Archibald the Grim's daughter Marjory. Outside the west end of the Victorian nave is a monument to **Joanna Baillie**, a playwright and poetess born at Bothwell manse in 1762. She was praised by Scott as being one of the finest writers of the 18th century. Her work, though at times filled with humour, is dark and sometimes violent, with murderous, paranoid characters, and more than one critic has wondered where a seemingly prim daughter of a minister found the material to write such stuff.

On the banks of the Clyde, some distance from the town, are the massive and impressive remains of **Bothwell Castle** (Historic Scotland), which historians have rated as one of the most important secular medieval buildings in Scotland. It was most likely built in the 13th century by Walter de Moravia who was granted the lands of Bothwell by Alexander II. It later passed to the Douglas family, who rebuilt and strengthened most of it. In the 15th century, when James II overthrew the Douglases, it passed to the crown.

Upstream is Bothwell Bridge, scene, in 1679, of the **Battle of Bothwell Bridge** between the Royalist forces of the Duke of Monmouth and a Covenanting army. The Covenanters were heavily defeated, with more than 500 being killed and 1200 taken prisoner. The bridge you see today is basically the same bridge, though much altered and widened. A memorial on the Bothwell side of the bridge commemorates the event.

BLANTYRE
3 miles NW of Hamilton on the A724

🏛 David Livingstone Centre

Blantyre is a former mining town, which nowadays is visited because of the **David Livingstone Centre** (National Trust for Scotland). Here, at Shuttle Row the African explorer and missionary David Livingstone was born in 1813. A great cotton mill once stood here, and Shuttle Row was a tenement block that housed some of the workers. The great man was born in a one-room flat, though the whole tenement has now been given over to displays and mementos about his life and work. Within the centre there is also an art gallery, social history museum, African play park, tearoom and gift shop.

Lanark

🦋 Lanimer Day 🦋 Whuppity Scoorie 🦋 Het Pint

🎭 William Wallace 🐿 Falls of Clyde

🏛 Royal Burgh of Lanark Museum

🐿 William Smellie 🏛 New Lanark 🐿 Robert Owen

🌱 Scottish Wildlife Trust Visitors Centre

Set above the Clyde Valley near the upper reaches of the Clyde, the ancient royal burgh of Lanark received its royal charter in about 1140, making it one of the oldest towns in Scotland. But even before this it was an important place, because, in 978AD, Kenneth II of Scotland held the very first recorded meeting of a Scottish parliament here.

This small town, with a population of just over 8000, keeps alive several old customs. Every year in June, the townspeople celebrate **Lanimer Day**, which originated as a ceremony of riding the boundaries of the burgh. And on March 1 each year, the

SHIRREFFS LTD.

5 Broomgate, Lanark, South Lanarkshire M11 9ET
Tel: 01555 660005

A little gem of a shop, **Shirreffs Ltd** stocks a dazzlingly diverse range if items. It is owned and run by June Shirreffs and her two daughters Lynn and Tracy, June and Tracy are both artists. So amongst the unusual stock you'll find some of their attractive oil paintings on display and for sale, picture framing is also available.

A popular choice in the shop is a range of stylish French ladies wear that includes blouses,

scarves, hats and Italian leather gloves. There are handbags by Fiorelli, Padavano, Kipling and Mary Francis, other designer names include Little Earth, Tony Perotti, Yoshi and Ciccia. There's also jewellery by Storm, Pilgrim, and Dyreberg Kern, there is also china pets by Pets with Personality, wall sconces and plaques, Woodwick candles, rainbow maker crystals, handmade glass coasters, Scottish cards and soaps and much much more.

A great place to browse and you can be sure, whatever your tastes, you will find something.

Whuppity Scoorie celebrations are held when the children of the town race round the 18th-century St Nicholas's Church waving paper balls above their head, then scrambling for coins thrown at them. Nowadays, it is the opening event in the Whuppity Scoorie Storytelling Festival, but it may have had its origins in pagan times, when it celebrated the arrival of Spring.

Another custom is the **Het Pint**, held on January 1 each year. Citizens of the town meet at 10am and are given a glass of mulled wine. Anyone wishing to do so, can also claim a pound. The tradition goes back to the 17th century, when Lord Hyndford gave money to the town to be used each year for pious or educational purposes.

High on a wall of St Nicholas's Church is a statue of **William Wallace** the Scottish freedom fighter. It recalls an event that took place when the town's castle (now gone) was garrisoned by English troops. Wallace committed some misdemeanour that brought him to the attention of the English sheriff of Lanark, Sir William Hesselrig. He fled, and when Wallace's wife Marion Braidfute (some versions refer to her as his lemman, or girlfriend) refused to divulge where he was,

Hesselrig killed her and her household. Wallace later returned and killed the sheriff in revenge. The supposed site of Wallace's House is now marked by a plaque near the church.

In the Westport you'll find the **Royal Burgh of Lanark Museum**, which explains the incident, as well as the town's history. Near the centre of the town are the ruins of **St Kentigern's Church**, the original place of worship. It is said that Wallace married Marion Braidfute within the church, though there is no proof of this. However, there certainly was a real Marion Braidfute living in the area at the time, referred to as the 'heiress of Lamington', a village to the south of Lanark.

In St Kentigern's kirkyard is buried **William Smellie** (pronounced Smillie), the father of modern midwifery. He was born in Lanark in 1697, and was the first obstetrician to teach midwifery on a formal basis as a branch of medicine. He also pioneered the use of forceps. He began life as a doctor in Lanark, but then studied in Glasgow and Paris before establishing a practise in London, where he also lectured. He was a kindly man, and frequently delivered the babies of the poor of London without charging them. He died in 1763.

On the banks of the Clyde below Lanark

TEA TIME

1 Hyndford Place, Lanark ML11 9EA
Tel: 01555 660484
e-mail: anareauil639@hotmail.com

Located in the heart of this ancient Royal Burgh, **Tea Time** is an inviting place to enjoy Scottish hospitality at its best. Here, in a relaxing environment, owner Andrea Wilson offers an excellent choice of home-cooked dishes based on fresh local produce. Try to get one of the window seats which provide grand views of the town. There are 8 tables, seating up to 34 customers, and a takeaway service is also available. Tea Time is open from 10am to 5pm, Monday to Saturday.

🏚 historic building 🏛 museum and heritage 🏛 historic site 🜨 scenic attraction 🌿 flora and fauna

Lesmahagow Priory, Lanark

technology. The 'ghost' of 18th-century mill girl Annie Macleod returns to tell the story of her life in the days of Robert Owen. Also in the village is a **Scottish Wildlife Trust Visitors Centre**.

The mills were at one time powered by the Clyde, and close by are the **Falls of Clyde** waterfalls, the most famous being Cora Linn and Bonnington. A hydroelectric scheme now harnesses the power of the water, and the falls are only seen at their most spectacular at certain times of the year.

lies the village and UNESCO World Heritage Site of **New Lanark**. It was here, in 1785, that David Dale founded a cotton mill and village of 2500 people that became a model for social reform. Under Dale's son-in-law **Robert Owen**, who was manager, there were good working conditions, decent homes, fair wages, schools and health care available.

The mills were still in production up to 1968. Under the care of the New Lanark Conservation Trust, it has become one of the most popular tourist destinations in Scotland, even though people still live in some of the original tenements and cottages.

Attractions include a Visitors Centre (including a Textile Machinery Exhibition and the New Millennium Ride that introduces you to Robert Owen's original vision), the Millworker's House, the Village Store Exhibition and Robert Owen's House. Other buildings have been converted into craft workshops, and there is also a hotel housed in a former mill. A presentation called Annie McLeod's Story is shown in what was Robert Owen's School, and uses the latest in 3-D

A few miles north of the town is Carluke, which stands above the Clyde Valley. It is noted for its orchards, introduced in medieval times by the monks of Lesmahagow Priory. The bell tower of the former parish church, built in 1715, still stands.

Around Lanark

BIGGAR
10 miles SE of Lanark on the A702

🏠 Biggar Gas Works Museum

🏠 Moat Park Heritage Centre

🏚 Greenhill Covenanter's House

🏠 Gladstone Court Museum

🏠 Albion Motors Archives 🐦 Hugh McDiarmid

🎨 Biggar Puppet Theatre 🏚 St Mary's Church

Biggar is a small, attractive market town that still has its original medieval layout. It sits

THE ELPHINSTONE HOTEL

145 High Street, Biggar, Lanarkshire ML12 6OL
Tel: 01899 220044
e-mail: robert@the-elph-fsworld.co.uk
website: www.elphinstonehotel.co.uk

Standing on Biggar's broad main street, the **Elphinstone Hotel** is a handsome whitewashed building with a long and illustrious history that goes back more than 400 years. The owners, Robert and Janette Allen, along with their son, Michael, have been at the heart of the business for more than twenty years and they offer a warm and homely welcome to all visitors and locals alike. The family pride themselves on the continued patronage of a busy local trade with a high level of repeat custom which clearly tells its own story.

A major attraction here is the quality of the food on offer. The menu is wide and varied with every effort made to source and utilise the best in fresh, local produce. Take your pick from two dozen starters and more than twice as many main courses. Delicious Cullen Skink, Black Pudding with a Smoked Bacon in a red wine jus, Smoked Salmon cornets are among the list of popular starters. Mains include tasty Chicken and Haggis with a wholegrain mustard sauce, Fishermans Pie and Stuffed Loin of Pork . Using local butcher, Jimmy Bogle, the chef will also cook you "the best steak you've had in years". Fresh haddock, and mince and tatties are also on the menu, as is a range of oriental dishes, thus ensuring every taste is catered for. A well balanced and reasonably priced wine list is also available.

The hotel lounge is in the style of a traditional old inn and is full of character. Here, as well as in the restaurant, meals are served or you can just sit in front of a roaring fire enjoying a glass of wine, a rusty nail or even a hot toddy.

The accommodation at 'The Elph' comprises 9 guest bedrooms, all bright and clean and all benefiting from recent complete refurbishment of the bathrooms. There's a choice of double, twin or single, and all rooms are equipped with en suite facilities digital television, direct dial telephone, broadband access, tea and coffee making facilities. Hairdryers and ironing facilities are available.

The hotel also has a first floor function room which can comfortably seat sixty for a full sit down meal and up to around ninety where a less formal buffet style of service is required.

🏛 historic building 🏛 museum and heritage 🏛 historic site ⚘ scenic attraction 🌱 flora and fauna

CORMISTON FARM

Cormiston Road, Biggar, ML12 6NS
Tel: 01899 221507
e-mail: info@cormistonfarm.com
website: www.cormistonfarm.com

Listed by Historic Scotland, **Cormiston Farm** is a 4 star
bed and breakfast surrounded by the rolling hills of the
Clyde Valley. It lies within 2 acres of mature garden and
woodland, 2 miles from the town of Biggar. Two large,
double bedrooms , one with a four poster, overlook the hills to the south. A full Scottish breakfast
is included: from fresh seasonal fruit, porridge and free range eggs laid by our own hens, to bacon,
sausage, home-made marmalade, and the finest teas and coffee. Dinner is a seasonal four-course
set meal and much of the produce is from the walled kitchen garden or from local markets. We
have a select wine list, as well as excellent beers from the local Broughton Brewery. All major
credit and debit cards accepted.

among the rich agricultural lands of South
Lanarkshire, and was granted its burgh
charter in 1451.

It must have more museums per head of
population than any other place in Britain.
The **Biggar Gas Works Museum**, housed in
the town's former gas works dating from 1839,
explains how gas was produced from coal in
former times, and the **Moat Park Heritage
Centre** has exhibits and displays about the
town and its immediate area from the time the
landscape was formed millions of years ago
right up to the present day. **Greenhill
Covenanter's House** used to stand at
Wiston, 10 miles away, but was transported to
Biggar stone by stone, and is now dedicated to
the memory of the Covenanters. These were
men and women who, in the 17th century,
resisted the Stuart monarchs' attempts to
impose bishops on the Church of Scotland.
They sometimes paid with their lives for their
convictions. The **Gladstone Court Museum**
has re-created a Victorian street, with a
dressmaker's shop, boot maker's shop and a
schoolroom.

The Albion Building houses the **Albion**

Motors Archives, the records of the Albion
Motor Company, which was started locally in
1899 by Norman Fulton and T B Murray
before moving production to Glasgow. It soon
grew to be the largest manufacturer of
commercial vehicles in the British Empire.

At Brownsbank Cottage, a mile and a half
from the town, lived the Scottish poet
Christopher Grieve, better known as **Hugh
McDiarmid**. He died in 1978, and his wife
Valda continued to live there until her death in
1989. The cottage has been restored to exactly
how it looked when the poet lived there, and it
is home to a writer-in-residence. It can be
visited by appointment only.

In Broughton Road is the professionally run
Biggar Puppet Theatre, which has a
Victorian-style theatre seating up to 100
people, plus a museum. Purves Puppets, which
owns it, is Scotland's largest puppet company
and regularly presents shows all over Britain.

St Mary's Church was founded in 1546 by
Malcolm, Lord Fleming, Chancellor of
Scotland. It was formerly collegiate, and is a
graceful, cruciform building. It was the last
church to be built in Scotland before the

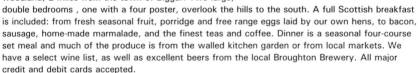

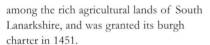

𝕗 stories and anecdotes 🐦 famous people ✐ art and craft 🖉 entertainment and sport 🚶 walks

HOLMLANDS COUNTRY HOUSE

22 Carlisle Road, Crawford, by Abington,
South Lanarkshire ML12 6TW
Tel; 01864 502753
e-mail: cerena_soances@btconnect.com
website: www.holmlandscountryhouse.co.uk

Beautifully located beside the River Clyde and
commanding some grand views of the Clyde Valley,
Holmlands Country House is a substantial Edwardian
property built in 1903 and set in an acre of land
surrounded by rolling hills. There is a pleasant garden
where guests can enjoy afternoon tea and homemade
cakes and admire the stunning views across the
valley. Inside, there is a spacious lounge with an
open fire for all to enjoy.

The owners of Holmlands, Verena and Graham
Soanes , extend a very warm welcome to their
guests on arrival. The house has a very comfortable
feel and visitors are able to relax and enjoy their stay
in a beautiful part of the Scottish countryside, great
for quiet walks by the river. The accommodation is reached by a handsome oak staircase and
comprises of 4 elegant bedrooms, all with en-suite or private facilities. The rooms are equipped
with colour TV, tea & coffee making facilities and all have pleasant views. Evening meals are
available from 6.30 pm to 9pm, a typical menu may include homemade soup and pate', Scottish
salmon and Game, a good cheeseboard and various delicious sweets. Meals are prepared on site
from local produce or from the kitchen garden. Holmlands is also a perfect setting for that special
celebration, catering for up to 20 guests, suitable for private dining, lunch or dinner, business or
pleasure.

There is also a Tearoom at Holmlands which is open daily, noon to 5pm except Tuesdays. The
menu is varied and offers good homemade food, such as soup, salads with gammon , beef or
salmon and bread made on the premises. Cakes and puddings are also available. Free Fly- Casting
tuition is on offer to residents, there is plenty of local fishing available, the Clyde River is fished for
Brown Trout in the summer and Grayling in the winter. There is ample off-road parking and secure
areas for cycles and motorbikes.

Holmlands is open throughout the year and is the ideal location
for that special quiet weekend in the country.

CABBAGE PATCH FABRICS

Coulter Park, Coulter, Biggar,
Lanarkshire ML12 6HN
Tel: 01899 221234

Are you looking for new curtains or just bits and pieces for upholstering a chair or making cushions, then Cabbage Patch Fabrics is the place to visit.

The farm steading conversion on the edge of Coulter village makes a wonderful setting for displaying our fantastic selection of fabrics.

Our opening hours are 10-5, Mon-Sat, if you need any further information please phone us.

Reformation. In the kirkyard is a gravestone commemorating the Gladstone family, forebears of William Ewart Gladstone, British prime minister during Victoria's reign.

To the west of the town, just off the M74, are the twin settlements of Abington and Crawford, which have a number of services, and make ideal stopping off places when heading north or south along the motorway.

LEADHILLS

18 miles S of Lanark on the B797

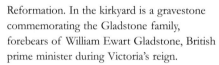 William Symington

Like its neighbour Wanlockhead (which is in Dumfriesshire), Leadhills is a former lead mining village. It has the highest golf course in Scotland, and is full of old 18th- and 19th-century lead miners' cottages. It forms one terminus for the Leadhills and Wanlockhead Light Railway.

The Allan Ramsay Library is the oldest subscription Library in Scotland, and is named after the famous poet born here in 1684. In the graveyard is the grave of John Taylor, a lead miner who lived to be 137 years old. Next to the cemetery is a monument to **William Symington**, who was born in the village in 1764. He worked as an engineer in the mines, and was a pioneer of steam propulsion in ships. His paddleboat the *Charlotte Dundas* was

launched at Grangemouth in 1802.

CARMICHAEL

4 miles S of Lanark on a minor road west of the A73

🏛 Carmichael Parish Church

🏛 Carmichael Visitor Centre

The small **Carmichael Parish Church** dates from 1750, and has an interesting laird's loft. One of the past lairds, the Earl of Hyndford, left a sum of money called the Hyndford Mortification to provide the local schoolmasters with a yearly pair of trousers and a supply of whisky. The **Carmichael Visitor Centre** is situated on the Carmichael Estate, and has a display of waxwork models (formerly housed in Edinburgh) that illustrate Scotland's history from the year 1000 to the present day. There are also displays about the history of the Carmichael family, which owned the lands of Carmichael since the 13th century, and others about wind energy.

DOUGLAS

8 miles SW of Lanark on the A70

🏛 Castle Dangerous 🏛 The Sun Inn

🏛 Old St Bride's 🏛 Douglas Heritage Museum

It was in Douglas, in 1968, that the Cameronians (Scottish Rifles), a proud

---

Scottish regiment, was disbanded. The ceremony took place in the grounds of **Castle Dangerous**, ancestral home of the Douglases, of which only a tower now survives. It was here, in 1689, that the regiment was raised by James, Earl of Angus. His statue now stands in the village.

The centre of Douglas is a conservation area, with many old cottages and houses. **The Sun Inn** of 1621 was once the village's Tolbooth, where justice was meted out. **Old St Bride's** is the choir of the former parish church dating from the 14th century. Within it are memorials to members of the Douglas family, including Archibald, the 5th Earl of Angus. He was killed at Flodden in 1513, and had the curious nickname of **Bell the Cat**. There is also a memorial to 'the Good Sir

James of Douglas', killed by the Moors in Spain while taking Robert the Bruce's heart to the Holy Land for burial. The clock in the clock tower was gifted to the church by Mary Stuart in 1565, and is the oldest working public clock in Scotland.

Douglas Heritage Museum, in Bell's Wynd, is situated in the former dower house of the castle. It is open on Saturdays and Sundays by prior appointment. It has displays on the Douglas family and on the Cameronians (Scottish Rifles).

CROSSFORD
4 miles NW of Lanark on the A72

🏛 Craignethan Castle

This lovely little village sits in the heart of the Clyde Valley, on the banks of the river. Above

Craignethan Castle, nr Crossford

it you'll find the substantial ruins of **Craignethan Castle** (Historic Scotland), where Mary Stuart once stayed. It was built in the 1530s by Sir James Hamilton of Finnart, illegitimate son of James Hamilton, 1st Earl of Arran and ancestor of the present Dukes of Hamilton. He was the master of works to James V, who gave him the lands of Draffan on which the castle was built. However, the king later suspected that Hamilton had been plotting against him (which was probably not true), and had him executed.

The castle then passed to the crown, and was subsequently given to the 2nd Earl of Arran, Sir James's half-brother and the Regent of Scotland.

Sir Walter Scott is reputed to have used the castle as a model for his Tillietudlem Castle in *Old Mortality*, though he later denied any link.

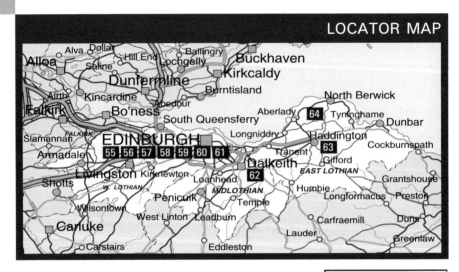

LOCATOR MAP

ADVERTISERS AND PLACES OF INTEREST

🏛 historic building   🏛 museum and heritage   🏛 historic site   🌀 scenic attraction   🌿 flora and fauna

5 | Edinburgh & The Lothians

The Lothians consist of the three former counties of East Lothian, Midlothian and West Lothian. The land is generally low-lying to the north, rising to moorland and hills in the south, with areas of industry to the west and expanses of good arable farmland to the east. Being close to Edinburgh, this area is at the heart of Scottish history, full of castles, grand houses and churches. It is also a place of quiet, pastoral villages and marvellous scenery. The only towns that could possibly be said to be industrial are Dalkeith, Bo'ness, Armadale and Bathgate, and even here industry never intrudes too much.

Dominating it all is the city of Edinburgh, which probably has more history per square mile than any other comparable place in the world. But it's a compact city, and its suburbs haven't yet gobbled up too much countryside. Behind the city are the Pentland Hills, a lonely area of high moorland stretching southwest towards the Lanarkshire boundary, and to the south and southeast are the Moorfoot and Lammermuir Hills respectively, which thrust down into the Borders.

East Lothian (formerly Haddingtonshire) is a farming county, a patchwork of fields and woodland dotted all over with small, neat villages. The quiet country lanes cry out to be explored by car, and though there is none of the grandeur of the Highlands here - indeed, the scenery has, like Ayrshire, an almost rural English feel to it - it is still a beautiful area. The land rises to the south where it meets the Lammermuir Hills. Here, the landscape changes though it never loses its gentle aspect. Haddington is the county town and is full of old buildings. The main Edinburgh-London railway line bypassed it, so it never developed as a place of industry. The town's main building is the cathedralesque St Mary's Church, the tower of which is sometimes called the Lamp of the Lothians. A succession of small resorts and golfing centres ring the coastline, though none have been commercialised to any great extent.

Mid Lothian was at one time called Edinburghshire. Towards the south it meets the Moorfoot Hills, and has a string of small towns sitting like satellites round Edinburgh itself. Coalmining was once important here, though all vestiges of the industry have now gone. It is home to such places as Dalkeith and Bonnyrigg, which have never been overwhelmed by industry. Plus, of course, it has the world-famous Rosslyn Chapel, which, people claim (and Dan Brown's novel *The Da Vinci Code* supported) conceals a mystery that goes right to the heart of Christianity.

Before 1975, the county town of West Lothian was Linlithgow. It is an ancient burgh with a royal palace where Mary Stuart, better known as Mary, Queen of Scots, was born. West Lothian is more industrial in character than the other two Lothians, and at one time had coal and shale mines, the latter being used to produce oil. Both industries have gone, though the occasional red shale spoil heap (called a bing hereabouts) can still be seen.

But there are still plenty of tranquil places to be visited, such as Torphichen, with its preceptory of St John, and South Queensferry, in the shadow of the two Forth bridges. A full day could be taken up exploring Linlithgow itself, with its royal palace, medieval church, canal basin and old stone buildings. Then there are the county's grand houses, such as Hopetoun and The Binns, which deserve to be visited and explored.

Edinburgh

- 🏛 Edinburgh Castle 🏛 St Margaret's Chapel
- 🖉 Edinburgh Military Tattoo
- 🏛 Ensign Ewart Tomb 🏛 Half Moon Battery
- 🏛 National War Memorial 🏛 King's Lodging
- 🏛 National War Museum of Scotland
- 🏛 Museum of the Royal Scots Dragoon Guards
- 🏛 Palace of Holyroodhouse 🏛 Tolbooth Church
- 🏛 Scotch Whisky Centre 🏛 Parliament House
- 🖉 Edinburgh International Festival
- 🏛 Gladstone's Land 🏛 Writer's Museum
- 🏛 St Giles Cathedral 🏛 Edinburgh City Chambers
- 🏛 Thistle Chapel 🏛 Museum of Childhood
- 🏛 John Knox House 🏛 Canongate Tolbooth
- 🏛 Museum of Edinburgh 🏛 Canongate Church
- 🏛 White Horse Close 🏛 Our Dynamic Earth
- 🖉 Queen's Gallery 🏛 Scottish Parliament Building
- 🏛 Royal Museum 🏛 Museum of Scotland
- 🏛 Surgeon's Hall Museum 🏛 Magdalen Chapel
- 🏛 Greyfriars 🖉 National Portrait Gallery
- 🏛 Greyfriars Bobby 🌱 Princes Street Gardens
- 🏛 Georgian House 🏛 St Mary's Cathedral
- 🖉 National Gallery of Scotland 🖉 Dean Gallery
- 🖉 Scottish National Gallery of Modern Art
- 🖉 City Art Centre 🖉 Talbot Rice Gallery
- 🖉 City Art Gallery 🏛 Edinburgh Dungeon
- 🏛 Register House 🏛 Scott Monument
- 🏛 Nelson Monument 🌱 Royal Botanic Gardens
- 🏛 Royal Yacht *Britannia* 🏛 Craigmillar Castle
- 🏛 Newhaven Heritage Museum
- 🌱 Edinburgh Zoological Gardens
- 🏛 Lauriston Castle 🏛 Royal Observatory

Edinburgh, the cultural and administrative capital of Scotland, is one of the great cities of the world. It used to be called the Athens of the North, and a full week would not be enough to see everything it has to offer the tourist. Whereas Glasgow has worked hard at building a new image, Edinburgh has never needed to do so, though this has led to a certain amount of complacency at times.

The UNESCO World Heritage Site at the heart of the city combines the medieval Old Town, the Georgian New Town, and some award-winning modern architecture.

With the advent of the Scottish Parliament, the world has rediscovered Edinburgh, and it now has all the feel and buzz of a great capital city once more. It is the sixth most important financial capital in Europe, and both the Church of Scotland and the Scottish law courts have their headquarters here.

The name Edinburgh has two possible origins. It either comes from the old Brithonic eiden burg, meaning fortress on the hill slope, or Edwin's Burgh, from a 7th-century Anglo Saxon king of Northumbria who built a fort where the castle now stands, though there was, no doubt, a fort here even before this.

Whatever the explanation, there's no denying that **Edinburgh Castle** (Historic Scotland) is where it all began. It sits on a volcanic plug (the core of a volcano that has solidified), with a narrow ridge running east from it on which sits the old town. There has been a fortification of some kind on the site for thousands of years, though the first stone castle was probably built by Malcolm III in the 11th century. The castle as you see it now dates from all periods, with the oldest part being **St Margaret's Chapel**, which was built in the 12th century. St Margaret was the wife of Malcolm III, and it was thanks to her that the Scottish Church came under the jurisdiction of Rome and swept away the last

---

🏛 historic building 🏛 museum and heritage 🏛 historic site 🌱 scenic attraction 🌱 flora and fauna

vestiges of Celtic monasticism. Her son David may have built the chapel in her memory. Every year in August, the Castle Esplanade is the setting for the **Edinburgh Military Tattoo**, an extravaganza of military uniforms, marching, music and spectacle that is known the world over. The **Ensign Ewart Tomb** on the esplanade contains the body of Charles Ewart of the 2nd (Scots Greys), who captured the eagle and standard of the French 45th Regiment of the Line at the Battle of Waterloo on June 18 1815. A story once circulated that the Castle Esplanade had become part of the Scottish colony of Nova Scotia, now in Canada, in the 17th century. This was so that the newly created barons of Nova Scotia could set foot in the colony and legally claim their titles. The story was completely untrue, though there is a plaque on the esplanade that states that in 1625 Sir William Alexander took possession of the colony of Nova Scotia 'by the ancient and symbolic ceremony of delivery of earth and stone'.

Overlooking the Esplanade and the entrance to the castle is the **Half Moon Battery**, built by Regent Morton in the 16th century, and behind it is the **National War Memorial**, designed by Sir Robert Lorimer and converted from an old barracks block between 1924 and 1927. The **King's Lodging** opposite originally dates from the 15th century, and it was here that the monarch had his personal apartments. One of the rooms, Queen Mary's Room, is where, in June 1566, Mary Stuart gave birth to her son James, who later became James VI of Scotland and I of Britain.

CHOCO-LATTE

39 South Clerk Street, Edinburgh EH8 9NZ
Tel: 0131 667 0091
e-mail: christine_davis@btconnect.com
website: www.choco-latte.co.uk

Choco-Latte is possibly one of the smallest shops in Edinburgh and is just utterly bursting with character. Although it is small it makes use of every square inch. There is literally chocolate hanging from the rafters. Choco-latte wafts flavours and smells into the busy main South Clerk Street which is only a 5-10 minute walk from Edinburgh's famous Royal Mile.

You walk into the shop and it holds delights from your childhood right through to your most secret adult indulgencies. It has just about every type of sweets available. If your preference is old school mixtures then the cola bottles, fizzy flying saucers and jelly snakes are there for you to mix it up. However if you have a more sophisticated pallet then the most amazing Belgium chocolates and fine chocolate delicacies are almost overflowing on the shelves.

Choco-latte is famous in Edinburgh for its amazing muffins.... These huge mountains of muffins are lashed with chocolate and topped with an array of goodies from maltesers to truffles. The tray bake biscuits are not to be missed - there is nowhere they are made better.

The girls at Choco-latte also do special gifts for occasions... There are fabulous chocolate lollies that you can have special messages put on such as *"Good luck in new job"* or *"Well done passing exams"* - anything you wish really, the girls love making special discs for your own occasion.

stories and anecdotes   famous people   art and craft   entertainment and sport   walks

RAGAMUFFIN

Edinburgh: The Canongate, Royal Mile,
Edinburgh EH8 8AA
Tel: 0131 557 6007

Ragamuffin is a 30-year-old, family-run business founded by Lesley Robertson on the Isle of Skye, with another branch in Edinburgh that sells the same collection of gorgeous knitwear, original clothes and fun accessories that can be found in Skye. From wild and funky, to simple and elegant, there is something for all ages, sizes and budgets. With heaps of hats, funky scarves, sparkly jewellery, things to make you smile and much, much more!

There's also a quirky in-house label too, this "Unruly Angels" collection is exceptionally well made and the quality shines through every garment, Lesley certainly has an eye for what is fashionable yet classic – pieces that will never date.

Lesley's shop in Edinburgh draws regular customers from near and far, visiting the famous Royal Mile but also making a beeline to her shop every time they visit this historic town. Often described as an Aladdin's cave, the shop is a riot of texture and colour with plenty of inspirational displays, showcasing how to layer the pieces together in interesting colour combinations. There is a wealth of experience about high quality women's fashions and accessories here, as well as friendly, helpful service and outstanding value for money.

There are two curious stories about this birth. One says that the Earl of Bothwell, and not Lord Darnley, Mary's husband, was the father of the baby, which would have made him illegitimate. The other says that Mary's baby was stillborn, and that another baby - the son of the Earl of Mar - was substituted in its place. At a later date, when the room was being refurbished, workmen are supposed to have found an infant's bones within the walls of the room.

In the Crown Chamber can be seen the Scottish crown jewels, known as the Honours of Scotland, and the Stone of Destiny, supposed to be the pillow on which Jacob slept, and on which the ancient kings of Ireland and Scotland were crowned. It was taken from Scone near Perth by Edward I in 1297 and lay in Westminster Abbey for 700 years. Some people claim, however, that it is merely a copy, and that the monks of Scone gave Edwrd a worthless drain cover and hid the real Stone. Others claim that, when the Stone was 'liberated' from Westminster Abbey in 1953 by Scottish Nationalists, the perpetrators substituted another stone in its place when it was returned. Whatever is the truth of the matter, there is no doubt that it is a potent symbol of Scottish nationhood.

The **National War Museum of Scotland** is also within the castle, and explores military service over the past 400 years. Another museum within the castle is the regimental **Museum of the Royal Scots Dragoon Guards**, which is at present based in Germany. The regiment is Scotland's only cavalry regiment, and was formed in 1971 when older regiments amalgamated.

From the castle every day except Sunday the One o' Clock Gun is fired. It booms out over the city, frightening tourists who are visiting the castle at the time. Another gun associated with the castle is Mons Meg. It is one of two huge siege guns presented to James II in 1457 by the Duke of Burgundy. Some people imagine that it is Mons Meg that is fired at one o' clock, but it is in fact a 25lb gun situated on Hill Mount Battery.

Leading from Edinburgh Castle down to the **Palace of Holyroodhouse** is the Royal Mile, one of the most famous streets in the world. It follows the crest of a ridge that slopes down from the castle, and was the heart of the old Edinburgh. It is actually four streets - Castlehill, Lawnmarket, the High Street and the Canongate - and each one had tall tenements on either side. The city was surprisingly egalitarian in the past. The gentry and the poor lived in the same tenement blocks, the rich at the top, the professional classes in the middle, and the poor at the bottom.

The **Tolbooth Church** was built in 1844, and was for a time the annual meeting place of the General Assembly of the Church of Scotland, the kirk's governing body. It was designed by James Gillespie Graham and Augustus Welby Pugin, and has a 240-foot spire, which is the highest point in the city centre.

The **Scotch Whisky Heritage Centre** on Castlehill tells the story of Scotch, and brings three hundred years of its history to life. You'll learn about how it's made, and every

CHIC & UNIQUE

8 Deanhaugh Street, Edinburgh,
Scotland EH4 1LY
Tel: 0131 332 9889
e-mail: moira.teale@homecall.co.uk
website: www.vintagecostumejewellery.co.uk

You can add more than a touch of romance to your wardrobe with vintage jewellery. A baroque vintage bracelet spells class like nothing else will. Vintage jewellery is the new must have in the fashion circuit. Chic & Unique offers a beautiful array of vintage costume jewellery and accessories, from a bygone era, where all items are hand picked and representative of the highest quality. Here, you can expect to find bracelets, brooches & clips, cufflinks and gentlemen's items, earrings, hair accessories, handbags/purses, hatpins, Masks - Venetian Carnival, necklaces, perfume bottles, compacts & bijoux items and tiaras (rental only).

If you are already a vintage devotee, you will know the attraction is that you are not buying something that is untouched and straight from a factory. Instead, you are dipping into the past, whether it is the far-off days of the 1920s flapper or the 1940s Hollywood glamour goddesses, to the more recently remembered 1970s disco era. Whenever you carry a vintage handbag or wear a piece of vintage costume jewellery or look into the mirror of a vintage powder compact, you can't help but wonder who it belonged to. It is this mystique, which is part of the allure of owning vintage. Chic and Unique is open Tuesday to Saturday - 10.30-2pm, 2.30-5pm.

CANONGATE JERSEYS & CRAFTS LTD

164 - 166 Canongate, Royal Mile, Edinburgh   EH8 8DD
Tel: 0131 557 2967
e-mail: canongatejandc@aol.com
website: www.canongatecrafts.co.uk

Canongate Jerseys was first established in Edinburgh in 1978
under the knitwear label 'Heather Knits'. Moving into the
Canongate in 1984, the shop soon expanded into crafts and
Heather and her daughter, Julie, continue to sell a unique
collection of Scottish Crafts and Kintwear to this day.

Heathers Knitwear, handmade locally in pure wools, is
inspired by Celtic and Pictish art and Fair-Isle Patterns. Walk in
to the shop and see a rich tapestry of colour. Along with
exclusive knitwear are garments from Shetland – the original
fair-isle – produced by the islanders for many years. Lace
hand-knitted gloves and scarves, colourful berets, and the
traditional "yoke" jumper and cardigans.

Harris Tweed, the famous tweed cloth woven on the island of Harris and Lewis on the Outer
Hebrides by individual wavers can be seen in a range of articles from purses, bags, scarves, wraps,
and hats some embroidered with the magical, intricate decorations of the Celts. A new collection
of Harris Tweed ladies jackets and hats in the old Scottish style beret and fedora abound, with the
roadkill pheasant feathers arriving soon.

The Crafts selection is mainly based on the art of the Picts and is the first shop of its kind to
sell such a range of Pictish Art. The Picts were indigenous people, various tribes living from the
Forth and Clyde to Orkney and Shetland, and the Western Isles. Very little remains of their culture,
they're meaning lost in time. Replica stones (Pictish and early Christian), painted glass, jewellery,
wall hangings, art carrels, pottery, books and many more interesting pieces can be found in the
craft section.

Sunday afternoon there is a tasting session.

Between July and September, Edinburgh
plays host to many festivals, the most important
being the **Edinburgh International Festival**
(with its attendant Fringe Festival) in August.
The Royal Mile then becomes a colourful open-
air theatre where Fringe performers and
buskers take over every inch of pavement to
present drama, juggling, classical music,
magicians, jazz, piping, folk music and a host of
other activities.

Edinburgh has often been called the
medieval Manhattan, as the 16th- and 17th-
century tenement blocks on the Royal Mile,
which looked no more than four of five
storeys high, were in fact up to 12 storeys

high, due to the steep slope on which they
were built. **Gladstone's Land** (National Trust
for Scotland), in the Lawnmarket, belonged to
Thomas Gledstone, a rich merchant. It was
built about 1620, has painted ceilings, and is
furnished in the way it would have been in the
17th century. In Lady Stair's House, off the
Lawnmarket, you'll find the **Writer's
Museum**, with displays on Scotland's trio of
great writers, Burns, Scott and Stevenson. The
house is named after Lady Stair, who owned
the house in the 18th century.

The glory of the Royal Mile is **St Giles
Cathedral**. Originally the High Kirk of
Edinburgh, it was only a cathedral for a short
while in the 17th century when the Church of

Scotland embraced bishops. It is now the spiritual home of Presbyterianism in Scotland. The first church in Edinburgh was built in the 9th century by monks from Lindisfarne, and St Giles is its direct descendant. It dates mainly from the 15th century and has a magnificent crown steeple, which is, along with the castle, one of Edinburgh's icons. At one time, in the Preston Aisle, an arm bone of St Giles was kept as a holy relic.

Attached to the cathedral is the ornate **Thistle Chapel**, designed by Sir Robert Lorimer and built in 1911. It is the home of the Most Ancient and Noble Order of the Thistle, which is said (erroneously, some people claim) to have been founded by Alexander II when he came to the throne in 1249. We do know, however, that James VII (James II of Britain) instituted the modern order in 1687, which consists of 16 knights (who may be female) and the sovereign. There is provision also for certain 'extra' knights, who may be members of the British or foreign royal families. Its motto is *nemo me impune lacissit*, which means 'no one provokes me with impunity'. However, it is usually expressed in Lowland Scots as 'wha daur meddle wi me?', or 'who dares meddle with me?' One of the delights of the chapel is a woodcarving of an angel playing the bagpipes.

Behind the cathedral is **Parliament House** where Scotland's parliament met up until the Treaty of Union in 1707. The building itself dates from the late 17th century, though the façade was added in 1829.

Across from the cathedral is the **Edinburgh City Chambers**, home to the city council. It started life as a royal exchange, built between 1753 and 1761 to designs by John Adam, brother of the better-known Robert. Though it appears to have only two or three storeys if seen from the Royal Mile, it actually has 12 storeys, which tumble down the slope at the back. Under the Chambers is the Real Mary King's Close, a narrow Edinburgh street was closed off and built over after the bubonic plague visited the city in 1645. Conducted tours of this most moving of places are available, though participants are advised to seek out a pub afterwards to steady the nerves, as the place is supposed to be haunted. The most poignant ghost is said to be that of a young girl. People still leave gifts for her, such as sweets and dolls.

The old Tron Church, built in 1648, was in use as a church up until 1952. It is now a visitor information centre. An archaeological dig inside the church in 1974 revealed the foundations of shops and cellars from a medieval street called Marlin's Wynd, which can now be viewed.

Further down the Royal Mile is the **Museum of Childhood**, a nostalgic trip down memory lane for most adults. It features toys, games and books, and even medicines such as castor oil. **John Knox House** is almost opposite. It dates from the 15th century, and though there is no real proof that he lived in the house, he may well have died here. Eastwards from John Knox's House the Royal Mile becomes the Canongate, so called because it is the gate or street, of the canons of Holyrood Abbey. Up until 1865, Canongate was a separate burgh with its own officials and councillors. The **Canongate Tolbooth** of 1591, which held the council chamber, courtroom and burgh jail, is a curious building with a clock that projects out over the pavement. It contains the **Museum of Edinburgh,** which gives an insight into the history of the city itself, and is packed with exhibits from its colourful past.

The **Canongate Church** of 1688 has Dutch influences, and in the kirkyard is buried Adam Smith the famous economist, Agnes McLehose for whom Burns wrote *Ae Fond Kiss*, and Robert Fergusson the poet. He was Burns's hero, and died aged 24 in a madhouse. When Burns visited his grave, he was disgusted to see that there was no grave marker, so he paid for the tombstone over the grave that we see now. **White Horse Close**, beyond the church, is the most picturesque of Edinburgh's closes, and it was from the White Horse Inn that the horse-drawn coaches left for London and York.

The **Palace of Holyroodhouse** is the Queen's official residence in Scotland. It grew out of the Abbey of Holyrood, of which only the ruined nave remains. Legend says that while out hunting, David I was injured by a stag. While he fought with it he found himself grasping, not the stag's antlers, but a holy cross or rood. As an act of thanksgiving he founded the abbey in 1128 for Augustinian canons. It became a favourite residence for Scottish kings, being much less draughty than the castle up the hill. It was here that Mary Stuart set up court on her return from France in the 16th century, and it was here that the murder of Rizzio, her Italian secretary took place.

The picture gallery contains portraits of over 100 Scottish kings. The recently opened **Queen's Gallery** is the first permanent exhibition space for the royal collection of paintings and sculpture in Scotland. It was designed by Benjamin Tindall Architects, and is housed in the former Holyrood Free Church and Duchess of Gordon's School at the entrance to the grounds.

Close to Holyrood is the new **Scottish Parliament Building**, designed by the late Catalan architect Enric Miralles. Officially opened in October 2004 by the Queen, it is a controversial building, having cost 10 times the original estimate and opening four years late. Its appearance has also divided the nation, with some people loving it and others loathing it. Guided tours are available and, while Parliament is in session, you can sit in the public galleries and watch the proceedings. In Holyrood Road is **Our Dynamic Earth**, an exhibition and visitors centre that takes you on a journey through the history of the universe, from the beginning of time and on into the future. It features dinosaurs, earthquakes, lava

Palace of Holyroodhouse, Edinburgh

🏛 historic building 🏛 museum and heritage 🏛 historic site ⚐ scenic attraction 🌿 flora and fauna

Greyfriars, Edinburgh

flows and tropical rainstorms.

To the south of the Royal Mile, in Chambers Street behind Edinburgh University, are the **Royal Museum** and the new **Museum of Scotland**. They house internationally important collections relating to natural history, science, the arts and history. On Nicolson Street is the **Surgeon's Hall Museum**, owned and run by the Royal College of Surgeons of Edinburgh.

One of Edinburgh's hidden gems can be found in the Cowgate - the **Magdalen Chapel** of 1547. It was built by Michael McQueen and his wife Janet Rynd, who are buried within it. It then passed to the Guild of Hammermen. The chapel contains pre-Reformation stained glass, and was where the very first General Assembly of the Church of Scotland was held in 1560, with 42 churchmen attending.

Another famous church south of the Royal Mile is **Greyfriars**. Built in 1612, it was here that the National Covenant rejecting bishops in the Church of Scotland was signed in 1638. From this, the adherents of Presbyterianism in the 17th century got the name Covenanters. In nearby Candlemaker Row is the famous **Greyfriars Bobby** statue. It commemorates a

terrier that faithfully kept guard over the grave of John Gray, his former master, who died in 1858 of tuberculosis. He did this for 14 years, until he too died in 1872. Bobby became famous after an American author, Eleanor Stackhouse Atkinson, wrote a book about it and Disney turned it into a film. However, she embellished the story somewhat by stating that Gray was a simple shepherd, when in fact he was a policeman.

North of the Royal Mile is Edinburgh's New Town. In the late 18th and early 19th centuries the medieval city was overcrowded and unhealthy, so the New Town was laid out in a series of elegant streets and squares to a plan by James Craig. Princes Street was one of these streets, and is now the city's main shopping area. It faces **Princes Street Gardens**, created from the drained bed of the old Nor' Loch.

Within the new town's Charlotte Square you'll find the **Georgian House** (National Trust for Scotland - see panel on page 178), which re-creates the interiors found in the New Town when it was being built. At No. 28 Charlotte Square is the National Trust for Scotland's headquarters and an art gallery. And within the Square gardens each August the Edinburgh Book Festival is held.

At the west end of the New Town is one of Edinburgh's most spectacular churches - **St Mary's Cathedral**. It was built in Victorian times as the cathedral for the Episcopalian diocese of Edinburgh and is as large and grand as a medieval cathedral, with three soaring spires that have become Edinburgh landmarks. It was designed by the eminent

The Georgian House

7 Charlotte Square, Edinburgh EH2 4DR
Tel/Fax: 0131 226 3318
or Tel: 0131 225 2160
e-mail: thegeorgianhouse@nts.org.uk
website: www.nts.org.uk

The Georgian House is part of Robert Adam's masterpiece of urban design, Charlotte Square. It dates from 1796, when those who could afford it began to escape from the cramped, squalid conditions of Edinburgh's Old Town to settle in the fashionable New Town. The house's beautiful china, shining silver, exquisite paintings and furniture all reflect the domestic surroundings and social conditions of the times. Video programme. New touchscreen programme featuring a virtual tour of the house.

architect Sir George Glibert Scott and built in the 1870s, though the spires were added in the early 20th century. Beside the cathedral is the much altered 17th-century manor house of Easter Coates House, now part of the choir school.

The **National Gallery of Scotland** on the Mound, the Scottish National Portrait Gallery (combined with the Scottish National Photography Collection) in Queen Street, the **Dean Gallery** and the **Scottish National Gallery of Modern Art** in Belford Road are all within, or close to, the New Town. A bus service runs between all four. The **City Art Centre** is in Market Street, behind Waverley Station. It houses the city's own art collection, and hosts major exhibitions, not just of art. The **Talbot Rice Gallery**, part of Edinburgh University, is in the Old College on South Bridge. Also in Market Street is **The Edinburgh Dungeon**, which aims to bring Scotland's bloody past to life.

The Scottish Genealogy Society Library and Family History Centre is in Victoria Terrace off George IV Bridge. At the east end of Princes Street you'll find **Register House**, where the National Archives of Scotland are

stored. It was designed by Robert Adam, with the foundation stone being laid in 1774. In front of it is an equestrian statue of the Duke of Wellington by Sir John Steel. Also in Princes Street is Scotland's official memorial to one of its greatest writers, the Gothic **Scott Monument**, which soars to over 200 feet, and offers a marvellous view from the top. It was designed by George Meikle Kemp, with work beginning in 1840. In August 1846, it opened to the public.

On Calton Hill, to the east of Princes Street is the 106-feet-high **Nelson Monument** from the top of which are views out over the city. It commemorates Nelson's death at the Battle of Trafalgar in 1805, and was designed by the architect Robert Burn. A time signal is installed at the top, consisting of a ball that drops at 12 noon in winter and 1pm in summer. It allowed ship's captains on the Forth to set their watches accurately.

Further north, off Inverleith Row, are the **Royal Botanic Gardens**, 70 acres of greenery and colour surrounded by the bustle of the city. They were founded in 1670 as a physic garden at Holyrood, but were transferred here in 1823. And at Leith, up

🏛 historic building 🏠 museum and heritage 🏛 historic site 🍃 scenic attraction 🌿 flora and fauna

until the 1920s a separate burgh, you'll find the **Royal Yacht Britannia** (see panel on page 180) moored at the Ocean Terminal, a leisure and entertainment complex. The ship is open to the public.

In Pier Place in Newhaven, to the west of Leith, is the **Newhaven Heritage Museum** explaining

Royal Botanical Gardens, Edinburgh

the history of this former fishing village. It was in Newhaven that the largest fighting ship of its day, the *Great Michael* was built between 1507 and 1513 for James IV's Scottish navy. It is said that the whole fleet that sailed to America with Columbus in 1492 could fit comfortably into her hull. It was the envy of Europe, and Henry VIII even demanded that it be handed over to him, as it was far too good for the Scots.

The Royal Yacht Britannia

Ocean Terminal, Leith, Edinburgh, Scotland EH6 6JJ
Tel: 0131 555 5566
e-mail: enquiries@tryb.co.uk
website: www.royalyachtbritannia.co.uk

For over forty years **The Royal Yacht** *Britannia* served the Royal Family, travelling over one million miles to become the most famous ship in the world. Travelling to every corner of the globe, in a career spanning 968 royal and official visits, she played a leading role in some of the defining moments of recent history. To Her Majesty The Queen and the Royal Family, *Britannia* proved to be the perfect royal residence for glittering State Visits, official receptions, honeymoons and relaxing family holidays. Since her decommissioning *Britannia* has now made Edinburgh's historic Port of Leith her final home and is open to the public throughout the year. Now owned by The Royal Yacht *Britannia* Trust, a non profit making charity, any proceeds go towards *Britannia's* maintenance.

Your tour of *Britannia* starts in the Visitor Centre on the second floor of Ocean Terminal. Here you can learn about *Britannia's* fascinating history through exhibits and photographs before you collect your complimentary audio handset and step on board *Britannia,* a privilege previously reserved for guests of Her Majesty The Queen and the Royal Family. Starting at the Bridge and finishing at the gleaming Engine Room, come and discover the reality behind life and work on board this Royal Yacht. Viewing five decks, using the lift or stairs for easy access, you will tour *Britannia* at your own pace and enjoy highlights that include the State Dining Room, the Drawing Room, the Sun Lounge, the Wardroom and the Chief Petty Officers' Mess. *Britannia* is furnished with artefacts from The Royal Collection, which are on loan from Her Majesty The Queen.

Granton sits further west, and at one time was a busy harbour and industrial area, with a huge gas works. It is now undergoing a major redevelopment, though one of the huge gasometers has been preserved. At its centre is Caroline Park (private), an elegant mansion dating from the 17th century.

Further to the west, at Corstorphine, are the **Edinburgh Zoological Gardens**, set in 80 acres. The zoo is famous for its penguins, and the daily penguin parade when they march round part of the zoo. However, the parade taking place or not depends on the weather and the whim of the penguins

themselves, who sometimes choose not to hold it.

Craigmillar Castle (Historic Scotland) is on the southeast outskirts of the city. The extensive ruins date from the 14th century, with many later additions. Mary Stuart stayed here for a short while after her Italian secretary Rizzio was murdered. **Lauriston Castle**, near Davidson's Mains, is also worth visiting. It is set in 30 acres of parkland. One of its owners was the father of John Napier, who invented logarithms. It now has a collection of furniture and decorative arts. The **Royal Observatory** sits on Blackford

---

🏛 historic building   🏛 museum and heritage   🏛 historic site   🝔 scenic attraction   🍃 flora and fauna

Hill, south of the city centre, and has displays and exhibits relating to astronomy.

Around Edinburgh

MUSSELBURGH
6 miles E of Edinburgh on the A199

🏛 Tolbooth   🌱 Inveresk Lodge Gardens

🏛 Battle of Pinkie

Musselburgh got its name from the beds of mussels that once lay at the mouth of the River Esk on which the town stands. Today, it is a dormitory town for Edinburgh. The **Tolbooth** dates from the 1590s, and was built of stones from the former Chapel of Our Lady of Loretto, which in pre-Reformation times was served by a hermit. **Inveresk Lodge Gardens** (National Trust for Scotland), with their terraces and walled garden, illustrates methods and plants that can be used in a home garden. The **Battle of Pinkie**, the last battle fought between Scottish and English national armies, took place near Musselburgh in 1547 during the Rough Wooing, when Henry VIII was trying to force the Scottish parliament to agree to a marriage between his son and the infant Mary Stuart. The Scots were defeated due to the incompetence of the Earl of Arran, Scotland's commander, though Mary herself eventually married the Dauphin of France, heir to the French throne.

PRESTONPANS
7 miles E of Edinburgh on the B1348

🏛 Battle of Prestonpans   🏛 Prestongrange Museum

At the **Battle of Prestonpans** in 1745, the Jacobite army of Charles Edward Stuart defeated a Hanoverian army under Sir John Cope. The whole battle only took 15 minutes,

with many of the Hanoverian troops being trapped against a high wall (which can still be seen) surrounding Prestongrange House. Contemporary accounts tell of terrified Hanoverian troops trying to scale the wall and dropping into the comparative safety of the house's grounds. Even though it took place in the early 18th century, the site was largely an industrial one, with even a primitive tramway for hauling coal crossing the battle field. The Jacobite song, *Hey Johnnie Cope,* lampoons the English commander, though he was not wholly to blame for the Hanoverian defeat.

The **Prestongrange Museum** is at Morrison's Haven, and tells the story of local industries through the ages.

PORT SETON
9 miles E of Edinburgh on the B1348

🏛 Port Seton Collegiate Church   🏛 Seton Castle

Port Seton Collegiate Church (Historic Scotland) was built, but never completed, in the 14th century as a collegiate church served by a college of priests. It is dedicated to St Mary and the Holy Cross, and has some tombs of the Seton family, as well as fine vaulting. In 1544, it was looted and stripped by the Earl of Hertford and his English army. **Seton Castle** dates from 1790, and was designed by Robert Adam. It replaced the former Seton Palace, one of the grandest Scottish buildings of its time. Mary Stuart visited the Palace after the murder of Rizzio by her second husband, Lord Darnley.

DALKEITH
7 miles SE of Edinburgh on the A68

🏛 Dalkeith Palace

🏛 St Nicholas Buccleuch Church

This pleasant town is nowadays a dormitory for Edinburgh, but at one time was an important market town on the main road south from Edinburgh to England. **Dalkeith Palace** was built around the medieval Dalkeith Castle for Anne, Duchess of Monmouth and Buccleuch, in the early 1700s. It became known as the 'grandest of all classical houses in Scotland', and its 2000-acre grounds are now a country park.

Anne's husband James Scott, Duke of Monmouth, was an illegitimate son of Charles II who had defeated a Covenanting army at Bothwell Bridge. However, he later plotted to usurp his father, and had himself declared king on June 20 1685. He was defeated at the Battle of Sedgemoor (the last battle fought on English, rather than British, soil) on July 6, and was executed on Tower Hill in London nine days later. Anne had been Duchess of Buccleuch in her own right, and was allowed to keep her title, though the Monmouth title was suppressed.

St Nicholas Buccleuch Church is a large building, formerly a collegiate church. Attached to it are the ruins of an old apse in which lie the remains of Anne, who died in 1732. Also buried there are the first Earl of Morton and his wife Joanna, daughter to James I of Scotland.

NEWTONGRANGE

8 miles SE of Edinburgh on the A7

🏛 Scottish Mining Museum

The monks of Newbattle Abbey started coal mining in the Lothians in the 13th century, so

---

NEWTONGRANGE PICTURE FRAMING GALLERY

website: www.scottisharthousegallery.co.uk

19 Station Road, Newtongrange,
Dalkeith EH22 4NB
Tel: 0131 660 9467

Some twelve kilometres southeast of the city of Edinburgh lies the small village of Newtongrange; here you will find the new **Newtongrange Picture Framing Gallery**. Owner, Carlo Veronese moved his work shop from Edinburgh to Newtongrange in 2008 and now offers 50% cheaper than Edinburgh high street prices.

When people walk into the shop they can view the whole shop and see the artwork being framed. Picture framing makes the perfect gift, be it an original painting, embroidery, tapestry, poster, or limited edition print. What about a love poem, a signed football shirt or picture of your hero/ heroine, car, cat or dog. It might be baby's first photograph, shoes, a lock of hair or mittens – put it in a picture frame and it will wow your loved ones. All types of frames available from resin to woods.

Pap of Glencoe; artist Colin Homes

The gallery also hosts a fabulous selection of fine art prints, contemporary prints and original paintings from local Scottish artists. One artist in particular is Raymond Murrary, who works from his studio on the Isle of Bute in the West of Scotland, his Giclee Fine Art is bold and eye-catching, perfect when you want to make a statement!

🏛 historic building   🏛 museum and heritage   🏛 historic site   ⌖ scenic attraction   🍃 flora and fauna

the industry has a long history in the area. The Lady Victoria Colliery in Newtongrange houses the **Scottish Mining Museum**, which tells the story of coal mining in Scotland from those days right up until the present. There is a re-created coalface, as well as the original winding engines and a visitor's centre. The Lady Victoria is one of the finest surviving Victorian collieries in Europe. It opened in the 1890s and closed in 1981. At its peak, it employed more than 2000 men.

ARNISTON
9 miles SE of Edinburgh off the A7

 Arniston House

Arniston House has been the home of the Dundas family for more than 400 years. It was built between 1726 and the 1750s to the designs of William and John Adam on the site of an old tower house. The interior detail is wonderful, and there is also a fine collection of paintings by artists such as Raeburn and Ramsay. In the 17th century, the Dundas family was one of the most powerful in Scotland, and held many important posts in the Scottish legal system. The house is open to the public, though dates and times should be checked, as they vary throughout the summer.

BORTHWICK
11 miles SE of Edinburgh off the A7

🏛 Borthwick Castle 🏛 Borthwick Parish Church

Borthwick Castle is a massive twin-towered castle built by Sir William Borthwick in about 1430 on the site of an earlier tower house. It was to this castle that Mary Stuart and Bothwell came after their marriage in 1567. It was a marriage that displeased the Scottish people, and more than a thousand Scottish nobles cornered the couple there. They demanded that Mary hand over Bothwell for his part in the murder of Lord Darnley, Mary's second husband. However, Bothwell escaped and fled to Dunbar.

On hearing of his escape, the nobles immediately retired from the Queen's presence, thinking that she had seen through his treachery. However, no sooner had they left her than she tore off her fine gowns and put on breeches and a pageboy's shirt, and made her escape so that she could rejoin her husband. The Red Room is said to be haunted by her ghost.

The Borthwicks were a powerful family, and when they took prisoners one of the games they played was to tie the prisoners' hands behind their backs and make them jump the 12 feet from the top of one tower to the other. If they succeeded, they were set free.

In 1650, the castle was attacked by Oliver Cromwell's Parliamentarian army, and it was abandoned not long after. In the early 20th century it was restored and, during World War II, it was secretly used to store national treasures. It is now a hotel.

The modern **Borthwick Parish Church** has a 15th-century aisle with effigies of the first Lord and Lady Borthwick.

CRICHTON
11 miles SE of Edinburgh on the B6367

🏛 Crichton Castle 🏛 Crichton Collegiate Church

🌿 Vogrie Country Park

Crichton Castle (Historic Scotland) was probably built in the late 1300s by John de Crichton. It consisted of a simple tower house typical of the period. This was added to by his son William, an ambitious and unscrupulous man who became Lord Chancellor of Scotland. During the minority of James II, Archibald, the 5th Earl of Douglas, was appointed regent, but he died two years after James ascended the throne. Both Crichton and Sir Alexander Livingstone competed to take Archibald's place, fearing that a Douglas might be appointed again. They invited the 6th Earl of Douglas, who was only 16, to a banquet at Edinburgh Castle in 1440, along with his brother and a friend. The head of a black bull was brought to the table, and at this sign the Earl, his brother and their friend were murdered. The affair became known as the Black Dinner.

Crichton Collegiate Church was built in 1449 by William Crichton. **Vogrie Country Park** lies to the north of the castle, and is centred on Vogrie House. It has woodland walks, picnic areas and a golf course.

SOUTRA

15 miles SE of Edinburgh off the A68

🏚 Soutra Aisle

From Soutra, high in the Lammermuir Hills, it is reckoned that you get the best view in central Scotland. On a clear day you can see the full sweep of the Firth of Forth with Fife beyond, and at least 60 Highland peaks. **Soutra Aisle** is all that remains of a medieval hospital. It was dedicated to the Holy Trinity, and it was here that Augustinian monks looked after travellers, pilgrims and the sick and wounded. A recent archaeological dig uncovered evidence of surgery and the treatment of patients by herbal remedies. Some pieces of bandage with human tissue still attached to them were even recovered.

ROSSLYN

7 miles S of Edinburgh on the B7006

🏚 Rosslyn Church   ⚜ Apprentice Pillar

🌿 Roslin Glen Country Park

Rosslyn (also known as Roslin), has gained world renown through *The Da Vinci Code*, a thriller written by American author Dan Brown. According to some people, it is the most important place in Christendom, all due to **Rosslyn Church**, an extravaganza of a building on which work began in 1446. Its founder was Sir William St Clair, third and last Prince of Orkney, who lived at nearby Rosslyn Castle. In the choir of this unfinished church (still in use) are carvings with both Masonic and Knights Templar associations.

The carving in the interior is spectacular, and shows plants that only grow in the New World, even though Columbus had not yet sailed across the Atlantic when it was built. There are also pagan carvings of The Green Man, as well as the famous **Apprentice Pillar**. This was said to have been carved by an apprentice when the master mason working on the church was on the Continent seeking inspiration. When he returned and saw the workmanship, the mason is supposed to have murdered the apprentice in a fit of jealousy.

Legends abound about the church. One theory says that the writings of Christ lie in its unopened vaults. Another says that the bodies of Knights Templar lie in the unopened crypt, fully dressed in armour. A third says that the Holy Grail is embedded in one of the pillars. And yet another says it is a re-creation of Solomon's Temple in Jerusalem.

There's even a theory that the body of Christ himself lies in the vaults. Whatever the truth of the matter, and the theories seem to get wilder and wilder with every new book written about it, there's no denying that it is one of the most beautiful buildings in Britain. There is certainly distinctive aura about the place.

Nearby is the **Roslin Glen Country Park**, with woodland walks that go past old gunpowder works.

🏚 historic building   🏛 museum and heritage   🏛 historic site   ⚜ scenic attraction   🌿 flora and fauna

PENICUIK
9 miles S of Edinburgh on the A701

🕊 Allan Ramsay   🏛 St Mungo's Parish Church

🎨 Edinburgh Crystal Visitor Centre

Penicuik was once a mining and paper-making town, founded in 1770 by its laird, Sir James Clerk of Penicuik. To the west of the town rise the Pentland Hills, with Scald Law being the highest peak at 1898 feet. In the grounds of Penicuik House stands the Allan Ramsay Obelisk, dedicated to the memory of the poet **Allan Ramsay** who was born in Leadhills in Lanarkshire in 1685. Ramsay visited the town often, as he was a friend of Sir James Clerk, who raised the obelisk, and had a house nearby.

St Mungo's Parish Church dates from 1771, and has a 12th-century detached belfry. The **Edinburgh Crystal Visitor Centre** at Eastfield has displays and exhibits about the history of crystal and glass-making in Scotland, plus factory tours.

CRAMOND
5 miles W of Edinburgh on a minor road off the A90

🏛 Parish Church

🏛 Roman Fort

Cramond is a charming village of old whitewashed cottages set on the banks of the River Almond where it enters the Firth of Forth. The **Parish Church** of 1656, with its medieval tower, sits within the ruins of a Roman Fort built about 142AD. The Rev Robert Walker, who was painted by Raeburn skating on Duddingston Loch in the 18th century, was minister here.

Cramond Tower (private) dates from the 15th century, while Cramond House (private) dates from 1680. At one time, the village was famous for the manufacture of nails. Cramond Island sits one mile offshore. It is possible to walk to it via a causeway at low tide, though walkers should heed the notices about tide times before setting off.

INGLISTON
7 miles W of Edinburgh off the A8

🏛 Cars of the Stars Motor Museum

Almost in the shadow of Edinburgh International Airport at Turnhouse is the Royal Showground, home each year of the Royal Highland Show, Scotland's premier country and farming fair. The **Cars of the Stars Motor Museum**, opened in 2003, features vehicles used in films, including two of the cars used in James Bond films.

Cramond Roman Fort

South Queensferry and Dalmeny

Distance: *5.2 miles (8.3 kilometres)*
Typical time: *120 mins*
Height gain: *60 metres*
Map: *Explorer 350*
Walk:*www.walkingworld.com ID:2522*
Contributor: *Fiona Dick*

ACCESS INFORMATION:

By car; leave Edinburgh on A90. After leaving the built-up area, take the second exit onto the B924, signposted Dalmeny. Follow signs to the village and drive to the west end (past the war memorial). Where the road swings round to the left into Standingstone Road, carry straight on into cul-de-sac and park opposite Wester Dalmeny Farmhouse.

By public transport: there are three buses an hour to Dalmeny Village from Princes Street in the yellow taxibus.

ADDITIONAL INFORMATION:

Dalmeny Village has a delightful small church (Norman doorway). Dalmeny House is home to the Earls of Rosebury and can be visited in the summer season (furniture, tapestries, paintings, small golf course). South Queensferry is a historic town that used to be the jumping-off point for travellers to the north of Scotland; there are still boat trips out to Inchcolm Island (birds, ruined abbey). As well as a museum and harbour, it can offer toilets (open even in winter), cafes, restaurants and pubs, of which the most famous is the Hawes Inn, featured in Robert Louis Stevenson's

"Kidnapped". Glorious views and the Forth Rail and Road Bridges, as well as down the estuary and back to Edinburgh. And all this within the boundaries of the City of Edinburgh.

DESCRIPTION:

A level walk passing through a country estate that juts out into the Forth Estuary, thus combining seashore and country. Easy going underfoot; you could just about get around with a buggy if you were prepared to lift it at a couple of places. Some walking on minor roads, but there is pavement throughout.

There are better views out to sea when the trees are bare, lots of daffodils in the spring and lovely mix of specimen trees in the summer.

FEATURES:

Sea, pub, toilets, church, stately home, birds, flowers, great views, café, food shop, good for kids, mostly flat, public transport, restaurant, woodland

WALK DIRECTIONS

1 | Walk straight ahead (west) to old railway bridge. At blue sign take path to the left alongside houses. Take steps down to old railway line.

2 | Turn right between three big stones onto the tarmac cycle path and go under the railway bridge.

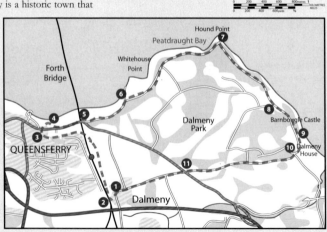

After the second bridge there is a view of the Forth Rail Bridge. Carry on under several bridges and round a left-hand bend.

3 | Just before the houses on the left-hand side, turn right onto an earth path towards a white house. At house, turn right down path onto shore road.

4 | Cross over and turn right towards the Forth Rail Bridge, passing underneath it, with the Hawes Inn on the opposite side of the road.

5 | As the road bends round to the right, take the lower path that runs alongside the water, with a low white building on the left-hand side (ices in summer). Carry on round the shore path - don't forget to look back for more great views of the rail bridge.

6 | At Long Craig Gate (white) and cottage, go through into the Dalmeny Estate (information board). Path now becomes hard-surfaced track. Carry on through the estate, following signs to Cramond Ferry, past the large tanker berth in the estuary. Ignore all side turnings.

7 | At Hound Point the track turns right. Here it is worth making a small detour onto the sand to admire the views.

8 | On meeting tarmac road coming in from the right, carry straight on towards Dalmeny House, which you shortly see.

19 | Ignore sign off to left to shore walk (although it is worth going to the edge of the golf course for the view). Instead, keep on the hard path curving round to the right past the house and the statue of a horse.

10 | At five-way junction, go straight ahead up the slope with a field and fence to your left. Shortly cross a cattle grid and make your way through the estate on the road (occasional cars).

11 | At the estate exit, cross the road with care and go straight ahead (signposted 'Dalmeny'). Pass farm with converted doocot on left and carry on into village, with more views of the road-bridge over the hedges. Continue through the village back to your car.

BALERNO
7 miles SW of Edinburgh off the A70

🌱 Malleny Garden

Malleny Garden (National Trust for Scotland) is a walled garden beside the 17th-. century Malleny House (private) extending to three acres and dominated by 400-year-old clipped yew trees. There are herbaceous borders, a fine collection of old-fashioned roses, and also the National Bonsai Collection for Scotland.

RATHO
8 miles W of Edinburgh on a minor road off the A8

🌿 Adventure Centre

Ratho sits on the Union Canal, and canal cruises are available from the Edinburgh Canal Centre. Parts of Ratho Parish Church date from the 12th century, though little of this can now be seen due to restorations over the years.

The **Adventure Centre** is billed as the 'gateway to adventure', with the National Rock Climbing Centre having 2400 square metres of artificial wall surfaces, the largest climbing arena in the world. One other feature is the Airpark, Europe's largest suspended aerial adventure ropes ride.

SOUTH QUEENSFERRY
9 miles W of Edinburgh city centre off the A90

🏛 Hawes Inn   🏛 Queensferry Museum

🏛 Carmelite Friary   🌿 Burry Man

🏛 Dalmeny House   🏛 Dalmeny Church

South Queensferry is named after St Margaret, Malcolm III's queen, who founded a ferry here in the 11th century to carry pilgrims across the Forth to Dunfermline Abbey and St Andrew's Cathedral. When she died she was buried in the abbey and later canonised, with her shrine becoming a place of pilgrimage as well. Now the ferry has been replaced by the Forth Rail Bridge and the Forth Road Bridge, two mammoth pieces of civil engineering. The rail bridge was built between 1883 and 1890 to link Edinburgh and Aberdeen, and the road bridge was completed in 1964. In the shadow of the Rail Bridge is the historic **Hawes Inn** of 1683, which features in R L Stevenson's *Kidnapped*. Opposite is the slipway from which the former ferry sailed.

The town has a glorious mix of cottages and houses dating from the 16th century onwards. Plewlands House (National Trust for Scotland) dates from 1643, and has been converted into private flats. The **Queensferry Museum**, in the High Street, has exhibits and displays on local history. There are also wonderful views of the two bridges from it. The church of the former **Carmelite Friary** in Rose Lane dates from the 15th century, and is now an Episcopalian church.

Each year in early August, the quaint custom of the **Burry Man** takes place. Dressed from head to toe in plant burrs, he spends nine hours walking about the town on a Friday. While everyone agrees it is an ancient custom, no on knows how it originated or what purpose it served.

Dalmeny House, to the east of the town, overlooks the Firth of Forth. It is the home of the Primrose family, who are Earls of Roseberry, and was built in the 1820s. There is an excellent collection of tapestries and furniture. **Dalmeny Church**, dedicated to St Cuthbert, is one of the best-preserved Norman churches in Britain. The south doorway is richly carved, as is the chancel and apse.

Haddington

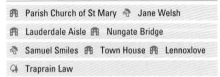

The royal burgh of Haddington received its royal charter in the 12th century from David I, and is thought to be the birthplace in 1505 of John Knox. It sits on the River Tyne (but not the one that flows through Newcastle), and at one time was the fourth largest town in Scotland. It was in St Martin's Church that the Scottish and French parliaments met in 1548 to sanction Mary Stuart's marriage to the Dauphin of France. Members of both the French and Scottish nobility attended, and put an end to Henry VIII's plans to have Mary marry his son Edward.

It is a quiet town of old buildings, including the quite superb cathedralesque **Parish Church of St Mary**, the longest parish church in Scotland. It was formerly collegiate, and dates from the 15th century. It stood outside the burgh boundaries at that time. When the parliament was meeting at St Martin's, the Scots were laying siege to the town, as it was then occupied by the English. Mary of Guise (Mary Stuart's mother) attended the parliament, and when she climbed to the top of St Mary's tower to view the English defences she was shot at. The ruined choir was restored in the early part of the 20th century. In the choir is the burial place of **Jane Welsh** (Thomas Carlyle's wife), who was born in the town in a house that can still be seen. The **Lauderdale Aisle**, owned by the Earls of Lauderdale, is unique in that it is a small Episcopalian chapel within a Presbyterian Church. This ecumenicalism

LETHAM HOUSE

Haddington, East Lothian EH41 3SS
Tel: 01620 820055
e-mail: stay@lethamhouse
website: www.lethamhouse.com

Nestled at the foot of a secluded rhododendron-lined drive on the outskirts of Haddington in East Lothian is **Letham House.** Only 16 miles from Scotland's capital city Edinburgh, this 17th century mansion boasts exceptional accommodation and dining in a magical setting. Each of the individually designed suites enjoys south facing views over ten acres of mature private gardens and grounds, while sumptuous fabrics, roaring fires and beautiful antiques evoke a sense of luxury and indulgence.

Elegant staircases and architectural features restored to their former glory reflect a bygone era and are complemented by wonderful, modern bathrooms and even a guest kitchen for midnight snacks!

Within the grounds you will find Hanka and Anya, two beautiful Haflinger horses. Further afield lies the rolling countryside of East Lothian, home to the finest selection of world class golf courses, golden beaches and a variety of local amenities. On return from a days outing, Letham invites you to unwind and indulge, offering absolute comfort and relaxation.

Letham is a nurturing retreat, offering privacy and tranquillity in majestic surroundings. This secret world can be enjoyed either for exclusive use or by individuals looking to escape for a night or two.

continues every year in May with the Whitekirk and Haddington Pilgrimage when people from all the main Christian religions in Scotland walk between the two towns.

St Mary's is one of the few Church of Scotland churches to have a full peal of bells, which were installed in 1999. The 16th-century **Nungate Bridge** over the Tyne is behind St Mary's and is named after the nunnery where the Scottish parliament met.

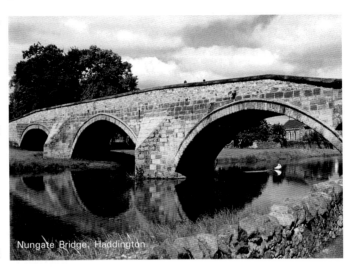

Nungate Bridge, Haddington

The writer **Samuel Smiles** was born in Haddington in 1812. Though he wrote many books, he is best known for *Self Help*. Several of his observations have become very familiar, amongst them 'A place for everything, and everything in its place', and 'He who never made a mistake, never made a discovery'.

The **Town House**, with its graceful spire, was designed by William Adam and built in the late 1740s, though the spire was added in 1831. Close to Haddington is **Lennoxlove**, home to the Dukes of Hamilton since 1946. Castle-like in appearance, the house dates back to the 1300s and was comprehensively restored in 2007. The house gains its name from Frances Theresa Stewart, Duchess of Lennox and Richmond, who bequeathed the house to her nephew, Lord Blantyre, with the dedication that it should be known as Lennox's Love to Blantyre. The house's most famous exhibit is the death mask of Mary

Stuart, which shows her to have been, as many contemporaries observed, an extremely beautiful woman.

About four miles east of Haddington is **Traprain Law** from the top of which there are superb views. The summit was occupied from Neolithic times right up until the Dark Ages, and the outline of a fort can clearly be seen. It was the capital of a tribe the Romans called the Votadini, which roughly translated means the farmers. More Roman finds have been made here, including a hoard of Roman silver, than anywhere else in Scotland.

Around Haddington

GULLANE
6 miles N of Haddington on the A198

🏛 Heritage of Golf   🏛 St Andrew's Church

This village sits inland from the Firth of Forth, but has fine views north towards Fife. Nowadays it is a small golfing resort with many large, imposing villas. The British Open is held here regularly, and the course at Muirfield is home to the Honourable Company of Edinburgh Golfers. The **Heritage of Golf** exhibition on the West Links Road traces the golfing history of the area.

The ruins of **St Andrew's Church** can be seen at the west end of the main street. They date from the 12th century, and were abandoned in 1612. On Gullane Bay, and signposted from the main street, is Gullane Bents, one of the best beaches on the Firth of Forth.

DIRLETON

6 miles N of Haddington off the A198

🏰 Dirleton Castle

The impressive ruins of **Dirleton Castle** (Historic Scotland) dominate this delightful village. The oldest parts date to the end of the 13th century, though there have been extensive additions and alterations over the years. To the west of the castle are some formal terraced gardens, which are in the *Guinness Book of Records* as having the longest herbaceous border in the world.

ABERLADY

6 miles N of Haddington on the A198

🦆 Aberlady Bay Nature Reserve   🦢 Nigel Tranter
🏛 Myreton Motor Museum   🏰 Mercat Cross
🏰 Aberlady Parish Church   🏰 Lufness Castle

This pleasant village was the port for Haddington until the bay silted up. The **Aberlady Bay Nature Reserve** covers 1439 acres of foreshore and dunes, and is popular with bird watchers. The village was home to one of Scotland's most popular historical novelists, **Nigel Tranter**, who died in the year 2000 at the age of 90. During his long life he published more than 130 books. There is a small cairn to his memory close to Quarry House where he used to live, and an exhibition of his life and works in the church in Athelstaneford.

Myreton Motor Museum contains displays of motorcars, cycles and military vehicles dating from 1899. There is also a large collection of period advertising, posters, enamel signs, and toy vehicles. **Aberlady Parish Church** was remodelled in the 19th century, though an interesting 16th-. century tower still stands. In the High Street is the old **Mercat Cross** of 1780. To the east of the village is **Luffness Castle**, a T-plan tower house with Norman origins that was once the ancestral home of the Earls of Hopetoun and is now a hotel.

ATHELSTANEFORD

2 miles NE of Haddington on the B1343

🏛 National Flag Heritage Centre

Athelstaneford has a special place in Scottish history. It was here that the Scottish flag, the Saltire, or St Andrew's Cross, was first adopted. Athelstan was a king of Northumbria who fought a combined army of Picts and Scots at Athelstaneford in 832AD. The Pictish leader, Angus mac Fergus, on the day before the battle, saw a huge white cross made of clouds in the sky, and took it as an omen. Athelstane was duly defeated, and a white cross on a blue background was adopted as the flag of Scotland, making it the oldest national flag in Europe.

This is why the Saltire on its own should be white and sky blue, whereas when it is incorporated into the Union Jack the blue darkens. The **National Flag Heritage Centre** in an old doocot (dovecot) behind the village church explains the story of the battle and the flag.

NORTH BERWICK
7 miles NE of Haddington on the A198

🦅 Scottish Seabird Centre   🏛 St Andrew's Auld Kirk

🎞 Gelie Duncan   🏛 Tantallon Castle

North Berwick is one of Scotland's best-known holiday and golfing resorts. It is a clean, attractive town, which was granted a royal charter by Robert II in 1373. North Berwick Law, a volcanic plug, rises to a height of 613 feet behind the town, and makes a wonderful viewpoint. Two miles off the coast rises the Bass Rock, another volcanic plug that broods over the waters of the Firth of Forth. More than 150,000 sea birds nest each year on the 350-feet-high cliffs and on other, smaller islands such as Fidra and Craigleith. From the **Scottish Seabird Centre**, on a promontory near the old harbour, you can use remote controlled cameras that are situated on the islands to study the birds without disturbing the colonies. There are also powerful telescopes on a viewing deck, a film about Scotland's sea birds, and a café restaurant.

In the 8th century, the Bass Rock was home to the hermit St Baldred, who evangelised this part of Scotland (though should not be confused with another St Baldred who succeeded St Mungo as Bishop of Glasgow, and who lived a century earlier). In later times it also served as a prison for Jacobites and Covenanters, and there are traces of old fortifications on it.

Also on the promontory are the scant ruins of **St Andrew's Auld Kirk**, which date from the 12th century onwards. It was finally abandoned in the 17th century due to coastal erosion. When the Seabird Centre was being

---

THE SCOTTISH ARCHERY CENTRE

Fenton Barns, North Berwick, East Lothian EH39 5BW
Tel: 01620 850401
e-mail: eric@scottisharcherycentre.co.uk
website: www.scottisharcherycentre.co.uk

Set in the beautiful countryside of East Lothian, the Scottish Archery Centre was the first Archery Centre in Scotland and was the brain-child of Eric Burn, who has some 30 years experience in archery. The Centre offers visitors the chance to try various shooting disciplines from Archery to Crossbow, from Air-Rifle to Air-Pistol. All the activities are mainly held indoors and under full supervision and instruction. All ages from very young to senior citizen are all welcome. As well as the wide range of activities at the Centre, Eric is also busy arranging

Corporate events devised around the various shooting activities, or organising Fun Highland Games that include Tossing the Caber, Putting the Stane and Haggis Hurling.

    The centre also holds a small archery museum with a selection of bows from around the world Another area contains war time memorabilia relating to the famed WW2 Drem airfield, in the X RAF buildings in which the archery centre is now located. As an introduction to this ancient skill, Eric and his Instructors with gives new visitors a fun hour at a, reasonable cost booked in advance of course, they will have you hitting the target and playing archery games in no time at all.

    Or if you are just passing and we are free you can try 8 arrows and bursting the balloon and scoring to earn a certificate. *Mission Statement* **(WE AIM TO PLEASE)**

🏛 historic building   🏛 museum and heritage   🏛 historic site   🏞 scenic attraction   🦅 flora and fauna

Bass Rock, off North Berwick

built, more than 30 well-preserved skeletons from the old graveyard were uncovered, the earliest one dating back to the 7th century.

In the 16th century the town was supposed to have been the home of a notorious witches coven, and a well-publicised trial took place in 1595. One of the accusations made was that the witches had caused a terrible storm to rise up when James VI's ship was returning from Denmark with his new bride.

It all started when a poor serving girl called **Gelie Duncan** was found to have remarkable healing powers, which aroused suspicion. Her master, David Seaton, tried to extract a confession of witchcraft from her using thumbscrews, and when this failed he had her body examined for the 'marks of the devil'. These were duly found on her throat, and she confessed and was thrown in jail.

On being tortured further, Gelie claimed to be one of 200 witches and warlocks in the town who, at the behest of the Earl of

Bothwell, David Seaton's sworn enemy, were trying to harm the king. At Hallowe'en in 1590, Gelie told them, the witches convened at the Auld Kirk, where Satan appeared to them and preached a sermon from the pulpit. King James had all the women identified by Gelie put to death, including one Agnes Sampson and a schoolmaster from Prestonpans called John Fian. Gelie herself was burnt on the Castle Esplanade in Edinburgh.

Though people have subsequently claimed that the Earl of Bothwell dressed up as Satan to take part in the Hallowe'en coven in the kirk, there's little doubt that Gelie made up the stories to save herself from further torture, and so many innocent people were executed. There is also no doubt that David Seaton had no interest in the women as such - he merely wanted to harm the Earl of Bothwell.

East of North Berwick is **Tantallon**

Castle (Historic Scotland). Its substantial and romantic ruins stand on a cliff top above the Firth of Forth, almost opposite the Bass Rock. It was a Douglas stronghold, built in the 14th century by William, first Earl of Douglas. It has a curtain wall 80 feet high.

WHITEKIRK
7 miles NE of Haddington off the A198

🏛 St Mary's Parish Church	🏛 Tithe Barn
🖼 Aeneas Sylvius Piccolomini	

St Mary's Parish Church dates from the 15th century and is the eastern end of the annual Whitekirk to Haddington Pilgrimage. Whitekirk had been a place of pilgrimage long before the church was built. In pre-Reformation times, people came to the village to seek cures at the Well of Our Lady, which used to be located nearby. An account of 1413 relates that more than 15,000 people of all nationalities visited yearly. Close to the church is the 16th-century **Tithe Barn**, built to store the tithes (a tithe being a 10th part) given to the church as offerings from the parishioners' agricultural produce.

The place's most famous pilgrim - but one who did not come seeking a cure - was a young Italian nobleman called **Aeneas Sylvius Piccolomini**. He had set out from Rome in the winter of 1435 as an envoy to the court of James I. During the sea crossing, his ship was blown off course by a raging gale. Aeneas vowed that if he made it to dry land he would offer thanksgiving at the nearest church dedicated to Our Lady. The boat was eventually shipwrecked between North Berwick and Dunbar, and Aeneas survived. He therefore set out on a 10-mile pilgrimage in a snowstorm to Whitekirk, where he duly offered prayers of thanks. While in Scotland,

he fell in love with a young woman, and pledged himself to her. However, he was ambitious, and soon gave her up. Twenty years later, Aeneas became Pope Pius II.

EAST LINTON
6 miles E of Haddington off the A1

🏛 Preston Mill	🏛 Phantassie Doocot
🏛 Prestonkirk	🏛 Hailes Castle
🖼 Scottish Museum of Flight	

Anyone travelling along the A1 should make a small detour to view this picturesque village. To the east is Phantassie, the mansion where John Rennie the civil engineer was born. He designed Waterloo, London and Southwark bridges over the Thames, and Rennie's Bridge at Kelso. Phantassie is now an organic market garden.

Preston Mill (National Trust for Scotland) is an old, quaint water mill that has been restored to full working order. It stands in an idyllic rural spot, and dates from the 18th century, though a mill has stood on the spot for centuries. With its conical roofed kiln and red pantiles, it is a favourite subject for painters and photographers.

Close by is **Phantassie Doocot** (National Trust for Scotland), which belonged to Phantassie House, and could hold 500 birds. Also nearby is **Prestonkirk**, a small, attractive church. It was built in 1770, though the 13th century chancel still stands, as it was used as a mausoleum for the Hepburn family.

The ruins of **Hailes Castle** lie to the west of East Linton in a beautiful location. Its earliest masonry dates from the 13th century, though it was much altered in later years by the Hepburns, who acquired the castle in the 14th century. It was to Hailes Castle that James Hepburn, Earl of Bothwell, brought Mary

Stuart after seizing her at Fountainbridge in 1567. He was later to become her third husband.

The **Scottish Museum of Flight** is situated at East Fortune, to the northeast of the village. Formerly a World War II airfield, it now has eight hangars housing a fascinating collection of aircraft, rockets, models and memorabilia. The most famous exhibit is Concorde, brought to the museum in 2004. Another is a Prestwick Pioneer, the only aircraft ever to have been wholly designed and built in Scotland. Also on display are a Soviet MIG, a Blue Streak rocket and a Lightning.

STENTON

7 miles E of Haddington on the B6370

🥾 Pressmennan Forest Trail 🏛 Stenton Kirk

This small conservation village still retains its old Tron, on which wool brought to the Stenton Fair by local sheep farmers was weighed. To the south of the village is Pressmennan Lake, one of the few lakes, as opposed to lochs, in Scotland (see also Lake of Menteith, Ellon and Kirkcudbright). This one, however, is artificial, created in 1819 by the local landowner. The **Pressmennan Forest Trail** runs along its southern shore, and from the highest point you can see Arthur's Seat in Edinburgh and the Bass Rock in the Firth of Forth.

Stenton Kirk is a handsome building designed by the noted architect William Burn in 1829. In the kirkyard is the Old Kirk, dating probably from the 14th century.

TYNINGHAME

7 miles E of Haddington on the B1407

Tyninghame is a small conservation village that formerly stood in what are now the grounds of Tyninghame House, which has been divided up into private flats. In 1761, the village was moved to its present position by the then Earl of Haddington to improve the view from his house, though the remains of the former parish kirk, dedicated to St Baldred, still stand there.

DUNBAR

11 miles E of Haddington on the A1087

🏛 Battle of Dunbar 🏰 Dunbar Castle
🏛 Town House 🏛 Torness Nuclear Power Station
🏛 John Muir Centre 🌿 John Muir Country Park
🏛 Doonhill Homestead

The Royal Burgh of Dunbar received its royal charter in 1445. It is a former fishing and whaling port, though its main industries are now brewing and tourism. It was near here, in 1650, that the **Battle of Dunbar** took place between the troops of Cromwell and a Covenanting army under General Leslie. The Covenanters were resoundingly beaten when General Leslie's advice not to confront Cromwell was ignored by the Scottish ministers. A stone commemorates the event.

The ruins of **Dunbar Castle** overlook the harbour, and date back to the 12th century. The castle was originally built for the Cospatrick family, which later changed its name to Dunbar. It was to Dunbar Castle that Edward II fled after his defeat at Bannockburn. He then boarded a boat for Berwick-upon-Tweed. In 1338, the Countess of Dunbar, known as Black Agnes, held the castle for five months against an English army before being relieved by a small contingent of Scots. On the orders of the Scottish Parliament, the castle was dismantled after Mary Stuart abdicated.

The old **Town House** in the High Street

dates from about 1620 and houses a small museum on local history and archaeology. A much newer attraction is situated south of the town, near the shore. **Torness Nuclear Power Station** was built in the early 1980s, and has a visitor centre that explains how electricity is produced from nuclear power.

John Muir, founder of the American national parks system, was born in Dunbar in 1838. His birthplace in the High Street is now the **John Muir Centre**, with displays on his travels and his work. The **John Muir Country Park** is to the northwest of the town. Established in 1976, this was the first park of its kind in Scotland, and covers 1760 acres.

Two miles south of the town, off the A1, is **Doonhill Homestead** (Historic Scotland), where once an Anglian hall dating from the 7th and 8th century stood. Its site is marked out on the grass, and shows that this area of Scotland was once part of the mighty Anglian kingdom of Northumbria.

GARVALD
6 miles SE of Haddington off the B6370

🏛 Garvald Parish Church

This tiny red sandstone village lies on the northern slopes of the Lammermuir Hills. **Garvald Parish Church** dates partly from the 12th century, and has a sundial dated 1633. It is surprisingly light and airy inside.

Southeast of the village is the mansion of Nunraw in whose grounds Cistercian monks, who arrived here in 1946, began building the Abbey of Sancta Maria in 1952. It was the first Cistercian monastery in Scotland since the Reformation, and was colonised by monks form Tipperary in Ireland. A Cistercian nunnery, founded by nuns from Haddington, had previously been founded here in about 1158.

GIFFORD
4 miles S of Haddington on the B6369

🏛 Yester Parish Church

Gifford was laid out in the 18th century, and is a pretty village with views of the Lammermuir Hills to the south. The whitewashed **Yester Parish Church**, which has Dutch influences, was built in 1708 and has a medieval bell. It was in Gifford that John Witherspoon, the only clergyman to sign the American Declaration of Independence, was born in 1723.

Southeast of the village is Yester House (private), designed by James Smith and dating from 1745. The interiors were later re-styled by Robert Adam in 1789. From the 1970s until his death in 2007, the house was the home of the Italian-American composer Gian Carlo Menotti. He was persuaded to buy the house because of the superb acoustics in the 28 feet by 45 feet ballroom. In 2008, the house was put on the market for £15 million, making it Scotland's most expensive property up to that time.

Beyond Yester House are the ruins of Yester Castle (private), built by Hugo de Gifford in the late 13th century. He was known as the Wizard of Yester. Beneath the castle is a chamber known as Goblin Ha' where he is supposed to have practised magic and called up goblins and demons. Scott mentions him in *Marmion*.

The narrow road from Gifford up into the Lammermuir Hills is a fine drive and takes you past Whiteadder reservoir and down into Berwickshire.

PENCAITLAND
6 miles SW of Haddington on the A6093

🏛 Pentcaitland

The oldest part of **Pencaitland Parish**

🏛 historic building 📷 museum and heritage 🏛 historic site 🗻 scenic attraction 🌿 flora and fauna

Church is the Winton Aisle, which dates from the 13th century. Close to the village is the 500-year-old Winton House. It was built for the Seton family by the king's master mason, and is famous for its twisted chimneys. It overlooks the Tyne, and has lovely terraced gardens. It is now a venue for private and corporate events. Glenkinchie Distillery, to the south of the village, was opened in 1837. It has a small exhibition and offers tours showing how whisky is distilled.

Linlithgow Palace

Linlithgow

- 🏛 Linlithgow Palace 🏛 King's Fountain
- 🏛 St Michael's Parish Church 🎬 James IV
- 🏛 Town House 🏛 Linlithgow Story
- 🏛 Linlithgow Canal Centre 🏛 Hopetoun House
- 🦶 Beecraigs Country Park 🏛 House of the Binns

This ancient royal burgh was granted its royal charter in 1138. It is a lovely place, with many historic buildings in its old High Street, and has played a central role in Scotland's history. **Linlithgow Palace** (Historic Scotland), situated on the banks of Linlithgow Loch, dates originally from the reign of James I, who ruled in the early 15th century. It became a favourite of many Scottish kings and queens, and it was here, in 1512, that James V was born. It was also the birthplace, in 1542, of his daughter, the tragic Mary Stuart. The birth

room was most probably the Queen's Bedchamber in the northwest tower. Mary's association with Linlithgow Palace lasted only seven months, as her mother, Mary of Guise, later took her to the more secure Stirling Castle. When Mary Stuart returned from France in 1561, after the death of her husband King Francis II, she only stayed briefly at the castle and it was allowed to decay.

Cromwell stayed here for a short time in 1650 when he invaded Scotland after its parliament had declared Charles II king of Britain. Then, in 1745, Charles Edward Stuart stayed in the palace. A year later the troops of the Duke of Cumberland moved in, and when they moved out they left their straw bedding too close to the fires. The place caught fire, and soon the whole building was ablaze, leaving it roofless and uninhabitable.

In the castle courtyard is the **King's**

🎬 stories and anecdotes 🐦 famous people 🎨 art and craft 🎭 entertainment and sport 🚶 walks

Fountain, built between 1536 and 1538 for James V. It is the oldest fountain in Britain, and is in three tiers, with elaborate carvings that symbolises his reign. It was badly damaged during the fire. A restoration scheme of the 1930s used concrete to replace some of the carvings, and this introduced salts into the structure, which began its decay. Now, following a five-year-long restoration project, the fountain has been restored to full working order.

The impressive Outer Gateway to the palace still stands. On it are the coats of arms of the four orders of chivalry to which James V belonged - the Garter of England, the Thistle of Scotland, the Golden Fleece of Burgundy and St Michael of France.

Opposite the Palace is **St Michael's Parish Church**, one of the most important medieval churches in Scotland. It dates from the 15th century, though a church had stood there long before that. Within the church, one of the most unusual incidents in Scottish history took place. The church was especially dear to **James IV,** who worshipped there regularly. In 1514, he had decided to take a large army into England in support of France, which had been invaded by Henry VIII's troops. Most of the Scottish court was against the idea, as was James's wife Margaret, sister of the English king.

But James held firm, and a few days before he and his army set out, he was at mass in St Michael's Church with his courtiers. A strange man with long, fair hair suddenly appeared in the church dressed in a blue gown tied with a white band and carrying a staff. Pushing aside the courtiers, he approached James and spoke to him. He had been sent 'by his mother', he said, to tell James that no good would come of the invasion of England. Furthermore, he

was not to meddle with other women.

Some of the courtiers tried to grab him, but before they could, the old man made good his escape. Confusion reigned, and people immediately took the man to be a ghost. The reference to his mother, they said, meant that he had been sent by Our Lady (to whom James was especially devoted). James took no heed, and marched into England. He, and all the flower of Scottish manhood, were wiped out on the field at Flodden. The 'ghost's' prophecy came true.

People nowadays discount the ghost theory, and say that the whole thing had been orchestrated by James's wife with the help of some of the court. The reference to the king's meddling with other women was the Queen's own contribution to the event, as James was renowned for his philandering.

One of the courtiers was Sir David Lyndsay, Lord Lyon, and a playwright, who knew all the tricks of the stage, and he may have been involved as well. There is a theory that says that Margaret had been put up to it by her brother Henry VIII, who was totally unprepared for a Scottish invasion, though this is now discounted. All she wanted to do was protect her husband from his own folly.

The **Town House**, in the centre of the town, dates from 1668, and replaces an earlier building destroyed by Oliver Cromwell in 1650. The Cross Well dates from 1807, and replaced an earlier structure.

It was in Linlithgow that the Earl of Moray, Regent of Scotland, was assassinated in the street by James Hamilton of Bothwellhaugh, who later escaped to France. A plaque on the old County Buildings commemorates the event. In Annet House in the High Street is the **Linlithgow Story**, with displays and exhibits explaining the history of the town.

There are also herb, fruit tree and flower gardens. At the **Linlithgow Canal Centre** in Manse Road is a small museum dedicated to the Union Canal, which links the Forth and Clyde Canal at Falkirk with Edinburgh. Trips along the canal are also available. **Beecraigs Country Park**, to the south of the town, is set in 913 acres of land near the Bathgate Hills. It has a loch where you can fish, a deer farm and a camping and caravan park.

To the north of the town is the **House of the Binns** (National Trust for Scotland), ancestral home of the Dalyell family, the best known member of which is Tam Dalyell, the former MP. In 1601 the Edinburgh butter merchant Thomas Dalyell married Janet, daughter of the first Baron Kinloss, and bought the lands of Binns. Between 1621 and 1630 he enlarged the house, and the present building has at its core that 17th-century structure. It represents possibly the best example of the transition from a fortified castle to a comfortable home in Scotland.

Thomas's son was also Thomas. He earned an unsavoury reputation as Bluidie Tam Dalyel, scourge of the Covenanters. He was every inch a king's man, and when Charles I was executed in 1649, he vowed never to cut his hair until there was a king on the throne once more. And indeed, Bloody Tam's portrait in The Binns shows a man with hair flowing down past his shoulders. Tam also helped the Tsar of Russia reorganise the Russian army and was made a nobleman of Russia. For that reason he also had another nickname - The Bluidie Muscovite.

Another stately home near Linlithgow is **Hopetoun House**, possibly the grandest 'big house' in Scotland, and certainly the best example of a Georgian house in the country. It sits almost on the banks of the Forth, and is home to the Marquis of Linlithgow. It was

House of the Binns, Linlithgow

started in 1699 by the first Earl of Hopetoun, ancestor of the present Marquis, and designed by Sir William Bruce with enlargements by William Adam, who introduced the sweeping curves. The inside is spectacular and opulent, with ornate plasterwork, tapestries, furnishings and paintings. Surrounding the house is magnificent parkland extending to 150 acres, with a deer park and spring garden. The main approach to the house is by the Royal Drive, which can only be used by royalty. George IV used it when he visited Scotland in 1822, and Elizabeth II used it in 1988.

Around Linlithgow

BO'NESS
3 miles N of Linlithgow on the A904

🏛 Kinneil Museum 🏛 Bo'ness Motor Museum

The town's real name is Borrowstoneness, though it is always referred to nowadays by its shortened name. It is an industrial town, and was formerly one of Scotland's leading whaling ports. It was near here that the eastern end of the Antonine Wall terminated. Near the town is the Kinneil Estate, with, at its centre, Kinneil House. It was built by the Hamilton family in the 16th and 17th centuries. It isn't open to the public, though it can be viewed from the outside. However, within the house's 17th-century stable block is the **Kinneil Museum**, which tells the story of Bo'ness over the past 2000 years. There is also an exhibition called Rome's Northern Frontier, which highlights the Antonine Wall and the Roman soldiers who manned it. The ruins of Kinneil Church lie near the house, and probably date from the 13th century with later additions. It was abandoned as a place of worship in 1669, when a new parish church was built at Corbie Hall. The church was accidentally destroyed by fire in 1745 by a troop of dragoons stationed at the house.

Bo'ness Motor Museum displays an interesting mix of classic cars and James Bond 007 memorabilia, including props from film and TV productions. There's also a soft play area ideal for keeping the children occupied whilst having a snack in Miss Moneypenny's or a refreshing drink in the Double O Bar.

The town's main attraction is the Bo'ness and Kinneil Railway, which has been developed since 1979 by the Scottish Railway Preservation Society. There is a Scottish railway exhibition, as well as workshops and a working station. Trips on the steam trains, which run between Bo'ness and Birkhill Station, are popular, and trains can be chartered for special occasions. At Birkhill are the caverns of the former Birkhill Fireclay Mine, which can be explored.

BLACKNESS
4 miles NE of Linlithgow on the B903

🏛 Blackness Castle 🏛 Archibald Douglas

Blackness Castle (Historic Scotland) must be the most unusually shaped castle in Scotland. It sits on a promontory jutting out into the Firth of Forth, and from the air looks like a huge ship. It was a Crichton stronghold, with the first castle on the site being built in about 1449 by Sir George Crichton, Sheriff of Linlithgow and Admiral of Scotland. However, there is an intriguing but untrue story about how the castle eventually came to look like a ship.

By the early 16th century, the castle had passed to the Douglases. James V appointed **Archibald Douglas** as Lord High Admiral of the Scottish fleet, but soon discovered that he had made a mistake, as every time Archibald went to sea he became sea sick.

The young James was enraged, and threatened to dismiss him. Archibald, who was making a fortune out of selling commissions in the navy, wanted to retain his position. So he promised his king that if he was allowed to keep his job, he would build him a ship that the English couldn't sink and on which he, Archibald, would never be sick. Mollified, the king agreed, and Douglas built Blackness Castle. However, a more mundane explanation of its shape is the restricted shape of the site on which it was built.

The castle was subsequently besieged by Cromwell's army in 1650, and was later used as a prison for Covenanters. During the Napoleonic wars, it was again used as a prison, this time for French prisoners-of-war. After that it was used as an ammunition dump but was finally restored in the 1920s and opened to the public.

TORPHICHEN
3 miles S of Linlithgow on the B792

- Torphichen Preceptory
- Torphichen Parish Church

The unusual name of this picturesque village comes from Gaelic Torr Phigheainn, meaning the hill of the magpies, and is pronounced Tor fichen. It is an ancient place, with its history going back to the founding of a church dedicated to St Ninian in the 6th century.

The Knights of the Order of St John of Jerusalem, or the Knights Hospitallers as they were more commonly called, was a monastic order of soldier monks formed in the 11th century to look after St John's Hospital in Jerusalem, and to offer hospitality and protection to pilgrims travelling to the Holy Land. **Torphichen Preceptory** (Historic

Scotland) was one of only two such establishments in Britain, the other one being in London. It was founded in about 1124, when the lands of Torphichen were given to the monks by David I. The head of a Knights Hospitaller monastery was called a preceptor, and for this reason a monastery was always known as a preceptory.

The only parts left standing of the original preceptory are the transepts and crossing of the monastic church. Above the crossing is a tower, which, no doubt because of the Knights' military role, looks more like a castle than a church tower. Within a small room is a display about the modern Order of St John, which was refounded in 1947 as a separate order in Scotland by George VI. Nowadays, it runs old folks homes, mountain rescue units and hospitals in Scotland. Where the nave once stood is now **Torphichen Parish Church**, which dates from 1756, though it incorporates masonry from the earlier building.

LIVINGSTON
6 miles S of Linlithgow off the M8

- Livingston Parish Church
- Almond Valley Heritage Centre
- Almondell & Calderwood Country Park

Livingston is one of Scotland's new towns, built round an historic village that has the **Livingston Parish Church** of 1732. At the 20-acre **Almond Valley Heritage Centre** in Millfield, visitors can find out about local history and the environment, including the Scottish shale industry, which once thrived in West Lothian. There is also an 18th-century water mill, a small railway line, a farm, a picnic area and teahouse.

The **Almondell and Calderwood Country Park** is three miles east of the town centre, and has woodland and riverside walks.

Almondell was originally a private estate, which belonged to the Erskine family, and many items from Kirkhill House, with which it was associated, have been relocated within the park, such as the entrance gates and the astronomical pillar. Calderwood was also a private estate, and belonged to the barons of Torphichen. This area has been deliberately left undeveloped to encourage wildlife.

The Oakbank Shale Bings are a reminder of the shale industry, and have been landscaped. A good view of the surrounding countryside, and even up into Fife, is available from the top.

Almond Valley Heritage Centre, Livingston

MID CALDER
8 miles SE of Linlithgow on the B8046

🏛 Kirk of Mid Calder

The **Kirk of Mid Calder** has an apse built in the 16th century. One of the 17th-century ministers of the church was Hew Kennedy, who was zealous in his persecution of witches. In 1644, several of them were burnt at the stake.

While staying at Calder House (private) in 1556 (four years before the Scottish Reformation), John Knox first administered Holy Communion using the new reformed liturgy. In 1848, the Polish pianist Frederic Chopin also stayed here.

BATHGATE
6 miles S of Linlithgow on the A89

🏞 Cairnpapple Hill　　🏛 Bennie Museum
🌿 Polkemmet Country Park

Bathgate is a substantial industrial town, and was formerly a centre for the shale oil industry. Sir James Young Simpson, who introduced chloroform into midwifery, was the son of a Bathgate baker, and was born here in 1811, as was James 'Paraffin' Young, who opened the world's first oil refinery in 1850, extracting paraffin from the local shale. **Cairnpapple Hill** (Historic Scotland), to the north of the town, is 1017 feet high, and was the site of a temple built about 2000 to 2500BC. Fragments of bone and pottery have been found here. The view from the top is magnificent, and on a clear day both the Bass Rock in the Firth of Forth and the mountains of Arran in the Firth of Clyde can be seen.

In Mansefield Street is the **Bennie Museum**, which contains collections relating to local history. **Polkemmet Country Park**, four miles west of the town, has a golf course, a driving range, bowling green and picnic sites. The whole area was owned at one time by the Baillie family, and a mausoleum, built by Robert Baillie, fourth Lord Polkemmet, can still be seen.

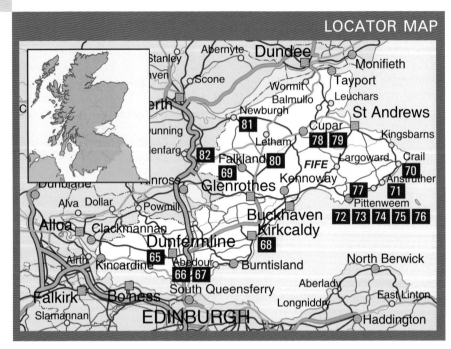

ADVERTISERS AND PLACES OF INTEREST

🏠 historic building 🏛 museum and heritage 🏚 historic site ⚘ scenic attraction 🌿 flora and fauna

6 | Fife

The county of Fife consists of a long peninsula bounded on the south by the Firth of Forth and on the north by the Firth of Tay. It is steeped in history, and for that reason is sometimes referred to as the Kingdom of Fife. James II, who ruled from 1437 to 1460, once called it a 'fringe of gold on a beggar's mantle', meaning that, in his day, it had prosperous coastal towns and a barren interior. During the Cold War years, Fife was where Scotland would be governed from in the event of a nuclear attack. The underground Secret Bunker, as it is now known, was located on a farm near St Andrews.

Dunfermline, still an important town, was Scotland's capital before Edinburgh took over, and on the coast there were small prosperous seaports that traded with Europe. You can still see the European influence today. Some of the older buildings in the coastal towns have a distinctly Low Countries feel to them, and some houses have red pantiles - brought in as ballast from the Netherlands and the Baltic countries - instead of slates. These ports, with names such as Crail, Pittenweem and Anstruther, are still there, though now they rely on tourism rather than trade.

Of all the towns on the county's east coast the most famous is surely St Andrews. Seen from a distance, it shimmers with spires and towers, and is crammed with ancient buildings and historical associations. It was formerly a place of pilgrimage because of

its great cathedral, the impressive ruins of which still overlook the shore. In it were kept the relics of St Andrew, Scotland's national saint, and this made it the country's ecclesiastical capital in pre-Reformation days.

It was also the seat of an archbishop and was where Scotland's first university was founded. Even today students can be seen dressed in their traditional red gowns as they scurry to lectures during term time. And the place still attracts pilgrims, though now they come in the name of sport, for the town - or perhaps we should call it a small city - is the recognised home of golf.

The county's largest town is Kirkcaldy, famous for the manufacture of linoleum. So much so that people used to say that you could always tell when you were approaching the town by its 'queer-like smell'. But this royal burgh has many historical associations. At one time it was known as the Lang Toun, because it appeared to consist of one long street, though it has now spread inland. And it can lay fair claim to being the birthplace of economics,

Dunfermline Abbey

Limekilns, Firth of Forth

was once a place of pilgrimage because of the tomb of St Margaret. It is now the resting place of one of Scotland's great heroes, Robert the Bruce. And, like Kirkcaldy, it too has its famous sons. Charles I was born here in 1600, as was, in 1835, Andrew Carnegie, the millionaire philanthropist.

Mining has given way to electronics as an employer, and this part of Fife is well and truly part of 'silicon glen'. But the area hasn't lost its attractiveness, and one of the places that must be visited is Culross, surely one of the loveliest and most historic small towns in Scotland.

because in 1728 Adam Smith was born here.

To the west of the county another industry held sway - coal mining. The Fife coalfields used to employ thousands of men, but now it has all but gone. Dunfermline is the largest town in this area - another Fife royal burgh whose roots go deep into Scotland's history, having been granted its royal charter in 1124. Its abbey, like the cathedral at St Andrews,

Since the opening of the Tay Road Bridge in 1966, the towns and villages of northern Fife across the firth, such as Newport-on-Tay, Tayport, Leuchars and Wormit, have become dormitory towns for Dundee. Even before this people were commuting, thanks to the Tay Rail Bridge, opened in 1887 after the first bridge collapsed into the firth in 1879 with much loss of life.

Dunfermline

- St Margaret of Scotland ⛪ Dunfermline Abbey
- Palace Visitors Centre ⛫ Malcolm's Tower
- Pittencrieff Park Pittencrieff House Museum
- Abbot House Heritage Centre
- St Margaret's Cave Andrew Carnegie
- Andrew Carnegie Birthplace Museum
- Dunfermline Museum
- Scottish Vintage Bus Museum

Now an important industrial town, Dunfermline was at one time the capital of Scotland, and still has many reminders of its past glories. It was here that Malcolm III (known as Malcolm Canmore, meaning bighead) and his second queen, later to become **St Margaret of Scotland**, held court in the 11th century.

Malcolm and Margaret married in 1070, and their reign was a turning point in Scotland's history. Margaret was the daughter of Edgar Aetheling, heir-apparent to the English throne, and was half Saxon and half Hungarian. When she came to the Scottish court in about 1067, she was shocked at what she found and, with her husband's consent, set about changing things. The Scottish church, though nominally subservient to Rome, was still observing the old Celtic rites, which she found abhorrent. So the church was the first thing she changed. A Culdee (from the Irish céli dé, meaning servants of God) monastery manned by Celtic/Irish priests had previously been established in Dunfermline. Margaret suppressed it and founded a Benedictine priory in its place and invited monks from Durham to serve in it. The priory later became Dunfermline Abbey, and when Margaret died in 1093, she was buried before its High Altar.

In 1250 she was canonised by Pope Innocent IV, and it is said that Mary, Queen of Scots owned her skull as a religious relic. It later passed to the monks of Douai in France but was lost during the French Revolution.

Scotland in the 11th century was a small kingdom, perched precariously on the edge of the known world. It was Margaret who brought refinement to the court and made the country think of itself as an integral part of Europe. Under Margaret and Malcolm, who was also a driving force, trade with the Continent flourished. Malcolm revelled in this, as though he could neither read nor write, he hankered after refinement and culture. He moved Scotland's capital from Perthshire to Dunfermline to be nearer the Fife ports that traded with Europe. Under Margaret, the centre of power shifted once more - this time to Edinburgh, which later became the nation's capital.

One other innovation is attributed to St Margaret - buttons on the sleeves of men's jackets. She had been disgusted to see that Scottish courtiers - in common with courtiers throughout Europe - wiped their noses on their sleeves, so set about making this habit as uncomfortable as possible. The buttons eventually became fashionable, and the fashion spread throughout Europe.

She died soon after her husband and son were killed in Northumberland in 1093 and was buried in the abbey she had founded. Soon a cult grew up round her, and her burial spot became a place of pilgrimage. The remains of her shrine, destroyed during the Reformation, can still be seen.

Dunfermline Abbey as we see it today is a mixture of dates. The heavily buttressed nave is Norman, and is reminiscent of Durham Cathedral. Beneath it lie the remains of the

🎭 stories and anecdotes famous people art and craft entertainment and sport walks

Abbot House Heritage Centre

Maygate, Dunfermline, Fife KY12 7NE
Tel: 01383 733266
e-mail: info@abbothouse.co.uk
website: www.abbothouse.co.uk

The award-winning Abbot House Heritage Centre is the oldest house in Dunfermline, dating from 1450, and stands in the centre of the historic area of the City and Royal Burgh of Dunfermline, Ancient Capital of Scotland. It is conspicuous, not only for its authentic pink livery....but for its enchanting and atmospheric visitor experience. Hardly an episode in Scotland's turbulant past has failed to leave its mark on the fabric of this treasure house of history, with its crow-stepped gables, turnpike stairs and barrel vaults. It has witnessed the intrigues of Church and State and even outlasted much of the great Abbey it once served. From caring for the sick and needy to training aircraft spotters to ward off the Luftwaffe.....Abbot House has seen it all.

Visit the displays on the two upper floors of the House which cover the history of Scotland, Kingdom of Fife and City of Dunfermline from the Picts to the opening of the Forth Road Bridge in 1964. Enjoy delicious home-baking or a light meal in the Abbot's Kitchen Café, browse in the Gift Shop or relax in the beautiful south-facing garden.

Open 7 days a week from 10am to 5pm (closed Christmas Day, Boxing Day and New Year's Day).

original church. The choir was rebuilt in the early 1800s as the parish church, and it was during its construction that workmen came across the skeleton of a man lying within a stone coffin and wrapped with gold cloth. It was immediately recognised as that of Robert the Bruce, King of Scots, since the breastbone and ribs had been sawn away. After he died, Bruce's heart had been removed from his body so that it could be taken to the Holy Land. The skeleton was re-interred with due reverence, and now a brass plate beneath the pulpit marks the spot. Around the battlements of the abbey tower are the words 'King Robert the Bruce'.

The **Dunfermline Abbey Nave and Palace Visitors Centre** (Historic Scotland)

tells the history of the abbey and of the later palace that was built on the site of the monastic buildings. A magnificent 200-feet long buttressed wall is all that now remains of the palace where Charles I was born.

To the west of the abbey is a great mound known as **Malcolm's Tower**, all that remains of Malcolm's fortress. The town takes part of its name from the mound, as Dunfermline literally means fort on the hill by the crooked stream.

It sits within **Pittencrieff Park** (famous for its peacocks), which was gifted to the town by Andrew Carnegie in 1908. The park had always fascinated him as a boy, and as it was privately owned at the time, he was always denied access. So when he had the money, he bought it and threw it open to the people of the town. Also in the park is **Pittencrieff House Museum** (free), based in a 17th-century mansion, which has an art gallery and displays on local history.

The **Abbot House Heritage Centre** (see panel opposite) is housed in a 14th to 16th century house to the north of the abbey in Maygate. It was formerly the Abbot's Lodgings for the great Benedictine monastery, as well as its administrative centre. Poets, kings and bishops visited, and it played its part in some of the great events in Scottish history.

St Margaret's Shrine has been reconstructed with its wall, showing just how rich the interior of the abbey was when it was at the height of its powers. In all, more than 1000 years of history can be seen, from the Picts right up until the present day.

Near Chalmers Street Car Park, about a quarter of a mile north of Abbot House, can be found **St Margaret's Cave** (free) where the pious queen prayed in solitude. A legend has it that Malcolm became suspicious of his wife's unexplained absences from court, and fearing that she had a lover, followed her to the cave one day, where he found her kneeling in prayer. It's fortunate that the cave still exists, as in the 1960s the local council wanted to cover it in concrete as part of a car park.

Andrew Carnegie was, in the 19th century, the richest man in the world. He was born in Dunfermline in 1835, and emigrated with his parents to the United States in 1848. By the 1880s, he had amassed a fortune through iron and steel-making, and retired from business in 1901 to distribute his wealth. His humble birthplace in Moodie Street, a former weaver's cottage, is now the central feature of the **Andrew Carnegie Birthplace Museum**. It tells the story of the great man from his humble origins to his death in 1919. In Pittencrief Park, close to the Louise Carnegie Gates (named after his wife), is a statue of the great man.

It is not only New York that has a Carnegie Hall - Dunfermline has one as well, housing a theatre and concert hall. It can be found in East Port, near the **Dunfermline Museum and Small Gallery** (free) in Viewfield. Here the history of the town is explained, including its time as a centre of manufacture for linen and silk, which continued right up until the 20th century. Special displays from the Dunfermline Linen Damask Collection are on view.

To the north of the town, at Lathalmond, is the **Scottish Vintage Bus Museum**, housed in a former Royal Navy Stores depot. Opened in 1995, it is possibly the largest collection of vintage buses in Britain. The museum is open on Sunday afternoons during the season.

Andrew Carnegie Birthplace Museum, Dunfermline

Around Dunfermline

COWDENBEATH
5 miles NE of Dunfermline, off the A909

🖉 Racewall Cowdenbeath

This small town was at the centre of the Fife coalfields, and though the mines have long gone, it still has the feel of a mining community about it. Its football team has perhaps the most unusual nickname of any senior team in Scotland - the Blue Brazils. **Racewall Cowdenbeath** has stock car racing every Saturday evening from March to November.

LOCHGELLY
7 miles NE of Dunfermline on the B981

🌾 Lochore Meadows Country Park 🦢 Ian Rankin

Lochgelly is a small mining town, famous throughout Scotland at one time for the manufacture of the Lochgelly, the leather strap used to punish children in school.

Loch Gelly itself, after which the town is named, has water sports facilities. At one time, the loch was famous for the quality of its leeches, used by doctors for bloodletting.

Near the town is the **Lochore Meadows Country Park**, set in 1200 acres of reclaimed industrial land. The last pits closed here in 1966, with the park being created on the site in the early 1970s. The area is now a haven for wildlife, and at the west end of the loch is a bird hide with disabled access. The 260-acre Loch Ore, created as a result of mining subsidence, is stocked with brown trout. It is also used for water sports.

The famous crime writer, **Ian Rankin**, was born at nearby Cardenden in 1960 and educated at Beath High School in Cowdenbeath.

SALINE
6 miles NW of Dunfermline on the B913

🖉 Knockhill Racing Circuit 🌾 Kirklands Garden

Knockhill Racing Circuit is Scotland's national motor sports centre for cars and motorbikes, and has meetings on most Sundays from April to October.

Kirklands Garden extends over two acres and is surrounded by 20 acres of woodland. In spring, it presents a spectacular display of rhododendrons, bluebells, wood anemones, hellebores and bulbs. There's also a walled terraced garden created in 1832, a bog garden, statues and a plant sales area.

ABERDOUR
6 miles E of Dunfermline on the A921

🏛 St Fillan's Church 🏛 Aberdour Castle
🖉 Aberdour Festival

Aberdour is a small coastal burgh that received its charter in 1500. The restored **St Fillan's Church** is partly Norman, with fragments that may date back to at least 1123, and has what is known as a 'leper window'. This was a window looking on to the altar through which lepers could see from a private room the mass being celebrated. It is said that Robert the Bruce, himself suffering from leprosy, used the window after his victory at Bannockburn in 1314. In 1790, the church was abandoned, and gradually fell into disrepair. However, in 1925 work began on restoring it, and it is now open for services once more. The town has two beaches, one of which, Silver Sands, has won a European blue flag for its cleanliness.

Aberdour Castle (Historic Scotland), close to the church, dates from the 14th century, when it was built by the Mortimer family, with later additions being made in the 16th and

ARTIS 33 / SHORELINE STUDIO

33 High Street, Aberdour, Fife KY3 0SH
Tel: 01383 860705
websites: www.artis-33.co.uk / www.shoreline.sco.fm

Located in the picturesque seaside conservation village of
Aberdour, **Artis 33 / Shoreline Studio** are housed in a
unique property that dates back to the 17th century. They
provides a light and airy exhibition space where you will
find a wide range of paintings, prints, ceramics, stained,
cast and fused glass pieces, jewellery, sculpture,
photographs and antiques. The gallerys are owned and
managed by Judith and Ian McCrorie. Judith is an
accomplished artist herself and works in a range of media
- oil, watercolours, fused, stained and cast glass,
printmaking and ceramics.

   Judith has tutored students of all ages and abilities for
more than 20 years and has worked as an examiner for
the Scottish Qualifications Authority and the Open College
of the Arts. At Artis 33, art workshops are offered
throughout the year and individual and small group tuition
is available.

   The studio is well equipped with printing presses, kilns for glass and ceramics and art, craft and
textile equipment. It is a colourful, fascinating place, full of great works of art that would adorn
any wall or shelf. The gallery space is available for hire.

MYSTIQUE MOMENTS
& THE GREEN WITCH

59-61 High Street, Aberdour, Fife KY3 0SJ
Tel/Fax: 01383 860106
e-mail: chris@greenwitch.co.uk
website: www.greenwitch.co.uk

As you open the door of **Mystique Moments & The Green
Witch**, you are greeted by the aroma of melting beeswax,
herbs and oils. You then notice the roaring fire and the
rocking chair which is a favourite with customers. The room
is crammed full of enticing herbs - crystals, jewellery, hand-
made incense and beeswax candles, creams, soaps and
home-made remedies. The magical atmosphere is enhanced
by witches and fairies, along with Tarot cards, runes and
pendulums. Also on display are various magical works and
prints by local artist Keli Clark.

   Owner Christine Quick established Mystique Moments in
1995 but her shop became known locally as The Green
Witch because of the magical elements of the stock on
display and because she recycled. She believes that her shop is unique in Scotland because she
makes many of the products herself and advises customers throughout the day or by e-mail.
Mystique Moments is certainly a great place to seek out unusual gifts whether it be the hand-made
soaps and hand creams or stylish gemstone jewellery.

Aberdour and Silversands Bay

Distance: *3.7 miles (5.9 kilometres)*
Typical time: *120 mins*
Height gain: *80 metres*
Map: *Explorer 367*
Walk: *www.walkingworld.com ID:1860*
Contributor: *Oliver OBrien*

ACCESS INFORMATION:

By train, there are regular services to Aberdour from Edinburgh (half-hourly via the 'Inner Circle' and the spectacular Forth Rail Bridge) and limited services from Aberdeen, Dundee and Perth. By bus, Stagecoach in Fife Service Number 7 runs past the walk start, at Aberdour Station. By road, the start is on the A921 Inverkeithing to Kirkcaldy road.

ADDITONAL INFORMATION:

Part of the walk follows the Fife Coastal Path, which stretches over many miles from the Forth Road Bridge at North Queensferry, to the Tay Bridge, across the water from Dundee. Aberdour has a castle and gardens owned by Historic Scotland and open for public visiting.

DESCRIPTION:

This walk takes in a short section of the Fife Coastal Path, passing through a picturesque Aberdour Village and its harbour, with views south over the Firth of Forth to Edinburgh. It continues past Hawkcraig Point with more spectacular views and passes the appropriately named Silversands Beach, which has an award for a 'Premium' British beach. The route then follows the railway line below 50m-high cliffs, the route passing through woodlands with a rocky beach only a few metres away, visiting a pleasant cascade at Bendameer, before striking uphill and returning on a smaller, pleasant high path through deciduous woodland The Heughs, back to Aberdour Village. There is a dramatic clifftop view at one point near the end.

FEATURES:

Sea, pub, toilets, play area, castle, wildlife, birds, flowers, great views, butterflies, café, gift shop, food shop, good for kids, public transport, nature trail, restaurant, tea shop, waterfall, woodland.

WALK DIRECTIONS:

1 | (If arriving on a train from Edinburgh, cross over by the footbridge). Leave the station car park and turn left off the main road, passing the entrance to Aberdour Castle, open to the public. Continue straight ahead, follow the road around to the right, pass a pub on your right and turn left, off Livingston Lane. Follow the narrow, walled road down to the seafront.

2 | There is a great view to Inchcolm Island here. The sign indicates the route of the Fife Coastal Path, so bear left and follow the promenade beside the road, to the harbour entrance.

3 | The road carries on down to the harbour. Bear left here onto the raised path, passing to the left of a gallery. Follow the path around the harbour, crossing a small bridge annd passing toilets.

4 | There is a choice here. Either head left, climb the steps and continue along the road, passing a large car park on your right, down into Silversands car park. Or carry straight on, following the path round (watching out for cliffs!) to Hawkcraig Point. Pick up the access road and follow it round to the left, leading into Silversands car park.

5 | Head along beside the appropriately named Silversands Beach, passing a playground at the far end. There are a couple of waymarks on the track beside the beach, indicating the continuation of the Fife Coastal Path.

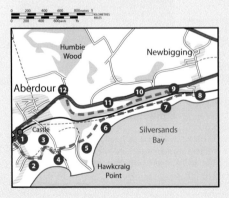

6|Pass through this gap in the wall, turn right and follow the path beside the railway line. This is the longest and most pleasant section of this walk, with the rocky beach never far away. There is a dramatic rock formation on your left at one point and later on a path down to a short, attractive section of the beach. The industry of Burntisland can be seen ahead on the horizon.

7|Follow the path underneath the railway sign and continue along the path, passing a turning to the left (you'll come back here shortly!).

8|This is a rather attractive cascade, best viewed from the bridge itself. Bendameer House is just ahead, but not visible from here. Although the Fife Coastal Path continues onwards, the next few miles are rather unpleasant as they thread through the industrialised Burntisland. So instead, turn around and retrace your steps back to that signpost you passed.

9|This signpost indicates 'Aberdour by The Heughs and Burntisland by the A921'. Turn right here and climb up the steep steps. The path becomes small but is easy to follow and continues upwards through very pleasant woodland, as views back down to the coastline become more impressive.

10|Turn left at the signpost here and follow the widening path, which begins gradually to descend through the woodland.

11|The view here, to the left of the path, opens out suddenly. There is a sheer 50m drop in front and Silversands and Hawkcraig Point can be clearly seen. The route continues along the path, descending slowly and bearing to the right. Ignore a small path to the left.

12|The path meets the main road here, at the edge of Aberdour. Turn left and continue along the pavement, through the village and back to Aberdour Station and the start of the walk.

17th centuries. It was later owned by James Douglas, 4th Earl of Morton and Regent of Scotland between 1572 and 1578. In 1580 he was executed for his part in the murder of Mary Stuart's second husband, Lord Darnley.

The **Aberdour Festival** is held every year at the end of July and offers 10 days of celebrations with arts, crafts, song, dance, puppetry, sports and much more.

DALGETY BAY
4 miles SE of Dunfermline off the A921

St Bridget's Church   2nd Earl of Moray

The ivy-clad ruins of **St Bridget's Church**, once the burial place of the Earls of Dunfermline, date from the 13th century. The church was first mentioned in a Papal Bull of 1178.

It was near Dalgety Bay that the murder of James Stewart, the **2nd Earl of Moray**, took place, an event that is remembered in one of the best-known of Scottish songs, *The Bonnie*

Earl o' Moray. Moray was the grandson of Regent Morton, regent of Scotland when Mary Stuart abdicated in favour of her infant son, later to be James VI. The earl was a popular nobleman, dashing and handsome, but he was also a staunch Protestant, and was engaged in a long feud with the Earls of Huntly, one of the great Catholic families of the time. The earl was implicated in a coup to overthrow James VI, though he probably had no involvement. But Huntly saw his chance and, armed with a king's warrant and a troop of soldiers, set out to seize the young earl. He eventually found him at his mother's castle at Donibristle, in what is now Dalgety Bay. He demanded that he give himself up, but Moray refused.

The troops therefore set fire to the building. Some men ran out from the front of the castle to distract Huntly's men while Moray ran out the back way, hoping to hide near the shore. Unfortunately, unknown to Moray, his

stories and anecdotes   famous people   art and craft   entertainment and sport   walks

bonnet had caught fire, and the smoke gave him away. He was hacked to death, with Huntly, it is said, striking the fatal blow. When James VI found out about the murder, he feigned outrage. When it later became known that Huntly had been armed with a king's warrant, James had to flee to Glasgow to escape the wrath of the public. Huntly spent a few weeks in Blackness Castle as a punishment, and was then released.

INCHCOLM
6 miles SE of Dunfermline, in the Firth of Forth

🏚 Inchcolm Abbey

This small island was at one time known as the Iona of the East. On it are the substantial ruins of **Inchcolm Abbey** (Historic Scotland), dedicated to St Columba. The story goes that Alexander I, son of Malcolm III and Queen Margaret, was crossing the Forth in 1123 when a storm blew up and the royal party had to seek refuge on the island, which had, for many years, supported a succession of hermits. The hermit of the time shared his meagre provisions with his guests for three days until the storm subsided. When Alexander reached the shore he vowed to build a monastery on the island dedicated to St Columba in thanksgiving for his safe passage, but before he could put his plans into effect he died. His younger brother, David I, who succeeded him, founded a priory, which eventually became the Abbey of Inchcolm in 1223.

A small stone building to the west of the abbey may have been the original hermit's cell, though it has been much restored over the years. The abbey buildings as we see them now date mainly from the 15th century, and represent the most complete medieval abbey in Scotland, with most of the buildings

remaining intact.

In the late 18th century, a military hospital was set up on the island to look after wounded sailors from the Russian fleet, which was using the Firth of Forth as a base. In the 20th century, it was fortified as part of the United Kingdom's sea defences, and some of these can still be seen. More than 500 troops were stationed on the island, and the first air raid of World War II took place close by in 1939 when German bombers dropped bombs not far from the Forth Rail Bridge.

INVERKEITHING
3 miles S of Dunfermline off the A90

🏛 Inverkeithing Museum 🏚 Battle of Inverkeithing

🐦 Admiral Sir Samuel Greig

Inverkeithing is an ancient royal burgh, which received its royal charter from William the Lion in about 1193. In medieval times it was a walled town with four ports, or gates, though the walls were pulled down in the 16th century. From the 1920s, the town became known for its shipbreaking yards. Amongst the famous ships that met their end here were the battleship *HMS Dreadnought* in 1921, the *Titanic*'s sister ships the *Homeric* and *Olympic* in 1932, and the *Mauritania* in 1965. Over the years, countless aircraft carriers, battleships, and vessels of every other shape and size were dismantled here.

The town lies close to the Forth Road and Rail Bridges, and has many old buildings. The Mercat Cross is 16th century, and the Old Town Hall opposite, with its outside staircase, dates from 1770. Of the 15th-century St Peter's Church, only the tower remains, as the rest dates from 1826. Two other old buildings are Thomsoun's House dating from 1617 and Fordell's Lodging dating from 1670. **Inverkeithing Museum**

🏚 historic building 🏛 museum and heritage 🏚 historic site 🐦 scenic attraction 🌱 flora and fauna

Inverkeithing Museum

the Clan MacLean, commemorates the event.

In the 14th century, Pitreavy Castle was owned by Christina Bruce, Robert the Bruce's sister. It later passed to the Kellock family and the Wardlaws, who rebuilt it. From World War II until 1996, a bunker beneath the castle was the naval operations HQ for Scotland. The castle is reputedly haunted by three ghosts: the Grey Lady, the Green Lady and a headless Highlander who is said to moan in anguish.

NORTH QUEENSFERRY
4 miles S of Dunfermline off the A90

📷 Forth Bridge Visitors Centre 🐟 Deep Sea World

🕴 Fife Coastal Path

This small town, huddled beneath the massive piers of the Forth Bridges, was the northern terminus for the ferry that plied across the Forth from South Queensferry in Edinburgh. The ferry was originally founded by Queen Margaret in the 11th century to enable her to travel from Edinburgh to her palace in Dunfermline. The town sits on a small peninsula, which juts out into the Forth where the river has its narrowest point until the Kincardine Bridge is reached.

The opening of the Forth Railway Bridge in 1890 meant that the ferries carried many fewer passengers across the river, but it was the building of the Forth Road Bridge in 1964 that finally put them out of business.

The **Forth Bridges Visitors Centre** is housed within the Queensferry Lodge Hotel, and tells the story of the two bridges spanning the Forth. There is a magnificent scale model of the Firth of Forth, as well as photographs, documents and artefacts.

Deep Sea World is billed as Scotland's Aquarium, and takes you on a walk along the 'ocean floor', thanks to the world's longest underwater tunnel made of specially

housed in the hospitium of an old friary, tells the story of Inverkeithing and of **Admiral Sir Samuel Greig**, a local man born in 1735 in what is now the Royal Hotel in the High Street. He entered the service of Tsarina Catherine of Russia in 1764, and is credited with creating the modern Russian navy, manning it initially with Scottish officers. He died in 1788 aged only 53.

Near the town, in 1651, was fought the **Battle of Inverkeithing** between a Royalist force under Sir Hector MacLean of Duart and the Parliamentarian forces of Cromwell. The result was a victory for the Parliamentarians, and the death of MacLean. As a result of the battle, the towns of Inverkeithing and Dunfermline were plundered, and Cromwell's ascendancy in Scotland rose. A small cairn by the roadside opposite Pitreavy Castle (private), erected by

toughened glass. Fish swim above and beside you in a specially made sea containing a million gallons of water. As you stand within it you can see sharks, stingrays and electric eels. A special touch pool allows you to touch sharks, sea urchins and anemones. One of the most popular experiences on offer at the aquarium is the chance to dive with sharks.

North Queensferry is the start of the **Fife Coastal Path**, a 78-mile-long pathway that passes through most of the small picturesque towns and villages on the Fife coast, ending at the Tay Bridge on the Firth of Tay.

CHARLESTOWN

3 miles SW of Dunfermline on a minor road off the A985

This small village was established in 1756 by Charles Bruce, 5th Earl of Elgin, to exploit the large deposits of limestone in the area, including an easily worked crag facing the sea. It was Scotland's first planned industrial village, though Bruce died before the work was finished. It was finally completed by the 7th Earl (of Elgin Marbles fame). There were nine kilns here at one time producing lime for building, agriculture and the making of iron and glass. It was a self-sufficient community,

with its own harbour, shops and school, and the houses were arranged in the shape of the founder's initials - CE, Charles Elgin.

The works closed in 1956, having produced more than 11 million tons of quicklime in their 200 years of existence. Now guided walks round the complex are available in the summer months thanks to the Scottish Lime Centre in the Granary Building in Rocks Road.

CULROSS

7 miles W of Dunfermline on a minor road off the A985

🏛 Mercat Cross 🏛 Sir George Bruce

🏛 Culross Palace 🏛 Town House 🏛 The Study

🌱 Torry Bay Local Nature Reserve

If you wish to see what a Scottish burgh looked like in the 16th, 17th and 18th centuries, then the royal burgh of Culross is the place to visit. It was granted its royal charter in 1592, and though having a population of no more than a few hundred, it had its own town council and provost up until local government reorganisation in 1975.

It is undoubtedly the most picturesque of Fife's old burghs - a situation that owes a lot to the town's relative poverty in the 18th, 19th and early 20th centuries when there was no money for modernisation. In the 16th century, it was a prosperous port that traded with the Low Countries, but when this trade dried up, it sunk into poverty. Now it is largely owned by the National Trust for Scotland.

It is a thriving and lively community, with most of the quaint crow-step gabled houses occupied. The streets

Culross Palace, Culross

are cobbled, and those around the old **Mercat Cross** (dating from 1588) have a feature known as the crown o' the causie, a raised portion in the middle where only the wealthy were allowed to walk, while the rest of the townsfolk had to walk on the edges where water and dirt accumulated.

The town's main industries were coal mining, salt panning and the making of baking griddles. Coal mining had been introduced by the monks of Culross Abbey at a time when coal was little known, and wondrous tales spread round Scotland about the 'stones that could burn'. After the Reformation, the mines were taken over by **Sir George Bruce**, a descendant of Robert the Bruce. Between 1575 and his death 50 years later, he revolutionised the industry. He was the first man to extend a coal mine beneath the sea, something that is taken for granted today. One of his mines had a tunnel that extended out under the waters of the Firth of Forth for more than a mile. James VI was fascinated by Culross's industry and paid a visit. Sir George took him on a tour of the mine, and led the unsuspecting king along the tunnel. When he emerged and found himself surrounded on all four sides by water, he panicked, shouting 'Treason!'

As an offshoot of the mining industry, salt panning became another major occupation in the town. It is reckoned that at one time there were 50 saltpans along the coast, all using inferior coal to heat salt water from the sea. Another industry was the making of iron griddles for cooking. Culross blacksmiths are said to have invented these round, flat utensils for frying and cooking after Robert the Bruce, in the 14th century, ordered that each one of his troops be given a flat pan for cooking oatcakes.

Nothing remains of Sir George's mining ventures. However, his home, now called **Culross Palace**, still stands, and is open to the public. Work started on it in 1597, and is a typical residence of its time for someone of Sir George's standing in society. It has splendid kitchen gardens. Along from it is the **Town House**, built in 1625 and gifted to the National Trust for Scotland in 1975 when Culross Town Council was wound up. At one time, the ground floor was a debtors' prison, while the attic was used as a prison for witches. It now houses the local tourist information centre.

Beside the Mercat Cross is **The Study**. It was built about 1610 and, after the Palace, is Culross's grandest house. When the Church of Scotland was Episcopalian, the town formed part of the diocese of Dunblane, and it was here that Bishop Robert Leighton stayed on his visits. The quaint Outlook Tower housed his actual study, hence the name of the house. If you continue past The Study, along Tanhouse Brae and into Kirk Street, you will eventually reach **Culross Abbey**, dedicated to St Serf and St Mary. The choir of the church (restored in 1633) still stands, and is used as the parish church, though the other buildings have either completely disappeared or are in ruins. It was founded in 1217 by Malcolm, Earl of Fife, and housed a Cistercian order of monks who left Kinloss Abbey. It is likely that the site of the abbey is where St Serf founded a monastery in the 6th century. Off the north transept is the Bruce Vault, where there is an impressive monument to Sir George Bruce of Carnock, his wife and their eight children.

Culross was the birthplace, in 514AD, of St Kentigern, patron saint of Glasgow. In 1503, Archbishop Blackadder of Glasgow erected a small chapel on the spot where the birth is supposed to have taken place, and its ruins can still be seen to the east of the village. The story goes that the saint was the son of Thenew (also known as Enoch), a princess of the kingdom of the Lothians. When her father Loth (after which the Lothians was supposedly named) discovered that she was pregnant, he banished her from his kingdom and she set sail in a boat across the Firth of Forth. She landed at Culross, where she gave birth to her son who was taken into care by a monk called Serf (later St Serf), who had established a monastic school there. It is now known that St Serf lived in the century following Kentigern's birth, so the story is doubtful.

But Culross's attractions aren't all historical. Close to the town is Longannet Power Station, one of Scotland's largest. There are organised tours (which have to be pre-booked), when you can see the huge turbine hall from a viewing platform, as well as tour the visitors centre, which shows how coal produces electricity.

Stretching from Longannet past Culross to Combie Point on the shores of the Firth of Forth, is the **Torry Bay Local Nature Reserve**, where there is a series of artificial lagoons built from the waste ash from Longannet. Here you can see many species of birds, such as shelduck, greenshank and great crested grebe.

KINCARDINE-ON-FORTH

10 miles W of Dunfermline, on the A985

This small burgh, which received its charter in 1663, sits at the north end of the **Kincardine Bridge**. Up until the Forth Road Bridge opened in 1964, this was the only road crossing of the Forth downstream from Stirling. Opened in 1936, the middle section used to swivel to allow ships to pass up the river. It was controlled from a control room

above the swivel section, and was, at the time, the largest swivel bridge in Europe. It allowed ships to sail up to Alloa, but has not opened since the 1980s, when Alloa declined as a port.

The town has plenty of small, old-fashioned cottages with red pantiled roofs, as well as the ruins of the 17th-century Tulliallan Church. The burgh's Mercat Cross also dates from the 17th century.

Sir James Dewar, inventor of the vacuum flask and co-inventor of cordite was born in the town in 1842. It was not until 1904, however, that the vacuum, or Thermos, flask was produced commercially by a firm in Germany. The term 'Thermos' was coined in Munich, and comes from the Greek word therme, which means hot.

To the west of the town is Tulliallan Castle, now the main police training college in Scotland. During World War II, it was the base of the Polish Free Forces under the command of General Wladislav Sikorski who was killed in an air crash in Gibraltar in 1943.

Kirkcaldy

🖉 Links Market	🏛 Kirkcaldy Museum & Art Gallery
🏛 Ravenscraig Castle	🐦 Adam Smith
🐦 Marjory Fleming	

Kirkcaldy is the largest town in Fife, and is famous for the manufacture of linoleum. At one time it was known as the Lang Toun, due to the fact that it appeared to stretch out along one main street. It was created a royal burgh in 1644, and one of the famous events held here every year in April is the **Links Market**, reckoned to be the longest street fair in Europe. The town's Esplanade is cordoned off from traffic and taken over by swings, roundabouts, dodgems, carousels,

Kirkcaldy Museum & Art Gallery

War Memorial Gardens, Kirkcaldy, Fife KY1 1YG
Tel: 01592 583213
e-mail: Kirkcaldy.museum@fife.gov.uk
website: www.friends-of-kirkcaldy-museums-and-art-gallery.org.uk

With an outstanding collection of Scottish Art, a visit to **Kirkcaldy Museum and Art Gallery** will inspire and entertain! Easy to find, it is next to the railway station, just five minutes walk from the busy shopping centre of Kirkcaldy – and absolutely free.

The gallery provides an oasis of calm where you can enjoy a fabulous range of art from the eighteenth century to the present day. Highlights include our nationally important collection of work by colourist S.J. Peploe and 'Scottish Impressionist' William McTaggart. Also on show are the only paintings by Jack Vettriano owned by a public gallery.

Not just an art gallery, we also have fascinating displays of local and natural history. After learning more about celebrated economist Adam Smith, and industries such as coal mining and linoleum, why not finish a visit to the gallery by stopping off at our popular café? Relax and enjoy delicious home cooking and baking amongst colourful displays of Kirkcaldy's prized Wemyss Ware pottery.

---

hoopla stalls and all the other attractions of a modern funfair. The very first Links Market took place in 1306 in Links Street in the town, hence its name.

Within **Kirkcaldy Museum & Art Gallery** (see panel above), in the War Memorial Gardens, is an exhibition devoted to Wemyss Ware, a form of earthenware pottery that was produced in the town by the firm of Robert Heron and Son between 1882 and 1930. It is now widley collected and is possibly the most sought after pottery ever made in Scotland. Its most distinctive feature is its decoration, which is bold, simple and direct. The firing methods caused a lot of waste, which meant that the pottery was always expensive. The museum also houses a local history collection, plus an extensive collection of Scottish paintings.

The ruins of **Ravenscraig Castle** stand on a promontory to the east of the town centre. It was built in the 15th century by James II for his queen, Mary of Gueldres, who died there in 1463. James had a passion for weaponry - especially guns - and had the castle built so that it could withstand the latest artillery. In 1470, it passed to William Sinclair, Earl of Orkney, who had to give up his earldom and Kirkwall Castle to acquire it.

Overlooking the town harbour is the 15th-century Sailor's Walk, the town's oldest house. The Old Parish Church sits at the top of Kirk Wynd, and dates from 1808. However, its tower is medieval.

Adam Smith, the founder of the science of economics, was born in Kirkcaldy in 1723. He went on to occupy the chair of moral philosophy at Glasgow University, and his

---

🎬 stories and anecdotes 🦅 famous people 🎨 art and craft 📖 entertainment and sport 🚶 walks

famous book, *The Wealth of Nations*, was partly written in his mother's house (now gone) in the town's High Street. Also born in the town were William Adam the architect, and his son, Robert Adam.

In the town's Abbotshall Kirkyard stands a statue to another person born in Kirkcaldy, but an unusual one. **Marjory Fleming** was a child writer whose nickname was Pet Marjory. She died in 1811, and yet her writings have intrigued and delighted people down through the ages. She kept a journal, in which she jotted down thoughts, poems and biographical scraps. She was, by all accounts, a handful, and when her mother gave birth to another girl in 1809, Marjory was sent to live with her aunt in Edinburgh. This is where her writing began, encouraged by her cousin Isa, and she eventually filled three notebooks. Nobody knows what she might have achieved in adulthood, because, one month short of her ninth birthday, and after she had returned to Kirkcaldy, she tragically died of meningitis. Her last piece of writing was a touching poem addressed to her beloved cousin. Her writings were subsequently published, and found great favour with the Victorians, though some frowned on the absolute honesty she displayed when it came to describing her tantrums and innermost thoughts.

Around Kirkcaldy

GLENROTHES
5 miles N of Kirkcaldy on the A92

🌿 Balbirnie Park

Glenrothes was one of the new towns established in Scotland in the late 1940s. In **Balbirnie Park**, which extends to 416 acres, is

a late Neolithic stone circle dating from about 3000BC. It was moved to its present site in 1971-1972 when the A92 was widened. The park was created in the estate of Balbirnie House, once owned by the Balfours.

Another attractive feature of Glenrothes is the array of modern sculptures dotted around the town. There are more than 130 of them, including giant flowers, totem poles and parading hippos.

FALKLAND
10 miles N of Kirkcaldy on the A912

🏛 Falkland Palace 🎾 Royal Tennis Court
🏛 Town Hall

This little royal burgh sits in the shadow of the Lomond Hills. There are two distinct peaks - East Lomond, at 1471 feet, and West Lomond at 1713 feet, the highest point in Fife. The town has quaint old cobbled streets lined with 17th- and 18th-century cottages and was the first conservation area established in Scotland.

Falkland Palace (National Trust for Scotland - see panel opposite) was a favourite place of the Scottish kings. It was built in the 15th century by the Duke of Albany on the site of an earlier castle owned by the Earls of Fife. James V later employed stonemasons to turn it into a magnificent Renaissance palace. It was never an important castle like Edinburgh or Stirling. Rather, it was a country retreat for Stuart kings to hunt deer and boar and get away from the affairs of state. James V died in Falkland Palace in 1542, and his daughter Mary Stuart, it is said, spent the best years of her tragic life at Falkland.

Mary was born a few days before James V died, and the story is told that when he was on his deathbed, aged only 30, and told about the birth of a daughter and heir, he exclaimed: 'It cam' wi' a lass, and it'll gang wi' a lass!',

Falkland Palace, Garden and Old Burgh

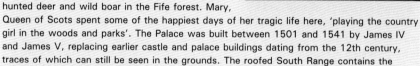

Falkland, Cupar, Fife KY15 7BU
Tel: 01337 857397 Fax: 01337 857980
Tel shop: 01337 857918
website: www.nts.org.uk

The **Royal Palace of Falkland** was the country residence of Stuart kings and queens when they hunted deer and wild boar in the Fife forest. Mary, Queen of Scots spent some of the happiest days of her tragic life here, 'playing the country girl in the woods and parks'. The Palace was built between 1501 and 1541 by James IV and James V, replacing earlier castle and palace buildings dating from the 12th century, traces of which can still be seen in the grounds. The roofed South Range contains the

Chapel Royal, and the East Range the King's Bedchamber and the Queen's Room, both restored by the Trust. The Keeper's Apartments in the Gatehouse are now also on display. The palace contains fine portraits of the Stuart monarchs and two sets of 17th century tapestry hangings.

The garden, designed and built by Percy Cane between 1947 and 1952, contains three herbaceous borders enclosing a wide lawn with many varieties of shrubs and trees. Here also is the original Royal Tennis Court the oldest in Britain still in use built in 1539. There is also a small herb garden border featuring quotations from John Gerard's book Herboll (1597). Exhibitions at Royal Tennis Court and at Town Hall.

meaning that the House of Stuart had started with Marjory, daughter of Robert the Bruce, and it would die out with his own daughter. In this prediction, he was both right and wrong. It did die out 'wi' a lass', but not Mary Stuart. The last Stuart monarch was Queen Anne, who died in 1715. The Palace is still nominally the property of the monarch, and its chapel, housed in what was the banqueting hall in the South Range, is the only Roman Catholic Church in Britain within royal property. In 1654, Cromwell burnt the Great Hall to the ground, and it was never rebuilt.

Both Charles I and Charles II visited Falkland, and it was in the Palace, in 1650, that Charles II founded the Scots Guards. His father Charles I had founded a regiment in 1642 called Argyll's Regiment to act as his personal bodyguard in Ireland, and this later merged with nine small regiments to form the Irish Companies. While at Falkland, Charles II renamed this regiment The King's Lyfeguard of Foot, and proclaimed it to be his bodyguard. It was later renamed the Scots Guards.

In the East Range can be seen the King's Bedchamber and the Queen's Room, and within the Gatehouse are the Keeper's Apartments. The gardens were laid out in the mid 20th century, and have magnificent herbaceous borders. Within the gardens is the **Royal Tennis Court**, which dates from the early 16th century, and is the oldest in the

🎬 stories and anecdotes 🦢 famous people 🎨 art and craft 🌿 entertainment and sport 🚶 walks

country still in use. Here real tennis is played, with the roofs of the 'lean tos' on either side of the court playing an integral part in the game. Tennis is still played here today, and there is a thriving club. The word 'real' simply means royal, and it was a favourite sport of kings throughout Europe at one time. It is said that it dates back to at least the 11th century, when monks played it in the cloisters of their abbeys and priories. In the 14th century, the Pope banned the playing of the game, but by this time it had become popular among the nobility.

At the beginning of the 19th century, the Keepership of the Palace was in the hands of Professor John Bruce of Edinburgh University. For six years he spent a lot of his own money on rebuilding and refurbishment, and when he died in 1826 he left the Keepership to his niece Margaret and an Indian lady. In 1828, Margaret married a Bristol lawyer with the delightful name of Onesiphorus Tyndall, who added Bruce to his name to become Onesiphorus Tyndall-Bruce. His statue stands in the town. The Keepership later passed to John Crichton Stuart, Marquis of Bute, and his descendants still hold it.

The burgh's **Town Hall**, which dates from 1805, houses an exhibition about the town. Close to it, in the square, is a house with a plaque thatcommemorates Richard Cameron, a local schoolmaster and Covenanter, who was killed at the Battle of Airds Moss in Ayrshire in 1680.

DYSART
NE suburb of Kirkcaldy on the A955

🏛 Pan Ha' 🏛 John McDouall Stuart Museum

🏛 St Serf's Tower 🏛 Harbourmaster's House

The harbour area of Dysart is very picturesque with whitewashed cottages and houses dating from the 16th, 17th and 18th centuries. At one time this was a salt panning area, and **Pan Ha'** (meaning Pan Haugh) is a group of particularly fine 17th-century buildings with red pantiled roofs (not open to the public). **St Serf's Tower** is the tower of the former parish church, and dates from the 15th century. It looks more like a castle than a tower, and reflects the area's troubled times when English ships prowled the Forth. In Rectory Lane is the **John McDouall Stuart Museum**, dedicated to the life of a locally born explorer who, in 1861-62, made the first return journey across the Australian continent.

The former **Harbourmaster's House** has been recently redeveloped and now provides visitors with an introduction to the features that make Fife's coastal area unique.

WEMYSS
4 miles NE of Kirkcaldy on the A955

🏛 MacDuff Castle

Below the substantial ruins of **MacDuff Castle**, near the shoreline, are some caves in the sandstone cliffs with old carvings on the walls. They date mainly from between 400AD to 800AD, though some may go back to before Christ. It has been claimed that there are more carvings within these caves than in all the other caves in Britain put together. Due to erosion and subsidence, most of the caves can no longer be entered, though they may be viewed from the shore.

BUCKHAVEN AND METHIL
7 miles NE of Kirkcaldy on the B931

🏛 Methil Heritage Centre 🏛 Buckhaven Museum

🌿 Wemyss Castle Gardens

Buckhaven and Methil constituted one burgh, which was created in 1891. Its motto was Carbone Carbasoque, which means By Coal and by Sail, reflecting the fact that it used to export coal. As with other Fife ports, it also had saltpans, and by 1677, three pans were in operation, fuelled by coal. The Methil docks were opened in 1887. In Lower Methil's High Street is the **Methil Heritage Centre**, a lively community museum that explains the history of the area.

Buckhaven, to the west, was never as industrialised as Methil. It was once a fishing port and ferry terminal, and has some old, quaint cottages. In College Street there is the **Buckhaven Museum**, which has displays about the town's industries, including fishing.

Wemyss Castle Gardens are open to the public during the summer months by prior arrangement. The six-acre walled garden in its present form dates from the mid 18th century, with new heated walls and an Orangery added before 1800. Set high atop cliffs looking out across the Firth of Forth, Wemyss Castle (private) dates from the 13th century, although most of the present structure was built in the 16th century. It was at the castle that Mary Stuart first met Lord Darnley, her second husband, in 1565.

LARGO
11 miles NE of Kirkcaldy on the A915

🕊 Sir Andrew Wood   🕊 Alexander Selkirk

There are two Largos - Lower Largo on the shores of the Forth, and Upper Largo about half a mile inland, where the Parish Church, some parts of which date from the early 17th century, stands. It was here that Scotland's greatest seafarer and one time Admiral of the Fleet, **Sir Andrew Wood**, had his home. He died in 1515, and was buried in the kirkyard. He oversaw the building in Newhaven of the largest and most magnificent fighting ship of its day, the *Great Michael,* flagship of the

Scottish fleet. All that remains of Wood's castle is a solitarytower.

Alexander Selkirk was another seafaring man who came from Largo. He was born in 1676, and was the seventh son of a local shoemaker. At the age of 19, the Kirk Session ordered him to appear before it after fighting with his brother, but instead of appearing he fled to sea where he eventually became a privateer, or legalised pirate, working for the British king.

By all accounts he was a short-tempered, unpleasant man, and while sailing on a ship called the *Cinque Ports* in 1704 he quarrelled with the captain who put him ashore (at Selkirk's request) on the uninhabited island of Juan Fernandez in the Pacific Ocean. He remained there until 1709, when he was rescued. Daniel Defoe, though he never met Selkirk, based his novel *Robinson Crusoe* on his adventures. A statue of Selkirk can be found near the harbour.

KINGHORN
4 miles SW of Kirkcaldy on the A921

🕊 Alexander III   🏛 Kinghorn Parish Church

🖉 Earthship Fife

This quiet little royal burgh saw one of the most decisive events in Scottish history. At the Pettycur Crags to the west of the town **Alexander III** was killed, throwing Scotland into turmoil. He was the last of the country's Celtic kings and had previously married Princess Margaret, daughter of Henry III of England, who had borne him two sons. But Margaret and the sons died; so, at the age of 45, Alexander married again, this time Yolande, daughter of the Count of Dreux in France, in the hope of continuing the direct royal line.

After a meeting of his nobles at Edinburgh in 1286, Alexander was anxious to return to his queen who was staying at Kinghorn Castle (now gone). The weather was stormy, and some of his men tried to dissuade him from crossing the Forth. However, he was adamant, and was taken across to Fife. But while riding along the Pettycur Crags, almost in sight of the castle where his wife awaited him, his horse stumbled, sending him over the cliffs to his death. It is said that the spot is haunted by the ghost of Yolande, still waiting for her husband to return to her arms.

The heir to the Scottish throne was now three-year-old Margaret, known as the Maid of Norway. She was the daughter of Alexander's own daughter, who had married Eric II of Norway. But while crossing from Norway to Scotland, Margaret also died, leaving the country without an heir. In the resultant vacuum, noblemen jockeyed for position, putting forward many claimants to the throne. Edward I of England was asked to intercede, and he saw his chance. He tried to incorporate Scotland into his own kingdom by installing a puppet king, and thus began the Wars of Independence. A tall monument at the side of the road, erected in 1886, marks the spot where Alexander was killed.

Kinghorn Parish Church dates from 1774, though there are partial remains of an earlier church dating from 1243 in the kirkyard. **Earthship Fife**, at Kinghorn Loch, is an unusual building made of used car tyres and soft drink cans. It has its own heating, lighting, water supply and sewage works, and explains all about eco-buildings and sustainable lifestyles.

BURNTISLAND
6 miles SW of Kirkcaldy on the A921

🏛 St Columba's Parish Church

🏛 The Museum of Communication

This small royal burgh, called Portus Gratiae, or Port of Grace by the Romans, is overlooked by a 632-feet-high hill called The Binn. In medieval times, Burntisland was the second most important port on the Forth after Leith, and in Victorian times exported coal from the Fife coalfields. It is now more of a resort with a popular Blue Flag sandy beach.

St Columba's Parish Church is a four square building dating from 1592, and is possibly based on a Dutch design. It was the first church built in Scotland after the Reformation that is still in use today, and has a wealth of detail inside, including elaborate lofts and pews. The nave sits at the centre of the church, with the altar, or Holy Table, sitting in the middle. The pews face it on four sides, emphasising the 'equality of all believers'. It is the birthplace of the Authorised Version of the Bible, as James VI attended a General Assembly of the Church of Scotland here in May 1601, and put forward the proposal for a translation of the Bible into English. The suggestion was enthusiastically received, but it was not until James had assumed the throne of Britain that work began.

James's son, Charles I, had good reason to remember Burntisland. In 1633, he lost most of his treasure, estimated to be worth more than £20m in today's money, when his baggage ship, the *Blessing of Burntisland*, foundered and sank just off the coast here. Nineteen witches who, it was claimed, had put a curse on the ship, were executed. In 1999, the wreckage was finally located, lying in a few metres of silt. Plans are afoot to explore it.

The Burntisland Edwardian Fair Museum is in the High Street, and features displays about Edwardian fairgrounds and local history. The highlight of the summer is the Highland Games in July, which attract around 30,000 visitors to the town. The annual Civic Week is held in June, and includes the crowning of the Summer Queen.

Open during the summer months, **The Museum of Communication** is the only museum in the UK that focuses on how our commuication systems have developed. It specialises in communications technology from the pre-electric telegraph to the present time. It has a major collection of artefacts covering Early Electrics, Telegraphy, Telephony, Radio, Television and Information Technology, together with a large number of supporting Printed Items.

The restored Rossend Castle, at the western end of the town, was the scene of a bizarre incident concerning Mary Stuart and a love-struck French poet who broke into her room to declare his undying love for her. As he had attempted it once before at Holyrood, he was later executed. The castle has recently been modernised and is now used as offices.

St Andrews

🏛 St Andrews Cathedral 🏛 St Rule's Tower

🏛 St Mary on the Rock 🏛 St Andrews Castle

🕯 Cardinal David Beaton

🕯 Archbishop James Sharp

🕯 Patrick Hamilton 🏛 St Salvator's Church

🏛 St Leonard's Chapel 🌿 Queen Mary's Thorn

🏛 Queen Mary's House ✏ Old Course

🏛 Museum of the University of St Andrews

🕯 Pierre de Châtelard 🏛 Dominican Friary

🏛 Holy Trinity Parish Church 🏛 West Port

🏛 St Andrews Preservation Trust Museum

🏛 St Andrews Museum 🌿 St Andrews Aquarium

🏛 Martyr's Monument 🏛 British Golf Museum

🕯 Tom Morris 🦶 Scottish Coast to Coast Walk

🎨 Crawford Arts Centre 🌿 Craigton Country Park

🌿 Cambo Gardens 🌿 St Andrews Botanic Garden

St Andrews is one of the most important and historic towns in Britain. Perhaps one should call it a city, as it was, in pre-Reformation times, Scotland's ecclesiastical capital on account of its huge cathedral, which was Scotland's largest building in medieval times. It is also a university town, and the home of golf.

St Andrews Cathedral (Historic Scotland) was begun by Bishop Arnold in 1160, though the magnificent ruins you see today date from many periods. The choir was the first part

St Andrews Castle

🎭 stories and anecdotes 🕯 famous people 🎨 art and craft ✏ entertainment and sport 🦶 walks

to be built, and shows both Norman and Gothic details. The nave was completed in the late 13th century, though the great west front was blown down in a gale and had to be rebuilt. The whole building was finally consecrated in July 1318 in the presence of Robert the Bruce. As well as being a cathedral, it was also a priory served by Augustinian canons.

This wasn't the first cathedral on the site. In about 1127, a more modest church was built, a remnant of which still remains. This is **St Rule's Tower** and its attached chancel, to the south of the ruins. From its top, there's a magnificent view of the town.

Legend tells us that St Rule (or Regulus) came from Patras in Greece in the 4th century, carrying with him the bones of St Andrew. He set up a shrine for them on the Fife coast, at what was then called Kilrimont - present day St Andrews. A more likely story is that the bones were brought here by Bishop Acca of Hexham in 732AD. The relics were eventually transferred to the later building, housed in a shrine behind the high altar. St Andrews soon became a place of pilgrimage, with people coming from all over Europe to pray at the shrine. However, in 1559 John Knox preached a fiery sermon in the town, which resulted in reformers sacking the cathedral and destroying the fittings and altars. Though there were plans to restore the building, by 1600 it was being used as a quarry for building material.

To the east of the cathedral and outside its precincts, are the scant ruins of another church, **St Mary on the Rock**. When the cathedral was being built, there were Culdee monks of the old Celtic church at St Andrews who refused to join the cathedral priory. In the 13th century they built this church for themselves, which became the first collegiate

church in Scotland. However, the monks gradually adopted the rites of the Catholic Church and its priests were soon allowed a place in the cathedral chapter.

St Andrews Castle was the archbishop's residence. It too sits on the coast, and its ruins are sturdy yet picturesque. The first castle on the site was probably built in the early 13th century, though this has been rebuilt and altered over the years. It was here, in 1546, that **Cardinal David Beaton**, Archbishop of St Andrews, was murdered. In March of that year, George Wishart the Protestant reformer had been burnt at the stake in front of the castle on Beaton's authority, which made him many enemies. In May, a group of Fife lairds broke into the castle and murdered the Cardinal in his bedroom, hanging the corpse from the window. There then followed a long siege of the castle, during which sappers working for the Earl of Arran dug a tunnel beneath the fortifications to gain entry. These tunnels can still be seen today.

Beaton was not the only Archbishop of St Andrews to have been murdered. The other one was **Archbishop James Sharp**, the Protestant archbishop when the Church of Scotland was Episcopalian. He had embarked upon a savage and bloody persecution of Covenanters, those people who wished the church to remain Presbyterian, and so was a hated man. In May 1679, he was returning to St Andrews from Edinburgh in a coach with his daughter. At Magus Muir, near the city, he was waylaid by Covenanters. Not averse to acts of unspeakable cruelty themselves when it suited them, they stabbed the archbishop to death in front of his daughter. This was not the first attempt on his life. In 1668, a man called James Mitchell had attempted to murder him. Mitchell was captured six years later and executed. Perhaps the most surprising thing about James Sharp was that he himself had once been sympathetic to the Covenanting cause.

Another Protestant who was executed in the town was **Patrick Hamilton**, who was burnt at the stake in 1528. The spot is marked by his initials incorporated into the cobbles outside **St Salvator's Church** in North Street, part of St Salvator's College. The church was founded in 1450 by Bishop James Kennedy, not only to serve the college, but as a place of worship for the people of the town.

It was on August 28 1413 that Pope Benedict XIII issued six papal bulls authorising the founding of the university, which is Scotland's oldest, and the third oldest university in the English-speaking world. At first the classes were held in the cathedral, but this was found to be unsatisfactory. In 1450, Bishop Kennedy founded St Salvator's College, and classes moved there. In the 16th century, two other colleges were founded, St Leonard's and St Mary's. **St Leonard's Chapel** was built long before the college came into being, its earliest parts dating from the 12th century.

St Mary's College is undoubtedly the loveliest of today's colleges. Step through the arch from South Street and you are in a grassed quadrangle surrounded by old, mellow buildings from the 16th century onwards. At the foot of the Stair Tower is **Queen Mary's Thorn**, said to have been planted by Mary Stuart in 1565. She visited the town five times, and possibly lodged at what is now known as **Queen Mary's House** in South Street. It dates from about 1525, and was built by one of the cathedral's canons. Charles II also stayed in it in 1650.

The most recent addition to the university's amenities is **The Museum of the University of St Andrews** (MUSA), which opened in October 2008. It puts on display to the public for the first time some of the real treasures amongst the University's collection of more than 112,000 artefacts. The museum has four galleries, a Leaning Loft and a viewing terrace with panoramic views over St Andrews Bay.

In February 1563, a French poet called **Pierre de Châtelard** was executed in Market Street. He had accompanied Mary when she returned from France, and swore undying love for her. However, he went too far, twice breaking into Mary's bedroom - once in Holyrood and once at Rossend Castle near Burntisland. He was taken to St Andrews Castle, and there imprisoned. On February 22 he was brought to trial and condemned to death. On the scaffold, he read out a poem called *Hymn to Death*, then cried out 'Farewell cruel dame!'.

Many people made political capital out of the incidents, saying Châtelard had been in the pay of the French, or that Mary had been his mistress. John Knox even claimed that when the poet had said 'cruel dame' he had actually meant 'cruel mistress', showing that Mary and he were closer than was proper for a queen and a commoner. However, there is little doubt that he was just a foolish young man who had unwisely fallen in love with a queen.

Further along South Street, in front of Madras College, one of the town's schools, is all that remains of the **Dominican Friary**. This is the 16th century north transept of the friary church, with some wonderful tracery in its windows. The friary was originally founded in the 13th century by Bishop William Wishart.

Almost across from it is **Holy Trinity Parish Church**. It was founded in the 15th

British Golf Museum, St Andrews

by is the **British Golf Museum**, which illustrates the history of a game that Scotland gave to the world, with a particular focus on St Andrews. It has an array of exhibits from over 500 years of golfing history, and gives an insight into 'surprising facts and striking feats'.

St Andrews and golf are inseparable. The town is still a place of pilgrimage, only today the pilgrims come wearing Pringle sweaters and weighed down by golf bags. The Royal and Ancient Golf Club is the world's ruling body on the game (with the exception of the United States), and formulates its rules as well as organising the yearly British Open Championship. The most famous of the town's courses is the **Old Course**, and it is here, in the clubhouse, that the Royal and Ancient has its headquarters.

century, though the building as we see it today dates largely from a rebuilding early in the 20th century. The only surviving parts of the medieval building are to be found in the west wall, some pillars and the tower. It contains a memorial to Archbishop Sharp, slain in 1679, though his body no longer rests under it. No doubt it had been removed and disposed of as soon as the Scottish church reverted to Presbyterianism.

At the west end of South Street can be found the **West Port**, one of the original gates into the town. It was built about 1589 on the site of an earlier port. In North Street is the **St Andrews Preservation Trust Museum and Garden**, housed in a charming building dating from the 16th century. It has displays and artefacts illustrating the town's history. The **St Andrews Museum** at Kinburn Park also celebrates the town's heritage.

At the Scores, down near the shore, you'll find the **St Andrews Aquarium**, which not only lets you see lots of fish and animals from sea horses to seals, and piranha to sharks, but lets you touch some as well. Also on the Scores is the **Martyr's Monument**, which commemorates the Protestant martyrs who were executed in St Andrews. It is a tall, needle-like monument, erected in 1842. Close

Two of the greatest names in golf were born in St Andrews - **Tom Morris** and his son, also called Tom. Old Tom was made green keeper at the Old Course in 1865, and was one of the best golfers of his day. His son, however, was even better, and won the Open Championship three times in a row while still a teenager. He died in 1875, aged only 24, some say of a broken heart after his wife died in childbirth. Memorials to both men can be seen in the cathedral graveyard.

The **Crawford Arts Centre**, originally part of the university, is in North Street, and has regular exhibitions of art and craftwork by living artists. **Craigton Country Park** sits about a mile outside the town to the southwest. It has a small boating loch, miniature railway, aviary, pets corner, glasshouses, restaurant and café. **Cambo Gardens** is a two-and-a-half acre walled garden within the Cambo estate at Kingsbarns.

🏚 historic building 🏛 museum and heritage 🏚 historic site 🎆 scenic attraction 🌱 flora and fauna

Cambo has been the home of the Erskine family since 1688, though the present mansion dates from 1881. There are also 70 acres of woodland, which is famous for its snowdrops.

The internationally recognised **St Andrews Botanic Garden** displays within its seven-hectare site an extensive range of rare and beautiful plants, both under glass and in the open.

Around St Andrews

CRAIL
8 miles SE of St Andrews on the A917

🏠 Tolbooth 🏛 Crail Museum & Heritage Centre

🏛 Secret Bunker 🎨 Jerdan Gallery

The royal burgh of Crail is one of the oldest ports in the East Neuk (East Corner), as this area of Fife is known. It is also possibly the most picturesque, and the small harbour has featured on countless calendars and postcards. Artists flock to the place because of the light and the quaint buildings. The **Tolbooth** dates from the early 16th century, with a tower dated 1776, and has Dutch influences. In the Marketgate is the **Crail Museum and Heritage Centre**, which traces the history of the town and its industries. During the summer months, the museum offers guided walks around the town.

At Troywood, three miles west of the town, off the B9131, is perhaps the most unusual visitor attraction in Scotland. The **Secret Bunker** was Scotland's underground command centre in event of a nuclear attack. It has an amazing 24,000 square feet of accommodation on two levels, 100 feet underground and encased in 15-feet-thick concrete walls. It was from here that the country was to have been run in the event of war with the Soviet Union. It is entered by an

CRAIL POTTERY

75 Nethergate, Crail, Fife KY10 3TX
Tel: 01333 451212
e-mail: sarah@crailpottery.com
website: www.crailpottery.com

The village of Crail is famed for it's picturesque and much photographed harbour, historic buildings and for Crail Pottery. The pottery is set amidst a beautiful pot and flower filled yard in the heart of the village. Established in 1965 by Stephen and Carol Grieve. In 1997 their daughter Sarah set up Crail Ceramics and son Ben and his wife Jane established Crail Earthenware. The businesses run along side each other and produce a diverse range of stoneware and brightly coloured earthenware. From cooking pots to mugs and salad sets to garden pots. Every item is hand thrown, decorated, glazed and fired here on the premises. All the pottery produced is sold in the packed showroom and quaint yard.

The two workshops are filled with potter's wheels, clay mixers and pug mills. The potters can be seen at work. The pottery boasts an Award for Excellence from Scotland the Best and it's famous customers include Tony Blair and Billy Connolly. The pottery is open from 9am - 5pm, Monday - Friday and 10am - 5pm, Saturday and Sunday. Open all year round.

📖 stories and anecdotes 🐦 famous people 🎨 art and craft 🎭 entertainment and sport 🚶 walks

THE SCOTTISH FISHERIES MUSEUM

The Scottish Fisheries Museum tells the story of Scottish fishing and its people from the earliest times to the present

OPEN: APRIL-SEPTEMBER
WEEKDAYS 10am-5.30pm SUN 11am-5pm

OCTOBER-MARCH
WEEKDAYS 10am-4.30pm SUN 12pm-4.30pm

The Scottish Fisheries Museum, St Ayles, Harbourhead, Anstruther, Fife KY10 3AB

Tel/Fax: 01333 310628

E-mail: info@scotfishmuseum.org
Website: www.scotfishmuseum.org

🏚 historic building 🏛 museum and heritage 🏛 historic site ♧ scenic attraction 🦜 flora and fauna

innocent looking farmhouse, and guarded by three tons of blast proof doors. As well as operations rooms, living quarters and six dormitories, it also contains two cinemas, a café and a BBC sound studio. Several similar bunkers were built around the country, but this is one of the largest. It came off the Official Secrets list in 1993 at the end of the Cold War.

The four star **Jerdan Gallery**, in Marketgate South, has a wide variety of paintings and craftwork from the 19th and 20th centuries, with exhibits changing on a monthly basis. There is a superb sculpture garden at the rear.

ANSTRUTHER
9 miles S of St Andrews off the A917

🏛 Scottish Fisheries Museum 🐟 Isle of May

Anstruther (sometimes pronounced Ainster) is a former herring fishing port. It comprises two ancient royal burghs, Anstruther Easter and Anstruther Wester, and is a picturesque place full of old white-washed cottages with red pantiled roofs and crow-stepped gables.

There is a story that, after the English defeated the Spanish Armada in 1588, one of the ships of the Spanish fleet put in at Anstruther and was civilly received by the people of the town. The ship's commander was one Jan Gomez de Midini, and he and his crew were offered hospitality (this at a time when Scotland and England were still independent countries). A few years later, the Spaniard repaid his debt when he discovered fishermen from Anstruther marooned in a foreign port after their boat had been wrecked. He re-equipped them and sent them homewards once more.

Located in 16th century St Ayles House, once a lodging house for the monks from Balmerino Abbey, is the **Scottish Fisheries Museum** (see opposite), which was opened in 1969. Here you can follow the fleet with the 'herring lassies', explore a typical fishing family's cottage, and see skilled craftsmen at work. Also on display are two boats - a 78-feet-long Zulu built in the early 1900s and based on an original African design, and the *Reaper*, a fifie herring drifter built in 1901. In a small private chapel is the poignant Memorial to Scottish Fishermen Lost at Sea.

Six miles southeast of Anstruther, in the Firth of Forth, is the **Isle of May**, measuring just over a mile long by a quarter of a mile wide at its widest. There are the scant remains of an old Augustinian priory, dedicated to St Oran and St Colman, which was founded by David I and colonised from Reading Abbey in England. In 1996, an archaeological investigation uncovered the remains of a 9th-century church - one of the oldest on Scotland's east coast. The whole place is now a national nature reserve managed by Scottish Natural Heritage. It was on this island that Scotland's first lighthouse was built in 1635.

Isle of May, off Anstruther

PITTENWEEM BUSINESSES -
OFFERING A WIDE RANGE OF PRODUCTS AND SERVICES.

Traquairs Village Shop & Studio - wines & wide range of convenience & fresh local produce. Open 08.00 - 19.00 Daily. **Photography & Art Studio:** Call 01333 310809. For Appoint to view/ discuss requirements. website: www.maureentraquair.com Tel: 01333 311498. e-mail: mtraquair@goldbraid.fsworld.co.uk 4/5 Market Place, Pittenweem, KY10 2P.

Pittenweem Pharmacy - Post office and Pharmacy offering stationary, gifts, cards, health products and health checks. Tel: 01333 311243. 7 Market Place, Pittenweem, KY10 2PH. Open 07:00-18:00 Mon-Sat (closed 1-2pm)

Donald Butchers - Traditional Butchery offering locally grown vegetables, in-house pies & cooked meats. Tel: 01333 311212. 14 High Street, Pittenweem, Fife, KY10 2LA. Open 07:00-17:50 Mon-Sat, Wed 07:00-14:00 (closed 1-2pm)

Stuart Barton Physiotherapy - Stuart has been the Scotland Rugby Team Physiotherapist since 1998 and has now opened his new clinic in Pittenweem specialising in sports injuries & spinal manipulations. website: www.stuartbartonphysiotherapy.com Tel: 01333 311651. 15 East Shore, Pittenween. Open 07:15-20:00 Mon-Fri.

Sea Fare (The FMA Shop) - Selling sailing and leisure wear, general hardware, nautical gifts and homeware. e-mail: admin@kindomseafood.co.uk Tel: 01333 311263. 23 East Shore, Pittenweem, KY10 2NH. Open 09:00-17:00 Mon-Wed, 08:00-17:00 Thurs & Fri, 09:00-12:00 Sat.

Fisherman's Mutual Association (Pittenweem) Ltd - Marketing of fresh shellfish. Tel: 01333 311263. e-mail: admin@kindomseafood.co.uk 23 East Shore, Pittenweem, KY10 2NH. Open 08:00-17:00 Mon-Fri.

The Royal Burgh of Pittenweem Arts Festival - 100 Artists, Exhibitions & Events in scenic seaside village. website: www.pittenweemartsfestival.co.uk Tel: 01333 313903. 47 High Street, Pittenweem, KY10 2PG. Open 1st Sat of August every year until 2nd Sunday.

The Coach House Pittenweem - Studio Gallery exhibiting contemporary craft & textiles. e-mail: jean@bradart.demon.co.uk. Tel: 01333 313700. School Wynd, Pittenweem, KY10 2PN. Open 11:00-17:00 daily, 14:00-17:00 Sun (closed Wed), Jan-1st April Weekends.

The Cocoa Tree Shop & Café - Specialist Chocolate Shop & Café serving hot chocolates & decadent chocolate cake as well as savoury snacks. websites: www.thecocoatreeshop.com / www.pittenweem.biz (Holiday-Let Apartment above shop) Tel: 01333 311495. 9 High Street. Pittwenweem. KY10 2LA. Open everyday 10.00–18.00 All Year Round.

Pittenweem Fish Bar - Traditional Fish & Chip Take-away. Tel: 01333 311-258. 5 High Street, Pittenweem, Fife. Open Tue-Thu 18:00-22:00 (closed Mon) Fri-Sat 17:00-22:00.

Fisher Studio & Gallery - Contemporary Art Gallery. website: www.fishergallery.co.uk e-mail: enquiry@fishergallery.co.uk Tel: 01333 312255. 11-13 High Street, Pittenweem, KY10 2LA. Open 10:00-17:00.

Rake Around - Bric-a-Brac store. e-mail: mwar7777@aol.com Tel: 01333 313763. 39 High Street, Pittenweem, KY10 2PG. Open Tue, Thu, Fri, Sat 09:00-16:00.

A.J.Nicholson - Traditional Sweet Shop on Harbour front with 170 types of sweets in jars - 11 types of ice-cream. Tel: 01333 310812. 17 Mid Shore, Pittenweem. Open afternoons Feb-Oct and also evenings throughout the summer.

G.H.Barnett & Son - Craft Baker, take-away hot snacks & sandwiches. e-mail: stewartbarnett@fsmail.net Tel: 01333 312052. 33 High Street, Pittenweem. Open 08:00-17:00. Mon-Fri, 08:00-14:00 Sat.

Art Extraordinary Gallery - Art Brut Gallery showing The Scottish Collection. 27 High Street. e-mail: artextraordinarytrust@yahoo.co.uk website: www.scottisharts.org.uk Sat & Sun May to Oct.

It was no more than a small stone tower with a brazier atop it, which burnt coal. Trips to the island are available from the pier at Anstruther.

KILRENNY
9 miles S of St Andrews on the A917

🏛 Kilrenny Parish Church

Kilrenny Parish Church has a tower dating from the 15th century, though the rest is early 19th century. In the Kirk yard is a mausoleum to the Scotts of Balcomie. There are many picturesque 18th- and 19th-century cottages, formerly the homes of fishermen. The name Kilrenny actually means the church of the bracken, and the village may be one of the earliest settlements in the area.

PITTENWEEM
9 miles S of St Andrews on the A917

🏛 St Fillan's Cave   🏛 Kellie Castle

The older houses in this small royal burgh crowd round the picturesque fishing harbour, which is now the busiest of all the fishing harbours in the area. Like most of the houses in the East Neuk, they are whitewashed with red pantiled roofs and crow-step gables. An Augustinian Priory was founded here in the 12th century by monks from the Isle of May, though very little of it now remains. The Parish Church has a substantial tower (which looks more like a small castle than a piece of ecclesiastical architecture) dating from the 16th century, while the rest is Victorian.

Pittenweem means the place of the cave,

THE LITTLE GALLERY

20 High Street, Pittenweem, Fife KY10 2LA
Tel: 01333 311227

The Little Gallery in Pittenweem is owned and run by Dr Ursula Ditchburn who hails from Zurich in Switzerland and came to Scotland in the 1950s. She was trained by an uncle who was an antiques dealer in Zurich and today her gallery displays a fascinating collection of antiques, paintings, rustica, small pieces of Edwardian furniture, and china from the 18th to 20th centuries. There's also lots of Art Deco items. Two to three times a year the Gallery hosts exhibitions of paintings by invited artists. The Gallery is open from 10am to 5pm, Wednesday to Saturday, and from 2pm to 5pm on Sunday.

G. DONALD (BUTCHERS)

16 High Street, Pittenweem, Fife KY10 2LA
Tel: 01333 311212   e-mail: gdonaldbutchers@btconnect.com

G. Donald (Butchers) are the real thing - a traditional family butcher's shop owned and run by local people who know their customers well and where each sale is accompanied by friendly chat and banter. All the beef, pork and lamb sold by Sandy and Derek Guthrie is Scottish. Their beef is matured for at least 14 days to ensure the best flavour. They make their own pies and sausage rolls and also sell potted meats, cooked ham, haggis, white and black puddings, and burgers, as well as vegetables from local farms.

📖 stories and anecdotes 🐦 famous people 🎨 art and craft 🎭 entertainment and sport 🚶 walks

ST ANDREW'S FARMHOUSE CHEESE COMPANY

Falside Farm, Pittenweem KY10 2RT
Tel: 01333 312580
website: www.standrewscheese.co.uk

Opened in January 2008, **St Andrew's Farmhouse Cheese Company** was established by Jane and Robert Stewart whose family have farmed at Falside for more than 50 years. The dairy had always been central to the business but as the price that farmers received for their milk sank to unsustainable levels, the Stewarts started to look at ways of adding value to their product.

Right from the start, cheese seemed an obvious option. There was nobody else in Fife making cheese from their own milk on the farm; there seemed to be public demand for, and interest in, locally produced food; and last, but not least, the Stewarts love cheese – "and you are much more likely to succeed if you have a passion for what you do!" they say.

So, early in 2008, their first cheese was born, and production has since continued three days each week. The Stewarts found it both exciting and immensely satisfying to taste, at last, their own 'Anster' cheese, named after the local term for the nearby fishing village of Anstruther. Anster' cheese is hand-made on the farm – to a traditional recipe – by Jane Stewart, using unpasteurised milk from her husband Robert's herd of home-bred Holstein Friesian cows. The cheese is fresh and dry, with an almost crumbly texture which dissolves in the mouth to leave a full-flavoured finish. Although Anster cheese is available through an increasing number of local delicatessens, farm shops and restaurants, you can go and see it being made at Falside Farm from a specially constructed Viewing Gallery.– a true 'try before you buy' experience!

As well as visiting the farm for 'the cheese experience', you can also take time to linger in the 'Butterpat' Coffee Shop with its splendid views down over the Firth of Forth. The Stewarts give the same care and attention to their home-baking and freshly prepared meals and snacks as they do to their cheese – so you can relax with a bowl of soup and an 'Anster' cheese scone, whilst enjoying the fantastic views down towards Anstruther and the sea.

'Anster' cheese is available to buy from the Coffee Shop, along with a selection of other British cheeses and a small selection of locally made gifts, crafts and speciality foods – and a large wall space hung with a constantly changing selection of delightful work by local artists.

Pittenweem Harbour

Picts, used to go for private prayer. It was renovated and re-dedicated in 1935. There are also many art galleries and antique shops, a testimony to the popularity of this area with artists and retired people.

Kellie Castle (National Trust for Scotland) dates from the 14th century, and is one of the best examples in the Lowlands of the secular architecture of the time. It contains superb plaster ceilings, murals, painted panelling, and furniture designed by Sir Robert Lorimer, who refurbished the place in the late 19th century. There are fine gardens with old roses and herbaceous borders.

and the cave in question is **St Fillan's Cave** in Cave Wynd, which is supposed to be where St Fillan, an 8th-century missionary to the

Every August since 1986, the Royal Burgh of Pittenweem in Fife has hosted a nine-day festival of visual arts. Houses, halls, galleries,

THE WEST END BAR AND GANTRY

West End Bar, 32 South Loan, Pittenweem,
Anstruther KY10 2QB
Tel: 01333 311587

With truly local food, real ales and a huge selection of whisky this is a well known venue yet retains its character of a village pub too. Visitors can expect not only the warmest of welcomes from owners Jonny and Margaret Pattisson, but also truly outstanding food, at a standard not normally associated with country pubs. Margaret's cooking has cemented **The West End Bar and Gantry** a firm favourite with local people and is deservedly attracting customers from far and wide, her cullen skink is highly regarded. Not only does Margaret operate the restaurant, she also teaches cooking classes that are great fun and have proved very popular too.

The restaurant can seat 30 comfortably or can be used as a function room where it can seat up to 24 around one table – it has a cocktail bar and a separate public bar, both of which can be used for eating. Throughout the building you can enjoy fine art work that is displayed by a successful local artist. There is also a beer garden at the back of the premises where food can be enjoyed.

Situated in a small working fishing village, it's only fitting that the food on offer includes local lobsters, crabs and fish from the local smokery. More interestingly, on the side of the pub, embedded in the wall, is the prow of a fishing boat – a sight not to be missed.

churches, the fishmarket and the harbour itself take on new roles. About 100 artists - resident, visiting and especially invited - show and sell their work, and more than 200,000 visitors thread their way through Pittenweem's cobbled wynds.

ST MONANS
10 miles S of St Andrews on the A917

🏛 Church of St Monans 🏛 Newark Castle

🏛 St Monans Windmill

This little fishing port's motto is Mare Vivimus, meaning "From the Sea we Have Life". It is famous for the **Church of St Monans**, built by David II, son of Robert the Bruce, in thanksgiving after he survived a shipwreck on the Forth. It stands almost on the shoreline, and is a substantial building consisting of a nave, transepts and stumpy spire atop a tower.

The chancel was never built.

The ruins of 15th century **Newark Castle** can also be seen near the shore. It originally belonged to the Newark family, but perhaps its most famous owner was General General David Leslie, who fought for Cromwell in the 17th century.

Salt panning was once an important industry in the town, and the 18th century **St Monans Windmill** at one time formed part of a small industrial complex, which produced salt from seawater.

EARLSFERRY AND ELIE
10 miles S of St Andrews off the A917

🏛 Gillespie House 🏛 Elie Parish Church

🏛 Lady's Tower

These two villages are small holiday resorts surrounding a sandy bay. The older of the two

---

FEATHER YOUR NEST

10-12 Station Road, St Monans, Fife KY10 2BJ
Tel: 01333 730033
Fax: 01333 730055
e-mail: feather.yournest@yahoo.com
website: www.featheryournestshop.co.uk

Located just off the harbour in St Monans, **Feather Your Nest** is a stylish gift and home wares shop run by the husband and wife team of Michael and Fiona Audsley. The shop opened in February 2008 and is already proving extremely popular. With editorial features in *Country Homes & Interiors* (which named them Shop of the Month in August 2008), *Scotland on Sunday* and *Homes & Interiors Scotland,* as well as celebrity shoppers like Lawrence Llewelyn Bowen, Michael and Fiona are obviously doing something right!

Their products come from all over the world and include Jersey Pottery, Ekelund of Sweden woven towels, McCalls candles from California and Authentic Models from Denmark. They also sell paintings, prints, cards, postcards and jewellery by local artists.

Being located so close to the sea many of the products have a nautical twist. You'll find fishing floats, model sail boats, tin signs and nautical instruments along with Emma Ball cards and paper featuring seagulls and puffins. So if you are looking for inspiration for a gift or for something to brighten your own décor, Feather Your Nest definitely has the answer.

🏛 historic building 📷 museum and heritage 🏚 historic site 🌄 scenic attraction 🌿 flora and fauna

is Earlsferry, which is a royal burgh. It was once the northern terminal for ferries that plied between it and ports on the south bank of the Forth. The earl in its name comes from an incident concerning Macduff, who was the Earl of Fife. In 1054, he escaped from King Macbeth, took refuge in a cave at Kincraig Point near the town, and was then ferried across the Forth to Dunbar.

Gillespie House, in Elie, dates from the 17th century, and has a fine carved doorway. **Elie Parish Church** dates from 1639, though the unusual tower was added in 1729. At Ruby Bay are the scant remains of **Lady's Tower**, built in the late 18th century as a changing room for Lady Anstruther, who bathed in the sea here.

At one time an old track called the Cadgers Road led from Earlsferry to Falkland, and it was along this that supplies of fresh fish were taken to feed the king when he stayed there.

CERES
7 miles W of St Andrews on the B939

🏛 Parish Church 🏛 Fife Folk Museum

🏛 Struthers Castle 🎨 Wemyss Ware Studio

Ceres gets its name from the family that once owned the lands surrounding the village - the de Syras family. It is a small picturesque village with a village green and the hump-backed, medieval Bishop's Bridge. In the **Fife Folk Museum** you can find out about what everyday life was like in Fife in the past.

The village's Bannockburn Monument is close by the Bishop's Bridge, and was erected in 1914, 600 years after the Battle of Bannockburn took place, to commemorate the archers of Ceres who fell in it. The **Parish Church** was built in 1806 on the site of a much older church. Its most unusual features are the communion tables, which run the full

length of the church. Built into a wall on the main street is a curious carving known as The Provost, said to have been the Rev Thomas Buchanan, the last holder of the title in 1578.

Pottery from the **Wemyss Ware Studio** provides visitors with highly collectable Scottish giftware. The range consists of beautifully hand-painted cats, pigs and other giftware, decorative tableware and tiles.

Two miles southwest of Ceres are the ruins of 14th-century **Struthers Castle**. It has been owned by the de Ochters, the Keiths, the Lindsays and the Crawfords. At one time the lands belonging to the castle were called Outhirothistrodyr, from which the word Struther comes.

CUPAR
8 miles W of St Andrews on the A91

🏛 Mercat Cross 🌿 Douglas Bader Garden

🏛 Hill of Tarvit Mansionhouse 🏛 Scotstarvit Tower

This small town, sitting on the River Eden, was once the county town of Fife. It is a pleasant place, and well worth strolling round just to see and appreciate its many old buildings. The **Mercat Cross**, topped with a unicorn, was moved from Tarvit Hill to its present location in 1897 to commemorate Queen Victoria's Diamond Jubilee. In Duffus Park is the **Douglas Bader Garden**, designed with the disabled in mind. The Old Parish Church dates from 1785, though the tower is medieval.

Hill of Tarvit Mansionhouse & Garden (National Trust for Scotland) is a fine Edwardian mansion that lies two miles south of the town, and was designed by Sir Robert Lorimer in 1906. It has French, Scottish and Chippendale furniture, a collection of paintings, an Edwardian laundry, and fine gardens. Close by is **Scotstarvit Tower**

FEMME FATALE

31 Bonnygate, Cupar, Fife KY15 4BU
Tel: *01334 655228*
website: www.femmefataleclothing.co.uk

Femme Fatale, situated in the heart of Cupar, is a very busy clothes shop that aims to offer you *'clothes you would die for'*. Femme Fatale has a wide spectrum of clothing for customers of all ages and sells wedding outfits, French designer casual ware, suits, knitwear and evening wear, ball gowns and cocktail dresses to that special party outfit.

Dressing to really impress? Evening wear is not as straightforward to buy as everyday clothing. Femme Fatale prides itself on offering a friendly, honest and helpful service, where you can browse and try out the outfits at your leisure. Mandy Seaton, the owner of Femme Fatale, has a wealth of experience in evening and occasional wear and looks forward to turning your dreams into reality.

Inside, Femme Fatale has one of the largest collections of special occasion wear you're likely to find, each outfit more dazzling and unusual than the one before. Femme Fatale are stockists of Serena Kay, Bernshaw, Cameron Dee, Solyne Kosmika (an Italian range) and many others. Mandy has now also started to stock a new Italian range named Peruzzi, which consists of wedding wear to lovely little casual t-shirts which are ideal for holidays. Their French designer wear is their most trendy range, and to suit all ages they stock beautiful tailored suits with complementing tops. They also have a large selection of jewellery and handbags to accompany many of the outfits they stock. Every item is handpicked from fashion shows all over the world, with special emphasis on the cut, colour and texture - which is all set to give women a rave look.

NUMBER FIVE

56 Bonnygate, Cupar, Fife KY15 4LD
Tel/Fax: 01334 657784
e-mail: jsh_bruce@yahoo.co.uk
website: www.clairedonald.com

Your eyes are always drawn to the windows of **Number Five**, a shop in Cupar's Bonnygate. It sells exquisite jewellery based on the designs of a number of jewellers, including internationally experienced designer, jeweller and goldsmith Claire Donald, who trained in Scotland, London and Paris.

Entering the shop is to step into a world where beauty, fashion and craftsmanship fuse to create objects both beautiful in themselves and which add elegance to any ensemble. Imagine entering a gallery where you see all the desirable pieces of jewellery in other galleries collected at one location. There is everything from simple stainless steel and titanium designs to bold acrylic pieces, traditional settings and truly inspiring pieces in the noble metals - gold, silver and platinum. They all represent remarkable value for money, and make the ideal gift for someone special, to mark a wedding, engagement or anniversary, or simply a unique token of love.

The pieces showcased are not limited to those produced by Claire Donald but also include the work of other top British designers from up and down the country. Their creations show a wide and varied range of different styles and techniques in traditional and contemporary materials.

To quote one admirer the designs are "deliciously seductive". The craftsmanship as you would expect is of the highest order. So successful has Number Five been that, having at first been renowned for its silverware, it now carries many fine pieces in 18 carat gold and other metals. Claire Donald has created many beautiful engagement and wedding rings, including white and yellow gold rings set with sparkling precious stones.

Claire likes to offer real choice to her customers, and not sell ranges that are too limited. Her pieces aren't just about shape or colour, but about the juxtaposition of textures and the contrast between various materials. For this reason, many pendants are sold separately from chains so that customers can bring their own tastes to an object, and stamp it with their own personality.

Number Five has a base of regular customers who return again and again. However, if you just want to buy one piece you are more than welcome to come along and browse in the shop. It is gaining a reputation throughout Scotland as a place where craftsmanship is showcased, keeping alive crafts that go deep into the heart of Scottish culture. It sells pieces that are at the top end of the range - the perfect accessories for any fashion conscious woman (or man!)

MUDDY BOOTS

The Old Manse, Balmalcolm,
Cupar, Fife KY15 7TJ
Tel: 01337 831 222
e-mail: tantrum.boarding@hotmail.co.uk

Muddy Boots is owned and run by the Samson family - Alec and Elise, their daughters Treina and Moira, Treina's son Fynn, in-laws Paddy and Price - and the family's golden Labrador, Berry. Together they provide a great way to entertain your children or grandchildren of all ages. In the Pottery area, they offer a fun range of animal ornaments, bowls, trinkets and money boxes for them to paint their own design on. Younger children can make a plate, mug or photo frame with their tiny foot and hand prints - it's a lovely way of capturing their baby days for ever.

For adults, there's a good selection of useful household items such as jugs, spoon rests, plates and bowls, vases and soap dishes. Using some very simple techniques and designs, you need not have any artistic ability to create a work of art you can be proud of.

You can also design the perfect present for any occasion - 'Sorry!', 'Thankyou', 'Well done', 'Congratulations' or 'Happy Anniversary' perhaps. The people at Muddy Boots will glaze and fire your pieces in their kiln ready to collect at a later date.

This is also a fantastic place for children's parties. Every guest can paint their own piece as well as enjoying a visit to the animals and other attractions such as the tractor trucks, gyro cars, play area and the Jumping Pillow! Adults, too, are welcome for parties and there are generous discounts for groups of 8 or more.

Muddy Boots also has its own café which offers a small but tasty choice based on home-grown produce or that you are able to buy in the farm shop. The menu offers home-made soup, Farm Specials such as Oatcake Platter, paninis and baguettes, and some wonderful desserts and cakes, including Elise's famed home-made Carrot Cake made to a secret recipe.

Before you leave, don't miss out a visit to the Farm Shop which sells top quality fresh local produce, much of it from the Samsons' own farm. The choice includes organic Aberdeen Angus beef and other meats, a range of cheeses from around the country, bread baked on the farm, jams, conserves and pickles, and those superb home-made cakes.

(Historic Scotland). It was built by the Inglis family around 1487 when they were granted the lands of Tarvit. In 1612, it was bought by Sir John Scott. He was an advocate who was deprived of his twin positions in the Scottish judiciary as judge and director of chancery by Cromwell in the 17th century, and retired to Scotstarvit, where he was visited by many eminent men of the time.

A few miles west of Cupar, at Rankeilor Park, is the Scottish Deer Centre and Raptor World. At the Deer Centre you can see - and even feed - both species of deer native to Scotland, the roe and the red deer, plus other species from around the world. At the Raptor Centre there are exhibitions about birds of prey, such as owls, hawks and falcons, plus there are spectacular flying demonstrations. There is also a small shopping court, an indoor adventure play area and picnic areas.

NEWBURGH
16 miles W of St Andrews on the A913

🏛 Lindores Abbey 🏛 Laing Museum

This small royal burgh stands on the banks of the Tay. Close to it are the red sandstone ruins of **Lindores Abbey**, founded by David I in 1178 for Tironenisan monks. It was the first abbey in Scotland to be sacked by Protestant sympathisers, 17 years before Scotland officially became a Protestant country. And the very first mention of whisky production in Scotland is contained in a document of 1494, when James IV commissioned John Cor, a monk at the abbey, to make the equivalent of 400 bottles of 'aquavitae' for the king's table.

The **Laing Museum** in the High Street has displays on Newburgh's history from medieval burgh to industrial town.

SUN GALLERY
154 High Street, Newburgh, Fife KY14 6DZ
Tel: 01334 842323
e-mail: sales@sungallery.co.uk
website: www.sungallery.co.uk

Conveniently located on the A913 Perth to St Andrews route, the **Sun Gallery** occupies an imposing building which had stood empty for 5 years until Nick Moss took it over, carried out an imaginative restoration and opened to the public in May 2006. He has always been passionate about art and decided he wanted to showcase the rich talents to be found in the local area and throughout Scotland. Accomplished artists such as Dylan Lisle, Rob Hain, Pat Kramek, John Johnstone and Ken Bushe are among those whose work is featured here.

The spacious gallery offers an inspired collection of painting, sculpture, ceramics, woodwork and jewellery from both established artists and exciting new talent. The work on show is constantly changing to show the wealth of creativity available in Scotland. Alongside the original pieces are a few carefully selected limited edition prints. There is also a fine selection of high quality greeting cards. The gallery also offers a bespoke picture framing service.

🎭 stories and anecdotes 🦅 famous people 🎨 art and craft 🎟 entertainment and sport 🚶 walks

AUCHTERMUCHTY

16 miles W of St Andrews on the A91

🏛 Tolbooth   🎵 Jimmy Shand

Auchtermuchty is a typical inland Fife town. It is small and compact, and sits in a fertile area known as the Howe of Fife (Hollow of Fife). It was here that the TV series *Dr Finlay* was filmed, its town centre being turned into a typical townscape of the 1930s. The **Tolbooth** dates from 1728.

Though born in East Wemyss, **Jimmy Shand**, the well-known Scottish dance band leader, lived in Auchtermuchty for many years. There is a statue of him, complete with kilt, at Upper Glens in the town.

LEUCHARS

4 miles NW of St Andrews, on the A919

🪶 Leuchars Air Show   🏛 Church of St Athernase

🌿 Tentsmuir Forest

Every September, the Royal Air Force puts on the **Leuchars Air Show**, held in one of Scotland's biggest RAF bases. The village is also famous for its **Church of St Athernase**, said by some to be the second finest Norman church in Britain. It was built in the late 12th century by Robert de Quinci, who lived in Leuchars Castle. The best parts are the finely carved chancel and apse, with the rather plain nave being Victorian. A bell tower was added to the apse in the 17th century. St Athernase is

---

SCARAMANGA

Gateside Mills, Gateside, Cupar, Fife KY14 7SU
Tel: 0845 2 591158
e-mail: info@scaramangadirect.co.uk
website: www.scaramangashop.co.uk

Offering stylish fashion accessories and home interior solutions Scaramanga occupies the former blacksmith's workshop in a old mill building, which still has a lot of the old mill equipment suspended from the blacken ceiling. The retro, post industrial look and feel works well with the naturally distressed retro furniture and vintage home accessories on display.

Scaramanga was established in 2006 by Carl Morenikeji who started selling men's and women's leather bags and leather journals and notebooks. Since then Scaramanga has developed a reputation for specialising in vintage styled leather messenger bags, men's and women's leather bags and satchels, and leather travel and weekend bags. They have also diversified into home interiors and other fashion accessories and now offer one of Scotland's widest ranges of antique wooden chests, trunks and old boxes.

You will also find a wide range of expertly crafted vintage and antique furniture, including: chairs, cupboards old kitchen cabinets and distressed mirrors. As well as: vintage cushions, hand-stitched bedspreads, old silver pendants, bracelets and chains, some of which are made in Scaramanga's on-site workshop. The shop also stocks a large range of gifts, including a range of more than 30 different hand-bound leather and sparkly sari journals and photo albums.

🏛 historic building 📷 museum and heritage 🏚 historic site 🌄 scenic attraction 🌿 flora and fauna

also known as St Ethernesc, and he was a companion of St Columba who travelled and preached throughout Fife.

Earlshall Castle (private) was started in 1546 by Sir William Bruce and completed by his descendant of the same name in 1617. It subsequently fell into disrepair, but was rebuilt in 1891 under the direction of Sir Robert Lorimer. **Tentsmuir Forest**, to the north of Leuchars, is a 3700-acre pine forest planted on sand dunes on the shores of the North Sea and the Firth of Tay. The whole area is rich in wildlife.

NEWPORT-ON-TAY

9 miles NW of St Andrews on the A92

🏛 Balmerino Abbey

This little town sits at the southern end of the Tay Road Bridge, and at Wormit, about a mile to the west, is the start of the Tay Rail Bridge. The ruins of **Balmerino Abbey** (National Trust for Scotland) stands five miles to the west. It was founded in 1229 by Queen Ermengarde, widow of William the Lion, king of Scotland, and colonised by Cistercian monks from Melrose. The ruins are not open to the public, but can be viewed from close by.

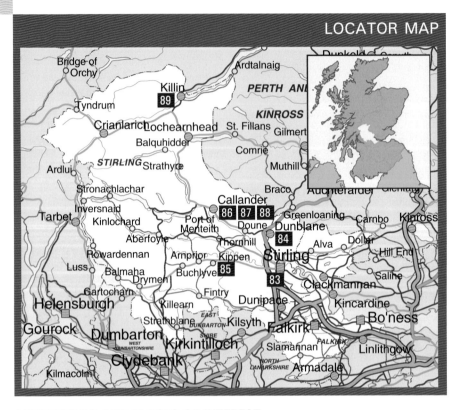

LOCATOR MAP

ADVERTISERS AND PLACES OF INTEREST

🏠 historic building 🏛 museum and heritage 🏚 historic site 🐾 scenic attraction 🌿 flora and fauna

7 | Stirlingshire & Clackmannanshire

The area of Scotland between the Firths of Clyde and Forth has always been strategically important. It is often referred to as Scotland's 'waist', and before the Kincardine Bridge was built in 1936, the bridge at Stirling was the lowest crossing point of the River Forth. To the west of the town are the Campsie and Kilsyth Hills, and these, along with marshy bogland such as Flanders Moss, formed another natural barrier, so the bridge at Stirling became the gateway to Perthshire and the Highlands.

That's why so many battles have been fought in and around Stirling and Falkirk, including Scotland's most important, the Battle of Bannockburn, which secured Scotland's future as an independent nation. It is also the reason why Stirling Castle was built. This royal castle stands sentinel on a great rocky outcrop, with the town of Stirling laid out below it to the west. In medieval times, it was almost impregnable, and from its top an approaching army could easily be seen even if it was miles away.

Clackmannanshire still proudly proclaims itself to be Scotland's smallest county, with an area of only 55 square miles. It lies in the shelter of the Ochil Hills to the north, which rise to well over 2000 feet in places, and was a centre for woollens and textiles. The string of hillfoot villages at the foot of the Ochils are all picturesque, and well worth visiting for this alone.

Around Falkirk and Grangemouth, Stirlingshire is unashamedly industrial. This is the heart of Scotland's petrochemical industry, with great refineries lining the shores of the Forth, which is still tidal at this point.

Travel northwest from Stirling however, and you enter another world - the Trossachs, one of Scotland's most beautiful areas. Though its hills are not as high as those of the Grampians or the Cairngorms, and don't have that brooding majesty we tend to associate with Highland scenery, it is still Highland in character. The hills slip down to the wooded banks of lochs such as Loch Katrine, Loch Venachar and the wonderfully named Loch Drunkie, which are among the most picturesque in Scotland, and the skies seem endless and sweeping. The Loch Lomond and Trossachs National Park takes in most of the Trossachs in its 720 square miles. It was the country's first national park, opened in 2002.

The town of Stirling is one of the most historic in Scotland, and has played a leading role in shaping the country's destiny. The castle has been fought over countless times by the Scottish and the English, and eventually became a favourite royal residence. Mary, Queen of Scots, stayed there, and her son, who became James VI, had his coronation in the town's Church of the Holy Rood. Falkirk, though more industrial in character, is also an ancient town, and has witnessed two important battles as Scotland's history was played out. Alloa, Clackmannanshire's largest town, is also industrial in character, though it too has history aplenty. At one time it was a thriving port, and Scotland's brewing capital, though only one brewery now remains.

For those interested in architecture, the whole area offers some memorable buildings. Stirling Castle itself was given a Renaissance makeover by James IV. Dunblane Cathedral, Alloa Tower, the ruins of Camubuskenneth Priory, the Wallace Monument, and both Doune Castle and Castle Campbell are also well worth visiting.

Clackmannan

🏛 Tolbooth 🏚 Mannau Stone 🏛 Mercat Cross
🏛 Clackmannan Tower 🏛 Parish Church
🌱 Gartmorn Dam Country Park

This small town was granted its burgh charter in 1550. It was once a small port on the Black Devon, a tributary of the Forth, but the river silted up years ago, leaving it high and dry. In the centre of the town is the belfry of the old **Tolbooth**, built by William Menteith in 1592. He was the sheriff of the town, and objected strongly to keeping felons in his own home, so he built the Tolbooth to hold them instead.

Beside it stands the **Mannau Stone**. Legend states that when St Serf came to this part of Scotland in the 6th century to convert it to Christianity, he found the locals worshipping the sea god Mannau, or Mannan, in the form of the stone (known as the clach mannau). From this, the town supposedly got its name. Another legend states that the name derives from an incident in the life of Robert the Bruce. It seems that he once rested close to the stone, and on remounting his horse, left his glove lying on it. He ordered one of his servants to return to the clach (stone) and retrieve his mannan (glove). The stone can still be seen on top of a column close to the Tolbooth and the **Mercat Cross**, which dates from the 1600s.

Clackmannan Tower, on King's Seat Hill, where once a royal hunting lodge built by David I stood, dates from the 14th century, with later alterations, and was once owned by Robert the Bruce. Though in the care of Historic Scotland, the interior can only be viewed by special arrangement. Robert Burns visited the area in 1787, and was 'knighted' by a direct descendant of Robert the Bruce, a

Mannau Stone and Tolbooth, Clackmannan

Mrs Bruce, who lived in a mansion house (demolished in 1791) near the castle. She was in her nineties at the time, and a woman of 'hospitality and urbanity'. She still possessed her ancestor's helmet and two-handed sword, and she used the sword to carry out the ceremony, declaring that she had a better right to confer knighthoods than 'some people' (meaning the Hanovarian kings who were on the throne in London).

Clackmannan's **Parish Church** dates from 1815. Inside is the beautiful Coronation Window, gifted to the church by its congregation to mark the coronation of Elizabeth II in 1953. The Queen visited the church specially to view it in 1997, so it seems that the loyalty of at least some Clackmannan people towards the monarchy in London is not in doubt any more.

Two miles north of the town is the **Gartmorn Dam Country Park**. It is centred on the 170-acre Gartmorn Dam, the oldest man-made reservoir in Scotland. It was constructed in the early 1700s by John Erskine, 6th Earl of Mar, to power the pumps that pumped water out of his coal mines at nearby Sauchie. Now a nature reserve, the park is popular with walkers and nature lovers, and the reservoir itself is stocked with brown trout.

Around Clackmannan

TILLICOULTRY
4 miles N of Clackmannan on the A91

⌇ Tillicoultry Glen

Tillicoultry is one of the hillfoot villages that relied on water tumbling down from the Ochils to power the mills in which most people were employed. It became a town in 1871, and behind it is the picturesque

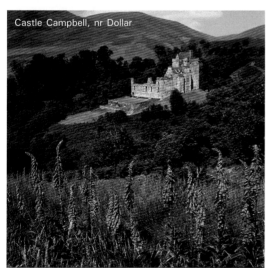

Castle Campbell, nr Dollar

Tillicoultry Glen, whose waters once powered eight mills in the town.

An old story says that the town got its unusual name from a Highlander who was driving some cattle along a road where the town now stands. He stropped at a stream to allow the cattle to drink. However, none of the cattle did so, and he exclaimed, 'there's tiel a coo try', meaning 'devil a cow is thirsty!' However, a more prosaic explanation of the name is that it comes from the Gaelic, and means hill in the back land.

DOLLAR
5 miles NE of Clackmannan on the A91

🏛 Dollar Museum   ⌇ Dollar Glen

🏰 Castle Campbell

Dollar is another hillfoot village, famous as the home of Dollar Academy. This private school (the equivalent of an English public school) was founded in the early 19th century thanks to a bequest by Captain John McNabb, a local herd boy born in 1732 who amassed a fortune in London as a merchant before his death in 1802. Eighteen years later, the academy had been built, though if he came back today he might be puzzled to see it. He had intended it to be a school for the children of the poor in Dollar parish. The elegant, colonnaded building was designed by the eminent architect William Playfair, and was opened in 1819. In the 1930s McNabb's coffin was rediscovered in a London crypt. The remains were cremated, and the ashes now rest in a niche above the bronze doors of the school.

Within an old woollen mill now called Castle Campbell Hall in Dollar is the small **Dollar Museum**, which has displays on the history of the village and on the Devon Valley railway. Above the town, and reached through the wooded **Dollar Glen** (National Trust for Scotland), is **Castle Campbell** (National Trust for Scotland). It was one of Clan Campbell's Lowland homes, and was formerly known as Castle Gloom. Close by are two burns called Care and Sorrow, and even the name Dollar itself is said to derive from dolour, meaning sadness. It seems strange that such a beautiful spot should have such depressing names. The castle dates essentially from the 15th century, with some later additions. Both John Knox and Mary Stuart have stayed there.

Alva Mill Town

ALVA
3 miles NW of Clackmannan on the A91

 Mill Trail Visitor Centre   ⚔ The Mill Trail

🍂 Ochil Hills Woodland Park   🍂 Alva Glen

🏛 St Serf's Parish Church

Alva sits at the foot of the Ochils, and is one of the hillfoot villages where weaving and spinning were the main industries. Its name means rocky plain, as does that of its near neighbour Alloa. To the northeast is the Ochil Hills' highest peak, the 2363-feet Ben Cleuch. At the **Mill Trail Visitor Centre**, housed in the former Glentana Mill building of 1887, there are displays and exhibits that explain what life was like in mill factories over the past 150 years. There is also a shop and a café. **The Mill Trail** itself is a signposted route taking you to many mills with retail outlets. **The Ochil Hills Woodland Park** has attractive walks and a visitor centre. It is centred on what were the

grounds of the long gone Alva House.

Alva Glen, also called the Silver Glen, is very picturesque. Silver was once mined here in the 18th century, and **St Serf's Parish Church**, which dates from 1815, has some communion vessels made from local silver. It was the Erskine family that mined the silver, and according to them it was a hit or miss affair. A story is told of one member of the family, Sir John Erskine, showing two of the mines to a friend. "Out of that hole there I earned £50,000," he told him. "And in that hole there I lost it all again."

BLAIRLOGIE
6 miles NW of Clackmannan on the A91

🍂 Dumyat

Blairlogie is possibly the most beautiful of the "hillfoot villages", and was the first conservation village in Scotland. It sits in the shadow of the 1373-feet **Dumyat**, which has the remains of a hilltop fort on its summit.

The name derives from Dun Maetae, meaning the fort of the Maetae, a Pictish tribe. At the summit there are memorials to the Argyll and Sutherland Highlanders, and superb views as far as Edinburgh.

MENSTRIE

4 miles NW of Clackmannan on the A91

- Sir William Alexander
- Menstrie Castle
- Sir Ralph Abercromby

Sir William Alexander, 1st Earl of Stirling, was born in Menstrie Castle in 1567. He was the founder of Nova Scotia, Scotland's only real colony in North America. The only part of the castle open to the public is the Nova Scotia Commemoration Room, which has displays about the colony. There are also the armorial bearings of the Nova Scotia baronetcies created in Scotland at the beginning of the 17th century. The baronetcies had nothing to do with chivalry or valour, but all to do with money, as they were offered for sale at 3000 Scots merks each.

In 1621, Sir William persuaded James VI to create the baronetcies, and when James realised how much money he could make from it, he readily agreed. In 1624, while at Windsor, he began the money-making scheme. A year later he was dead, and his son Charles I, not unnaturally, continued the practice. By the end of 1625, the first 22 titles had been conferred. Even today there are 109 titles still in existence. Sir William died penniless in London in 1644, and now lies buried in the Church of the Holy Rood in Stirling.

Menstrie Castle itself was built in the late 16th century and was a stronghold of Clan McAllister, a family that changed its name to Alexander as it adopted English customs. It gradually fell into a state of disrepair, but was refurbished in the 1950s.

Sir Ralph Abercromby, who commanded the British troops at the Battle of Alexandria in 1801, was born in Menstrie in 1734. He died at Alexandria in 1801 of wounds received during the battle.

ALLOA

2 miles W of Clackmannan on the A907

- St Mungo's Parish Church
- Alloa Tower
- Mary Stuart
- Alloa Museum & Gallery

With a population of about 15,000, Alloa is the largest town in Scotland's smallest county. Though an inland town, it sits on the River Forth at a point where it is still tidal, and its name is supposed to mean rocky plain. It was traditionally an engineering, brewing and glass-making town, though today these industries are less important than they once were.

St Mungo's Parish Church dates from 1817, though it incorporates the 17th-century tower of an earlier church. **Alloa Tower** (National Trust for Scotland) dates from the 14th century, and is all that is left of the ancestral home of the Erskines, one of the most important families in Scotland. They eventually became the Earls of Mar, and as such were (and still are as the Earls of Mar and Kellie) Hereditary Keepers of Stirling Castle. The tower was built for Alexander Erskine, the 3rd Lord Erskine, in the late 15th century, and later remodelled by the 6th Earl of Mar in the 18th century. It has the original oak roof beams, medieval vaulting and a dungeon.

The Erskines were custodians of **Mary Stuart** during her infancy, and she lived in the tower for a time. An old story says that when Mary gave birth to James VI in Edinburgh Castle in 1566, the baby was stillborn, and the Earl of Mar's infant son was substituted. Certainly, while still a boy,

James stayed here, as did his mother.

The 6th Earl was an ardent Jacobite, and after the 1715 Uprising he was sent into exile. The story of the Erskines is told within the tower, and the present Earl has loaned a superb collection of paintings, including works by Raeburn and Kneller.

Alloa Museum and Gallery, in the Speirs Centre in Primrose Street, has exhibits tracing the history of the town.

TULLIBODY
4 miles W of Clackmannan on the B9140

🏚 Tullibody Auld Brig 🏚 Tullibody Auld Kirk

🦋 Robert Dick

Legend says that Tullibody was founded by King Kenneth MacAlpine, the first king of Scots, who united the kingdoms of Dalriada and the Picts in 843AD. He called it Tirlbothy, meaning the oath of the crofts, as he and his followers made an oath there that they would not lay down their arms until their enemies or themselves were killed. A stone once stood at Baingle Brae where the oath was made.

Tullibody Auld Brig, which spans the River Devon, was built about 1535 by James Spittal, tailor to the royal family. In January 1560, the easternmost arch of the bridge was dismantled by Kirkcaldy of Grange to impede a French army that was in Scotland in support of Mary of Guise, mother of Mary Stuart and widow of James V. However, the French army dismantled the roof of **Tullibody Auld Kirk**, which dated from the early 16th century, and made a new bridge. In 1697, Thomas Bauchop, a local mason, was commissioned by John, 6th Earl of Mar, to build a new eastern arch.

Robert Dick, the eminent, but self-taught, botanist, was born in Tullibody in 1811.

Falkirk

🏚 Old Parish Church 🏚 Town Steeple

🎦 Bonnybridge Triangle 🏚 Rough Castle

🏚 Callendar House 🖈 Park Gallery

🏛 Falkirk Wheel

Falkirk is Stirlingshire's largest town, and received its burgh charter in 1600. It sits at an important point on the road from Edinburgh to Stirling, and nearby Stenhousemuir was once the meeting place of various drove roads coming down from the Highlands. Here great herds of cattle were kept before being sold at 'trysts', then taken further south to the markets of Northern England. It has been estimated that more than 24,000 head of cattle were sold annually at the three trysts held each year.

Falkirk, like Stirling, is located in an important part of Scotland. Here the country narrows, with the Firth of Forth to the east and the Campsie and Kilsyth Hills to the west. This meant that any army trying to march north from the Lowlands or south from the Highlands had to pass close to the town. For that reason, there have been two battles fought at Falkirk. One was in 1298, when William Wallace and his Scottish army were defeated by the English army of Edward I.

The second Battle of Falkirk was fought in 1746, when a Jacobite army defeated a Hanovarian army led by Lieutenant General Henry Hawley. After the defeat, Hawley was replaced by the notorious Duke of Cumberland.

The name of the town means the kirk of mottled stone, a reference to its first stone-built medieval church. The present **Old Parish Church** dates from 1810, and incorporates fragments of an earlier church. Its tower dates from 1734. The church was the burial place for many prominent local families, and in the churchyard is said to be Sir John de Graeme, who was killed at the Battle of Falkirk fighting in William Wallace's army.

The **Town Steeple** was built in 1814, and was designed by the famous architect David Hamilton. It replaced an earlier building, which dated from the 17th century, and has traditionally been a meeting place for the people of the town. In 1927, the upper portion of the steeple was struck by lightning and had to be rebuilt.

The Falkirk Wheel

Near Falkirk the two great Lowland canals - the Forth and Clyde and the Union Canal - meet. Thanks to the £84.5 million Millennium Link Project, they have recently been restored, and the magnificent new 120-feet-high **Falkirk Wheel** at Rough Castle, which has become a tourist attraction in its own right, carries boats between one canal and the other (which are on different levels), within water-filled gondolas. It is the world's first (and as yet only) rotating lift for boats. It replaced a series of locks built in the early 19th century, but which had been abandoned as the canals fell into disuse.

Centred on the village of Bonnybridge, two miles west of Falkirk, is the **Bonnybridge Triangle**, so called because there have been more sightings of UFOs and unexplained phenomena in this area than anywhere else in the UK. It all started in 1992, when a cross-shaped cluster of lights was seen hovering above a road, and it has continued up until the present day, with mysterious football-sized lights, delta-shaped craft and even spaceships with opening doors being sighted.

The town sits on the line of the Antonine Wall, a massive turf wall on a stone base built on the orders of the Roman emperor Antonius Pius just after 138AD. It stretched the 38 miles from the Firth of Clyde at Bowling, to the Firth of Forth west of Bo'ness. **Rough Castle** (National Trust for Scotland) five miles from the town, is one of the best preserved of the wall's fortifications. Parts of the wall can be seen in the town's Callendar Park, in which you will also find **Callendar House**. This magnificent building, modelled on a French château, has played a major role in Scotland's history. In 1293, Alexander II granted land to one Malcolm de

Rough Castle, nr Falkirk

Kalynter, and he may have built a wooden castle here. A descendant of Malcolm became involved in plots against David II in 1345, and the estates were forfeited and given to Sir William Livingstone, whose descendants lived there until the 18th century.

The Livingstones were close to Mary Stuart, and the queen visited the estate many times. In 1600, James VI rewarded the family by making them Earls of Linlithgow. But with the rise of the Jacobites, the family's fortunes went into decline. The 5th Earl was forced into exile for siding with the Old Pretender in 1715, and his daughter, Lady Anne, married the ill-fated Earl of Kilmarnock, who was beheaded in London for his part in the 1745 Uprising. A story is told that on the evening before the Battle of Falkirk, the commander of the Hanovarian troops, General Hawley, dined at Callendar House with Lady Anne. He so enjoyed her company that he ignored requests to leave early to be appraised of the Jacobite movements. His troops were soundly beaten the following day.

In 1783, the house and estate were bought by the businessman William Forbes, whose

descendants lived there for almost 200 years. It has now been restored by the local council as a heritage centre and museum, with a working Georgian kitchen, printer's and clockmaker's workrooms and a general store. In the Victorian library is an extensive archive of books, documents and photographs on the history of the area, and the Major William Forbes Falkirk exhibition traces the history of the town. The **Park Gallery**, which runs a series of art exhibitions and workshop activities, is also located in Callendar Park.

Around Falkirk

AIRTH
5 miles N of Falkirk on the A905

🏛 The Pineapple 🏛 Airth Castle

It is hard to imagine that a huge royal dockyard founded by James IV once stood close to this small village in the 15th and 16th centuries. Now it is visited mainly because of one of the most unusual buildings in Scotland - **The Pineapple** (National Trust for Scotland) in Dunmore Park. It is a summerhouse, built in 1761, and on top of it is a huge, 45-feet-high pineapple made of stone. The house is heated using an early form of central heating, as passages and cavities within the stone walls carry hot air through them. Now owned by the Landmark Trust, The Pineapple can be rented as a holiday home. Also at Dunmore are 16 acres of gardens.

Parts of the nearby **Airth Castle** (now a hotel and spa) date from the 14th century. An earlier castle stood on the site and it was here that William Wallace's uncle, a priest, was held prisoner by the English before Wallace rescued him. The castle frontage as seen today dates from 1810, and was designed by David Hamilton. Close to the castle are the ruins of a 16th-century church.

GRANGEMOUTH

3 miles E of Falkirk on the A904

- 🏛 Grangemouth Museum
- 🌱 Jupiter Urban Wildlife Garden

Grangemouth is a modern town, and the centre of Scotland's petrochemical industry. It was one of the country's first planned towns, having been established by Sir Laurence Dundas in the late 18th century to be the eastern terminus of the Forth and Clyde Canal. His son, Thomas, continued the work.

On Bo'ness Road is the **Grangemouth Museum**, which traces the history of the town up to the present day. The **Jupiter Urban Wildlife Garden** is off Wood Street, and was established in 1990 by Zeneca (formerly ICI) and the Scottish Wildlife Trust on a piece of land that was once a railway marshalling yard. Surrounded by industrial buildings and smokestacks, this oasis of green shows how derelict industrial land can be cleaned up and reclaimed for nature. It has four ponds, an area of scrub birch known as The Wilderness, a wildlife plant nursery and a formal wildlife garden, as well as meadows, marshland and reed beds.

Zetland Park is the town's main open area, and offers putting, crazy golf, an adventure playground, a boating pond and tennis courts.

Stirling

- 🏰 Stirling Castle 🎭 Frenzied Friar of Tongland
- 🏰 Church of the Holy Rude 🏰 Cowane's Hospital
- 🏛 Old Town Jail 🏰 Mar's Wark
- 🏰 Argyll's Lodging 🏰 Bastion
- 🏰 Tolbooth 🏰 Mercat Cross
- 🏰 Old Stirling Bridge 🏯 Battle of Bannockburn
- 🏛 Bannockburn Heritage Centre
- 🏰 National Wallace Monument
- 🏰 Cambuskenneth Abbey 🎨 Smith Art Gallery

Stirling is one of the most strategically placed towns in Scotland, and was granted its royal charter in 1226. It sits astride the main route north from the Lowlands at Scotland's narrowest point, which is why it is so important. On the craggy plug of an ancient volcano a fort was built in prehistoric times. This evolved over the years to become a castle and royal residence. At the same time, a settlement grew on the eastern slope of the hill to cater for its needs. Now it is Scotland's newest city, as in 2002, it was granted city status as part of the Queen's Golden Jubilee celebrations.

A good introduction to the town is to follow the Back Walk, a scenic pathway around the castle and Old Town that takes in the medieval Church of the Holy Rude, the castle and Stirling Old Jail.

The old town is a mixture of buildings dating from the 15th century onwards, and a day could be spent walking about and admiring them. **Stirling Castle** (Historic Scotland) is a mixture of styles and dates. Some form of fortification has no doubt stood here from at last pre-Christian times, and it is one of the many sites in Scotland associated with King Arthur. It entered recorded history in the early 12th century, when Alexander I dedicated a chapel here. There must also have been a palace of some kind, as Alexander died here in 1124. We next hear of it in 1174, when William the Lion was compelled to hand over various Scottish castles to Henry II of England, Stirling included.

During the Wars of Independence in the 13th and 14th centuries, Stirling Castle played a leading role. By this time it was back in Scottish hands, and Edward I was outraged by the fact that it was the last Lowland castle to hold out against his conquest of the country and was a barrier to further conquest in the north. So, in 1304, he set out to besiege it, and it eventually fell. For the next 10 years the English garrisoned it. In 1313, Edward Bruce, brother of Robert I, laid siege to it, and its commander, Sir Philip Mowbray, agreed to surrender the castle on June 24 1314 if it was not relieved by an English army.

By this time Edward I was dead, and his son Edward II was on the throne. He did not want to lose Stirling, so he came north with a great army to relieve it. The Scots met this army at Bannockburn, and secured a great victory - one that sealed Scotland's independence.

All traces of the castle as it was at the time of Bannockburn have long gone. Most of the buildings now date from the 15th century and later. James III was the first of the Scottish kings to take an interest in its architecture, and built the Great Hall as a meeting place of the Scottish parliament and for great ceremonial occasions. James IV then began building a new palace in the Renaissance style, with his son James V finishing the work. In 1594, James VI had the Chapel Royal built, and these three buildings represent the most important architectural

elements in the castle. It was within the Chapel Royal, on September 9 1543, when she was barely nine months old, that Mary Stuart, later known as Mary, Queen of Scots, was crowned in a ceremony that was curiously lacking in pomp or majesty.

In recent years extensive restoration has been carried out at the castle and James IV's magnificent Great Hall now looks just as it would have donewhen it was completed in 1504, alongwith the impressive King's Gold outer rendering, which makes it visible for miles around.

A curious tale is told of Stirling Castle. It concerns James IV and John Damien, the Abbot of Tongland in Kirkcudbrightshire, who earned the nickname of the **Frenzied Friar of Tongland.** He was an Italian, and a learned man who spent a lot of time at court. In 1507 he convinced James IV that man could fly, and to prove it, he told him that he would jump from the walls of the castle and soar like a bird.

A date was set for the flight to take place, and James IV and his court assembled on the battlements. Meanwhile, Abbot Damien had told his servants to amass a large collection of feathers from flying birds and construct a large pair of wings from them. However, his servants could not collect enough feathers of the right kind in time, so incorporated some chicken feathers as well. The Abbot duly presented himself on the battlements of the castle with the wings strapped to his back and wrists. No mention is made in contemporary accounts of how the king and the court viewed this unusual sight, but there must have been a few suppressed sniggers.

Damien stood on the battlements, made a short speech, and began flapping his wings. He then jumped - and fell like a stone, landing in the castle midden, on which more than the castle's kitchen scraps were deposited. His fall couldn't have been that far, as all he succeeded in doing was breaking a leg. When he later discovered that his servants had incorporated chicken feathers in the wings, he blamed this for the failure of his flight. The court poet William Dunbar was present at this attempt at the world's first manned flight, and wrote some verses about it.

The **Church of the Holy Rude** on St John Street is Stirling's parish church. The word rude in this context means cross, and is also found in Holyrood Abbey in Edinburgh. It dates from the 15th century, and was built on the site of an earlier place of worship at the command of James IV, who, tradition says, worked alongside the masons during its construction. It is one of the finest medieval churches in Scotland and still has its original oak roof. Within the church, in 1567, the infant James VI was crowned King of Scotland in a Protestant ceremony at which John Knox preached a sermon. His mother, Mary Stuart, was unable to attend as she was being held prisoner in Loch Leven Castle. What is not generally known is that James (who later became James VI and I of England and Great Britain) had been christened Charles. James was chosen as his 'royal' name to continue the tradition of having a James on the Scottish throne.

It is one of only two still functioning churches in Great Britain to have witnessed a coronation, the other one being Westminster Abbey. From just after the reformation until the 1930s, a wall divided the church in two, with two independent congregations worshipping at the same time.

The kirkyard was once the castle's tilting ground, where great tournaments of jousting and horsemanship were held. One of the monuments in the kirkyard is the Star Pyramid, which commemorates the Covenanting martyrs of the 17th century. A local legend says that a man was interred within it, sitting at a table laden with food. Lady's Rock is next to the kirkyard, and was where the ladies of the court sat and watched staged events take place on the fields below. Close by is **Cowane's Hospital**, on which work started in 1637 and finished in 1649. It is named after John Cowane, a Stirling merchant, who bequeathed funds to establish an almshouse for 12 unsuccessful merchants, or 'decayed guildsmen' of the town. It was later used as a school and an epidemic hospital, and is now a venue for ceilidhs and concerts. Above the door is a statue of Cowane himself.

The King's Knot sits beneath the castle and church, on the south side, and is all that is left of a formal garden, originally planted in the 1490s, though the knot itself is much older - possibly early 14th century. It is in the shape of an octagonal stepped mound nine feet high, now grassed over. Near it used to be the King's Park (where houses now stand), once a favourite hunting ground for the Scottish kings.

The **Old Town Jail**, down the slope in the city itself, was opened in 1847 to take the prisoners that were formerly held in the Tolbooth. From 1888 until 1935, it was used as a military prison. Now it has been reopened as a tourist attraction, and shows what life was like for prisoners and wardens in the 19th century. You'll also meet a character called Jock Rankin, who was the town's hangman. If, during your visit, a prisoner should try to escape, you should remain calm and follow the advice of the warden!

Also in the town centre, in front of the

Corn Exchange, is a memorial to another Scottish folk hero, Rob Roy Macgregor. The Rob Roy Statue faithfully depicts his famously long arms.

The intriguingly named **Mar's Wark** is in Broad Street, close to the parish church. It was the wark (meaning work, or building) of the sixth Earl of Mar, Regent of Scotland and guardian of the young James VI. In 1570, he began building a new Renaissance palace using French masons that would reflect his status and power, and Mar's Wark was the result. In the 18th century it became a military hospital, but soon after fell into disrepair. Now all that is left of the building is a façade along the street front.

On the opposite side of the street is **Argyll's Lodging** (Historic Scotland), a Renaissance-style mansion built about 1630 by Sir William Alexander, the founder of Nova Scotia. It was further enlarged by the 9th Earl of Argyll in the 1670s, and is possibly the best example of a 17th-century town house in Scotland. Most of the rooms have been restored, showing what life would have been like when the Earl lived there.

Stirling is one of the few Scottish towns with parts of its Town Wall still standing. It was built in 1547 as a defence against the English armies of Henry VIII when he was trying to force a marriage between his son Edward and Mary Stuart (a time known as the Rough Wooing). The remaining parts stretch along the south side of the town, from near the Old Town Jail to Dumbarton Road. Incorporated into the Thistle Shopping Mall is the 16th-century **Bastion**, one of the wall's defensive towers. It contains a vaulted guardroom above an underground chamber, and has a small display about the history of the town. There was no wall to the north of the town, as attacks never came from that quarter, though people who lived there were supposed to build thick, high walls at the backs of their gardens as a defence, and keep them in good repair.

One bloody association with Scotland's past is to be found at the Beheading Stone, well to the north of the castle. It was here, in 1425, that James I took his revenge on Murdoch, Duke of Albany, his two sons, and the Earl of Lennox, his father-in-law, by having them beheaded. The duke's father had controlled Scotland for 18 years while the English held James captive, and he and his cronies had brought the country to its knees by their greed and cruelty. Their lands were forfeited to the crown, and James gave them to his supporters.

The **Tolbooth** sits at the heart of the old town. It was built in 1704 by Sir William Bruce, and was where the town council met and

Argyll's Lodgings, Stirling

🏠 historic building 🏛 museum and heritage 🏛 historic site 🗻 scenic attraction 🌸 flora and fauna

Bannockburn Heritage Centre

Glasgow Road, Whims of Milton, Stirling,
Stirlingshire FK7 0LJ
Tel: 01786 812664
website: www.nts.org.uk

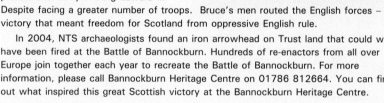

This atmospheric spot is the site of Robert the Bruce's famous victory over the English. Here, in 1314, Bruce gathered his men to take on the professional army of King Edward II. Despite facing a greater number of troops. Bruce's men routed the English forces – a victory that meant freedom for Scotland from oppressive English rule.

In 2004, NTS archaeologists found an iron arrowhead on Trust land that could well have been fired at the Battle of Bannockburn. Hundreds of re-enactors from all over Europe join together each year to recreate the Battle of Bannockburn. For more information, please call Bannockburn Heritage Centre on 01786 812664. You can find out what inspired this great Scottish victory at the Bannockburn Heritage Centre.

---

looked after the affairs of the burgh. A courthouse and jail were added in 1809. It is now used as a venue for concerts and rehearsals. The **Mercat Cross**, close to the Tolbooth, has the figure of a unicorn on top, and this is known locally as the 'puggy'.

Two famous battles have been fought near Stirling. The Battle of Stirling Bridge took place in 1297, when William Wallace defeated an English army under John de Warenne, Earl of Surrey, and Hugh de Cressingham. Wallace, who was a guerrilla fighter and a master tactician, used the bridge to divide the English forces - leaving one contingent on each bank - before launching his attack. It was a major setback for Edward I, who more or less had to start his conquest of the country all over again. The bridge in those days was a wooden one, and the present **Old Stirling Bridge**, which stands upstream from the original, was built in the late 15th century. Up until 1831, when Stirling New Bridge was built

downstream, this was the lowest crossing point of the Forth, which made it one of the most important bridges in Scotland.

The other famous battle was the **Battle of Bannockburn**, fought to the south of the town in 1314. The actual site of the battle still causes much debate, but there is no doubt that it was a defining moment in Scotland's history. Edward I had died by this time, and his son Edward II, a much weaker man, was in charge of the English army, which was trying to reach Stirling Castle to relieve it. Robert the Bruce, one of Scotland's great heroes, achieved a stunning victory - one that secured the country's status as an independent nation. The **Bannockburn Heritage Centre** (National Trust for Scotland - see panel above), on the A872 two miles south of the town, commemorates this victory. There are exhibitions, an audiovisual display and a huge statue of Bruce on his warhorse.

Scotland's other national hero, of course, is

Around Stirling

Distance: *6.5 miles (10.4 kilometres)*
Typical time: *195 mins*
Height gain: *180 metres*
Map: *Explorer 366*
Walk: *www.walkingworld.com ID:2938*
Contributor: *Tony Brotherton*

ACCESS INFORMATION:

Park in one of the streets behind the Tourist
Information Centre in Dumbarton Road (Allan Park,
Park Road, Glebe Road, Victoria Square, Clarendon
Place etc). These are beautifully laid out incidentally,
prime examples of fine town planning and worth an
admiring stroll around in their own right.

DESCRIPTION:

'Scotland's newest city' says the blurb (and surely
more deserving than other contenders I've heard
proposed for city status recently, in what has
become an unseemly 'dash for cash'!). Given its
historical and strategic importance, it is surprising
that Stirling wasn't a city long before now. The walk
follows part of the Historic Trail around the Old
Town and visits Stirling Castle and the Beheading
Stone, crosses the Forth via Stirling Auld Brig and
takes in the Wallace Monument and
Cambuskenneth Abbey.

FEATURES:

Hills or fells, river, pub, toilets, museum, play area,
church, castle, wildlife, birds, flowers, great views,
butterflies, café, gift shop, food shop, good for kids,
industrial archaeology, public transport, nature trail,
restaurant, tea shop, woodland, ancient monument.

WALK DIRECTIONS

1 | Starting from the TIC in Dumbarton Road,
cross and turn left to reach Robert Burns's statue
standing this side of Albert Halls. Turn right up
road (Corn Exchange) to find statue of Rob Roy.
Passing Rob Roy, turn left into Back Walk.

2 | Walk uphill alongside town wall ('best
preserved in Scotland').

3 | Divert to visit Old Town at this sign for Church
of the Holy Rude. Opposite church is Cowane's

Hospital, with this representation of its founder
above entrance. It originally provided
accommodation for 'twelve decayed guild
brethren'. Continue to road and turn left. On left
is ruinous Mar's Wark, former palace built in 1570s
by Earl of Mar. Turn downhill along Broad Street,
centre of Old Town. Here is found Darnley's
House, Tolbooth (music and arts centre) and
Mercat Cross.

4 | Walk down to pair of cannons. Turn left into St
Mary's Wynd. Walk down to Settle Inn of 1733.
To resume route along Upper Back Walk, retrace
your steps to Waymark 4 and turn right. Continue
up to Ladies' Rock. Here castle ladies would sit to
watch tournaments (so 'tis said). Alternatively, you
can take short cut to castle at Waymark 6 by
turning back up St Mary's Wynd for a few yards
and then cutting up steep alleyway on right. This is
unsigned but leads directly onto Castle Esplanade.

5 | By nearby seat on left, one may look down on
The King's Knot. This was a formal garden laid
out for King Charles I. Now it is grassed over, but
symmetrical earthworks remain. Continue uphill
through cemetery to reach Stirling Castle, 'the Key
to the Kingdom'. Seven battle sites may be seen
from its ramparts. Mary, Queen of Scots, once
lived here, as did many Stuart kings. There are
displays and exhibitions, guided tours and Argyll
and Sutherland Highlanders' Regimental Museum.

6 | Now take Castle Esplanade downhill to just
before visitors centre (free). Turn left down steps
and along footpath to meet road. Here turn left.
Walk down road with castle on left, to arrive at
Ballengeich Cemetery gates. Pass through gates
and bear right. Walk across cemetery and exit at
far side onto gravel track curving downhill.

7 | Keep on main path and aim for cannons on top
of Mote Hill ahead. Climb hill to reach cannons
and find Beheading Stone.

8 | Retrace steps and turn left to descend to road.
Cross with care into Union Street straight ahead. At
large roundabout, turn left. With Laurencecroft
Roundabout ahead, take underpass and bear right
to reach Stirling Auld Brig. This was setting for
William Wallace's victory in Battle of Stirling Bridge
in 1297. Present-day bridge dates from the late 15th
century.

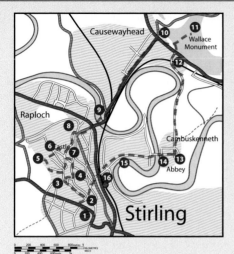

9 | Cross River Forth via Auld Brig. At road ahead, cross at lights and pass under railway bridge to walk along A9 road towards Wallace Monument, prominent atop its crag. Continue to Causewayhead Roundabout, then turn right along A907 for short distance, to reach children's play area in park.

10 | Walk across playground and take path leading to steps uphill.

11 | Climb Abbey Craig to reach Wallace Monument. Resuming walk, retrace steps to road and turn left. Cross and turn right into Ladysneuk Road.

12 | On reaching this level crossing, keep on along the road soon to meet loop of river and distant view of castle.

13 | Continue into Cambuskenneth Village and reach abbey, founded in 1147 for David I. Robert the Bruce held a parliament here in 1326, and James III and Margaret of Denmark are buried in the grounds. Today only its 14th-century belfry survives.

14 | Retrace steps and turn left along South Street to reach footbridge over river.

15 | Back in Stirling, bear left and follow road, forking left to meet river again. Keep ahead along the pathway and then along road to reach Stirling Station.

16 | Cross railway bridge. Now cross road in front of station and turn left to reach main shops and enter pedestrianised area. Follow signs for tourist information centre along Port Street and turn right into Dumbarton Road.

William Wallace, and on Abbey Craig, to the east of the town and across the river, is the **National Wallace Monument**. This spectacular tower is 220 feet high, with 246 steps, and from the top you get a panoramic view that takes in the Forth Bridges to the east and Ben Lomond to the west. Here you can learn about the Battle of Stirling Bridge, plus see a re-creation of Wallace's travesty of a trial at Westminster, when he was charged with treason, even though he wasn't English. You can even gaze on his great two-handed broadsword, which is five feet six inches long.

The scant ruins of **Cambuskenneth Abbey** (Historic Scotland) also lie on the eastern banks of the Forth. David I founded it

as an abbey in 1140 for Augustinian monks, and in 1326, Robert the Bruce held an important parliament here. It suffered greatly at the hands of various English armies, and by 1378 was in ruins. It was rebuilt in the early 15th century through royal patronage. The detached bell tower of the abbey is more or less complete, though only the foundations of the rest of the buildings survive. James III and his queen, Margaret of Denmark, are buried before the high altar, and a monument marks the spot. In 1488, the king had been assassinated near Bannockburn after his defeat at the Battle of Sauchieburn, where his son, the future James IV, was on the opposing side.

The **Smith Art Gallery and Museum** in

Albert Place chronicles Stirling's long history through displays, exhibitions and artefacts. It has a fine collection of paintings, including works by Naysmith and Sir George Harvey, who painted great works depicting Scottish history. One of the more unusual exhibits in the museum is the world's oldest football, found in Mary Stuart's bedchamber in Stirling Castle and dated to the late 16th century.

Around Stirling

BRIDGE OF ALLAN
2 miles N of Stirling off the M9

🏛 The Fountain of Nineveh

🏛 Bridge of Allan Parish Church

Bridge of Allan, which is almost a suburb of Stirling nowadays, was once a small spa town and watering place with a pump room and baths. Now it is chiefly known for being the home of Stirling University, based in the grounds of the Airthrie Estate, with its picturesque loch. In 1617, James VI wanted to establish a college or university at Stirling, but it was not until 1967 that his wish came true, when the first 180 students enrolled. Now it has more than 9000 students, and is one of the premier universities in Scotland.

Airthrie was owned by Sir Robert Abercrombie, who was instrumental in setting up the village as a spa, having had the waters of a local spring analysed. In 1844, the estate was bought by a Major Henderson, who developed the town even further. The **Fountain of Nineveh** (now dry) on Fountain Road was built by him in 1851 to commemorate the archaeological excavations going on at Nineveh at the time. Though healing waters are no longer taken, other, equally interesting, liquids are most certainly

consumed. The Bridge of Allan Brewery Company, a microbrewery in Queens Lane, has tours showing how beer is produced.

Bridge of Allan Parish Church (formerly know as Holy Trinity Church) was built in 1860, and inside it are some furnishings by the Glasgow architect, designer and artist, Charles Rennie Mackintosh.

DUNBLANE
5 miles N of Stirling off the M9

🌾 Dunblane Memorial Garden

🏛 Cathedral Church of St Blane   🏛 Dean's House

🏛 Bishop Leighton's Library   🏚 Battle of Sheriffmuir

Before local government reorganisation, Dunblane (and most of the area north and northwest of Stirling) was in Perthshire. This small town, or more properly city, is famous for two things. The first is the horrific shooting that took place here in 1996 when 16 schoolchildren and their teacher were killed in a local school. The **Dunblane Memorial Garden**, built in 1998, commemorates the victims, and is within Dunblane Cemetery.

The second is the **Cathedral Church of St Blane and St Lawrence** (Historic Scotland), which stands on the site of a Celtic monastery founded by St Blane in about 602AD. He had been born on Bute where he had founded a great monastery. Dunblane monastery would have been a cleared space surrounded by a low wall, or rath, within which would have been wooden churches, monks' cells, school rooms, brewhouses and workshops.

What you see nowadays dates mainly from the 13th century, and was built by Bishop Clement who was elected bishop in 1233. He decided that the only part of the previous 12th-century Norman church that would be left standing was the tower, though two extra storeys were added to it in the 15th century. It is not a cathedral in the style of Elgin, St Andrews or any of the great English establishments. Rather, it is an intimate church with no side aisles or transepts.

In the 16th century, with the arrival of Protestantism, only the choir was used for worship, and the nave fell into decay, with the roof collapsing about 1600. The city also declined and became a small weaving centre. In 1898, the whole building was restored under the direction of Sir Rowand Anderson, a noted Scottish architect. In 1914, Sir Robert Lorimer did further work on the choir with the present choir stalls - one of the glories of the cathedral - being designed by him.

Within the **Dean's House**, built in 1624 by Dean James Pearson during the time the Church of Scotland was episcopal, is a small museum, which explains the history of the city and its cathedral. **Bishop Leighton's Library** is housed in a building that dates from 1681 and contains more than 4000 books, some of them priceless.

With the coming of the railways, Dunblane became a popular place in which to holiday and the city regained some of its former prosperity. Dunblane Hydro was built in 1875 to cash in on the tourist boom, and it is still a luxury hotel to this day.

About three miles northeast of the town is the site of the **Battle of Sheriffmuir**, one of the deciding battles in the 1715 Jacobite Uprising. It took place on November 13 1715, and was an unusual battle in that the outcome was a stalemate. The Jacobite forces were led by John Erskine, 11th Earl of Mar, and the government forces by John Campbell, 2nd Duke of Argyll.

FINTRY

12 miles SW of Stirling on the B818

 Loup of Fintry 🏛 Culcreuch Castle

🏛 Fintry Parish Church

This charming village sits on the northern slopes of the Campsies, that great range of hills that forms a northern backdrop for the city of Glasgow. There are some fine walks on the hills, which are popular with Glaswegians at weekends and holidays. The **Loup of Fintry**, east of the village, is a fine waterfall caused by the Endrick Water tumbling down a 94-feet-high slope.

Culcreuch Castle (now a country house hotel) is a 700-year-old tower house within a large estate that was once owned by the Galbraiths. The last Galbraith chieftain to live there was Robert Galbraith, who fled to Ireland in 1630 after killing a guest in his home. Carron

Valley Reservoir, to the east of the village, was built in the 19th century to supply Falkirk and Grangemouth with a water supply. It now offers trout fishing (permit required).

Fintry Parish Church dates from 1823, and its method of building was unusual. The former church was too small for the growing congregation, so the present church was built around it. Only when it was complete was the earlier church, which had continued in use, demolished.

KIPPEN

9 miles W of Stirling on the B822

🏛 Kippen Parish Church 🏛 Kippen Vine

This attractive little village sits to the south of that expanse of flat land called Flanders Moss. At one time it was a peat bog, then, in the 18th century, Lord Kames, a law lord and agricultural improver, began removing the

peat to get at the fertile bands of clay beneath. There are still a few remnants of the original peat bog left; these have been declared Areas of Special Scientific Interest.

In **Kippen Parish Church**, built in 1825, is one of the finest post-Reformation churches in Scotland. The Carmichael Memorial Window was installed in 1985, and is the work of John K Clarke. The ruins of the old church, built in 1691, still survive, surrounded by an old graveyard.

In 1891, a man called Duncan Buchanan planted a vineyard in Kippen within a glasshouse, and one of the vines, later to be called the **Kippen Vine**, grew to be the largest in the world. When fully grown, it had an annual crop of more than 2000 bunches of table grapes, and in 1958 created a record by producing 2956 bunches. By this time it was enormous, covering an area of 5000 square feet and stretching for 300 feet within four large greenhouses. It became a tourist attraction, and people came from all over Scotland - and abroad - to see it.

But alas, the vinery closed down in 1964 (when it could also boast the second and third largest vines in the world) and the Kippen Vine was unceremoniously chopped down by Selby Buchanan, Duncan's son. The land was later used for housing.

ARNPRIOR
10 miles W of Stirling on the A811

King of Kippen

In the early 16th century, a man called John Buchanan, who had styled himself the **King of Kippen**, lived in this small village. One day a party of hunters was returning to Stirling Castle with some venison for James V's court, and passed John's castle. John captured them and confiscated the venison. The hunters told

him that the meat was for the king, but John merely replied that if James was King of Scotland, then he was King of Kippen.

The king was duly informed of this, and instead of being angry, found the incident amusing. He and some courtiers rode out from Stirling one day to pay the King of Kippen a visit. He approached John's castle, and demanded that he be allowed to enter. His demand was refused by a guard, who told the king that John Buchanan was at dinner, and could not be disturbed.

James V had a habit of dressing up in peasant's clothes and slipping out of his palaces alone to meet and speak to his subjects and gauge their opinions of their king and country. When he did this, he assumed the guise of the Guidman of Ballengeich (meaning The Goodman of Ballengeich), Ballengeich being the name of a pathway he always took down from Stirling Castle when in disguise.

He therefore told the guard to tell Buchanan that the Guidman of Ballengeich was at his door, and he humbly requested an audience with the King of Kippen. When informed, John Buchanan knew who his visitor was, and rushed out in trepidation. But James greeted him cordially, and laughed at the escapade of the venison. Buchanan invited the king into his home to dine, and the king agreed. Soon the company was merry, and the king told Buchanan that he could take as much venison as he liked from the royal hunters that passed his door. He also invited the King of Kippen to visit his brother monarch at Stirling any time he liked. The 'king' was later killed at the Battle of Pinkie in 1547.

To the east of Kippen, and off the A811, is the village of Gargunnock, with a picturesque parish church built in 1774.

PORT OF MENTEITH
14 miles W of Stirling on the B8034

🏴 Lake of Menteith 🏛 Inchmahome Priory

This little village sits on the shore of the **Lake of Menteith**, sometimes erroneously called the only lake (as opposed to loch) in Scotland. However, there are several bodies of water in Scotland - some natural, some man-made - that are referred to as lakes.

But there is no doubting that the Lake of Menteith is one of Scotland's most beautiful stretches of water. It is only a mile wide by a mile-and-a-half long, with low hills sloping down towards it northern shores. Its name is probably a corruption of Laigh (meaning a flat piece of land) of Menteith, as the land to the south of the lake, Flanders Moss, is flat.

On the island of Inchmahome are the beautiful ruins of **Inchmahome Priory** (Historic Scotland), within which Mary Stuart was kept after the Battle of Pinkie in 1547.

Inchmahome Priory, Port of Menteith

Within the re-roofed chapter house are many carved effigies and tombstones. The priory was founded in 1238 by Walter Comyn, Earl of Menteith, for Augustinian canons. In 1306, 1308 and 1310, Robert the Bruce visited the place, as the then prior had sworn allegiance to Edward I of England. No doubt Robert was pressurising him to change his mind. The priory can be reached by a small ferry from the jetty at Port of Menteith.

On the nearby Inchtulla, the Menteiths had their castle, and on Dog Island, the Earl kept his hunting dogs.

ABERFOYLE
17 miles W of Stirling on the A821

🌿 Poker Tree 🏛 Scottish Wool Centre

🎞 Rev Robert Kirk 🌿 Scottish Sheepdog School

🏛 Cunninghame Graham Memorial

Aberfoyle has been called the Gateway to the Trossachs, and sits beside the River Forth after it emerges from beautiful Loch Ard. The six-mile-long Duke's Road (named after a Duke of Montrose who laid out the road in 1886) goes north from the village to the Trossachs proper, and has some good views over Lochs Drunkie and Venachar.

Standing close to the village's main road is a gnarled oak known as the **Poker Tree**. In Scott's novel *Rob Roy*, Baillie Nicol Jarvie, a Glasgow magistrate and cousin of Rob Roy, gets involved in a fight with a Highlander at a local inn, and draws the red hot poker from the fire to defend himself. A poker was later hung from the tree to remind people of the escapade.

The **Scottish Wool Centre** is situated within the village, and tells the story of Scottish wool. You can visit the Spinner's Cottage, and have a go at spinning wool into yarn. There are also occasional visits from

Loch Drunkie, Trossachs

local shepherds, who put on sheepdog demonstrations. There is a shop where woollen items - from coats to blankets - can be bought. The Wool Centre is also the home of the **Scottish Sheepdog School** where you can watch local shepherds putting the dogs through their paces as they round up sheep and Indian Runner Ducks.

It was in Aberfoyle that the famous and mysterious disappearance of the **Rev Robert Kirk**, minister at Aberfoyle Parish Church, took place. He was born in 1644, and had an abiding interest in fairies, even writing a book called *The Secret Commonwealth of Elves, Fauns and Fairies*.

Legend states that the fairies were none too pleased that Robert had revealed their secrets. In 1692, while walking on Doon Hill, well known in the area as one of the entrances to the fairy realm, Robert disappeared. People claimed that he had been taken to the fairy kingdom, and that one day he would come back, looking no older than he did when he disappeared. To this day, he has not returned.

Another legend states that Robert's wife was given the chance of getting her husband back. He would appear, she was told, during Sunday service in the kirk, and she had to throw a knife at him, which should penetrate his flesh. Robert did appear during the service, but his wife could not bring herself to throw the knife, so he disappeared once more.

Robert Kirk was indeed a minister in Aberfoyle in the 17th century, and he did indeed disappear one day while out walking. Did the fairies take him? Or was he the victim of a more earthly crime? No one will ever know - unless he turns up again to give his account of what happened!

South of Aberfoyle, near the conservation village of Gartmore, is the **Cunninghame Graham Memorial** (National Trust for Scotland). Robert Cunninghame Graham of Ardoch (born Robert Bontine) was a Scottish author and politician who died in 1936. The memorial once stood at Castlehill in Dumbarton, but was moved here in 1980.

KILLEARN
18 miles W of Stirling on the A875

Killearn Glen

Killearn Glen is a picturesque area of deciduous woodland over 250 years old with narrow footpaths. The village was the birthplace, in 1506, of George Buchanan, Protestant reformer and tutor to James VI, who greatly admired him. He was a noted linguist, and could speak Latin, Greek, French, Gaelic, Spanish, Hebrew and Italian. He also wrote plays, mostly in Latin, and now lies buried in the Greyfriars kirkyard in Edinburgh. The Buchanan Monument, built in 1788, commemorates him.

DRYMEN
20 miles W of Stirling off the A811

Buchanan Castle

During World War II, **Buchanan Castle** was a military hospital. Its most famous patient was Rudolph Hess, Hitler's deputy, who was kept here after he parachuted into Scotland in 1941 on a secret mission to see the Duke of Hamilton. The castle itself dates from 1855, and was built by the 4th Duke of Montrose after the former castle was destroyed by fire three years previously. The roof was removed in 1955 to prevent the paying of taxes on it, and it is now partly ruinous, though it can be viewed from the outside.

Drymen is on the West Highland Way, the footpath that stretches from Milngavie on the outskirts of Glasgow to Fort William. It is also the gateway to the eastern, and less busy, shores of Loch Lomond, which lie three miles away. The small village of Balmaha (also on the West Highland Way) sits on the shore of the loch, and should be visited for the wonderful views it gives of Britain's largest sheet of water. Balfron, four miles east of Drymen, is an attractive village with a parish church that dates from 1832. Alexander 'Greek' Thomson, the noted architect whose work can be seen in Glasgow, was born in Balfron in 1817.

BLAIR DRUMMOND
6 miles NW of Stirling on the A84

🐾 Blair Drummond Safari & Leisure Park	
🐾 Briarlands Farm	

Blair Drummond Safari and Leisure Park is one of the most visited tourist attractions in Scotland. You can tour the 1500-acre park by car or coach, and see animals such as elephants, lions, zebras, giraffes, white rhino and ostriches in conditions that allow them plenty of freedom. You can take a boat trip round Chimp Island, watch the sea lion show or glide above the lake on the Flying Fox.

Right next door to the Safari Park, **Briarlands Farm** promises a great day out for

all the family. Attractions include Giant Jumping Pillows, a Straw Mountain, go-karting and an Amazing Maize Maze, Also on site are a tearoom and gift shop.

DOUNE
6 miles NW of Stirling on the A84

🏛 James Spittal	🏛 Doune Castle	
🏛 Mercat Cross	🐾 Argaty Red Kites	
⛲ Sir David Stirling Memorial Statue		

The bridge across the River Teith in this picturesque village was built by **James Spittal**, tailor to James IV. Legend has it that he arrived at the ferry that once operated where the bridge now stands without any money, and the ferryman refused to take him across. So, out of spite, he had the bridge built to deprive the ferryman of a livelihood.

Doune Castle (Historic Scotland) is one of the best preserved 14th-century castles in Scotland, and was the seat of the Earls of Moray. It stands where the River Ardoch meets the Teith, and was originally built for Robert Stewart, Duke of Albany, son of Robert II and Regent of Scotland during the minority of James I. When James had the Duke's son executed for plotting against the crown, the castle passed to him. Later, the castle was acquired by Sir James Stewart, the first Lord Doune, and then by the Morays. It has two main towers connected by a Great Hall with a high wooden ceiling. In 1883, the 14th Earl of Moray restored the castle. It is visited each year by many fans of Monty Python, as some of the scenes in *Monty Python and the Holy Grail* were filmed here.

The village itself gained its burgh charter in 1611, and originally stood close to the castle. In the early 1700s, however, the village and its 17th-century **Mercat Cross** were moved to their present position. The village was, at one time, famous as a centre of pistol making. The industry was started in about 1646 by a man called Thomas Cadell, and so accurate and well made were his guns that they soon became prized possessions. By the 18th century, Cadell's descendants were all involved in making guns, and began exporting them to the Continent. It is said that the first pistol fired in the American War of Independence was made in Doune.

Just north of the village, **Argaty Red Kites** is central Scotland's only red kite viewing station. More than 100 bird species have been spotted at this wildlife friendly farm. Advance booking is recommended.

On the B824 between Doune and Dunblane is the **Sir David Stirling Memorial Statue**, commemorating the founder member of the Special Air Services (better known as the SAS) during World War II.

DEANSTON
8 miles NW of Stirling on the B8032

Deanston is a village on the banks of the River Teith, built round the Adephi Cotton Mill, founded in 1785 and designed by Sir Richard Arkwright. It passed through several hands before finally closing in 1965. Now the mill houses the Deanston Distillery, which makes a range of whiskies, using the same water that once powered the weaving machines. It is not open to the public.

CALLANDER
13 miles NW of Stirling on the A84

🖉 Kilmahog Woollen Mill

🏠 Rob Roy and Trossachs Visitor Centre

This pleasant holiday town stands to the east of the Trossachs, and has some wonderful walking country on its doorstep. It is a

---

THE TREEHOUSE

4 Main Street, Callander, Perthshire FK17 8BB
Tel: 01877 330414
e-mail: mail@trossachstreehouse.co.uk
website: www.trossachstreehouse.co.uk

The Treehouse is a small, family-run business specialising in quality wooden products at affordable prices, providing some wonderful gift ideas for the whole family. Owner Janet Michael has personally selected the items for their quality and carefully ensures that all the timber is sourced from sustainable forest sources. If you are looking for something different, and need some inspiration for that unusual gift that you can't get at home, The Treehouse is well worth a visit.

There are hand-made boxes in all shapes and sizes for trinkets, keepsakes and jewellery; some stunning wooden carvings and wooden ornaments; wooden photo frames; Scottish wood-turning; wooden kitchenware; good quality traditional toys and games; ornaments and carvings; door nameplates - and much, much more, all at unbelievably low prices. Other popular ranges include dolls' houses, furniture and dolls, and for the garden a selection of windmills and swings. There truly is something for everyone at The Treehouse. The Treehouse is conveniently located near the main car parks in the picturesque village of Callender.

🎭 stories and anecdotes 🪶 famous people ✒ art and craft ♪ entertainment and sport 🚶 walks

DELI ECOSSE

10 North Ancaster Square, Callander FK17 8ED
Tel: 01877 331220
e-mail: deli.ecosse@yahoo.co.uk

Occupying a former Church Hall with a wonderful ceiling, **Deli Ecosse** was established in 2003 by Julie Carmichael who has put together an enticing range of appetising food and drink. Much of the stock has been sourced locally including the ham, beef, turkey and dried meats, and you will also find jams and chutneys from Mrs Bridge, Arbroath, Galloway Lodge Preserves, Uncle Roy's savouries and Gilles Fine foods. There's a selection of some 30, mostly Scottish, cheeses, and Black Pudding from Stornoway. The Deli is licensed and offers an excellent variety of wines and Scottish beers.

Much of the fresh produce can be enjoyed in the pleasant licensed café where the menu offers a choice of All Day Breakfasts, home-made soup, freshly made sandwiches, baguettes and paninis, jacket potatoes and daily specials. And don't miss out on the scrumptious home-made cakes. All the food is available to take away. The café has seating for 18 people with a further 10 places outside for fair-weather dining. Deli Ecosse has good disabled access throughout and there's plenty of free parking.

GALLERIA LUTI

16 Ancaster Square, Callander,
Perthshire FK17 8BL
Tel: 01877 339577
e-mail: info@gallerialuti.co.uk
website: www.gallerialuti.co.uk

Occupying a sturdy stone building in Callander's Ancaster Square, the **Galleria Luti** is owned and run by the mother and daughter team of Sandie and Marsha Luti. The idea of opening and running a small gallery in their home town of Callander was conceived by the pair through a shared enthusiasm for contemporary art, in particular paintings, jewellery and ceramics. Both felt that there was a significant need for a gallery in the area. In December 2005, the Lutis purchased a terraced house in the centre of Callander which was converted into a beautiful gallery space where exhibitions take place every 2 months.

In the 1980s Sandie and her husband Pete owned and ran Callander based 'PL Pottery' which sold high quality Scottish pottery directly to the public. A graduate in ceramics from Duncan of Jordonstone, Pete produced pottery to sell in the shop. Lately, he has discovered a passion and talent for painting and has been exhibiting and selling his paintings in several Scottish Art Galleries. Galleria Luti is open from 10.30am to 5pm, Monday to Saturday, and from 1pm to 5pm on Sunday.

planned town, laid out in the 1770's, though it dates back to plans prepared by the Duke of Perth in 1735. Being an ardent Jacobite, the Duke forfeited his lands after 1745.

Callander is home to the **Rob Roy and Trossachs Visitor Centre**, housed in a former church in Ancaster Square, and, as the name suggests, it tells the story of both the Trossachs and its most famous son, Rob Roy MacGregor (1671-1734). Even today, people cannot agree on whether he was a crook, a freedom fighter or the Scottish Robin Hood. The Duke of Montrose confiscated his lands in 1712, and he was imprisoned by the English in the 1720s. He was made famous by two books - Daniel Defoe's *Highland Rogue* and Sir Walter Scott's *Rob Roy* - as well as by the recent film starring Liam Neeson and Jessica Lange. An earlier film, *Rob Roy the Highland Rogue*, was made in 1953, starring Richard Todd and Glynis Johns.

There's no denying that the man was an outstanding leader who could read and write in English and Gaelic, and possessed a large library. It was Sir Walter Scott who described him as behaving dishonourably at the Battle of Sheriffmuir when in fact he acquitted himself with courage and honour fighting for the Jacobites. At his funeral on New Year's Day 1735, people came from all over Scotland to pay their respects.

Also in Callander is the Hamilton Toy Museum, five rooms of model cars, planes, dolls, teddy bears and such TV collectables as Thunderbird, Star Trek and Star Wars figures.

The **Kilmahog Woollen Mill**, to the west of the town, is more than 250 years old and still has its original water wheel. A shop sells a wide range of Tweed and woollen garments.

LOCH KATRINE
23 miles NW of Stirling close to the A821

Rob Roy Falls of Leny

There is no doubt that Loch Katrine is one of the most beautiful lochs in Scotland. It is surrounded by craggy hills, which in autumn blaze with orange and gold. But the loch as you see it today has more to do with man than nature. In the mid 19th century, the loch became a huge reservoir for the city of Glasgow, and the depth of the water was increased considerably. In 1859, Queen Victoria opened the new reservoir, and 90 million gallons of water a day flowed towards Glasgow, over 30 miles away.

The engineering that made this happen was well ahead of its time, and consisted of tunnels and aqueducts that relied purely on gravity to carry the water towards the city. The engineering surrounding the loch was equally as spectacular. The water from Loch Arklet, high in the hills between Lochs Katrine and Lomond, used to flow west into Loch Lomond. By the use of dams, this was changed so that it flowed east into Loch Katrine. The whole scheme was the largest of its kind in the world for many years, and even today, Glasgow still gets its water from Loch Katrine.

The loch's name comes from the early Welsh cethern, meaning furious, a reference to the many mountain torrents found in the area. It was made famous by Sir Walter Scott, who set his poem, *The Lady of the Lake*, here. And at Glengyle, at the western end of the loch, Rob Roy MacGregor was born. It is still a remote place, and cannot be reached by car.

The steamer *Sir Walter Scott* has been sailing the waters of the loch from the beginning of the 20th century, and it still does so today. It was built in Dumbarton, and people always wonder how it got from there to the loch, The

stories and anecdotes famous people art and craft entertainment and sport walks

answer is that it was transported by barge up the river Leven onto Loch Lomond, then dragged overland by horses from Inversnaid. When it reached Loch Katrine, the engines were fitted.

The steamship takes you from the pier at the east end of the loch towards Stronachlachar, six miles away. The small islet at Stronachlachan is known as the Factor's Island, and recalls one of **Rob Roy's** exploits. He captured the Duke of Montrose's factor, who was collecting rents in the area, and imprisoned him on the island. He then sent a ransom note to the duke, but none came. So Rob Roy calmly relieved the man of the £3000 he was carrying and sent him on his way.

This is the heart of the Trossachs (the name translates as bristly or prickly), and there are other equally as attractive lochs nearby. Loch Lubnaig, to the east, is the largest. Loch

Venachar, Loch Achray and Loch Drunkie (which can only be reached by a footpath through the forest) are well worth visiting. At the southern end of Loch Lubnaig are the spectacular **Falls of Leny**.

BALQUHIDDER
24 miles NW of Stirling on a minor road off the A84

 Rob Roy MacGregor's Grave

This small village sits to the east of the picturesque Loch Voil. It lies in that area of Scotland known as Breadalbane (uplands of Alban -  Alban is the ancient name for Scotland), and in the heart of Clan MacGregor country. In the kirkyard of the roofless kirk is **Rob Roy MacGregor's Grave**, plus those of some of his family including his wife.

Rob's real name was Robert McGregor, the 'Roy' coming from the Gaelic ruadh, meaning

---

BREADALBANE HOUSE B&B
Killin, Perthshire FK21 8UT
Tel: 01567 820134
e-mail: info@breadalbanehouse.com
website: www.breadalbanehouse.com

Located on the border of Perthshire and Stirlingshire, Killin is ideally situated for exploring both. With Loch Tay, the Trossachs, mighty Ben Lawers, Glen Lyon and Glen Ogle virtually on the doorstep (not to mention the Falls of Dochart within the village), the options for excursions are limitless. Add some majestic castles and a number of whisky distilleries within less than an hour's spectacular drive, and you will find yourself spoilt for choice! To others, the boating, fishing, hillwalking, cycling, wildlife or plant spotting will be the top attractions. The region has it all.

Désirée and Wouter strive to bring you comfort in a warm, friendly atmosphere, starting with a hearty breakfast in the morning, with a vegetarian option if you are so inclined. To end the day, you can enjoy a relaxing wind-down in the spacious guests' lounge - and a subsequent good night's rest in one of the five comfortable rooms. All rooms have en-suite facilities and everything else you will have come to expect like television, hair drier and facilities for making tea and coffee.

Even in the busiest periods you will have no trouble parking, because Breadalbane House has a spacious off-street parking for cars and motorbikes. Bicycles can be locked away if you wish.

Wir sprechen Deutsch – on parle français – wij spreken Nederlands

🏛 historic building 🏛 museum and heritage 🏚 historic site 🍃 scenic attraction 🌿 flora and fauna

red-haired. He died in 1734 a free man, having received a royal pardon for his misdeeds (if indeed they were misdeeds) in 1726.

KILLIN
30 miles NW of Stirling on the A827

- Falls of Dochart
- Breadalbane Folklore Centre
- Falls of Lochay
- Moirlanich Longhouse
- Finlarig Castle

Killin sits close to the western end of Loch Tay, which stretches for 15 miles north-eastwards into Perthshire. The best views of the loch are from the wooded south shore road, though the northern road is wider and straighter.

The **Falls of Dochart**, a series of cascades on the River Dochart as it enters Loch Tay, are within the village, and next to them is the **Breadalbane Folklore Centre**, housed in an old mill, which gives an insight into the life and legends of the area. Three miles north on a minor road are the **Falls of Lochay** on the River Lochay, though care should be taken when approaching them. The **Moirlanich Longhouse** (National Trust for Scotland) on the Glen Lochay road dates from the 19th century, and is a rare surviving example of a cruck-frame Scottish longhouse, where a family and their livestock lived under the one roof. In an adjacent shed is a display of working clothes found in the longhouse, along with displays, that explain the building's history and restoration.

The ruins of **Finlarig Castle**, which date from the late 16th century, are to the north of the village. The castle was once a Campbell stronghold, and was built by Black Duncan, one of the most notorious members of the clan. Within its grounds are the remains of a beheading pit and a Campbell mausoleum built in 1829.

LOCHEARNHEAD
21 miles NW of Stirling on the A84

This small, attractive village is at the western end of Loch Earn, and is a centre for such pursuits as sailing, fishing, water skiing and diving. East of the village is Edinample Castle (private), owned by Black Duncan Campbell of Glenorchy in the 16th century. It was originally a McGregor stronghold, and is associated with tales of black deeds, doom and gloom. It is said that in the 6th century St Blane cursed the lands around the castle. Another tale says that the castle was doomed as it was built using old gravestones.

CRIANLARICH
32 miles NW of Stirling on the A82

- Falls of Falloch

The name of this small village comes from the Gaelic for low pass, and sits on the southern edge of Breadalbane. Surrounding it is some marvellous walking and climbing country, with the West Highland Way passing close to the village. The twin peaks of Ben More (3843 feet) and Stobinian (3821 feet) are to the southeast, while the picturesque **Falls of Falloch** (with a small car park close by) lie four miles to the southwest on the A82.

TYNDRUM
40 miles NW of Stirling on the A82

- Dalrigh

This little village has a population of no more than 100 people, and yet has two railway stations - one on the line from Glasgow to Oban, and the other on the line from Glasgow to Fort William. It sits at the head of rugged Strath Fillan, which snakes south towards Crianlarich, carrying the West Highland Way. At **Dalrigh** (meaning the field of the king), in 1306, Robert the Bruce was defeated in battle.

2

The Country Living Guide to Rural Scotland

ADVERTISERS AND PLACES OF INTEREST

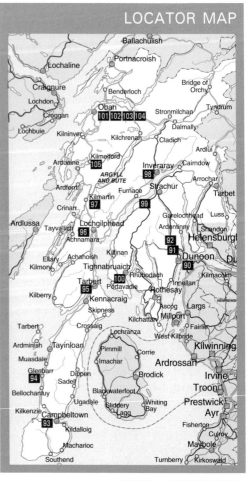

LOCATOR MAP

Accommodation, Food and Drink

90 | The Craigen Hotel & Tearoom, Dunoon — pg 277
93 | Craigard House Hotel, Campbeltown — pg 280
95 | Made In Italy, Tarbert — pg 283
96 | Edo Restaurant, Lochgilphead — pg 284
100 | Millcroft Lavender, Millhouse, Tighnabruaich — pg 292
102 | Julie's Coffee House, Oban — pg 294
104 | The Barriemore, Oban — pg 296
105 | The Cuilfail Hotel, Kilmelford, Oban — pg 300

Arts and Crafts

91 | Atelier 23 Art Studio, Sandbank, Dunoon — pg 278
99 | Fyne Studios (The Hidden Gallery), Strathlachlan, Cairndow — pg 291
101 | The Wool & Needlecraft Centre, Oban — pg 294

Place of Interest

92 | Benmore Botanic Garden, Dunoon — pg 279
94 | Glenbarr Abbey, Glenbarr, Tarbert — pg 282
97 | Kilmartin House, Kilmartin, Lochgilphead — pg 287
98 | Inveraray Maritime Museum, Inveraray — pg 289
100 | Millcroft Lavender, Millhouse, Tighnabruaich — pg 292

Specialist Food and Drink Shops

95 | Made In Italy, Tarbert — pg 283
100 | Millcroft Lavender, Millhouse, Tighnabruaich — pg 292
103 | Willie-Fish, Oban — pg 296

🏛 historic building 🏛 museum and heritage 🏛 historic site 🍂 scenic attraction 🌱 flora and fauna

8 | Argyll

Argyll (sometimes also called Argyllshire) is one of the most diverse and beautiful counties in Scotland. It sits on the country's western seaboard, where long sea lochs penetrate deep into the interior and mountains tumble down towards fertile glens.

The name Argyll comes from the Gaelic *Earraghaidheal*, meaning the coastline of the Gaels. It can truly claim to be the cradle of Scotland, for this was at one time the kingdom of Dalriada, founded by the Scotti who originally came from Ireland in the 6th century. Here, at the fortress of Dunadd, they established their capital. From Dunadd, in AD843 Kenneth MacAlpin, King of Dalriada, set off towards Scone in Perthshire (taking the Stone of Destiny with him) to claim the throne of the Picts through his mother's family, thus uniting the two great northern kingdoms and creating an embryonic Scotland, at that time called Alba. In the 11th century, the Lothians (centred on Edinburgh) and Strathclyde (centred on Dumbarton) were absorbed, and Scotland as we largely know it today was formed.

The other great Dalriadan centre was at what is now Dunstaffnage, north of Oban. The site is nowadays occupied by Dunstaffnage Castle, one of the most spectacular fortifications on Scotland's western seaboard. And the 12th-century Castle Sween, on the shores of Loch Sween, is reckoned to be the oldest surviving stone built castle on the Scottish mainland.

Though it has attractive towns, such as Oban, Lochgilphead, Inveraray and Campbeltown, Argyll is sparsely populated. There are few clogged highways (though Oban can get very busy in the summer months), and driving is a pleasure. The climate is mild, thanks to the Gulf Stream, and the place has many fine gardens to explore, such as Ardkinglas, Crarae and Arduaine, some with palm trees and other species you would not expect to thrive so far north.

Man has lived in Argyll for centuries. Around Kilmartin there are cairns and standing stones built long before the ancient Egyptians built the pyramids. A museum in the village of Kilmartin itself records the history of the area, and explains the many cairns, standing stones, stone circles, graves and henges that abound in the area.

The Argyll coastline is rugged and rocky, though there are some marvellous, glistening beaches, which are invariably empty. And, while the landscapes are rugged and romantic, there are also lush meadows and farmlands where heavily-horned Highland cattle can be seen.

The island of Bute, in the Firth of Clyde, also forms part of Argyll. Along with Arran and the Cumbraes, it used to form the county of Bute, but local government reorganisation in the 170s meant its demise as an administrative unit, sharing out its islands between Argyll and Ayrshire.

That great peninsula known as the Mull of Kintyre, which hangs down into the Atlantic like an arm, is also in Argyll. This is a remote part of Scotland. It forms part of the mainland yet is as isolated as any island. Though Glasgow is only 60 miles from Campbeltown as the crow flies, it takes the average driver three or four hours over twisting, loch-girt roads to reach it. This is the area made famous by Sir Paul McCartney's song *Mull of Kintyre*, where he sings of *mists rolling in from the sea*.

Bute

🌿 Ardencraig Gardens 🌄 Canada Hill

🏛 Rothesay Castle 🏛 Bute Museum

🏛 Church of St Mary 🏚 Dunagoil Vitrified Fort

🏚 Isle of Bute Discovery Centre 🚻 Victorian Toilets

🚶 West Island Way 🏛 St Blane's Chapel

🏛 St Ninian's Chapel 🏛 St Macaille's Chapel

🏛 Mount Stuart House

🌿 Ascog Hall Fernery & Garden

The island of Bute is the second largest of the islands in the Firth of Clyde, and used to be part of the small county of the same name, which also took in Arran and the Cumbraes. It is about 15 miles long by five miles wide, and though it now comes under Argyll, the Highland Boundary Fault passes right through the island's capital, Rothesay, and the 175-acre Loch Fad in the heart of the island. This means that the larger northern part is in the Highlands while the smaller southern part is in the Lowlands. The scenery reflects this, with the north being rugged, while the south is pastoral, with many small farms and settlements.

There are two ferries connecting Bute to the mainland. The main one is from Wemyss Bay in Renfrewshire to Rothesay, while another, smaller one, runs between Ardentraive on the Cowal Peninsula and Rhubodach on the north east tip of the island. The latter crossing takes only about five minutes, with the distance being just a third of a mile. At one time cattle, instead of being transported between Bute and the mainland, were made to swim the crossing.

The main town Rothesay, is an ancient royal burgh that was given its charter in 1401. It is one of the most famous holiday resorts on the

Firth of Clyde, and at one time attracted thousands of Glasgow tourists during the Glasgow Fair, which is always the last two weeks in July. Fine Victorian mansions line the front, built to take Glasgow merchants who would descend on the town, along with family and servants. There were also more modest B&Bs and guest houses that took in the working classes for what was their one and only holiday of the year. It eventually earned the nickname of Scotland's Madeira, not just because it was on an island, but because palm trees flourish here due to the influence of the Gulf Stream.

The gentleness of the climate can best be appreciated at **Ardencraig Gardens** in Ardencraig Lane, which were bought by Rothesay Town Council in 1970. They formed part of the original gardens designed by Percy Cane for the owners of Ardencraig House. Every summer it shimmers with colour, and is a popular spot with holidaymakers. Another popular spot is **Canada Hill**, to the south of the town, where there are spectacular views of the Firth of Clyde. From here, people used to watch ships sailing down the Clyde taking Scottish emigrants to a new life in North America, hence its name. On the sea front is a memorial to people who left Rothesay but never returned - the six hundred Bute bowmen who fought alongside William Wallace at the Battle of Falkirk in 1298.

Rothesay Castle (Historic Scotland) is one of the oldest in Scotland. It is a royal castle with an unusual circular curtain wall and a water-filled moat, and was probably built in the 13th century by Walter, third steward of the royal household. Not long after, the Vikings besieged it. King Haakon of Norway took it in 1263, but was later defeated at the Battle of Largs. The Treaty of Perth, signed in 1266, gave Scotland the Inner Hebrides and the island of Bute, and it became a favourite residence of the first Stuart king, Robert II, and his son, Robert III, who may have died there. The courtyard contains the remains of a royal chapel, dedicated to St Michael the Archangel.

It was Robert III who created the dukedom of Rothesay (the first such dukedom in Scotland), and conferred it on his eldest son. Ever since, all royal heirs bear the title, with Prince Charles being the present duke. The whole building was in a ruinous state until 1816, when it was partly rebuilt by the 2nd Marquis of Bute.

In Stuart Street, close to the castle, is the **Bute Museum**, which has displays and artefacts about Rothesay, the Firth of Clyde and the island of Bute itself. The ruins of the **Church of St Mary** (Historic Scotland), on

Rothesay Castle, Bute

the southern outskirts of the town, is next to the present High Kirk built in 1796. It dates mainly from the 13th and 14th centuries and has two canopied tombs. One contains the effigy of a woman and child, and the other the effigy of a man. There is also the grave slab of an unknown Norman knight on the floor. The church has been recently re-roofed to protect them.

The **Isle of Bute Discovery Centre** is housed in the town's Winter Garden (built in 1924) on the front. It features an exhibition highlighting life on the island through interactive displays and plasma screens, as well as a cinema/theatre.

Rothesay has more unusual attractions, such as the ornately designed mens **Victorian Toilets** at the end of the pier, which date from 1899. They still work perfectly, and were recently voted the second best place in the world to spend a penny. If you want the best place, you'll have to go to Hong Kong. Women can view the toilets at quiet times.

Scotland's first long distance island footpath, the 30-mile **West Island Way**, starts at Kilchattan Bay and finishes at Port Bannatyne. Full details of the trail are available from the Isle of Bute Discovery Centre in Rothesay.

Close to Kilchattan Bay, at Kingarth, is **St Blane's Chapel**. The ruins of this Norman structure sit within what was a Celtic monastery, founded by St Blane in the sixth century (see also Dunblane). The whole area shows how such a monastery would have been laid out. The rath, or cashel, a low wall surrounding the monastery, can still be seen, as can the foundations of various beehive cells in which the monks lived. There are two old graveyards - one for men and one for women. Close by is the **Dunagoil Vitrified Fort**,

---

[K] stories and anecdotes ☙ famous people ✗ art and craft ✎ entertainment and sport ☿ walks which dates from the Iron Age. Vitrified forts are so called because at one time they were exposed to great heat, turning the surface of the stone used in their construction to a glass-like substance.

There are lots of other religious sites on Bute, some dating from the Dark Ages. At Straad (a name that tells you that the island once belonged to the Vikings) there are the scant remains of **St Ninian's Chapel**, which may go back at least 1500 years, and at Kilmichael there are the ruins of the old **St Macaille Chapel**.

Mount Stuart House, near the lovely village of Kerrycroy, is the ancestral home of the Marquis of Bute. In 1877 a fire destroyed most of the old house, built during the reign of Queen Anne, and the third Marquis employed Robert Rowand Anderson to design the present Victorian Gothic one. It is an immense house, full of treasures, and reflects the history and importance of the family who owned it. When built, it was full of technological wonders. It was the first house in Scotland to be lit by electricity, and the first private house to have a heated indoor swimming pool. Surrounding the house are 300 acres of delightful gardens. The house achieved international fame in 2003 when designer Stella McCartney, daughter of Sir Paul, got married here.

Near Port Bannatyne, north of Rothesay, is Kames Castle, dating from the 14th century. Neither it nor its beautiful gardens are open to the public, but they can be viewed from the road. One place, which can be visited, however, is **Ascog Hall Fernery and Garden**, three miles south of Rothesay. It was built about 1870, and has a sunken fern house with over 80 sub-tropical fern species. It was awarded the first ever Scottish prize by the

Historic Gardens Foundation, which promotes historic gardens and parks throughout the world.

Off the west coast of Bute is the small privately owned island of Inchmarnock, no more than two miles long by half a mile wide. Its name means Marnock's island, the Marnock in question being a Celtic saint whose name is also found in other Scottish place names such as Kilmarnock. There are the ruins of an ancient chapel here.

Dunoon

🐚 Cowal Highland Gathering ⋔ Adam's Grave
🏛 Castle House Museum ⋐ Highland Mary
🏛 Dunoon Castle 🏛 Ardnadam Heritage Trail
🌱 Cowal Bird Garden 🏛 Cowal Way

Dunoon is one of the best-known Clyde holiday resorts. It sits opposite the Renfrewshire coast, and an all-year ferry connects it to Gourock, with a further ferry going from Hunter's Quay, to the north of the town, to the mainland. Each year in August the town hosts the **Cowal Highland Gathering**, one of the largest in Scotland, where competitors take part in tossing the caber, throwing the hammer and other traditional Scottish events.

The **Castle House Museum** in the Castle Gardens features an exhibition entitled Dunoon and Cowal Past and Present. There are models, artefacts and photographs, which bring the Dunoon of yesteryear to life. There are also furnished Victorian rooms and a shop. The statue of **Highland Mary**, erected in 1896, is close by. She was a native of Dunoon, and worked as a maid in a large house near Mauchline in Ayrshire. Burns met her there, and asked her to accompany him to the West

THE CRAIGEN HOTEL & TEAROOM

85 Argyll Street, Dunoon, Argyll PA23 7DH
Tel: 01369 702307
e-mail: bookings@craigenhotel.co.uk
website: www.craigenhotel.co.uk

Occupying a superb position in Argyll Street and just a few minutes from the ferry, pier and promenade, **The Craigen Hotel and Tearoom** offers very reasonably priced food and comfortable accommodation.

Dating back to the turn of the 18th to 19th century it was at one time owned by the daughter of the Lord Provost of Glasgow , whose summer residence was the become the Castle House Museum. Originally trading as The Royal Hotel as far back as 1870, it became the Craigen around 1917. For the past 5 years, it has been owned by Les and Mary Bishop, a friendly and welcoming couple who have been married for 30 years.

In the Tearoom, the extensive menu offers a good selection of enticing dishes, based wherever possible on locally sourced produce. The choice ranges from an All Day Breakfast or the Belly Buster Breakfast for the really hungry, home-made soup, snacks such as Scrambled Egg or Beans on Toast, fresh made cold or toasted sandwiches, a Fish Tea, and other hot dishes.

The accommodation comprises 6 attractively firnished and decorated rooms, 2 with en-suite.

Indies when he was thinking of emigrating. She agreed, but on a trip home to Dunoon to make arrangements, she died and was buried in Greenock.

Little now remains of **Dunoon Castle**. It was built in the 12th century, and Mary Stuart is said to have stayed in it for a short while. On Tom-a-Mhoid Road, in West Bay, is the Lamont Memorial, erected in 1906 to commemorate the massacre of the Lamonts by the Campbells in 1646. Three miles north of Dunoon, on the A815, is **Adam's Grave**, the popular name for a 3500-year-old neolithic burial cairn, which still has two portals and a capstone intact at its entrance. It sits close to the Holy Loch, at one time an American nuclear submarine base. It was chosen as a base not only because of its deep water, but also because this part of Argyll has a cloud covering for most of the year, thwarting satellite and aerial photography. The Americans left in 1992, taking with them their large American cars and their accents, which were once common on the streets of the town.

At Sandbank, on the shores of the loch, is the two-mile long **Ardnadam Heritage Trail**, with a climb up to a viewpoint at Dunan. The **Cowal Bird Garden** at Sandbank is open from Easter to October every year, and has parrots, exotic birds, donkeys, rabbits and other birds and animals. Details of the 47-mile long **Cowal Way**, a footpath that runs from Portavadie to Artgartan, can be had at the local tourist office.

Around Dunoon

KILMUN
3 miles N of Dunoon on the A880

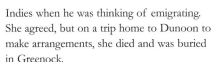

Kilmun Church   Elizabeth Blackwell

Revd Alexander Robinson   Kilmun Arboretum

Kilmun Church, dedicated to St Munn, was a

stories and anecdotes   famous people   art and craft   entertainment and sport   walks

collegiate church founded in 1442 by Sir Duncan Campbell of Lochawe, ancestor of the present Dukes of Argyll. All that remains is the tower, now roofless. In 1794, a Campbell mausoleum was built close to the present church of St Munn, which was built in 1841 to designs by Thomas Burns. In the kirkyard is the grave of **Elizabeth Blackwell** who, in 1849, was the first woman to graduate in medicine. Born in Bristol in 1821, she studied in Geneva (where she graduated), in the United States and in Paris and London. After returning to the United States, she opened (despite intense opposition) the first hospital staffed entirely by women. She died in 1910, and was buried in the churchyard as she regularly holidayed in the area. Close by is the grave of the **Revd Alexander Robinson**, a former minister who was deposed after writing *The Saviour in the Newer Light*, a book

that put forward opinions that brought accusations of heresy.

On a hillside is the **Kilmun Arboretum**, extending to 180 acres. First planted in 1930, it has a wide range of trees - some rare - from all over the world, and is maintained by the Forestry Commission, which does research work here.

BENMORE
6 miles N of Dunoon off the A815

🌿 Benmore Botanic Garden 🧍 Puck's Glen

Benmore Botanic Garden (see panel opposite) enjoys a magnificent mountainside setting on the Cowal Peninsula. This enchanting 120-acre garden boasts more than 300 species of rhododendron, Bhutanese and Chilean plantings, and a spectacular avenue of Giant Redwoods. Within the Glen Massan Arboretum are some of the tallest trees in

---

ATELIER 23 ART STUDIO

Holy Loch Marina, Sandbank, Dunoon, Argyll PA23 8QB
Tel: 01369 704817
e-mail: info@ronnieford.com website: www.ronnieford.com

Established in 2004 and occupying a superb position overlooking Holy Loch, **Atelier 23 Art Studio** is the working studio of Ronnie and Carol Ford. Ronnie holds a BA Honours degree from the Glasgow School of Art and has been teaching art, latterly in Hong Kong. There he became recognised as an accomplished artist and exhibited regularly with the top gallery, Amelia Johnson Contemporary. He returned to Scotland in 2003 and set up his working studio and gallery which began as a messy creative space and has evolved into a stylish gallery.

Ronnie is best known for his romantic visions of the landscapes in which he explores texture and colour in a highly original style. His uniquely Textured Canvasses have evolved from his studies of sculpture and optical art. His time in the Far East also encouraged him to challenge Western perspectives and to explore the Chinese idea of taking a journey through the landscape. The Gallery displays a selection of affordable original artwork as well as high quality signed giclée prints by the artist.

Also on sale are Carol's limited edition cushions made with Asian fabrics; exclusive woodcraft by Trevor Fenwick; jewellery by Rosemary Graham and photography by Alan Forsyth.

Benmore Botanic Garden

Dunoon, Argyll PA23 8QU
Tel: 01369 706261 website: www.rbge.org.uk

In the natural woodland setting of the Eachaig Valley lies **Benmore**, a garden famous for its magnificent collections of trees and shrubs including some of the tallest trees in Britain. Surrounded by dramatic scenery, the garden's west coast climate provides the ideal growing conditions for the cultivation of some of the finest Himalayan rhododendrons.

On entering the garden, visitors are welcomed by an impressive avenue of Giant Redwoods over 40 metres tall and established in 1863. There is a fine living collection of rhododendron, with over 250 species represented, from the rare to the familiar.

With its delicious home baking, the James Duncan Café is a welcome resting place for visitors. Keen gardeners will also appreciate the selection of books, gifts and plants on offer at the Botanics Shop, and the Courtyard Gallery which offers exhibitions and events.

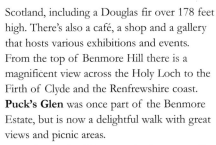

Scotland, including a Douglas fir over 178 feet high. There's also a café, a shop and a gallery that hosts various exhibitions and events. From the top of Benmore Hill there is a magnificent view across the Holy Loch to the Firth of Clyde and the Renfrewshire coast. **Puck's Glen** was once part of the Benmore Estate, but is now a delightful walk with great views and picnic areas.

To the north of Benmore is the seven-mile-long Loch Eck, with the A815 following its eastern shores towards Strachur on Loch Fyne. Near the head of the loch is Tom-a-Chorachasich, a low hill where, legend says, a Viking prince was once slain.

ARDENTINNY

7 miles N of Dunoon on a minor road

🚶 Flowers of the Forest Trail

Ardentinny sits on the shores of Loch Long, and is a small, attractive village made famous by the Sir Harry Lauder song *O'er the Hill to Ardentinny*. The mile-long **Flowers of the Forest Trail** takes you through oak woodland, where you can discover some of the native flowers and plants of the area.

TOWARD

6 miles S of Dunoon on the A815

🏰 Toward Castle 📷 Tom-a-Mhoid

The ruins of **Toward Castle** date mainly from the 15th century. It was a stronghold of the Lamonts, who supported the MacDonalds and Charles II in his attempts to impose bishops on the Church of Scotland, while the Campbells were Covenanters, and bitterly opposed to episcopacy. Mary Stuart stayed at the castle in 1563.

An episode in 1646 shows just how the Scottish clans took matters into their own hands when dispensing justice. The Campbells laid siege to the castle and, after unsuccessfully trying to blow it up, offered safe passage as far as Dunoon to the Lamonts sheltering within. The Lamonts duly left the castle, but were immediately rounded up and taken to **Tom-a-Mhoid** (Hill of Justice) in Dunoon, where 36

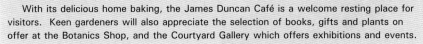

🎥 stories and anecdotes 🐥 famous people ℘ art and craft 📖 entertainment and sport 🚶 walks

Toward Castle

clansmen were hanged. It wasn't just political or religious differences that prompted the massacre. Previously, the Lamonts themselves had slaughtered Campbells at Strachur and attacked and massacred the villagers of Kilmun who were hiding in their church.

Campbeltown

- 🏠 Campbeltown Heritage Centre
- 🏠 Campbeltown Museum 🏛 Campbeltown Cross
- 🌱 Lady Linda McCartney Memorial Gardens

Campbeltown has the reputation of being the most isolated town on the British mainland. It sits on the Mull of Kintyre, that great peninsula hanging down from the main body of Argyll. It received its royal charter in 1700, making it the second youngest royal burgh in Scotland. Though 140 miles from Glasgow by

CRAIGARD HOUSE HOTEL

Low Askomil, Campbeltown, Argyll PA28 6EP
Tel: 01586 554242 Fax: 01586 551137
e-mail: info@craigard-house.co.uk
website: www.craigard-house.co.uk

Craigard House Hotel was originally built in 1882 for a prosperous whisky distiller. It's a striking building in honey sandstone with a Florentine tower and huge bay windows. The house stands in an acre of land bordering Campbeltown Loch and close to the harbour. The original family stayed at Craigard until 1942 after which the house suffered variable fortunes and by 1995 it was semi-derelict. It was then lovingly restored and opened as a bijou hotel in 1997. Today it offers twelve comfortable and well-appointed rooms, many with glorious sea views. Amongst them are a four poster room with a super king double, five family rooms (double or king size double) with one single bed (all but one with sea view); one family room with king size double and two single beds (front and side sea view); four double rooms (two with sea view); and one single room.

The hotel is well-known for its outstanding food. The Lochside Restaurant serves excellent cuisine lovingly prepared by the renowned local celebrity Chef, Joanne Baird, and her team with freshly caught seafood and home-made produce a speciality.

🏛 historic building 🏠 museum and heritage 🏚 historic site 🝤 scenic attraction 🌱 flora and fauna

road, it is only 30 miles from Ballycastle in Northern Ireland. It also has the distinction of being the most southerly town in the Scottish Highlands, and is 25 miles further south than Berwick-upon-Tweed.

At one time the main industries were fishing and distilling, but the fishing fleet has gone now, and only three distilleries remain of the 30 or so that once produced more than two million gallons of whisky a year. There are conducted tours, by appointment only, round Springbank Distillery, established in 1828. At the **Campbeltown Heritage Centre**, in an old kirk, there are displays and exhibits about South Kintyre, including photos of the light railway that once connected the town with Machrihanish on the peninsula's west coast, where the town's airport now stands. The airport has one of the longest runways in Europe, though only one flight uses it - a Loganair flight to Glasgow. The **Campbeltown Museum** in Hall Street has exhibits on the geology, wildlife and archaeology of the Kintyre Peninsula.

The town sits beside Campbeltown Loch, which is guarded by the small island of Davaar. Within a cave on the island is a famous painting of the Crucifixion by local artist David MacKinnon, dating from 1887. The island can be reached on foot at low tide by a long shingle beach known as The Doirlinn. **Campbeltown Cross**, erected near the harbour, dates from the 14th century. It was used as the mercat (market) cross after the town became a royal burgh. In the grounds of Campbeltown Library are the **Lady Linda McCartney Memorial Gardens**, named after the late wife of Sir Paul McCartney who has a holiday home on Kintyre. Campbeltown Picture House was built in 1913, and is the oldest cinema still functioning in Scotland.

Around Campbeltown

SOUTHEND
8 miles S of Campbeltown on the B842

🏛 Knockstapple Standing Stone

This is the most southerly village in Argyll. It was near here, at Keil, that St Columba is supposed to have first set foot on Scottish soil before sailing north towards Iona. In the ancient churchyard at Keil are footprints that are said to mark the spot. It was near here, too, that a massacre of 300 MacDonald clansmen under Sir Alasdair MacDonald took place in 1647. The nine feet tall **Knockstapple Standing Stone** can be seen from the Campbeltown to Southend Road. The remote Sanda Island, two miles south of the village, can be reached by boat from Campbeltown. Though remote, it still has a pub - the Byron Darnton Tavern, built in traditional style and opened in 2003. It is named after the largest vessel to have been wrecked on the island, in 1946.

SADDELL
9 miles N of Campbeltown on the B842

🏚 Saddell Abbey

Saddell Abbey (Historic Scotland) was founded by Somerled, Lord of the Isles, in 1148 for Cistercian monks, and completed by his son Reginald, who also founded Iona Abbey and Nunnery. Only scant remains can now be seen, most notably the presbytery and the north transept. As at other places in Argyll, stone carving once flourished here, and no fewer than 11 beautiful grave slabs, each one showing a monk or a knight in full armour, can be seen. After the Battle of Renfrew in 1164, the bodies of Somerled and his heir were brought to Saddell for burial. Saddell Castle (private) was

GLENBARR ABBEY

Macalister Clan Visitor Centre, Glenbarr,
by Tarbert, Argyll PA29 6UT
Tel: 01583 421247
e-mail: jeannemacalister@tiscali.co.uk

Located on the west coast of the Kintyre peninsula, **Glenbarr Abbey** is a marvellous Gothic structure which is the family seat of the Macalisters of Glenbarr. Tours of the house are conducted personally by Lady Glenbarr and the treasures on display include a pair of gloves worn by Mary, Queen of Scots, 19th century fashions, antique toys, an original Spode dinner service, Sevres and Derby china collection, family jewellery, a unique thimble collection and some wonderful patchworks.

The oldest part of the house dates back to the late 1700s but the most impressive part is the Gothic Revival wing constructed during the second decade of the 19th century. The most recent alterations to the house took place in 1844 when a court of offices was added on the south side of the house. In 1984, Glenbarr Abbey was formally presented to the Macalister clan, as a clan centre, by its owner Angus C. Macalister, 5th Laird of Glenbarr. A museum recounts the centuries-long history of the clan and other facilities include a gift shop, tea room and some lovely forest walks. Glenbarr Abbey is open to the public from 11am to 4pm, Wednesday to Sunday, Easter to October.

built in 1508 for the Bishop of Argyll.

CARRADALE

12 miles N of Campbeltown on the B879

🏛 Network Carradale Heritage Centre

🏛 Carradale House

This quiet fishing village lies opposite Arran, on the east coast of the Mull of Kintyre. The **Network Carradale Heritage Centre**, in a former school, has displays about fishing, farming and forestry in the area, as well as hands-on activities for children. **Carradale House** dates from the 18th century, but was extended in 1804 for the then owner Richard Campbell. In its grounds are gardens noted for their rhododendrons, of which there are more than 100 varieties.

Torrisdale Castle, which has been converted into holiday accommodation, was built in 1815, and has a tannery open to visitors.

GLENBARR

10 miles N of Campbeltown on the A83

🏛 Macalister Clan Centre

At the **Macalister Clan Centre** (see panel above) in Glenbarr Abbey (not an abbey but a mansion house) are exhibits tracing the history of the Macalister Clan as far back as Somerled, Lord of the Isles, nearly 900 years ago. The castle was presented to the clan in 1984 by Angus C Macalister, 5th Laird of Glenbarr. The mansion house itself is open to the public between Easter and mid-October each year.

TARBERT

31 miles N of Campbeltown on the A83

🏛 An Tairbeart 🏛 Tarbert Castle

🌿 Stonefield Castle Garden 🏛 Skipness Castle

🏛 Kilbrannan Chapel

This small fishing port sits at a point where

Kintyre is no more than a mile wide, and is the gateway to the peninsula. To the east is the small East Loch Tarbert, and to the west is the eight-mile-long West Loch Tarbert, where, at Kennacraig, ferries leave for Islay and Jura. In 1093 King Magnus Barelegs of Norway is said to have been dragged in his galley across the narrow isthmus, proving to his own satisfaction that the Mull of Kintyre was an island and he was entitled to add it to his empire. **An Tairbeart**, to the south of the village, is a heritage centre that tells of the place's history and people. **Tarbert Castle**, which is now a ruin, dates originally from the 13th century. Robert the Bruce later added further defences. The ruins that we see today date from the late 15th century. It can be reached along a footpath from Harbour Street.

North of the village is Stonefield Castle, built in 1837 and now a hotel. Attached is **Stonefield Castle Garden**, which is open to the public. As with so many gardens in the area, it is famous for its rhododendrons. There are also plants from Chile and New Zealand, and conifers such as the sierra redwood.

Seven miles south of Tarbert is **Skipness Castle** (Historic Scotland), which dates originally from the 13th century. The first historical mention of it is in 1261 when the McSweens owned it, though it later came into the possession of Walter Stewart, Earl of Menteith. It finally came into the possession of the Campbells, and was abandoned in the late 17th century when a newer, more comfortable house was built close by. The ruins of **Kilbrannan Chapel** near the foreshore, which was dedicated to St Brendan, date from the 13th century. Five medieval grave slabs are to be found inside the chapel walls and in the kirkyard. The

MADE IN ITALY

Harbour Street, Tarbert, Highland PA29 6UD
Tel: 01880 821464

Located on the harbour at Tarbert, **Made in Italy** is unusual in that it offers authentic Italian cuisine to take away. Owner Davide Agosti from Milan and his wife Alessandra from Venice first came to know the Tarbert area while visiting friends in Scotland. They fell in love with the people, the scenery and the lifestyle. So, in 2006, they and their children moved to Tarbert.

Davide's family has a background of working as bakers and Alessandra has experience in restaurant ownership, so it was natural for them to stay in the food business and open Made in Italy. The staff here use only the freshest local produce for their food, including fresh local fish. They have a dedicated pasta chef so all the pasta is home-made, along with the ravioli, lasagne and pizzas. The kitchen is open with a traditional large pizza oven so customers can see the staff preparing the food.

For a genuine sampling of quality Italian cuisine,
Made in Italy is definitely the place to go to.

church replaced an earlier building dedicated to St Columba.

Lochgilphead

🌱 Kilmory Woodland Park ♨ Crinan Canal

Lochgilphead, as the name suggests, stands at the head of Loch Gilp, a small inlet of Loch Fyne. It is a planned town, laid out in about 1790, and is now the main shopping centre for a wide area known as Knapdale, that portion of Argyll from which the long 'arm' of the Mull of Kintyre descends. Knapdale is steeped in history, and though it now seems to be on the edge of things, at one time it was at the crossroads of a great communications network. Ireland was to the southwest, the Isle of Man was to the south, the Hebrides were to the north, the bulk of Scotland itself was to the east, and all could be easily reached by boat.

Kilmory Woodland Park, off the A83, surrounds Kilmory Castle, which has been turned into local government offices. The park contains many rare trees, plus a garden and woodland walks.

The **Crinan Canal** (known as Scotland's most beautiful shortcut) starts at Ardrishaig, a couple of miles south of Lochgilphead, and skirts the town as it heads across the peninsula towards the village of Crinan on the west coast. Work started on the canal in 1794. However, it was beset with problems, and didn't open, albeit in an incomplete form, until 1801. By 1804 it still wasn't complete and had debts of £140,000. Then, in 1805, some of the canal banks collapsed and had to be rebuilt. It was finally reopened in 1809, though in 1815 Thomas Telford, the civil engineer, inspected it and declared that even more work needed doing. In 1817 it reopened again, this

---

EDO RESTAURANT

1 Argyll Street, Lochgilphead PA31 8LZ
Tel: 01546 606163

Edo Restaurant is a small friendly family establishment situated in the Argyll town of Lochgilphead and is owned and run by Michael and Sandra Staniland. Edo Restaurant was opened on 14th March 2008. The restaurant has a simple yet comfortable ambience and has already picked up 'Best New Restaurant' and 'Gourmet Menu under £50' awards from the Scottish Chef Awards 2008. And is shortlisted for 2009 Scottish Chef Awards – 'Rural Chef of the Year' and 'Gourmet Menu under £50.00'.

Delicious Scottish concoctions, with a twist of classical flavours, are created in here by the chefs, who know how to tingle the taste buds. The menu features only the freshest of ingredients from local and organic suppliers throughout Argyll & Islands. The restaurant is an unlicensed BYO, for which there is a nominal corkage charge, and it is soaking in praise heaped on by well-satisfied patrons - *"The scallops, (served in their half shells in garlic butter!), were to die for as were the starters of asparagus and mint risotto and the goat's cheese crostini".*

Lunch is served from 12.00pm-2.30pm, and dinner from 6.00pm -9.00pm. Closed Sunday and Monday. Edo is situated at the bottom end of Argyll Street 20 yards from the roundabout. Look out for their sign on the gable end of the restaurant.

🏛 historic building 🏛 museum and heritage 🏚 historic site ♨ scenic attraction 🌱 flora and fauna

time to everyone's satisfaction.

It is nine miles long, has a mean depth of nine feet six inches, and rises to 65 feet above sea level. It has, in this short length, 15 locks. In 1847 it got the royal seal of approval when Queen Victoria sailed its full length as she was making a tour of the Highlands. Perhaps the most unusual craft to have used it were midget submarines during World War II.

Around Lochgilphead

DUNADD

4 miles N of Lochgilphead off the A816

🏛 Dunadd 🕊 St Columba

Dunadd (Historic Scotland) is one of the most important historical sites in Scotland. This great rock rises to a height of 175 feet from a flat area of land called Crinan Moss, and is where the ancient kings of Dalriada had their royal fort and capital. From here, they ruled a kingdom that took in all of modern day Argyll. It was founded by immigrants from Antrim, in present day Northern Ireland, in the 5th century, and gradually grew in importance. With them from Ireland they brought that great icon of Scottish nationhood, the Stone of Destiny.

A climb to the top of Dunadd gives a wonderful view over the surrounding countryside, which is the reason the fort was established here in the first place. Parts of the ramparts can still be seen, and near the top, on a flat outcrop of rock, are some carvings of a boar, a footprint, a bowl and some ogham writing, which may have been connected to the inauguration of the Dalriadan kings.

The kings of Dalriada were special. Before this time, kings were looked upon more as great tribal leaders and warriors than as men

set apart to rule a kingdom. But one man changed all that - **St Columba.** His monastery on Iona was within Dalriada, and on that island he conducted the first Christian 'coronation' in Britain. In 574AD he anointed Aidan king of the Dalriadans in a ceremony that relied on Biblical precedents. It also contained an element that is still used in today's coronations, when the assembled crowds shouted out 'God Save the King!' in unison. There is no doubt that Aidan sat on the Stone of Destiny during the ceremony.

Though it may now look austere and lonely, Dunadd, in its heyday, would have been a busy place. Excavations have shown that it traded with the kingdoms of present day England and the Continent. When the king was in residence, great flags would have fluttered from the wooden buildings, colourful banners and pennants would have hung from the ramparts and soldiers would have stood guard at its entrance. The River Add, no more than a couple of feet deep nowadays, winds its way round the base of the rock before entering the sea at Loch Crinan. In olden days, before Crinan Moss was drained for agriculture, the river would have been navigable right up to the rock itself. Boats would have been tied up at its banks, and there would have been a small township to house the king's retainers. There would also have been storerooms, stables and workshops where jewellery and weapons were crafted, cloth woven and pots made.

The other great kingdom north of the Forth of Clyde was the kingdom of the Picts, and for years it and Dalriada traded, fought, mingled and intermarried. Eventually, in 843AD, because of this intermarriage, Kenneth MacAlpin, king of Dalriada, also inherited the throne of the Picts. By this time the centre of power had moved to the west because of constant Norse raids, so Kenneth MacAlpin set off for Scone in present day Perthshire (taking the Stone of Destiny with him) and established his capital there. Thus was born the kingdom of Scotland, or Alba as it was known then, though it would be another 200 years before the kingdoms of the Lowlands - the Angles of the Lothians and the British of Strathclyde - were incorporated as well.

Dunadd survived for a few years after Kenneth left, but it was no longer an important place, and by the 12th century was largely abandoned.

KILMICHAEL GLASSARY

4 miles N of Lochgilphead on a minor road off the A816

🏛 Parish Church 🏛 Cup and Ring Rock

In common with many other kirkyards in this part of Argyll, the kirkyard of the attractive 19th-century **Parish Church** has a fine collection of carved, medieval and later, grave slabs.

The **Cup and Ring Rock** (Historic Scotland) lies within a small fenced-off area in the village, and has some ancient cup and ring markings carved into it. No one knows the significance of such carvings, though there are many throughout Scotland.

KILMARTIN

8 miles N of Lochgilphead on the A816

🏛 Parish Church 🏛 Glebe Cairn

🏛 Temple Wood Circles 🏛 Carnassarie Castle

🏛 Kilmartin House Museum

The area surrounding Kilmartin is said to be Scotland's richest prehistoric landscape. Within a six-mile radius of the village over 150 prehistoric and 200 later monuments are to be found. The whole place is awash with standing stones, stone circles, cairns, henges, burial mounds, forts, crannogs, cup and ring markings, castles, carved grave slabs and crosses.

A church has stood in the village for centuries, though the present **Parish Church** was only built in 1835. Its former dedication to St Martin indicates that a church has stood here since at least the Dark Ages, as St Martin was a favourite saint of Celtic monks. a decorated cross in the church dates from about the 9th century, and within the kirkyard are three further crosses, also dating from the 9th century. Also in the kirkyard is the finest collection of carved medieval grave slabs in Western Scotland. Most date from the 14th or 15th century, though there are some thatmight be older. They might come as a surprise to those who imagine Scottish warriors to be wild Highlanders in kilts, who brandish broadswords as they dash across the heather. These warriors are dressed in the kind of sophisticated armour found all over Europe at the time. Only the well-off could have afforded it. The other carvings on the slabs, such as swords, coats-of-arms and crosses, bear out their aristocratic lineage.

Some people have suggested that the carvings show Knights Templar, those warrior monks whose order was suppressed by Pope Clement V in 1307, egged on by Philip le Bel, king of France, who wanted to get his hands on the order's fabled treasure.

A great Templar fleet left La Rochelle in France soon after the order was suppressed - supposedly carrying the Templar's treasure - and were never heard of again. Not long before, the Pope had excommunicated Robert the Bruce for the murder of the Red Comyn in a friary in Dumfries, and people believe the Templars were heading for Scotland. The

Kilmartin House

Kilmartin, Lochgilphead, Argyll Scotland, PA31 8RQ
Tel: 01546 510278
website: www.kilmartin.org

**A Museum of Ancient Culture,
where Argyll's Ancient Past Comes Alive!**

Artefacts from nearby sites are on display in this internationally-acclaimed archaeological museum. Reconstructions, interactive models and unique recordings of prehistoric instruments explore the intricate relationship between Scotland's richest prehistoric landscape and its people.

Over 5,000 years of human history are traced across the Kilmartin valley. At least 150 prehistoric sites lie within six miles of this quiet village: burial cairns, rock-carvings, standing stones and the fortress of the earliest Scottish Kings.

This extraordinary concentration and diversity of ancient monuments is celebrated at Kilmartin House, and is well worth a visit.

Pope's influence in the country was minimal, indeed the clergy, ignoring the Pope, were still giving communion to Bruce. So it would certainly have made sense for the Templars to make for Scotland, bringing their treasure with them. Edward I continually bemoaned the fact that the Scots seemed to have unlimited funds to defend themselves.

An even more intriguing theory has been put forward that the treasure was in the form of a great secret regarding Jesus, who either survived the crucifixion or married Mary Magdalene. Whatever the truth, many books have been written linking this part of Argyll - and other parts of Scotland - with the Knights Templar.

Behind the church is the **Glebe Cairn**, a circular mound of stones dating from 1500-2000BC. It forms part of what is known as the linear cemetery, a collection of such cairns, that stretches for a mile along the floor of Kilmartin Glen. The others are Nether Largie North Cairn, Nether Largie

Mid Cairn, Nether Largie South Cairn and Ri Cruin Cairn. All are accessible by foot. In addition, there is the Dunchraigaig Cairn, just off the A816, which doesn't form part of the linear cemetery.

The **Temple Wood Circles**, south of Kilmartin, date from about 3500BC. There are two of them, with the northern one possibly being used as a solar observatory when agriculture was introduced into the area. Burials were introduced at a later date. The Nether Largie Standing Stones are close to the Temple Wood Circle, and the Ballymeanoch Standing Stones are to the south of them. Of the seven stones, only six now survive in their original positions.

To the north of Kilmartin are the substantial ruins of **Carnassarie Castle** (Historic Scotland), dating from the 16th century. It was built for John Carswell, Protestant Bishop of the Isles and the man who translated Knox's Book of Common Order (his liturgy for the reformed church)

into Gaelic. It was the first book ever to be printed in that language.

If you find all these stone circles, cairns, castles, carvings and burial mounds hard to comprehend, then you should visit the award-winning **Kilmartin House Museum** (see panel on page 287) next to the church in the village. Using maps, photographs, displays and artefacts it explains the whole chronology of the area from about 7000BC right up until AD1100.

KILMORY

13 miles SW of Lochgilphead on a minor road off the B8025

🏛 Castle Sween   🏛 Kilmory Sculptured Stones

🏛 Keills Chapel

North of Kilmory, on the shores of Loch Sween, stands the bulky ruins of **Castle Sween**, mainland Scotland's oldest surviving stone castle. Four massive, thick walls surround a courtyard where originally wood and thatch lean-tos would have housed stables, workshops and a brewery. It was started by one Suibhne (pronounced Sween), ancestor of the MacSweens, in about 1100, and in later years became a centre of craftsmanship and artistry. This is shown by the **Kilmory Sculptured Stones**, at the 700-year-old Kilmory Knap chapel, a few miles south west of the castle. There was a thriving settlement here in medieval times, and within the ruins of the chapel is a remarkable collection of carved stones collected from the kirkyard, some dating back at least 1000 years. The symbols on them include men in armour, blacksmiths' and woodworkers' tools, swords and crosses. They probably all marked the graves of craftsmen and warriors associated with Castle Sween over the years.

The most spectacular stone is MacMillan's Cross, which dates from the 15th century. On one side it shows the Crucifixion, and on the other a hunting scene. There is a Latin inscription that translates, 'This is the cross of Alexander MacMillan'. Across Loch Sween, at the end of the B8025, is **Keills Chapel**, which has another fine collection of grave slabs.

KILBERRY

10 miles SW of Lochgilphead on the B8024

At Kilberry Castle you'll find some late medieval sculptured stones (Historic Scotland), gathered from the Kilberry estate.

KILMARIE

On the B8002 10 miles NW of Lochgilphead

🏛 Kilmarie Old Parish Church

If you take the B8002 a few miles north of Kilmartin, you will find yourself on the Craignish Peninsula. Beyond the attractive village of Ardfern, a popular haven for yachtsmen, is **Kilmarie Old Parish Church**. This roofless ruin, dedicated to St Maelrubha, dates from the 13th century, and contains a wonderful collection of carved grave slabs dating from the 14th and 15th centuries.

Inveraray

🏛 Inverary Castle   🏛 Parish Church

🏛 Church of All Saints   🏛 Inverary Jail

🏛 Inverary Maritime Museum   🐟 Neil Munro

Standing on the western shores of Loch Fyne, Inveraray is a perfect example of a planned Scottish town. It was built between 1753 and 1776 by the 3rd Duke of Argyll, who had pulled down his decaying castle and replaced it with a grander one, which would reflect his important position in society. At that time the small clachan, or hamlet, of Inveraray stood in

Inveraray Maritime Museum

Arctic Penguin, Inveraray, Argyll PA32 8UY
Tel: 01499 302213

A unique Maritime experience on one of the world's last iron sailing ships. Enjoy the fascinating collection of Clyde Maritime displays, memorabilia, stunning archive film and entertaining hands-on activities gathered from far and wide on board our unique three masted schooner. Marvel at the skill of the ancient mariner who lovingly crafted shell valentines for his sweetheart, or engraved walrus tusks and whales teeth with the tragedies and events which touched his life. Relive the horrors on emigrant and slave ships. Graphic tableaux in the lower hold depict the hardships suffered aboard ship during the Highland Clearances when landowners callously evicted whole communities to empty the land for sheep. Savour the luxury of steam yacht accommodation and uncover the most intimate secrets of the Victorian lady afloat. Be amazed at the famous Pepper's ghost illusion. Witness the terrible end of Scotland's most notorious pirate. Bring his grizzly remains back to life – if you dare.

And way, way down in the bowels of the ship lies Davy Jones Locker with it's own attractions specially created for our younger visitors.

front of the castle, and the duke wanted to improve the castle's view out over Loch Fyne, so he had the old township, which stood east of the castle, demolished. He then built a new town to the immediate south, which became a royal burgh thanks to a charter of 1648 granted by Charles I. The result is an elegant town with wide streets and well-proportioned, whitewashed houses. It is actually no bigger than a village, but so well-planned, that it has the feel of a busy metropolis. In the summer months tourists flock to Inverary, making it an extremely busy place.

Inveraray Castle stands to the north, and is an elegant, foursquare stately home. With its four turrets - one at each corner of the building - it looks more like a grand French

château than a Highland castle, but this was the intention. It was designed to tell the world that the Campbells, Dukes of Argyll, belonged to one of the most powerful families in the land - one that had always supported the Protestant cause and the Hanovarian dynasty against the Jacobites. It was designed by Roger Morris and Robert Mylne, and contains a famous armoury, French tapestries, Scottish and European furniture, and a genealogy room that traces the history of Clan Campbell.

There are two churches within the town - the **Parish Church**, which dates from 1794, and the Episcopalian **Church of All Saints**. The Parish Church was designed by Robert Mylne, and is divided in two so that services could be held in both English and Gaelic, though this is seldom done nowadays. All Saints Church, which dates from 1886, has a bell tower with the second heaviest ring of 10 bells in the world. Each bell is named after a saint, and has the name inscribed on it. Ringers can sometimes be watched in action, while visiting ringers can practise by appointment.

Being the main town for a large area, Inveraray was the place where justice was meted out. **Inveraray Jail** takes you on a trip through Scotland's penal system in the 1800s, and here you can see what the living conditions would have been like in cells that housed murderers and thieves. There are two prison blocks, one built in 1820 and one in 1848, the latter having more 'enlightened' conditions. You can also see the branding irons, thumb screws and whips that passed for justice before the 18th century. There is also a courtroom where a tableau, complete with sound, shows how a trial was conducted before a High Court judge.

Within the Arctic Penguin, a three-masted schooner built in 1911, is the **Inveraray Maritime Museum** (see panel on page 289). Here the maritime history of Scotland's western seaboard is vividly brought to life. There's an on-board cinema with an archive of old film, and a re-creation of what conditions were like aboard a ship taking emigrants to a new life in America. The latest addition to the museum is the *Eilean Eisdeal,* a typical puffer built in Hull in 1944.

One of the area's most famous sons was **Neil Munro** (1863-1930), the writer and journalist who wrote the ever-popular *Para Handy* books. On the A819 through Glen Aray towards Loch Awe is a monument that commemorates him. It stands close to his birthplace at Carnus.

Around Inveraray

CAIRNDOW
6 miles NE of Inveraray across the loch on the A83

🌿 Arkinglas Woodland Garden

🚶 Clachan Farm Woodland Walks

This small village stands at the western end of Glen Kinglas, on the shores of Loch Fyne. Within the Arkinglas Estate is the 25-acre **Arkinglas Woodland Garden**. High annual rainfall, a mild climate and light, sandy soil have created the right conditions for a collection of coniferous trees. The Callander family established the collection in about 1875, and it has seven champion trees that are either the tallest or widest in Britain. There is also one of the best collections of rhododendrons in the country. Arkinglas House itself, designed by Robert Lorimer in 1907, is not open to the public.

At Clachan Farm near Arkinglas you'll find the **Clachan Farm Woodland Walks**, which allow you to see many species of native tree, such as oak, hazel and birch. The walks vary from a few hundred yards in length to two-and-a-half miles, and take in the old burial ground of Kilmorich.

STRACHUR
4 miles S of Inveraray across the loch on the A815

🏠 Strachur Smiddy 🚶 Glenbranter

🦅 Sir Fitzroy MacLean 🏛 St Finan's Chapel

🏛 Glendaruel 🏛 Kilmodan Sculptured Stones

Strachur sits on the shores of Long Fyne, on the opposite bank from Inveraray. **Strachur Smiddy** (meaning 'smithy') dates from 1791, and finally closed in the 1950s. It has now been restored as a small museum and craft shop,

FYNE STUDIOS (THE HIDDEN GALLERY)

Newton, Strathlachlan, Cairndow, Argyll PA27 8DB
Tel/Fax: 01369 860379
e-mail: info@fyne-studios.com
website: www.fyne-studios.com

Occupying a two studio cottage in the village of Newton on the shores of Loch Fyne, **Fyne Studios (The Hidden Gallery)** is the base for two Scottish artists with international reputations, Don McNeil and Jean Bell. Their works express the emotional aspect of the wild and rugged Scottish landscape along with the ever-changing weather and dramatic light of the West of Scotland.

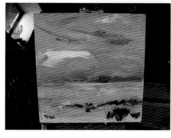

Don prefers to work outside, and, by setting himself a time limit, he seeks to bring about an emotional charge and expression of being Scottish through physical gesture. Jean, on the other hand, as her background is movement and art, likes to encourage the paint to dance and move over the canvas, creating unique and exciting shapes and colours. She also enjoys the challenge of painting 'en plein air'.

The two artists also have an unusual event when they get a group of people to produce a composite painting at a wedding, for example, Hen Party, Stag party, special birthday or whatever. Once everyone has added a bit to the painting they all sign it and present it to the appropriate person. They use acrylic paint and a box canvas so there is no need to get the final result framed.

and has some original tools and implements used by blacksmiths and farriers. **Glenbranter**, which was once owned by Sir Harry Lauder, has three short walks through mature woodlands. In the kirkyard at Strachur is buried **Sir Fitzroy MacLean**, diplomat and spy, who died in 1996, and was said to be the inspiration for Ian Fleming's James Bond.

Lachlan Castle (private), ancestral home of the MacLachlans, lies six miles south of Strachur on the B8000. The older 15th-century castle, which is in ruins, is close by. Nine miles south of the castle, still on the B8000, is Otter Ferry. As the name implies, this village was once the eastern terminal of a ferry that crossed Loch Fyne, but it is long gone. The word 'otter' comes from the Gaelic 'oitir', meaning a gravel bank, and has nothing to do with the animal.

A single lane track, the Ballochandrain, leaves Otter Ferry and rises to more than 1000 feet before descending to Glendaruel. It has some wonderful views towards the Inner Hebrides.

South of Otter Ferry is the small, peaceful clachan of Kilfinan. The ruined **St Finan's Chapel**, dedicated to St Finian, a 6th-century Irish saint, dates from about the 12th century and has some old burial stones. Five miles further on at Millhouse is a turn off to the right along an unmarked road for Portavadie, where the Portavadie-Tarbert ferry will take you onto the Mull of Kintyre (summer only). If you turn left at the same junction and head north again, you pass through Tighnabruaich on the Kyles of Bute, and eventually arrive at **Glendaruel**, the site of a battle in about 1110

MILLCROFT LAVENDER

Millhouse, Tighnabruaich, Argyll PA21 2BW
Tel/Fax: 01700 811110   e-mail: info@millcroftlavender.co.uk
website: www.millcroftlavender.co.uk

Nestled in the lovely little hamlet of Millhouse Argyll, Millcroft Lavender is the most northerly grower of lavender in the UK. Since 2001, Isobel and Alistair Lindsay have opened up their croft to the public from March 1st until 24th December each year.

The original barns have been transformed into a well stocked shop offering customers an opportunity to buy anything from lavender plants to stems, filled lavender bags made from Harris Tweed woven on the Isle of Harris to moreish preserves and truffles. Alongside these products Isobel has had a chance to use her creative talents and make an array of colourful cushions, rag rings, floral decorations and working with the changing seasons wreaths from Spring through to Christmas.

There is also a small Heritage display depicting early farming and croft house memorabilia which the public can view for no charge. The conservatory area and summer house serve coffee, tea and home -baking. Lavender scones are served with Raspberry and Lavender Jam, lavender ice -cream or sample the Whisky Mac fruit cake. Visitors are welcome to walk around the garden whilst enjoying the stunning views of Arran.

Millcroft Lavender was featured on the BBC Landward Programme, has appeared in many papers and magazines and in 2008 was choosen as one of 6 Scottish finalists for the British Small Business Awards.

between Norsemen led by Mekan, son of Magnis Barefoot, and native Gaels, in which the Vikings were defeated. The name translates from the Gaelic as the 'glen of red blood', as the defeated Norsemen were thrown into a local burn whose water turned red with their blood. The road hugs the shoreline most of the way, and gives some wonderful views of sea and hill. At Glendaruel are the **Kilmodan Sculptured Stones**, within the graveyard of Kilmodan Parish Church

ARROCHAR

13 miles E of Inveraray on the A83

🏛 Arrochar Parish Church ⚲ Cruach Tairbeirt Walks

Arrochar sits at the head of Loch Long. Two miles to the west is the small village of Tarbet, which sits on the shore of Loch Lomond. It sometimes surprises people who don't know

the area that Britain's largest sheet of fresh water is so close to the sea. From the jetty at Tarbet small ships offer cruises on the loch. **Arrochar Parish Church** is a whitewashed building dating from 1847. It was recently saved from demolition by the concerted effort of the villagers.

Some of Argyll's finest mountains are to be found close by, such as Ben Narnain (3036 feet) and Ben Ime (3318 feet). This area could fairly claim to be the homeland of Scottish mountaineering, as the first mountaineering club in the country, the Cobbler Club, was established here in 1865. The road westwards towards Inveraray climbs up past the 2891-feet-high Ben Arthur, better known as The Cobbler, and over the wonderfully named Rest and Be Thankful, until it drops down again through Glen Kinglas to the shores of Loch Fyne. It is a wonderful drive, with the floor of

Glen Croe several hundred feet below the road at some points.

Near the Jubilee Well in Arrochar are the **Cruach Tairbeirt Walks**. These footpaths (totalling just over a mile and a half in length) give some wonderful views over Loch Lomond and Loch Long. Though well surfaced, they are quite steep in some places.

AUCHINDRAIN
5 miles S of Inveraray on the A83

🏚 Auchindrain Township

Auchindrain Township is an original West Highland village that has been brought back to life as an outdoor museum and interpretation centre. Once common throughout the Highlands, many of these settlements were abandoned at the time of the Clearances, while others were abandoned as people headed for cities such as Glasgow and Edinburgh to find work. Queen Victoria visited Auchindrain in 1875 when it was inhabited, and you can now see the town as she saw it. Most of the cottages and other buildings have been restored and furnished to explain the living conditions of the Highlanders in past centuries. The visitor centre also has displays on West Highland life, showing many farming and household implements.

CRARAE
10 miles S of Inveraray on the A83

🌿 Crarae Garden

Crarae Garden (National Trust for Scotland) was started by Lady Campbell in 1912, and includes the national collection of southern beech, as well as eucalyptus and *Eucryphia*. It is one of the finest woodland

Crarae Garden, nr Inveraray

gardens in Scotland, with rare trees and exotic shrubs thriving in the mild climate, and over 400 species of rhododendron and azaleas providing a colourful display in spring and summer. A fine collection of deciduous trees adds colour and fire to autumn. There are sheltered woodland walks and a spectacular gorge. The Scottish Clan Garden features a selection of plants associated with various Argyll clans.

Oban

🏛 Cathedral of St Columba 🏛 McCaig's Folly

🏛 Dunollie Castle 🌿 Armaddy Castle Garden

🏛 Oban War & Peace Museum

🌿 Oban Rare Breeds Farm Park

🌿 Oban Zoological World 🤿 Puffin Dive Centre

Seeing Oban nowadays, it is hard to imagine that in the 18th century this bustling holiday resort was no more than a village, with only a handful of cottages built round a small bay. It received its original burgh charter in 1811, but even then it was an unimportant place. With the coming of the railway in 1880, the town blossomed as people discovered its charms. Grand Victorian and Edwardian villas were built by prosperous Glasgow merchants, and

THE WOOL AND NEEDLECRAFT CENTRE

13 Argyll Square, Oban, Argyll PA34 4AU
Tel/Fax: 01631 564469
e-mail: sales@woolandneedlecraftcentre.co.uk

Linda Wilson established **The Wool and Needlecraft Centre** more than 20 years ago when she realised the opportunity to create the best wool shop in the region. She was joined by Philip Cooper who brought a modern twist to the shop with his personal gift for printing and designing needlework kits.

Their shop displays a huge selection of hand-knitting yarns - anything from basic to luxury pure wool - silk mixes, alpaca and more. The speciality wools include beautiful naturally dyed wool from the Isle of Harris and the Shetland Isles; undyed pure wool from a local conservation flock of Hebridean sheep, as well as quality yarns from Debbie Bliss, Sirdar, Wendy and others. There's also an extensive range of needlework kits, including their own exclusive designs featuring local scenes and Celtic emblems.

Also on sale are haberdashery and paper crafting supplies. And if you would like a memento of your holiday in the area, consider one of the exclusive range of gifts made on the premises and printed with local views - painted and embroidered T-shirts, sweatshirts, aprons and bags, mugs, mouse mats, fridge magnets and more. Customers can have items printed on the premises and personalised with their own photos.

JULIE'S COFFEE HOUSE

33 Stafford Street, Oban, Argyll PA34 5NH
Tel: 01631 565952

Located right next door to the famous Oban Distillery and just a 2-minute walk to the terminal for ferries to the islands, **Julie's Coffee House** is well-known for its friendly staff and atmosphere. It is also renowned for its excellent coffees which have been voted the best in Oban, and is highly regarded for the quality of its home baking, with fresh scones baked each day.

Established more than 20 years ago, Julie's has been owned and run since 2001 by Ann Smith and Janet Thom. Their menu also offers light lunches based on ingredients that are sourced locally wherever possible. Options include freshly made sandwiches, soups, salads, toasties, baked potatoes and a specials board that changes each month.

There's seating for 30 people in the cosy café with its central fireplace, and in summer a further 16 customers can occupy pavement tables on quiet Stafford Street which is something of a suntrap.

Dunollie Castle, Oban

that has been fortified since the Dark Ages, and was a MacDougall stronghold. It was finally abandoned as a dwelling house in the early 1700s, when a new McDougall mansion was built. It soon became a quarry for the people of the area. North of the ruins, near the beach at Ganavan, is the Clach a' Choin, or Dog's Stone, where, legend has it, the giant Fingal tied up his dog Bran. The groove at the base is supposed to be where the leash wore away the stone.

Armaddy Castle Garden, eight miles south of Oban off the B844 road for Seil Island, is another of the local gardens that benefit from the area's mild climate.

The pier is where most of the ferries leave for the Western Isles. From here you can sail for Lismore, Mull, Coll, Tiree, Colonsay, Barra and South Uist, and one of the joys of Oban is sitting on the pier watching the graceful ferries entering and leaving Oban Bay.

The **Oban Distillery** in Stafford Street produces a whisky that is one of the six 'classic malts' of Scotland, and offers tours showing the distillery at work. This is one of the smallest distilleries in the country, with just two pot stills. The whisky is a lightly peated malt, and the tour includes a free dram. On the Corran Esplanade is the **Oban War and Peace Museum**, which has photographs and military memorabilia. There is also a model of a flying boat with a 14-feet wingspan.

The **Oban Rare Breeds Farm Park** at Glencruitten has, in addition to rare breeds, a pets corner, a woodland walk, tearoom and shop. And at Upper Soroba is the **Oban Zoological World**, a small family-run zoo

local people began to open hotels, guest houses and B&Bs.

Now it is the capital of the Western Highlands, and known as the 'Gateway to the Western Isles'. It has two cathedrals, the Roman Catholic **Cathedral of St Columba**, built in 1930 of granite and the town's largest church, and the Episcopalian Cathedral Church of St John the Divine in George Street, built in the 19th century but never fully completed.

Dominating the town is **McCaig's Folly**, a vast coliseum of a building that was begun in 1897. To call it a folly is a misnomer, because the man who built it, Oban banker John Stuart McCaig, wanted to establish a museum and art gallery inside it, but he died before it was completed. As the town had a lot of unemployed people at the time, he also wanted to create work for them. In his will he left money for a series of large statues of himself and his family to be erected around the parapet, but this never happened.

The oldest building in Oban is **Dunollie Castle**, the ruins of which can be seen on the northern outskirts of the town beyond the Corran Esplanade. It was built on a site

📖 stories and anecdotes 🐦 famous people 🎨 art and craft 🎭 entertainment and sport 🚶 walks

WILLIE-FISH

8 Stevenson Street, Oban, Argyll PA34 5NA
Tel: 01631 770670
Fax: 01631 770670/01631 562503
e-mail: info@williefishoban.co.uk
website: www.williefishoban.co.uk

Willie-Fish, owned and run by William and Karen MacDonald, has become very well-known in the local region for supplying top quality seafood. They both take pride in providing quality produce with a personal service. William (Willie) is exceptionally expert at filleting fish and customers enjoy watching him at work in the back part of the shop.

Karen spends most of her time at their recently opened Feochan Mhor Smoke-house just outside Oban where they smoke their own fish and shellfish. In their town centre shop hey sell a wide range of seafood and shellfish, including scallops, mussels, razor clams, oysters, smoked salmon and trout, as well as smoked fish pâté. As far as possible, all their fish is sourced locally but they are happy to track down any variety not readily available.

Their shop is conveniently close to the quay where local boats land their catches and there's parking right outside. If you aren't able to visit, Willie-Fish operates a mail order service available by phone or through their website.

THE BARRIEMORE

Corran Esplanade, Oban, Argyll PA34 5AQ
Tel: 01631 566356 Fax: 01631 571084
e-mail: reception@barriemore-hotel.co.uk
website: www.barriemore-hotel.co.uk

The Barriemore enjoys a splendid location as the last hotel on the Oban seafront heading north towards Ganavan on Corran Esplanade. From its superior vantage point, it commands magnificent panoramas towards the islands of Kerrera, Lismore and Mull. The house was built in 1895 for John Stuart McCaig, a wealthy Oban banker who financed the construction of the famous local landmark known as McCaig's Tower. The house exudes an opulence in keeping with its late-Victorian origins.

There's an elegant and comfortable residents' lounge with a range of books and magazines relating to local places of interest. The lounge leads into the bar with its warm, cosy atmosphere and attractive lighting. The eye-catching dining room has picture windows overlooking Oban Bay and provides the perfect spot in which to enjoy full Scottish Breakfasts which include such delights as locally produced smoked haddock and kippers.

All the bedrooms at The Barriemore are beautifully and individually furnished, and all have the added convenience of full en suite facilities, colour television, and hospitality tray. Some rooms enjoy a magnificent outlook over Oban Bay.

specialising in small mammals and reptiles. The **Puffin Dive Centre** at Port Gallanach is an award-winning activity centre where you can learn to scuba dive in some remarkably clear water.

Around Oban

CONNEL BRIDGE
4 miles NE of Oban off the A828

Falls of Lora

Connel Bridge is a one-time railway bridge that now carries the A828 over the entrance to Loch Etive. The entrance to this sea loch is very shallow, and when the tide ebbs, the water pours out of the loch into the Firth of Lorne over the **Falls of Lora**.

DUNSTAFFNAGE
3 miles N of Oban off the A85

Dunstaffnage Castle Ell Maid

Dunstaffnage Chapel

On a promontory sticking out into Ardmuchnish Bay, in the Firth of Lorne, is the substantial **Dunstaffnage Castle** (Historic Scotland). Seen from the east, it has a glorious setting, with the island of Lismore and the hills of Morvern behind it. And the setting is not just beautiful. This must be one of the most strategic places in Argyll as far as sea travel is concerned, as many important sea routes converge here. The castle was originally built in the 13th century by either Ewan or Duncan MacDougall, Lords of Lorne, on the site of a Dalriadan royal fort and settlement, though the castle as seen today dates from all

The Harbour, Oban

periods up to the 19th century. In 1309, the castle fell into the hands of Robert the Bruce, and he gave it to the Stewarts. In 1470, Colin Campbell, the first Earl of Argyll, was created hereditary captain, or keeper of Dunstaffnage.

In 1363 a dark deed was carried out here. The then Stewart owner was set upon outside the castle and murdered by a troop of MacDougalls, who still considered the castle theirs. The troop then attacked the castle and it fell into their hands once more. A few months later a force of men sent by David II, Robert the Bruce's son, retook it. In 1746, Flora MacDonald was held captive here for a short while.

The castle's resident ghost is called the **Ell Maid**, and sometimes on stormy nights she can be heard wandering through the ruins, her

stories and anecdotes famous people art and craft entertainment and sport walks

footsteps clanging off the stone as if shod in iron. If she is heard laughing, it means that there will be good news for the castle. If she shrieks and sobs, it means the opposite.

Dunstaffnage Chapel stands outside the castle and also dates from the 13th century. It is unusual in that chapels were usually within the defensive walls of a castle. A small burial aisle, built in 1740 for the Campbells of Dunstaffnage, forms an eastern extension.

BARCALDINE
10 miles N of Oban on the A828

🐾 Scottish Sealife Sanctuary 🏛 Barcaldine Castle

The **Scottish Sealife Sanctuary** is Scotland's leading marine animal rescue centre, and it looks after dozens of injured or orphaned seal pups before returning them back into the wild. The sanctuary is set within a mature spruce forest on the shores of beautiful Loch Creran and is home to some of the UK's most enchanting marine creatures. In crystal clear waters you can explore more than 30 fascinating natural marine habitats containing everything from octopus to sharks. Every day there is a range of talks and feeding demonstrations from the team of marine experts.

Barcaldine Castle has associations with the Appin murder and the Massacre of Glencoe. There are secret passages and a bottle dungeon, and the castle is said to be haunted by a Blue Lady. Though not open to the public, it offers B&B accommodation. Tralee Beach is one of the best beaches in the area. It lies off the unmarked road to South Shian and Eriska.

ARDCHATTAN
8 miles NE of Oban on a minor road on the north shore of Loch Etive

🏛 Ardchattan Priory 🐾 Ardchattan Priory Garden

Ardchattan Priory (Historic Scotland) was built in about 1230 by Duncan McDougall, Lord of Lorne, for the Valliscaulian order of monks. The ruins of the church can still be seen, though the rest of the priory, including the nave and cloisters, was incorporated into Ardchattan House in the 17th century by John Campbell, who took over the priory at the Reformation. There are some old grave slabs that mark McDougall graves. **Ardchattan Priory Garden** is open to the public, and has herbaceous borders, roses, a rockery and a wild flower meadow.

KINLOCHLAICH GARDENS
11 miles N of Oban on the A828

This old walled garden was created in 1790 by John Campbell. It sits on the shores of Loch Linnhe, in an area known as Appin, and it has one of Scotland's largest plant and nursery centres.

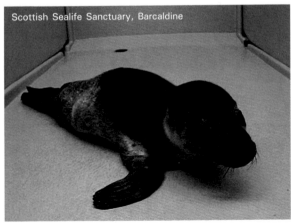
Scottish Sealife Sanctuary, Barcaldine

DRUIMNEIL HOUSE GARDEN

10 miles N of Oban on a minor road off the A828

The garden has a fine display of rhododendrons, shrubs and trees, plus a garden centre. It is open from Easter to October each year under the Scottish Gardens Scheme. Teas and coffees are available.

Bonawe Furnace, Taynuilt

TAYNUILT

9 miles E of Oban on the A85

🚶 Coast to Coast Walk   🏛 Bonawe Furnace

🌱 Barguillean's Angus Garden

Taynuilt lies close to the shores of Loch Etiven and is on the 128-mile-long **Coast to Coast Walk** from Oban to St Andrews. Nearby, at Inverawe, is the **Bonawe Furnace**, which dates from 1753. Ironworking was carried out here for over 100 years, and the furnace made many of the cannonballs used by Nelson's navy. In 1805, the workers erected a statue to Nelson, the first in Britain, and it can still be seen today near Muchairn Church.

At Barguillean Farm you will find **Barguillean's Angus Garden**, established in 1957 on the shores of Loch Angus. It extends to nine acres, and was created in memory of Angus Macdonald, a journalist who was killed in Cyprus in 1956.

LOCH AWE

16 miles E of Oban on the A85

🏰 Kilchurn Castle   🏰 St Conan's Kirk

If you take the road east from Dunstaffnage Castle, passing near the shores of Loch Etive and going through the Pass of Brander, you will come to Scotland's longest loch, Loch Awe. This is its northern shore, and it snakes southwest for a distance of nearly 25½ miles until it almost reaches Kilmartin. Twenty crannogs, or artificial islands, have been discovered in the loch. On them defensive houses were built of wood, with a causeway connecting them to the mainland. They were in use in the Highlands from about 3000BC right up until the 16th century. Near the village of Lochawe are the impressive ruins of **Kilchurn Castle** (Historic Scotland), right on the shores of the loch. It was built by Sir Colin Campbell, who came from a cadet branch of the great Campbell family, in about 1450. They were eventually elevated to the peerage as the Earls of Breadalbane. In the 1680s Sir John Campbell converted the castle into a barracks to house troops fighting the Jacobites. However, it was never used as such.

St Conan's Kirk, also on the banks of the loch, is reckoned to be one of the most beautiful churches in Scotland, though it dates only from the 1880s, with later additions. It was built by Walter Douglas Campbell, who had a mansion house nearby. The story goes that his mother disliked the long drive to the parish church at Dalmally, so, in 1881, Walter decided to built a church on the shores of Loch Awe. Not only did he commission it, he designed it and carved some of the woodwork. The church was completed in 1887, but it proved too small for him, so in 1907 he began extending it. He died in 1914 before he could complete it, and it was finally finished in its present state in 1930. The kirk has a superb chancel, an ambulatory, a nave with a south aisle, various chapels and, curiously for a small church, cloisters. The Bruce Chapel commemorates a skirmish near the church, when a small force of men loyal to Robert the Bruce defeated John of Lorne, who had sworn allegiance to Edward I of England. The chapel contains a small fragment of bone from Bruce's tomb in Dunfermline Abbey.

The waters of Loch Cruachan, high on Ben Cruachan above Loch Awe, have been harnessed for one of the most ambitious hydroelectric schemes in Scotland. Not only does the Cruachan Power Station produce electricity from the waters of Loch Cruachan as they tumble down through pipes into its turbines and then into Loch Awe, it can actually pump 120 tons of water a second from Loch Awe back up the pipes towards Loch Cruachan by putting the turbines into reverse. This it does during the night, using the excess electricity produced by conventional power stations. In this way, power is stored so that it can be released when demand is high. It was the first station in the world to use the technology, though nowadays it is commonplace.

The turbine halls are in huge artificial caves beneath the mountain, and there is an exhibition explaining the technology. Tours are also available taking you round one of the wonders of Scottish civil engineering - one that can produce enough electricity to supply a city the size of Edinburgh.

THE CUILFAIL HOTEL

Kilmelford, by Oban, Argyll PA34 4XA
Tel: 01852 200274 Fax: 01852 200264
e-mail: mail@cuilfail.com
website: www.cuilfail.co.uk

The Cuilfail Hotel is a large stone "landmark" building with a specimen Virginia creeper growing along its façade. It was built in the mid-1850s onto an existing drover's inn that is believed to be about 250 years old. The Victorian hotel owned most of the surrounding land and lochs and attracted guests interested in hunting and fishing.

Today, the hotel is owned and run by Simon Fletcher and Yvonne O'Shea who have made the hotel a welcoming place that lives up to its Gaelic name "Cuilfail" which means "sheltered corner". The interior of the hotel retains many of its Victorian features - open fires, coving, wainscoting, large feature staircase all add to the charm. There's a unique cosy bar with a vast collection of bank notes from around the world. Bar meals are served here and there's also a restaurant. The guest bedrooms are spacious, and individually decorated to give a light, airy feel. All 12 of them are en suite and they include 2 family suites. Outside, there is seating space at the front and a peaceful riverside space ideal for drinks on sunny afternoons.

KILMELFORD
11 miles S of Oban on the A816

🏛 Parish Church

In the kirkyard of the small **Parish Church**, dated 1785, are some gravestones marking the burial places of people killed while making the "black porridge".

It was at Loch Melfort, in 1821, that one of Scotland's most unusual weather phenomenons occurred - it rained herrings. The likeliest explanation is that the brisk south-westerly that was blowing at the time lifted the herring from the loch and deposited them on dry land.

ARDUAINE
15 miles S of Oban on the A816

🌱 Arduaine Gardens

The 50-acre **Arduaine Gardens** (National Trust for Scotland) are situated on a south-facing slope overlooking Asknish Bay. They are another testimony to the mildness of the climate on Argyll's coast, and have a wonderful collection of rhododendrons. There are also great trees, herbaceous borders and a diversity of plants from all over the world. They were laid out by James Arthur Campbell, who built a home here in 1898 and called it Arduaine, which means 'green point'. It was acquired by the NTS in 1992.

ARDANAISEIG GARDEN
14 miles E of Oban on a minor road off the B845 on the banks of Loch Awe

Ardanaiseig is a large, 100-acre woodland garden with a large herbaceous border. The garden is closed from January to mid February each year.

DALAVICH
13 miles SE of Oban on a minor road off the B845 on the banks of Loch Awe

🚶 Dalavich Oakwood Trail

If you follow the B845 south from Taynuilt, then turn south west onto a minor road near Kilchrenan, you will eventually reach the **Dalavich Oakwood Trail**. It is a two-mile-long walk laid out by the Forestry Commission, with not only oaks, but also alder, hazel, downy birch and juniper. There are also small sites where 18th- and 19th-century charcoal burners produced charcoal for the Bonawe Iron Furnace near Taynuilt. Other woodland trails include the Timber Walk and the Loch Avich.

🎬 stories and anecdotes 🐦 famous people 🎨 art and craft ✏ entertainment and sport 🚶 walks

ADVERTISERS AND PLACES OF INTEREST

LOCATOR MAP

🏠 historic building   🏛 museum and heritage   🏛 historic site   🝔 scenic attraction   🌿 flora and fauna

9 | Inner Hebrides

The Inner Hebrides, unlike the Western Isles, is not a compact geographical unit. Rather, it is a collection of disparate islands lying off the Argyll coast and forming part of that county (apart from Skye, which is part of the Highlands). Each island has its own distinct character, with sizes ranging from the 87,535 hectares of Mull (the third largest of Scotland's islands) to the 33 hectares of Staffa and the 877 hectares of Iona.

Not all the islands are inhabited, and of those that are, most have seen a drop in population over the years. On some that were once inhabited, the remains of cottages and even old chapels are still to be found. The names trip off the tongue like a litany, and some, to English speakers, are decidedly unusual. Mull; Muck; Rum; Eigg; Coll; Canna; Tiree; Islay; Jura; Colonsay. Most have their origins in Gaelic, and in some cases Norse.

Each island is different. Lismore, for instance, is flat and fertile, while Jura is mountainous. Mull is easily accessible from the mainland, while Canna, beyond Rum, is remote. Islay (pronounced 'Eyelah') and Jura are the most southerly and lie off the western coast of the Mull of Kintyre, from where they are reached by ferry. Islay is where you will find, at Finlagan, the capital of the ancient Lordship of the Isles. It is

also an island famous for its distilleries, which make a peaty, dark malt. Tiree is said to be the sunniest spot in Britain, though it is also one of the wettest and windiest. It is low lying, so much so that its name in Gaelic, Tir an Eorna actually means the land below the sea. It is now famous for its surfing beaches, and many championships are held here.

Even though most of the islands lie well away from the mainland, they have still been influenced by Lowland Scots and English sensibilities. Rum has changed its name three times since the 1880s. Originally it was Rum, then, when the Bullough family bought it in the late 19th century, they changed it to Rhum in deference to their teetotal beliefs. In 1957 the island was bought by Scottish Natural Heritage and the name changed back to Rum.

Places like Mull and Skye are proving to be popular retirement spots, with the local people having a name for the Lowland Scots and

Tobermory, Isle of Mull

Iona Abbey

English who settle there - white settlers. Though there has been some grumbling in the past about incomers seeking to impose English values on what is essentially a Gaelic culture, they are generally welcomed.

The Inner Hebrides can also claim to have the most sacred place in Scotland, if not Britain. Iona, off the west coast of Mull, was where St Columba established his great monastery, and from where missionaries set out to convert the northern lands. St Columba wasn't the first man to bring Christianity to Scotland - that honour goes to St Ninian - but he was the most influential, and we know a lot about his life, thanks to a biography written by St Adamnan, ninth abbot of Iona, almost one hundred years after he died. Though some of it is uncritical hagiography, there is enough to learn about the man behind the venerated saint that is Columba. He tells of a man who was all too human - vengeful yet forgiving, impetuous yet thoughtful, arrogant yet unassuming and boastful yet modest. Today Iona is still a place of pilgrimage, though most people now come as tourists to see and admire the later abbey buildings and experience that feeling of calm for which the island is famous.

Gigha

17 miles NW of Campbeltown off the west coast of Kintyre

🚶 Gigha Path Network 🏛 Kilchattan Church

🏛 Ogham Stone 🌿 Achamore Gardens

This small island, no more than six miles long by two miles wide at its widest, is reached by ferry from Tayinloan. It is best to see the island on foot, and the **Gigha Path Network** makes this easy. The name Gigha (pronounced gee-yah, with a hard 'g') was given to the island by the Norse king Hakon, and means God's island. It seems to have a climate of its own, and while the rest of Argyll is enveloped in cloud, Gigha is sometimes bathed in sunshine due to the Gulf Stream washing its shores. Its highest peak, at 330 feet, is Creag Bhan, where you can see a 4th-century inscribed stone.

The scanty ruins of **Kilchattan Church**, behind the hotel, date from medieval times. In the kirkyard are some old grave slabs showing knights in armour. One is possibly of Malcolm MacNeill, Laird of Gigha, who died in 1493.

Behind the church, atop the Cnoc A'Charraidh (Hill of the Pillar), is the **Ogham Stone**, dating from the time the island formed part of the kingdom of Dalriada. It carries a carving that reads "Fiacal son of Coemgen", and probably marks a burial.

The 50-acre **Achamore Gardens**, near the ferry port at Ardminish, are open to the public. They were founded by Sir James Horlick, of bedtime drink fame, after he bought the island in 1944. They are famous for their rhododendrons and camellias. In 2001, the inhabitants of Gigha bought the island, and it is now managed by a trust.

Around Gigha

ISLAY
35 miles SW of Inveraray in the Atlantic Ocean

🏛 Dunyveg Castle 🏛 Coll Ciotach

🏛 Kildalton Cross & Chapel 🏛 Dun Nosebridge

🏛 American Monument 🏛 Museum of Islay Life

🏛 Cultoon Stone Circle 🏛 Kilchiaran Chapel

🏛 Kilchoman Church & Cross

Islay's relatively mild, wet climate has meant that the island has been inhabited for thousands of years. Clan Donald, which claims descent from Somerled, made the island the centre of their vast Lordship of the Isles,which at one time was almost a separate kingdom beyond the reach of Scottish monarchs. It is a truly beautiful island, with a range of hills to the east rising to 1500 feet, and low, fertile farmland. It is famous for its distilleries, with more than four million gallons of whisky being produced each year. Most of them have tours explaining the distilling process, and offer a dram at the end. An Islay malt has a peaty taste all of its own, due to the grain being dried over peat fires.

On islands in Loch Finlaggan, west of Port Askaig (where there is a ferry to Feolin Ferry on Jura and West Loch Tarbert on the Mull of Kintyre) you will find the ruins of the medieval centre of the Lordship of the Isles, with a visitor centre close by. The important remains are to be found on two of the islands in the loch, Eilean Mor (the Great Island) and Eilean na Comhairle (the Council Island). Ancient burial slabs are thought to mark the graves of important women and children, as the chiefs would have been buried on Iona. Close to Port Askaig itself are the Bunnahabhain and the Caol Ila distilleries. To the east of Port Ellen (which also has a ferry to Tarbert) are the distilleries of Lagavulin, Laphroaig and Ardbeg.

The ruins of **Dunyveg Castle**, a MacDonald stronghold, sit near Lagavulin. At one time it was owned by a man called **Coll Ciotach,** or left-handed Coll. While he was away on business, the castle was captured by his enemies the Campbells, and his men taken prisoner. They then waited for Coll to return so that they could overpower him. But one of the prisoners was Coll's personal piper, and when he saw his master approach the castle, he alerted him by playing a warning tune. Coll escaped, but the piper had his right hand cut off and never again could play the pipes. It's a wonderful story, though whether it is true or not is another matter, as the legend is also associated with other castles in Argyll, notably Duntroon.

At Ardbeg is the **Kildalton Cross and Chapel**. The incised cross dates from the 9th century, and is one of the finest in Scotland. Staying on a religious theme, Bowmore, on the A874 beside the shores of Loch Indaal, has one of only two round churches in Scotland. It was built in 1767 by Daniel Campbell, who reckoned that, having no corners, the devil could not hide anywhere within it. Bowmore Distillery - the oldest (founded in 1779) and one of the most famous on the island - is open to visitors. North of Bowmore, near Bridgend, is an Iron Age fort with the wonderful name of **Dun Nosebridge** (Landrover trips can be arranged to visit and view it), and to the southwest of the village, at the tip of the Mull of Oa (pronounced 'oh'), is the **American Monument**, which commemorates the 266 American sailors lost when *Tuscania* sank after being torpedoed in

---

AN TIGH SEINNSE

11 Queen Street, Portnahaven, Isle of Islay PA47 7SJ
Tel: 01496 860224

Fancy a relaxing afternoon watching the seals sunbathe whilst eating a pint of prawns on the shore? Then visit **An Tigh Seinnse**! It is tucked away at the bottom of Portnahaven village on the right hand-side of the bay - you are sure to agree that it is probably the best pub/restaurant in the village. It is open from 10 am serving tea/coffee and home baking (from Easter), with food served from 12 noon till 8pm.

Sample startersmight inclusde Porthnahaven crab soup with homemade bread, smoked haddock, parmesan and spinach fishcakes served with mayonnaise or a smoked fish platter (Braden Orach, Braden rost & mackerel). Main mealscould include Islay beef lasagne with garlic bread & side salad, diver caught scallops served with a lime dressing, salad & baby potatoes or half a Portnahaven lobster served with garlic butter & salad (24 hr notice required). Baguettes served with side salad are available as a lighter option.

The menu changes regularly. If you have any special requests or food allergies etc please phone and they promise to do their best to accommodate your needs. Children are welcome, however, no dogsare allowed inside the pub - there is, however, a beer garden.

The Mull of Oa, Islay

Distance: *1.9 miles (3.0 kilometres)*
Typical time: *60 mins*
Height gain: *60 metres*
Map: *Explorer 352*
Walk: *www.walkingworld.com ID:1837*
Contributor: *Colin & Joanne Simpson*

ACCESS INFORMATION:

From Port Ellen an unclassified road leads west past the old distillery and is signposted to the Mull of Oa. Follow this with a final left turn along a track signposted to the American monument to reach the parking area.

ADDITONAL INFORMATION:

The American monument atop the cliffs commemorates two troopships from the First World War which sank in these waters. HMS Tuscania was torpedoed by a German submarine on 5th Feb 1918 and sank off the Mull of Oa. HMS Otranto was involved in a collision with HMS Kashmir on 6th Oct 1918 and sank off Machir Bay.

DESCRIPTION:

Much of the coastline of the Isle of Islay is low-lying, with rocky shores interspersed with beaches and only in the south-west are there cliffs of any note. This walk crossed the moors to the most dramatic section of cliffs, from where there are views over much of the island and across the North Channel to Northern Ireland.

FEATURES:

Sea, Wildlife, Birds, Great Views, Moor, Ancient Monument.

WALK DIRECTIONS:

1 | From the parking area, go through the gate and follow the track. A short distance down the track a signpost points to the right, to a recently built path that runs up the side of the field.

2 | The path is obvious here, following the fence uphill.

3 | At the top of the field the new path traverses rightwards and crosses a stile onto the open moorland. From here the route follows the old unmade path which can be indistinct at times, but the American monument on the skyline means there is always something to aim for. Another fence is crossed by a stile immediately before the first cliffs are reached. From here it is only a couple of hundred metres to the monument.

4 | From the monument there are some views along the coast in both directions to the adjacent cliffs. It is possible to follow a faint track beyond the monument towards the headland, allowing you to look back at the nearest cliffs. In good conditions this is quite straightforward but could be quite dangerous if the grass is wet. To the south are more dramatic cliffs, including the highest on Islay at almost 200 metres. On a good day (not as hazy as the one here) Northern Ireland can be clearly seen across the North Channel about 30km away.

5 | The return can be made by the same route, passing this trig point just below the monument, but a longer alternative heads towards the bay at Port nan Gallan before returning past Upper Killeyan Farm.

Lower Killeyan

Kinnabus

Upper Killeyan

Monument

Mull of Oa

1918 and the *Otranto* was wrecked. Many of the bodies were washed up at the foot of the cliff here.

On the opposite side of the loch is a peninsula called the Rhinns of Islay, and it is here that you will find the Bruichladdich Distillery, which, in 2003, found itself under surveillance by American intelligence agents as the whisky distilling process is similar to the one used in making certain kinds of chemical weapons. At Port Charlotte is the Islay Natural History Trust, housed in a former whisky bond. It has a wildlife information centre where you can learn about the natural history and wildlife of Islay. Also in the village is the **Museum of Islay Life**, which tells of everyday life on the island through the ages, and has a special display on the many shipwrecks that have taken place off Islay's rugged coastline. Continue past

Port Charlotte on the A874 and you will come to Portnahaven. About four miles from the village, and situated on the west side of the Portnahaven to Kilchiaran road, is the **Cultoon Stone Circle**. Not all the stones have survived, but three are still standing and 12 have fallen over at the point where they once stood. The ruins of **Kilchiaran Chapel**, on the west coast of the Rhinns, can be reached by car via a narrow track. Though its fabric is basically medieval, its origins go right back to the time of St Columba, who founded it in honour of his friend St Ciaran. There is an old baptismal font and some carved gravestones. The nearby beach is a favourite place for seals to sun themselves. Further north is the **Kilchoman Church and Cross**, accessed by another narrow track, which leaves the B8018 and goes past Loch Gorm. The cross dates from the 15th

---

ISLAY CELTIC CRAFT SHOP

Main Street, Bowmore, Isle of Islay PA43 7JH
Tel: 01496 810262 / 860319

Tucked away in the top part of Bowmore's Main Street, next to the Post Office, the **Islay Celtic Craft Shop** offers a fascinating range of crafts with a Celtic theme. The shop was established more than ten years ago by Mairi Clark from the Rhinns of Islay.

Mairi does leather work as her main craft, specialising in Celtic designs among others. Her repertoire includes key rings, bookmarks, whisky coasters, belts, bracelets and much more. All items are made totally by hand from real leather. Mairi also does paintings and other crafts. Although difficult to source, the shop tries to have as many local products for sale as possible.

The shop also stocks an unusual range of gift items, some with Gothic and fantasy themes and silver jewellery, as well as a good range of gift gadgets for men and souvenirs. The shop also offers a leather repair service.

Customers are welcome to come in and browse. The shop is open from 10.30am to 5pm, Monday to Saturday.

---

century, and was erected by 'Thomas, son of Patrick'. The church is no longer in use and has lost part of its roof.

JURA

24 miles W of Inveraray in the Atlantic Ocean

🐦 Jura House Garden	🏛 Claig Castle
🏛 Chapel of St Earnadail	📖 Mary MacCrain
🏛 Cille Mhoire an Caibel	📖 Breachkan
🕯 George Orwell	

Jura is an island of peat bogs, mists and mountains, notably the Paps of Jura, to the south. The highest mountain in the range, at over 2500 feet, is Ben an Oir. The island's only road, the A846, takes you from Feolin Ferry, where there is a ferry to Islay, north along the east coast, where most of the island's population lives. You will pass **Jura House Garden** at Cabrach, with its collection of Australian and New Zealand plants. They thrive in this mild and virtually frost- and snow-free environment. Craighouse, with its distillery, is the island's capital. Behind the parish church, dated 1776, is a room with some old photographs and artefacts of life on Jura through the ages. On the small island of Am Fraoch Eilean, south of the village, are the ruins of **Claig Castle**, reputed to be an old MacDonald prison.

A mile or so north of Craighouse is the ruined **Chapel of St Earnadail**. St Earnadail was St Columba's uncle, and the story goes that he wanted to be buried on Jura when he died. When asked where on the island, he replied that a cloud of mist would guide the mourners to the right spot. On his death, a cloud of mist duly appeared and settled where the ruins now stand.

The road then takes you north to Ardlussa, where it peters out. Within the old burial ground is the tombstone of **Mary MacCrain**, who died in 1856, aged 128. They seem to have been long-lived on Jura, for the stone goes on to say that she was a descendant of Gillouir MacCrain, 'who kept one hundred and eighty Christmases in his own house, and died during the reign of Charles I'.

Just under a mile off Jura's north cost is the small island of Scarba. It has been uninhabited since the 1960s, though in the late 18th century it managed to support 50 people. It rises to a height of 1473 feet, and has many Iron Age sites on its west coast. On the east coast are the ruins of **Cille Mhoire an Caibel**, surrounded by an old graveyard. Many miracles were supposed to have taken place within the kirk in early medieval times.

Between Jura and Scarba, in the Gulf of Corryvreckan, is the notorious Corryvreckan whirlpool. The name comes from the Gaelic Coire Bhreacain, meaning speckled cauldron, and it is best viewed from the safety of the cliff tops on Jura (even though you have to walk about five miles from just beyond Ardlussa to get there) as it has sent many boats to the bottom. It is caused by the combination of an immense pillar of rock rising from the seabed and a tidal race, and the best time to see it is when a spring tide is running westward against a west wind. The sound of it can sometimes be heard at Ardfern on the mainland, more than seven miles away.

Legend tells us that the whirlpool's name has a different derivation. A Norwegian prince called **Breachkan** was visiting the Scottish islands and fell in love with a beautiful princess, a daughter of the Lord of the Isles. Her father disapproved of the young man, but declared that he could marry his daughter providing he could moor his galley in the whirlpool for three days.

Breachkan agreed to the challenge, and had three cables made - one of hemp, one of wool and one from the hair of virgins. He then sailed into the Gulf of Corryvreckan, and while there was a slack tide, moored his boat in the whirlpool. The tides changed, and the whirlpool became a raging monster. The hemp cable snapped on the first day and the wool one snapped on the second. But Breachkan wasn't worried, for he knew that the one made from virgins' hair would keep him safe.

But on the third day it too snapped, sending the prince to his death. It seems that some of the virgins from whom the hair had come were not as innocent as they had made out.

The whirlpool almost claimed the life of the writer **George Orwell** who lived in a cottage, Barnhill, on the north of the island while writing his novel *1984*. One day in 1947, Orwell (real name Eric Blair) had taken a day off from writing to sail with his nephews and nieces. They ventured too close to the whirlpool and their boat was sucked under the water. Fortunately, Orwell and the youngsters managed to reach a small rock where they were later picked up by a fishing boat.

COLONSAY AND ORONSAY
40 miles W of Inveraray in the Atlantic Ocean

| 🏛 Sanctuary Cross | 🌿 Kiloran Valley |
| 🌿 Colonsay House | 🏛 Oronsay Priory |

The twin islands of Colonsay and Oronsay are separated by an expanse of sand called The Strand, which can be walked across at low tide. Half way across the strand are the remains of the **Sanctuary Cross**. Any law-breaker from Colonsay who passed beyond it and stayed on Oronsay for a year and a day could escape punishment. Colonsay is the bigger of the two islands, and has a ferry service connecting its

main village of Scalasaig to Oban.

It is a beautiful place, full of rocky or sandy coves and areas of fertile ground. Perhaps the most beautiful part is **Kiloran Valley**, which is sheltered and warm. So warm that palm trees and bamboo grow quite happily here. It is where **Colonsay House** stands. It is said that the builder, Malcolm MacNeil, used stones from an old chapel that stood close by when building the house in 1722. Its gardens are open to the public.

Oronsay is famous for the substantial ruins of **Oronsay Priory**, perhaps the most important monastic ruins in the west of Scotland after Iona. Tradition gives us two founders. The first is St Oran, companion to St Columba, who is said to have founded it in 563AD. The second is St Columba himself. When he left Ireland, the story goes, he alighted first on Colonsay, and then crossed over to Oronsay where he established a small monastery. However, he had made a vow that he would never settle where he could still see the coastline of Ireland. He could from Oronsay, so he eventually moved on to Iona.

John, Lord of the Isles, founded the present priory in the early 14th century, inviting Augustinian canons from Holyrood Abbey in Edinburgh to live there. The church is 15th century, and the well-preserved cloisters date from the 16th century. A series of large carved grave slabs can be seen within the Prior's House, and in the graveyard is the early 16th-century Oronsay Cross, intricately carved, and carrying the words *'Colinus, son of Christinus MacDuffie'*. Another cross can be found east of the Prior's Chapel, with a carving of St John the Evangelist at its head.

EILEACH AN NAOIMH
29 miles W of Inveraray in the Atlantic Ocean

This small island is part of the Garvellochs,

and is famous for its ancient ecclesiastical remains dating from the Dark Ages, which include chapels, beehive cells and an ancient graveyard. A monastery was founded here in about 542AD by St Brendan, better known as Brendan The Navigator. This was before St Columba founded the monastery on Iona. In the 10th century the monastery was destroyed by Norsemen, and the island has remained unihabited since then. It is reputed to be the burial place of both Brendan and Columba's mother, Eithne. There is no ferry service to Eileach an Naoimh.

Bridge Across the Atlantic, Seil

SEIL AND LUING
9 miles S of Oban on the B844

- 🏛 Bridge Across the Atlantic
- 🏛 House of Trousers
- 🌿 An Cala Garden
- 🏛 Ellenabeich Heritage Centre
- 🏛 Easdale Island Folk Museum

These two islands are known as the slate isles due to the amount of slate that was quarried here at one time. Seil is a genuine island, but is connected to the mainland by the **Bridge Across the Atlantic**, designed by Thomas Telford and built in 1792. It is more properly called the Clachan Bridge, with the channel below being no more than a few yards wide. It is a high, hump-back bridge to allow fishing boats to pass beneath.

It got its nickname because at one time it was the only bridge in Scotland to connect an island with the mainland. Now the more recent Skye Bridge dwarfs it. On the west side of the bridge, on the island itself, is a late 17th-century inn called the Tigh na Truish, or **House of Trousers**. This recalls when the wearing of the kilt was forbidden in the aftermath of the Jacobite Uprising. The islanders, before crossing onto the mainland by ferry, which preceded the bridge, would change out of their kilts here and into trousers.

On the west coast of the island is the village of Ellenabeich with, facing it, the small island of Easdale. Ellenabeich was itself an island at one time, but the narrow channel separating it from the mainland was gradually filled up with waste from the local slate quarries. One of the biggest quarries was right on the shoreline, with its floor 80 feet below the water line. It was separated from the sea by a wall of rock. During a great storm, the wall was breached and the quarry filled with water. Now it is used as a harbour for small craft.

An Cala Garden dates from the 1930s, and is behind a row of cottages that was turned into one home. There are meandering streams, terracing built from the local slate, and wide lawns. A 15-feet-high wall of grey brick protects the garden from the worst of the gales that occasionally blow in from the Atlantic.

One of the former quarries' cottages in the village has been turned into the **Ellenabeich Heritage Centre** with a number of displays connected with the slate industry.

Offshore lies the small island of Easdale, connected to Ellenabeich by a small passenger ferry. This too was a centre of slate quarrying, and in the **Easdale Island Folk Museum** you can see what life was like when the industry flourished. It was founded in 1980 by the then owner of the island, Christopher Nicolson.

On Seil's southern tip is the small ferry port of Cuan, where a ferry plies backwards and forwards to Luing, to the south. This is a larger island than Seil, though is more sparsely populated. Here too slate quarrying was the main industry. It is a quiet, restful place where seals can be seen basking on the rocks, as well as eagles and otters. Above the clachan of Toberonochy are the ruins of Kilchattan Chapel, complete with slate gravestones. One commemorates a Covenanter called Alex Campbell.

KERRERA
1 mile W of Oban, in Loch Linnhe

🏛 Gylen Castle

Offshore from Oban is the small rocky island of Kerrera, which can be reached by passenger ferry from a point about two miles south of the town. At the south end of the island are the ruins of 16th-century **Gylen Castle**, another former MacDougall stronghold. It was built by Duncan MacDougall, brother (or son) of the clan chief, Dougal McDougall. It was sacked by a Covenanting army under General Leslie in 1647 and all the inhabitants were slaughtered.

LISMORE
7 miles N of Oban, in Loch Linnhe

🏛 Commann Eachdraidh Lios Mor	
🏛 Lismore Cathedral	🏛 St Moluag
🏛 Tirefour Castle	🏛 Achadun Castle
🏛 Coeffin Castle	

Lismore is a small island, no more than a mile and a half wide at its widest and ten miles long. It's name means great garden, and it is a low-lying, fertile island connected to Oban by a daily ferry. The main village and ferry terminal is Achnacroish, though a smaller pedestrian ferry plies between Port Appin on the mainland and the north of the island in summer. In the village is the **Commann Eachdraidh Lios Mor** (Lismore Historical Society), situated in an old cottage that re-creates the living conditions of the past.

Lismore, before the Reformation, was the centre of the diocese of Argyll. **Lismore Cathedral** stood at Kilmoluaig, near the small village of Clachan. It was destroyed just after the Reformation, but the choir walls were lowered and incorporated into the present church in 1749. The site had been a Christian one for centuries, and was where St Moluag set up a small monastery in 564AD.

Lismore was a prized island even in those days, and it seems that **St Moluag** and another Celtic saint, St Mulhac, had a quarrel about who should found a monastery there. They finally agreed to a race across from the mainland in separate boats, with the first one touching the soil of Lismore being allowed to establish a monastery. As the boats were approaching the shore, Moluag realised that he was going to lose, so took a dagger, cut off one of his fingers and threw it onto the beach. As he was the first to touch the soil of the island, he was allowed to build his monastery.

This was supposed to have taken place at Tirefour, where there are the remains of a broch now called **Tirefour Castle**, whose walls still stand to a height of 16 feet.

On the west coast of the island, facing the tiny Bernera Island, are the ruins of the 13th-century **Achadun Castle**, where the Bishops of Argyll lived up until the 16th century, and further up the coast are the remains of **Coeffin Castle**, built by the MacDougalls in the 13th century.

The highest point on the island, at a mere 412 feet, is Barr Morr (meaning 'big tip'), but from the top there is a wonderful panoramic view in all directions.

MULL

8 miles W of Oban, in the Atlantic Ocean

🏛 Torosay Castle	🐦 Wings Over Mull	
🏛 Duart Castle	🎬 Chief MacLean	
🐦 William Black	🏛 Moy Castle	🏛 Mull Museum
🏛 Macquarie's Mausoleum	🏛 St Kenneth's Chapel	
🐦 Diana Mitford	🏞 Mackinnon's Cave	
🏛 Hebridean Whale & Dolphin Trust		

🎬 San Juan de Sicilia	🏛 Aros Castle	
🎨 Mull Little Theatre	🏛 Old Byre Heritage Centre	
🏞 Carsaig Arches	🏛 Ross of Mull Historical Centre	

The island of Mull, with more than 300 miles of coastline and 120 miles of roads, is the third largest island in Scotland (only Lewis/Harris and Skye are bigger). Within its 87,535 hectares is a wild divergence of scenery, from rugged coastline to pasture and high mountains. The soils are, unlike some other rugged islands off Scotland's west coast, very fertile, so there is very little heather in the late summer and early autumn. However, it is still one of the most beautiful islands in the country, and it has the added advantage of being easy to reach, as a car ferry plies between the pier at Craignure and Oban all day.

On its north east side Mull is separated from Morvern on the mainland by the Sound of Mull, a deep sea trench that offers some of the best diving in Scotland. So much so that sometimes the wrecks can get very crowded with divers! One of the favourite dives is to the *Hispania*, sunk in 1954 and now sitting at a depth of 30 metres. She was sailing to Sweden

Torosay Castle & Gardens

Torosay, Craignure,
Isle of Mull PA65 6AY
Tel: 01680 812421
e-mail: torosay@aol.com

A beautiful and welcoming Victorian family home surrounded by 12 acres of spectacular gardens. Visitors are invited to wander round principal rooms, in a relaxed atmosphere and browse through family scrapbooks, memorabilia and portraits.

The woodland garden with pool, is home to a wide collection of smaller gardens; Alpine garden, Rhododendron collection, Eucalyptus walk, old walled garden, rock and bog gardens and the Japanese Garden with its impressive sea view.

Torosay is a working farm so why not keep the children entertained and introduce them to some of the natives – our herd of pedigree highland cattle!

🎬 stories and anecdotes 🐦 famous people 🎨 art and craft 🎨 entertainment and sport 🚶 walks

from Liverpool with a cargo of steel and asbestos when she hit Sgeir Mor reef. A story is told that the captain refused to leave the sinking ship, thinking that he might be blamed for the accident. As the crew were rowing to safety in high seas, the last they saw of him was a figure standing on the ship saluting as it slowly submerged.

Another, unusual, wreck is of the *Rondo*. It sits vertically beneath the water, and though it is in two parts, its bow is 50 metres below the surface, embedded in the sea bed, and its stern just six metres below the surface.

The island's name comes from the Gaelic Meall, meaning a rounded hill. It is steeped in history, and was known to the Romans and Greeks. Even Ptolemy wrote about it, calling it Maleus. The highest peak, at 3140 feet, is Ben More, the island's only Munro (a Scottish mountain above 3000 feet).

The island is home to 816 species of plants and trees, including 56 varieties of ferns, 247 varieties of seaweed, 22 species of orchid and 1787 species of fungi. This diversity has made it popular with botanists, who visit the island throughout the year. In April, many parts of Mull are carpeted with bluebells with Grasspoint, a few miles south of Craignure, being a favourite place to see them. Mull is also famous for its primroses.

Its wildlife is just as diverse. You can see birds of prey such as golden eagles, sea eagles and buzzards (the UK's commonest bird of prey), as well as polecats, mountain hares, badgers, pine martens, adders, slow worms, otters, mink (that escaped from captivity) and red squirrels. The lonely coastal cliffs are home to wild goats. Take a sea trip and you can see bottlenose dolphins, porpoises, seals and even Minke whales.

Close to Craignure is **Torosay Castle** (see panel on page 313) with its spectacular gardens. The castle sits in 12 acres of grounds, and is a fine Victorian mansion built in 1858 to the designs of David Bryce in the Scottish Baronial style. The walls of the front hall are crowded with red deer antlers. Though it is open to the public, Torosay is still the family home of the Guthrie Jones family, who live on the upper floors. It was a favourite place of Winston Churchill in his younger years, and on display are photographs of him in the grounds. The castle is open to the public from April to October, while the gardens are open all year round. From the castle grounds a miniature railway connects Torosay to nearby Craignure.

Wings Over Mull is at Auchnacroish House, close to the castle, and brooded over by the island's second highest mountain, Dun da Ghaoithe. It is a conservation centre for birds of prey, with owls being especially well represented, though you can also see hawks, kites, eagles and even vultures. There are flying demonstrations every day during the season, and a display on the history of falconry.

The Mull and West Highland Railway, a one-and-a-quarter mile long narrow gauge line, connects the castle with the pier. It has a gauge of 26cm, and was opened in 1984 specifically to link the pier at Craignure with Torosay Castle. It passes through woodland and coastal scenery, and at one point it even crosses over a peat bog, which brought special problems when it was being built. The tiny engines that pull the carriages are a mixture of steam and diesel, with possibly the *Lady of the Isles* being the prettiest of the lot. It was the first engine on the line, though there are now six operating.

To the east of Torosay Castle, on a small promontory, is **Duart Castle**, perched on the cliffs above Duart Point. It is the ancestral home of the Macleans, and still houses the clan chief. Parts of it go back to the 13th century, though it is such a well defended position that there was certainly a fort here long before that. The keep dates from the 14th century, and was built by Lachlan Lubanach Maclean. The buildings in the courtyard were added in the 16th century by Lachlan Mor (Great Lachlan). In 1688 the castle was sacked by the Campbells.

Duart Castle, Isle of Mull

Duart was confiscated after Culloden, as the Macleans had fought alongside Charles Edward Stuart, but in 1911 the 26th MacLean chief, Sir Fitzroy MacLean, bought it back and restored it. Maclean means son of Gillean, who is better remembered as Gillean of the Battleaxe. The name means follower, or servant, of John, and he was said to have descended from the ancient kings of Dalriada. The Macleans of Duart had the world's first recorded tartan - the Hunting Duart.

Some Maclean chieftains were unsavoury characters. The 11th chief was one such man. He detested his wife, as she could not provide him with an heir. Unfortunately for **Chief Maclean**, she was a sister of the Earl of Argyll, the most powerful man in the Western Highlands. Maclean hatched a plot. In 1497, he had her tied up and marooned on a rocky island below the castle that flooded at each high tide. He left her there for a whole night, and next morning noted that she had gone. Seemingly distraught, he later reported her sad death to the earl, saying that she had been washed out to sea and drowned.

The Earl was sympathetic and overcome with emotion. He immediately invited him to his castle in Inveraray and, when the chief got there, he discovered his wife alive and well and seated at the top of the table beside her brother. A passing fisherman had rescued her. Nothing was said during the chief's visit, and the meal passed pleasantly, with much small talk and smiles all round. Maclean and his wife eventually went home together, and still nothing was said. By this time the chief was terrified, as he knew that retribution would eventually come. However, the event was never mentioned again, even by Maclean's wife, and when she eventually died of natural causes, the chief heaved a great sigh of relief. He married again, and his second wife died also of natural causes, again without bearing him an heir. So he married a third time, his new wife eventually giving birth to a son. After the birth, in 1527, Maclean had to go to Edinburgh on business. While there, he was murdered in mysterious circumstances and for no apparent reason. Retribution had come 30 years after the event.

Near Duart Point is the William Black Memorial, erected in memory of the 19th-century writer **William Black,** who died in 1898. He wrote such books as *Macleod of Dare*, *A Princess of Thule* and *Prince Fortunatus*. They were extremely popular in their day, though they are hardly ever read now. However, a new version of *Macleod of Dare* was recently published.

A single track road leaves the A849 at Strathcoil, and heads south and then east towards Lochbuie. **Moy Castle** sits on the shore of Loch Buie, 10 miles south west of Craignure, at the head of a small track leaving the A849 at Strathcoil. This was the family seat of the Macleans of Lochbuie, and was built in the 15th century. Inside is a dungeon that floods twice a day with the incoming tide. In the middle of the dungeon is a stone platform where the prisoners had to huddle to keep dry. Because of ongoing restoration work it is not possible to view the interior.

A small island a few miles to the south, off the coast, has possibly the most unusual name of any island in the Western Isles - Frank Lockwood's Island. It was named after the

brother-in-law of a Maclean of Duart in the 19th century. During the Jacobite Uprising in 1745, the castle on the island was garrisoned by a troop of Campbells. In 1752 it was finally abandoned, and though it is still in a fine state of preservation, it is not open to the public. Close to the castle is one of the very few stone circles on Mull. There are nine stones, with the circle having a diameter of 35 feet.

To the west of Craignure, on the A849, is Fishnish Pier, where a ferry connects the island to Lochaline on the mainland, across the Sound of Mull. At Salen the road becomes the A848, and if you turn southwest along the B8035 you can visit **Macquarie's Mausoleum** at Gruline, where lies Major General Lachlan Macquarie, Governor General of New South Wales between 1809 and 1820, and sometimes called the Father of Australia. It is a square, cottage-like building of local stone surrounded by a high wall. Also buried there is his wife Elizabeth and their son, also called Lachlan. Born on the island of Ulva in 1762, Macquarie joined the army at he age of 14 and quickly rose through the ranks, serving in America, Egypt, Nova Scotia and India. In April 1809 he was appointed Governor of New South Wales. However, he suffered frequent bouts of ill health, and in 1820 he resigned, having turned New South Wales from a penal colony into a prosperous state.

He died in London in 1824, and his wife built the memorial above his grave in 1834. Now it is owned and maintained by the National Trust of Australia. In the year 2000, the Australian

Waterfall, Isle of Mull

MULL POTTERY

Baliscate Estate, Tobermory,
Isle of Mull PA75 6QA
Tel/Fax: 01688 302347
e-mail: info@mull.pottery.com
website: www.mullpottery.com

Located just outside the picturesque town of Tobermory, **Mull Pottery** makes high-fired, hand-thrown ceramics, the designs of which are inspired by the landscapes and seascapes of Scotland's rugged west coast.

All the pottery is made by skilled craftspeople who are dedicated to producing pieces that are beautiful and unique. The pottery makes all its own glazes, and refines its own clay to a secret recipe that was first used in 1982. If you visit the well-stocked gallery, you can see the pots being made in the workshop before choosing a pot from the complete range of products on display. Seconds at bargain prices, and the work of other craftspeople can also be purchased. Crafts showcased here include glassware, textiles, jewellery prints, original paintings and other ceramics. The gallery was recently awarded a 4-star shopping award from Visit Scotland.

After you've made your purchase, why not relax in the Mull Pottery's licensed Café/Restaurant which has an outdoor balcony with fantastic views overlooking the Sound of Mull. The restaurant serves great snacks, meals and drinks using the pottery's own tableware. There is local seafood, game and farm produce, as well as great Costa coffee, tea and home baking.

---

government spent $A70,000 on its refurbishment. So famous was he in Australia that there are many towns, schools, universities, streets and even teashops named after him.

At this point Mull is no more than three miles wide, thanks to Loch na Keal, which drives deep into the island in a north easterly direction. Its shores are famous for their bird life, particularly ducks, which includes wigeon, Slavonian grebe, teal, goldeneye, mallard, black-throated diver and shelduck. At the entrance to the sea loch is the 130-acre island of Inch Kenneth. Curiously enough, its geology is unlike that of Mull, and it is flat and fertile. The 'Kenneth' in question is supposed to be St Cannoch, a contemporary of St Columba. The ruins of **St Kenneth's Chapel** date from the 13th century, and in the kirkyard are many wonderfully carved grave slabs. A tradition says that ancient Scottish kings were buried here if the weather was too rough for the royal barges to travel to Iona. One of the best grave slabs is that of an armed man lying with his head on a cushion and his feet on an unnamed animal of some kind. In one hand is a cannonball and in the other a shield. The shield once had a coat of arms on it, but it has long since been weathered away.

Inch Kenneth was a favourite haunt of **Diana Mitford,** whose father Lord Redesdale owned the island. She married the infamous Oswald Mosley, leader of the British Nazi party. When her sister Unity was recovering from a suicide bid (she had tried to shoot herself in the head), she stayed on the island until she died of meningitis, brought on by the shooting, in 1948.

Another owner at one time was Sir Harold

🎬 stories and anecdotes 🐚 famous people 🎨 art and craft 🎭 entertainment and sport 🥾 walks

Boulton, who wrote perhaps the most famous Jacobite song ever - *The Skye Boat Song*. Many people believe it is a traditional song, but it was written in 1884.

When Johnson and Boswell were making their Highland tour in the 18th century, they were entertained on the island by Sir Alan Maclean, chief of the Macleans of Duart. Johnson described it as a 'pretty little island' - praise indeed from a man who disliked most things Scottish.

Mull only has two large fresh water lochs. One is the wonderfully named Loch Ba, close to Gruline, which has the remains of a crannog. The other, Loch Frisa, sits in inaccessible country in the north west of the island and is famous for its bird life. Like Loch Ba, it has some good fishing.

Mackinnon's Cave, on the Ardmeanach Peninsula near Balnahard, can only be reached at low tide, and great care should be taken if you visit. The cave goes hundreds of feet into the cliff face, and you'll need a torch if you want to explore it. It was visited by Dr Johnson, and is said to be the largest cave in the Hebrides, being over 90 feet high. A legend tells of a piper and his dog entering the cave, and while the piper was killed by a witch who lived there, his dog escaped. At the back of the cave is Fingal's Table, a flat rock used as an altar by early Celtic saints. Also on the Ardmeanach Peninsula is McCulloch's Tree, a huge fossil over 36 feet high and three feet in diameter. It is believed to be over 50 million years old. There is another fossil in a nearby cave. Part of the land here, including the fossils, is owned by the National Trust for Scotland. The cave can be reached by a track that branches off the A849. To the south of the Ardmeanach Peninsula is Loch Scridain, the largest of the island's sea lochs. Like other locations on Mull, it is famous for its bird life.

Tobermory, Mull's capital, sits on the A848 to the north west of the island. Its name means 'Mary's Well', and it is an attractive small burgh with many brightly-painted houses and buildings fronting Tobermory Bay. Up until 1788 it was a small village, but in that year a fishing station was established that changed its fortunes forever. The houses date from that time, though they were not painted until many years later. St Mary's Well, which gave its name to the town, can be found in Dervaig Road. At one time its waters were thought to

Tobermory, Isle of Mull

have healing qualities.

Tobermory is the setting for the popular children's TV programme *Balamory,* though the houses you see on the programme are even more brightly painted than the real ones thanks to the magic of television. **Mull Museum** is situated in the Columba building in Main Street, and has displays explaining the history of the island. There is also a small exhibition explaining Boswell and Dr Johnson's visit in 1773. Also in Main Street is the headquarters of the **Hebridean Whale and Dolphin Trust**, a research, education and conservation charity. There is a small visitors centre with displays on whales and dolphins. Here you can watch videos of whales and dolphins in the Hebrides, as well as, in some cases, listen to their 'songs'. The Tobermory Distillery is the only distillery on the island, and is one of the oldest in Scotland. It dates

from 1798, when a local merchant called John Sinclair was granted a license to distil spirit from the local grain. It now makes five distinct single malts; there is a visitor centre and shop.

At the bottom of Tobermory Bay lies the famous wreck of the 800-ton **San Juan de Sicilia**, (though some say it was the *Florida*) part of the Spanish Armada fleet. Fleeing in September 1588 from the English ships, she anchored in the bay to repair her hull and take on provisions. Being part of the Spanish fleet that had tried to attack Scotland's old enemy England, the local people made her welcome. Donald Maclean of Duart Castle agreed to supply the ship with provisions if its captain agreed to pay for them and give him 100 soldiers to attack his enemies on Coll. The Spanish captain agreed, and provisions were taken on board while repairs were carried out. However, Maclean suspected that the captain

ULVA HOUSE

Tobermory, Isle of Mull PA75 6PR
Tel/Fax: 01688 302044
e-mail: info@ulva-house.co.uk
website: www.ulva-house.co.uk

Built in 1864 by a successful businessman as a wedding present for his daughter, **Ulva House** occupies a superb location in an acre of ground in the conservation area of Tobermory with breathtaking views over the harbour, the distant mountains and the town. Ulva House, the owners' private residence, now offers a choice of exclusive self-catering accommodation, all within easy walking distance of the busy fishing harbour, pubs and restaurants.

Ulva Cottage (4 Star) is detached and situated within the gardens of Ulva House and has been completely renovated. It sleeps up to 6 guests in 3 bedrooms. Columba Apartment (5 Star) is luxurious, with period style furniture and original paintings, an open fire and spa bath and opens to the garden terrace. Shuna Apartment (4 Star), is in a modern, contemporary style and is on the first floor. Both apartments can accommodate 2 people and both has its own private exterior door and open views and offer total relaxation in a quite, private location, yet only minutes from the sea front.

would try to sail from the harbour without honouring his part of the bargain. He therefore boarded the ship and blew it up, making good his own escape. She sank in 60 feet of water, taking 350 Spaniards with her. Stories started to circulate that she had 30 million gold ducats aboard her, and though some items were recovered (which can now be seen in the local museum), successive dives to locate the ducats failed. The first dive was in the early 17th century, when the Earl of Argyll sent men down to the wreck. Successive dives, including one by the Royal Navy, have recovered small items such as a skull, cannon shot, pieces of wood and even a gold coin. Another rumour had it that the ducats had actually been recovered in secret, and lay hidden at Aros Castle. Sir Walter Scott owned a writing case made of wood from the wreck, and it is said that the

Queen owns a snuff box made from the ships wood. The ship now lies completely covered in silt, and it is unlikely that anything will ever be recovered from her again.

Protecting Tobermory Bay is Calve Island, close to which there is plenty of good diving. Tobermory has one of the island's three ferry links with the mainland, this one plying to Kilchoan on the Ardnamurchan Peninsula.

Glengorm Castle lies a few miles west of Tobermory, at the end of a single track road. It was built in 1860 for local landowner James Forsyth, who instigated the Clearances in the area, removing crofters from their land and replacing them with the more profitable sheep. The castle is not open to the public, though there is both a flower garden and a market garden here where you can buy plants and vegetables. There is also a coffee shop. At Bloody Bay, about a mile east of the castle, a

ISLE OF MULL CHEESE

Sgriob-ruadh Farm Dairy, Tobermory, Isle of Mull,
Scotland PA75 6QD
Tel: 01688 302235 Fax: 01688 302546
e-mail: mull.cheese@isleofmullcheese.co.uk
website: www.isleofmullcheese.co.uk

The home of 'Isle of Mull Cheese' is a small family farm situated on the beautiful Isle of Mull, off the west coast of Scotland. Isle of Mull Cheddar (also known as Reade's Cheddar) is the pride of Scotland and the Scots' cheddar of choice. An unforgettable bite and slightly bitter finish distinguishes this cheese from English cheddars. The texture and flavour are rich.

Fine cheese, of course, cannot be made with out the very best of milk. No cheese is made with fresher milk than that used at Sgriob-ruadh Farm. Here, in the morning, as the cows are milked, their milk is taken directly from the milking parlour to the cheese-making vat. The Isle's cattle feed on the spent barley from the whiskey-making process - essentially a high-protein cattle feed - and it shows in this cheese's distinct overtones of peat and smoke.

Visitors to the Farm are always most welcome. You can watch the cows being milked, inspect the cheeses in the underground cellar or simply relax over a Ploughman's lunch in the Garden Barn. Those who know Isle of Mull will tell you that of all the Scottish Islands it is the most beautiful - discover some of its magic and mystery through its cheese!

🏛 historic building   🏛 museum and heritage   🏛 historic site   ꕯ scenic attraction   🌱 flora and fauna

battle was fought in 1480 between the last Lord of the Isles and the mighty Crawford and Huntly families, aided by the Lord of the Isle's son Angus.

The ruins of **Aros Castle** lie a mile or so north west of the village of Salen, south east of Tobermory. They date mainly from the 13th and 14th centuries. Originally built by the MacDougalls, it later became the Mull base for the Lords of the Isles, and was the most important place on the island up until the mid 18th century. In 1608, clan chiefs were invited to the castle by Lord Ochiltree, lieutenant to James VI. The chiefs, suspecting nothing, boarded Ochiltree's ship, *The Moon*, and sat down to dine. However, Ochiltree had an ulterior motive. He calmly stood up and announced that they were all prisoners of the king, as they had plotted against James VI and were rebellious and disloyal. The chiefs tried to leave the ship, but it was too late. It had weighed anchor and was now sailing south. The chiefs were later imprisoned in Blackness, Stirling and Dumbarton castles until they agreed to swear undying loyalty to the king.

The narrow B8073 rises up from Tobermory and passes through Dervaig, said to be the loveliest village on the island. It is home to the 38-seat **Mull Little Theatre**, which puts on a season of plays every year to packed audiences. According to the Guinness Book of Records, it is the smallest professional working theatre in the world. It opened in 1966 in the converted coach house of a Free Church manse and was established by Barrie and Marianne Hesketh, professional actors who had settled on Mull to bring up their children. Now it not only presents plays within the tiny theatre, it tours the Highlands and Islands as well.

stories and anecdotes famous people art and craft entertainment and sport walks

TURUS MARA

Penmore Mill, Dervaig,
Isle of Mull PA75 6QS
Tel/Fax: 01688 400242/297
e-mail: info@turusmara.com
website: www.turusmara.com

Wildlife & Seabird Cruise-tours   **Turus Mara.**   Treshnish Isles ~ Staffa ~ Iona

The waters and islands around the Isle of Mull are astonishingly rich in wildlife and **Turus Mara** provides the opportunity to explore this natural wonderland. During the season, there are daily landing cruises from Ulva Ferry to Staffa and the Treshnish Isles Seabird and Seal Sanctuary. Lunga, largest of the Treshnish Isles, has one of the most varied and accessible seabird colonies on the Western Seaboard. Dun Cruit (the Harp Rock stack), is home to more than 6000 guillemot, razorbill, puffin, kittiwake, fulmar, shag, skua and many more. The puffins are so tame you can get very close to them without frightening them. Owner Iain Morrison says "We provide a unique therapy in puffin watching at close quarters. This is much cheaper than a shrink!"

Passengers land on the world renowned Island of Staffa to experience the unique and awesome wonder of Fingal's Cave. It takes little imagination to hear Mendelssohn's music amongst the massive basaltic columns which create this natural cathedral. Amongst the many possible sightings on your day's journey on the edge of the Atlantic are Golden and Sea Eagles, otters, whales, basking sharks, dolphins and porpoises - and the scenery is second to none,

Another trip takes in both Staffa and Iona, "The Sacred Isle", historic cradle of Christianity. Passengers can visit the Abbey, wander in the ruined Benedictine Nunnery and the Rielig Oran, burial place of 48 Scottish kings, including the infamous Macbeth and numerous French, Irish and Norwegian monarchs.

An alternative option is a cruise to Staffa and the island of Ulva which is a paradise of tranquil woodland walks and unspoilt scenery. It's large enough to get lost in but without modern trappings. Here you can see otters, seals, red deer and some of the 100 + bird species that have been recorded on the island.

Turus Mara, which means "sea journey", has more than 30 years experience in operating these cruises. The company offer a cultural aspect to their cruises. It is one of few tourism activity operations run by an indigenous family – part of the commentary will usually be in Gaelic, the original language of the West Highlands and Islands of Scotland. Sailings are from Easter to October, subject to weather conditions.

The B8073 continues on to the small village of Calgary, on Calgary Bay. The name in Gaelic means the harbour by the dyke, the dyke being a natural basalt formation, which can still be seen. Here you will find what is possibly the best beach on the island, with vast stretches of white sand. In 1883, Colonel J F Macleod of the Royal North West Mounted Police holidayed in Calgary, and was so impressed by the scenery that he named the Canadian city after it.

At the **Old Byre Heritage Centre**, which is about a mile from the village, Mull's visitors can learn about the island's history and heritage. There are also displays on natural history, and a half-hour video.

The road continues in a south-easterly direction along the shores of Loch Tuath, giving views across to the islands of Ulva, visited by Boswell and Johnson in 1773, and Gometra. The ancestors of David Livingstone, the African explorer and missionary, came from Ulva. From the 10th century until the 19th century, when it was sold to pay off debts, the island was owned by the MacQuarries. When Boswell and Johnson visited Ulva, they were entertained by the then MacQuarrie chief. Though they found their host to be a charming, intelligent man, Boswell wrote that the house was 'mean', and that the chief was burdened with debts. At one time, there was a popular piping school on the island.

To summon the privately-owned ferry to Ulva, visitors slide back a small white panel to uncover a red panel that can be seen from the island. At the ferry point on the island is the small Ulva Heritage Centre, housed in a restored thatched cottage, with attached tearoom. To the west of Ulva is the smaller

CALGARY HOTEL

Calgary, Isle of Mull PA75 6QW
Tel: 01688 400256
e-mail: calgary.hotel@virgin.net website: www.calgary.co.uk

Now in its 21st year, the **Calgary Hotel** has been created out of farmsteadings and is just up the hill from the stunning white sands of Calgary Bay. This small family hotel occupies a truly idyllic location, flanked by mature woodland to the east and west, and Calgary Bay to the south.

The hotel accommodation comprises 10 comfortable rooms, each individually designed in a modern, but cosy style. Some of the rooms have views out over woodland towards the beach, as do the lounge terrace and restaurant. As an alternative to these rooms, the Calgary Cottages provide contemporary-styled self-catering accommodation. The hotel lounge is cosy and warm, with a wood-burning stove and separate TV room. The Dovecote is a unique restaurant with ash and elm tables handcrafted by a local artist and woodworkers. The restaurant serves quality local and Scottish produce daily, with local shellfish being a speciality.

Across from the farm square there is an Art Gallery and Tearoom, and also an Art Gallery with visitor centre and carving studio - a good source of local artwork. A Sculpture Trail through mature woodland leads down to the beach with plenty of wild flowers and sculptures to discover along the way.

island of Gometra, connected to Ulva by a causeway. It has been uninhabited since 1983, though Gometra House can still be seen. Since early times, Gometra was owned by the monastery of Iona, and indeed was known as Iona's granary on account of the crops grown there. Later it was acquired by the Campbells when James VI abolished the title of Lord of the Isles.

The B8073 then swings northeast along the northern shores of Loch na Keal before joining the B8035, which, if you turn right, takes you along the southern shore of Loch na Keal and on to the A849.

The Treshnish Islands are a small chain of islands well to the west of Gometra. The main islands are Lunga, Fladda, Bac Mor, Cairn na Burgh Mor and Cairn na Burgh Beg. Now uninhabited, they are a haven for wildlife, with Lunga especially being a favourite nesting site for puffins, shags, guillemots, razorbills and kittiwakes. On Cairn na Burgh are early Viking and Iron Age fortifications. Autumn is the breeding season for grey Atlantic seals, and many can be seen on all the islands' beaches at that time. Boat trips to the Treshnish Islands leave from various ports on Mull and from Iona.

Pennyghael, gateway to the Ross of Mull, sits just off the A849, on the way to Fionnphort and the ferry for Iona. Nearby is the Beaton Cairn, which commemorates the hereditary doctors of the Lord of the Isles. A narrow road branches south at Pennyghael, taking you to the southern shore of the Ross of Mull at Carsaig. If you walk westwards along the beach you will reach the Nun's Cave, which has Celtic Christian carvings. The cave got its name because the nuns of Iona Nunnery are supposed to have hidden here during the Reformation. The spectacular

Carsaig Arches is further on, at Malcolm's Point. They were once caves, but the sea has eroded the 600-feet high cliffs behind them and left the arches standing.

Bunessan, nine miles west of Pennyghael, sits on the small Loch na Lathaich, which is a favourite anchorage for small boats and yachts. Next to the village hall, in a Portacabin, is the **Ross of Mull Historical Centre**, which gives information about the history, wildlife and people of the area. At the end of the A849 is Fionnphort (pronounced 'Finnafort', meaning fair port), the ferry terminal for Iona. Before crossing, a visit to the four-star Columba Centre should prepare you for what you'll find on the island. On the shore stands Fingal's Rock, supposedly thrown by the giant Fingal while in a bad temper.

IONA

36 miles W of Oban off the coast of Mull

🏛 Iona Abbey	🏛 Ridge of the Chiefs	
🏛 Ridge of the Kings	🏛 St Oran's Chapel	
🏛 St Mary's Nunnery	🏛 Chapel of St Ronan	
🏛 Iona Heritage Centre		

No tourists' cars are allowed on Iona (National Trust for Scotland), but it is so small (no more than three miles long by a mile and a half wide) that everything on it can easily be visited on foot. It is one of the most sacred spots in Europe (and unfortunately, during the summer months, one of the busiest), and was where St Columba set up his monastery in 563AD. From here, he evangelised the Highlands, converting the Picts to Christianity using a mixture of saintliness, righteous anger and perseverance.

Columba's monastery would have been built of wood and wattle, and little now survives of it apart from some of the cashel, or surrounding wall. The present **Iona Abbey**,

Reilig Odhrain (St Oran's Chapel), Iona

on the site of the original monastery, was founded in 1203 by Reginald, son of Somerled, Lord of the Isles, though the present building is early 16th century. It was a Benedictine foundation, and later became a cathedral. By the 18th century it was roofless, and the cloisters and other buildings were in ruins. In the 20th century they were restored by the Rev George MacLeod, a Church of Scotland minister who went on to found the Iona Community.

Beside the cathedral is the Reilig Odhrain, or St Oran's Cemetery. Within it is the **Ridge of the Chiefs**, which is supposed to contain the bodies of many West Highland chiefs who were buried here in medieval times. Close by is the **Ridge of the Kings**, where, it is claimed, no less than 48 Scottish, eight Norwegian and four Irish kings lie buried, including Macbeth. However, modern historians now doubt if any kings are buried there at all apart from some from ancient Dalriada. They say that the claims were a 'marketing exercise' by the monks to enhance their abbey.

One man who does lie within the cemetery is John Smith the politician, who was buried there in 1994. **St Oran's Chapel**, near the cemetery, was built as a funeral chapel in the 12th century by one of the Lords of the Isles.

The ruins of **St Mary's Nunnery** are near the jetty, and date from the 13th century. It too was founded by Reginald, and he placed his sister Beatrice in charge as prioress. A small museum has been established in the **Chapel of St Ronan** close to the ruins.

Just west of the cathedral is the Tor Ab, a low mound on which St Columba's cell may have been situated. Of the many crosses on the island, the best are the 10th-century St Martin's Cross, outside the main abbey door, and the 16th-century MacLean's Cross.

In the former parish church manse (designed by Telford) is the **Iona Heritage Centre**, which traces the history of the people who have lived on the island throughout the years.

STAFFA
34 miles W of Oban in the Atlantic Ocean

🔾 Fingal's Cave

The most remarkable feature of this small uninhabited island is **Fingal's Cave**, which was visited in August 1829 by the composer Felix Mendelssohn. Though he found Edinburgh delightful, he was less enamoured of the Highlands, which he declared to be full of 'fog and foul weather'. When he made the boat trip to see the cave, he was violently seasick and called the cave 'odious'. However, it later inspired one of his most famous works, the Hebrides Overture. The cliffs are formed from hexagonal columns of basalt that look like wooden staves, some over 50 feet high. The Vikings therefore named the island Stafi Øy (Stave Island) from which it got its modern name. Boat trips to the island are available from Mull and Iona.

COLL AND TIREE

50 miles W of Oban in the Atlantic Ocean

- 🏚 Great Exodus 🜄 Ceann a'Marra
- 🏛 Sandaig Island Life Museum
- 🏛 Skerryvore Lighthouse Museum

These two islands, lying beyond Mull, can be reached by ferry from Oban. They are generally low lying, and can be explored by car in a few hours. The ferry first stops at Arinagiour, Coll's main village before going on to Scarinish on Tiree.

Robert the Bruce granted Coll to Angus Og of Islay, and it was Angus who was responsible for building Breachacha Castle (not open to the public) to the south of the island. Later it was owned by the MacLeans, the MacNeils and the MacDonalds. The present castle, which is largely 15th century, was restored in 1965.

It was in Coll that an incident called the **Great Exodus** took place. In 1856, the southern part of the island, which was the most fertile, was sold to one John Lorne Stewart. In spite of protests from the crofters who farmed there, he raised their rents to a level they could not afford. So the tenants took matters into their own hands. Overnight, they all left their crofts and moved north to the less hospitable lands owned by the Campbells, where the rents were reasonable. Lorne Stewart was powerless to stop them leaving, and was left with no rent income whatsoever.

Tiree means the land of corn, as it is one of the most fertile of the Inner Hebridean islands. It is sometimes called Tir fo Thuinn, meaning the land beneath the waves, because of its relative flatness. Its highest peaks are Ben Hynish (460 feet) and Ben Hough (387 feet). In the south eastern corner of the island is the spectacular headland of **Ceann a'Marra**, with its massive sea cliffs. They are home to thousands of sea birds, and on the shoreline you can often see seals basking in the sun.

Tiree has the reputation of being the sunniest place in Britain, though this is tempered by the fact that it is also the windiest. This has made the island the windsurfing capital of Scotland. Near Vaul to the north east of the island is a curious marked stone called the Ringing Stone, which, when struck, makes a clanging noise. Legend says that if it is ever broken the island will disappear beneath the Atlantic. At Sandaig is the tiny **Sandaig Island Life Museum**, housed in a restored thatched cottage.

The **Skerryvore Lighthouse Museum** at Hynish tells the story of the Skerryvore lighthouse, 10 miles to the south on rocks surrounded by open sea. It was designed by Alan Stevenson, uncle of Robert Louis Stevenson, and completed in 1842. The museum is within houses built for the Skerryvore workers.

SKYE

50 miles NW of Oban in the Atlantic Ocean

- 🏰 Castle Moil 🜄 Cuillin Hills
- 🐦 Skye Serpentarium Reptile World
- 🎨 An Tuireann Art Centre 🏚 Dun Gerashader
- 🜄 Old Man of Storr 🜄 Lealt Falls
- 🜄 Kilt Rock Waterfall 🏛 Staffin Museum
- 🏰 Flodigarry House 🏛 Skye Museum of Island Life
- 🏰 Dunvegan Castle 🏚 Fairy Flag
- 🏛 Colbost Croft Museum 🏛 Glendale Toy Museum
- 🏛 MacCrimmon Piping Heritage Centre
- 🐦 Armadale Castle Gardens 🏛 Museum of the Isles
- 🏰 Dunscaith Castle

The Skye Road Bridge opened in 1995 amid controversy about its tolls, although it is now

---

🏰 historic building 🏛 museum and heritage 🏚 historic site 🜄 scenic attraction 🐦 flora and fauna

Isle of Skye Bridge from Mainland

place names with them.

At Kyleakin, near the bridge, is the Bright Water Visitor Centre, which offers tours to the island nature reserve of Eilean Ban (White Island) beneath the bridge. This was where Gavin Maxwell, author of *Ring of Bright Water*, once lived. Nearby are the ruins of **Castle Moil**, which was a stronghold of Clan Mackinnon. In the 17th century they abandoned the castle and it gradually fell into disrepair.

free. Skye is one of the most beautiful and haunting of the Inner Hebrides, and the place has beauty and history aplenty.

Its name may come from the Norse word skuy, meaning misty, and it is an apt description of an island that seems to get more beautiful the cloudier and mistier it becomes. Another possible derivation of the name is from the Gaelic sgiath, meaning winged, and a glance at a map will show you that the island does indeed look as if it has wings. Nowadays, Gaelic speakers know it as Eileen à Cheo, meaning the Misty Isle. It is one of the few Inner Hebridean islands that has seen an increase in population over the past few years, due to people from the mainland settling here to find a better quality of life.

The island has been inhabited for thousands of years and has many ancient cairns, standing stones, stone circles and burial mounds. St Columba is said to have visited and baptised a Pict there by the name of Artbranan. He was an old man - a chieftain of a Geona tribe - and Columba had to talk to him through an interpreter. Later, the Vikings raided the island, and then settled, bringing many Norse

Perhaps the most famous feature on Skye are the **Cuillin Hills**, a range of mountains in the south east of the island. They are divided into the Black Cuillin and the Red Cuillin. The former are made from hard rock that has been shaped into jagged peaks and ridges by the last Ice Age, while the latter are of soft granite, which has been weathered by wind and rain into softer, more rounded peaks. Though not the highest, they are perhaps the most spectacular mountains in Scotland, and present a challenge to any climber. The highest peak is Sgurr Alasdair, at 3257 feet.

The A87 leaves the Skye Bridge and heads to the west of the island, passing through Broadford, one of its main settlements. At Harrapool is the **Skye Serpentarium Reptile World**, an award winning reptile exhibition. It suffered a serious fire in 2006 in which 149 reptiles perished, but since then it has been re-stocked. There are now more than 50 animals on display, ranging from White's Tree Frogs to Large Green Iguanas.

From Broadford, the road passes through

Duncan·House

Strathaird Steading, Strathaird,
Isle of Skye, IV49 9AX
Tel: 01471 866366 website: www.duncan-house.com

Garth Duncan - Master Goldsmith, maker of fine jewellery, traditional knives, and precious objects. The single track to Elgol is one of Scotlands secret treasures, truely awe inspiring with mountains and sea. If you are not too distracted by the scenery, you will find the Duncan House workshop and Gallery just four miles before Elgol. With all life's many disappointments, this is a promise kept.

Open: 11am-5pm, Monday to Friday and some Saturdays.
During off season please phone ahead to avoid disappointment.

CREELERS OF SKYE

Lower Harrapool, Broadford, Isle of Skye IV49 9AQ
Tel: 01471 822281
e-mail: skyegumbo@aol.com
website: www.skye-seafood-restaurant.co.uk

"The little restaurant with the big reputation"

At **Creelers of Skye** we use the very freshest of local produce to cook the kind of world-class dishes you would expect to find in Nice or Marseille.

Our local seafood is among the very best in the world and most of it finds its way to the top restaurants in London, Paris, Rome and Madrid.

Along with Aberdeen Angus beef, Scottish lamb and Angus chicken, you will find nothing but the very best on your plate at Creelers of Skye.

David Wilson's cooking is famous all over the world and many of our customers return year after year from all points of the planet.

Add to this one of the best wine lists in the north of Scotland, and the fact that we always try to keep prices as low as possible, and you have a truly rare experience. Try our famous traditional Marseille Bouillabaisse and our winter cookery school.

Creelers of Skye is a small, family run restaurant and has been established for 11years.

🏛 historic building 🏛 museum and heritage 🏛 historic site ⛲ scenic attraction 🌿 flora and fauna

Cuillin Hills, Isle of Skye

in 1540 by James V. Before that it was called Kiltaragleann, which in Gaelic means the Church of St Talicarin in the Glen. Across the bay is Ben Tianavaig, which gives good views out towards the island of Raasay. The Aros Experience on Viewfield Road on the south side of the town incorporates a theatre, cinema, shops and exhibition area. **An Tuireann Art Centre**, on Struan Road off the A87 to Uig, is a gallery that presents exhibitions of contemporary art and crafts

The town is the gateway to the Trotternish Peninsula, which juts out for 20 miles into the

Sconser, the southern terminus of a ferry linking Skye to the smaller island of Raasay, before reaching the island's main settlement of **Portree**.

Its name (port an righ, meaning king's harbour) comes from a visit made to the place

BEN TIANAVAIG B&B

5 Bosville Terrace, Portree,
Isle of Skye IV51 9DG
Tel: 01478 612152
e-mail: info@ben-tianavaig.co.uk
website: www.ben-tianavaig.co.uk

Ben Tianavaig B&B occupies a superb position overlooking Portree harbour, Loch Portree, the Red Cuillins and Raasay. The name is a mixture of Gaelic and Norse and means "harbour (vaig) at the foot of the hill (ben)" which owners Bill & Charlotte Johnson feel is very appropriate given their location. They moved to Portree in the summer of 2008 after some years of being holiday visitors to Skye. This means they know from personal experience what the island has to offer and also what's been important to them when staying in a B&B. "We offer a warm friendly welcome; comfortable, clean rooms and a great breakfast! We want our visitors to enjoy Skye and that means making their stay with us a really good one. So, we will also give guests what help they want to plan their stay at Ben Tianavaig." The house has a large dining room on the first floor with great views and there is a selection of maps and books which guests are welcome to use during their stay.

The accommodation at Ben Tianavaig comprises 2 large double rooms upstairs (1 of them a family room) and 2 double/twin rooms on the ground floor. All rooms are en suite and are equipped with television, hairdryer, hospitality tray and a good selection of books. There is wi-fi.
Ben Tianavaig is open all year round.

VANILLA SKYE

1 Wentworth Street, Portree, Isle of Skye IV51 9EJ
Tel: 01478 611295
e-mail: info@vanillaskye.co.uk
website: www.vanillaskye.co.uk

Skye is one of the most beautiful islands, full of dramatic scenery and replete with stirring history. It is also home to **Vanilla Skye** who specialise in exclusive hand-made chocolates. It can be found in Portree and you only have to ask a native of the place for the "chocolate shop" and you'll be directed straight away.

Absolutely no artificial preservatives, colourings or flavourings are used in making the chocolates. They are hand tempered the old fashioned way on marble slabs and the chocolate is poured by hand into moulds and left to set before being filled with Vanilla Skye's own delicious centres. Only high percentage cocoa solids are used in the manufacture of the centres and coverings, making them rich and full of flavour. You are assured of the very best quality, as every stage in the process is carefully watched. All the products will make you mouth water. So, when you're in Portree, you really can't afford to miss Vanilla Skye. The company was established in 2001 and moved to its present premises in 2006. Owner Lesly Harper took advantage of the new building to also sell local produce and other fine Scottish foods.

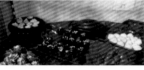

CAFÉ ARRIBA

Quay Brue, Portree, Isle of Skye IV51 9DB
Tel: 01478 611830
e-mail: arriba@cafearriba.co.uk
website: www.cafearriba.co.uk

Café Arriba is a lively bistro/café located in the heart of Portree. Traditional on the outside and modern, funky and smart inside, it is more than just a café - it is a great eating place where creative food and value for money go hand in hand.

By day, you can relax and enjoy great teas and coffees, as well as light snacks and lunches. In the evening, from 6pm onwards during the season, the ambiance changes and it becomes an intimate yet spacious restaurant serving some of the best food on the island. The cuisine is always imaginative and based on local produce wherever possible, and although there is a strong vegetarian influence to many of the dishes, the food is sure to appeal to everyone.

There is always an informal feel to the place and the service is efficient while still remaining friendly. You can choose from a menu or from the specials board which has been known to change two or three times a day as popular dishes run out and are replaced by something else!

Café Arriba is open six days a week from 7am to 10pm in the summer, and from 8am to 5 or 6pm in the winter.

GIVENDALE GUEST HOUSE

Heron Place, Portree, Isle of Skye IV51 9GU
Tel: 01478 612183
e-mail: givendale@gmail.com website: www.givendale.co.uk

Located just a 10-minute walk from Portree town centre, **Givendale Guest House** occupies a stunning position with a great view of the bay and the surrounding countryside. There's a comfortable guest lounge which also enjoys a view of the bay and is equipped with a TV with VHS and DVD systems. The 3-star accommodation comprises 3 rooms with en suite facilities, and a further two rooms which have a private bathroom. In the morning, the much-travelled owner Jurriaan Dijkman offers a choice of Continental or full Scottish breakfast, served in the conservatory overlooking a lovely garden.

THE ISLES INN

Somerled Square, Portree, Isle of Skye IV51 9EH
Tel: 01478 612179
Fax: 01478 612528
e-mail: info@accommodationskye.co.uk
website: www.accommodationskye.co.uk

A charming white-washed building, **The Isles Inn** is located in a quiet corner of Somerled Square, only minutes away from the shops, harbour and the town's swimming pool. The inn is especially noted for the food served in its recently refurbished restaurant which has been decorated in a Jacobean style and offers the best of Highland hospitality. Good food, using locally sourced ingredients wherever possible is served in a true Celtic atmosphere by staff dressed in the family tartan. Diners can enjoy freshly prepared dishes such as Langoustines which were landed on the Pier perhaps ten minutes earlier, or Sconser Scallops hand-dived just down the road and brought straight to your table. There's also Scottish beef and venison, or why not try the local haggis, neeps and tatties. Vegetarians are most certainly not forgotten with choices ranging from creamy home-made lasagne to mushroom tagliatelle and goat's cheese and onion flan. After dinner, why not partake of 'the Golden Spirit of Skye', Talisker Whisky, in the thatched traditional Skye Black Crofthouse Bar in front of a roaring open fire and listen to the live Ceilidh Music which is played throughout the year.

Minch, the sea channel separating the Outer Hebrides from the mainland. A road from Portree follows its coastline right round until it arrives back at the town. **Dun Gerashader**, a prehistoric hill fort, lies about a mile north of Portree just off the A855. The fort still has some of its stone ramparts intact. Also off the A855, about seven miles north of Portree, is the 160-feet-high pinnacle of rock known as the **Old Man of Storr**.

To the north, the **Lealt Falls** are possibly the most spectacular on the island. Though not visible from the road, there is a lay-by where you can park your car, then walk the hundred yards or so to the gorge and the falls themselves. A few miles away is Kilt Rock, a formation of basalt rocks above the shore that resembles the folds of a kilt. **Kilt Rock**

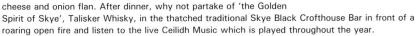

Old Man of Storr, Isle of Skye

North of Staffin, within the grounds of the Flodigarry Country House Hotel, is **Flodigarry House**, where Flora MacDonald and her husband Allan MacDonald settled in 1751. Some people imagine Flora was a simple, Highland lass who helped Charles Edward Stuart, disguised as her Irish maid Betty Burke, cross from the Western

Waterfall, which plunges down some cliffs into the sea, can also be seen here. The village of Staffin has the **Staffin Museum**, famous for its collection of dinosaur bones, the first ever discovered in Scotland. At An Corran, close to Staffin Bay, is a prehistoric rock shelter dating back 8000 years.

Isles to Skye by boat. She came, in fact, from a wealthy family who were tenant farmers on South Uist, though she herself was brought up on Skye and went to school in Edinburgh. Her husband, Allan MacDonald of Kingsburgh, was an officer in the Hanoverian army who later fought on the British side in

🏛 historic building   🏛 museum and heritage   🏛 historic site   ⌘ scenic attraction   🌿 flora and fauna

the American War of Independence.

The sea crossing from Benbecula to Skye is remembered in the famous *Skye Boat Song*. However, it is not, as some people imagine, a traditional Jacobite song. It was written by an Englishman, Sir Harold Boulton, in 1884.

The **Skye Museum of Island Life** at Kilmuir is near the northern tip of the Trotternish Peninsula, and is a group of seven thatched cottages furnished very much as they would have been in the past. Here you can also learn about the crofter rebellions of the 19th century, plus exhibits connected with Charles Edward Stuart and Flora MacDonald.

Loch Chaluim Chille was at one time one of Skye's largest lochs, being over two miles long. It was drained in the early 19th century to create grazing land, and now you can walk across the old loch bed to what used to be islands to see the remains of a Celtic monastery.

Fifteen miles west of Portree along the A850 is Dunvegan, famous for **Dunvegan Castle**, perched above the waters of Loch Dunvegan. It has been the home of Clan MacLeod for 800 years and though much of it is Victorian, parts date back to the 13th century. In the drawing room is the famous **Fairy Flag**, revered by members of Clan MacLeod, which was supposed to bring success in battle. It is one of the Clan's most important possessions, and legends abound about its origins. Experts have examined the flag and say that the cloth is Middle East silk from either Rhodes or Syria. For this reason, some people have connected it to the Crusades. But the fabric dates from about 400AD to 800AD, many years before the

---

HILLCROFT BED & BREAKFAST

2 Treaslane, By Portree, Isle of Skye, IV51 9NX
Tel: 01470 582304
e-mail: hillcroft_skye@btinternet.com
website: www.hillcroftskye.co.uk

Hillcroft is a traditional croft house built circa 1920, which has been extended and modernised over the years. Robin and Janet bought Hillcroft in September 2007 and since then have refurbished the whole house, in particular the bedrooms and ensuites have been updated to provide well appointd guest accommodation. There is a comfortable sitting room with an open fire to sit round if the evenings are chilly, and a bright sunny dining room for morning breakfast. Hillcroft has spectacular views across Loch Snizort beag to the Trotternish hills in the east with glimpses of the spectacular black Cuillin ridge to the south.

Hillcroft is situated on the A850, midway between Portree, the capital of Skye, and Dunvegan with its historic castle, home to the clan MacLeod, and just a few minutes further on you come to the coral beaches passing quite a large seal colony on the way. Hillcroft is just a short walk from the rocky shore line where you can often see seals, otters, cormorants, oyster catchers and herons. The Trotternish ridge, the Quirang and the Old Man of Storr are just a short drive away, and the famous Cuillin is about a 40 minute drive. There is a 9-hole golf course at nearby Skeabost Hotels where a day's fishing can also be arranged, and pony trekking is available at Suledale. For those interested in arts and crafts there is the Edinbane pottery and the galleries and craft shops in Waternish. There are several fine eating places nearby, including The Lodge at Edinbane, Greshornish House, The Stein Inn and The Loch Bay Fish Restaurant, with the renowned Three Chimneys a 20minute drive away.

🎬 stories and anecdotes 🗣 famous people 🎨 art and craft ✏ entertainment and sport 🚶 walks

STEIN INN

Macleod's Terrace, Waternish, Isle of Skye IV55 8GA
Tel: 01470 597362
e-mail: angus.teresa@steininn.co.uk
website: www.stein-inn.co.uk

Located on the shore of Loch Bay, renowned for its
breathtaking views, the **Stein Inn** dates back to around 1790
when it was part of a village commissioned by the British
Fisheries Society and designed by the celebrated architect
Thomas Telford. Much of the original village has survived and
is now a Conservation Area. The inn has been owned since
1993 by Angus and Teresa MacGhie who proudly run it in the
time-honoured, but now rare, tradition of Highland inn
keeping. The inn serves a variety of delicious home-cooked
food, including the freshest local seafood and Highland lamb
and beef. The cosy Bar boasts more than 125 malt whiskies
and keeps a fine selection of real ales, including many from
the Isle of Skye Brewery. A children's area adjacent to the bar
ensures that Mum and Dad can enjoy a quiet drink, and to
complete the scene, a peat fire burns all year round. The
accommodation at the inn comprises 2 king-sized double/twin/
family rooms, 2 standard double and one single room. All are
en suite and enjoy wonderful sea views. Also available is a
self-catering apartment with its own private access.

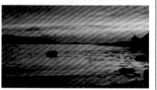

THE SHILASDAIR SHOP

THE SHILASDAIR SHOP

10 Carnach, Waternish, Isle of Skye IV55 8GL
Tel: 01470 592297
website: www.shilasdair-yarns.co.uk

If you enjoy colour, knitting or hand-knitted garments, you must visit **The Shilasdair Shop**. Situated
at the north-west corner of the island, the shop is a modern extension to a 100-year-old byre from
which there are the most spectacular views across to the Western Isles. Inside you will find yarn in
all colours of the rainbow to meet all needs in pure wool, hand-spun cashmere and baby camel, as
well as cashmere/angora mix and cord silk and cotton. The yarns are hand-dyed on site using only
dyes created from natural substances such as meadow-sweet, indigo, cochineal and logwood.

You can purchase ready-made designer garments or select your own yarn to take home a knit kit.
See the dye house and examples of dyestuffs
used in the production of the colours by
following the road signs.

Crusades took place. Another theory says it was the battle flag of King Harold Hardrada of Norway, who was killed in 1066. But how did he get hold of a flag from the Mediterranean?

Others are content to attribute a fairy origin on it, citing the old legend about a MacLeod who fell in love with a fairy princess. He asked the fairy king for his daughter's hand in marriage, but the king refused, declaring that MacLeod would eventually bring her great sorrow through his death, as he was mortal and fairies lived forever. His daughter openly wept so the father relented, saying that they could be married, but only for a year and a day. Nine months after the marriage, a son was born to the couple, and there was great rejoicing.

A year and a day after the marriage, the fairy princess returned to her people, leaving behind her husband and son. Their farewells took place on the Fairy Bridge near Dunvegan, and the princess made the heartbroken chief promise that he would never give their son cause to cry, as she could hear him from Fairyland and would grieve.

After she had gone, the chief was inconsolable, and his clansmen decided to organise a great party to cheer him up. The chief took part, leaving his son in the care of a nurse. However, when she heard the laughter and music, she stole out of the nursery to take part, leaving the child alone. He began to cry, and no one could hear him apart from the fairy princess. She came back to the castle and lifted the child from his cradle, soothing him and singing fairy songs. When the nurse returned to the nursery, she heard the magical singing, and knew at once who it was. She burst into the room and found the child wrapped in a silk shawl.

ULLINISH COUNTRY LODGE

Ullinish, Struan, Isle of Skye IV56 8FD
Tel: 01470 572214 Fax: 01470 572341
e-mail: ullinish@theisleofskye.co.uk
website: www.theisleofskye.co.uk

Built as a farmhouse in the early 1700s, **Ullinish Country Lodge** enjoys dramatic views of the Black Cuillin and MacLeod's Tables, and is surrounded by Lochs on three sides. In its time, the Lodge has provided hospitality for some distinguished guests. The celebrated Samuel Johnson and James Boswell stayed here in 1773 and the Lodge is favourably mentioned in the book of their travels through the Hebrides. More than 200 years later, owners Brian and Pamela Howard continue to provide hospitality at the highest level. Guests are assured of not only the finest cuisine but also extremely comfortable and relaxed 5-star accommodation. In the restaurant, the award-winning chef presents dishes based on fish and seafood from the surrounding waters, as well as meat and game from the hills. The contemporary cuisine is complemented by fine wines from the extensive cellar. All of the Lodge's public rooms enjoy stunning views across lochs and hills, as do many of the bedrooms, all of which are en suite and many feature traditional roll top baths. And for a very special experience, why not stay in the room originally occupied by Dr Johnson? AA 5 Star 'Inspector's Choice' AA 3 Rosette for Food, Gold Award Eat Scotland, 5 Star Visit Scotland.

BALMEANACH HOUSE B&B

Balmeanach, Struan, Isle of Skye IV56 8FH
Tel: 01470 572320 Fax: 01470 521482
e-mail: info@skye-holiday.com website: www.skye-holiday.com

Commanding an elevated view of Loch Caroy and enjoying panoramic views across to the MacLeod Tables, **Balmeanach House B&B** is the main croft house of the glen. It was recently renovated to a very high standard and has a very attractive garden with ponds, water features and seating areas. Inside, guests have the use of a spacious lounge/breakfast room with a huge fireplace where log and peat fires burn in the cooler months. The 4-star accommodation comprises 3 individually decorated rooms, all of which have colour TV, DVD player, radio/alarm clock, electric blanket and many extras such as fresh fruit. John & Arlene also run the **Atholl Filling Station** which, as well as serving fuel, has a well-stocked forecourt shop selling groceries, wines and beers, DVDs for hire and sale, and much more. Adjacent to the service station, **Plants 'n Stuff** offers a large range of perennial plants, roses, shrubs and garden sundries. Also leading from the shop is a recently opened **Café**, with stunning views of Loch Dunvegan, serving home-baking, and hearty home-cooked meals. It is licensed and has a small but well-chosen wine list as well as speciality Isle of Skye brewed beers.

She told the chief about the shawl, and he placed it in a locked case, vowing to take it with him wherever he went. Years later the son told his father that he miraculously remembered his mother returning. He told him that if Clan MacLeod ever needed help, he was to wave the shawl three times and a fairy army would rush to its aid.

Across the loch, and reached by the B884, is the **Colbost Croft Museum**, based on a 'black house' (a small traditional cottage of turf or stone, topped with a thatched roof). It shows the living conditions of islanders in the past, and features an illicit still. Black houses got their name, not because they were blackened inside by the peat fire, but to differentiate them from the 'white houses' that were built in Victorian and later times, which were more modern and usually painted white.

Travelling north from Colbost along a minor road brings you to Boreraig and the **MacCrimmon Piping Heritage Centre.** The MacCrimmons were the hereditary pipers to the MacLeods and reckoned to be the finest pipers in the country.

West of Colbost is the **Glendale Toy Museum** (see panel below), which as well as featuring antique toys, also has displays of modern ones from films such as *Star Wars*, *Barbie* and *Action Man*.

To the southeast of the island, on the Sleat (pronounced Slate) Peninsula at Armadale, is the **Armadale Castle Gardens** and **Museum of the Isles**. It sits within a 20,000-acre Highland estate, once owned by the MacDonalds of Sleat, and was purchased by the Clan Donald Land Trust in 1971. The earliest parts of the castle date from the 1790s, when it was built by the first Lord MacDonald on the site of a farm and gardens where Flora

GLENDALE TOY MUSEUM

Holmisdale House, Holmisdale, Glendale,
Isle of Skye IV55 8WS
Tel: 01470 511240
e-mail: crafts@toy-museum.co.uk
website: www.toy-museum.co.uk

Fully restored after a disastrous fire in 2002, the **Glendale Toy Museum** occupies Holmisdale House, one of the most famous Victorian mansions on Skye with wonderful views of the Outer Hebrides. It stands in 3 acres of garden, complete with a waterfall, just 7 miles from Dunvegan. This family-friendly museum is unique in that not all the toys are hidden behind glass. Many of the games can be enjoyed, demonstrated and played with.

Owners Terry and Paddy Wilding also make their own hand-made games, traditional toys and crafts which are on sale in the wee shop which stocks a wide range of collector's items and well-known stocking fillers. The front two rooms of the museum are filled with an amazing collection of toys, games and dolls from Victorian times to Star Wars. Terry and Paddy opened the museum in 1987. Paddy, a teacher from Blackpool, had collected toys since her childhood. Terry, from Wigan, was a design draughtsman for Leyland Bus. They abandoned the rat race to move to Glendale and establish the most remote Toy Museum in Europe. The museum is open from 10am to 6pm, Monday to Saturday.

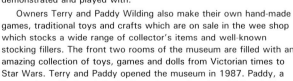

🎭 stories and anecdotes 🦢 famous people 🎨 art and craft ✒ entertainment and sport 🚶 walks

RAGAMUFFIN

Isle of Skye: on the pier @ Armadale, Sleat,
Isle of Skye IV45 8RS
Tel: 01471 844 217
e-mail: ragamuffin@madasafish.com
website: www.ragamuffinonline.co.uk

Established over 30 years ago, Lesley Robertson originally founded **Ragamuffin** whilst she was still at school – making jewellery and clothes and selling them to friends. Her love for beautiful apparel inspired her to open two wonderful stores, which sell the very best collection of designer knitwear, original clothes and accessories from the UK, Ireland and beyond. From wild and funky, to simple and elegant, there is something for all ages, sizes and budgets. With heaps of hats, funky scarves, sparkly jewellery, things to make you smile and much, much more! There's also a quirky in-house label too, this "Unruly Angels" collection is exceptionally well made and the quality shines through every garment, Lesley certainly has an eye for what is fashionable yet classic – pieces that will never date.

The shop is a pretty little, white washed building that sits overlooking the sea to Mallaig. On entering, you are subject to a glorious visual feast of colour and textures. The fabulous displays are so cleverly put together, the colours and fabrics so tempting and unusual, that when you see an 'outfit' on display you realise the possibilities immediately. The staff here sells what is termed "wearable art," the apparel here is unique. Well, not exactly: Ragamuffin also has a shop in Edinburgh.

MacDonald married in 1750.

Dunscaith Castle, the ruins of which lie on the western side of the peninsula near Tokavaig, was abandoned by the MacDonalds in the 18th century. Legend says that the castle was built by fairies in one night, and subsequently protected by a pit full of snakes. It was the home, the legend continues, of the Queen of Skye, who taught the arts of war.

EIGG

42 miles NW of Oban in the Atlantic Ocean

An Sgurr   Massacre Cave

In 1997, the island of Eigg was bought on behalf of its inhabitants by the Isle of Eigg Heritage Trust from the German artist who called himself Maruma. Its most famous feature is the 1277-feet-high **An Sgurr**, which

slopes gently up to a peak on one side, and dramatically plunges on the other.

Southwest of the main pier is St Francis's Cave, also known as the **Massacre Cave**. It got its name from a gruesome event in 1577, when nearly 400 MacDonalds took refuge there when pursued by a force of MacLeods. The MacLeods lit fires at the entrance, and every one of the MacDonalds was suffocated to death. The story was given some credence when human bones were removed from the cave in the 19th century and buried. A nearby cave, MacDonald's Cave, is also known as the Cathedral Cave, as it was used for secret Catholic church services following the 1745 rebellion.

At Kildonnan, on the west coast, are the ruins of a 14th-century church, built on the site of an ancient Celtic monastery founded by St Donan. The saint and his 52 monks were massacred in 617AD by a band of pirates.

MUCK
39 miles NW of Oban in the Atlantic Ocean

🏚 Dun Ban

The tiny island of Muck's improbable name comes from eilean nam muc, meaning island of pigs, though in this case the pigs may be porpoises, which are called sea pigs in Gaelic. It is reached by ferry from Mallaig, and is a low-lying island with good beaches. Port Mor is the main settlement and harbour, with, above it, an ancient graveyard and ruined church. On the south side of the Port Mor inlet are the scant remains of **Dun Ban**, a prehistoric fort. The highest point, at 445 feet, is Beinn Airein, and from the top there is a good view of the whole of the island.

RUM
47 miles W of Fort William

🏚 Kinloch Castle 🏚 Bullough Mausoleum

When Sir John Bullough bought the island of Rum in 1888 he arrogantly changed its name to Rhum, as he disliked the association it had with alcohol. However, when the Nature Conservancy Council took over the island in 1957, they changed the name back to the more correct Rum, meaning wide island, and it has been that ever since. Nowadays it is a Special Site of Scientific Interest and a Specially Protected Area, as its plant life has remained almost unchanged since the Ice Age.

The main settlement is Kinloch, on the east coast. **Kinloch Castle**, overlooking Loch Scresort, was built by Sir George Bullough, John's son, as his main home, between 1901 and 1902. The **Bullough Mausoleum** in Glen Harris, to the south of the island, was built to take the bodies of Sir George, his wife Monica and his father John.

Kilmory, on the north coast of the island, has a fine beach and an old burial ground.

CANNA
60 miles NW of Oban in the Atlantic Ocean

Canna means the "porpoise island", and has been owned by the National Trust for Scotland since 1981 when it was given to them by Gaelic scholar John Lorne Campbell. It is about five miles long by just over a mile wide at its widest, and is usually sunny and mild. The remains of St Columba's Chapel, dating from the 7th or 8th centuries, with an accompanying Celtic cross, stand opposite the small island of Sanday, and have been excavated. An Corghan, on the east coast, is all that is left of a small tower house where a Clanranald chief imprisoned his wife who was having an affair with a MacLeod clansman. At Uaigh Righ Lochlain can be seen remnants of Viking occupation, and at Camas Tairbearnais, a bay on the western side of the island, a Viking ship burial was uncovered. Sanday is a small island that lies off the south east coast and is joined to Canna by a bridge and, at low tide, a sand bar. Canna is reached by ferry from Mallaig.

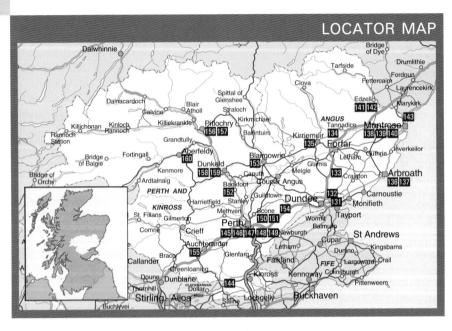

LOCATOR MAP

ADVERTISERS AND PLACES OF INTEREST

🏛 historic building   🏚 museum and heritage   🏛 historic site   🍃 scenic attraction   🌿 flora and fauna

10| Perthshire, Angus & Kinross

The two counties of Perthshire and Angus straddle the Highland Boundary Fault, which separates the Highlands from the Lowlands, while Kinross, once Scotland's second smallest county, is wholly Lowland in character. So there is a wide variety of scenery within this area, from mountains, glens and lochs, to quiet, intensely cultivated fields and picturesque villages.

Perthshire is a wholly inland county, a place of agriculture, high hills and Highland lochs. It is the county of Loch Rannoch and Loch Tummel, and of possibly the loneliest railway station in Britain, Rannoch, deep within the bleak expanse of Rannoch Moor. It is also the county of the Gleneagles Hotel, one of Britain's most luxurious, and of rich farmland surrounding Perth itself. Blairgowrie is the centre of Scotland's fruit growing industry - and once supplied the Dundee jam makers.

The A9 from Perth heads north towards the Drumochter Pass, which reaches its highest point of 1505 feet at the Perthshire/Inverness-shire border, overlooked by four Munros. On the way, it passes deeply wooded glens and skirts such historic towns and villages as Dunkeld, Pitlochry and Blair Atholl. In fact, Perthshire likes to call itself the Big

Tree Country, as it has some of the most remarkable woodlands anywhere in Europe.

Perth is a city, and before local government reorganisation in the 1970s, had a lord provost, one of only six places in Scotland that could claim that distinction, the others being Edinburgh, Glasgow, Dundee, Aberdeen and Elgin. No legal document has ever specifically taken that honour away, so it remains a city still. It is often referred to as the Fair City of Perth, and this is no idle description. It may be in the Lowlands, but it was never scarred by the industrial developments of the 19th century. It remains a confident, attractive place with many fine buildings and a good quality of life.

Angus has a coastline that takes in high cliffs and sandy beaches. The coastal towns are famous. Carnoustie, where the British Open is sometimes held; Montrose and its almost land-locked basin where wildfowl can be seen; and of course Arbroath, with the ruins of an abbey where one of the momentous documents in Scottish history was signed - the Declaration of Arbroath. Inland, the countryside is gentle and pastoral, with the particularly beautiful glens of Angus, such as Glen Prosen, Glen Clova and Glen Doll,

ADVERTISERS AND PLACES OF INTEREST (CONT)

🎦 stories and anecdotes 🐦 famous people 🎨 art and craft 🎭 entertainment and sport 🚶 walks

Lochleven Castle, Kinross

Pictish army under King Nechtan defeated the Northumbrians and secured independence from Anglian rule. The Battle of Killiecrankie in 1689 was the first of the Jacobite battles in Scotland.

Scone, outside Perth, was where the medieval Scottish kings were crowned as they sat on the Stone of Destiny; at Blair Atholl the Duke of Atholl keeps the only private army in Britain; Glamis Castle was the childhood home of the late Queen Mother; and Mary Stuart was held captive in a castle on an island in Loch Leven, frm where she made a daring escape.

At Crook of Devon in Kinross, a coven was discovered in 1662, and the witches put on trial and subsequently executed. At Scotlandwell we have yet another place of pilgrimage. A friary once stood here, along with a holy well, and people came from all over Scotland seeking cures for their ailments. The well is still there, and the waters may still be drunk.

Then there are the literary associations. JM Barrie was born at Kirriemuir, and Violet Jacob was born near Montrose. The Dundee publisher D C Thomson has given us a host of comic characters that have delighted children (and adults) for years, such as Desperate Dan, Korky the Cat, Biffo the Bear, Beryl the Peril, Denis the Menace, Lord Snooty, The Bash Street Kids and Oor Wullie.

winding their way into the foothills of the Cairngorms.

Dundee is the area's largest settlement, and the fourth largest city in Scotland. It sits on the north bank of the Firth of Tay and is a place of industry. At one time it was one of the powerhouses of Scotland, relying on its three traditional industries of jute, jam and journalism. But it is an ancient place as well, and its roots go deep into Scottish history. One of Scotland's famous historical characters, John Graham of Claverhouse, adopted its name when he became 1st Viscount Dundee.

Kinross sits to the south east of Perthshire in a great saucer-shaped depression with, at its heart, Loch Leven. The main industry is farming, and the gentle countryside, ringed by hills, is well worth exploring. Loch Leven is famous for its fishing, and Vane Farm Nature Reserve was the first educational nature reserve in Europe.

History resonates everywhere in Perthshire, Angus and Kinross. The medieval cathedrals at Dunkeld and Brechin are well worth exploring. In 685AD, at Nechtansmere, a

Dundee

Dundee is Scotland's fourth largest city, and sits on the banks of the Firth of Tay. It is a manufacturing town, at one time famous for the 'three Js' of jam, jute and journalism. It also brims with history and heritage, and was granted royal burgh status in the 12th century, when it was one of the largest and wealthiest towns in Scotland. **Dundee Law** (571 feet) looms over the city, and from its summit there is a superb view south towards the Tay Bridges and Fife. A road and separate footpath (with a series of steps) take you to the summit, where there is a war memorial, an observation point and fact panels.

Dundee is joined to Fife by two bridges across the Tay: the Tay Road Bridge, opened in 1966, and the Tay Rail Bridge, opened in 1887. The road bridge (which replaced a ferry) opened up a huge area of north Fife to commuters wishing to work in Dundee, and made it the main shopping centre for the area . The rail bridge replaced an earlier bridge, built in 1878. On the evening of 28 December 1879, during a violent westerly gale, the bridge collapsed while a train was crossing it. All the 75 train passengers were killed.

One of Dundee's best-known sons, **William Topaz McGonagall**, later wrote a poem to commemorate the disaster, which has became almost as famous as the disaster itself:

Beautiful Railway Bridge of the Silv'ry Tay!
Alas! I am very sorry to say
That ninety lives have been taken away
On the last Sabbath day of 1879,
Which will be remember'd for a very long time.

It has been called, rather unfairly perhaps, the worst poem ever written. McGonagall was born in Edinburgh in 1830, the son of Irish immigrants, and came to Dundee with his parents after having lived in Paisley and Glasgow. In 1877, he took to writing poetry, having felt 'a strange kind of feeling stealing over me', and then wrote until he died in September 1902.

The **Old Steeple** of St Mary's Church, in the heart of the

Tay Rail Bridge, Dundee

🎬 stories and anecdotes 🐦 famous people 🎨 art and craft 🏃 entertainment and sport 🚶 walks

McManus Galleries, Dundee

city, dates from the 15th century, and is reckoned to be one of the finest in the country. The rest of the building dates from the 18th and 19th centuries, and was once divided into four separate churches. Until the 1980s, when they finally amalgamated, there were still three churches within the building - the Steeple Church, Old St Paul's and St David's.

Another reminder of Dundee's past is the **Wishart Arch** in the Cowgate. It is one of the city's old gateways, and from its top, George Wishart, the religious reformer, is said to have preached to plague victims during the plague of 1544. Near the arch is the Wishart Church, where **Mary Slessor** used to worhip. She was born in Aberdeen in 1848 and moved to Dundee when she was 10. Inspired by David Livingstone, she went to Africa as a missionary, and died at Calabar in 1915.

RSS Discovery, Captain Scott's ship, was built in Dundee and launched in 1901. It now forms the centrepiece of the five-star **Discovery Point**, at Discovery Quay. It was one of the last wooden three-masted ships to be built in Britain, and the first to be built

solely for scientific research. You can explore the ship, 'travel' to Antarctica in the Polarama Gallery and learn more out about this great voyage of exploration and courage.

At Victoria Dock you'll find **HM Frigate Unicorn**, the oldest British-built wooden frigate still afloat. It was built at Chatham in 1824 for the Royal Navy at a time when iron was beginning to replace wood in ship building, and carried 46 guns. The ship re-creates the conditions on board a wooden sailing ship during Nelson's time, with officers' quarters, cannons, and the cramped conditions within which the crew lived.

In 1999, **The Verdant Works**, in West Henderson's Wynd, was voted Europe's top industrial museum. Jute was once a staple industry in Dundee, employing over 40,000 people. Here, in a former jute mill, you are taken on a tour of the industry, from its beginnings in India to the end product in all its forms. You will see the processes involved in jute manufacture, the original machinery, and the home conditions of people both rich and poor who earned their living from the trade. There are interactive displays, film shows, and a guided tour.

Sensation is Dundee's science centre. Located in the Greenmarket, it is a place where science is brought to life using specially designed interactive and hands-on exhibits. Here you can find out how a dog sees the world, how to use your senses to discover where you are, and why things taste good or bad. The latest exhibition is Roborealm, the only one of its kind in the world. It will give visitors a chance to interact with a team of robots. **The Mills Observatory** in Balgay Park, a mile west of the city centre and accessed from Glamis Road, also deals with matters scientific. It is Britain's only full time public observatory, and houses a 25mm Cooke telescope. It also has a small planetarium and display area.

The McManus Galleries are housed within a Gothic building in Albert Square, and contain many 18th- and 19th-century Scottish paintings. Within it there is also a museum of more than local interest, with a particularly fine collection of artefacts from Ancient Egypt. The **Dundee Contemporary Arts Centre** in the Nethergate specialises in contemporary art and film, and has galleries, cinemas and workshops.

Dudhope Castle, at Dudhope Park in Dundee, dates originally from the 13th century, and was once the home of the Scrymageour family, hereditary constables of Dundee. The present building dates from the late 16th century. In its time it has also been a woollen mill and a barracks. It now forms part of the University of Abertay and is not open to the public, though it can be viewed from the outside. And at the junction of Claypotts Road and Arbroath Road is the wonderfully named **Claypotts Castle** (Historic Scotland), built between 1569 and 1588 by John Strachan. It can be viewed by prior appointment with Historic Scotland.

On the Coupar Angus Road is the **Camperdown Wildlife Centre**, with a fine collection of Scottish and European wildlife, including brown bears, Scottish wildcats, wolves and bats. **Clatto Country Park** is to the north of the city, and is centred on a 24-acre former reservoir. It has facilities for water sports and fishing. The ruins of **Mains Castle**, sometimes called Mains of Fintry, is in Cairds Park, and was once owned by John

Broughty Castle Museum

Castle Approach, Broughty Ferry, Dundee DD5 2TF
Tel: 01382 436916
website: www.dundeecity.gov.uk/broughtycastle

This amazing 15th century coastal fort has faced many battles and seiges, and was rebuilt in the 19th century as part of the River Tay's coastal defence system. It now houses a fascinating museum featuring displays on the life and times of Broughty Ferry, it's people, the environment and the wildlife that lives close by. Take a journey through time in Broughty Ferry, 400 million years ago to the present day. Follow the delightful 'Brochtie' family as they travel through the ages. Come face to face with a woolly mammoth, as you explore the geology and natural history of the area! Don't miss the spectacular views over the River Tay from the observation post - you may even be able to spot a dolphin or two! There is a refreshment area and gift shop. Opening Times: April - September; Mon to Sat 10am-4pm, Sun 12.30-4pm: October - March; Closed Mon, Tue to Sat 10am-4pm, Sun 12.30-4pm. Admission is free.

📖 stories and anecdotes 🐦 famous people 🎨 art and craft 🎭 entertainment and sport 🚶 walks

DUNTRUNE HOUSE BED AND BREAKFAST

Duntrune, Dundee DD4 0PJ
Tel: 01382 350239
e-mail: info@duntrunehouse.co.uk
website: www.duntrunehouse.co.uk

At **Duntrune House Bed & Breakfast,** just 20 minutes by car from Glamis Castle, your fellow guests come from all corners of the world to experience the best of Scottish hospitality in the relaxed atmosphere of a historic house. Whether you wish to explore the ancient county of Angus, to play golf at any of the many beautiful courses in the area, including St Andrews and Carnoustie, to paint under the nurturing eye of Liz McCarthy whose studio is at the end of the drive, to research family history (a particular passion of your hosts), to enjoy pampering at the nearby Retreat Salon, to wander in the garden and see the spectacular views over the Tay Estuary, or to browse an eclectic collection of books, you can be assured of lively conversation round the dinner or breakfast table, or with a wee dram in the cosy study.

Your hosts, Olwyn and Barrie Jack, have carefully restored this elegant, 1820s house to ensure the en suite guest rooms have kept their character while providing the high standard expected by today's travellers. Modern touches include a fridge for guests' use and a broadband, wireless connection. A roving TV is available and there is also one in the guest sitting room but overall, guests are encouraged to share experiences of their own countries and of their visit to Scotland.

The present house was built on the foundations of the 16th century house owned by Walter Graham who styled himself Graham of Duntrune. His great-great-great-granddaughter, Clementina Stirling Graham, has left an interesting legacy. She was the author of Mystifications, an account of how, in the guise of Lady Pitlyal, she entertained the elite of 19th century society, regaling them with the most outrageous stories. A copy of this book is in every guest bedroom.

In Clementina's time, fruit and vegetables were grown in the walled garden and honey came from the hives in the bee boles. Today, fruit and vegetables are organically grown in a fruit cage and poly tunnel and honey is provided by the gardener's bees and fresh eggs from his hens.

A stay at Duntrune House - 4-star Visit Scotland and Silver Green Tourism accredited - is an experience not to be missed.

🏛 historic building 🏛 museum and heritage 🏛 historic site ♨ scenic attraction ☘ flora and fauna

Graham, a cousin of Viscount Dundee.

To the east of the city is Broughty Ferry, once called the 'richest square mile in Europe' because of the many fine mansions built there by the jute barons. The **Broughty Ferry Museum** (see panel on page 345) is at Castle Green, and housed within a castle built by the Earl of Angus in 1496 as a defence against marauding English ships. It has displays on local history, and tells the story of Dundee's former whaling fleet, at one time Britain's largest. If you visit Broughty Ferry at New Year, you can see the annual **N'erday Dook** (New Year's Day Dip), when swimmers enter the waters of the Firth of Tay. It is organised by Ye Amphibious Ancients Bathing Association, one of the country's oldest swimming clubs, and is done for charity. It attracts about 100 to 150 swimmers a year, and it is not unknown for the crowd of spectators, which can be over 2000 strong, to be wrapped up in warm woollens, scarves and gloves as the swimmers enter the water dressed only in swimsuits.

To the west of the city, on the north bank of the Tay, is the Carse of Gowrie, one of the most fertile areas of Scotland.

Around Dundee

MONIFIETH
6 miles E of Dundee on the A930

🏛 St Rule's Church

This little holiday resort sits at the entrance to the Firth of Tay, and has some good sandy beaches. Its golf courses were used in the qualifying rounds of the British Open. At one time it was an important Pictish settlement, and some Pictish stones, discovered at **St Rule's Church**, are now in The National Museum of Scotland in Edinburgh.

CARNOUSTIE
11 miles E of Dundee on the A930

🏛 Barry Mill 🏛 Carlungie and Ardestie Souterrains

Golf is king in Carnoustie. This small holiday resort on the North Sea coast hosted the British Open Championships in 1931 and 1999, and is a favourite destination for golfing holidays.

But it has other attractions. **Barry Mill** (National Trust for Scotland) is a 19th-century working corn mill, though a mill has stood here since at least the middle of the 16th century. You can see the large water wheel turning and find out how corn is ground. There is an exhibition explaining the historical role of the mill, as well as a walkway along the mill lade.

Three miles north west of the town are the **Carlungie and Ardestie Souterrains** (Historic Scotland), underground earth houses dating from the 1st century AD.

BALGRAY
4 miles N of Dundee off the A90

Four miles north of the city centre, near Balgray, is the Tealing Souterrain (Historic Scotland), an underground dwelling dating from about 100AD. It was accidentally discovered in 1871, and consists of a curved passage about 78 feet long and seven feet wide with a stone floor.

FOWLIS EASTER
6 miles W of Dundee on a minor road off the A923

🏛 Parish Church of St Marnan

This small village has one of the finest small churches in Scotland. The **Parish Church of St Marnan** dates from about 1453, and still has part of its rood screen, as well as medieval paintings dating to about 1541 and a sacrament house that is reckoned to be the finest in Scotland. Lord Gray built it in 1453 on the site of an earlier church, built in about 1242 by a member of the local Mortimer family whose husband was in the Holy Land fighting in the Crusades.

GLAMIS
10 miles N of Dundee on the A94

🏛 Glamis Castle 🏛 Angus Folk Museum

🏛 St Orland's Stone

Glamis Castle is famous as being the childhood home of the late Queen Mother and the birthplace of her daughter, the late Princess Margaret. The lands of Glamis (pronounced Glams) were given to Sir John Lyon in 1372 by Robert II, the first Stewart king and grandson of Robert the Bruce, and still belongs to the family, who are now the

Earls of Strathmore and Kinghorne. In 1376 Sir John married Robert's daughter, Princess Joanna, and the castle has had royal connections ever since. The present castle was built in the 17th century to resemble a French château, though fragments of an earlier 14th-century castle still survive in the tower.

Shakespeare's *Macbeth*, which he wrote in 1606, is set in Glamis, and Duncan's Hall, the oldest part of the castle, is said to have been built on the spot where Macbeth murdered Duncan. Shakespeare, like most playwrights, was more interested in drama than historical fact, and history tells us that Duncan most probably died in battle near Elgin. It may even be that Shakespeare visited Glamis, as he and his troupe of actors were sent to Aberdeen in 1599 by Elizabeth I to perform before James VI.

Tragedy seems to stalk Glamis Castle. In

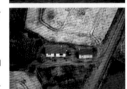

CRAWFORD COTTAGES

Foreside of Cairn, by Forfar, Angus DD8 3TQ
Tel: 01575 572655 Mobile: 0780 1492531
e-mail: kathleen@crawfordcottages.co.uk
website: www.crawfordcottages.co.uk

If your vision of Scotland includes deep lochs, bonny glens, turreted castles and welcoming hospitality, then you won't be disappointed by the Angus District. It's a very picturesque part of a beautiful country, where the people are warm, friendly and welcoming.

You won't be disappointed by **Crawford Cottages** either. There are three of them, all fully equipped and comfortably furnished to very high standards. Clova Cottage can sleep up to 6 people; Prosen up to 7, and Esk up to 8. The cottages are adjoining and share a large back garden with built in barbeque, making them ideal for parties of up to 20.

The cottages are available all year round, normally from 3pm. on Saturday until 10am the following Saturday, although alternative days or times may be possible, especially during the winter season when 3 or 4 night short breaks are available. Electricity is supplied free of charge to all cottages as well as logs or coal, for cottages which have an open fire. And while you are staying at Crawford Cottages, you can be sure that owner Kathleen Smith will do everything she can to make your stay in Angus a holiday to remember.

1537, Lady Glamis, Janet Douglas, was burnt as a witch in Edinburgh for plotting to murder James V, and the crown seized the lands. It was a trumped up charge, as James V hated the Douglas family, and Lady Glamis was later declared innocent of all the charges, with the lands being restored to her son. Glamis has the reputation of being one of the most haunted castles in Scotland. There is a Grey Lady who haunts the chapel, a Black Page, and a window that looks out from a room that doesn't appear to exist. Legend has it that in the room, which might be within the thickness of the walls, one of the Lords of Glamis and the Earl of Crawford played cards with the devil, and were sealed up because of it.

The castle is also noted for its gardens, and in springtime the mile-long driveway is lined with daffodils. In summer there are displays of rhododendrons and azaleas.

Within the village of Glamis, at Kirkwynd, is the **Angus Folk Museum** (National Trust for Scotland), housed in a row of 18th-century stone cottages. It contains one of the finest folk collections in Scotland, including a Life on the Land exhibition baesd in an old courtyard, and a restored 19th-century hearse.

A few miles north of the village is Pictish **St Orland's Stone**, with, on one side, the carving of a cross and on the other, a carving of a boat containing several men.

FORFAR
13 miles N of Dundee on the A932

🌶 Forfar Food Festival 🏛 Restenneth Priory
🏛 Meffan Museum & Art Gallery
🌿 Balgavies Loch 🌿 Forfar Loch Country Park
🌿 Mountains Animal Sanctuary

Once the county town of Angus, Forfar is now a small royal burgh and market town. It

🎭 stories and anecdotes 🐦 famous people 🎨 art and craft 🎟 entertainment and sport 🚶 walks gives its name to one of Scotland's culinary delights - the Forfar Bridie. This confection of meat and vegetables within a pastry crust used to be popular with the farm workers of Angus as it was a self-contained and easily portable meal. Appropriately enough, the Bridie plays a prominent role in the **Forfar Food Festival**, which takes place annually at the beginning of July.

The **Meffan Museum and Art Gallery** in West High Street gives you an insight into the town's history and industries. It was built in 1898 after a daughter of a former provost left a sum of money to the town. During the Dark Ages this part of Scotland was inhabited by the Picts, who, as far as we know, had no alphabet. However, they were expert carvers, and in the museum is a superb display of carved stones. You can also walk down an old cobbled street and peer into shops and workshops. A more unusual display is one about witchcraft in Angus.

Five miles east of Forfar is **Balgavies Loch**, a Scottish Wildlife Trust reserve, where you can see great crested grebe, whooping swans, cormorant and other birds. Keys to the hide are available from the ranger at the Montrose Basin Wildlife Centre. There is a hide that is open on the first Sunday of each month. **Forfar Loch Country Park**, to the west of the town, has viewing platforms where wildfowl can be observed feeding.

The ruins of **Restenneth Priory** (Historic Scotland) sit about a mile-and-a-half from the town, on the B9113. It once stood on an island in Restenneth Loch, but this was drained in the 18th century. The priory was founded by David I for Augustinian canons on the site of a much earlier church and its square tower, which is surmounted by a later spire, has some of the earliest Norman - and possibly Saxon - work in

Scotland. The priory was sacked by Edward I, but under the patronage of Robert the Bruce it soon regained its importance. Prince John, one of Bruce's sons, is buried here.

A few miles north of Forfar, near Tannadice, is the **Mountains Animal Sanctuary**, for rescued ponies, horses and donkeys.

KIRRIEMUIR
15 miles N of Dundee on the A926

🏛 JM Barrie's Birthplace 🏛 Camera Obscura

🏛 Kirriemuir Aviation Museum ❧ Lintrathen Loch

At 9 Brechin Road is **J M Barrie's Birthplace** (National Trust for Scotland). The creator of *Peter Pan* (first performed in 1904) was born here in 1860, the son of a handloom weaver, and the building's outside washhouse was his first theatre. The house next door has an exhibition about Barrie's life. He was a bright child, attending both Glasgow Academy and Dumfries Academy before going on to Edinburgh University. He wrote many stories and novels, setting them in a small town called Thrums - a thinly disguised Kirriemuir.

In 1930, when he was given the freedom of the town, Barrie donated a **Camera Obscura** (National Trust for Scotland) to Kirriemuir, one of only three such cameras in the country. It is situated within the cricket pavilion on top of Kirriemuir Hill, and is open to the public. The **Kirriemuir Aviation Museum**, at Bellie's Brae, has a private collection of World War II memorabilia. It was established in 1987, and largely confines itself to British aviation history.

Kirriemuir is the gateway to many of the beautiful Angus glens, and in the Gateway to the Glens Museum in the former town hall in the High Street you can find out about life in the glens and in the town itself. The glens lie north of the town, and go deep into the Cairngorms. They are extremely beautiful and

THRUMS HOTEL

25 Bank Street, Kirriemuir, Angus DD8 4BE
Tel/Fax: 01575 572758
e-mail: enquiries@thrumshotel.co.uk
website: www.thrumshotel.co.uk

South from the foothills of the Cairngorms, within the fertile plain of Strathmore, you'll find the charming town of Kirriemuir and, at its heart, the **Thrums Hotel** which offers quality accommodation and a welcoming, friendly atmosphere within charming surroundings. The 'Thrums' is fully licensed and in the lounge you'll find an extensive range of drinks, including a wide selection of some of Scotland's finest malt whiskeys. If you prefer, meals can be enjoyed here in the lounge rather than the dining room which offers an excellent, varied dishes, many of which contain local produce such as fresh Scottish Salmon, marvellous local game and excellent seafood fresh from the East Coast.

The guest bedrooms at the Thrums have recently undergone a major refurbishment and are now of the highest standard you would expect. The tastefully decorated rooms are bright and airy, and each has full en suite facilities, colour TV and tea and coffee making facilities.

The Thrums Hotel is a favourite with shooting parties and the management are happy to arrange shooting and stalking on nearby estates subject to the season. Fishing, hill walking and climbing are all available locally, as is golf with more than 30 courses within a one-hour drive!

well worth a visit. The B955 takes you into Glen Clova, then, at its head, forms a loop, so you can travel along one side of the glen and return along the other for part of the way. A minor road at the Clova Hotel takes you up onto lonely Glen Doll before it peters out. At Dykehead you can turn off the B955 onto a minor road for Glen Prosen and follow it as it winds deep into the mountains. A cairn close to Dykehead commemorates the Antarctic explorers Robert Falcon Scott and Edward Adrian Wilson. Wilson was born in Cheltenham, the son of a doctor, but lived in Glen Prosen, and it was here that some of the Antarctic expedition was planned. He died along with Scott in Antarctica in March 1912.

Glen Isla is the southernmost of the Angus glens, and you can follow it for all of its length along the B951, which eventually takes you

onto the A93 at Glenshee and up to Braemar if you wish. You will pass the **Lintrathen Loch**, which is noted for its bird life. A couple of miles further up the glen a minor road takes you to lonely Backwater Reservoir and its dam.

DUNNICHEN

13 miles NE of Dundee on minor road off the B9128

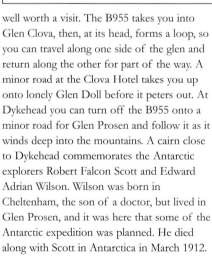 Battle of Nechtansmere

Close to the village the **Battle of Nechtansmere** was fought in 685AD between the Picts, under King Nechtan, and the Northumbrians. It was a turning point in early Scottish history, as it was decisive in establishing what was to become Scotland as an independent nation, and not part of an enlarged Northumbria and later England.

Northumbria was aggressively trying to

extend its boundaries, and had already taken the Lothians and Fife, when they came north. The Northumbrians, under King Ecgfrith, were roundly beaten, and Ecgfrith himself and most of the royal court were killed. The Pictish battle plan, according to Bede, was to lure the Northumbrians into a piece of land between Dun Nechtan, a hill fort, and an area of swamp close to the loch, where they were trapped. At the crossroads in the village is a cairn that commemorates the battle. A newer one was erected in 1998 close to the actual battlefield. Some people claim to have seen a ghostly re-enactment of the fighting take place in modern times. The mere, or loch, which gave its name to the battle, was drained many years ago.

The picturesque village of Letham, which is close by, was founded in 1788 by George Dempster, the local landowner, as a settlement for farm workers who had been forced to leave the land because of farming reforms. It became a centre of weaving and spinning, though the introduction of power looms in nearby towns killed it off.

ARBROATH
15 miles NE of Dundee on the A92

🏛 Arbroath Abbey 𝔪 Battle of Arbroath

🏛 Arbroath Museum 𝔐 Arbroath Smokie

🏃 Cliffs Nature Trail 🐚 Kerr's Miniature Railway

The ancient town of Arbroath is special to all Scots. It was here, in 1320, that the nobles of Scotland met and signed the Declaration of Arbroath, which stated that the country was an independent kingdom, and not beholden to England. It was sent to a sceptical Pope John XXII in Rome and in it they claimed that they were not fighting for glory, riches or honour,

---

ALEX SPINK & SONS

24 Seagate, Arbroath DD11 1BJ
Tel: 01241 879056 Fax: 01241 439540
e-mail: sales@alexspinkandsons.co.uk
website: www.arbroathsmokiesonline.co.uk

Alex Spink & Sons is a family business originally established in 1977 by Alex and Mary Spink who bought a second-hand Hillman car and adapted it for selling fish by removing the back seats. Later, they were joined by their sons, Andrew, Alex and Norman. Alex travels to Aberdeen every morning to buy fresh fish direct from the market at Aberdeen and Peterhead.

In 1987, Alex Snr. retired but the company goes from strength to strength and now has a workforce of 25, supplying numerous restaurants and hotels as well as delivering fish to their customers doors throughout Angus, Tayside and Fife.

Naturally, a speciality of the business is making Arbroath Smokies in the traditional way over an oak-wood fire, something the company has been doing since 1977. But their retail outlets in Blairgowrie and Dundee also offer an extensive range of fish that includes smoked and unsmoked haddock, lemon sole, kippers, smoked mackerel, hot smoked salmon and fresh salmon. Their products are also available by mail order and are sent vacuum-packed to ensure you receive them in the very best condition.

🏛 historic building 🏛 museum and heritage 𝔪 historic site 🜚 scenic attraction 🌱 flora and fauna

SMITHIES

16 Keptie Street, Arbroath DD11 1RG
Tel: 01241 873344
e-mail: smithiesdeli@google mail.com

An outstanding delicatessen and coffee shop, **Smithies** was established in 2000 by Pattie Smith, an enthusiastic lady with a passion for good food. Her business occupies a striking building of 1900 which, appropriately, was originally Lipton's Food Hall. Most of its colourful décor is still in place. Inside, you'll find a huge range of wholesome and appetising food, including between 30 and 40 different types of cheese and 6 kinds of coffee which is freshly ground to order. To carry your purchases away, Smithies sells some wonderful, eco-friendly jute bags which are made in India. The shop is also an off licence, runs a bespoke hamper service all year round and sells an attractive range of tableware such as cheese boards, butter dishes, egg cups and so on.

In the wood-panelled coffee shop the menu offers an excellent selection of sandwiches (almost 20 different fillings available, including a tasty Brie & mango chutney); a variety of light meals such as home-made soup, baked potatoes and salads. And don't miss out on the wide selection of delicious home-made cakes that includes Malteser cake, carrot cake and various sponges.

---

but for freedom. They also, in no uncertain terms, claimed that they would remain loyal to their king, Robert the Bruce, only as long as he defended Scotland against the English. It was a momentous declaration to make in those days, when unswerving loyalty to a sovereign was expected at all times.

The Declaration was drawn up in **Arbroath Abbey** (Historic Scotland), with Bernard de Linton, the abbot of the abbey, being the writer. The ruins of the abbey still stand within the town, and sometimes a re-enactment of the signing is held there. A Visitor Centre tells the story of the abbey and the Declaration.

The abbey ruins date from the 12th century and later, and are of warm red sandstone. The abbey was founded in 1176 by William the Lion for the Tironensian monks of Kelso and dedicated to St Thomas of Canterbury.

Portions of the great abbey church remain, including the south transept with its great rose window. In 1951, the abbey was the temporary home of the Stone of Destiny after it was removed from Westminster Abbey by students with Scottish Nationalist sympathies.

In 1446, the **Battle of Arbroath** took place around the abbey. It had been the custom for the abbot to nominate a baillie to look after the peacekeeping and business side of Arbroath. He appointed Alexander Lindsay to the lucrative post but later dismissed him for 'lewd bahaviour', appointing John Ogilvie in his place. Lindsay took exception to this and arrived at the abbey with an army of 1000 men. The ensuing battle, fought in the streets of the town, killed more than 600 people with Lindsay's army emerging triumphant. However, it was a hollow victory, as Lindsay himself was killed.

The award-winning **Arbroath Museum**, at Ladyloan, is housed in the elegant signal tower for the Bellrock Lighthouse, and brings Arbroath's maritime and social history alive through a series of models, sounds and even smells.

Arbroath has had a harbour at the 'Fit o' the Toon' (Foot of the Town) since at least the 14th century, and it supported a great fishing fleet. The town gave its name to that delicacy called the **Arbroath Smokie** (a smoked haddock), though the supposed origins of the delicacy are to be found not in the town, but in Auchmithie, a fishing village four miles to the north. The story goes that long ago it was the practice to store fish in the lofts of the fishermen's cottages. One day, a cottage burned down, and the resultant smoked fish was found to be delicious. Not only that, it preserved them.

The **Cliffs Nature Trail** winds for one and a half miles along the red sandstone cliffs towards Carlinheugh Bay. There is plenty of bird life to see, as well as fascinating rock formations. The town is also a holiday resort, and at West Link Parks is the 10¼ inch gauge **Kerr's Miniature Railway**, always a favourite with holidaymakers. It is open during the summer months, and is Scotland's oldest miniature railway, having been built in 1935. It runs for over 400 yards alongside the main Aberdeen to Edinburgh line.

ST VIGEANS
17 miles NE of Dundee on minor road off the A92

🏛 St Vigean's Museum

When the 12th-century parish church of St Vigeans was being refurbished in the 19th century, 32 sculptured Pictish stones were discovered. They are now housed in the

St Vigean's Museum, converted cottages close to the small knoll where the church stands. The most important stone is the St Dristan Stone, dating from the 9th century.

St Fechan, or St Vigean, was an Irish saint who died in about 664AD. The village of Ecclefechan in Dumfriesshire is also named after him.

ABERLEMNO
18 miles NE of Dundee on a minor road off the B9134

🏛 Aberlemno Sculptured Stones

Within the village are the Pictish **Aberlemno Sculptured Stones** (Historic Scotland). One is situated in the kirkyard of the parish church, and the others are within a stone enclosure near the roadside north of the church. The one in the kirkyard shows a fine cross on one side surrounded by intertwining serpents and water horses, and a typical Pictish hunting scene on the other. It dates from the 8th or 9th century. The other two have crosses, angels, and battle or hunting scenes. Because of possible frost damage, the stones are boxed in between October and May.

BRECHIN
22 miles NE of Dundee off the A90

🏛 Brechin Cathedral 🏛 Round Tower

🏛 Maison Dieu 🏛 Brechin Museum

🌿 Brechin Castle Centre 🏛 Pictavia 🏛 Caterthuns

🖉 Caledonian Railway 🌣 Glen Lethnot

If the possession of a cathedral makes a town a city, then Brechin is indeed a city, even though it has a population of only 6000. **Brechin Cathedral** dates from the 12th century, though most of what we see today is 13th century and later. In 1806, the nave, aisles and west front were remodelled, and between 1901 and 1902

Harp at Pictavia Exhibition, Brechin

were restored to their original design. Adjacent to the cathedral, and now forming part of its fabric, is an 11th-century **Round Tower**, which rises to a height of 106 feet. These towers are common in Ireland, though this is the only one of two to have survived in Scotland. From the top a monk rang a bell at certain times during the day, calling the monks to prayer. It was also used as a place of refuge for the monks during troubled times. In Maison Dieu lane is the south wall of the chapel of the **Maison Dieu** almshouses founded in 1267 by Lord William de Brechin.

Brechin Museum has exhibits and displays about the cathedral, the ancient city crafts and local archaeology. Brechin Castle (private) is the seat of the Earls of Dalhousie, and within the **Brechin Castle Centre** are a garden centre, walks and a model farm. There is also **Pictavia**, an exhibition that explains about the enigmatic Picts, who occupied this part of Scotland for centuries. One of the displays explains the Battle of Nechtansmere. Their name means the painted people, and they fought the Romans, the Vikings and the Angles. The various tribes eventually amalgamated, forming a powerful kingdom, which ultimately united with the kingdom of the Scots of Dalriada in 843AD to form an embryonic Scotland.

At Menmuir, near the town, are the White and Brown **Caterthuns**, on which are the well-preserved remains of Iron Age forts. The hills also give good views across the surrounding countryside.

The **Caledonian Railway** runs on Sundays during summer and also on Saturdays during the peak season, when passengers can travel between the Victorian Brechin Station on Park Road and the nearby Bridge of Dun. The railway has 10 steam engines and 12 diesels, and is run by the Brechin Railway Preservation Society. The Brechin branch line, on which the trains run, was closed in 1952.

To the north west of Brechin is **Glen Lethnot**, one of the beautiful Angus glens. Flowing through it is the West Water, and near the head of the glen is an old trail that takes you over the Clash of Wirren into Glen Esk. Once used as a route by illicit distillers who hid their casks in the corries among the hills, it became known as the Whisky Trail.

MONTROSE
27 miles NE of Dundee on the A92

🐦 Montrose Basin Wildlife Centre
📷 Montrose Air Station Heritage Centre
✒ William Lamb Studio 🏠 House of Dun
🦅 1st Marquis of Montrose 🦅 George Wishart

Montrose is an ancient royal burgh, which received its charter in the early 12th century. It sits on a small spit of land between the North Sea and a shallow tidal inlet called the Montrose Basin, which is a local nature reserve founded in 1981 and famous for its bird life. The **Montrose Basin Wildlife Centre** (see panel on page 356) is visited by thousands of bird watchers every year who come to see the many migrant birds.

At the old Montrose Air Station, where some of the Battle of Britain pilots trained, is

🎭 stories and anecdotes 🦅 famous people ✒ art and craft 🎭 entertainment and sport 🚶 walks

GREENBANK BED & BREAKFAST

50 Redfield Road, Montrose, Angus DD10 8TW
Tel: 01674 678430
e-mail: info@greenbankbedandbreakfast.com
website: www.greenbankbedandbreakfast.com

A warm welcome from Ishbel and Duncan awaits you upon your arrival at their comfortable family home. **Greenbank Bed & Breakfast** is a detached, recently extended family home, centrally located in a quiet residential area of Montrose with open views across Montrose Basin and the surrounding countryside. Those views are also seen from the dining room where breakfast is served with a wide choice on the menu. Evening meals may be available by prior arrangement.

The accommodation at Greenbank comprises twin, double and family bedrooms, each with en suite shower facilities or a private bathroom situated immediately outside the room. All rooms are equipped with multi-channel TV with DVD & video, hospitality tray, hairdryer, alarm clock and bathrobes. In addition, a selection of DVDs & books are available for guests. Internet access is available for those who require it and for relaxation guests can use the landscaped garden. Greenbank is a non-smoking establishment, but provision is made outside for those who have yet to give up! An ideal base from which to explore the North East of Scotland, Greenbank is just a short walk from Montrose town centre.

LUNAN LODGE B&B

Lunan, Montrose, Angus DD10 9TG
Tel: 01241 830679
e-mail: via website
website: www.lunanlodge.co.uk

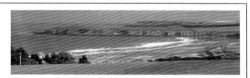

Set in two acres of secluded grounds and enjoying outstanding views over the spectacular Lunan Bay, **Lunan Lodge B&B** offers quality accommodation in a friendly, informal atmosphere. The oldest part of the house dates back to the 18th century, and retains many period features. The best-preserved room in the house is the Penthouse, with the original plaster cornices still visible. All guest bedrooms enjoy spectacular sea views.

Lunan Lodge is very child friendly! There are two family rooms and owners Samantha and Jules (whose motto is "Your whim is our command!") can supply single beds (guaranteed bounce-proof) for children. The beach at Lunan Bay is a short, safe walk away, and children from ages 3 to 80 will love the park and the soft toy library! And, what child wouldn't love a picnic under the "secret tree", in the safety of the kitchen garden?

The Lodge is surrounded by castles, both ruined and inhabited. At night you can see, flashing over the headland, the world-famous Bell Rock lighthouse. From this quiet and secluded B&B you can explore the nearby towns or you might prefer to just relax in the peaceful gardens and spacious rooms.

Montrose Basin Wildlife Centre

Rossie Braes, Montrose, Angus, DD10 9TJ
Tel: 01674 676336

Come and see magnificent wildlife and enjoy a superb panorama from the comfort of this unique centre. Montrose Basin is the 750 hectare enclosed estuary of the South Esk river. Virtually untouched by industrial development and pollution, the Basin provides a rich feeding ground for thousands of resident and migrant birds.

The daily tidal cycle and passing seasons, each with its own characteristic pattern of birds – winter and summer visitors and passage migrants – ensure something new and different every month of the year. In summer the Basin is home to curlews, oystercatchers, eider ducks and lots more. In autumn, the Basin resounds with the calls of thousands of migrant geese.

The Centre shop is a delight, with exciting and unusual gifts, including a good selection of bird feeders, bird food and a full range of binoculars and telescopes. You can test them out on site. Our full time Education and Information Officer welcomes enquiries and visits from schools. The fully-equipped classroom enables children to enjoy a range of activities linked to the 5-14 Curriculum Guidelines.

the **Montrose Air Station Heritage Centre**. In 1912, the government planned 12 such air stations to be operated by the Royal Flying Corps, later called the Royal Air Force. Montrose was the first, and became operational in 1913. Now it houses a small collection of aircraft, including a full size replica of the famous Sopwith Camel, plus mementoes, documents and photographs related to flying.

The **William Lamb Studio** is in a close off Market Street and is open to the public during the summer. The working studio of the famous Montrose sculptor who died in 1951 includes displays of his sculptures, etchings, paintings and drawings. Also featured are his workroom and tools and his living room with furniture he designed and made. In 1932, Lamb was commissioned by

the Duchess of York to make busts of her daughters, Princess Elizabeth and Princess Margaret. So impressed was she that she then commissioned a bust of herself.

To the west of the town, beyond the Basin, is the **House of Dun** (National Trust for Scotland). From 1375 until 1980 the estate was home to the Erskine family, with the present house being designed by William Adam in 1730 for David Erskine, 13th Laird of Dun. It contains good plasterwork, sumptuous furnishings and a collection of embroidery carried out by Lady Augusta Kennedy-Erskine, natural daughter of William IV by his mistress Mrs Jordan. There are also formal gardens and woodland walks.

Montrose was adopted as the title of the Graham family when it was ennobled. The most famous member was James Graham,

RUSHIEMYRE COTTAGE

Burn Estate, Edzell, Brechin,
Angus DD9 7XU
Tel: 01356 648523

This delightful, semi-detached, two bedroom stone property
enjoys a very peaceful location, on the Burn Estate, one mile
north east of the beautiful village of Edzell, which has been
described as the 'Jewel in the Crown of Angus'. It benefits
from both seclusion and accessibility in an area renowned for
its scenery and the many country pursuits that take place in
the vicinity. Tarfside and Glenesk offer excellent walks, or
travel along the Victorian Heritage Trail, passing through
Fettercain and Deeside, ending at Balmoral Castle.
Alternatively there are stately homes warranting a visit,
notably House of Dunn or Clamis Castle.

The property is equipped to a high standard and offers
exceptionally warm and welcoming accommodation for up to
four people. The interior was redecorated in Spring 2009
complete with carpets throughout and a wood burning stove.
The dining room/kitchen is well-appointed, and there is a separate back entrance room with
washing and drying machines, and a deep freeze. Cooking is by electricity. The bathroom has both
bath and shower, and is on the ground floor. Pets are not permitted in the cottage, though there is
an outhouse, which is weatherproof and suitable for their keep.

BEL'S BUTCHERS

25a High Street, Edzell, Angus DD9 7TE
Tel: 01356 648407

The unspoilt village of Edzell is noted for two
attractions in particular: one is the impressive
shell of Edzell Castle; the other, a fine old
traditional butcher's shop - **Bel's Butchers.**
Annabel Forbes bought the business in the
summer of 2007 after previously owning a
catering enterprise. Since her arrival, she has
maintained its status as a high class butcher's
shop specialising in local meats wherever
possible.

You'll find fresh free range poultry from local
farmers, meats from Aberdeenshire pigs, privately
bought Scottish beef which is fully matured, as well as
Aberdeen Angus beef. Local ducks, geese. pheasant in
season, and Scottish smoked salmon are also available.

The sausages and the black and white puddings are
all made on the premises, as are the pies, pasties and
clootie dumplings - the latter being sweet puddings, full
of currants or raisins, that have been boiled in a cloth or
'cloot'. It is rather like a Christmas pudding. Other local
produce on sale includes preserves and honey.

5th Earl and **1st Marquis of Montrose**, who was born in 1612 and succeeded to the earldom in 1625. At first he was a Covenanter, then changed sides. He was made Lieutenant-General of Scotland by the king, and unsuccessfully tried to invade the country with an army. He later went to the Highlands in disguise to raise a Royalist army. During a succession of skirmishes, he defeated Covenanting forces due to his brilliant leadership and almost reckless courage. Charles's defeat at Naseby, however, left him powerless, and his forces were eventually soundly beaten at Philiphaugh in 1645. Afterwards he fled to the Continent but returned in 1650 in support of Charles II. Charles, however, disowned him and he was hanged.

Though not born in Montrose, **George Wishart** the religious reformer has close associations with the town. He attended the grammar school here in the 1520s, and went on to Aberdeen University. He later returned and taught at the grammar school, where he used the Greek translation of the Bible while teaching his pupils. For this he was accused of heresy and had to flee to England. In 1546, he was burnt at the stake in St Andrews on the orders of Cardinal Beaton.

EDZELL
27 miles NE of Dundee on the B966

🏰 Edzell Castle 🏰 Dalhousie Arch

🏛 Glen Esk Folk Museum

There has been a castle at Edzell since at least the 12th century, when one was built by the Abbot family. The present ruins of **Edzell Castle** (Historic Scotland) date from the early 16th century. It was a seat of the Lindsays and reckoned to be the finest castle in Angus. At Edzell there is evidence that life in a Scottish castle was not the cold, draughty experience that people imagine from seeing bare, ruined walls. They could be places of refinement and comfort.

The gardens were especially tasteful and elegant, laid out in 1604 by Sir David Lindsay, though he died in 1610 before they could be completed. The walled garden has been described as an 'Italian Renaissance garden in Scotland', and featured heraldic imagery and an array of carved panels representing deities, the liberal arts and the cardinal virtues.

The castle was added to in 1553 when David Lindsay, 9th Earl of Crawford and a high court judge, built the west wing. In 1562 Mary Stuart spent two nights here, and held a meeting of her Privy Council in her house.

In 1715, the Jacobite Lindsays sold the castle to the Earl of Panmure, who were also Jacobite sympathisers, so that they could raise a Jacobite regiment. After the rebellion, the castle and lands were forfeited to the crown and sold to an English company called the York Building Company, which went bankrupt in 1732. The castle gradually became a ruin, but in the 1930s the gardens were restored to their former glory. The summerhouse contains examples of the carved panelling that was in the castle in its heyday.

One of the delights of Edzell village is the **Dalhousie Arch**, erected in 1887 over a road into the village as a memorial to the 13th Earl of Dalhousie and his wife, who died within a few hours of each other.

Edzell is the gateway to Glen Esk, the longest and most northerly of the glens. You can drive the 19 miles to Invermark Lodge, close to Loch Lee, where the road peters out. Along the way stop at the Retreat, where you will find the **Glen Esk Folk Museum**, which traces the life of the people of the glen from about 1800 to the present day.

ST CYRUS

32 miles NE of Dundee on the A92

🎁 Laird of Bridgeton

St Cyrus is a small village boasting three miles of glorious sandy beaches and an adjacent Nature Reserve. Fishing is still a significant element in the local economy with lobster being particularly important.

Back in the mid-1800s a certain John Orr, the **Laird of Bridgeton**, saw a young couple struggling through snow drifts near St Cyrus and, rather curiously, this inspired him to establish a dowry valued at £1000. The interest was to be divided into five equal parts with one part devoted to helping old folk. The remaining four amounts were to be paid to the youngest, oldest, tallest and shortest brides of the year who had married in St. Cyrus. The dowry is still in place.

Kinross

🏛 Tolbooth 🏛 Kinross House 🦅 Loch Leven

🦅 Vane Farm Nature Reserve 🏛 Lochleven Castle

🖼 Mary, Queen of Scots 🐑 Cashmere at Lochleven

🦅 Scottish Raptor Centre 🌿 T in the Park

Once the main town in the tiny county of Kinross, which measures no more than 15 miles by nine, this small burgh now sits quietly on the shores of Loch Leven. The opening of the M90 motorway has put it within half an hour of Edinburgh, and over the past two decades it has expanded to become a peaceful haven for commuters.

COUNTRY ESSENTIALS GIFT AND COFFEE SHOP

Roadside, St Cyrus, Montrose, Angus DD10 0BA
Tel: 01674 850850
e-mail: countryessentials@btinternet.com
website: www.countryessentials.org.uk

Located in the heart of the village of St Cyrus and fully refurbished in 2009, **Country Essentials Gift and Coffee Shop** provides the opportunity of browsing through the enticing range of gifts on display before passing through to the coffee shop with its alluring aroma of fresh coffee.

Owner Joanne Ashton has gathered together a fascinating range of gifts, many with a local connection. There's beautiful jewellery from the Isle of Bute, Isle of Arran Aromatics, cards and prints by Alex Clark, and an eclectic mixture of paintings by local artists. Children's wooden toys, quizzes and educational items, Yankee candles, Flame Home-ware, quality Taurus handbags - the list goes on and on.

The 38-place coffee shop is notable for its home baking and its range of Italian-style coffees. The home-made cakes, scones, shortbread, biscuits and cookies are all delicious and the menu also offers a good choice of light lunches - soup, sandwiches, baked potatoes and hot toasted pannini served with fresh side salad and home-made coleslaw. Country Essentials is open 7 days a week and has its own very large car park.

🏛 historic building 🏛 museum and heritage 🏛 historic site 🌿 scenic attraction 🦅 flora and fauna

The town's **Tolbooth** dates from the 17th century, and was restored by Robert Adam in 1771. On the Mercat Cross are the 'jougs', an iron collar placed round the neck of wrongdoers. **Kinross House,** built on a slight rise overlooking Loch Leven, dates from the late 17th century, and was built for Sir William Bruce, Charles II's surveyor and master of works. Bruce had been responsible for the fabric of the Palace of Holyrood in Edinburgh. Kinross House is an elegant Palladian mansion, which is still a family home and not open to the public. However, the wonderful formal gardens are open from April to September. An unusual feature within the grounds is the decorative Fish Gate. Between a pair of overflowing cornucopias is an upstanding basket of fish containing, it is said, the seven varieties of fish that could be caught in the loch at that time. They have been listed as being salmon, char, grey trout, speckled trout, blackhead, perch and pike.

Loch Leven is one of Scotland's most famous lochs, not because of its size (it covers 3500 acres) or its spectacular beauty, but because of its wonderful trout fishing. Though this has gone into decline in recent years, the trout are still highly prized for their delicate pink flesh, a by-product of the small fresh water shellfish on which they feed. The whole loch is a National Nature Reserve, and on the south shore of the loch, close to the B9097, is the **Vane Farm Nature Reserve**, administered by the Royal Society for the Protection of Birds and part of the Loch Leven National Nature Reserve. It hosts a programme of events throughout the year, and was the first educational nature reserve in Europe.

The loch has seven islands. On St Serf's Island, the largest, a small Augustinian priory once stood, though all that remains now are the scant walls of the chapel and the ruins of a small priory and chapel.

On another island are the ruins of **Lochleven Castle** (Historic Scotland). It was a Douglas stronghold, the surrounding lands and the loch having been gifted to the family by Robert III in 1390. From June 1567 until May 1568, **Mary, Queen of Scots,** was held prisoner here, having been seized in Edinburgh for her alleged part in the murder of her husband, Lord Darnley. She was 25 years old at the time and married to Bothwell, who was also implicated in Darnley's murder. While kept prisoner in the castle, she was constantly pressurised to abdicate and divorce Bothwell, but this she refused to do, as she was already pregnant by him. However, after giving birth to stillborn twins, she eventually signed the deeds of abdication. But it was not her stay on the island that made the castle famous; rather it was the way she escaped.

The castle was owned by the Dowager Lady Douglas, mother of Mary's half brother, the Earl of Moray, who became regent when Mary abdicated. Both she and her other sons, Sir William and George Douglas, looked after Mary during her imprisonment. But George gradually fell under Mary's spell, and hatched various plans for her to escape. All failed, and he was eventually banished from the island.

But someone else had also fallen under Mary's spell - 16-year-old Willie Douglas, who was thought to be the illegitimate son of Sir William, and who was kept as a page. After the various attempts at escape, Mary was being held in the third storey of the main tower, above the Great Hall where the Douglas family dined. One evening young Willie ,accidentally, dropped a napkin over the castle keys, which his father had placed on the table

Lochleven Castle, Kinross

season stock. There's also a small exhibition called **Cashmere at Lochleven,** which traces the history of this luxury cloth. The **Scottish Raptor Centre** at Turfhills has falconry courses and flying displays. Close to Kinross, in July every year, Scotland's biggest outdoor rock festival is held, **T in the Park.** And don't miss the Kinross Market, the largest indoor market in Scotland, held every Sunday. The Heart of Scotland Visitor Centre gives you a general introduction to the area, and is to be found near Junction 6 of the M90 motorway.

while dining. On picking up the napkin, he picked up the keys as well.

As the meal progressed, Mary and one of her attendants crept out of her room and made for the main doorway, where Willie met them. He unlocked the door, and they both slipped out. He then locked the door behind him and threw the keys into the water before rowing the two women ashore. There they were met by George Douglas, Lord Seton, and a troop of loyal soldiers, and taken to the safety of Niddrie Castle.

In those days, the loch was much bigger and deeper than it is now, and the water came right up to the doors of the castle. Between 1826 and 1836 it was partially drained, reducing its size by a quarter, and the keys were recovered from the mud. Nowadays, trips to the island leave from the pier at Kinross.

Set beside the loch are the premises of Todd and Duncan, probably the best place in Scotland for cashmere bargains. The mill produces knitwear for Ballantyne, Chanel, Clements Ribeiro, Daks, Mulberry, Shelley Fox and others, and its shop is stocked with almost faultless seconds, samples and out-of-

Around Kinross

MILNATHORT
2 miles N of Kinross off the M90

🏛 Burleigh Castle 🏚 Orwell Standing Stones

Milnathort is a small, former wool-manufacturing town. To the east are the striking ruins of 15th-century **Burleigh Castle,** built of warm red stone, which was a stronghold of the Balfour family. All that remains nowadays is a curtain wall and a substantial four-storey tower, which is said to be haunted by the ghost of a woman called Grey Maggie.

There is an interesting story attached to the castle. In 1707 the heir to the castle fell in love with a servant girl, which so displeased his father that he sent him abroad. However, he declared his undying love for her, and swore that if she married someone else while he was away, he would kill him when he returned.

After a year or so he returned, only to find that she had married a schoolmaster. True to his word, he shot him dead. He then fled, but was captured and sentenced to death. However, he escaped the gallows by changing places with his sister and donning her clothes. He later fought in the Jacobite army during the 1715 Uprising. For this, his castle and lands were taken from the family and given to the Irwins.

The **Orwell Standing Stones** are just off the A911. Two huge stones, dating to about 2000BC, stand on a slight rise. One of them fell down in 1972, and during restoration work cremated bones were discovered buried at its foot.

SCOTLANDWELL
5 miles E of Kinross, on the A911

🏯 Arnot Tower 🏯 Holy Well 🦅 Scottish Gliding Centre

Scotlandwell takes its name from the springs that bubble up to the surface in this part of the county, which is on the western slopes of the Lomond Hills. In the early 13th century, the Bishop of St Andrews set up a hospice here, and his successor gave it to the Red Friars, or Trinitarians, a monastic order that had originally been founded to raise money for the release of captives in the Holy Land during the Crusades. They exploited the springs and established a **Holy Well**. Soon it became a place of pilgrimage, bringing huge revenue to the monks. Robert the Bruce came to find a cure for his leprosy, and, while here, held a parliament.

On the slopes above the village are the Crooked Rigs, remnants of a medieval runrig field system.

The local landowners, the Arnots of **Arnot Tower,** the ruins of which can still be seen, gazed enviously at the wealth of the

Trinitarians, and decided to 'muscle in' on the venture. They placed younger sons of the family within the order as fifth columnists, and when enough of them were in place, they occupied the friary and ejected those friars who weren't Arnots. They established Archibald Arnot, the Laird of Arnot's second son, as minister (the name given to the head of the friary), and began creaming off the vast wealth. At the Reformation, the lands and income of the friary were given to them, and the takeover was complete.

The **Holy Well** still exists. In 1858 the Laird of Arnot commissioned David Bryce to turn it into a memorial to his wife Henrietta, and this is what can be seen today. The friary has completely disappeared, though a small plaque in the graveyard marks the spot where it once stood.

At Portmoak near Scotlandwell there's the **Scottish Gliding Centre**, where the adventurous can try a flight.

CROOK OF DEVON
5 miles W of Kinross on the A977

🕌 Lamblaires

This small village has twice won an award for being the Best Kept Village in Kinross. An earlier claim to fame occurred in the 1660s, when it achieved notoriety as a centre of witchcraft. A coven of witches had been discovered in the area, and in 1662 three women were tried and sentenced to be strangled to death and their bodies burnt at a 'place called **Lamblaires**'. A few weeks later four women and one man were executed in the same manner, and not long after two women were tried, one of them escaping death because of her age. The other was burnt at the stake.

By this time the other members of the

COUNTY FABRICS

Watermill, Crook of Devon Village, Kinross KY13 0UL
Tel: 01577 840529
Fax: 01577 840626
e-mail: info@county-fabrics.com
website: www.county-fabrics.com

Offering quality curtain and upholstery fabrics at affordable prices, **County Fabrics** carries stock from many of the major global manufacturers and also from smaller, lesser known suppliers. The fabrics are a combination of tried and tested favourites, mixed in with more eclectic selections, giving a wonderful range of materials from which to choose. There are also more than 200 pattern books for you to browse through. Some of the fabrics are discontinued or slight seconds from many leading suppliers which are on sale at a fraction of their regular retail price.

Designed and produced exclusively for County Fabrics is the Bird Fabric range based on watercolours by Iona Buchanan, the niece of owner Moray Wallace. Her next design will feature freshwater fish. A making-up service is available for curtains, pelmets, blinds, tiebacks, bedspreads and all other soft furnishing requirements, and there is also an upholsterer on site who can provide a quotation, or the helpful staff can suggest someone in your own area. County Fabrics is open from 10am to 5pm, Monday to Saturday.

---

coven had fled from the area. But in July, two further women were put on trial, one of whom was executed and the other, Christian Grieve, acquitted. The acquittal was regarded as an affront by the local people - especially the clergy - and she was retried and eventually executed.

There is no doubt that the trials were a travesty, and that many old scores were settled by naming people - especially old women - as witches. It was also not unknown in Scotland at that time for the accused, knowing their fate was sealed, to get their own back on the accusers by naming them as witches and warlocks as well. Thus Scotland seemed to be awash with devil worship, when, in fact, it was very rare.

Today Lamblaires is a small grassy knoll in a field adjoining the village. It looks peaceful enough, with nothing to remind you of the horrible stranglings and burnings that took place there.

Perth

- 🏛 St Ninian's Cathedral ⚜ James
- 🏛 St John's Kirk
- 🏛 Black Watch Regimental Museum
- 🏛 Perth Museum & Art Gallery
- ⚜ Fergusson Gallery 🖼 Catherine Glover
- 🏛 Fair Maid's House
- ⚜ Caithness Glass Visitor Centre
- 🌿 Bell's Cherrybank Gardens
- 🌿 Branklyn Garden ⛰ Kinnoull Hill

The Fair City of Perth sits on the Tay, and in medieval times was the meeting place of Scottish kings and parliaments. Though a large place by Scottish standards, having a

---

🏛 historic building 🏛 museum and heritage 🏛 historic site ⛰ scenic attraction 🌿 flora and fauna

population of about 43,000, its location away from the Central Belt ensured that it was never overwhelmed by the intense industrialisation that many other towns experienced. But it did succumb to the ravages of modernisation, and many of the ancient buildings that played a part in Scotland's story have been swept away.

The city centre lies between two large open spaces, the North Inch and the South Inch, and is filled with elegant 18th and 19th century buildings. Up until the local government reorganisations of the mid 1970s, it had a lord provost and was truly a city. It even has **St Ninian's Cathedral**, which dates from the 19th century, was designed by Wiliam Butterfield and consecrated in 1850. It was the first cathedral to be built in Britain aftre the Reformation.

Perth has played a large part in the history of Scotland. **James I** chose it as his capital, and if he had not been murdered in the city in 1437, it might have been Scotland's capital to this day. The story of James's murder has been embellished over the years, but the facts are simple. He was an unpopular monarch, and when he was staying in the city's Dominican Friary (now gone), he was attacked by a group

of nobles under the Earl of Atholl, who hoped to claim the crown. James tried to make his escape through a sewer that ran beneath his room, but was caught and stabbed to death. An embellishment to the story is that one of his Queen's ladies-in-waiting stuck her arm through the boltholes of the door as a bar to prevent the entry of the assassins. However, that is probably a later invention.

In the centre of the city is **St John's Kirk**, one of the finest medieval kirks in Scotland. From this church, the city took its earlier name of St Johnstoune, which is remembered in the name of the local football team. The Kirk was consecrated in 1243, though the earliest part of what you see nowadays, the choir, dates from the 15th century, with the tower being added in 1511. It has some Renaissance glass, and it was here, in May 1559, that John Knox first preached after his return from exile in Europe. It more or less launched the Reformation in Scotland.

After the Reformation of 1560, the building was divided into three churches, with three distinct congregations. It was not until the early 20th century that the church housed one congregation again. The architect for the scheme was Sir Robert Lorimer, and the

---

THE BEAN SHOP

67 George Street, Perth PH1 5LB
Tel: 01738 449955
e-mail: sales@thebeanshop.com
website: www.thebeanshop.com

Located opposite the Perth Museum and Art Gallery, **The Bean Shop** specialises in gourmet coffees and teas. Its traditional Georgian shop front, painted in duck egg blue, has windows full of tea and coffee goods, Espresso machines and designer cafetières. The interior is beautifully decorated and here you'll find a marvellous choice of coffees and teas. Owners Lorna and John Bruce have created a haven for the coffee and tea connoisseur, a great place with a welcoming atmosphere in which to enjoy your choice of organic, Rainforest Alliance and Fairtrade coffees.

WHISPERS OF THE PAST

15 George Street, Perth PH1 5JY
Tel: 01738 635472

As Perth's original fine gifts boutique, **Whispers of the Past** has been serving this vibrant city for over 25 years. A family business throughout, it was started by Christine Wilson. Nowadays her two daughters, Laura and Sarah run the business offering an eclectic mix of both old and new, covering all the seasons. Modern and antique jewellery, ranging from costume baubles to quality gold and silver pieces sit alongside linen, china, silk flowers, cards and French candles. A gift wrapping service is available. Styles may change but impeccable craftsmanship is timeless. The shop is well known as the place to go for Easter and Christmas gifts and decorations.

A visit to Whispers of the Past is a must when visiting Perth. You will find an extensive range of quality items to fit most budgets and a warm welcome always.

THE SMART GOOD FOOD SHOP

8 Bridge Lane, Perth PH1 5JJ
Tel: 01738 451591
e-mail: sales@thesmartgoodfoodshop.com
website: www.thesmartgoodfoodshop.com

Overlooking the entrance to the new Perth Concert Hall, the Smart Good Food Shop is tucked in the corner of Bridge Lane and the town lade. The shop was established in 2005 by James and Eva Smart, both of them lovers of good food and wines. With fresh fruit, vegetables and herbs outside the shop, we welcome you to explore two floors of delicatessen products. On the ground floor you will find an amazing selection of olives and antipasti, as well as local and continental cheeses, smoked and home roasted meats, own made pies, terrines and quiches. All our own made products are made on the premises in small batches and the range also includes chutneys, relishes, oatcakes and shortbread. We also make our own hand made chocolates from the finest Belgium

chocolate. Too good to miss. The first floor boasts a selection of fine wines, including many organic ones, Italian pastas, a large range of olive oils, sauces and pickles and well as chocolates, Indonesian and Dutch goodies. The Smart Good Food Shop also offers a bespoke outside catering service and caters from office lunches to weddings, celebrations, barbecues and parties or any other event that demands high quality food. All food is freshly prepared on the premises and menus are tailored to your specific event requirements.

furnishings in the nave are mostly his work.

In Balhousie Castle in Hay Street near the North Inch you'll find the **Black Watch Regimental Museum**. Raised in 1725 from the ranks of clans generally hostile to the Jacobites, such as the Campbells, Frasers and Grants, its purpose was to patrol or 'watch' the Highlands after the first Jacobite Uprising, the Black Watch is now the senior Highland regiment (see also Aberfeldy).

The **Perth Museum and Art Gallery** is in George Street, and is one of the oldest in Britain. It houses material whose scope goes beyond the city and its immediate area, as well as a collection of fine paintings, sculpture, glass and silver. The **Fergusson Gallery** in Marshall Place is dedicated to the painter John Duncan Fergusson (1874-1961) who, along with Peploe, Cadell and Hunter formed a group called the Scottish Colourists. The gallery, which opened in 1992, is housed in a former waterworks dating from 1832.

In 1928 Sir Walter Scott's novel *The Fair Maid of Perth* was published, the heroine of which was **Catherine Glover**, daughter of Simon Glover, who lived in Curfew Row. It was set in the 14th century, and tells of how Catherine, a woman noted for her piety and beauty, was sought after by all the young men of the city. David Stewart, Duke of Rothesay and son of Robert III, also admired her, though his intentions were not honourable. He was thwarted by Hal Gow, who came upon the duke and his men trying to enter Catherine's house in the dead of night.

The ensuing skirmish resulted in one of the duke's retainers having his hand hacked off by Hal before they fled in disarray. Catherine slept through it all, though Hal wakened her

stories and anecdotes 🐦 famous people 🎨 art and craft 🎭 entertainment and sport 🚶 walks

LICKWID

35 George Street, Perth PH1 5LA
Tel: 01738 444140
e-mail: lickwid@hotmail.com

Lickwid Ice Cream Parlour is a modern style gelato shop situated half way down historic George Street. The shop has been open a number of years and has won prestigious awards for their Dairy Ice Cream which is made using organic milk & cream from Scottish dairies. The shop is friendly with attentive staff who enjoy spending time with customers of all ages. During sunny days you can sit outside and bask in the sunshine. Lickwid offers customers free samples of the 24 delicious dairy ice cream flavours, superb knickerbocker glories, sensational sundaes, hot waffles with that WOW factor. Lickwid has professionally trained barista staff offering a smooth locally roasted quality coffee and imported fine tea, they also offer other hot and cold drinks along with sandwiches & homemade soup for those colder days or perhaps try their porridge with honey, cream or raisins which can be made to order.

The parlour is within minutes walk from Perth museum, North Inch Park and the beautiful River Tay. "We offer indoor & outside seating, toilet facilities, we are very much child and dog friendly, so show us your guide book and we will show great hospitality."

father and showed him the severed hand. The story ends happily when Hal subsequently marries Catherine.

The present **Fair Maid's House** (private) does not go back as far as the 14th century. However, it is more than 300 years old, and incorporates some medieval walls, which may have belonged to the original house that stood on the site. In 1867 Bizet wrote his opera *The Fair Maid of Perth,* based on Scott's book, and the story became even more popular.

The **Caithness Glass Visitor Centre** at Inveralmond has viewing galleries from which you can see glass being blown into beautiful glass ornaments and vases. There is also a shop. **Bell's Cherrybank Gardens** is an 18-acre garden on the western edge of the city. It incorporates the National Heather Collection, which has over 900 varieties of

heather. On the Dundee road is the **Branklyn Garden** (NTS), developed by John and Dorothy Rentonn, who bought the house in 1922. One of its more unusual plants is the rare blue Himalayan poppy. **Kinnoull Hill**, to the east of Perth, rises to a height of 729 feet above the Tay. If you are reasonably fit, you can walk to the summit, where there is a folly, and get some wonderful views across the Tay to Fife, over to Perth and beyond, and down over the Carse of Gowrie.

Around Perth

SCONE PALACE
2 miles N of Perth off the A93

🏛 Moot Hill 🏰 Scone Palace

Historically and culturally, Scone (pronounced Scoon) is one of the most important places in

Scotland. When Kenneth MacAlpin, king of Dalriada, also became king of the Picts in 843AD, he quit his capital at Dunadd and moved to Scone. He made the move to be nearer the centre of his new kingdom and to escape from the constant Norse raids on the western seaboard. This was the beginning of the kingdom of Scotland as we know it, though it would be another 170 years before the Lowland kingdoms of Strathclyde and the Lothians were absorbed.

Scone Palace

Scone Abbey, (now gone) was built by Alexander I in 1114 for the Augustinians but was totally destroyed after the Reformation. Outside of it, on **Moot Hill** (which can still be seen) the Scottish kings were crowned sitting on the Stone of Destiny. It was here that Robert the Bruce was crowned king of Scotland in 1306, in defiance of Edward I of England. Traditionally, the Earl of Fife placed the crown on the monarch's head, but as he was being held in England, he could not perform the duty. Therefore his sister, Isobel MacDuff, Countess of Buchan, took his place, incurring the wrath of both Edward I and her own husband who supported Edward's claim to the throne.

A replica of the Stone of Destiny is to be found at the summit of Moot Hill, along with a small chapel. The last king to be crowned at Scone was Charles II in 1651. The stone is also called Jacob's Pillow, and is supposed to have been the pillow on which the Biblical Jacob slept, though the present one, housed in Edinburgh, was almost certainly quarried in Perthshire. However, there are those who say that when Edward I seized the stone in 1296, he was given a worthless copy by the monks of the abbey.

FOR ART SAKE

10 Angus Road, Scone, Perth PH2 6QU
Tel/Fax: 01738 552187
website: www.forartsake.info

Are you feeling creative? Do you fancy a new hobby? Would you like to make a unique and heartfelt gift? For Art Sake opens up a whole new world for children and adults alike – whether you are artistic or not. The friendly staff specialise in helping you to paint beautiful ceramic pieces. Should you choose a glaze project, they will fire your work and it will be ready within a couple of days, alternatively, you may wish to paint using Acrylics, which can be finished and taken home on the same day. Try something new – you may surprise yourself!

🎭 stories and anecdotes 🐦 famous people 🎨 art and craft ✏ entertainment and sport 🚶 walks

ANN DAVIDSON

31 Perth Road, Scone, Perth PH2 6JJ
Tel: 01738 551313

Ann Davidson has been a butcher since leaving school. She learnt the trade working in her father's shop, founded during World War II, and then established her own business in June 2007. Her stand-alone shop looks very appealing from the outside with its pink and white striped awning and life-size figure of a friendly butcher standing by the window.

Inside, the full length counter is packed with an array of appetising edibles, all of it from the Davidsons' own farm. Amongst them are Ann's own home-made pies, meat loaf, haggis and sausages made from meat that has been hung for 3½ weeks to ensure the fullest flavour. The chickens are all free range and in addition to the meat products, Ann also offers her own delicious apple pies and there's a separate cabinet stocked with jars of local produce - jams, preserves, pickles and more. A typical country village butcher's, the shop is just a 5-minute walk from historic Scone Palace.

THE BANKFOOT INN

Main Street, Bankfoot, Perthshire, PH1 4AB
Tel: 01738 787243
e-mail: info@bankfootinn.co.uk website: www.bankfootinn.co.uk

Offering a great atmosphere, this traditional 18th century coaching inn is located in the scenic village of Bankfoot, right in the heart of Perthshire. Situated just south of Dunkeld and near to the villages of Kenmore, Pitlochry and Aberfeldy, the inn is an ideal base for weekends, short breaks and longer stays, and is only short drive from many main sights with great walks right on the door step.

Rab and Susan Wallace took over in 2007, and have restored its historic charm back to what it is today. With their personal approach, you will be assured a warm welcome and comfortable stay.

The inn offers six well-appointed rooms, recently redecorated for 2009. The recently restored restaurant is open for lunch and dinner, serving locally-sourced, home-cooked food. The bar, with open fires, is the ideal place to sample an ever-growing collection of single malts or a wide range of ales from various Scottish breweries.

Live music is available at the end of each month (check website for details) and the inn also hosts weekly musicians "open session" every Wednesday evening – all are welcome, bring an instrument if you like! The Bankfoot Inn is very close to the River Tay (we're only 1 mile from Stanley). Popular for fly fishing, many famous salmon beats are only a few minutes from our door. We can cater for fishing parties and have facilities to freeze caught salmon and provide locked storage for assembled rods.

The Bankfoot Inn can cater for shooting parties and offers an ideal position for any groups wishing to enjoy the Glorious Twelfth and can store birds in our outbuildings.

Scone Palace itself is the home of the Earls of Mansfield and dates from the early 19th century. The State Rooms contain a magnificent collection of objects d'art, including pieces that once belonged to Marie Antoinette. There are paintings by Reynolds, Zoffany and Wilkie, and the Library has one of the finest collections of porcelain, including pieces from Sèvres, Ludwigsburg and Meissen. Within the grounds of the palace are some wonderful collections of shrubs and woodland walks through the pinetum which, contains David Douglas' original fir.

STANLEY
6 miles N of Perth on the B9099

🏚 Kinclaven Castle

The picturesque small village of Stanley sits on the River Tay, and is a former mill village. Sir Richard Arkwright had an interest in the mills here, the first of which was founded in 1786. Three large mills were built in the 1820s, powered by seven waterwheels. Four miles away are the ruins of 13th-century **Kinclaven Castle**, once a favourite residence of Alexander II, who had built it. William Wallace ambushed a small force of English troops near here in 1297, and when they took refuge in the castle Wallace besieged it, forcing it to surrender.

BANKFOOT
7 miles N of Perth on A9

🔏 The Macbeth Experience

This small village sits just off the A9. The **Macbeth Experience** is a multi-media show that explains all about one of Scotland's most famous kings. It debunks the Macbeth of Shakespeare's play and instead concentrates on the actual man and his achievements.

MEIKLEOUR
10 miles N of Perth on A984

🌱 Meikleour Hedge

The **Meikleour Hedge**, just outside the village on the A93, is the world's largest. It borders the road for more than 600 yards, and is now over 85 feet high. It is of pure beech, and was supposed to have been planted in 1745 by Jean Mercer and her husband Robert Murray Nairne, who was later killed at the Battle of Culloden. Jean immediately left the area, and the hedge was allowed to grow unattended for many years.

BLAIRGOWRIE
14 miles N of Perth on the A93

🔏 Cateran Trail 🏚 Craighall Castle

This trim town, along with its sister town of Rattray, became one burgh in 1928 by an Act of Parliament. It is noted as the centre of a raspberry and strawberry growing area. It sits beside the Ericht, a tributary of the Tay, and the riverside here is very attractive. Cargill's Visitor Centre, housed in a former corn mill, stands on its bank and has Scotland's largest water wheel. Within the library in Leslie Street is the Blairgowrie Genealogy Centre where you can carry out research on the old families of the area.

The **Cateran Trail** is named after medieval brigands from beyond Braemar who used to descend on Perthshire to wreak havoc and steal cattle. It is a 60-mile-long circular route centred on Blairgowrie, and uses existing footpaths and minor roads to take you on a tour of the area. It has been designed to take about five or six days to complete, with stops every 12 or 13 miles, and takes in parts of Angus as well as Perthshire.

Craighall Castle, the earliest parts of

GALLIMAUFRY

58 High Street, Blairgowrie, Perthshire PH10 6DF
Tel: 01250 875550

If you are in search of interesting and unusual gifts, or for something to add distinction to your own decor, then the place to visit is **Gallimaufry** on Blairgowrie's High Street. According to the dictionary, 'gallimaufry' is a collection of varied things, a hotchpotch, a description that doesn't really do justice to the fascinating array of items that owner Noreen Philip has gathered together in her colourful shop.

A former tourism officer for Wester Ross, Noreen opened Gallimaufry in the autumn of 2008 and has quickly established a reputation for offering quality items at reasonable prices. You'll find an enticing range of jewellery, a range of linens, some interesting pottery, and a selection of aromatics, decorative pieces, candles and spices. Specifically for ladies, there's a range of stylish tartan handbags and hand-made felted jackets and knitted goods.

October sees Gallimaufry transformed into a Christmas emprorium bursting with traditional, quirky and bespoke seasonal goodies!

Gallimaufry is just a 1-minute walk from the town centre car park and the shop is open from 9.30am to 5.30pm, Monday to Saturday.

KINNAIRD CERAMICS

Bankfoot Cottage, Kinnaird by Inchture,
Perthshire PH14 9QY
Tel: 01828 686371
e-mail: janekirakira@aol.com
website: www.kirakiraceramics.com

Located near the top of a hill village overlooking the beautiful Carse of Gowrie, **Kinnaird Ceramics** was established by Jane Woodford who studied at Duncan of Jordanstone College of Art and Design in Dundee. Specialising in ceramics and printmaking, she graduated with a B. Des (Hons) in Design in 1999. Her studio is housed in an ancient outhouse above Kinnaird Castle, "probably where hunting dogs were kennelled some 200 years ago!" she says. It has been transformed into a lovely, light work space behind her cottage.

Kinnaird Ceramics makes contemporary ceramics for the home. Jane's speciality pieces are beautiful In-glaze Reduction Lustre - the glazes contain silver! So if you fancy a shimmering bowl, jug, vase, or table lamp in gold or turquoisy blues, come and visit. You can watch pots of all sizes being thrown on the wheel, and courses are available for both adults and children.

Jane's new work mixes the old and the new. Decorative pieces incorporate old family lace, yet have a fresh contemporary look to them. Lacy platters in aqua and indigo glazes look very striking mixed with plain white china. Jane always welcome commissions - a unique design can be made for your home or as a special wedding gift.

which date from the 16th century, is perched on a cliff above the Elricht. Sir Walter Scott visited it, and he used it as a model for Tullyveolan in his book *Waverley*. It now offers B&B accommodation.

COUPAR ANGUS
12 miles NE of Perth on the A94

🏛 Coupar Angus Abbey 🏛 Tolbooth

Situated in Strathmore, Coupar Angus is a small town that was given its burgh charter in 1607. The scant remains of the gatehouse of **Coupar Angus Abbey**, founded by Malcolm IV for the Cistercians in the mid-12th century, stand in the kirkyard. At one time it was the wealthiest Cistercian abbey in Scotland. The town's **Tolbooth** dates from 1702, and was used as a courthouse and prison.

MEIGLE
16 miles NE of Perth on the b954

🏛 Meigle Museum

The finest collection of Pictish stones in Scotland was found in and around Meigle, and they are now on display at **Meigle Museum** (Historic Scotland), in a converted schoolhouse. The largest stone, at eight feet tall, is Meigle 2, and shows a fine carved cross on the side and mounted horsemen and mythical animals at the bottom. The central panel shows what appears to be Daniel surrounded by four lions, but some people have put another intrepretation on it. They say it depicts the execution of Queen Guinevere. It seems that she was captured by Mordred, king of the Picts, and that when she was released Arthur ordered her execution by being pulled apart by wild animals. The museum is open from April to September.

ERROL
8 miles E of Perth on a minor road off the A90

🏛 Parish Church 🎨 Tayreed Company

🎨 Errol Station Trust

Set in the Carse of Gowrie, a narrow stretch of fertile land bordering the northern shore of the Firth of Tay, Errol is a peaceful village with a large **Parish Church** designed by James Gillespie Graham in 1831, which is sometimes called the 'cathedral of the Carse'. It gives its name to an earldom, which means that there is an Earl of Errol (see Slains Castle). A leaflet is available that gives details of most of the old kirkyards and kirks in the Carse. The **Tayreed Company**, based in an industrial estate, harvests reeds for thatching from reedbeds on the nearby Tay. In the 1990's the **Errol Station Trust** opened the former railway station as a heritage centre. It is now a coffee and craft shop.

ELCHO
3 miles SE of Perth on a minor road

🏛 Elcho Castle

Elcho Castle (Historic Scotland) was the ancient seat of the Earls of Wemyss. The present handsome and complete castle was built by Sir John Wemyss in the 16th century on the site of an earlier fortification dating from the 13th century. By about 1780, the castle had been abandoned, and it gradually became a ruin. It was re-roofed in 1830.

ABERNETHY
6 miles SE of Perth on the A913

🏛 Abernethy Round Tower 🏛 Abernethy Museum

The pleasant village of Abernethy stands on the banks of the River Earn where it joins the River Tay. It is best known for the 75-feet-high **Abernethy Round Tower**

(Historic Scotland), which is one of only two round towers in Scotland (see also Brechin). It dates from the end of the 9th century and was used as a place of refuge for priests during times of trouble. At the foot of the tower is a carved Pictish stone.

In 1072, Malcolm III met William the Conquerer here and knelt in submission, acknowledging him as his overlord. This act had repercussions down through the ages - Edward I used it to justify his claim that Scottish kings owed allegiance to him. The **Abernethy Museum**, founded in the year 2000, explains the village's history, and is housed in an 18th-century building.

In Main Street the oddly named Tootie House is a reminder of the days when the cowherd blew his horn as a signal for the villagers to release their cows to be driven to the common grazing.

FORTEVIOT
6 miles SW of Perth on the B935

This little village was at one time the capital of a Pictish kingdom. In a field to the north of the River Earn stood the Dupplin Cross, erected, it is thought, in the 9th century by King Constantine I, who died in 877AD. It was taken to the National Museum of Scotland in 1998 for restoration.

DUNNING
8 miles SW of Perth on the B934

🎦 Maggie Wall   🏛 St Serf's Parish Church

This quiet village is mainly visited because of **St Serf's Parish Church**, with its fine early 13th-century tower. The original church was probably built by Gilbert, Earl of Strathearn, in around 1200. A couple of miles outside the village, near the road, is a monument topped with a cross that marks the spot where, according to its inscription, **Maggie Wall**, a witch, was burned in 1657. It is the only memorial to a witch in Scotland, though no record has ever been found about the trial or execution of someone called Maggie Wall. The whole thing - including who actually built the cairn - remains a mystery.

AUCHTERARDER
12 miles SW of Perth on the A824

🎦 Auchterarder Heritage   🏛 Tullibardine Chapel

Situated a couple of miles north of the Gleneagles Hotel, Auchterarder is a small royal burgh with a long main street. It has been bypassed by the busy A9, and retains a quiet charm. At **Auchterarder Heritage**, within the local tourist office in the High Street, there are displays about local history. It was in Auchterarder in 1559 that Mary of Guise, Mary Stuart's mother, signed the Treaty of Perth acknowledging that Scotland was a Protestant country.

About three miles west of the town, near the A823, is the cruciform **Tullibardine Chapel** (Historic Scotland), one of the few finished collegiate chapels in Scotland that have remained unaltered over the years. It was founded by Sir David Murray of Tullibardine, ancestor of the Dukes of Atholl, in 1446.

The village nestles at the foot of the Ochil Hills whose springs are noted for the purity of their waters. Presumably this was why Scotland's first public brewery was built here. Records have survived showing that at James IV's coronation in 1488, beer from Tullibardine brewery was drunk. The site of the brewery is now occupied by the Tullibardine Distillery, which produces a fine single malt whisky. It has a visitors centre, which is open from May to September each year.

D & R JOHNSTON

173 High Street, Auchterarder, Perthshire PH3 1AD
Tel/Fax: 01764 662762
e-mail: info@johnstonshoes.co.uk
website: www.johnstonshoes.co.uk

D & R Johnston is that rarity nowadays - a genuine, family-run footwear specialist. You just can't afford to miss the shop - it sits in Auchterarder, just off the A9, so be sure to call in when visiting the town or passing by. It is a totally independent business with a huge range of shoes and accessories, so you are sure to find something that is just right for you, whether formal or casual.

The staff are friendly, informal and very knowledgeable. Customers come from far and wide to buy their footwear here, and return again and again. Most ladies shoes are stocked in sizes 3 to 8, with a selection of size 2s. 'Dressy' brands such as Van Dal, HB and Lotus are available, most with matching bags. These are complemented by the German styling of Gabor and Ara which usually suit people wanting a wider fitting. For the finishing touch to any outfit there are fabulous bags from Gabor, Bulaggi and Rieker.

Finally, don't forget comfort when relaxing at home. D & R Johnston also stocks a wide range of high quality slippers, including leading brand Nordika for both ladies and gents.

MUTHILL

15 miles SW of Perth on the A822

🏛 Muthill Parish Church 🏛 Muthill Village Museum
🏛 Innerpeffray Library 🏛 Innerpeffray Chapel
🏛 Innerpeffray Castle 🌿 Drummond Castle Gardens

Within Muthill (pronounced Mew-thill) are the ruins of the former **Muthill Parish Church** (Historic Scotland), which date mainly from the early 15th century, though the tower was probably built four centuries earlier. The **Muthill Village Museum** is housed in a cottage built about 1760. It is open on Wednesdays, Saturdays and Sundays from June to September each year.

Three miles east of Muthill, at Innerpeffray, is **Innerpeffray Library**, one of the oldest libraries in Scotland. It was founded in 1680 by David Drummond, 3rd Lord Maddertie and brother-in-law of the Marquis of Montrose,

and is housed in a building specially built for it in 1750. It contains many rare books, such as a copy of the 16th-century Treacle Bible, so called because the translation of Jeremiah chapter 8 verse 22 reads, 'Is there not triacle (treacle) at Gilead'. There is also a 1508 *Ship of Fools*, a medieval satire written by a German writer called Simon Brant. Before moving to its present building it was housed in **Innerpeffray Chapel** (Historic Scotland), built in 1508. The ruins of **Innerpeffray Castle** are nearby. It is a simple tower house dating from the 15th century, which was heightened in 1610 for the 1st Lord Maddertie.

Drummond Castle Gardens are regarded as amongst the finest in Europe. They were first laid out in the 17th century, improved and terraced in the 19th, and replanted in the middle of the 20th. There's a magnificent Italianate parterre and a mile-long beech-lined avenue leading to an imposing ridge-top tower

Drummond Castle & Gardens, Muthill

HUNTINGTOWER

2 miles W of Perth on the A85

🏛 Huntingtower Castle

Huntingtower Castle (Historic Scotland) is a restored 15th-century tower house once owned by the Ruthvens, Earls of Gowrie, and then the Murrays. The interior of the castle is notable for its striking painted ceilings. Mary Stuart visited the castle twice and, in 1582, the famous Raid of Ruthven took place here, when the Earl of Gowrie and his friend the Earl of Mar tried to kidnap the young King James VI. Justice in those days was sometimes swift, as the perpetrators were first executed, and then tried for treason. The castle has no connection with the John Buchan spy yarn, also called Huntingtower, which was set in Ayrshire.

FOWLIS WESTER

12 miles W of Perth on a minor road off the A85

🏛 Parish Church of St Bean

The first name of this small village (pronounced fowls) comes from the Gaelic foghlais, meaning stream or burn. However, there is another, more intriguing derivation. It seems that long ago three French brothers settled in Scotland - one at Fowlis Wester, one at Fowlis Easter near Dundee and one at Fowlis in Ross-shire. They each named their village after the French word for leaves, feuilles. Above an archway in the **Parish Church of St Bean** in Fowlis Wester is a carving showing three leaves.

The church stands on a spot where a place of worship has stood since at least the 8th century. The present one dates from the 15th-century, and is dedicated to an 8th century Irish saint, grandson of the King of Leinster, who preached in the area. The church has a leper's squint, a small window

house (private). In 1842, Queen Victoria visited the castle and its gardens and planted two copper beech trees, which can still be seen.

To the east of the village are the sites of two Roman signal stations - the Ardunie Signal Station and the Muir O'Fauld Signal Station. They were two of a series of such stations running between Ardoch and the Tay, and date back to the 1st century AD.

BRACO

19 miles SW of Perth on the A822

Half a mile north of the village are the Blackhall Camps, two Roman marching camps that date back to the 3rd century AD.

that allowed lepers to see the chancel area without coming into contact with the congregation. Two Pictish cross slabs from the 8th or 9th centuries are housed within the church - a 10-feet high cross slab and a smaller one. The larger one shows two horsemen and some animals on one side and a man leading a cow and six men on the other. The smaller slab shows two men - possibly priests - seated on chairs. A replica of the larger one stands on the village green. Also in the church is a fragment of the McBean tartan, taken to the moon by American astronaut Alan Bean. He was the lunar module pilot on Apollo 12 during the second mission to the moon in November 1969, and the fourth man to walk on its surface.

CRIEFF
15 miles W of Perth on the A85

 Falls of Turret Lady Mary's Walk

The second largest town in Perthshire with a population of around 6000, Crieff is an inland holiday resort and the 'capital' of that area of Scotland known as Strathearn. At the centre of the town is St James's Square with an elaborate Victorian fountain. At the Crieff Visitor Centre on Muthill Road, in addition to copious information about the area, you can also see a display of paperweights, pottery and miniature animal sculptures. The Glenturret Distillery at the Hosh, home of the famous Grouse Experience, is Scotland's oldest, and tours (with a dram at the end) are available.

Lady Mary's Walk, a mile-long beech-lined avenue beside the River Earn, was gifted to the town in 1815 by Sir Patrick Murray of Ochtertyre in memory of his daughter Mary. Another popular feature is Macrosty Park, opened in 1902 and named after its benefactor, James Macrosty, who was provost of the town. The park is one of the most picturesque in Scotland, with a fine collection of mature specimen trees and the Turret Burn flowing through it. The Victorian bandstand, gifted by the brother of James Macrosty, has brass band concerts in summer.

Crieff stands at the beginning of Glen Turret, within which are the picturesque **Falls Of Turret**. The 3480-feet-high Ben Chonzie, eight miles north west of Crieff, has been described as the 'most boring Munro in Scotland', though this is doing it an injustice. It can be climbed via a route leaving the car park at Loch Turret dam.

The Baird Monument stands on a hill to the west of the town, and was erected by his widow in memory of Sir David Baird (1757-1829), the distinguished general whose achievements included taking South Africa from the Dutch.

MADDERTY
10 miles W of Perth off the A85

 Inchaffray Abbey

To the north east of this village is the site of **Inchaffray Abbey**, of which nothing now remains apart from a low mound. The name means island of the smooth waters, as at one time the mound was an island within a small loch.

COMRIE
21 miles W of Perth on the A85

 Melville Monument De'ils Cauldron Waterfall

This village is often called the earthquake capital of Scotland and the shaky toun as it sits right on the Highland Boundary Fault. James Melville, writing in his diary in July 1597, mentions an earth tremor, though the first fully recorded one was in 1788. A 72-feet-high monument to him - the **Melville Monument** - stands on Dunmore Hill. In 1874, it was struck by lightning, and the man who climbed to its top to repair it swore he could see Edinburgh Castle.

In 1839, a major earthquake took place, causing the world's first seismometers to be set up in the village. The recently refurbished Earthquake House, built in 1874, now houses an array of instruments to measure the tremors.

North of the village, in Glen Lednock, is the **De'ils Cauldron Waterfall**, overlooked by a granite obelisk commemorating Henry Dundas, 1st Viscount Melville (1742-1811).

To the south of the village, off the B827, is the **Auchingarrich Wildlife Centre**, with a wide variety of animals, including Highland cattle, wallabies, llamas, raccoons, porcupines, otters, meerkats, maras, prairie dogs, chipmunks, deer and birds of prey. There's also a wild bird hatchery, woodland walks and an adventure playground.

ST FILLANS
26 miles W of Perth on the A85

🏰 Loch Earn Castle

St Fillans stands at the eastern end of Loch Earn, where the River Earn exits on its way to join the Firth of Tay, and is a gateway to the new Loch Lomond and Trossachs National Park. It is named after the Irish missionary St Fillan. Two relics of the saint - his bell and his pastoral staff - are now housed within the National Museum of Scotland.

On an island in Loch Earn stand the scant ruins of **Loch Earn Castle**, which belonged to Clan MacNeish. From here they plundered the surrounding countryside before retreating to the safety of their castle. The McNabs, whom they attacked in 1612, gained their revenge by

carrying a boat over the mountains, unseen by the MacNeishes, and mounting a surprise attack. The MacNeish clan chief was killed, as were most of his followers. Since then, the McNab crest has featured the head of the chief of Clan McNeish.

At the top of Dunfillan Hill (600 feet) is a rock known as St Fillan's Chair. To the southwest, overlooking Loch Earn, is Ben Vorlich (3224 feet).

Pitlochry

🌱 Salmon Ladder 🎭 Pitlochry Festival Theatre
🏞 Road to the Isles 🏞 Queen's View
🏞 Loch Faskally 🏛 Dunfallandy Standing Stone

Set amidst some of the most beautiful scenery in Europe, Pitlochry has been a popular holiday resort for more than a 100 years. It is said to be at the geographical heart of the country, and is as far from the sea as it is possible to be in Scotland. It was the 2003 winner of the Best Small Country Town in the Britain in Bloom contest.

Though not a large town, Pitlochry relies heavily on tourism, and is full of hotels and guest houses, making it a good stopping off point for those travelling further north. At the Pitlochry Visitor Centre, near the dam, there is the famous **Salmon Ladder**, which allows salmon to enter the loch from the River Tummel below. There is a viewing gallery, which allows you to watch the salmon, and displays about how electricity is produced from flowing water. Beside the loch is a picnic area with an archway called the Clunie Arch. It has the exact dimensions of the tunnel that brings the waters from Loch Tummel to the Clunie Power Station.

Another place not to be missed is the **Pitlochry Festival Theatre**. It was founded in 1951 and presented its first plays in a tent. It continued like this until 1981 when a purpose-built theatre was opened at Port-na-Craig on the banks of the Tummel. It presents a varied programme of professional plays every summer, and is one of Scotland's most popular venues.

From Pitlochry, the B8019, the famous **Road to the Isles**, goes west towards beautiful Loch Tummel, whose waters have been harnessed for electricity. It passes the Forestry Commission Visitor Centre, which interprets the wildlife of the area. From the **Queen's View** there is a magnificent view west towards Loch Tummel and beyond. Queen Victoria stopped at this point during her Highland tour in 1866 and praised the scenery, though it is said that it was Mary Stuart who originally gave the place its name when she visited in 1564.

Loch Faskally is close to Pitlochry, and is a man-made loch. It is still a lovely stretch of water and forms part of the Tummel hydroelectric scheme.

The Edradour Distillery, situated among the hills to the east of Pitlochry, is Scotland's smallest, and possibly its most picturesque distillery. It was established in 1837 and produces handcrafted malt using only local barley. Conducted tours, finished off with a tasting, are available. Bell's Blair Atholl Distillery is the oldest working distillery in Scotland, and is also in Pitlochry.

The A924 going east from Pitlochry takes you up into some marvellous scenery. It reaches a height of 1260 feet before

---

MACDONALD BROS

6/8 Bonnet Hill Road, Pitlochry PH16 5BS
Tel: 01796 472047
Fax: 01796 472267
e-mail: rory-macdonalds@msn.com
website: www.macdonald-bros.co.uk

Macdonald Bros. is an award-winning traditional butcher's shop and delicatessen that boasts an impressive display of the finest cuts of meat in the area. For breakfast, there are home-made sausages, black and white pudding, lorne sausage, bacon and free range eggs. For lunch, how about a home-made pie, lasagne or macaroni cheese. And for dinner, the choice includes stewing steak, mince, chicken portions or whole chicken, steaks, joints of beef, lamb, pork or venison, or home-made family size steak pies. All of the beef, lamb, pork and venison are raised on local farms and estates. If the season is right, you could try pheasant, pigeon, partridge, grouse or guinea fowl.

In the delicatessen area you'll find a wide range of cooked meats as well as a choice of delicious salads. The home-made potted meat, lasagne, apple pies, quiches and various pies, bridies and sausage rolls are all handy for an easy meal. The deli also carries a fine selection of cheeses, along with smoked salmon and salami, pepperoni and pastrami. Macdonald Bros. is open from 7am to 5pm, Monday to Saturday, apart from Thursday when it closes at 2pm.

Pitlochry - Edradour - Moulin

Distance: *3.6 miles (5.8 kilometres)*
Typical time: *110 mins*
Height gain: *110 metres*
Map: *Explorer 386*
Walk: *www.walkingworld.com ID:1113*
Contributor: *Ian Cordiner*

By car or by foot from the centre of Pitlochry. Pitlochry is well served by trains and coaches on the Perth to Inverness routes and also by a number of local bus services.

If travelling on foot from the cente of Pitlochry, start at Waymark 13. Please note that the walk crosses a stream now without a bridge at Waymark 9.

This walk starts in an oakwood and rises to a viewpoint overlooking an impressive waterfall. It then continues to rise and, after leaving the wood, passes along the side of fields to reach Edradour Distillery. This is the smallest distillery in Scotland and is open most of the year to visitors.

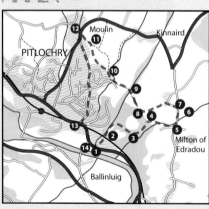

On leaving the distillery, the walk returns via a path between fields before branching out northwards. It passes through open fields near the ruins of The Black Castle, on the way to Moulin. Next it continues through the streets of Pitlochry, passing a small wildlife garden and another distillery before returning to the start.

Please note that at Waymark 9 the bridge over the stream has been washed away. If the water level is high or fast-flowing the route may be impassable at this point.

Sea, toilets, wildlife, birds, gift shop, good for kids, mostly flat, nature trail, ancient monument.

1 | To start the walk, turn left as you leave Pitlochry (going east along the A924 Perth road). If you are leaving Pitlochry on foot, start the walk at Waymark 13. The narrow road to the left here passes underneath the railway line, then leads to a car park.

2 | This is the real start to the walk. As you leave the car park, turn right up the hill. Keep to the right and then again go right.

3 | Continue up the hill following the signs to Black Spout. When you reach the waterfall, continue along the same path. Take the right fork here and continue towards the field.

4 | There is a fenced-off path, which separates you from the field. Continue onwards.

5 | The path eventually leads to a tarred road, which you will follow to the left.

6 | This is Edradour Distillery. It offers free tours from March to mid-December (although opening hours are more restricted in November and December). You may wish to break your walk and enjoy a tour, which takes about 40 minutes. There is also a shop that is open all year and toilets are available.

7 | After the distillery, continue up the narrow tarred road until you come to a passing place. Look out for the path between the road and the field and follow it.

8 | When you reach a junction, turn right. Cross a small bridge and take a short cut across the field (or

follow the path to the left, round the field). Rejoin the path at the other side of the field.

9 | At this point there used to be a bridge but it has been washed away and may not have been replaced. You may still be able to proceed, provided the water level is low, but this should not be attempted if the water is deep or fast-flowing. At the other side of the stream, continue up to the gate and into the next field. The path continues on through this field where animals may be present. Leave the field and move straight on along the tarred road. At the end turn right, then at the end of the wooden fence turn left and walk alongside a small stream.

10 | Go through the gate and follow the path as best you can. It is not very well-marked here, but you are heading in the general direction across the diagonal of the field towards the church spire, which is visible in the distance. On the way you will pass the ruins of Black Castle (marked Caisteal Dubh on the map). This was originally built on a crannog (man-made island) at the time of Robert the Bruce, but became uninhabited in the 15th century when the inhabitants were killed by the plague.

11 | Cross this stile in the northwest corner of the field and head for the building in the distance (which has a shored-up gable wall). It is here that you exit the field onto a short narrow lane.

12 | At the end of the lane turn left. Turn left again into East Moulin Road. Follow this road all the way down to Waymark 13.

13 | At the bottom of the road, turn left along the main road (the A924 towards Perth). Continue on under the railway bridge.

14 | Just opposite the grounds of the next distillery, there is a small wildlife garden on the south side of the road. As you continue on the north side of the road you pass the Blair Athol Distillery gates. The visitor centre entrance is a little farther on. Again, tours are available but this time there is a small charge, which contains a discount voucher redeemable towards a purchase of a bottle of whisky. The distillery is open all year and there are also toilets here. Continue eastwards until you again reach Waymark 1.

Loch Tummel from Queen's View, nr Pitlochry

THE CHRISTMAS EMPORIUM

119 Atholl Road, Pitlochry,
Perthshire PH16 5AG
Tel: 01796 470470
e-mail: enquiries@thechristmasemporium.co.uk
website: www.thechristmasemporium.co.uk

Situated at the north end of the main street in Pitlochry is a fascinating place not to be missed – **The Christmas Emporium**. Don't worry about coming to visit outside the festive season, The Christmas Emporium is open every day throughout the year! The shop stocks hundreds of different styles of Christmas tree decorations from elegant Victorian to retro-kitsch. Christmas ornaments, wreaths, indoor and outdoor lights

If you're looking for something special a selection of traditional hand-blown glass ornaments from Germany and Poland can be found, together with exquisite hand-carved Russian dolls in a range of Christmas styles. Also on offer is a wonderful range of tartan and Scottish themed ornaments and tree hangers so that you can take back a little reminder of your visit to Highland Perthshire.

Visit during Pitlochry's Autumn Festival, from late October to early November and join in the shop's yearly anniversary celebrations complete with warm mulled wine and mince pies. The great thing is that if you have enjoyed your visit you can log-on to the web site any time and shop on-line using the great easy to navigate pages at www.thechristmasemporium.co.uk. If you're not a confident surfer, postal and telephone orders are also welcome.

dropping down into Kirkmichael and then on to Bridge of Cally. On the way, at Enochdhu, you will pass Kindrogan, a Victorian country house where the Scottish Field Studies Association offer residential courses on Scotland's natural history. The **Dunfallandy Standing Stone** lies south of the town near Dunfallandy House, and west of the A9. It dates from Pictish times, and has a curious legend attached to it. A nun called Triduana was being forced into marriage with the son of a Scottish king, but escaped to a small chapel at Dunfallady, where she erected the 'praying stone' in gratitude.

There are many fine guided walks in the area, some organised by such bodies as National Trust for Scotland, the Scottish Wildlife Trust and the Forestry Commission. A small booklet about them is available.

Around Pitlochry

SPITTAL OF GLENSHEE
13 miles NE of Pitlochry on the A93

🏛 Four Poster Stone Circle

As the name suggests, a small medieval hospital, or spittal, once stood close to this village, which lies in the heart of the Grampian Mountains at a height of 1125 feet. It sits on the main road north from Perth to Braemar, and surrounding it is some marvellous scenery. The Glenshee skiing area (Britain's largest) lies six miles north of the village, and is dealt with in the North East Scotland section of this guidebook.

The Devil's Elbow on the A93 lies about five miles north. A combination of steep inclines and double bends made it a notorious place for accidents in days gone by, though it has been much improved. At Cairnwell the road reaches a height of 2199 feet, making it the highest public road in Britain. During the winter months the road can be blocked by snow for weeks on end. The **Four Poster Stone Circle** at Bad an Loin is unusual in that it only has four stones. From it there are fine views of Glen Shee.

DUNKELD

11 miles S of Pitlochry off the A9

🏛 Dunkeld Cathedral 🏛 Battle of Dunkeld

🎦 Count Roehenstart 🌿 Beatrix Potter Gardens

Though it has all the appearance of an attractive town, Dunkeld is in fact a small cathedral city. **Dunkeld Cathedral** sits on the banks of the Tay and consists of a ruined nave and a restored chancel, which is now used as the parish church.

The cathedral as we see it today dates from many periods. The choir (the present parish church) was built mainly in the early 14th century, while the nave (now ruined) was built in the early 15th century. Within the church is the tomb of Alexander Stewart, son of Robert II and known as the Wolf of Badenoch, the man who sacked Elgin Cathedral in the 14th century after a disagreement with the Bishop of Moray. After the Reformation, the cathedral fell into disrepair and it was not until 1600 that the choir was re-roofed and used as the parish church.

In 1689, the town was the scene of the **Battle of Dunkeld**, when Jacobite forces were defeated by a force of Cameronians under William Cleland. This was an unusual battle, as the fighting and gunfire took place among the streets and buildings of the town, and not in open countryside. William Cleland

KETTLES OF DUNKELD

15/17 Athold Street, Dunkeld, Perthshire PH8 0AR
Tel: 01350 727556
website: www.kettlesdunkeld.com

Kettles of Dunkeld is actually two adjacent shops: one selling quality kitchen and house wares; the other is stocked with a range of quality original knitwear.

In the kitchenware shop you'll find a huge range of items from the all the top names - Le Creuset, Highland Stoneware, Bridgewater, Nicholas Mosse, Analon, Circulon, SKK, Stellar, Ekelundand Walton Burleigh kitchen textiles. You'll also find every gadget you'd ever need.

In the knitwear shop, the designer's include Sophie's Wild Woollens, Linda Wilson, Spirit of the Andes, Hume Sweet Hume, Carraig Donn and Quernstone. So if you want to brighten up your wardrobe, Kettles of Dunkeld is certainly the place to seek out.

🎦 stories and anecdotes 🐿 famous people 🎨 art and craft 🎭 entertainment and sport 🚶 walks

MENZIES OF DUNKELD

1 Athol Street, Dunkeld PH8 0AR
Tel: 01350 728028

Menzies of Dunkeld is the kind of traditional grocers you wish you could find in every town. It's owned by Alec Cruikshank whose three Perthshire stores specialise in providing shoppers with the very best of Perthshire and Scottish produce.

Alec is particularly proud of his cheese selection - more than 60 at the last count. The Scottish cheeses alone range from 'Anster', made at Anstruther, to 'Swinzie' which comes from Ayrshire. You'll also find a good choice of other UK and European cheeses. The cheese counter is beautifully displayed with information about each cheese, and the staff are pleased to hand cut the cheeses to your own requirements. Cheeses are only part of the story. You'll also find their own smoked hams along with a full range of deli items.

A recent addition is their own range of ready meals which they make in small batches using the best local ingredients. So why not give yourself a break from the kitchen and enjoy one of these tasty dishes.

Alec's two other delicatessens are The Scottish Deli in Pitlochry, and The Scottish Farm Shop at Dull near Aberfeldy.

was fatally wounded during the encounter, and now lies in the ruined nave of the cathedral.

Another, but not so famous, man lies in the nave of the cathedral. Curiously enough he lies beside William Cleland, and yet he was the grandson of the greatest Jacobite of them all, Charles Edward Stuart. The Prince's illegitimate daughter Charlotte had an affair with the Archbishop of Rouen, the result being two daughters and a son - Charles Edward Maximilien de Roehenstart, better known as **Count Roehenstart** (a name made up from Rouen and Stuart). On a trip to Scotland in 1854 he was killed in a carriage accident.

Most of the 'little houses' in Dunkeld date from the early 18th century, as they were built to replace those that had been destroyed in the

battle. Now the National Trust for Scotland looks after most of them. On the wall of one house in the square, the Ell Shop, is portrayed an old Scottish length of measurement, the ell, which corresponds to 37 inches. Also in the square is the Atholl Memorial Fountain, erected in 1866 in memory of the 6th Duke of Atholl.

At the Birnam Institute is the **Beatrix Potter Gardens**, and within the Institute itself there is a small exhibition, which tells the story of the young Beatrix. She used to holiday in the area, and gained some of her inspiration from the surrounding countryside.

This is the heartland of the 'big tree country', and it was in Dunkeld, in 1738, that the first larches were planted in Scotland.

GRANDTULLY

7 miles SW of Pitlochry on the A827

🏠 St Mary's Church

Grandtully is pronounced Grantly. Grandtully Castle, to the west of the village, dates from the 15th century, and was a Stewart stronghold. It is not open to the public but can be seen from the road.

St Mary's Church (Historic Scotland) was built by Sir Alexander Stewart in 1533, and was remodelled in 1633 when a painted ceiling was added that shows heraldic motifs and coats-of-arms of families connected with the Stewarts.

ABERFELDY

8 miles SW of Pitlochry on the A827

🐾 Falls of Moness 🏛 General Wade's Bridge
🏛 Black Watch Memorial 🏠 Castle Menzies

In 1787, Robert Burns wrote a song called *The Birks of Aberfeldy*, and made famous this small town and its surrounding area. Birks are birch trees, and the ones in question can still be seen to the south of the village, as well as the **Falls of Moness**. Some people claim, however, that Burns was actually writing about Abergeldie near Crathie in Aberdeenshire, though this is doubtful.

The village sits beside the River Tay, and crossing it is **General Wade's Bridge**, built in 1733 by Major-General George Wade, Commander-in-Chief of North Britain from 1724 until 1740 ('Scotland' was not a name that was liked by the English establishment at the time). It is 400 feet in length, with a middle arch that spans 60 feet, and was part of a road network used to police the Highlands during the Jacobite unrest. It was formally opened in 1735, and cost £3596, which in today's terms in close to £1m.

At about the same time, six independent regiments were raised to 'watch' the Highlands

General Wade's Bridge, Aberfeldy

🎭 stories and anecdotes 🐦 famous people 🎨 art and craft 🎪 entertainment and sport 🚶 walks

FERNBANK HOUSE

Kenmore Street, Aberfeldy PH15 2BL
Tel: 01887 820486
e-mail: enquiries@fernbankhouse.co.uk
website: www.fernbankhouse.co.uk

Located close to Aberfeldy's many attractions, **Fernbank House** is a charming Victorian villa that was once owned by the Earl of Breadalbane. It is now the home of Rory and Annette Macdonald and their family who all extend a warm welcome to their bed & breakfast guests. They offer a high standard of service, comfort and a commitment to ensure that their guests have a great night's sleep and a hearty breakfast. The 4 guest bedrooms are spacious and elegantly decorated to a high standard, have a wealth of original Victorian features and are all equipped with en suite facilities, TV, and Welcome Tray.

Fernbank is situated in its own grounds with private off road parking and with an attractive walled garden to the rear of the property, ideal for relaxing on a summer's evening. You could relax even more by treating yourself to a session of Reflexology or Indian Head Massage with Annette in the new Fernbank treatment facilities. Both therapies are used to relax, de-stress and restore and maintain your body's natural equilibrium, by encouraging the body to work naturally to restore its own healthy balance and is suitable for all ages.

for signs of unrest. These six regiments later amalgamated to form the 43rd Highland Regiment of Foot under the Earl of Crawford, and it paraded for the first time at Aberfeldy in May 1740. The regiment later became the Black Watch, and the **Black Watch Memorial**, built in 1887, near the bridge commemorates the event.

Right on the A827 is Dewar's World of Whisky. Here you will find out about one of Scotland's most famous whisky firms, located in the distillery where Aberfeldy Single Malt is made.

A mile or so northwest of the village, near Weem, is **Castle Menzies**, home to Clan Menzies (pronounced Ming-iz in Scotland). The clan is not Scottish in origin, but Norman, with the name coming from Mesnieres near Rouen. James Menzies of Menzies, son-in-law

of the then Earl of Atholl, built the castle in the 16th century. In 1665, the clan chief was created a baron of Nova Scotia. The last member of the main line died in 1918, and the clan was left without a chief. In 1957, the descendants of a cousin of the first baron were recognised as clan chiefs, and the present one is David Steuart Menzies of Menzies.

The castle is now owned by the Menzies Charitable Trust. Parts of it are open to the public, and it houses a Clan Menzies museum. Charles Edward Stuart spent two nights within its walls in 1746 on his way to Culloden.

KENMORE
13 miles SW of Pitlochry on the A827

🏛 The Scottish Crannog Centre

Kenmore sits at the eastern end of Loch Tay, and was founded in about 1540 by the Earls of Breadalbane. The loch is the source of the River Tay, one of the most picturesque in Scotland. The loch is 14-and-a-half miles long, less than a mile wide, and plunges to a maximum depth of more than 500 feet. Overlooking it, on the northern shore, is Ben Lawers (4033 feet), with the Ben Lawers Mountain Visitor Centre (National Trust for Scotland) on a minor road off the A827. There is a nature trail, and a booklet is available at the centre.

The Scottish Crannog Centre, run by the Scottish Trust for Underwater Archaeology, explains how people in the past lived in crannogs, which were dwelling houses situated in the shallow waters of a loch that offered defence against attack. They were either built on artificial islands or raised on stilts above the water, and were in use from about 2500BC right up until the 17th century. Off the north shore of the loch is Eilean nan Bannoamh (Isle of the Holy Women) where once stood a small Celtic nunnery. Alexander I's wife Queen Sybilla, died here in 1122, and Alexander founded a priory in her memory.

FORTINGALL

15 miles SW of Pitlochry on a minor road off the B846

🐦 Pontius Pilate 🌿 Fortingall Yew

🏛 Cairn of the Dead 🐾 Glen Lyon

🌿 Glengoulandie Country Park

This little village has a unique claim to fame. It is said to be the birthplace of **Pontius Pilate**, the governor of Judea at the time of Christ's execution. It is said that his father, a Roman officer, was sent to Scotland by Augustus Caesar to command a unit that kept the local Pictish clans in check. Whether Pontius was born of a union between his father and a local woman, or whether his father had brought a wife with him, is not recorded. There is no proof that the story is true, but there was certainly a Roman camp nearby.

Sir Donald Currie laid out Fortingall as a model village in the 19th century and it has some picturesque thatched cottages that would not look out of place in a South of England village. In the kirkyard of the early 20th-century parish church is the **Fortingall Yew**, said to be the oldest living thing in Europe. The tree looks rather the worse for wear nowadays, but as it may be as much as 3000 years old (a plaque next to it says 5000 years, but this is doubtful), perhaps this is not surprising.

In a field next to the village is the **Cairn of the Dead**, which marks the mass grave of plague victims during the galar mhor, or great plague. It is said that one old woman, who was still sufficiently healthy, carried the bodies to the field on a horse-drawn sledge.

The village sits at the entrance to **Glen Lyon**, at 25 miles long, Scotland's longest, and perhaps loveliest, glen. Tumbling through it is the River Lyon, which rises at Loch Lyon, part of a massive hydroelectric scheme. At Bridge of Balgie a minor road strikes south, rising into some wild scenery and passing Meall Luaidhe (2535 feet) before dropping down towards the Ben Lawers Mountain Visitor Centre and the shores of Loch Tay. Bridge of Balgie is also home to a gallery that houses prints and original paintings by renowned artist Alan Hayman.

On the B846, four miles north of Fortingall, is the **Glengoulandie Country Park** within which is the Glengoulandie Deer Park with its herd of red deer, Highland cattle, goats and rare breeds of sheep.

KINLOCH RANNOCH
17 miles W of Pitlochry on the B846

🐾 Schiehallion 🌳 Dugald Buchanan

🐾 Rannoch Moor

This small village, laid out in the 18th century by James Small, a government factor, sits at the eastern end of Loch Rannoch, which has roads on both the northern and southern sides. It is overlooked by the conically shaped **Schiehallion** (3547 feet), from the summit of which there is a wonderful view as far south as the Lowlands.

An obelisk in the centre of the village commemorates **Dugald Buchanan**, who died here in 1786. He was one of the Highland's greatest religious poets, and was buried at Balquidder. The Parish Church is one of Telford's parliamentarian churches, and was built in 1829. Usually a parliamentarian church was nothing but a plain, T-shaped preaching box, but Kinloch Rannoch is more like a conventional church, with the Holy Table at the east end.

The B846 carries on westward past Kinloch Rannoch and skirts the northern shores of Loch Rannoch. It eventually comes to an end at Rannoch Station. This station, on the Glasgow/Fort William line, is the loneliest railway station in Britain. Beyond it is **Rannoch Moor**, said to be the most desolate spot in Scotland, and 'Europe's last great wilderness'. In the winter, when snow covers it, it is treacherous, and no one should venture out onto it unless they're experienced. Even in summer, when it is hauntingly beautiful, the moor should still be treated with respect.

But the moor's landscape isn't a natural one. Even here, man has made his mark. The whole of the moor was once covered with the trees of the old Caledonian Forest, but man

gradually cleared them to use as fuel and for building. The whole of the moor is littered with large boulders, debris carried by the glaciers that once covered this area.

KILLIECRANKIE
3 miles N of Pitlochry off the A9

🏛 Battle of Killiecrankie

📷 Killiecrankie Visitors Centre 🌳 Soldier's Leap

The rather unusual name comes from the Gaelic Coille Creitheannich, meaning the aspen wood. It was here, in 1689, that the **Battle of Killiecrankie** took place. The Pass of Killiecrankie is a narrow defile, and as government troops under General Mackay passed gingerly through it, they were attacked from above by Jacobite forces under Bonnie Dundee. The government troops had the River Garry behind them, so escape was impossible, and it ended in a victory for the Jacobites. However, Bonnie Dundee himself was killed. The **Killiecrankie Visitors Centre** (National Trust for Scotland) has displays explaining the battle.

At the north end of the pass is a spot known as the **Soldier's Leap**, high above the River Garry. It is said that, after the battle, a government trooper called Donald McBean leapt across the 18-foot-wide gap to escape from the Jacobites who were chasing him.

BLAIR ATHOLL
6 miles NW of Pitlochry off the A9

🏛 Blair Castle 📷 Atholl Highlanders

📷 Clan Donnachaidh Museum 🐾 Falls of Bruar

Blair Castle is one of the most famous castles in Scotland. It sits above the village, and with its whitewashed walls looks more like a great fortified mansion house than a castle. It is the ancestral home of the Murrays,

Dukes of Atholl, and originally dates from 1269, though what you see nowadays is mainly from the 18th and 19th century refurbishments. About 30 furnished rooms are open to the public, with fine furniture, paintings, china and armour on display. The Duke of Atholl is the only person in Britain who is allowed to have a private army, the **Atholl Highlanders**, and a small museum has displays of uniforms, weapons and musical instruments. It was raised in 1778 by the 4th Duke of Atholl to fight the colonists in the American War of Independence. However, after a posting to Ireland they were disbanded. The regiment as we know it today dates from 1839. In 1844, Queen Victoria stayed at Blair Atholl and a year later presented the regiment with two sets of colours

In the kirkyard of St Bride's Kirk is the grave of John Graham, 1st Viscount Dundee, known as Bonnie Dundee, who was killed at the Battle of Killiecrankie in 1689 (see also Killiecrankie). At Bruar, four miles north of Blair Atholl, is the **Clan Donnachaidh Museum**. Though the name translates into English as Donnachie, it traces the history of the Clan Robertson, and shows their place in local and Scottish history. **The Falls of Bruar** are close by, and descend through a picturesque ravine with footbridges over them.

PERTHSHIRE, ANGUS & KINROSS

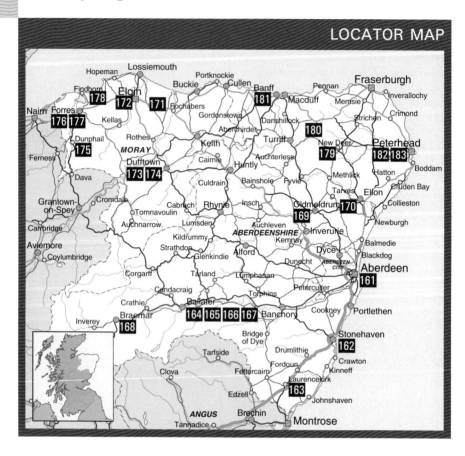

LOCATOR MAP

ADVERTISERS AND PLACES OF INTEREST

🏠 historic building 🏛 museum and heritage 🏚 historic site 🌿 scenic attraction 🌱 flora and fauna

11 | North East Scotland

High mountains, wooded glens, cityscapes, beaches, rich farmland, towering cliffs and moorland - North East Scotland has the lot. And yet it is relatively unknown by those outside Scotland, apart from the city of Aberdeen and along Deeside. The beaches are quiet and uncrowded, the country lanes are a joy to drive in, and there is history and heritage aplenty.

And always in the background are the Grampians, which reach their highest peaks here. Queen Victoria popularised Deeside, a glen that goes deep into the heart of the mountains, and it has remained firmly on the tourist trail ever since. But, as with many parts of Scotland, the tourist traps swarm with people, while other places, equally as interesting and picturesque, are bypassed.

To go off the beaten track in the North East is to be rewarded with some wonderful discoveries. Nowhere else in Europe is there such a concentration of historic castles - around 1000 at the last count. The local tourist board has organised a Castle Trail, with a leaflet that explains their history and how you get to them. And then there are the distilleries. The industry is centred mainly on Banffshire and Moray, where the streams are swift flowing and the water pure. It's amazing that two distilleries a mile or so apart can make whiskies that are totally different in character. The local tourist board has laid out a Whisky Trail and, like the Castle Trail there's a leaflet to guide you as you explore it.

The inland villages are quiet and peaceful, and the market towns, such as Inverurie, Forres and Huntly, are packed with history and charm. The coastline is as dramatic as anywhere in Britain. Yet another trail, the Coastal Trail, takes you on a tour from St Cyrus in the south to Findhorn in the west.

For all its crowds (especially in late summer

ADVERTISERS AND PLACES OF INTEREST (CONT)

🎞 stories and anecdotes 🐦 famous people 🖋 art and craft 🎭 entertainment and sport 🥾 walks

Leith Hall, Huntly

and subsequent monarchs, fell in love with Royal Deeside in the first place.

Aberdeen is Scotland's third largest city and Europe's oil capital. The name, which means at the mouth of the Dee and the Don, sums up its location exactly, as the two rivers enter the North Sea here. The oil industry has brought money to the city, and it has also brought a cosmopolitan lifestyle that includes smart restaurants, boutiques, nightclubs and stylish pubs.

when the Queen is there), Deeside should not be missed. This long glen follows the Dee up into the heart of the Grampians with Braemar, at its heart, being officially Britain's coldest place (though summer days can be balmy and long). Balmoral, Crathie, Aboyne, the names are familiar to us all through news programmes, and yet the reality of seeing them makes you realise why Queen Victoria,

The other city in the region is Elgin, at one time one of the most important places in Scotland. It has lost some of that importance now, but not any of its charm. It is still a busy place, and is the shopping and administrative centre for a large fertile area called the Laigh of Moray.

Aberdeen

With a population of about 220,000, Aberdeen is Scotland's third largest city. Its nickname is the Granite City because of the predominant building material, which has created a stylish and attractive place that seems to glisten in the sun. It prides itself on being Scotland's most prosperous city, due to the oil fields that lie beneath the North Sea. For this reason it is also known as the Oil Capital of Europe, and the docks and harbours, which were once full of fishing boats, now pulse with supply ships ferrying men and machines out to the oil rigs. It also has the ferry terminal for the Shetland ferry.

But Aberdeen has two more nicknames -

Scotland's Garden City and the Flower of Scotland. Both derive from the many gardens and colourful open spaces that can be visited. The city has won awards for its floral displays (including many Britain in Bloom awards), with Johnston Gardens, Hazelhead Park, Union Terrace Gardens, Duthie Park and the Cruickshank Botanic Gardens offering particularly fine examples. In 2003, Aberdeen took silver in the Nations in Bloom competition, beaten only by Seattle, USA, and Quanzhou, China.

It is also a centre of learning, administration, shopping and business. But it has never been scarred by industry in the way that some Scottish central belt towns have. It has managed to remain above such things, and its quality of life is among the best in Britain.

And for all its bustle and modern office blocks, it is an ancient city, having been granted a charter as a royal burgh in 1175. Even then it was an important and busy port, trading with the Baltic States as well as the Netherlands and France. During the Wars of Independence it was sacked three times by the English, and finally razed to the ground by Edward III in 1337. One unexpected visitor to Aberdeen was William Shakespeare who, with his troupe of actors, was sent by Elizabeth I in 1601 to perform before the court of James VI.

There are two Aberdeens - the original one, and Old Aberdeen, which was at one time a separate burgh. Perversely, Old Aberdeen was only granted its charter in 1489, and is a captivating area of old, elegant buildings and quiet cobbled streets.

Provost Scene's House, Aberdeen

🎬 stories and anecdotes 🕊 famous people 🎨 art and craft 🎭 entertainment and sport 🚶 walks

The buildings you see throughout the city nowadays however, are mainly Georgian, Victorian and later, with some older buildings among them to add historical depth. The **Cathedral Church of St Machar's** in Old Aberdeen was founded in about 1131, and is dedicated to a saint who was the son of Fiachna, an Irish prince. He was also a companion of St Columba, and came over from Ireland with him to found the monastery on Iona. Legend states that Columba sent Machar to convert the Picts in the area, and had a vision from God to build a church at a point where a river bends in the shape of a bishop's crosier just before it enters the sea. As the Don bends in this way, he established

his church here in about 580AD. It's a fascinating tale, but probably untrue, as a bishop's crosier in those days was not curved, but straight.

St Machar's as we see it today dates from the 14th century and later. The choir has completely disappeared, and what you see now was the nave of the original cathedral with the ruins of the two transepts, which are in the care of Historic Scotland. In 1688, the central tower collapsed, leaving a rather truncated building with a beautiful west front with two towers. Perhaps its most famous bishop was William Elphinstone, Chancellor of Scotland and producer of the first book of liturgy in the country, the *Aberdeen*

Aberdeen Maritime Museum

Aberdeen Maritime Museum,
Shiprow, Aberdeen AB11 5BY
Tel: 01224 337700 Fax: 01224 213066
e-mail: johne@aberdeencity.gov.uk
website: www.aagm.co.uk

Situated on the historic Shiprow and incorporating Provost Ross's House - built in 1593 - **Aberdeen Maritime Museum** tells the story of the city's long relationship with the Sea. This award-winning museum houses a unique collection covering shipbuilding, fast sailing ships, fishing and port history, and is the only place in the UK where you can see displays on the North Sea oil industry.

The exhibitions include fine ship's portraits, fishing equipment, information on the 3,000 ships built in the port and the world's largest oil platform model which stand nine metres tall.

Aberdeen Maritime Museum also offers a spectacular viewpoint over the busy harbour filled with powerful offshore supply vessels and modern cargo and passenger ships. There is an exciting programme of special exhibitions and a vibrant education programme. Aberdeen Maritime Museum is fully accessible to visitors with disabilities.

Excellent café and shop complete the range of services. Admission is free and the museum is open Monday to Saturday 10am-5pm, Sunday 12noon-3pm.

Breviary. Its heraldic ceiling is magnificent, the work of Bishop Gavin Dunbar, who succeeded Elphinstone in 1518. Dunbar also erected the two west towers.

The **Brig o' Balgownie** over the Don, near the cathedral, dates from the early 14th century, and has a single, pointed arch. It is said to have been built using money given by Robert the Bruce, and is reckoned to be the finest single arch structure in Scotland. Aberdeen's other old bridge, to the south of the city, is the **Bridge of Dee**, built by Bishop Dunbar in the early 1500s.

At Bridge of Don is Glover House, the family home of **Thomas Blake Glover**, the Scotsman who, it is said, inspired Puccini's opera *Madame Butterfly*. Born in Fraserburgh in 1838, his family moved to Bridge of Don in 1851, when he was 13 years old. When he left school, he began working for a trading company and got a taste for overseas travel.

When he first went to Japan aged 21, he was entering a feudal society that had been closed to the west for over 300 years. However, within one year he was selling Scottish-built warships and arms to Japanese rebels during the country's civil war. At the same time he sent young Japanese men to Britain to be educated.

Glover was called the Scottish Samurai, and helped found the Mitsubishi shipyards, the first step Japan took to becoming a great manufacturing power. He also helped found the famous Kirin Brewery, and his picture still appears on Kirin labels to this day. A grateful government presented Glover with the Order of the Rising Sun, Japan's greatest honour. He later built himself a house at Nagasaki, and married a Japanese woman called Tsura, who invariably wore kimonos decorated with butterfly motifs. When Puccini came across a short story and subsequent play based on this relationship, it sowed the seeds for *Madame Butterfly*.

The **Church of St Nicholas** stands in St Nicholas Street. The first mention of a church on the site is a Papal Bull dated 1157. Of the original church only the transepts and the crypt survive. Its carillon of 48 bells is the largest of any church in Britain. There are six entrances to the kirkyard, the grandest being the granite colonnade in Union Street, designed in 1830 by John Smith, Aberdeen's city architect. Beneath what was the East Kirk is St Mary's Chapel, built by Lady Elizabeth Gordon. When she died in 1438 she was buried within it.

Union Street, Aberdeen's main thoroughfare, is more than a mile long, and thronged with shops. It was laid out in the early 1800s to celebrate the union of Britain and Ireland. At one end, in Castle Street, is the city's 17th-century **Mercat Cross**, standing close to where Aberdeen's long gone medieval castle stood.

Provost Skene's House, off St Nicholas Street, dates from about 1545, and is named after a former lord provost of the city, Sir George Skene, who bought it in 1669. It is a tall, solid building of turrets and chimneys, and has wonderful painted ceilings and period furniture, as well as displays on modern history. Provost Ross's House is in Shiprow, said to be Aberdeen's oldest street still in use. The house was built in 1593, but is named after its most famous owner, John Ross, lord provost of Aberdeen in the 18th century. It now houses the **Aberdeen Maritime Museum** (see panel opposite), with exhibits and displays on Aberdeen's maritime history, plus a re-created helicopter ride out to an offshore oilrig.

Aberdeen University was founded by Bishop Elphinstone in 1494 under a Papal Bull from Pope Alexander IV. **King's College** stands in Old Aberdeen, and its chapel, built in 1505, forms one side of a quadrangle in the middle of which is a 20th-century monument to its founder. The chapel's crown steeple, built in honour of James VI, was blown down in a storm in 1633, and there were dark mutterings all over Aberdeen that witchcraft was involved. The following year work started on rebuilding it.

Marischal College, another university, was founded in 1593, 99 years after King's College, which meant that the city had two universities - exactly the same number as the whole of England at that time, as locals gleefully point out. It was founded by George Keith, 5th Earl Marischal of Scotland, as a Protestant alternative to the Catholic-leaning King's College. The present imposing granite building in Broad Street dates from the 19th century, and is the second largest granite building in the world. In 1860, the two universities united to form Aberdeen University.

The **Aberdeen Art Gallery and Museum** are at Schoolhill, near Robert Gordon's College. Apart from a fine collection of paintings and sculpture by such artists as Degas, Reynolds, and Epstein, it houses displays on Aberdeen's history, including finds made at various archaeological digs throughout the city.

The **Gordon Highlanders Museum** on Viewfield Road tells the story of what Sir Winston Churchill called 'the finest regiment in the world'. There is an audiovisual theatre, gardens, a children's handling area, a shop and a café. One of Aberdeen's newest attractions is **Stratosphere** in The Tramsheds in Constitution Street, a hands-on science centre where children can explore all aspects of science, and watch a show that explains things like colour and bubbles.

At one time there were well over 100 quarries in the city mining granite. Rubislaw Quarry, near the Gordon Highlanders Museum, was one of the biggest. It was still being worked right up until 1971, when it was about 465 feet deep and 900 feet across. Now it has been filled with water to a depth of 180 feet and fenced off. During 230 years of quarrying, it is said to have produced more than six million tonnes of granite, not just for Aberdeen, but for places like London, Russia and Japan.

In King Street is the Aberdeen and North East Scotland Family History Society, which has a wide range of reference material for family and genealogical research. At Blairs, on South Deeside Road, there was once a catholic seminary, which closed in 1986. The **Blairs Museum** now holds the Scottish Catholic Heritage Collection, and is open to the public. There are objects connected with the Stuart line (including Mary Stuart and Charles Edward Stuart) on display, as well as a collection of rich vestments, church plate and paintings.

On the north bank of the Dee, where it enters the North Sea, is an area called Footdee, or, as it is known by Aberdonians, Fittie. This is where Aberdeen's original fishing community lived, in rows of cottages that have now been renovated and smartened up.

Around Aberdeen

STONEHAVEN
16 miles S of Aberdeen off the A90

🏚 Mercat Cross 🏚 Steeple 🏛 Tolbooth Museum

🏚 Dunnottar Castle   🔥 Fireball Festival

Stonehaven was once the county town of Kincardineshire. It is a fishing community,

GLENCAIRN B&B

9 Dunnotter Avenue, Stonehaven, Aberdeenshire AB39 2SD
Tel: 01569 762612
e-mail: mosangster@hotmail.com
website: www.theglencairn.co.uk

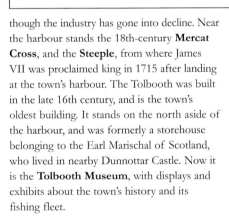

Located in the heart of Stonehaven, just 500 yards from the beach. **Glencairn** offers 3-star bed & breakfast accommodation in a pleasant and relaxing atmosphere. Guests receive a warm welcome from owner Maryann Sangster who has been welcoming visitors here and extending traditional Scottish hospitality since 2003'.

In Glencairn's dining room, which has a superb fireplace feature, you can enjoy your choice of a full hearty Scottish, Continental or vegetarian breakfast. The accommodation comprises 3 attractively furnished and decorated en suite rooms, plus another with its own private bathroom. All rooms have recently been refurbished to a high standard, have full central heating and are equipped with colour TV.

Stonehaven itself is a pretty little town with many local attractions including the magnificent Dunnottar Castle which can be reached from Glencairn on foot. A few minutes walk away there is the very picturesque harbour, and an open air heated swimming pool is nearby. The area is suitable for golfers, walkers, cyclists and birdwatchers, and during the summer months there are Boat Trips available along the coast to Catterline and the Fowlsheugh Bird Sanctuary.

though the industry has gone into decline. Near the harbour stands the 18th-century **Mercat Cross**, and the **Steeple**, from where James VII was proclaimed king in 1715 after landing at the town's harbour. The Tolbooth was built in the late 16th century, and is the town's oldest building. It stands on the north aside of the harbour, and was formerly a storehouse belonging to the Earl Marischal of Scotland, who lived in nearby Dunnottar Castle. Now it is the **Tolbooth Museum**, with displays and exhibits about the town's history and its fishing fleet.

Two miles south of the town is **Dunnottar Castle**. It is magnificently sited, as it stands on a promontory 160 feet above the sea and is guarded on three sides by the North Sea and on the fourth by St Ninian's Den, a steep ravine. It dates from the 13th century and later, and has seen some gruesome episodes in

Scotland's history. In 1297, William Wallace torched it, burning to death every English soldier within its walls. In 1652, Cromwell's troops laid siege to it to capture Scotland's Crown Jewels. However, they were foiled by the wife of the minister of Kinneff Church, who smuggled them out under the very noses of the troops.

In 1685, 167 Covenanters were imprisoned in an underground cellar. Those that tried to escape were killed, while most of those that remained succumbed to disease and starvation. Those that survived were sent to the colonies.

Each year at Hogmanay the traditional **Fireball Festival** is held in Stonehaven. It takes place in the 'Auld Toon' area of the town, with up to 60 men parading at midnight while swinging huge fireballs on the end of stout wires. The origins are rooted in paganism,

Stonehaven - Dunnottar Woods - Dunottar Castle

Distance: *4.5 miles (7.2 kilometres)*
Typical time: *110 mins*
Height gain: *75 metres*
Map: *Explorer 396*
Walk: *www.walkingworld.com ID:864*
Contributor: *Ian Cordiner*

Stonehaven, 15 miles south of Aberdeen, is served by frequent rail and bus services. It can be reached from the south by the A90 and A92.

DESCRIPTION:

This walk starts in the town centre where there is a car park. It soon leaves the streets and leads through the quiet deciduous Dunnottar Woods in which there is an old building known as the Shell House, because the interior is picturesquely decorated with seashells. Continuing past the high walls of what is now a garden centre, it crosses a small road to proceed once more through deciduous woodland. On the way through the woods it passes the ruins of a stone structure known as Lady Kennedy's Bath.

After leaving this section, the walk follows quiet roads before reaching Dunnottar Castle. From here there is a cliff path that leads back to Stonehaven, but because of erosion this part may not be accessible and it may be necessary to follow a pavement back to the town.

The route gives spectacular views over the town and its harbour. A steep path leads down to the harbour area where hotels, shops and toilets are found. Also in this part of town is one of the oldest buildings in Stonehaven, the Tolbooth, now a museum.

Finally, the walk continues along a boardwalk by the seashore and leads back to the town centre.

FEATURES:

Sea, pub, toilets, museum, castle, great views, food shop, public transport, nature trail, woodland, ancient monument.

WALK DIRECTIONS

1 | The walk starts at the south corner of the square in the town centre. Leave the square by going south along Barclay Street. At the end of Barclay Street, turn right. Cross to the south side of the street, then cross this pedestrian bridge.

2 | Immediately over the bridge, take the path to the right. Turn right here.

3 | At this junction, turn left. Continue to the far corner between the houses to enter the woodland. Follow the route to the right as you pass through this gate.

4 | At the steps, keep left and follow the sign to Glasslaw Gate. Bear left here. You are going to take the route to the right, but first stop at this building. It is called the Shell House and has its interior decorated with seashells. It was in fact, once an ice house. Follow the track to the right until you come to the tarred road.

5 | Continue straight across the road here and continue to folllow the woodland path. At the first Y-junction bear left. Cross the bridge, then turn right. Continue past this bridge until you reach a similar one further on.

6 | From the next bridge you look down into a stone structure known as Lady Kennedy's Bath.

After a short incline turn left and follow the main track until you reach the Glasslaw car park.

7 | At the exit of the car park keep left. At the main road turn left.

8 | Continue along the pavement until you reach a junction, where you turn right. The walk now continues along a tarred country lane and eventually reaches the coast.

19 | When you reach the main road at Mains of Dunnottar Farm, turn right. Continue south for about 100m. Immediately to the south of a small lodge there is a small car park for Dunnottar Castle. Enter the castle grounds via a gate in the corner of the car park.

10 | At this point the route leads to the right of the castle. If you keep left, there is a path that is a cliff path back to Stonehaven. There may, however, be a problem here. Due to costal erosion, this part may be closed as repairs to the path may be in progress.

11 | There is an entrance fee to visit the castle itself. This castle was the hidingplace for the Scottish Regalia (crown jewels) in 1652. More recently, the castle was used in the filming of *Hamlet*, starring Mel Gibson. If the coastal path is closed, retrace your steps to Waymark 9 and follow the pavement back to Stonehaven.

12 | On the skyline you will see Stonehaven's war memorial. If you were able to take the cliff path, you will be able to reach the war memorial quite easily. When you leave the memorial site, turn left.

13 | Across from the 'Welcome to Stonhaven' sign and where the road narrows, look out for a narrow path leading to the right. Follow this steep path down towards the harbour. When you reach this narrow lane follow it to to the end, where it comes out at the harbour. There are popular pubs and food sources along the seafront. Continue along the seafront, keeping right past the white building.

14 | The building on the left is the oldest in Stonehaven. A former tolbooth (jail), it is now a small museum. Continue past this and take the road to the left, past a toilet block and into a car park. Continue through the car park until you come to a boardwalk, which skirts the water and leads back to the town centre.

15 | When you reach the end of the boardwalk, turn left to get to the town square. On the other hand, you could continue along the path ahead, which eventually leads to an open-air swimming pool, passing amusements and sports facilities on the way. Turning left leads up to the town centre.

16 | Cross the main road back to the car park in the square.

with the light from the balls supposedly attracting the sun, ensuring its return after the dark days of winter. Today, the whole ceremony lasts about half an hour, but the past it could last for up to an hour or more.

INVERBERVIE
25 miles S of Aberdeen on the A92

Mercat Cross Kinneff Church

Though no bigger than a village, Inverbervie is in fact a royal burgh, having been granted its charter in 1341 by David II who, along with his queen, was shipwrecked off the coast as he returned from imprisonment in France, and was 'kindly received' by the people of the village. John Coutts, whose son Thomas Coutts founded the famous bank, was born here in 1699. Hallgreen Castle (private) stands close to the sea and has associations with the Dunnet family. The village's **Mercat Cross** dates from 1737.

Three miles north, at Kinneff, is **Kinneff Church**, built in 1738. The previous church on the site, built in about 1242, has a unique place in Scotland's history. In 1651, the Scottish Crown Jewels were used at the coronation of Charles II at Scone, then hidden in Dunnottar Castle so that Parliamentarian troops could not find them. But when their whereabouts became known to

stories and anecdotes famous people art and craft entertainment and sport walks

Cromwell, they were smuggled out by the wife of Kinneff's minister, and placed within the church. There they lay for 10 years, beneath the floor. Every three months the minister and his wife dug them up, cleaned them and aired them before a fire. With the Restoration of Charles II in 1660, they were taken to Edinburgh Castle. Though no longer used for worship, the church is still open to the public and under the care of the Kinneff Old Church Preservation Trust.

ARBUTHNOTT

23 miles S of Aberdeen on the B967

- Arbuthnott Collegiate Church
- Lewis Grassic Gibbon Arbuthnott House
- Lewis Grassic Gibbon Centre

The village of Arbuthnott lies in what is called The Mearns. **Arbuthnott Collegiate Church** is dedicated to St Ternan, a Pictish saint. The

choir was consecrated in 1242, with the rest of the church following later. It was here that James Sibbald, priest of Arbuthnott, wrote the *Arburthnott Missal* in 1491. It laid out the form of service to be used at masses celebrated within the church, and can now be seen in Paisley Museum. The Arbuthnott Aisle contains the tomb of Hugo le Blond of Arbuthnott, whose effigy can be seen above it. Another tomb is of a later period, and is of James Arbuthnott.

The ashes of James Leslie Mitchell the author, otherwise known as **Lewis Grassic Gibbon**, lie within the kirkyard, where there is a memorial to him. He was born in The Mearns and, when he had settled in Welwyn Garden City near London, wrote dark brooding novels about Mearns farm life, far removed from the couthy stories about simple Scottish country folk that had been published before. The **Lewis Grassic Gibbon Centre**,

MUFFINS COFFEE SHOP

63 High Street, Laurencekirk,
Aberdeenshire AB30 1BH
Tel: 01561 377636
e-mail: muffins63@hotmail.co.uk

Good wholesome and appetising fare is the order of the day at **Muffins Coffee Shop** in Laurencekirk's High Street. Everything on the menu is cooked on the premises using top quality local produce. Naturally, there's a Muffin of the Day along with various dishes such as paninis, wholesome filled baguettes, home-made soup and baked potatoes. There's also a good selection of espresso based coffees, speciality teas, fresh smoothies and milk shakes made to order. Owner Lauren Smith took over here in 2007 and has seen the shop grow in popularity. There are 35 seats as well as some comfy sofas where customers can settle down with a grand caffe latte perhaps, and a newspaper.

Muffins is open from 9am to 5pm, Monday to Friday, and from 10am to 4pm on Saturday. There's good disabled access throughout and a disabled toilet. Children are welcome.

Drum Castle, Maryculter

next to the parish hall, traces the life and works of a man who became one of the most important British writers of the 20th century.

The area has other literary associations. Robert Burn's father was born here before setting up home in Ayrshire, and in the kirkyard of the church at Glenbervie, four miles to the northwest, is the grave of Burns's great grandfather, James Burnes (the 'e' in the name was dropped after Burns's father moved to Ayrshire).

Arbuthnott House, home to the Arbuthnott family for 800 years, dates mainly from the 18th and 19th centuries, and is open to the public on certain days of the year. The gardens, including a formal 17th-century walled garden, are open all year round.

MARYCULTER
6 miles SW of Aberdeen on the B9077

🏛 Drum Castle ⚘ Storybook Glen

The land surrounding Maryculter was granted to the Knights Templar by William the Lion in the 12th century. The order of monastic soldiers established a church and preceptory, dedicating it to St Mary. Pope Clement V suppressed the order in 1312, and at trials held at Holyrood Abbey in Edinburgh in 1319, the last Preceptor of the house at Maryculter was given as William de Middleton of the 'tempill house of Culther'. The lands formerly owned by the Knights Templar were then granted to

the Knights of the Order of St John. On the opposite bank of the Dee a church had been established and dedicated to St Peter, and this parish became known as Peterculter. It now lies within the City of Aberdeen, while Maryculter is in Kincardineshire.

Four miles west of the village is **Drum Castle** (National Trust for Scotland), built in the late 13th century, probably by the wonderfully named Richard Cemantarius, king's master mason and provost of Aberdeen. In 1323, it was given to William de Irwyn by Robert the Bruce, and the Irvines lived in it from that date right up until 1975. It was enlarged in 1619 by the creation of a grand Jacobean mansion and later by some Victorian additions.

Storybook Glen, also in Maryculter, and is a 28-acre children's park where fairy tale and nursery rhyme characters can be found.

FETTERCAIRN
27 miles SW of Aberdeen on the B974

🏛 Mercat Cross 🏛 Fettercairn Arch 🏛 Fasque

On the edge of the fertile Howe of the Mearns, Fettercairn is an attractive village with, at its heart, the **Mercat Cross** of 1670. In 1861, Queen Victoria and Prince Albert visited the village and the **Fettercairn Arch** commemorates the event.

The B974 north to Strachar and Banchory on Royal Deeside has many fine views. Close

🎬 stories and anecdotes 🐟 famous people 🎨 art and craft ⚘ entertainment and sport 🚶 walks

Mercat Cross, Fettercairn

power this wauk mill, which finished off woven cloth. The mill is open to the public, and there are displays giving information about its history and machinery.

The **Cullrelie Stone Circle**, close to the village just off the B9125, dates from the Bronze Age, and consists of eight stones placed in a 33-feet diameter circle. The shallow **Loch of Skene**, to the north of the village, is a special protection area and supports an important colony of Icelandic greylag geese. Three miles to the west of the village, near Echt, is the **Barmekin of Echt**, an ancient fortified hill settlement.

BANCHORY
17 miles W of Aberdeen on the A93

> 🏛 Banchory Museum　🏛 Crathes Castle

This attractive little 19th-century burgh stands at the point where the River Freugh enters the Dee, and is often called the 'Gateway to Royal Deeside'. It once stood on the Deeside railway line that closed in 1966, and there are now plans to reopen a section between the town and Crathes, three miles to the east. In Bridge Street is the **Banchory Museum**, which has collections featuring tartans, royal commemorative china and the natural history of the area. The Scottish musician and composer James Scott Skinner, the Strathspey King, was born at Arbeadie, just outside the town, in 1843, and a further display in the museum is dedicated to his life. He now lies buried in Allenvale Cemetery in Aberdeen.

Three miles east of the town is **Crathes Castle** (National Trust for Scotland), which dates from the 16th century. Some of the rooms retain their original painted ceilings, which were only rediscovered in 1877. The first castle was built by the Burnetts of Ley who were granted the lands of Ley by Robert

to the road, about a mile north of the town, is **Fasque**, home of William Gladstone, prime minister in the late 19th century. It was built in 1829 by his father, Sir John Gladstone, son of a Leith corn merchant, and has a deer park. It is open for groups of more than 12 by prior arrangement.

Fettercairn Distillery sits to the northwest, and has guided tours (with a free dram at the end) and a visitor centre.

GARLOGIE
10 miles W of Aberdeen on the B9119

> 🏛 Garlogie Mill Power House Museum
> 🏛 Cullrelie Stone Circle　🍃 Loch of Skene
> 🏛 Barmekin of Echt

The **Garlogie Mill Power House Museum** has a rare beam engine - the only one to have survived intact in its location - which used to

the Bruce in 1323.
The ancient Horn of
Leys hangs in the
Great Hall. It is
made of ivory and
encrusted with
jewels, and was
presented to the
Burnetts by Bruce at
the time of the land
grant. The family's
coat-of-arms
includes the horn.
On the main stairway
there is a 'trip stair',
which tripped up

Crathes Castle Rope Bridge, Banchory

attackers who didn't know about it. Watch
out also for the castle's ghost - the Green
Lady. The house remained with the family
until 1951, when Sir James Burnett presented
it to the National Trust for Scotland. Eight
themed gardens have been laid out within the
old walled garden, separated by yew hedges.
There is also a shop and restaurant.

KINCARDINE O'NEILL

23 miles W of Aberdeen on the A93

🏚 Kirk of St Mary

This little village, with its Irish sounding name,
claims to be the oldest village on Deeside. It is
in fact a small burgh, having been granted its
charter in 1511. It was here, in 1220, that the
first bridge was constructed across the Dee
beyond Aberdeen, so it became an important
place. The ruins of the **Kirk of St Mary** date
from the 14th century. It may have been the
chapel for a hospital that stood here before
the Reformation. It was in use up until 1862
when a new church was built. St Mary's was
thatched up until 1733, when someone shot at
a pigeon perching in its roof and it caught fire.

ALFORD

26 miles W of Aberdeen on the A944

🏛 Grampian Transport Museum

🚲 Alford Valley Railway 🏚 Craigievar Castle

🌴 Haughton House Country Park

Alford (pronounced Afford locally, with the
accent on the first syllable) is a pleasant village
within a fertile area known as the Howe of
Alford. The **Grampian Transport Museum**
has displays and working exhibits about
transport in the Grampian area. Major exhibits
include the world's oldest Sentinel Steam
Wagon from 1914, a giant Mack Snowplow,
and a Jaguar XKR used in the James Bond
film, *Die Another Day*. Visitors can even
clamber aboard some of the exhibits. Each
year the Eco Marathon takes place at the
museum, where vehicles have to travel as far
as possible on a set amount of fuel. The
current record, established in 2008, is
6603 miles per gallon of petrol.

The **Alford Valley Railway** is a two-mile
long narrow gauge passenger railway with
steam and diesel locomotives that runs

between the Transport Museum and **Haughton House Country Park**, where there are woodland walks, a wildflower garden and a caravan park.

Four miles south of Alford, on the A980, is one of Aberdeenshire's finest castles, **Craigievar Castle** (National Trust for Scotland). With its many turrets and small windows, it looks like something from a fairy tale. It was built by William Forbes, who bought the land in 1610 and completed the castle in 1626. It has a fine collection of 17th- and 18th-century furniture, as well as family portraits. William Forbes was also known as Danzig Willie, and was a rich Aberdeen merchant who traded with the Baltic countries. The castle is currently closed for major reharling work, but is scheduled to re-open some time in 2009.

LUMPHANAN
24 miles W of Aberdeen on the A980

🏛 Peel Ring of Lumphanan

Lumphanan was founded when the Deeside railway was constructed, and was the highest point on the line. The **Peel Ring of Lumphanan** (Historic Scotland) is a huge motte and bailey where a castle built by the Durward family once stood.

ABOYNE
27 miles W of Aberdeen off the A93

🏇 Aboyne Highland Games

🏇 Aboyne and Deeside Festival 🏃 Glen Tanar

🏛 Culsh Earth House 🏛 Tomnaverie Stone Circle

This small Royal Deeside town is famous for the **Aboyne Highland Games**, held in August each year. The village prospered with the coming of the railway in the 19th century, and is now a quiet settlement, popular with

tourists. It is also the home of the **Aboyne and Deeside Festival**, held in July and August, which features music, drama and art. There is a lovely, but in places difficult, walk up **Glen Tanar**, two miles west of Aboyne.

Five miles north of the town, and two miles northeast of Tarland, is the **Culsh Earth House**, a souterrain, or underground chamber, which is over 2000 years old. It is a long, doglegged tunnel, which was probably not used as a house, but as a store for foodstuffs. A torch is needed to explore it. The **Tomnaverie Stone Circle** (Historic Scotland) is a mile to the southwest, and dates to about 1600BC.

BALLATER
34 miles W of Aberdeen on the A93

🏛 The Old Royal Station

🏃 Muir of Dinnet Nature Reserve 🏃 Glen Muick

Set among the spectacular scenery of Royal Deeside, Ballater is surrounded by wooded hills of birch and pine, and makes an excellent base for exploring an area of outstanding beauty. It is a comparatively modern settlement and, like Aboyne, owes its growth to the coming of the railways in the 19th century. In fact, this was as far as the Deeside line came, as Prince Albert stopped a proposed extension as far as Braemar. **The Old Royal Station** has been restored to how it would have looked like in Victorian times, when used by the Royal Family. The **Muir of Dinnet Nature Reserve** lies between Ballater and Aboyne, and covers 2000 acres around Lochs Kinord and Davan.

There is plenty of good walking country around the village, and **Glen Muick**, to the south of Ballater, has a narrow road that you can drive up towards Loch Muick (the road ends before the loch is reached, so you have to

CAMBUS O'MAY HOTEL

Ballater, Aberdeenshire AB35 5SE
Tel: 013397 55428   Fax: 013397 55428
e-mail: mckechnie@cambusomay.freeserve.co.uk
website: www.cambusomayhotel.co.uk

Situated four miles east of the picturesque Deeside Village of Ballater, the **Cambus O'May Hotel** provides a haven of peace and tranquillity, yet affords direct access to the A93 Aberdeen to Perth road. Set in sixteen acres of attractive wooded grounds the hotel overlooks the River Dee and the hills beyond.the hotel, which has been owned and run by the McKechnie family for over quarter of a century, provides warm and friendly service with cuisine and comfort to match. Great emphasis is placed on the personal attention shown to guests, which allows them to enjoy a memorable and relaxing stay.

Originally a Victorian hunting lodge built in 1874 this Country House has been carefully modernised to provide 12 tastefully furnished bedrooms, all different and in keeping with the ambience of the building. All rooms have en-suite facilities, colour television, hair dryer and individually controlled heating. The elegant residents lounge with comfortable seating and open fire overlooks the front gardens and the valley beyond. It is here that guests may relax, enjoy a chat with friends, perhaps take afternoon tea or finish off their meal with coffee, mints and liqueurs. The small dining room which has panoramic views across the Dee Valley is the ideal place to enjoy the excellent cuisine offered from the table d'hote menu which changes daily. The hotel welcomes families, the large grounds offering children scope to explore in safety.

HM SHERIDAN

11 Bridge Street,
Ballater AB35 5QP
Tel: 013397 55218
Fax: 013397 56042
e-mail: info@hmsheridan.co.uk

Within this business there is a huge range of products made on site making the shop very unique as so many businesses buy in ready prepared products now. The aim is to keep the business successful by giving customers the best of quality with local farm beef, Aberdeenshire lamb and pork. Venison, pheasant, pigeon, partridge, rabbits, hares and mallard duck come from local estates. Pies are made daily - the pastry is also made on the premises - from your everyday steak pie to venison and cranberry pie. Gammons, beef, pork and meat roll are all cooked to perfection for beautiful sliced meat. A mail order service is available delivering fresh goods on a next day delivery throughout the UK.

New products introduced have been ready meals; either to be microwaved or re-heated in the oven. These range from mince, tattie and meallie to fish pie or Lasagne. There are a large range of sausages -over 40 different varieties - including beef and horseradish, pork and leek, lamb and rosemary, and venison. The burgers are not far behind, with varieties such as pork and apple, chicken, spicey lamb burger, venison burger or smoked salmon fishcakes. Coleslaw, carrot and cheese salad and tattie salad are all made on site. And let's not forget the fabulous Haggis, Black Pudding, Meallie Pudding, Fruit Pudding. A new service being provided is the hire of spit roasts or barbecues with or without a butcher cooking.

And last but not least Granny Munro's Dumpling you have to taste it to believe it!!!

MCEWAN GALLERY

Ballater (Royal Deeside) on A939, Aberdeenshire AB35 5UB
Tel: 013397 55429 Fax: 013397 55995
e-mail: dot@mcewangallery.com

The McEwan Gallery, a family business, specialising in quality

paintings of the last three centuries, was founded over forty years ago. Although dealing primarily in works by Scottish artists, including contemporary examples, the Gallery also carries a small selection of English and Dutch works. With a lifetime of experience in the art world, Peter, Dorothy and Rhod welcome you to browse through their collection at leisure. Peter wrote the definitive *Dictionary of Scottish Art & Architecture*, available from the Gallery, and produces a quarterly catalogue of antiquarian books.

Valuations for insurance and probate are undertaken as well as providing a restoration service. We pride ourselves on offering London quality at provincial prices.

Samples of our changing stock can be seen on our website *www.mcewangallery.com*. Enquiries are always welcome. There is parking space beside the imposing house, originally built in 1902 by the Swiss artist Rodolphe Christen.

GLEN LUI HOTEL

14 Invercauld Road,
Ballater, AB35 5PP
Telephone: 013397 55402
e-mail: infos@glen-lui-hotel.co.uk
website: www.glen-lui-hotel.co.uk

The Glen Lui is quietly located within two acres of private wooded grounds offering the most spectacular panoramic views over Ballater's golf course, towards the Cairngorm mountains and famous Lochnagar. This family run business is a perfect place for relaxing in the heart of this Royal Deeside setting. The seasons spring to life before your eyes with deer, red squirrel and an abundance of bird life to watch.

While outdoor activities are numerous the other option of course is relaxing on the terrace or in one of the lounges with a 'dram' in front of an open fire. The Castle Trail and Malt Whisky Trail are situated nearby and Balmoral Castle and Royal Lochnagar Distillerty are only 10 miles away. For the more adventurous there is pony trekking, fishing, shooting, gliding and of course golfing, all amongst our breathtaking scenery.

We carry a good choice of Single Malt Whiskies in the bar and we offer an extensive menu to suit all tastes and our chefs use locally sourced high quality fresh produce to prepare the dishes. We are happy to cater for larger parties and functions, and also have conference facilities for our business clientele. Weddings of up to 30 people can be accommodated and we have a Wedding License should you wish to be married at the hotel.

walk part of the way), in the shadow of Lochnagar, which, notwithstanding its name, is a mountain rising to a height of 3786 feet. It gave its name to Prince Charles's book, *The Old Man of Lochnagar*. The drive is a particularly fine one, and takes you past Birkhall (not open to the public), which was bought by Edward VII before he became king. It was the Deeside home of the late Queen Mother.

BALMORAL

42 miles W of Aberdeen off the A93

> 🏰 Balmoral 🏰 Crathie Kirk 🦢 John Brown
> 🎐 Victorian Heritage Trail

Balmoral, the Queen's private home in Scotland, was purchased by Prince Albert in 1852. Four years previously, Queen Victoria had visited the area and fallen in love with it. Though the castle as you see it today only dates from that time, a castle has stood here for centuries. The grounds are closed when the Royal Family is in residence. The present castle is in Scots Baronial style, and built from local granite.

A quarter of a mile east of the castle is the small **Crathie Kirk**, where the Royal Family worship while at Balmoral. It dates from 1895 and overlooks the remains of the original 14th-century kirk. Many of the fittings and furnishings have been donated over the years by members of the Royal Family. **John Brown**, Queen Victoria's controversial ghillie, lies in the adjoining cemetery. The Royal Lochnagar Distillery, established in 1845, is near the kirk, and has a visitors centre. It was given a Royal Warrant by Queen Victoria in 1864.

A **Victorian Heritage Trail** has been laid out (with distinctive brown signs) that traces the footsteps of Queen Victoria, not just on Deeside, but throughout the area, and a leaflet is available from most tourist offices.

BRAEMAR

50 miles W of Aberdeen on the A93

> 🔲 Braemar Highland Games 🏰 Braemar Castle
> 🌿 Mar Lodge Estate 🔲 Glenshee

This little village high in the Cairngorms is officially Britain's coldest place. Between 1941 and 1970 its average temperature was only 6.4 degrees Celsius. On two occasions, in 1895 and 1982, it experienced the lowest temperature ever officially recorded in Britain - minus 28.2 degrees Celsius.

It sits at an altitude of 1100 feet, and is famous for the **Braemar Highland Games**, held every September, which is attended by the Royal Family. **Braemar Castle** is the seat of the Farquharsons of Invercauld, and was built in 1628 by the Earl of Mar on the site of an older castle. It was used as a base by Hanoverian troops during the 1745 Rebellion. In the drawing room can be seen the world's largest Cairngorm (a semi-precious stone) weighting 52 pounds. And in the morning room display is a collection of Native American items from the great Lakes area of Canada. They were sent back to this country by two members of the family who went there seeking their fortunes.

The 72,598-acre **Mar Lodge Estate** (National Trust for Scotland) lies five miles west of Braemar on a minor road, and is part of the Cairngorms National Park, which came into being in September 2003. The estate has been described as the most important nature conservation landscape in Britain, and contains four out of its five highest mountains. In medieval times, when the estate was owned by the Earls of Mar, it was one of Scotland's most important hunting estates. It displays many of the features normally associated with Highland landscapes, and has a wealth of wildlife, plants, trees and

CALLATER LODGE GUEST HOUSE

9 Glenshee Road, Braemar, Aberdeenshire AB35 5YQ
Tel: 01339 741275
e-mail: info@hotel-braemar.co.uk
website: www.callaterlodge.co.uk

Callater Lodge Guest House is a traditional stone-built Victorian villa
dating from 1861. The guest house offers six guest rooms each
with its own bathroom with shower; two rooms also have bath
tubs. All bedrooms have the following: colour television, tea and
coffee making facilities, thermostatically controlled heating, hair
dryer, bathrobe, luggage rack and complementary quality toiletries.
A choice of cooked breakfast, or a continental style breakfast, is
served in the large airy dining room. There is also a comfortable
residents' lounge with a Victorian fireplace available for guests use
throughout the day, where you can enjoy a drink at the end of a
hard day sightseeing, walking etc. There is also a large garden for
guests to enjoy during the summer months, home to several red squirrels and numerous birds.

Braemar is a pretty village on Royal Deeside, situated within the Cairngorm National Park,
surrounded by superb hills and stunning scenery. The village is close to Balmoral Castle, the
Glenshee Ski Centre and many other attractions. Callater Lodge is about 400 metres from the
village centre and is an ideal base for walking, cycling, climbing, touring, golf and other activities.
Packed lunches are available on request and there is a snack menu available from 5pm until 8pm
daily. For guests, returning from the hills or ski slopes, there is a drying room available to hang up
wet clothing and boots. There is also a secure shed available for those requiring storage (bicycles,
golf clubs, skis etc).

archaeological sites. The estate is open daily,
and the Lodge itself has special open days that
are well advertised.

To the south of Braemar, on the A93, is one
of Scotland's most popular winter sports areas,
Glenshee. The snowfields stretch over three
valleys and four Munros, with about 25 miles
of marked pistes as well as off-piste skiing.

KINTORE
10 miles NW of Aberdeen off the A96

🏯 Kintore Tolbooth 🏯 Kintore Parish Church

🏛 Battle of Mons Graupius

Kintore is a small picturesque royal burgh four
miles southeast of Inverurie. **Kintore
Tolbooth** dates from 1747, when the Earl of
Kintore was the provost. **Kintore Parish
Church** was built in 1819, and incorporated
into the west staircase is a piece of the

sacrament house of the pre-Reformation Kirk
of Kinkell.

To the west of the town stood a Roman
Camp known as Devona. The slopes of
Bennachie, also to the west, is one of the
likely locations for the **Battle of Mons
Graupius**, fought in 84AD and no doubt
Devona played a major part. It was fought
between a confederation of Caledonian tribes
and the army of Agricola, with no clear
victor emerging.

INVERURIE
15 miles NW of Aberdeen city centre off the A96

🏛 Battle of Harlaw 🏛 Carnegie Inverurie Museum

🏛 Bennachie Visitors Centre 🏯 Castle Fraser

🏛 Easter Aquhorthies Stone Circle 🏯 Kinkell Church

The royal burgh of Inverurie sits where the
River Urie meets the Don. A legend tells of

how a Roman soldier who came to this area exclaimed 'urbi in rure!' (a city in the countryside) when he first saw the settlement. The town adopted the words as its motto and it is inscribed on the coat of arms of the burgh. However, in reality, the town's name has a more prosaic meaning - the mouth of the Urie. Mary Stuart visited the town in 1562, and stayed in the royal castle, which once stood where the mound known as the Bass is situated. The **Battle of Harlaw** was fought near the town in 1411, and a monument now marks the spot. A Lowland army fought a Highland army under Donald, Lord of the Isles, and while the result was an honourable draw, it did stop the Highlanders from moving into the Aberdeenshire lowlands and controlling them. It was one of the bloodiest battles fought on Scottish soil, which earned it the nickname of Red Harlaw.

In 1805, the Aberdeenshire Canal was opened, linking Inverurie with Aberdeen. Designed by John Rennie, it was never a great success, and in 1845 it was sold to the Great North of Scotland Railway Company, who drained it and used part of its route to carry their railway line. Port Elphinstone, to the south east of the town, recalls the canal, and part of its channel can still be seen there. It was the only canal in Britain to be closed down every winter in case of ice and snow. Within the **Carnegie Inverurie Museum** in the Square is a small display dedicated to the canal, as well as displays on local history.

To the west of the town is the area's best-known hill, Bennachie. Though not particularly high (1600 feet) it has a distinctive conical shape and is sometimes called Aberdeenshire's Mount Fuji, as it can be seen from all round the area. Near the Chapel of Garrioch is the **Bennachie Visitors Centre**, where the natural and social history of the hill

is explained. Also nearby is the **Easter Aquhorthies Stone Circle,** well-signposted from the A96.

Two miles south of the town are the ruins of the 16th-century **Kinkell Church,** which has a particularly fine sacrament house. The ornate grave slab of Gilbert de Greenlaw, who was killed at the Battle of Harlaw, can also be seen. **Castle Fraser** (National Trust for Scotland) lies six miles southwest of the town, near the village of Craigearn. Work started on it in 1575 by Michael Fraser, the sixth laird, and was finished in 1636. It has a traditional Z plan, and contains many Fraser portraits, fine carpets, linen and curtains.

OLDMELDRUM
15 miles NW of Aberdeen on the A920

Built mostly in an attractive grey stone, Oldmeldrum has a large open square at its heart, which is dominated by grand Town Hall built in 1877. Around this square, there's a number of family-run shops, including an unusual petrol station. Just downhill from the square is Morris's Hotel, which has a sign stating that it opened in 1673, as well as plaques commemorating some of the famous people who have stayed there.

On the north side of Oldmeldrum is Glen Garioch distillery. Built in the same grey stone as much of the rest of the town, the distillery has a four-storey malt barn, two pagodas, a still house and a visitor centre. The distillery, pronounced Glen Geery can trace its origins back to 1797.

MONYMUSK
17 miles W of Aberdeen off the B993

🏛 Parish Church of St Mary

Monymusk was once the site of an Augustinian priory, founded in 1170 by the

RAINBOW FABRICS
& NEEDLECRAFTS

Urquhart Road, Oldmeldrum,
Aberdeenshire AB51 0EX
Tel: 01651 873280
e-mail: probins@rainbow-fabrics.co.uk
website: www.rainbow-fabrics.co.uk

Pat Robins has had a lifelong interest in
needlework and in 2000 she decided to
convert a hobby into a new career. Her
customers and friends describe
Rainbow as an Aladdin's Cave because
of its extensive stock that includes more than 2000 patchwork fabrics from most of the major
manufacturers. Also in stock are threads, including specialist threads for machinery and hand
embroidery; books and patterns; beads; needlecraft and embroidery kits and supplies for both
traditional and contemporary techniques; and fibres and yarns for felting, knitting, crochet and
embellishing. You'll also find an excellent range of haberdashery, fabric paints, tools and textile art
supplies. The shop is open from 10am to 5pm, Tuesday to Saturday.

Rainbow Fabrics also hosts a wide range of classes and workshops run by Meldrum Craft
Workshops. These cater for a wide range of abilities from City & Guilds courses to taster sessions
for absolute beginners.

Earl of Mar. The Monymusk Reliquary, in which was kept a bone of St Columba, was one of its treasures. It dates from the 8th century, and is a small wooden box covered in silver and bronze and decorated in semi-precious stones. It was paraded before Bruce's troops at the Battle of Bannockburn, and is now in the Museum of Scotland.

The **Parish Church of St Mary**, which formed part of the priory, dates from the early years of the 12th century. In 1929, it was restored to its original condition, and it is now one of the finest parish churches in Scotland. Inside it is the Monymusk Stone, on which are carved Pictish symbols.

OYNE
21 miles NW of Aberdeen on the B9002

🏛 Archaeolink Prehistory Park

More than 7000 ancient sites have been identified in Aberdeenshire, from Pictish

carvings to stone circles, and these form the basis for the **Archaeolink Prehistory Park**, which bridges the gap between ancient history and modern times by way of exhibits and hands-on displays, both indoor and out. It has some of the finest collections of ancient remains in Europe.

FYVIE
23 miles NW of Aberdeen city centre off the A947

🏰 Fyvie Castle 🏰 Parish Church
🐾 Cosmo Gordon Lang

The oldest part of **Fyvie Castle** (National Trust for Scotland) dates from the 13th century, and was once a royal stronghold. There are 17th-century panelling and plaster ceilings, as well as a portrait collection that includes works by Raeburn, Romney and Gainsborough. One of the legends attached to the castle is that its five towers were built by the five great families in the northeast who owned it - the Gordons, the Leiths, the Meldrums, the Prestons and the Setons. Both Robert the Bruce and and his descendant Charles I stayed here.

The **Parish Church** dates from the 19th century, and has a fine laird's pew and wine glass pulpit. **Cosmo Gordon Lang** was born In Fyvie Old Manse in 186. He became Archbishop of York in 1908 and Archbishop of Canterbury in 1928.

HUNTLY
33 miles NW of Aberdeen on the A96

🏰 Huntly Castle   🗿 Standing Stones of Strathbogie

🏛 Brander Museum   🖋 George MacDonald

🏰 Leith Hall

Huntly is an old burgh, which was granted its charter in 1488. It sits in an area called Strathbogie, and is famous for the ruins of **Huntly Castle** (Historic Scotland). It was originally called Strathbogie Castle, and was built by the Earl of Fife in the late 12th century. While in the area in the early 1300s, Robert the Bruce took ill, and spent some time in the castle, as the then earl, David, was one of his supporters. However, the earl changed sides and joined the English just before Bannockburn, and subsequently forfeited the lands of Strathbogie.

They were subsequently given to Sir Adam Gordon of Huntly who lived in the Scottish Borders. He moved north to claim them in 1376. In the 16th century, the name of the castle was changed to Huntly, and in the early 1550s it was rebuilt by George, 4th Earl of Huntly.

During the Reformation, the Gordons of Huntly were one of the most important Catholic families in Scotland, and fought on the side of Mary Stuart. James VI, her son, had the castle demolished when the 6th Earl, George, was implicated in an uprising against him. George fled to France, but returned, made his peace with James, and had the castle rebuilt. During the turbulent Covenanting times, the castle changed hands many times until it finally fell into the hands of the Covenanters in the early 17th century.

From about the early 18th century, the castle fell into decay. But even today you can see just how stately and comfortable the place must have been in its heyday. It entertained many famous people, including Mary of Guise, mother of Mary Stuart, and Perkin Warbeck, pretender to the English throne.

In the town square is a statue to the 4th Duke of Richmond, and beneath it are the **Standing Stones of Strathbogie**, or as they are known in Huntly, the Stannin Steens o Strahbogie. At one time they formed part of a stone circle.

The **Brander Museum** in

Leith Hall, Huntly

the Square has collections dealing with local history, arms and armour, and the works of local author **George MacDonald**, who died in 1905. His most popular stories were of fantasy and fairies, with a strong religious message. He rejected the Calvinist view, still held by some people in the Church of Scotland at the time, that art was self-indulgent and iconoclastic. Instead, he argued that God could be understood through art and imagination.

Six miles south of Huntly, on the B9002 near Kennethmont, is **Leith Hall** (National Trust for Scotland). It was the home of the Leith (later Leith-Hay) family from 1650 onwards, and contains many of their possessions. The family had a tradition of military service and its most famous member, Andrew Hay, fought for Charles Edward Stuart.

Not far from here is Rhynie, known for its Celtic sites, Pictish stone circles, vitrified forts and castles. The village is situated on crossroads from which there is easy access to the distilleries, Deeside, Aberdeen and the coast. The local hill, Tap O'Noth, is a favourite spot for hang-gliders, while mountain bikers and anglers are also well catered for.

ELLON
15 miles N of Aberdeen on the A920

- 🏛 Parish Church
- 🏛 Moot Hill Monument
- 🏛 Museum of Farming Life
- 🏛 Haddo House
- ⚘ Formartine Buchan Way
- ⚘ Pitmedden Garden
- 🏛 Tolquhon Castle

Situated within an area known as the Formartine, Ellon is a small burgh or barony, which was granted its charter in 1707. It was one of the places burned down during what became known as the Harrying of Buchan in 1308 soon after Robert the Bruce defeated John Comyn, Earl of Buchan at Old Meldrum.

The town sits on the River Ythan, with a **Parish Church** that dates from 1777. It's hard to imagine nowadays that this little town, five miles from the coast, was once a port with a small steamer that took goods up and down the river. It is also one of the stops on the **Formartine Buchan Way**, based on disused railway tracks from Dyce, just outside of Aberdeen, to Fraserburgh. The **Moot Hill Monument** stands on Moot Hill, from where justice was dispensed by the Earls of Buchan in the 13th and early 14th centuries.

Five miles west of the town, on the A920 is the **Pitmedden Garden** (National Trust for Scotland - see panel opposite). The centrepiece is the Great Garden, laid out by Sir Alexander Seton, 1st Baronet of Pitmedden, in 1675. In the 1950s, the rest of the garden was re-created using elaborate floral designs. Four parterres were created, three of them being inspired by designs possibly used at the Palace of Holyrood in Edinburgh, and

Forbes Tomb, Ellon

Pitmedden Garden

Ellon, Aberdeenshire AB41 7PD
Tel: 01651 842352
website: www.nts.org.uk

The heart of this property is the formal walled garden originally laid out in 1675 by Sir Alexander Seton. In the 1950s, the Trust set about re-creating the gardens following designs dating from the 17th century. Today, Pitmedden features over 5 miles of box hedging arranged in intricate patterns to form six parterres. Each parterre is filled with some 40,000 plants bursting with colour in the summer months.

Extensive herbaceous borders provide an abundance of colour and texture throughout the season and the spectacular lupin border is not to be missed. Honeysuckle, jasmine and roses create a succession of fragrances, while fountains, topiary, sundials, and a fascinating herb garden add to the sense of discovery around the walled garden. There are over 80 varieties of apple trees offer a spectacular show of blossom and scent in spring. On the last Sunday in September the garden holds harvest celebrations with dancing and music, and visitors can buy fruits harvested from the gardens.

The adjacent Museum of Farming Life boasts an extensive collection of domestic and agricultural artefacts of a bygone era. For the more adventurous, the woodland walk extends for a mile and a half round the estate and takes in ponds, rhododendrons, a lime kiln and a nature hut with information about the wider estate. The picnic area is an ideal spot to stop for lunch, and visitors can even enjoy a game of boules on the petanque piste.

the fourth based on Sir Alexander's coat of arms. There is also a visitor centre and a **Museum of Farming Life**, which has a collection of old farming implements once used in this largely farming area.

Near the gardens are the substantial ruins of **Tolquhon Castle**, built by William Forbes, 7th Lord of Tolquhon in the 1580s. In 1589 James VI visited the house, and both his and the Forbes' coats of arms were carved over the doorway. William Forbes and his wife Elizabeth were buried in an elaborately carved tomb in the south aisle of the parish church at Tarves. The church has since been demolished, but the

Forbes Tomb survives to this day.

Haddo House (National Trust for Scotland), one of the grandest stately homes in Aberdeenshire, lies six miles northwest of Ellon. It was designed by William Adam for the 2nd Earl of Aberdeen in the early 1730s, and restored in the 1880s. It is noted for its Victorian interiors within an elegant Georgian shell, and features furniture, paintings and objets d'art. It also has a terraced garden with rose beds and a fountain. In the grounds is Kelly Lake, one of the few natural (as opposed to man-made) sheets of water called 'lake' rather than 'loch' in Scotland.

Elgin

🏚 St Giles Church 🏚 Muckle Cross
🏚 Thunderton Hotel 🏛 Elgin Museum
🏛 Moray Motor Museum 🌱 Elgin Cathedral
🏚 Bishop's Palace 🏚 Old Mills 🏚 Spynie Palace
🏚 Greyfriars Monastery
🌱 Johnston's Cashmere Visitor Centre

Situated in the fertile Laigh of Moray, Elgin is a charming city with the ruins of what was one of the finest cathedrals in Scotland. Before the local government reforms in the mid-1970s, there were only six towns - or cities - in Scotland that were allowed to have lord provosts, and Elgin was one of them.

The city's layout is still essentially that of the medieval burgh, with a High Street that goes from where the royal castle once stood on Lady Hill to the cathedral. It widens in the middle into a market place called the Plainstanes, and close to it stands **St Giles Church**. It is in neoclassical style, and was built in 1828 to replace a medieval building. In the square at its east end is the **Muckle Cross**, a Victorian rebuilding of a medieval one. On Lady Hill is a monument to the 5th Duke of

Richmond, dating from 1839, with the statue added 16 years later. At the far east end of the High Street is another cross. It marks the spot where Alaxander MacDonald of the Isles did penance for despoiling the cathedral. It also marks the western limit of the sanctuary area of the cathedral.

Just off the High Street is the **Thunderton Hotel**, housed in what was a grand medieval town house. It was once the royal residence of the town, where the monarch stayed when he visited. It was surrounded by orchards, gardens and a bowling green. In 1746, Charles Edward Stuart stayed here while on his way to Culloden.

Three 17th-century arcaded merchants' houses are to be found in the High Street, one of which at one time housed the bank of William Duff, a member of the family thatwent on to become substantial landowners in the area. The award-winning **Elgin Museum** is also in the High Street, and has many important collections, including natural history, archaeology, and the social history of the area. Another museum worth visiting is the **Moray Motor Museum** in Bridge Street, with its collection of old cars and motorcycles from 1904 to the 1960s. The centrepiece of the collection is a 1928 Rolls-Royce Phantom I.

Work was started on **Elgin Cathedral**, or to give it its proper name, the Cathedral of the Holy Trinity, in about 1224. It was one of Scotland's grandest churches, and could compare to the great cathedrals of Europe. There had been three

Elgin Cathedral, Elgin

THE STEADING

Greenfields, Lhanbryde, Elgin, Moray IV30 8LN
Tel: 01343 842633
Mobiles: 07795 236623 or 07798 725845

Hilary Anderson and Maggie Brown, partners in the Steading Café, have backgrounds in education and training, but realised their shared passion for good home cooked food and rural life when they established the café and country store in June 2008. Building on the success of Hilary's previous business, The Whole Horse Tack Shop in Keith, and utilising their culinary skills and rural knowledge, they have since added a deli counter and an outside catering service, and provide a range of rural-themed courses and holiday breaks too.

THE CAFÉ:

The café is situated in a relaxed rural setting and places its emphasis on ethically sourced products, using local producers and fair trade goods wherever possible. Eggs are free range, meat is free range/outdoor reared and many ingredients are organic. Bread is freshly baked each morning and different freshly cooked special dishes are offered each day with vegetarian and vegan options always available. A mouth-watering array of Steading Café home baking is on offer and the Café is already well known for its excellent coffee and teas. Food is freshly cooked to order and, although it takes a little extra time, customer feedback confirms that the results are worth waiting for.

THE DELI & COUNTRY STORE:

Under their own Bothy Bakehouse label, the Steading Café's deli counter offers home produced breads, baking, chutneys and salad dressings for sale, in addition to seasonal quality produce from local artisan producers. Paintings and crafts from local artists are for sale, and countrywear, clothing and gifts complete the range.

COURSES AND ACTIVITY BREAKS:

From 2 hour courses to mid-week or weekend breaks, Hilary and Maggie share their passion for good food and their keen interest in rural skills through cookery classes and a range of other rural-themed leisure and personal development courses. Maggie's husband, Angus, passes on the secret of his Steading bread, shortbread and clootie dumpling in the introductory rural cookery class, and other course options include natural horsemanship, animal care, rural crafts and painting and drawing. Breaks can be tailored to suit particular interests. Refreshments are included and accommodation and evening meals can be arranged where required.

ROOM TO BLOOM

28 Thunderton Place, Elgin, Moray IV30 1BG
Tel: 01343 548677
e-mail: roomtobloom@fsmail.net

Kevin Shand became a florist in 2000 and opened his own shop, **Room to Bloom,** on Valentine's Day the following year. Those premises, in an old sea captain's house, measured about 8ft square. Successful trading meant that he and his 4 staff moved to the present, larger shop. Kevin now offers top quality fresh flowers for all occasions and will create tailor-made wedding packages as well as beautiful floral tributes for any occasion. Room to Bloom also stocks silk flowers, chocolates, cards, balloons and candles.

cathedrals in the dioceses before this one, at Birnie, Spynie and Kinneder, but the locations had all been unsuitable. By the end of the 13th century, building work was complete, but in 1390 the Wolf of Badenoch set fire to it after a violent quarrel with the Bishop of Moray, who had ordered him to give up his mistress and return to his wife.

The fire did a lot of damage, and work on repairing it continued right up until the Reformation in 1560. After the Reformation, the cathedral became a quarry for the people of the town. In 1807, a keeper of the ruins was appointed, and from then on what was left was cared for and preserved. The east gate to the cathedral precincts, known as the Panns Port, still stands.

To the northwest of the cathedral are the ruins of the so-called **Bishop's Palace**. It had nothing to do with the bishop, but was instead the manse of the cathedral's preceptor, who looked after the sacred music. It was one of about 20 such manses around the cathedral that housed the cathedral staff. And to the northeast of the cathedral is the Brewery Bridge, built in 1798 and so called because a brewery stood close by until 1913.

Off Greyfriars Street stands the restored **Greyfriars Monastery**, now reckoned to give the best idea of what a medieval Scottish friary looked like. It was built in 1479, then, in the late 19th century, was restored by John Kinross, who built new walls on the foundations of the old ones.

At ther west end of the high street is the imposing façade of Dr Gray's Hospital, the town's main infirmary. It was founded by Dr Alexander Gray, who amassed a fortune in India, and was built between 1816 and 1819.

Johnston's Cashmere Visitor Centre is at Newmill. There are tours round the mill, an exhibition and audiovisual devices that explains the making of the luxury material. There is also a shop where Johnston products can be bought, as well as a coffee shop.

The **Old Mills** is the last remaining meal mill on the River Lossie. Its history goes back to the 13th century, when it was owned by Pluscarden Abbey.

North of the city are the impressive ruins of **Spynie Palace** (Historic Scotland), the home of the bishops of Moray. The palace stands on the shores of tiny Loch Spynie, and dates from the 14th century and later. David's Tower, the main part of the building, dates from the 16th century.

Around Elgin

DUFFUS

5 miles NW of Elgin on the B9012

🏛 Church of St Peter 🏛 Duffus Castle

The ruins of the **Church of St Peter** (Historic Scotland) stand near the village. Though mainly 18th century, it incorporates work that is much older. Opposite the porch is the medieval Parish Cross.

Close by are the ruins of **Duffus Castle**, founded in the 12th century by Freskin, Lord of Strabrock, who later took the title and name of Lord of Duffus and Freskin or Moravia. He is the ancestor of the great Moravia, (later Moray, or Murray), family, which has played such a prominent part in Scotland's history. The castle would originally have been a wooden tower surrounded by a wooden palisade, which not only encompassed the castle on top of its motte, or hill, but a bailey as well, where a small settlement would have flourished. The castle as we see it today dates from the 14th century onwards, and still has the finest motte and bailey of any castle in the north of Scotland.

Gordonstoun School, attended by both Prince Philip and Prince Charles, is close to Duffus, and is housed in an 18th-century mansion. It was founded by the German educationalist Dr Kurt Hahn in 1934.

LOSSIEMOUTH

5 miles N of Elgin on the A941

🏛 Lossiemouth Fisheries & Community Museum

🐟 James Ramsay Macdonald

This holiday resort sits at the mouth of the River Lossie, and was established as a small port for the city of Elgin in the 18th century after Elgin's original port at Spynie was cut off from the sea as the River Lossie silted up. There are fine sandy beaches, and the **Lossiemouth Fisheries and Community Museum**, in a former net mending loft at Pitgaveny Quay, traces the history of the town and its fishing industry. There is also a reconstruction of the study used by **James Ramsay Macdonald**, Britain's first Labour prime minister, who was born illegitimate in a small cottage in the town in 1866.

FOCHABERS

8 miles E of Elgin on the A96

🏛 Fochabers Folk Museum 🏛 Bellie Church

🏛 Milne's High School

Fochabers dates from 1776, when the then Duke of Gordon decided that he didn't like the dilapidated huddle of cottages that was old Fochabers within his parkland. He therefore built a new village further north with a large spacious square. The architect was John Baxter, an Edinburgh man who had already worked on Gordon Castle. Within the former Pringle Church in the High Street is the **Fochabers Folk Museum**, and in the square is the elegant, porticoed **Bellie Church**. Its rather quaint name comes from the Gaelic *beul-aith*, meaning the mouth of the ford.

The imposing **Milne's High School** dates from 1844, and was built using money gifted by a native of the town who made his fortune in New Orleans.

West of the village centre and overlooking the Spey is Baxter's Highland Village, home to one of the best-known food firms in Scotland. It all started in 1868, when George Baxter, who worked for the Duke of Gordon, opened a small grocery shop in Fochabers. This is one of the most fertile areas in Britain, famed for its fruit, vegetables and cattle, and soon

🎬 stories and anecdotes 🐟 famous people 🎨 art and craft 🚲 entertainment and sport 🚶 walks

George's wife was making jams and conserves in the back shop. Now the factory and associated shops, restaurants and kids' play areas are tourist attractions in their own right.

BUCKIE
13 miles E of Elgin on the A990

🏛 Buckie District Fishing Heritage Museum	
🏛 Buckie Drifter 🌿 Fordyce Joiner's Workshop	
🌿 Peter Anson Gallery 🏛 Deskford Church	
🏛 St Mary's Church 🏛 Findlater Castle	

Buckie is a major fishing port, based in Cluny Harbour. In the **Buckie District Fishing Heritage Museum** in Clunie Place and the **Buckie Drifter** in Freuchny Road are displays that tell the story of the fishing industry on the Morayshire coast. The **Peter Anson Gallery** is within the town's library, and has a collection of paintings by the maritime artist Peter Anson.

Four miles west of the town is the mouth of the River Spey. It is half a mile wide, though no great port sits here. The village of Kingston dates from 1784 and was founded by Ralph Dodworth and William Osbourne. They came from Kingston-upon-Hull in Yorkshire and named the village after their home town. It was near here that Charles II alighted after a trip from Holland on June 23 1650. His ship grounded in shallow water, and he had to be taken ashore piggyback style on the back of a villager.

The small fishing communities round about, such as Findochty and Portnockie, are very attractive, and well worth visiting. Five miles southwest of the town are the ruins of **Deskford Church**, within the village of the same name. It is noted for its ornately carved sacrament house. The 16th-century **St Mary's Church** stands in the small fishing village of Cullen, to the north of Deskford, and was formerly collegiate. Cullen, a former fishing village, gives its name to one of Scotland's best known dishes - Cullen skink, a fish soup enriched with potatoes, onion and cream. The word skink comes from the Gaelic word for essence.

One of the most dramatically situated castles in the area is **Findlater Castle**, which sits on a small promontory jutting into the sea. It was built by the Ogilvie family and the ruins you see now date from the 15th century. Care should be taken when approaching or exploring it. The name comes from the Norse *fyn*, meaning white and *leitr* meaning cliff, as the cliffs in this part of the country are studded with quartz.

In the village of Fordyce, southeast of Cullen, is the **Fordyce Joiner's Workshop and Visitor Centre** in Church Street, dedicated to the skills and tools of carpentry in northeast Scotland. Fordyce Castle was built in 1592 by Sir Thomas Menzies of Durn, a provost of Aberdeen. It is an L-plan tower, and is not open to the public.

CRAIGELLACHIE
12 miles S of Elgin off the A95

🏛 Craigellachie Bridge 🌿 Speyside Cooperage	
🏛 Ballindalloch Castle	

The **Craigellachie Bridge** dates from 1814, and is Scotland's oldest iron bridge. It was designed by Thomas Telford, and has one single graceful arch spanning the Spey. The village sits in the heart of the Malt Whisky Trail, and most of the distilleries organise tours round the premises, with a tasting at the end. The **Speyside Cooperage**, on the Dufftown road, has a visitor centre where you can learn about the skills involved in making and repairing whisky casks.

Craigellachie Distillery lies within the village, as does the Macallan Distillery, and four miles north is the Glen Grant Distillery. The Glenfarclas Distillery is seven miles southwest, near **Ballindalloch Castle.** The castle dates from the 16th century, and is the home of the McPherson-Grant family who have lived there continuously since it was built. It is open to the public during the summer months. About four miles south of Ballindalloch is the Glenlivet Distillery, which again has organised tours.

A couple of miles southwest is the village of Aberlour, where the Aberlour Distillery has a visitor centre.

Tolbooth Clock Tower, Dufftown

DUFFTOWN

16 miles S of Elgin on the A941

| 🏚 Clock Tower | 🎭 McPherson of Kingussie |
| 🏚 Mortlach Church | 🏰 Balvenie Castle |

Founded in 1817 by James Duff, the 4th Earl

FLORAL OCCASIONS

15 Fife Street, Dufftown, Moray AB55 4AL
Tel: 01340 820567

For everything to do with flowers and floral displays, you should head for **Floral Occasions** in the whisky town of Dufftown. Established in 2002, the shop is owned and personally managed by Margaret Brown, a knowledgeable lady who is happy to discuss your requirements and advise.

Located next to the town square so that you can't miss it, the shop's colourful displays include an excellent variety of flowers, including roses, lilies, orchids and flowering plants, silk flowers, baskets and vases. You'll also find a host of products to do with floral displays, chocolates, balloons, teddies and candles.

If you're in Morayshire, make sure you call in!

🎭 stories and anecdotes 🐦 famous people 🎨 art and craft ✏ entertainment and sport 🚶 walks

original building still survive. In the graveyard is an old Pictish cross, and inside the church is the Elephant Stone, again with Pictish associations. An old story tells of how Malcolm II extended the church in thanks for his victory over the Vikings in 1010. **Balvenie Castle** (Historic Scotland), lies a mile north, and was once home to the Comyns and later the Stewarts and the Douglases. In the 13th century it was visited by Edward I of England, and Mary Stuart spend two nights here in 1562.

The Keith and Dufftown Railway connects Dufftown to the market town of Keith, 11 miles away. It was reopened in 2000/2001 by a group of enthusiasts, and runs services between the two towns.

The 18-hole Dufftown Golf Club boasts the highest hole in the UK. Besides golf, the town caters for all types of outdoor activities including walking, fishing, shooting and cycling.

KEITH
15 miles SE of Elgin on the A96

🏚 Packhorse Bridge 🏚 Milton Tower

🏛 Scottish Tartans Museum

Keith is divided into two communities, separated by the River Isla. The old Keith was founded in the 12th century on the west bank of the river as a market centre for the selling of cattle. The newer, and larger, Keith was laid out in 1755 by the Earl of Findlater on the east bank.

The town is home to the Glenisla Distillery, which is open to the public. The old **Packhorse Bridge** dates from 1609, though the town's oldest building is **Milton Tower**, dating from 1480. It was a stronghold of the Ogilvie family, whose most famous member

---

GOWANBRAE GUEST HOUSE

19 Church Street, Dufftown, Banffshire AB55 4AR
Tel: 01340 821344
e-mail: bedbreakfast@gowanbrae-dufftown.co.uk
website: www.gowanbrae-dufftown.co.uk

Gowanbrae Guest House is a handsome Victorian property with spacious rooms, tastefully modernized and decorated. Guests are assured of a warm welcome and every effort is made to make your stay comfortable and enjoyable. There is a comfortably furnished lounge where you can relax and enjoy a selection of videos, DVDs, CDs and board games. In the morning, a hearty Scottish breakfast is served in the cosy dining room and a packed lunch service is also offered. Special diets are catered for and children are welcome. From the ground floor, an impressive Victorian staircase leads to the first and second floor bedrooms. There is one double room and also three family rooms. Every room is en-suite with TV, tea/coffee-making facilities, hairdryer and central heating. Guests are provided with their own key and are free to come and go as they please.

Dufftown itself is a small country town located midway between Aberdeen and Inverness, and is ideally located for touring the North East of Scotland. The mountains are about half an hour's drive away and the coast is the same.

🏚 historic building 🏛 museum and heritage 🏚 historic site 🌂 scenic attraction 🌠 flora and fauna

was John Ogilvie. Raised a Protestant, he later converted to Roman Catholicism on the Continent, and was sent back to Scotland to promote the faith, posing as a horse dealer and soldier called John Watson. He was eventually hanged in Glasgow in 1615, and was made a saint in 1976. There is a **Scottish Tartans Museum** in Keith's Institute Hall. The town is the eastern terminus of the Keith and Dufftown Railway.

TOMINTOUL
27 miles S of Elgin on the A939

🏛 Tomintoul Museum 🏰 Corgarff Castle

Tomintoul dates from 1775, when the 4th Duke of Gordon decided to lay out a new village in the aftermath of the Jacobite Uprising. It is situated at a height of 1160 feet and is said to be the highest village in the Highlands (but not in Scotland). The A939 southwest to Cockbridge is called The Lecht, and is notorious for being blocked by snow in winter. The ski area of the same name lies six miles from Tomintoul. The small **Tomintoul Museum**, in the village square, has displays on local history and wildlife.

At Cockbridge, **Corgarff Castle** (Historic Scotland), is a tower house set within a curious star-shaped walled enclosure. It was built in about 1550 by John Forbes of Towie. There was a long running feud between the Forbes and the Gordons. During a siege of the castle in 1571, John Forbes's wife Margaret held out against a force led by Adam Gordon. Eventually, the castle was burned down, killing everyone in it, including Margaret.

PLUSCARDEN
6 miles SW of Elgin on a minor road

🏰 Pluscarden Priory

Pluscarden Priory was founded in 1230 by

Alexander II and settled firstly by the Valliscaulian and then the Benedictine monks. In the 19th century, the Bute family acquired the ruined buildings, and in 1943 presented them to the monks of Prinknash in England, who took up residence in 1948. This means that it is the only medieval abbey in Britain still used for its original purpose. At first it was a priory, but became an abbey in its own right in 1974. It is open to the public, and has a small gift shop.

FORRES
12 miles W of Elgin on the A96

🗿 Sueno's Stone 🏛 The Falconer Museum

🏰 Nelson Tower 🏰 Brodie Castle

🌿 Culbin Sands 🏛 Findhorn Heritage Centre

🏛 Dallas Dhu Distillery

This small royal burgh, which was granted its charter in the 13th century, was once one of the most important places in Scotland, and is mentioned in Shakespeare's *Macbeth*. The ground plan of the medieval settlement still forms the basis of the town today, though it is much more open and green than it was then, thanks to some large areas of parkland.

The 20-feet high **Sueno's Stone** (Historic Scotland) dates from the 9th or 10th century, and is the largest known stone with Pictish carvings in Scotland. One side shows a cross, while the other shows scenes of battle. One of the scenes might be the battle fought at Forres in 966AD where the Scottish king, Dubh, was killed. It is now floodlit, and under glass to protect it from the weather. **The Falconer Museum** in Tolbooth Street was founded in 1871, and highlights the history and heritage of the town and its surroundings. It was founded using money from a bequest from two brothers who left Forres for India. One was Alexander Falconer, a merchant in

LOGIE STEADING

Dunphail, Forres, Moray IV36 2QN
Tel: 01309 611275 Fax: 01309 611300
e-mail: panny@logie.co.uk website: www.logie.co.uk

*Located in the beautiful Findhorn Valley, 6 miles south of Forres, **Logie Steading** is an interesting complex of small businesses promoting Scottish craftsmanship and local produce throughout the year. They occupy sandstone farm buildings which were converted into workshops in 1992.*

The Art Gallery - The Art Gallery specialises in contemporary Scottish art and exhibits a wide range of individual original work. Artists include oil painters, watercolourists, printmakers, jewellery craftsmen, ceramicists, sculptors and textile designers. Exhibitions change regularly.
Tel: 01309 611 378 e-mail: gallery@logie.co.uk

Giles Pearson Antiques & Country Furniture - Giles and Margaret Pearson offer a range of superb antique country furniture, folk art pieces and general high quality objets d'art. They specialise in the restoration of cane and rush-seated chairs and customers can view work in progress in the shop.
Tel: 01309 611280 e-mail: gilespearson@btinternet.com

Logie Steading Bookshop - A firm favourite of book-lovers from near and far, the Logie Steading Bookshop stocks more than 20,000 volumes which means that there is something to suit most tastes. Now in its tenth year, the bookshop is well-established as one of Scotland's leading Antiquarian and Secondhand Bookshops. Helen Trussell's staff will travel to advise, and to buy quality books and libraries.
Tel: 01309 611 373
e-mail: logiesteadingbookshop@btinternet.com

Archie's Furniture and Gifts - In Archie's Furniture and Gifts you'll find carefully sourced gifts for your friends or for your own house - interesting, timeless pieces which look as well amongst antiques as in modern surroundings. *Tel: 01309 611722*

Diva Designs - Diva Designs offers a selection of bags, scarves, jewellery and interior accessories designed and made by three talented textile designers using sumptuous silks, velvets, merino wool and Scottish tweeds. Creative course and workshops run throughout the year.
e-mail: cawthra.hewitt@btinternet.com

Farm and Garden Shop - Open seasonally, the Farm and Garden Shop sells a wide range of unusual hardy perennials, herbs and shrubs; strong plants grown in Scotland for Scottish gardens. Friendly, knowledgeable staff can suggest suitable plants for your garden. Local produce includes the renowned Longhorn beef from the Logie herd.
Tel: 01309 611 222 e-mail: farmandgarden@logie.co.uk

The Café - The Café is open daily at 10.30am for coffee with freshly made scones, followed by delicious home-made soups, salads, tarts and filled ciabattas for lunch to satisfy both vegetarians and meat-eaters. After a breathtaking riverside walk, come back for afternoon tea with a great range of irresistible cakes from which to choose. Everything is made on the premises with finest quality ingredients sourced locally wherever possible, and as much as possible is organic.
Tel: 01309 611733

MURDOCH BROTHERS

10-12 High Street, Forres,
Moray IV36 1DB
Tel: 01309 672805
Fax: 01309 676667
e-mail:
murdochbros@moraybroadband.co.uk

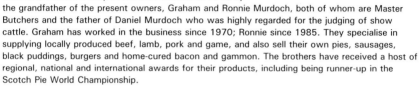

Murdoch Brothers, Butchers is a long-established
traditional butcher's shop which was founded in 1916 by
the grandfather of the present owners, Graham and Ronnie Murdoch, both of whom are Master
Butchers and the father of Daniel Murdoch who was highly regarded for the judging of show
cattle. Graham has worked in the business since 1970; Ronnie since 1985. They specialise in
supplying locally produced beef, lamb, pork and game, and also sell their own pies, sausages,
black puddings, burgers and home-cured bacon and gammon. The brothers have received a host of
regional, national and international awards for their products, including being runner-up in the
Scotch Pie World Championship.

A major refurbishment in 2006 has given the shop a very welcoming and friendly atmosphere.
Traditional meets modern with the elegantly curved refrigerated displays offering a wide selection
of fresh meats, sausages, pies and convenience products.

The brothers have also recently opened a new processing unit at the rear of the premises which
has greatly increased their capacity to fulfil the growing demand for the award-winning produce
from the Royal Burgh of Forres! If you are unable to visit the store, you need not miss out, the
website offers online shopping and a nation wide delivery service is also available.

Calcutta, and the other was Hugh Falconer, a botanist and zoologist.

Dominating the town is the **Nelson Tower**, opened in 1812 in Grant Park to commemorate Nelson's victory at Trafalgar seven years before, the first such building to do so in Britain. If you're fit enough to climb its 96 steps, you'll get spectacular views over the surrounding countryside and the Moray Firth.

Brodie Castle lies four miles west of the town. It is a 16th-century tower house with later additions, which give it the look of a comfortable mansion. In about 1160, Malcolm IV gave the surrounding lands to the Brodies, and it was their family home until the late 20th century. It contains major collections of paintings, furniture and ceramics, and sits in 175 acres of ground. Within the grounds is Rodney's Stone, with Pictish carvings.

A couple of miles northeast of Forres is Kinloss, with an RAF base and the scant remains of an old abbey. It was founded in about 1150 by David I, and colonised by Cistercian monks from Melrose. It is said that the abbey David founded in thanks after getting lost in a dense forest. Two doves led him to an open space where shepherds were looking after their sheep. They gave him food and shelter and, as he slept, he had a dream in which he was told to build an abbey on the spot. Before the Reformation, it was one of the wealthiest and most powerful abbeys in Scotland.

On the coast north of Forres is perhaps Scotland's most unusual landscape, the **Culbin Sands**. In 1694 a storm blew great drifts of sand - some as high as 100 feet - over an area that had once been green and fertile, causing people to flee their homes. The drifts covered

SHERSTON HOUSE

Hillhead, Forres, Moray IV36 2QT
Tel/Fax: 01309 671087

Sherston House is an impressive-looking property, built in Moray stone in 1930 by a local farmer. A notable feature of the house is the generous use of Oregon pine with its warm and welcoming colour. Most of the house's original fixtures and fittings have also survived. This beautiful period house is the home of Hazel and Robbie Newlands who have been running the guest house since they retired from their farm in 1997. Their guests have the use of a comfortable sitting room and there's also a large well-tended garden with swings and picnic table. The 4-star accommodation comprises 3 tastefully decorated en suite rooms with all mod. cons. As well as 1 single room with a separate bathroom. A hearty breakfast is included in the tariff and evening meals are available by arrangement. If you prefer to eat out, there are several good eating places within easy reach. The house is just 2 miles from Forres with its historic Brodie Castle and only 8 miles from Elgin whose manifold attractions include the remarkable ruins of what was once one of the grandest cathedrals in Scotland.

cottages, fields, even a mansion house and orchard, and eventually created eight square miles of what became known as Scotland's Sahara. Occasionally, further storms would uncover the foundations of old cottages, which were then covered back up again by succeeding storms. The sands continued to shift and expand until the 1920s, when trees were planted to stabilise the area. Now it is a nature reserve.

At Findhorn, on the Moray Firth coast, is the Findhorn Foundation, one of the most successful centres in Britain for exploring alternative lifestyles and spiritual living. It was founded by Dorothy Maclean and Peter and Eileen Caddy in 1962 in a caravan park. The **Findhorn Heritage Centre and Museum** has displays on the history and heritage of the place. The village of Findhorn itself was once a busy port, trading with the Low Countries and Scandinavia. Now it is a sailing and wildlife centre.

Dallas Dhu Distillery (Historic Scotland) sits to the south of Forres, and here you can learn about the making of whisky. It was built between 1898 and 1899 to produce a single malt for a firm of Glasgow blenders called Wright and Greig.

Fraserburgh

- Kinnaird Lighthouse Old Kirk
- Fraserburgh Heritage Centre Wine Tower
- Sandhaven Meal Mill Memsie Burial Cairn

Fraserburgh sits on the coastline just at that point where the Moray Firth becomes the North Sea. It is one of the main fishing ports in northeast Scotland, and the largest shellfish port in Europe. It was founded in the 16th century by Alexander Fraser, eighth laird of Philorth, who built the first harbour in

 historic building museum and heritage historic site scenic attraction flora and fauna

THE OLD KIRK

Dyke by Forres, Morayshire IV36 2TL
Tel/Fax: 01309 641414
e-mail: enquiries@oldkirk.co.uk
website: www.theoldkirk.co.uk

Built in 1856 as the "East Kirk", this Presbyterian church remained in use until 1941. For the next 40 years it was used a storage barn for potatoes before being converted into a striking residence in 1998 with many original features, such as the stained glass window, still in place.

The Old Kirk is now the home of Herby and Hilary McFarland who are originally from Northern Ireland. They came to the village to be close to their son and daughter-in-law after the birth of the couple's first baby. They moved into The Old Kirk in the spring of 2008 and began welcoming bed and breakfast guests in May of that year. Guests have the use of a spacious and comfortable lounge with a wood-burning stove and the accommodation comprises 3 attractively furnished and decorated rooms, two of which are en suite while the third has a private bathroom. One of the en suite rooms has a 4-poster bed and all bedrooms are equipped with a television, hairdryer and tea/coffee making facilities.

The Old Kirk is just 3 miles from historic Forres, close to Brodie Castle and Cawdor Castle, and is also on the Malt Whiskey Trail.

1546. Between 1570 and 1571 he also built Fraserburgh Castle. A powerful lantern was added on top of it in 1787, and it became a lighthouse, known as **Kinnaird Lighthouse**, owned by Historic Scotland. It is now a museum dedicated to Scotland's lighthouses.

The **Old Kirk** in Saltoun Square isn't as old as its name would suggest. It was built in 1803 to replace the original church built by Alexander between 1570 and 1571. Beside it is the Fraser Burial Aisle.

One of Alexander's grander schemes was the founding of a university in the town, and he even went so far as to obtain James VI's permission to do so. The Scots Parliament gave it a grant, and the Rev Charles Ferme became its first principal. Unfortunately, the Rev Ferme was later arrested for attending a general assembly of the Church of Scotland in defiance of the king. The embryonic university subsequently collapsed, though one

street in the town, College Bounds, still commemorates the scheme.

The **Fraserburgh Heritage Centre** in Quaerry Road, has exhibits about the history of the town, including some haute couture dresses designed by the late fashion designer Bill Gibb, who hailed from Fraserburgh. The most unusual building in Fraserburgh is the **Wine Tower**, next to the lighthouse. It too was built by Alexander Fraser, possibly as a chapel. It has three floors, but no connecting stairways. The Tower probably got its name because it was the wine cellar of those who at one time lived in the nearby castle. Under the tower is a cave more than 100 feet long.

At Sandhead, to the west of the town, is the **Sandhaven Meal Mill**, dating from the 19th century. Guided tours and models show how oatmeal used to be ground. At Memsie, three miles south of Fraserburgh on the B9032, is the **Memsie Burial Cairn**, dating from about

🎭 stories and anecdotes 🦜 famous people 🎨 art and craft 🖊 entertainment and sport 🎿 walks

Kinnaird Lighthouse, Fraserburgh

1500BC. At one time three stood here, but only one is now left.

Around Fraserburgh

OLD DEER
12 miles S of Fraserburgh on the B9030

🏛 Deer Abbey

In a beautiful location on the banks of the River South Ugie, are the ruins of **Deer Abbey** (Historic Scotland), founded in 1219 by William Comyn, Earl of Buchan, for the Cistercian order of monks. Little remains of the abbey church, but the walls of some of the other buildings are fairly well preserved. It

is said that it was built on the site of a Celtic monastery founded by St Columba and his companion St Drostan in the 6th century.

MINTLAW
11 miles S of Fraserburgh on the B9030

🏛 Aberdeenshire Farming Museum

In the village you'll find the 230-acre **Aberdeenshire Farming Museum** (free), which sits within Aden Country Park. The museum traces the history of farming in this fertile area of Aberdeenshire through three separate themes - the Aden Estate Story, the Weel Vrocht Grun (well worked ground) and the country park itself. Hareshowe Farm has been restored to what it would have been like in the 1950s.

MAUD
12 miles S of Fraserburgh on the B9029

🏛 Maud Railway Museum

Maud grew up around a junction in the railway line that once connected Aberdeen to Fraserburgh and Peterhead. In the **Maud Railway Museum**, housed in the village's former station, you can relive the days of the Great North of Scotland Railway through exhibits, sound effects, photographs, artefacts and displays.

TURRIFF
20 miles SW of Fraserburgh on the A947

🏛 Turriff Parish Church   🏛 Delgatie Castle

🏛 Turra Coo

Set on the River Deveron in the heart of the Buchan farmlands, Turriff is an ancient burgh that was given its charter in 1512 by James IV. The Knights Templar once owned land in the

FOOD FOR THOUGHT

The Brae, New Deer, Turriff AB53 6TG
Tel: 01771 644366

Occupying a quaint wooden building in the centre of New Deer,
Food for Thought was the joint brainchild of friends Jane
Hodgson and Karen Woodhouse who have worked together
since 2000. Both love good food and are enthusiastic cooks so
they can confidently advise customers on culinary matters.

Their delicatessen sells a huge range of produce. There's a wide selection of Scottish and
international cheeses, Highland beef, home-cured pork and free range chicken and eggs. Wherever
possible they go to local producers for their stock, but from further afield they also sell olives,
antipasti, nuts and wines. Naturally, there's a good choice of fresh fruit and vegetables, and the Veg
in a Box delivery service is available throughout the Buchan area and parts of Aberdeen. Charcuterie,
smoked fish, fresh bread, oils, vinegars, dried fruits, preserves - the list goes on and on and the range
is continually expanding. Oh, and they also serve freshly made sandwiches and home-made soup.

The village of New Deer
itself is a busy little
place. It has its own
bank, convenience
stores, hairdresser, fish
and chip shop, even a
kilt shop and, of course,
an outstanding deli in the
form of Food for
Thought.

area, and a Templar chapel stood here. **Turriff
Parish Church** was built in 1794, and there
are some good carvings on its belfry and
walls from the previous kirk that stood on
the site. In 1693, a Covenanting army
controlled Turriff, but in May of the same
year a force led by the Marquis of Huntly put
them to flight, an event which became
known as the Turriff Trot.

Delgatie Castle, close to the town, was
founded in about 1050, though the castle as
you see it today dates from the 16th century. It
is the ancestral home of Clan Hay, and has
been in the Hay family for just under 700
years. It belonged to the Earls of Buchan until
after the battle of Bannockburn in 1314, when
Robert the Bruce gave it to the Hays. In 1562,
Mary Stuart stayed in the castle for three days
after the Battle of Corrichie, which took place

to the west of Aberdeen. The Queen's troops
easily defeated a force of men led by the 4th
Earl of Huntly who was killed in the battle.

Turriff was the scene of a famous incident
concerning the **Turra Coo** (Turriff Cow),
which received widespread publicity throughout
Britain. New National Insurance Acts were
passed in 1911 and 1913, which required
employers to pay 3d per week for each of their
employees. The farmers of Aberdeenshire, in
common with others all over Britain, did not
want to pay, as they reckoned that farm workers
had a healthy lifestyle and would not need
much medical treatment. Curiously enough, the
farm workers themselves supported the
farmers on this issue.

One Turriff farmer in particular, Robert
Paterson, refused to comply with the new
regulations, so one of his cows was taken to

be sold at auction to pay off his arrears. However, the auction, held in Turriff, turned into a fiasco, as the cow, which had slogans painted all over its body, took fright and bolted through the streets of the town. Meanwhile, the auctioneer was pelted with raw eggs and bags of soot. Three days later, the cow was taken to Aberdeen where it was sold for £7.

It was a hollow victory for the authorities, which had spent nearly £12 in recovering the sum. And they were further annoyed to hear that Paterson's neighbours had clubbed together and bought the cow so that it could be returned to him. So, while the authorities were out of pocket over the whole affair, it had not cost Robert Paterson a penny. There are now plans to erect a statue of the Turra Coo to commemorate the event.

Seven miles southwest of Turriff, along the B9024, is the Glendronach Distillery, situated on the banks of the Dronach Burn. Tours are available, and there is a visitor centre and shop.

PENNAN
9 miles W of Fraserburgh on the B9031

Pennan is possibly the most spectacular of the little fishing villages on the northern coast of Aberdeenshire. It is strung out along the base of a high cliff, with many of the cottages having their gable ends to the sea for protection. It is a conservation village, and is famous as being the setting, in 1983, for the film *Local Hero*. The red telephone box, famously used in the film, was a prop. However, Pennan's real telephone box, about 15 yards away from where the prop stood, is still a favourite place for photographs.

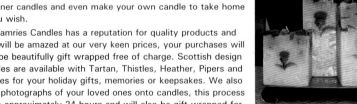

BANFF

20 miles W of Fraserburgh on the A98

Banff Museum Duff House

Macduff Marine Aquarium

A small fishing port close to the mouth of the River Deveron, Banff was once the county town of Banffshire. It is an ancient royal burgh, having been granted its charter in 1163 by Malcolm IV. The **Banff Museum** in the High Street is one of Scotland's oldest, having been founded in 1828. It has a nationally important collection of Banff silver.

Duff House (see panel below) is a unique country house art gallery run by a unique partnership between Historic Scotland, the National Galleries of Scotland and Aberdeenshire Council, with a fine collections of paintings by such artists as Raeburn and El Greco, as well as tapestries and Chippendale furniture. The house was designed by William Adam and built between 1735 and 1740 for William Duff of Braco, who later became Earl of Fife. After a bitter wrangle with Adam, William Duff abandoned the house, and it was left to James, the 2nd Earl Fife, to complete the grand plan, including the grounds. Over the years it has had a chequered career, having been a hotel, a sanatorium, a prisoner-of-war

Duff House Country Gallery

Banff, Banffshire AB45 3SX
Tel: 01261 818181

Duff House was designed by William Adam and built between 1735-40 as the seat of the Earls Fife. A treasure house with an extraordinary history, it contains masterpieces from the National Galleries of Scotland. The outstanding collections consist of furniture, including chairs by Chippendale, tapestries and paintings by artists such as Sir Henry Raeburn and El Greco.

Story-tellers, musicians and artists are at home at Duff House. The House organises a regular artistic programme of exhibitions, music, theatre, dance and other live performances, some in conjunction with the Macduff Arts Centre.

Come and enjoy the popular tea-room with its range of fresh food and home baking. Visitors can also browse in our shop with its wide range of quality gifts and books.

Families are welcome as there are facilities for parents and small children, children's quizzes and an adventure playground to explore.

With extensive grounds and woodland walks by the river Deveron you will find a day is not enough. Other things to do and see in the area are the whisky and castle trails, scenic coastal routes and towns, or visit the Macduff Marine Aquarium and the Museum of Scottish Light Houses at Fraserburgh.

Call 01261 818181 to find out what we can offer your school, educational or community group.

Educational visits are free.

 stories and anecdotes famous people art and craft entertainment and sport walks

camp, and the scene of an attempted murder, when a Countess of Fife tried to do away with her husband.

The small town of Macduff sits on the opposite shores of the small bay where the Deveron enters the Moray Firth. The lands were bought by the 1st Earl of Fife in 1733, and in 1783, the 2nd Earl founded the town as a burgh or barony. It contains the **Macduff Marine Aquarium** at High Shore, which has a central tank open to the sky surrounded by viewing areas so that you can see fish and marine mammals from all angles. This deep central exhibit, which displays a living kelp reef, is the only one of its kind in Britain, and divers hand-feed the fish on a regular basis. The aquarium has a wave-making machine, which adds to the experience of seeing underwater life in its true condition.

Six miles west of Banff, on the A98, is the attractive little fishing port of Portsoy, which is well worth visiting if only to soak in the atmosphere. Though its burgh charter dates from 1550, it was Patrick Ogilvie, Lord Boyne, who realised its potential and developed it as a port to export marble from the nearby quarries. Portsoy marble was used on Louis XIV's palace at Versailles.

PETERHEAD
16 miles SE of Fraserburgh on the A982

🏚 Arbuthnot Museum 🏛 Slains Castle

🏛 Peterhead Maritime Heritage Museum

Peterhead is the largest town (as opposed to city) in Aberdeenshire, and one of the chief fishing ports in the northeast. It was founded by George Keith, the 5th Earl Marischal of

---

GLENDAVENY TEDDY BEARS

41 Broad Street, Peterhead, Aberdeenshire AB42 1JB
Tel: 01779 481608 Fax: 01779 838406
e-mail: di.faithfull@aberdeenshire.gov.uk
website: www.glendaveny.co.uk

Glendaveny Teddy Bears forms part of an Aberdeenshire Council project to give adults with learning disabilities training opportunities in various crafts. The bears are traditionally crafted, based on an original design and made with loving care using the finest quality Mohair with board and pin jointing. Each bear has its own personality and they come in a variety of sizes, with a choice of more than 20 different Mohairs. Examples of the Glendaveny range of teddy bears can be seen on display and for sale in the shop at 41, Broad Street. Most of the teddy bears can be personalised with embroidered text on paw pads. Limited

editions, as a matter of course, carry the limited number of the requested bear sewn on to a paw pad. The opening times for the shop are Mon - Fri 9am - 3.30pm.

The same council project also produces **Glendaveny Jams and Chutneys**, made in the traditional manner using home-grown and local sources of fruit. No artificial preservatives or flavours are employed. A third element of the project is **Glendaveny Garden Furniture** which produces high quality, substantial, hand-crafted pieces such as garden benches, love seats, tables, bird boxes and more.The opening times for the Day Service are Mon - Fri 9:00am - 4:00 pm. Tel: 01779 838301

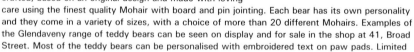

🏚 historic building 🏛 museum and heritage 🏚 historic site 🔱 scenic attraction 🌿 flora and fauna

THE FLOWER SHOP

14, Thistle Street, Peterhead, Aberdeenshire AB42 1TD
Tel: 01779 474318
website: www.theflowershop.org.uk

In 2003 Amy Buchan started work in the Flower Shop as a Saturday girl. Having found her passion for floristry, she left school at 17 and started work in the shop as a full-time trainee florist. She went on to gain her certificates to become a top florist, whilst also achieving the much sought after Interflora certificate. She also achieved first and second places in national competitions.

In 2008 at the age on 19 years Amy bought the business from the existing owner and started to build her own business. In 2009 after a complete shop renovation Amy now runs a very busy shop in the heart of Peterhead with her team of four florists, three delivery assistants and two part time florist assistants. The Flower Shop flowers come direct from the markets in Holland and the three deliveries a week ensure that the flowers that customers receive are as fresh as can be.

For weddings the team at the Flower Shop strive to make the brides day a beautiful occasion and as well as delivering the bridal party flowers to the brides home on time they can arrange for the church or wedding venue to be decorated to the brides requirements. The church flowers can be picked up and taken to the reception if required.

For funeral flowers a home visit can be arranged for the deceased's family, so that choosing a loved one's floral tributes can be done in privacy...

NO JOB IS TOO BIG OR SMALL. All floral designs can be tailored to the customer's budget.

Scotland in 1587, and is Scotland's most easterly burgh. In the mid-1980s, it was Europe's largest white fish port, landing 120,000 tonnes of fish in 1987 alone. Now that fishing has declined, it benefits from being one of the ports that services the offshore gas industry. The **Arbuthnot Museum** in St Peter Street tells the story of the town and its industries, and has a large collection of Inuit artefacts. It was given to the town of Peterhead in 1850 by Adam Arbuthnot, a local man who had acquired a huge collection of antiquities.

In South Road, in a purpose-built building, **Peterhead Maritime Heritage Museum** tells of the town's connections with the sea over the years. It traces its history, from its fishing fleet (which went as far as the Arctic in search of fish) to its whaling fleet (in its day,

the second largest in Britain), and finally, to the modern offshore gas and oil industries. The building was shaped to resemble a scaffy, a kind of fishing boat once used in the area.

A few miles south of the town, at Cruden Bay, are the ruins of **Slains Castle**, built by the 9th Earl of Errol in 1597. Perched on top of the cliffs looking out over the North Sea, the castle has been rebuilt and refurbished several times since then, and the ruins you see date from the early 19th century. Now there are plans to restore it yet again, this time as holiday flats. It has literary associations of an unusual kind. While staying at the nearby village of Cruden Bay in 1895, Bram Stoker began writing *Dracula*, and based the vampire's Transylvanian castle on Slains. In an early draft of the novel he even has the Count coming ashore at Slains rather than Whitby.

LOCATOR MAP

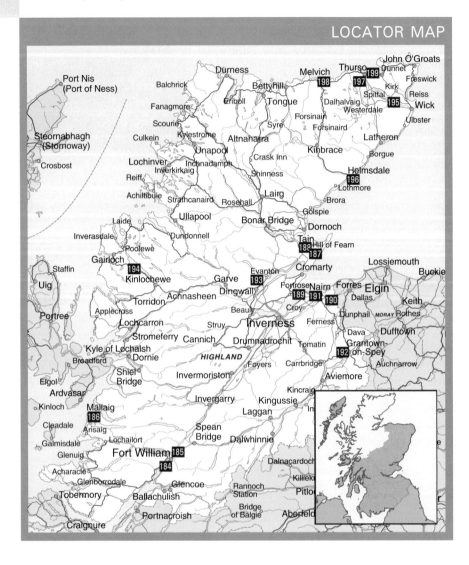

John O'Groats
Durness
Melvich
Thurso **199** Dunnet
Port Nis
(Port of Ness)
Balchrick
Bettyhill
Freswick
198 **197**
Kirk
Spittal
Reiss
Fanagmore
Eriboll
Tongue
Dalhalvaig
Westerdale
195 Wick
Scourie
Syre
Forsinain
Forsinaird
Ulbster
Steornabhagh
(Stornoway)
Culkein
Kylestrome
Altnaharra
Latheron
Crosbost
Lochinver
Inchnadamph
Unapool
Crask Inn
Kinbrace
Borgue
Reiff
Inverkirkaig
Shinness
Helmsdale
Achiltibuie
Strathcanaird
Rosehall
Lairg
196
Lothmore
Laide
Ullapool
Bonar Bridge
Brora
Golspie
Inverasdale
Dundonnell
Dornoch
Poolewe
Tain
Hill of Fearn
Gairloch
188 **187**
Staffin
194
Kinlochewe
Garve
Evanton
Cromarty
Lossiemouth
Uig
193
Fortrose
Nairn
Forres
Elgin
Buckie
Dingwall
189 **191** **190**
Dallas
Keith
Torridon
Achnasheen
Croy
Dunphail
MORAY
Rothes
Applecross
Beauly
Portree
Lochcarron
Struy
Inverness
Ferness
Dava
Dufftown
Stromeferry
Cannich
Drumnadrochit
Tomatin
Grantown-
Kyle of Lochalsh
Dornie
HIGHLAND
192
on-Spey
Broadford
Foyers
Carrbridge
Auchnarrow
Elgol
Shiel
Invermoriston
Aviemore
Ardvasar
Bridge
Invergarry
Kincraig
Kinloch
Mallaig
Kingussie
Cleadale
186
Arisaig
Laggan
Galmisdale
Lochailort
Spean
Glenuig
Bridge
Dalwhinnie
Fort William **185**
Acharacle
184
Dalnacardoch
Glenborrodale
Glencoe
Killiek
Tobermory
Ballachulish
Rannoch
Station
Pitlo
Bridge
Portnacroish
of Balgie
Aberfeld
Craignure

12| The Highlands

When people talk of Scottish scenery, they inevitably mean the scenery of the Highlands - mountains, deep glens and dark, brooding lochs. The Highlands area has no set boundaries, and some places described in earlier chapters, such as Aberdeen and Grampian, Argyllshire and parts of Perthshire, can lay claim to being in the Highlands as well. But the area described in this chapter has the same boundaries as the local government area, and can legitimately be called the true heart of the Highlands.

The capital of the Highlands is Inverness. It is a thriving city with an enviable quality of life, and its environs are reckoned to be the most rapidly growing areas in Britain, if not Europe. Seen from the A9 as you head over the Kessock Bridge, it has all the appearance of a large metropolis, with suburbs that sprawl along the Moray and Beauly Firths. But in fact, its population is no more than 50,000, though this is growing almost daily, with plans recently announced for the building of a huge new suburb to the west of the city. And some of the countryside surrounding it looks more like the Lowlands than the Highlands, though this notion is soon dispelled if you head southwest along the A82 towards Loch Ness.

ADVERTISERS AND PLACES OF INTEREST

🎭 stories and anecdotes 🦅 famous people 🎨 art and craft 🎭 entertainment and sport 🥾 walks

Within the Highlands you'll find Scotland's most famous features. Ben Nevis, Scotland's highest mountain, is here, as is Loch Morar, the country's deepest loch. The northern tip of Loch Ness, undoubtedly the most famous stretch of water in

Eilean Donan Castle, Kyle of Lochalsh

Europe, is a few miles from Inverness, and the last full battle on British soil was fought at Culloden. Here too, is Glencoe, scene of the infamous massacre, as well as John O' Groats, Aviemore, Skye, Fort William, Cape Wrath and Plockton, the setting for the books and TV series *Hamish Macbeth*.

The west coast is rugged, with sea lochs that penetrate deep into the mountains. Settlements are few and far between, and most of them are to be found on the coast. Some visitors to the west coast of the Highlands are amazed at the sub-tropical plants, such as palm trees, that seem to thrive here. It's all down to the Gulf Stream, which warms the shores and makes sure that snow is not as common as you would imagine.

The east coast, from Nairn to Inverness then north to John O' Groats, is gentler, with many more settlements. Dornoch, though

small, has a medieval cathedral, so is more of a city than a town, and Strathpeffer was once a thriving spa town, with regular trains connecting it to Edinburgh and London.

Between the east and west coasts are the mountains, the lochs, the tumbling streams and the deep glens. The scenery can be austere and gaunt, but never anything less than beautiful. No Gulf Stream here, and in some sheltered corners, snow lies on well into the year. Glencoe, Nevis and Aviemore take advantage of this by being skiing centres, though of late, snow has been in short supply.

In Caithness and Sutherland - Scotland's two northernmost counties - you'll find the Flow Country, mile upon mile of low peaks, high moorland and small lochans. This is not the dramatic scenery of the West Highlands where mountain seems to pile on mountain, but it has a ruggedness and grandeur of its own.

Fort William

🏃 West Highland Way ⛰ Ben Nevis ⛰ Glen Nevis

🏛 Glen Nevis Visitor Centre 🐟 Underwater Centre

🏛 West Highland Museum 💎 Treasures of the Earth

🏰 Inverlochy Castle 🏃 Great Glen Way

🎞 Neptune's Staircase ⛰ Jacobite Steam Train

The small town of Fort William lies at the western end of Glen Mor (meaning the Great Glen), in an area known as Lochaber. Though it is small, in the summer months it can paradoxically get crowded with visitors all seeking the genuine, uncrowded Highlands. It is the northern terminus of the 95-mile long **West Highland Way**, which snakes through Western Scotland from Milngavie on the outskirts of Glasgow. The fort referred to in the town's name was built by General Monk in the 1650s, then rebuilt during the reign of William III to house a garrison of 600 troops to keep the Highland clans in order. At that time it was renamed Maryburgh, after William's queen. Only parts of the town wall survive, as most of it was dismantled in the 19th century to make way for the West Highland Railway.

It was from Fort William that thousands of Scots sailed for the New World during that time known as the Clearances. In the early 19th century, landowners could squeeze more profit from their estates if it had sheep on it instead of people, so Highlanders were evicted from their cottages and small parcels of land. Some settled on the coast, and some emigrated.

It was the coming of the railway in 1866 that established Fort William as one of the Highland's main centres for tourism, and it has remained so to this day. A few miles east of the town is **Ben Nevis**, at 4406 feet, Britain's highest mountain. The five-mile climb to the top, along a well-trodden path, is fairly easy if you're reasonably fit. It can also get crowded at times. The summit is reached by way of **Glen Nevis**, often called Scotland's most beautiful glen, though there are other contenders for the title. The rewards of the climb are immense. The Cairngorms can be seen, as can the Cuillin range on Skye and the peaks of Argyllshire. On an exceptionally clear day even the coast of Northern Ireland can be glimpsed through binoculars. At the **Glen Nevis Visitor Centre** there are exhibits about local heritage and wildlife, and, importantly, information about the weather on the mountain.

Aonach Beag (4058 feet) and Aonach Mor (3999 feet) are Ben Nevis's little brothers, rising just over a mile to the east. In the winter this is a skiing area, but it is equally popular in the summer. Britain's only mountain gondola takes you half way up the range to a

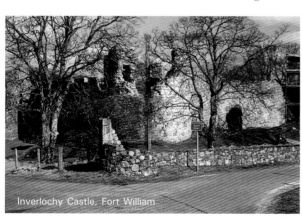
Inverlochy Castle, Fort William

🎞 stories and anecdotes 🗣 famous people 💎 art and craft 🎭 entertainment and sport 🏃 walks

TORLINNHE GUEST HOUSE

Achintore Road, Fort William PH33 6RW
Tel: 01397 702583
e-mail: info@torlinnhe.co.uk
website: www.torlinnhe.co.uk

Set on the shore of Loch Linnhe, just over a
mile from Fort William's town centre,
Torlinnhe Guest House is owned by Andy
and Sue Keen who purchased the property in
February 2008 and after an initial 3-month refurbishment
opened the new style guest house in June. They have
completely re-modelled the ground floor with a brand new
kitchen and the creation of a large oak-floored guest lounge
which enjoys spectacular views of the loch. An eco-friendly
wood pellet burning stove in the lounge provides all their hot
water and heating. Andy and Sue also refurbished three of
their six rooms to Visit Scotland 4-star standard. All of the
rooms have a 26-inch digital TV, DVD player, hospitality
tray and there is wi-fi access throughout.

Breakfast at Torlinnhe is definitely something to look forward to. To start, there is a substantial
buffet with the usual cereals, fruit juices etc., plus Highland muesli, fruit dishes and usually
pastries, croissants and yoghurts. These are followed by either a freshly cooked traditional
breakfast, a creamy Scottish Salmon Scramble & oatcakes, or Sue's breakfast twist on Cranachan,
Scottish Raspberries & Oatmeal, heather honey and thick Greek-style yogurt. Irresistible!

restaurant and bar, and there are several
walks to enjoy when you get there.

Within the town, in Cameron Square, is
the **West Highland Museum**, with exhibits
and displays about the area. The most
famous exhibit is the 18th-century Secret
Portrait of Prince Charles Edward Stuart. It
is a meaningless swirl of colours, which,
when reflected onto a polished cylinder, gives
a likeness of the Prince. There are also some
pieces of eight brought up from the Spanish
galleon that sank in Tobermory Bay. On the
A830 at Corpach, northwest of the town, is
the award-winning **Treasures of the Earth**,
one of Europe's finest collections of crystals
and gemstones.

The **Underwater Centre**, on the banks of
Loch Linnhe. was opened in 2003, and cost
£2.3m. It features marine life (including
more than 42 species of fish) and diving

shows in a large aquarium. You can even take
dives yourself and get guided tours round
the adjacent diver training centre.

The impressive ruins of 13th-century
Inverlochy Castle (Historic Scotland) stand
one-and-a-half miles north east of Fort
William. It was built by the Comyn family in
the 13th century on the site of an even
earlier fort, though the ruins you see now
date from much later. It was here that
Montrose had an important victory over the
Campbells, who were Covenanters, in 1645.

Not far away, on the A82, is the 174-year-
old Ben Nevis Distillery and Whisky Centre,
which has conducted tours. One of its
products is a blend of whiskies called The
Dew of Ben Nevis.

Fort William is the northern terminus of
the West Highland Way, a long distance
footpath that starts at Milngavie just outside

🏚 historic building 🏛 museum and heritage 🏚 historic site ⚜ scenic attraction 🌱 flora and fauna

LOCHABER FARM SHOP, CRAFTS & CAFÉ

Aonach Mhor Road, Torlundy,
Fort William PH33 6SW
Tel: 01397 708 686
e-mail: info@lochaberfarmshop.com
website: www.lochaberfarmshop.com

Set in the shadow of Ben Nevis, 5 miles north of Fort William, **Lochaber Farm Shop, Crafts & Café** occupies a smart modern building and was established by Alison and Alasdair Macintosh in June 2004 to sell their home-reared lamb, mutton, beef and free range pork. The lamb is naturally reared and is either Blackface, Texel or Charollais. The animals are grazed only on grass and heather as nature intended. Similarly, their Tamworth pigs are free to dig and forage, living outside with access to shelter when needed. Most of the beef on sale comes from the Arisaig Estate where they rear Luing bullocks for the shop. The beef is beautifully marbled and tender, having been hung for at least 17 days.

The ethos of the Farm Shop carries through to the café where local, Fairtrade, organic and free range produce is used wherever possible. The café serves morning coffee/brunch, lunches and afternoon tea.

Glasgow. It is also the western terminus for the **Great Glen Way**, which opened in 2002. This is another long distance footpath that follows the Great Glen and Loch Ness, ending at Inverness, 73 miles away.

Fort William is also where the Caledonian Canal begins. It is not one uninterrupted canal, but a series of canals connecting Loch Lochy, Loch Oich and Loch Ness (see Drumnadrochit for details of Loch Ness). **Neptune's Staircase** at Banavie, near Fort William, was designed and built by Thomas Telford in the early 1800s, and takes the canal through a series of eight locks while raising it over 60 feet.

In the summer months, the **Jacobite Steam Train** travels the famous Fort William to Mallaig line. It passes along the northern shores of Loch Eil - a continuation of Loch Linnhe after it turns westward - on a 45-mile journey that has some of the most beautiful scenery in Britain.

Around Fort William

SPEAN BRIDGE
8 miles NE of Fort William on the A82

🏛 Commando Memorial 🏛 Spean Bridge Mill

🏛 Battle of Mulroy

It would seem logical to assume that this attractive village was named after the bridge over the River Spean that Thomas Telford built here in 1819. In fact it is actually named after the bridge, a mile and a half to the west, that was built by General Wade in the 1740s. That bridge survived until 1913 when part of it collapsed into the river 100 feet below.

It was around Spean Bridge that commandos trained during World War II, and they are remembered by the **Commando Memorial**. It was designed by the sculptor Scott Sutherland, and depicts three commando soldiers. It was unveiled by the late Queen Mother in 1952. The **Spean Bridge Mill,** which is nearby, has demonstrations of tartan weaving as well as a clan tartan centre. At Roy Bridge the **Battle of Mulroy** was fought in 1688 between the MacDonnells and the Macintoshes, with the MacDonnells being the victors. It was the last great inter-clan battle fought in the Highlands, and the last one on British soil where bows and arrows were used. A cairn marks the spot.

ACHNACARRY

9 miles NE of Fort William on a minor road off the B8005

🏛 Clan Cameron Museum 🐾 Loch Arkaig

From 1665 Achnacarry Castle was the home of Cameron of Locheil, known as Gentle Locheil, one of Charles Edward Stuart's most ardent supporters. After 1745, it was burned down by Hanoverian troops. Locheil's family was banished from the country, but they were allowed to return in 1784 when they built a new home nearby. In 1942, the Cameron chief had to leave his home once again, when it was taken over by the British army as a training centre for commandos.

A 17th-century white-washed single storey croft house close to where the original Achnacarry once stood now houses the **Clan Cameron Museum**, which has displays, charts and exhibits relating to the history of the clan and to the commandos who trained here during the Second World War. A minor road takes you past the museum and along the lovely banks of **Loch Arkaig,** finally petering out near its western end.

LAGGAN

19 miles NE of Fort William on the A82

🏛 Battle of the Shirts

Laggan sits between Loch Lochy and Loch Oich, two of the lochs that make up the Caledonian Canal. It was here, in 1544, that the **Battle of the Shirts** took place, fought between Clan Fraser and the combined forces of Clan Ranald and Cameron. It was fought on a hot summer's day, and the clansmen removed their plaids and fought in their shirts. There were many casualties, including the chief of Clan Fraser and his son.

FORT AUGUSTUS

28 miles NE of Fort William on the A82

🏛 Caledonian Canal Heritage Centre

🐾 Highland and Rare Breeds Croft

🏛 Clansman Centre

This small village on the shore of Loch Ness was originally named after St Cummein who built a church here. The current name followed the building of a fort, Fort Augustus, as part of the government's attempt to quash all further opposition from Jacobite supporters after the defeat of the 1715 uprising. The fort took its name from King George II's younger son, Prince William Augustus, who became better known as the Duke of Cumberland, or 'Butcher' Cumberland, because of the ruthless carnage at the bloody battle of Culloden. Today, almost nothing remains of the original fort, parts of which were incorporated into Fort Augustus Abbey when it was built in 1876. The community of monks was unable to sustain itself and left in 1998. Surrounded on three sides by waters of the Caledonian Canal, Loch Ness and the river Tarff, the abbey is

Pleasure Boat on Caledonian Canal, Fort Angustus

Leven and is on the West Highland Way. It was developed as an industrial village in the early 20th century when the North British Aluminium Company built the Blackwater reservoir and a hydro electric scheme to power an aluminium smelter, which was the largest in the world at the time. Before that, it had been two small villages called Kinlochmore and Killochbeag. The **Aluminium Story Visitor Centre** on Linnhe Road at the library tells the story of the smelting works right up until the year 2000. Outside the centre is a giant sundial designed by blacksmith Robert Hutcheson that takes its inspiration from the area's history and scenery.

currently being converted into self-catering holiday apartments.

Fort Augustus is bisected by the Caledonian Canal and within the village itself is a flight of locks that provide a fascinating place to watch the world go by. The **Caledonian Canal Heritage Centre** is located in a converted lock keeper's cottage near these locks through which boats pass into Loch Ness. The Centre explains the history and uses of the canal.

The **Highland and Rare Breeds Croft** is on Auchterawe Road, and here you can see Highland cattle, red deer and rare breeds of sheep; at the **Clansman Centre**, housed in an old school, there are presentations on ancient Highland life.

KINLOCHLEVEN
10 miles SE of Fort William on the B863

🏛 Aluminium Story Visitor Centre 🏊 Ice Factor

This little town sits at the head of Loch

The **Ice Factor** on Leven Road is Britain's premier indoor mountaineering centre, and features the world's largest indoor ice climbing wall, as well as Britain's largest articulated rock climbing wall. There is also a children's activity zone, audiovisual lecture theatre, steam room, plunge pool and hot tub, and a cafeteria and restaurant.

BALLACHULISH
10 miles S of Fort William on the A82

🎭 James of the Glen 🎭 Massacre of Glencoe

👤 Three Sisters 🏛 Glencoe Visitor Centre

🏛 Glencoe and North Lorn Folk Museum

The area surrounding Ballachulish ("settlement near the narrows") was once famous for its slate quarries. There are actually two villages separated by the waters of Loch

🎭 stories and anecdotes 👤 famous people 🎨 art and craft 🏊 entertainment and sport 🚶 walks

Leven - North Ballachulish and Ballachulish itself. They were once connected by ferry, which stopped running in 1975 when a bridge was built.

Ballachulish straggles along the southern shore of Loch Leven. To the west of the village a cairn marks the spot where Jacobite sympathiser **James of the Glen** was hanged for a crime he did not commit. He was found guilty of the murder of Colin Campbell, known as the Red Fox and a government agent, by a Campbell judge and jury. Robert Louis Stevenson used the incident in his book *Kidnapped*. Another cairn marks the site of the murder.

To the east of Ballachulish, on the A82, is one of the most evocative places in Scotland - Glencoe. It was here, in 1691, that the infamous **Massacre of Glencoe** took place. Because of bad weather, McIan of Clan MacDonald had failed to take the oath of allegiance to William III before the deadline, and a party of Campbell troops were sent to Glencoe to massacre his people. They pretended at first to come in peace, and were offered hospitality. But in the early hours of February 13th, they set about systematically killing McIan's people - men, women and children - with few escaping. A monument in the shape of a tall Celtic cross commemorates the gloomy event.

Glencoe, further east than the village, is a wild, beautiful place though it does get crowded in summer months with hikers and climbers. On the north side is Aonach Eagach, a long ridge, and on the south side, the three peaks of Beinn Fhada, Gearr Aonach and Aonach Dhu, known as the **Three Sisters**. About 14,000 acres within Glencoe are now owned by the National Trust for Scotland, and it has set up the **Glencoe Visitor Centre**,

which tells the story of the massacre. In Glencoe village itself, the **Glencoe and North Lorn Folk Museum** has exhibits about the history of the area and its people.

About nine miles east of Glencoe, on a minor road off the A82, is the Glencoe skiing area with a chair lift that is open in the summer months, and gives wonderful views over Glencoe and Rannoch Moor.

ARDNAMURCHAN
30 miles W of Fort William

🏰 Mingary Castle   🏰 Castle Tioram

🌾 Seven Men of Moidart

The B8007 leaves the A861 at Salen (where a small inlet of Loch Sunart is usually crowded with picturesque yachts) and takes you westwards onto the Ardnamurchan Peninsula. It is single track all the way, so great care should be taken. It heads for Ardnamurchan Point and its lighthouse, the most westerly point of the British mainland, and in doing so passes some wonderful scenery.

At Glenborrodale you can see the late-Victorian Glenborrodale Castle, the home from 1933 to 1949 of Jesse Boot, founder of the chain of chemists. It was built in the early 20th century for C D Rudd, who made his fortune in diamonds in South Africa. The castle is now available for weddings and other functions.

At Kilchoan there are the ruins of **Mingary Castle**, a stronghold of Clan MacIan before passing to the Campbells. It was visited by James IV in 1493 on one of his expeditions to subdue the Western Isles. It was briefly used in the 2002 movie *Highlander: Endgame*. Kilchoan is Britain's most westerly mainland village, and up until 1900, when the B8007 was constructed, it was also Britain's most inaccessible, as it could only be reached by boat. Nowadays, in summer, a ferry connects it to Tobermory on Mull.

A few miles North of Salen, on the edge of the area known as Moidart, are the ruins of **Castle Tioram** (pronounced Chirrum). The castle stands on a small island and was originally built in the 14th century by Lady Anne MacRuari, whose son Ranald gave his name to Clan Ranald. It was burnt by the Jacobites in 1715 to prevent it being used by Hanoverian forces, and has been a ruin ever since.

At the head of Loch Moidart is a line of five beech trees. Originally there were seven, which were known as the **Seven Men of Moidart**. They commemorate the seven men who landed with Charles Edward Stuart and sailed with him up Loch Shiel. They were originally planted in the early 19th century.

STRONTIAN
20 miles SW of Fort William on the A861

🌱 Ariundle Oakwoods

Strontian (pronounced Stron - teeh - an, and meaning point of the fairies) sits in an area known as Sunart, which lies to the south of Loch Shiel. The village gave its name to the metal strontium, which was discovered in 1791 in the local lead mines by a chemist called Adair Crawford. A few years later, Sir Humphrey Davie gave it its name.

To the north of the village are the **Ariundle Oakwoods**, a national nature reserve.

MORVERN
24 miles SW of Fort William

🏚 Ardtornish Castle

Morvern is that area of the mainland that lies immediately north of the island of Mull. The A884 leaves the A861 east of Strontian and travels down through it as far as Lochaline,

on the Sound of Mull. The restored Kinlochaline Castle (private) stands at the head of Loch Aline, and was once the ancestral home of Clan MacInnes. The clan takes a special pride in being one of the few clans in Scotland without a chief. The last one, and all his family, was butchered by John, Lord of the Isles, in 1354 at **Ardtornish Castle**, the ruins of which can still be seen a few miles from Lochaline.

The narrow B849 from Lochaline (with passing places) follows the shores of the Sound of Mull as far as Drimmin, and makes a wonderful drive.

SALEN
27 miles W of Fort William on the A861

🌱 Claish Moss

Salen sits on the shore of Loch Sunart. Three miles east (not accessible by road) is **Claish Moss**, a good example of a Scottish raised bog. Water is held in the peat, and the landscape is dotted with lochans, or pools. The peat has preserved seeds and pollen for thousands of years, so it is of interest to biologists researching the flora of the Western Highlands.

GLENFINNAN
13 miles W of Fort William on the A830

🏚 Charles Edward Stuart Monument

📷 Glenfinnan Station Museum

It was here, at the northern tip of Loch Shiel, Scotland's fourth longest freshwater loch, that Charles Edward Stuart raised his standard in 1745, watched by 1200 Highland followers, after having been rowed a short distance up the loch from the house of MacDonald of Glenaladale on the western shores. The **Charles Edward Stuart Monument** (National Trust for Scotland) was erected in

1815 by Alexander MacDonald of Glenaladale to commemorate the event. A small visitors centre nearby tells the story.

The **Glenfinnan Station Museum**, which lies on the Fort William to Mallaig line, tells of the building of the line by Robert McAlpine (known as Concrete Bob) in the late 19th and early 20th centuries. The museum's restaurant and tearoom is a restored 1950s' railway carriage.

ARISAIG
29 miles W of Fort William on the A830

🏛 Land, Sea and Islands Centre

The tiny village of Arisaig has wonderful views across to the islands of Rum and Eigg. Southeast of the village is Loch nan Uamh, where, on July 25 1745, Charles Edward Stuart first set foot on the Scottish mainland. After his campaign to restore the Stuart dynasty

failed, he left for France from the same shore. A cairn now marks the spot.

Purpose-built in 1999, the **Land, Sea and Islands Centre**, set in a stunning location in the village, has exhibits and displays about the history and wildlife of the area including information on crofting, fishing, church history, marine life, the SOE and the films made here - *Local Hero* being one of the most famous.

MALLAIG
31 miles NW of Fort William on the A830

🏛 Mallaig Heritage Centre

🌿 Mallaig Marine World Aquarium

Mallaig, Britain's most westerly mainland port, is a busy fishing port and the terminal of a ferry connecting the mainland to Armadale on Skye. It is also the end of the Road to the Isles and the western terminus for the Jacobite Steam Train. The **Mallaig Heritage Centre**

GINGER

Morar, Highland PH40 4PA
Tel: 01687 462655
e-mail: anna@ginger-morar.com
website: www.ginger-morar.com

Anna Skea has been designing and manufacturing knitwear since 1980 and now retails her high quality hand-finished clothes at **Ginger** in the coastal village of Morar. Anna's work is very individual, aimed at the customer who likes to wear something a little bit different. Her inspiration comes from the rock formations, seashore and living environment of the Highlands, with colours and textures reflecting these sources.

Anna's knitwear and clothes are designed and crafted in the workshop, using colour and texture in a distinctive way. Some of the work is hand-painted or printed. The yarns are natural and sustainable and are spun from wool, silk, linen, viscose and cotton in various mixes. Felted pieces use wool sourced in the Highlands. Most of the work is hand-crafted and all pieces are hand finished and washed. Customers often remark that the quality of craftsmanship means that a Ginger piece remains a favourite for many years. The business occupies what was once a car showroom but has now been transformed into a colourful work and display area where clothing, mostly knitwear, is designed, manufactured and sold to the public. The showroom is open all year round, from Monday to Saturday.

🏛 historic building 🏛 museum and heritage 🏛 historic site 🍃 scenic attraction 🌿 flora and fauna on Station Road has displays and exhibits featuring the districts of Morar, Knoydart and Arisaig. The **Mallaig Marine World Aquarium and Fishing Exhibition** sits beside the harbour, and tells the story of Mallaig's fishing industry and the marine life found in

Eilean Donan Castle, Kyle of Lochalsh

the waters of Western Scotland. Most of the live exhibits were caught by local fishermen.

Southeast of the town is water of another sort - Loch Morar, which is Britain's deepest fresh water loch. It plunges to a depth of 1077 feet - if you were to stand the Eiffel Tower on the bottom, its top would still be 90 feet below the surface. A minor road near Morar village, south of Mallaig, takes you to its shores. Like Loch Ness, it has a monster, nicknamed Morag, which, judging by people who have claimed to see it, looks remarkably like Nessie.

KYLE OF LOCHALSH
40 miles NW of Fort William on the A87

🌿 Lochalsh Woodland Garden 🌿 Seaprobe Atlantis
🏠 Eilean Donan Castle 🌿 Five Sisters of Kintail
🏛 Battle of Glen Shiel 🏠 Strome Castle
🌿 Craig Highland Farm

Kyle of Lochalsh was once the mainland terminus of a ferry that made the short journey across Loch Alsh to Skye. Now the graceful Skye Bridge has superseded it (for Skye see the Inner Hebrides chapter). Three

miles east of the village, on the A87, is the Balmacara Estate and **Lochalsh Woodland Garden** at Lochalsh House, with sheltered walks beside the shores of Loch Alsh, as well as mature woodlands and a variety of shrubs, such as rhododendrons, bamboo, ferns, fuchsias and hydrangeas. There is a small visitors centre at the square in Balmacara, just off the A87. Also centred on Kyle of Lochalsh is **Seaprobe Atlantis**, a glass-bottomed boat that takes you out into the Marine Special Area of Conservation and shows you the rich diversity of marine life in the waters surrounding Scotland.

Six miles east of the village is one of the most photographed castles in Scotland, **Eilean Donan Castle**, which stands on a small island connected to the mainland by a bridge. Its name (Donan's Island) comes from the legend that St Donan lived on the island as a hermit. He was killed during a Viking raid on the island of Eigg in 617AD. Parts of the castle date back to 1220 when it was built by Alexander II and given to an ancestor of the Mackenzies who fought beside him at the Battle of Largs. The castle was left in ruins for

200 years until it was purchased in 1911 by Lt-Col John Macrae Gilstrap who spent some 20 years carrying out a complete restoration before opening it to the public in 1932. It is now the ancestral home of Clan MacRae, and has a small clan museum. The castle has also featured in many films, most notably *The World is Not Enough* and *Highlander*.

If you continue eastwards along the A87 you will eventually arrive at Shiel Bridge, at the head of Loch Duich. To the southeast is Glen Shiel, where five peaks, called the **Five Sisters of Kintail** (National Trust for Scotland) overlook the picturesque glen. Close by is the site of the **Battle of Glen Shiel**, fought in 1719 between a Hanoverian Army and a force of Jacobites (which included 300 Spaniards). It was the last battle fought on British soil between British and foreign soldiers, and it had no clear victor. There is a Countryside Centre (National Trust for Scotland) at Morvich Farm, off the A87, and it makes a good starting point for walking on some of the surrounding hills and mountains.

Northeast of Kyle of Lochalsh is the conservation village of Plockton, with its palm trees and idyllic location. This was the Lochdubh of *Hamish Macbeth* fame, as it was here that the TV series was filmed. It sits beside Loch Carron, and on the opposite bank, opposite Strome Ferry and a few miles inland off a minor road, are the ruins of **Strome Castle** (National Trust for Scotland). It was built in the 15th century, and was a stronghold of the MacDonalds, Lords of the Isles. On **Craig Highland Farm**, near the village, you can view rare breeds, as well as feed the farmyard animals

Kyle of Lochalsh is the western terminus for the famous Dingwall to Kyle of Lochalsh railway line (see Dingwall).

Inverness

🏚 Inverness Castle	🐟 Fiona MacDonald		
🏚 Town House	🏚 Tolbooth Steeple		
📷 Inverness Museum & Art Gallery			
🏚 Abertarff House	🏚 Dunbar's Hospital		
🏚 Inverness Cathedral	🏚 Old High Church		
🏚 Old Gaelic Church	🏚 Victorian Market		
🐟 Dolphins and Seals Centre			

Inverness is the capital of the Highlands. It is said to be the most rapidly expanding city in Britain, if not Europe, and though it only has a population of about 50,000, its hinterland supports a further 20,000. The town has all the feel and bustle of a much larger place, and its shopping - especially in the pedestrianised High Street, where the Eastgate Shopping Centre is located - is superb.

The city sits at the northeast end of the Great Glen, at a point where the River Ness enters the Moray Firth. It was once the capital of the Northern Picts, and it was to Inverness that St Columba came in the 6th century to confront King Brude MacMaelcon and convert him and his kingdom to Christianity. The doors of Brude's fort were firmly closed, but Columba marked them with the sign of the cross and they flew open of their own accord.

The present **Inverness Castle** dates from 1835, and houses the local courthouse. Castles have stood on the site since at least the 12th century. However, Macbeth's castle, where Shakespeare set the murder of Duncan, stood some distance away, where people have claimed to have seen the ghost of Duncan in full kingly attire close to the River Ness. General Wade enlarged Inverness

---

🏚 historic building 📷 museum and heritage 🏛 historic site 🐟 scenic attraction 🐦 flora and fauna

Castle after the uprising of 1715, and its garrison surrendered to Charles Edward Stuart when he occupied the town in 1745. Wade then ordered the castle to be blown up. Close to the present castle is a statue of **Flora MacDonald**, who helped Charles Edward Stuart evade capture.

Near the castle, in Bridge Street, is the **Town House**, which was completed in 1882. It was in the council chamber here, in 1921, that the only cabinet meeting ever held outside London took place, when Lloyd George, the Prime Minister, wanted to discuss the worsening Ireland situation. Across from it is the **Tolbooth Steeple**, dating from the late 18th century. It was once part of a complex of buildings that contained a courthouse and jail. In Castle Wynd, in a modern building, is **Inverness Museum and Art Gallery**, which has a large collection relating to the history of the Highlands and the town in particular. Within the library, behind the bus station, is the Highland Archives and Genealogy Centre, where you can research your forebears.

The oldest secular building in the city is **Abertarff House** in Church Street (National Trust for Scotland), which dates from 1593. It was built as a town house for the Frasers of Lovat, and is now the local headquarters for the National Trust for Scotland. **Dunbar's Hospital** is also on Church Street, and dates from 1668. It was founded by provost Alexander Dunbar as a hospital for the poor. It has now been divided into flats.

Inverness Cathedral, dedicated to St Andrew, is a gem of a building in pink sandstone designed by Alexander Ross and consecrated in 1874. It was supposed to have had two large spires, but these were never built. The interior is more spacious than the exterior suggests, and is notable for a beautiful oak choir screen separating the nave from the choir. The Eden Court Theatre, next to the cathedral, incorporates parts of the old Bishop's Palace.

The **Old High Church** in Church Street, dedicated to St Mary, is Inverness's parish church and was built in 1770, though parts of the tower may date from medieval times. After the battle of Culloden, the church was used as a jail for Jacobite soldiers, some of whom were executed in the kirkyard. It is said to be built on a site where St Columba once preached. The **Old Gaelic Church** was originally built in 1649, though the present building dates from a rebuilding of 1792.

Inverness is one of the few Scottish towns to have retained its traditional market, and the indoor **Victorian Market** in the Academy Street building dates from 1890, when it was rebuilt after a disastrous fire.

The magnificent Kessock Bridge, opened in 1982, carries the A9 over the narrows between the Moray and Beauly Firths and connects Inverness to the Black Isle. At North Kessock is the **Dolphins and Seals of the Moray Firth Visitor and Research Centre**. The Moray Firth is famous for its bottlenose dolphins, and boats leave from many small ports so that you can observe them. This visitor centre gives you one of the best opportunities in Europe to learn about the creatures, and to listen to them through underwater microphones.

A few miles west of the town at Kirkhill is the Highland Wineries, based around Moniack Castle, an old Fraser stronghold dating from 1580. There are country wines, liqueurs, preserves and sauces.

Around Inverness

CROMARTY

16 miles NE of Inverness on the A832

🏛 Hugh Miller's Cottage

🏛 Cromarty Courthouse Museum

This picturesque small royal burgh, which received its charter in the 13th century, sits on a small headland near the mouth of the Cromarty Firth. It is probably the best-preserved 18th-century town in Scotland, and was where many Highlanders embarked for Canada during the clearances of the early 1800s.

Cromarty was the birthplace, in 1802, of Hugh Miller, writer and the 'father of geology'. **Hugh Miller's Cottage** (National Trust for Scotland), where he was born, is open to the public. It has a collection of fossils and rock specimens, as well as some of his personal possessions, including his geological hammer and microscope. The major part of his fossil collection of more than 6000 specimens provides the core of today's Scottish national collection in the Royal Scottish Museum in Edinburgh.

The **Cromarty Courthouse Museum**, as its name suggests, is housed within the old courthouse. There is a reconstruction of an 18th-century trial in the courtroom itself, plus you can see the old cells, children's costumes, a video presentation giving 800 years of Cromarty history and an audio tape tour of the old part of the town.

The Cromarty Firth has always been a safe anchorage for British ships. On December 30 1915 *HMS Natal* mysteriously blew up here, with the loss of 421 lives. Many of those killed lie in the kirkyard of the Gaelic Chapel.

Ross and Cromarty was one of the counties of Scotland lost in the local government reforms of 1975. Originally, it was two counties, which were amalgamated in 1889.

FORTROSE

8 miles NE of Inverness on the A832

🏛 Fortrose Cathedral 🌱 Chanonry Point

🗓 Brahan Seer 🏛 Groam House Museum

Fortrose Cathedral (Historic Scotland) was founded by David I as the mother church of the diocese of Ross. Building began in the 1200s, though the scant remains you see nowadays date from the 14th century. One of the three fine canopied tombs is of Euphemia Ross, wife of the Wolf of Badenoch (see also Dunkeld, Grantown-on-Spey and Elgin). The other two are of bishops, possibly Robert Cairncross and John Fraser.

Nearby **Chanonry Point** is one of the best places to observe the Moray Firth dolphins. Here, where the Firth is at its narrowest, you can sometimes see up to 40 of these graceful creatures glide through the waters or put on a fine display of jumping and diving. It was at Chanonry Point that Kenneth Mackenzie, better known as the **Brahan Seer**, was executed in 1660. He had the gift of second sight, and when he was asked by the 3rd Countess of Seaforth why her husband was late returning home from Paris, he said that he was with a lady. She was so enraged that she had Kenneth executed. A cairn marks the spot.

In nearby Rosemarkie is the **Groam House Museum**, with exhibits and displays that explain the culture of the Picts, those mysterious people who inhabited this part of Scotland in the Dark Ages.

TAIN

23 miles N of Inverness on the A9

📷 Tain Through Time   🏛 Tain Tolbooth

Glenmorangie Distillery, Tain

In medieval times, Tain was a great Christian centre, drawing pilgrims from all over Europe to the shrine of St Duthac within St Duthac Collegiate Church. One of the finest medieval buildings in the Highlands, the church is now an exhibition and visitors centre called **Tain Through Time.** The exhibits explain about St Duthac himself, the pilgrimage, and the people who made it. A regular pilgrim was the devout King James IV who made many offerings to the shrine including, on one particularly parsimonious occasion, some broken silver plates for the adornment of St Duthac's relics.

Within the centre there's a museum that has displays about Clan Ross.

FEARN HOTEL

Main Street, Fearn, Tain,
Highland IV20 1TJ
Tel: 01862 832234
e-mail: info@fearnhotel.co.uk
website: www.fearnhotel.co.uk

Following a long career in the civil service, Graeme Cousins and his partner Denise McIntosh, a qualified nurse, took the opportunity to purchase the **Fearn Hotel** which presented the chance to develop an establishment which provided a warm and friendly welcome in cosy surroundings. The hotel has a small bar with a good range of wines and spirits, and a restaurant with spectacular views over the countryside. Meals are served in the restaurant from 6pm to 9pm, and during the busy summer period, lunch is served from noon until 2.00pm. There's also a 16-cover breakfast room with a truly magnificent view of nearby Fearn Abbey. The hotel has 6 guest bedrooms - 3 singles, 2 doubles and 1 twin - all with either en suite or private facilities, and some with lovely views over the surrounding countryside.

Nearby attractions include the Blue Flag beaches at Shandwick and Portmahomack, as well as Dornoch, and the Tarbat Discovery Centre is a short drive away at Portmahomack, as is the Anta pottery centre. The Glenmorangie Distillery is at Tain, 4 miles away, and there are numerous golf courses in the area, including the Tom Morris-designed course at Tain.

THE TAIN POTTERY

Aldie, Tain, Ross-shire IV19 1LZ
Tel: 01862 894112 Fax: 01862 893306
e-mail: robert@tainpottery.co.uk
website: www.tainpottery.co.uk

Now firmly established as one of the largest Scottish ceramic manufacturers, **The Tain Pottery** offers an inspiring range of products created by traditional craft techniques and skills. The pottery and visitor centre is located on the A9, just south of the Royal Burgh of Tain, and is easily located by following the brown and white tourist board signs. It is an ideal place to break your journey and a popular venue for those seeking refuge from inclement weather! The working pottery is housed in a renovated farm steading and has ample parking facilities. Visitors will be welcome to wander freely and discover how the raw clay is transformed into desirable objects.

This durable stoneware is all crafted on site, before being fired to a temperature of 1280 degrees centigrade and can therefore be used in microwaves, ovens, freezers and dishwashers. The original designs are inspired by the surrounding area which is rich in natural beauty and the colours used will complement most décor. 'Glenaldie' - our 'flagship design' depicts the national emblem, whereas flowers, berries and crustacean are also very popular. In addition, we create a selection of tartan designs. Each piece is individually hand painted by one of a team of talented artists and is therefore unique.

Our shop offers the full Tain Pottery range, which is highly collectable, functional and popular for giftware. Whether you wish to purchase a single egg cup or full dinner service, table lamp or clock there should be something to suit most tastes. You will also find some special 'one off' pieces, and commissions can be undertaken, for those seeking that extra special gift, we can put names or inscriptions on any piece. We offer a wedding list service for the bride who is looking for something a little different. Visitors have the unique opportunity to browse our vast array of seconds, which are available at discounted prices, exclusively from our shop.

Opening Times:

April – October
Monday: Saturday 9.00 – 5.30 pm,
Sunday 10.00 – 5 pm
November – March
Monday – Saturday 9.30 – 5.00 pm,
Sundays by appointment only.

Tain Tolbooth was built in 1707, replacing an earlier building. Half a mile north of the town is the Glenmorangie Distillery, which has guided tours and a museum, with a tasting at the end of the tour.

DORNOCH

30 miles N of Inverness on the A949

🏛 Dornoch Cathedral 🏛 Dornoch Castle

📖 Witch's Stone

Dornoch Cathedral dates originally from the early 13th century. However, the church as we see it today is largely a rebuilding of the early 19th century, though there are some old features still visible, mostly in the chancel and crossing. Sixteen Earls of Sutherland are said to be buried within it. It was also where, in December 2000, the son of pop star Madonna and her husband Guy Ritchie was baptised. **Dornoch Castle** stands opposite the cathedral, and was built in the 15th century with later additions. It is now an hotel.

Dornoch was the scene in 1727 (though the stone says 1722), of Scotland's last execution for witchcraft, when an old woman called Janet Horne was burned for supposedly turning her daughter into a pony. The judge at the trial was later reprimanded for his handling of the case. The **Witch's Stone**, within a garden in Littletown, marks the spot where Janet was executed.

BRORA

45 miles NE of Inverness on the A9

🏛 Brora Heritage Centre

Brora is a picturesque coastal village at the mouth of the River Brora. The **Brora Heritage Centre** on Coalpit Road has a hands-on guide to the history and wildlife of the area. At one time it was the location of the

Highland's only coal mine, with the coal being shipped out from the local harbour until the railways took over. The Clynelish Distillery has a visitors centre and shop.

GOLSPIE

40 miles NE of Inverness on the A9

🕊 Duke of Sutherland 🏛 Dunrobin Castle

🏛 Carn Liath

A steep hill path takes you to the summit of Ben Bhraggie, on which there is a statue by Chantry of the first **Duke of Sutherland**, who died in 1833. Locally, it is known as the Mannie, and was erected in 1834 by 'a mourning and grateful tenantry to a judicious, kind and liberal landlord'. The words ring hollow, however, as the duke, owner of the biggest private estate in Europe at the time, was one of the instigators of the hated Clearances of the early 19th century. There have been continued calls to have the statue removed, and in some cases blown up. Others have argued that the statue should stay as a reminder of those terrible times.

Dunrobin Castle, the seat of the Dukes of Sutherland, is the most northerly of Scotland's stately homes and one of the largest in the Highlands. Though the core is 14th century, it resembles a huge French chateau, thanks to a

Drawing Room, Dunrobin Castle, Golspie

📖 stories and anecdotes 🕊 famous people 🎨 art and craft 🎭 entertainment and sport 🚶 walks

spare-no-expense remodelling in 1840 by Sir Charles Barry, designer of the Houses of Parliament. Some of the castle's 189 rooms are open to the public, and there is a museum in the summerhouse.

North of Golspie, on the road to Brora, is **Carn Liath** ("the Grey Cairn"). It overlooks the sea, and is all that is left of a once mighty broch. The walls are still 12 feet high in places.

Fort George

Fort George, Inverness, Inverness-Shire IV2 7TD
Tel: 01667 462777 / 01667 460232
website: www.historic-scotland.gov.uk/properties

Following the 1746 defeat at Culloden of Bonnie Prince Charlie, George II created the ultimate defence against further Jacobite unrest. The result, Fort George, is the mightiest artillery fortification in Britain, if not Europe. Its garrison buildings, artillery defences bristling with cannon, and superb collection of arms – including bayoneted muskets, pikes, swords and ammunition pouches – provide a fascinating insight into 18th century military life.

Fort George was intended as an impregnable army base – designed on a monumental scale using sophisticated defence standards. Today, it would cost nearly £1 billion. Within almost a mile of boundary walls was accommodation for a governor, officers, artillery detachment, and a 1600-strong infantry garrison. It also housed a magazine for 2,500 gunpowder barrels, ordnance and provision stores, a brewhouse and chapel. When the fortress was completed in 1769, the Highlands were peaceful but it was maintained in readiness for action that never came, and has remained virtually unaltered. Visitors today can see historic barrack rooms which are a time capsule of the domestic life of the Scottish soldier.

Fort George is the only ancient monument in Scotland still functioning as intended – a working army barracks – but still welcoming visitors. A gift shop and café (seasonal) are among the attractions. There is also a summer events programme.

🏠 historic building 🏛 museum and heritage 🏚 historic site 🌲 scenic attraction 🌱 flora and fauna

LAIRG

40 miles N of Inverness on the A836

⛲ Falls of Shin 🏰 Ord Hill

🏛 Ferrycroft Countryside Centre

Lairg is an old village that sits at the south-eastern tip of Loch Shin, which, since the 1950s, has been harnessed for hydroelectricity. The loch, which is famous for its fishing, is over 18 miles long by no more than a mile at its widest, with the A838 following its northern shoreline for part of the way. Due to the hydroelectric scheme, it is 30 feet deeper than it used to be.

The village became important because it stands at the meeting point of various Highland roads that head off in all directions. Five miles south are the picturesque **Falls of Shin**, which has a visitor centre and a Harrod's shop. **Ord Hill**, west of the town, has an archaeological trail, which takes you round a landscape rich in ancient sites. **Ferrycroft Countryside Centre** explains land use in this part of Sutherland since the end of the last Ice Age.

FORT GEORGE

10 miles NE of Inverness on the B9006

🏰 Fort George

🏛 Queen's Own Highlanders Museum

Fort George (Historic Scotland - see panel opposite) was designed by Major General William Skinner, the King's Military Engineer for North Britain (the name given to Scotland after the Jacobite Uprising). He originally wanted to build it at Inverness, but the councillors of the town objected, saying it would take away part of the harbour. The fort was named after George II, and sits on a headland that guards the inner waters of the Moray Firth near Ardersier. Work started on

building it in 1748 as a direct result of the Jacobite Uprising of 1745, and it was subsequently manned by government troops. It covers 42 acres, has walls a mile long, and the whole thing cost over £1bn to build at today's prices. It has been called the finest 18th-century fortification in Europe, and has survived almost intact from that time. The **Queen's Own Highlanders Museum** is within the fort.

NAIRN

16 miles NE of Inverness on the A96

🏛 Nairn Museum 🏛 Fishertown Museum

🏰 Boath Doocot 🏰 Battle of Auldearn

🏰 Auldearn Parish Church

Nairn is a small, picturesque holiday and golfing resort on the Moray Firth. Local people will tell you that the name is a shortened version of 'nae rain' ('no rain'), and indeed this area is one of the driest in Britain. It has a fine, clean beach and a large caravan park. The River Nairn, which flows through the town, is supposed to mark the boundary between the English speaking areas to the east and the Gaelic speaking areas to the west. A great royal castle once stood here, built by William the Lion in 1179, but it is long gone. The **Nairn Museum** on Viewfield Drive has collections on local history, archaeology and wildlife. There is also the **Fishertown Museum**, in the heart of the fisher town area. As its name implies, this is where the fishermen that manned the town's former fishing fleet lived. There are displays and artefacts highlighting the industry.

At Auldearn, two miles east of the town (now bypassed), is the **Boath Doocot** (National Trust for Scotland), which stands within what was a small medieval castle built in the late 12th century by William the Lion.

BOATH STABLES HOLIDAY ACCOMMODATION

Boath Steading, Auldearn, by Nairn, Inverness-shire IV12 5TE
Tel: 01667 451500
Fax: 01667 451301
e-mail: maxwell_ellen@hotmail.com
website: www.boathstables.co.uk

Set in lovely gardens in a peaceful rural setting, **Boath Stables** offers luxury self-catering accommodation in a beautifully converted 18th century property. There are two similar luxury apartments. Each has a cosy lounge with an open fire, digital TV and DVD player with surround sound and wifi connection is available in the property. In colder weather there is full central heating with adjustable under-floor heating on the ground floor.

The kitchens are modern and well-equipped, with a washing machine and tumble dryer located in the adjacent converted Hen House. This small building also provides separate storage place for bicycles, golf clubs and wet gear.

Each apartment sleeps up to 6 people. The two upstairs bedrooms have the flexibility of zip and link beds, for either double or twin occupation. The small bedroom has an en suite shower; the larger room has an en suite bathroom and plenty of room for a cot or child's bed/ Downstairs, the lounge has a comfortable sofa-bed with its own shower facilities in the downstairs bathroom. For larger groups, the two apartments can be united to comfortably house up to 12 people, plus children.

CALEDONIAN CRAFT CONNECTIONS

115 High Street, Nairn IV12 4DB
Tel: 01667 452423

e-mail: info@caledoniancraftconnections.com
website: www.caledoniancraftconnections.com

Located on the "Brae" of the High Street, Pat and Marie have run their Studio/Craft shop/workshop since December 2007, when they identified a lack of outlets for local handcrafters/ artisans, of which they included themselves. This enables original pieces to be shown in an eclectically displayed style, with an ambiance of past times when the pace was slower and the individual needs of the customer were uppermost. Due to the nature of the shop, pieces change frequently, (some being unique, others limited), but include locally handcrafted pottery, ceramics, glass, woodturning, jewellery, photography, art, soaps, cards and a range of felt, tweed and textile items.

After the local Wool shop closed in February 2008 Pat and Marie added a wool and haberdashery department, featuring locally produced wools, as well as popular yarns Collinette and Sirdar. The studio at the rear of the craft shop is where Pat and Marie make their full range of hand-crafted, bespoke wedding and special occasion stationery under the name of Temparia. The studio also hosts classes and workshops throughout the year on a variety of craft techniques, details can be found on website.

The **Battle of Auldearn** was fought here in 1645 between 1500 Royalist troops of the Marquis of Montrose and a 4000-strong Covenanting army under Sir John Hurry. Even though they outnumbered the Royalist troops, the Covenanters were routed, and some of the dead were buried in the kirkyard of **Auldearn Parish Church**, built in 1757.

CAWDOR
12 miles NE of Inverness on the A96

🏰 Cawdor Castle

Cawdor Castle was made famous by Shakespeare in his play *Macbeth*, though the core of the present castle was built in the 14th century by the then Thane of Cawdor, who was sheriff and hereditary constable of the royal castle at Nairn. He built the core - essentially the central tower - round a thorn tree that can still be seen today. The story goes that the thane loaded a donkey with gold, and let it wander round the district. The thane vowed to built the castle where it finally rested. This it did beside a thorn tree, which was incorporated into the building. Recent carbon dating suggests the tree was planted in about 1372. With its fairy tale looks and its turrets, Cawdor is said to be one of the most romantic castles in Scotland.

CULLODEN
5 miles E of Inverness on the B9006

🏛 Battle of Culloden   🏰 Leanach Cottage

🏛 Culloden Visitor Centre   🏛 Clava Cairns

The **Battle of Culloden** was fought in 1746, and was the last major battle to take place on British soil. It lasted less than an hour and left 349 government troops dead and 1000 Jacobites. The hopes of the Jacobites to return a Stuart king to the British throne were dashed on that cold April day, and the clan system was smashed forever. The battlefield is on Drumossie Moor, which in the 18th century was a lonely, wild place.

Now it has been drained and cultivated, though the battlefield itself has been returned to the way it was. There is still a sadness about the place, and it was once said that no birds ever sang here. That's not quite true, but no one who visits can fail to be moved. You can still see the stones that mark the graves of various clans, and there is a huge memorial cairn at the centre of the battlefield. **Leanach Cottage**, which survived the battle, has been restored, and the **Culloden Visitor Centre** (National Trust for Scotland) has displays and exhibits that explain the battle. The Cumberland Stone marks the place where the 25-year-old Duke of Cumberland, third son of George II and commander of the Royalist troops, watched the battle. He earned the nickname Butcher Cumberland for his unspeakable acts of cruelty after the battle.

Not far from the battlefield are the **Clava Cairns** (Historic Scotland), a fascinating group of three burial cairns of the early Bronze Age.

TOMATIN
13 miles SE of Inverness off the A9

Tomatin sits on the River Findhorn, just off the A9. The Tomatin Distillery, north of the village, is one of the highest in Scotland, and was founded in 1897. Now owned by a Japanese company, it has 23 stills, and draws its water from the Alt-na-Frithe burn. It has tours, a visitor centre and tastings.

NETHY BRIDGE
24 miles SE of Inverness on the B970

🌿 Dell Wood National Nature Reserve

Dell Wood National Nature Reserve is in

Abernethy Forest. It is famous for its rare bog woodland, which has largely disappeared from the area because of drainage and agricultural improvements.

GRANTOWN-ON-SPEY
26 miles SE of Inverness off the A939

🏛 Inverallan Parish Church

🌱 Revack Country Lodge 🏛 Lochindorb Castle

This beautiful and elegant tourist centre is situated in the heart of Strathspey (never, ever the Spey Valley), and sits at a height of 700 feet above sea level. It was built by James Grant of Grantcastle in the late 18th century and laid out in a grid plan. The **Inverallan Parish Church** in Mossie Road was completed in 1856, and commemorates the 7th and 8th Earls of Seaforth.

The 15,000-acre **Revack Country Estate**

lies to the south of the town, on the B970 to Nethy Bridge. It has gardens, woodland trails and an adventure playground. Revack Lodge was built as a shooting lodge in 1860.

Six miles northwest of the town are the ruins of **Lochindorb Castle**, built on an island in Lochindorb, on bleak Dava Moor. This was the home of the infamous Alexander Stewart, son of Robert II, known as the Wolf of Badenoch.

CARRBRIDGE
21 miles SE of Inverness on the A938

🌱 Landmark Forest Heritage Park

🌱 Speyside Heather Centre

The arch of the original packhorse bridge still stands and dates from 1717 when it was built by Brigadier-General Sir Alexander Grant of Grant. It carried funeral processions to Duthil

---

DUNALLAN HOUSE

Woodside Avenue, Grantown-on-Spey, Moray PH26 3JN
Tel: 01479 872140
e-mail: enquiries@dunallan.com
website: www.dunallan.com

Enjoying a peaceful location, yet only a short walk from local shops and a wide range of excellent restaurants and cafes, **Dunallan House** was built in 1898 as a handsome country retreat for aristocrats and is now a family-run traditional Victorian Guest House with a friendly and relaxing atmosphere. Owners Jayne Osgood and David Graham have kept many of the villa's original features, including the lovely stained glass windows, cornices and the original fireplaces in the dining room and guest's lounge. Awarded a 4-star rating by the Scottish Tourist Board, Dunallan House offers a choice of 4 double rooms, 2 twin rooms and one multiple bed room. All the rooms are en suite and individually decorated and include a popular Victorian room and a honeymoon suite.

At breakfast time, guests are very well looked after with a choice that includes porridge, fresh fruit, organic yoghurts, Dorset cereal, local smoked salmon and a full Scottish breakfast. Dunallan's other facilities include a

drying room, laundry
service, lockable storage
and private off-road parking.
Mountain bike and Nordic
walking instruction, hire and
guiding are all available.

🏛 historic building 🏛 museum and heritage 🏚 historic site 🏞 scenic attraction 🌱 flora and fauna

Church, and for this reason was given the nickname of the Coffin Bridge.

South of the village is the **Landmark Forest Heritage Park**. It is carved out of woodland, and has such attractions as a Red Squirrel Trail, Microworld (where you can explore the world of tiny insects) and the Tree Top Trail, where you take a walk through the high branches of the trees. The Timber Tower gives amazing views over the surrounding countryside. At Dulnain Bridge, six miles east of the village on the A95, is the **Speyside Heather Centre**, with over 300 species of a plant that has become synonymous with Scotland.

AVIEMORE
30 miles SE of Inverness off the A9

- Cairngorm Reindeer Centre
- Rothiemurchus Highland Estate
- Strathspey Steam Railway

Once a quiet Inverness-shire village, Aviemore has now expanded into one of the main winter sports centres in the Highlands. The skiing area and chair lifts lie about nine miles east of the village, high in the Cairngorms. This is also the starting point of the Cairngorm Mountain Railway, which carries passengers all year round to the Ptarmigan Station, within 400 feet of the summit of the 4084-feet-high Cairngorm itself. On the road to the skiing area is the **Cairngorm Reindeer Centre**, where Britain's only permanent herd of reindeer can be seen.

The **Rothiemurchus Highland Estate** is a magnificent area with spectacular views, deep forests and woodland trails. You can try hill walking and mountain biking, and there are guided walks and safari tours in Land Rovers. The estate contains some of the last remnants

Cairngorm Mountain Railway, Aviemore

of the great, natural Caledonian Pine Forest, which once covered all of the Highlands. Parts of *Monarch of the Glen* were filmed here (see also Kingussie). Details of all the activities are available from the visitor centre on the B970, southeast of the village.

Aviemore is one of the termini of the **Strathspey Steam Railway**, which runs through Boat of Garten to Broomhill, 10 miles away. Broomhill station featured as Glenbogle Station in the popular TV series *Monarch of the Glen*. The line was once part of the Aviemore to Forres line, which was closed in the early 1960s.

KINGUSSIE
28 miles S of Inverness off the A9

- Highland Folk Museum
- Clan MacPherson House Ruthven Barracks
- Highland Wildlife Park

Kingussie (pronounced King - yoosy) sits in Strathspey with good views of the Cairngorms to the east, while to the west lie the Monadhliath Mountains, rising to over 3000 feet.

At Newtonmore, three miles south of Kingussie, is the **Highland Folk Museum**, which gives an insight into the history and lifestyle of the ordinary people of the

stories and anecdotes famous people art and craft entertainment and sport walks

Aviemore - Boat of Garten

Distance: *5.6 miles (9.0 kilometres)*
Typical time: *150 mins*
Height gain: *100 metres*
Map: *Explorer 403*
Walk: *www.walkingworld.com ID:1009*
Contributor: *D B Grant*

DESCRIPTION:

On the map this looks like a boring straight line; but in fact nowhere is it straight for more than 100 metres. Part of the Speyside Way, it has been well planned and laid out. It's wide and well surfaced (but good shoes, or boots, recommended). It's full of variety and offers good views to the northern Cairngorms. The walk is 5.5 miles from one railway station to the other, to take advantage of a return journey on the steam train; it can be shortened to four miles if you use two cars. Food, drink etc are available in the two villages and there is a licensed diner on the train (timetables available at the Tourist Information Centre, any hotel, guesthouse etc).

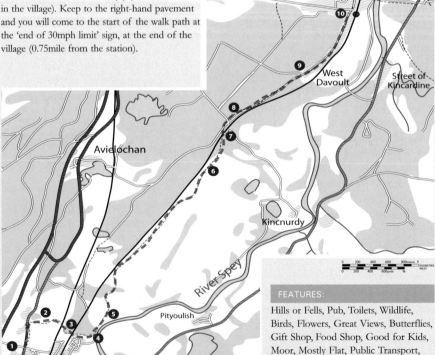

FEATURES:

Hills or Fells, Pub, Toilets, Wildlife, Birds, Flowers, Great Views, Butterflies, Gift Shop, Food Shop, Good for Kids, Moor, Mostly Flat, Public Transport, Restaurant, Tea Shop, Woodland.

WALK DIRECTIONS:

1 | The path starts, on the northern edge of Aviemore, at the '30mph' sign. After following the A95(T) for a short distance the track turns right, to reach double gates.

2 | Go through the gates, and under the Perth to Inverness railway. After that cross three wooden bridges, then under the Strathspey Railway bridge.

3 | After going under this bridge you soon come to a fork. Here keep left and you'll soon reach another fork.

4 | At this fork, keep left and go on through open birch woods and old Scots pines. Where you emerge from the woodland there is another fork.

5 | Keep left here, onto open moorland. Continue, alternating between open woodland and moor, with views behind to the Cairngorms.

6 | Continue on to reach a gate.

7 | Immediately through the gate, turn left on to a farm road (waymarked Speyside Way). The route soon goes under the Speyside Railway again, and a few metres on there is a junction.

8 | Go straight on here. Stay on this farm road; it becomes tarred on the outskirts of Boat of Garten.

9 | Here, where the road becomes tarred, is where you can park your car if not using the train. Continue into Boat of Garten; on reaching the main road turn right for a few metres to arrive at the station.

10 | Railway station and parking.

Highlands over the years by means of a reconstruction of an 18th-century Highland township. Also in the village is the **Clan MacPherson House and Museum**, which, as its name implies, recounts the history of the MacPhersons.

The ruins of **Ruthven Barracks** (Historic Scotland) lie to the south of Kingussie, on the other side of the A9. The barracks were built in 1719 to house government troops when Jacobite sympathies were strong in the area. Charles Edward Stuart's army seized the barracks in 1746 and burnt them. After the Jacobite defeat at Culloden, more than 3000 Jacobite troops mustered here to continue the fight. However, Charles Edward Stuart saw that further fighting was useless and sent a message saying that each man should return home. Four miles north of Kingussie is the **Highland Wildlife Park**, which has an array of Scottish wildlife, plus some animals that once used to roam the Highlands freely.

A few miles south west of Kingussie, along the A86, is Loch Laggan, where scenes for the BBC series *Monarch of the Glen* were filmed.

The Adverikie Estate, with its large house, played the part of Glenbogle.

DRUMNADROCHIT
16 miles SW of Inverness on the A82

🎞 Nessie   🏛 Loch Ness Exhibition Centre

🏛 Original Loch Ness Exhibition

Drumnadrochit sits on the shore of Loch Ness at Drumnadrochit Bay. It is a quaint place, though it can get overcrowded in the summer, due to tourists flocking here to catch a glimpse of the Loch Ness Monster, nicknamed **Nessie**. Whether a monster actually exists or not has never been proved, but that has never deterred the crowds. The loch measures just less than 23 miles long by a mile wide at its widest, and contains more water than any other loch in Britain.

The first mention we have of a monster - though in this case it was in the River Ness and not in the loch - occurs in Adamnan's *Life of St Columba*, written in the 7th century. In the year 565AD, St Columba was heading up the Great Glen towards Inverness, when he

🎞 stories and anecdotes 🐦 famous people 🎨 art and craft 🎭 entertainment and sport 🚶 walks

encountered a monster attacking a man in the River Ness at the point where it enters the loch. He drove it back by prayer and the man's companions fell on their knees and were converted to Christianity.

Nowadays, the monster is a bit more timid. Most sightings have been made at **Urquhart Castle** (Historic Scotland), about a mile from Drumnadrochit. Curiously enough, this is where the loch is at its deepest at 754 feet. The castle is one of the largest in Scotland and stands on a promontory that juts out into the water. A fortification has stood here for centuries, but the present ruins date from the 16th century when the Grants occupied it. Urquhart Castle has nothing to do with Clan Urquhart, whose homeland was on the Black Isle, north of Inverness, though there may have been early links. After the Jacobite Uprising of 1689, the castle was blown up and never rebuilt. A visitor centre contains a model of the castle, which shows what it was like in its heyday.

Two exhibitions vie for attention in the village, the **Original Loch Ness Exhibition** and the **Loch Ness Exhibition Centre**. They each have displays about the Loch Ness Monster, but the latter was designed by scientist Adrian Shine who has spent more than 30 years investigating the Loch Ness phenomenon.

BEAULY
7 miles W of Inverness on the A862

🏚 Beauly Priory 🏛 Beauly Centre ⌘ Strathglass

🏚 Wardlaw Mausoleum

Within this picturesque village are the ruins of **Beauly Priory** (Historic Scotland), founded by the Bisset family in 1230 for monks of the Valliscaulian order, though what can be seen nowadays dates from between the 14th and 16th centuries, when the Frasers of Lovat

were the dominant family. The north transept, which is more or less complete, is the burial place of the MacKenzies of Kintail.

It is said that the village got its name when Mary Stuart stayed in the priory in 1564 on her way to Dingwall and declared it to be a beau lieu, or beautiful place. However, it was called Beauly long before she arrived, though the name may indeed come from the French for beautiful place.

The **Beauly Centre**, next to the priory, has displays about the history of the area. There is also a reconstructed village store, a weaving centre and a Clan Fraser exhibition.

To the southwest is **Strathglass**, one of the most beautiful glens in the area. It was here, in the early 19th century, that the Sobieski Stuarts lived in some style, claiming to be the legitimate grandsons of Charles Edward Stuart. Their claims were believed by many people, notably the Earl of Moray, Lord Lovat and the Earl of Dumfries. There is no doubt, however, that they were charlatans.

The **Wardlaw Mausoleum**, built on to the east end of Kirkhill Parish Church, is one of the burial places of Clan Fraser. It was built in 1634, and in 1998 was restored by Historic Scotland.

DINGWALL
11 miles NW of Inverness on the A862

🏛 Sir Hector MacDonald 🏛 Dingwall Museum

⌘ Rogie Falls

Dingwall's name derives from the Norse thing vollr, meaning the place of the parliament, which shows that even in ancient times it was an important settlement. It is a royal burgh, having received its charter from Alexander II in 1227. Its castle, now long gone, was the birthplace of Macbeth in 1010. Another famous son is **Sir Hector MacDonald**, a crofter's son who was born in 1853 and joined the army as a private, rising through the ranks to become a major general and national hero. He was known as Fighting Mac, and eventually commanded the British Army in Ceylon. In 1903, on his was back to Ceylon after a trip to London, he committed suicide in Paris after unproved accusations of homosexuality from those who objected to his lowly birth. After his death, it was discoverd that he had a secret wife and child. A monument to him, known as the Mitchell Tower, stands on a hill to the south of the town on Mitchell Hill.

Within the old Tolbooth of 1730 is the award-winning **Dingwall Museum**, where the town's history is explained by way of displays and exhibits.

Dingwall is the eastern terminus for the famous Dingwall to Kyle of Lochalsh railway line, which runs through some of the most beautiful scenery in Scotland as it crosses the country.

The Dingwall Canal (now closed) is Britain's most northerly canal, and was designed by Thomas Telford in 1817, though by 1890 it had closed. It is just over a mile in length. At the end of the canal is the Ferry Point, which has a picnic area.

Eight miles west of the town, off the A835, are the **Rogie Falls** on the Blackwater, reached by a footpath from a car park on the main road. A fish ladder has been built to assist salmon to swim upriver. There are also woodland walks in the surrounding area.

STRATHPEFFER
14 miles NW of Inverness on the A834

🏛 Spa Pump Room

📷 Highland Museum of Childhood 🏛 Eagle Stone

At one time, this small village was one of the

KILTEARN HOUSE

Evanton, Ross-shire IV16 9UY
Tel: 01349 830617
e-mail: info@kiltearn.co.uk website: www.kiltearn.co.uk

Occupying a superb position on the foreshore of Cromarty Firth, **Kiltearn House** is a 4* guest house offering hotel luxury with the personal touch. Built in 1894, this imposing Victorian sandstone house was a former Church of Scotland Manse. It is now the home of Lin and Paul Houlden who offer an irresistible combination of luxury accommodation, super food and a wonderful location. Many of the major east coast rivers are within a very short drive and there are 23 of Scotland's finest golf courses within easy reach.

Guests at Kiltearn House have the use of a spacious, double aspect but cosy lounge which has comfortable down-filled sofas and a wood-burning stove for those chilly evenings. Here you can relax and watch TV, DVDs or videos, listen to the radio or the vast selection of CDs.

There's also a drawing room with a large picture window enabling guests to enjoy the panoramic view over the Firth. There is no TV in this room but guests are welcome to read any of the books or newspapers provided.

The 5 guest bedrooms are all en suite and all enjoy views over the Firth or gardens. They have new, ultra-comfortable beds, individual soft furnishings and large, fluffy towels.

🎬 stories and anecdotes 🐦 famous people ✏ art and craft 🖌 entertainment and sport 🚶 walks

most famous spa resorts in Britain, and trains used to leave London regularly carrying people who wanted to 'take its waters'. For this reason, it is full of hotels, B&Bs and genteel guest houses. So fashionable was it that the local paper used to publish a weekly list of the crowned heads and aristocratic families who were 'in town'.

The spa days are over now, though the **Spa Pump Room** has been refurbished and re-creates the halcyon days of the village when the cream of society flocked here. You can even sample the curative waters yourself. The adjacent Victorian gardens, where Victorian society used to promenade and play croquet, have also been restored.

Within the disused railway station is the **Highland Museum of Childhood**, with photographs, toys, games and videos. The Angela Kellie Doll Collection is particularly fine. There's also a gift shop and coffee shop.

On the eastern outskirts of the village is the **Eagle Stone**, with Pictish symbols. Scotland's own Nostradamus, the Brahan Seer (Kenneth Mackenzie, born in the early 17th century)

Eagle Stone, Strathpeffer

predicted that if the stone fell over three times, the waters of the Cromarty Firth, five miles to the east, would rise so that ships could drop anchor near where the stone stood. The stone has fallen over twice so far, and as some of the Seer's other predictions have come true, it is now embedded in concrete to be on the safe side.

Ullapool

🏛 Ullapool Museum 🌱 Leckmelm Gardens

This fishing port and ferry terminal on Loch Broom was founded by the British Fisheries Society in 1788 and laid out in a grid plan to designs by Thomas Telford. By 1792, much of the work on the port buildings and some houses was completed, settlers having been given a plot of land, free stone to build a home, and land for a garden. Over the years the fortunes of the village fluctuated as the fishing industry prospered or went into recession.

Now the town is a tourist resort, and a centre for hill walking, sightseeing, wildlife study and fishing. It is also the mainland terminus for the Stornoway ferry, and can be a busy place during the summer months. The award-winning **Ullapool Museum and Visitor Centre** is housed in a former church designed by Thomas Telford - one of the so-called parliamentary churches".

In 1773, before the town was established, the very first settlers bound for Nova Scotia left Loch Broom in the *Hector*, and there is a scale model of the ship within the museum.

One of the hidden jewels of the West Highlands are the **Leckmelm Gardens**, three miles south of the town just off the A835. They were planted in about 1870, but by 1985 had become overgrown. In that year work began on re-establishing them and revealing the beauty that had been lost for so long. The area surrounding Ullapool is famous for its golden beaches, the best ones being at Achnahaird, Gruinard Bay and Achmelvich.

Around Ullapool

GAIRLOCH
22 miles SW of Ullapool on the A832

- Inverewe Gardens
- Beinn Eighe Nature Reserve

This little village, on the shores of Loch Gairloch, has one of the loveliest settings in Scotland. The Gairloch Heritage Museum, housed in old farm buildings, has an illicit still, village shop, lighthouse interior and other displays that explain how life was lived in northwest Scotland in the past.

A passenger ferry service runs two return crossings daily to Portree on the Isle of Skye.

Five miles northeast, on the banks of Loch Ewe are the famous **Inverewe Gardens** (National Trust for Scotland). They have plant collections from all over the world, which thrive in these northern latitudes due to the Gulf Stream. The gardens were founded by Sir Osgood Mackenzie, third son of the Laird of Gareloch. He bought the Inverewe and Kernsary estate in 1862, when he built Inverewe House and surrounded it with gardens. The most amazing thing about Inverewe is that it is further north than some parts of Greenland, yet still manages to grow some exotic species.

Sixteen miles south east of Gairloch, and beyond beautiful Loch Maree, is the quiet village of Kinlochewe. It is in the heart of what is recognised to be some of the finest mountain scenery in Scotland. The **Beinn**

THE OLD MILL HIGHLAND LODGE

Loch Maree, Wester Ross IV22 2HL
Tel: 01445 760271
e-mail: plbyrne@aol.com
website: www.theoldmillhighlandlodge.co.uk

Set beside the magnificent island-dotted Loch Maree within the National Scenic Area of Wester Ross, **The Old Mill Highland Lodge** enjoys a panoramic view from its lovely garden that takes in the unforgettable sight of Slioch, the finest mountain landmark in Wester Ross. On one side of the lodge is the crystal clear mountain stream which brings the cleanest water in the land and on the other is a restful summer house beside a tinkling burn. The 2 acres of landscaped grounds have matured into a true paradise of flowers, heathers, trees and shrubs.

The Lodge was completed as a purpose-built Highland lodge in 1976, on the site of a former grain store and horse mill. It offers visitors a warm welcome, good food and wine, and the chance to enjoy complete tranquillity in one of the most spectacular areas of Scotland. There's a choice of accommodation in 6 spacious en suite bedrooms (3 twin and 3 double), all with hairdryer and tea/coffee making facilities.

The Old Mill is situated in Talladale, a tiny hamlet named by Norsemen, in whose language 'talla' meant 'hall' and 'dal' meant 'flat field'. With only three permanent residents, it is one of the smallest communities in the British Isles.

Eighe Nature Reserve, Britain's first, has a visitor centre and nature reserve. It sits just west of Kinlochewe, along the A832.

LOCHINVER

17 miles N of Ullapool on the A837

🏚 Ardvreck Castle   🏛 Assynt Visitor Centre

⛰ Suilven   🌿 Hydroponicum

This small fishing port sits on Loch Inver, at the end of the A837. A few miles east is Loch Assynt on whose shore you will find the ruins of **Ardvreck Castle**, built in the 16th century by the MacLeods of Assynt. It was here, in 1650, that Montrose was kept prisoner before being taken to Edinburgh for execution. The **Assynt Visitor Centre** has small displays and exhibits about local history.

Four miles southeast of the village is what has been called the most beautiful mountain in Scotland - **Suilven**. At a mere 2389 feet, it is not even a Munro, nor is it the highest in the area. Seen from Lochinver, it appears to be a solitary mountain that rises sheer on all sides. It's name comes from the Norse, and means the Mountain Pillar. However, it is the western end of a high ridge, and makes for some superb walking and climbing country.

At Achiltibuie, 10 miles south of Lochinver, and reached by a narrow road, is the **Hydroponicum**, a 'garden' where plants grow without soil. It calls itself the garden of the future and kits are available so that you too can start growing plants without soil. It was set up in the mid-1980s to show that some of the problems found in this part of Scotland - poor soil, a short growing season and high winds - could be overcome. It now provides high quality produce (from lettuces to bananas) for homes and businesses in the area. It also features renewable sources of energy and green technologies.

DURNESS

50 miles N of Ullapool on the A838

⛰ Smoo Cave   🌿 John Lennon Memorial Garden

Durness, in Sutherland, is one of the most northerly villages in Scotland, and sits close to Cape Wrath - one of only two capes in Great Britain, the other being Cape Cornwall. To reach it, you have to cross the Kyle of Durness from Durness itself on a small ferry and walk or take a minibus to the cape, 10 miles away. The peculiarly named **Smoo Cave** is in the cliffs a mile and a half west of the village. It consists of three chambers, and goes underneath the coast road. The name may come from the Old Norse smjugga, meaning rock. A walkway with railings takes you down to the cave, which has had lights fitted.

There are many clean, golden beaches in the area, most of them uncrowded. The best ones are Balnakeil, Ceann na Beinne, Sango Beag and Sango Mor.

The village has associations with John Lennon of The Beatles, who used to spend holidays here with his family when he was young. The **John Lennon Memorial Garden** commemorates his stays, and there is a small display of Lennon letters in the village hall.

Wick

🏛 Wick Heritage Centre   🏚 Old Parish Kirk

🗿 George Sinclair   🏚 Castle of Old Wick

🏚 Girnigoe Castle   🏚 Sinclair Castle

Wick is a an ancient royal burgh on the North Sea coast, and was once the leading herring port in Europe. Up until 1975, it was also the administrative capital of Caithness, Scotland's most northerly mainland county. The name comes from the Old Norse word vik meaning bay, and this whole area owes more to Norse culture than it does to the culture of the

Gaels. Parliament Square near the Market place recalls the fact that James V held a parliament at Wick as he made a royal progress through Scotland in 1540.

The award-winning **Wick Heritage Centre** in Bank Row has exhibits and displays about life in Wick and Caithness. In Huddart Street in Pulteneytown on the south bank of the River Wick is the Pulteney Distillery, which makes the world-famous Old Pulteney single malt whisky. It has a visitor centre and shop, and there is a tour of the distillery, plus tastings.

The **Old Parish Kirk**, dedicated to St Fergus, dates from 1830, though a church has stood here since medieval times. In the kirkyard is the Sinclair Aisle, burial place of the old Earls of Caithness.

An old story featuring **George Sinclair**, the 4th Earl, explains just how bloodthirsty times were in the 16th century. He was suspected of

murdering the Earl and Countess of Sutherland so that he could marry off his daughter to their heir, and thus claim the Sutherland lands. However, in 1576, the heir left the country, and Sinclair's plans were thwarted. In revenge, he ordered his son John to lay waste to the Sutherland lands, but when he refused, Sinclair had him thrown into a dungeon.

With the help of his jailer, John hatched a plot to escape. John's brother William found out about this and told his father, who executed the jailer. When William went down to the dungeon to goad his brother, John killed him with his chains. For this, his father punished him by denying him food for five days, then feeding him salt beef without giving him anything to drink. John died in agony, his tongue swollen through lack of water. His father had him buried in the Sinclair Aisle, and years later, just before he too died, full of

🏠 stories and anecdotes 🐦 famous people 🎨 art and craft 🎭 entertainment and sport 🚶 walks

GILBERT'S

10 Dunrobin Street, Helmsdale,
Sutherland KW8 6JA
Tel: 01431 821090
e-mail: info@gilbertsofhelmsdale.co.uk
website: www.gilbertsofhelmsdale.co.uk

Gilbert's opened in the autumn of 2004 as an antique and furniture centre, offering middle range collectables, furniture and jewellery items, with an accompanying coffee and homemade cake selection. This combination proved so successful that proprietors Mel and Russ went on to develop a lunchtime menu, specialising in daily sourced seafood, meat and game, available from local suppliers and cooked to suit individual requirements. Today, the café restaurant with its stylish modern interior, offers a wide ranging and appetising, 'Taste of Scotland' menu, that changes weekly and is based on fresh local, organic produce where available and good home cooking.

Throughout the day Gilbert's is filled with the lovely aroma of fresh baking and friendly staff create a warm and welcoming atmosphere. Although the restaurant is not licensed customers are welcome to bring their own beverages. In the summer months Gilbert's is open on Friday and Saturday evenings and out of season offers special themed evening events, such as classic Italian cuisine or a Medieval night.

Children are welcomed at Gilbert's and there is full disabled access in the restaurant. Gilbert's own handmade 'Highland Posh Nosh' products are also available, including jams, chutneys, truffles and ice cream sauces, with fresh breads and homemade pies lovingly produced for sale. Much of the restaurant's success is undoubtedly due to the owners, Mel and Russ with their attention to detail and undoubted passion for freshly prepared food made with quality, local ingredients.

When visiting Gilbert s do leave time to browse around the interesting selection of antiques, collectables and items of furniture that are displayed in the 50 feet warehouse.

Or if you are planning to stay in this delightful seaside village, Mel and Russ have a fully modernised self catering apartment to let for short breaks and holiday lets. This can accommodate up to 5 people and is available all year round.

🏛 historic building 🏛 museum and heritage 🏛 historic site ♧ scenic attraction 🌿 flora and fauna

remorse for what he had done, he asked that his heart be buried beside his son.

One mile south of the town, on a cliff top, are the ruins of the **Castle of Old Wick** (Historic Scotland), built by Harald Maddadson, Earl of Caithness, in the 12th century.

On a hill to the south of Wick Bay is a memorial to the engineer James Bremner, who was born in Wick and who died in 1856. He collaborated with Brunel, and salvaged the *SS Great Britain* when it ran aground off Ireland.

North of Wick, the two castles of **Girnigoe** and **Sinclair** stand above Sinclair Bay. They were strongholds of the Earls of Caithness. Girnigoe is the older of the two, dating from the end of the 15th century, and it was in its dungeons that George Sinclair had his son incarcerated. Sinclair Castle dates from about 1606.

On the northern edge of the town is Wick Airport, Scotland's most northerly mainland commercial airport. It currently has scheduled flights to and from Aberdeen and Edinburgh.

Around Wick

LATHERON
15 miles SW of Wick on the A9

🏛 Clan Gunn Heritage Centre

🏛 Laidhay Croft Museum

🏛 Dunbeath Heritage Centre 🐦 Neil Gunn

Latheron, unlike other villages in the area, has a name derived from Gaelic, làthair roin, meaning resort of seals. Within the old church, which dates from 1735, is the **Clan Gunn Heritage Centre**. It traces the history of the clan from its Norse origins right through to the present day. At Dunbeath, three miles south of Latheron, is the thatched

Laidhay Croft Museum, which shows a typical Highland house with living quarters, byre and stable all under the one roof. And in an old schoolhouse at Dunbeath is the **Dunbeath Heritage Centre**, managed by the Dunbeath Preservation Trust. It has displays, photographs and documents about the village.

Neil Gunn, one of Scotland's finest writers (author of *The Silver Darlings,* 1941), was born in Dunbeath and attended the school in which the Heritage Centre is located.

HELMSDALE
30 miles SW of Wick on the A9

🏛 Timespan 📖 Isobel Sinclair

📖 Gold Rush of 1868

The name Helmsdale comes from the Norse Hjalmundal, meaning dale of the helmet. A great battle is supposed to have been fought here between two Norse chiefs, Swein and Olvir. Swein was victorious, and Olvir fled and was never heard from again.

Within this little fishing port is **Timespan**, a visitor centre that tells the story of Helmsdale and its surrounding communities. There are exhibits about the Clearances, Picts, Norse raids, witches and much more. Helmsdale Castle once stood in Couper Park, but the last vestiges of it were demolished in the 1970s due to the unstable state of the ruins. In 1567, a famous tragedy - said to have inspired Shakespeare to write *Hamlet* - was enacted here. **Isobel Sinclair** had hopes that her son would claim the earldom of Sutherland. She therefore invited the then Earl and Countess and their heir to dinner one evening. And poured them poisoned wine. The Earl and Countess died, but the heir survived. Unfortunately, Isobel's own son drank the wine and died also.

The Strath of Kildonan, through which flows the River Helmsdale, was the scene of a famous **Gold Rush of 1868**. A local man called Robert Gilchrist, who had been a prospector in Australia, began searching for gold in the river. He eventually found some, and once his secret was out, the Duke of Sutherland began parcelling off small plots of land to speculators. At its height, more than 500 men were prospecting in the area, and a shanty town soon sprung up. But in 1870, when sportsmen complained that the prospectors were interfering with their fishing and hunting, the Duke put a stop to it all, and the gold rush was over. There is still gold there today, and it is a favourite spot for amateur gold panners.

TONGUE
50 miles W of Wick off the A838

🏛 Varrich Castle 📷 Hazard

📷 Strathnaver Museum 🏃 Strathnaver Trail

🌄 Loch Loyal

Tongue is a small village situated near the shallow Kyle of Tongue. Its name means exactly what it says, as it comes from the Norse *tunga*, meaning a tongue, in this case a tongue of land. In 1972, a causeway was built across it to take the A838 westwards towards Loch Eribol and Durness.

The ruins of **Varrich Castle** (Caisteal Bharraich in Gaelic) sit on a rise above the loch, with a footpath taking you to them. It dates from the 14th century, and was once a Mackay stronghold. It is said to be built on the foundations of a Norse fort.

The 16th-century House of Tongue, overlooking the Kyle of Tongue, was also a Mackay stronghold. It was destroyed in the 17th century, with the Mackays building a new house sometime in the 18th century. The gardens are open to the public.

In 1746 a ship - the *Hazard* - carrying gold

coinage for Charles Edward Stuart's Jacobite army tried to take shelter in the Kyle of Tongue to escape *HMS Sheerness,* a government frigate. The crew took the coinage ashore for safekeeping, but were followed and captured by some Mackay clansmen, who were supporters of the government. The crewmen threw the coins into a loch, but most were later recovered.

Nine miles northeast of the village, within the old St Columba's Church at Bettyhill, is the **Strathnaver Museum**, with exhibits about local history, most notably the Clearances and Clan Mackay. Strathnaver was probably the most notorious area in the Highlands for the eviction of tenants so that they could be replaced with the more profitable sheep. The whole area abounds with prehistoric archaeological sites, and within the kirkyard of the museum is a burial stone dating to the 8th or 9th century. The £190,000 **Strathnaver Trail** to the east of the village opened in May 2003 and takes you round 16 sites, which date from 5000BC to the 20th century.

The A836 south from Tongue to Lairg passes alongside beautiful **Loch Loyal** for part of the way, and has some beautiful views.

ALTNAHARRA
51 miles W of Wick on the A836

🏛 Dun Dornaigil Broch

Sitting close to the western tip of Loch Naver, Altnaharra is a small village famous as a centre for game fishing. Loch Naver is the source of the River Naver, one of the best salmon rivers in Sutherland, which flows northwards through Strathnaver to the sea (see also Tongue).

On a narrow, unclassified road from Altnaharra to Strath More and Loch Hope are the remains of the **Dun Dornaigil Broch**. Some of its walls rise to 22 feet, and over the entrance is a strange triangular lintel. A few miles beyond the broch is Ben Hope, at 3041 feet Scotland's most northerly Munro.

The B873 strikes east from Altnaharra along Strathnaver, following the loch and then the river, until it joins the B871, which joins the A836 south of Bettyhill. It is a superb run, with magnificent scenery.

THURSO
19 miles NW of Wick on the A9

🏛 St Peter's Church 🏛 Scrabster Castle
🎭 Graycoat 🏛 Thurso Heritage Museum
🏛 Thurso Castle 🏛 St Mary's Chapel
🏛 Dounreay Visitor Centre

Thurso is a former fishing port on Caithness's northern coast, and is the most northerly town on mainland Britain. It was once a Norse settlement, with its name meaning river of the god Thor. The ruins of **St Peter's Church** sit in the old part of the town, and date from the 16th century. It was once the private chapel of the Bishop of Caithness, whose summer retreat was **Scrabster Castle**, of which only scant remains survive. In the early 17th century, a witch called **Graycoat** was held in the church's tower. The story goes that a man was having difficulty getting his whisky to ferment properly, and blamed a stray cat that had dipped its paw in it. He attacked the cat and cut off its paw, which fell into the whisky. When he drained the barrel, he found, not a paw, but a human hand. Graycoat was then seen nursing a bandaged hand, and people quickly put two and two together, making five. She was summoned before the kirk elders and

TEMPTATIONS
1 Rotterdam Street, Thurso, Caithness   KW14 8AA
Tel/Fax: 01847 893255
e-mail: katie@temptations.wanadoo.co.uk

The large display windows at **Temptations** do indeed look very inviting. Step inside and on the ground floor you'll find a ravishing array of imaginative gifts for all to enjoy. Owner Katie Gunn has put together a wonderful collection with a choice that includes wall hangings, candles, collectable teddy bears, photo frames, mugs, bags, mirrors, trinket boxes, wooden animals and much much more. There's also a selection of local flagstone products.

The first floor is dedicated to a large selection of toys ranging from traditional farm animals and construction kits to dolls, soft and wooden toys and a Sylvanian collectors centre. Whether it's a gift for a loved one, a christmas present for a nephew or a treat for yourself, you are sure to find it at Temptations.

🎭 stories and anecdotes 🐦 famous people 🎨 art and craft 🎭 entertainment and sport 🚶 walks

HALLADALE INN

Melvich, by Thurso, Caithness KW14 7YJ
Tel: 01641 531282
e-mail: mazfling@tinyworld.co.uk
website: www.halladaleinn.co.uk

The Halladale Inn is not just a welcoming hostelry but also
offers a restaurant with a varied menu, bed & breakfast or
self-catering accommodation and a camping park. In the inn
itself there's a bar lounge with a real fire, a well-equipped
games room and a spacious restaurant that is bright and
cheery with its colourful tablecloths and serviettes. Here
you will find an appetising menu based on local produce and
supplemented by daily specials such as local brown trout.

Just one hundred metres from the inn, the Chalet Park
has 4 self-catering chalets each of which can sleep up to 4
people and comprises one double bed and 2 single beds.
The Park has private parking within a fenced garden and
guests have the option of using the laundry service in the
caravan site - a small charge applies.

The caravan park, which has been awarded a 4-star rating by the Scottish Tourist Board, has 14
pitches, six caravans or motor homes with optional electric hook-up, and there are also 8 tent
pitches. The site is conveniently located next to the inn which is open during normal licensing hours
with extended times on Friday evenings (until 1am) and on Saturday evenings (until 12 midnight).

VALLEYVIEW HOUSE
BED & BREAKFAST

Murkle, by Thurso, Caithness KW14 8YT
Tel: 01847 895546
e-mail: antoinetterc@tiscali.co.uk
website: www.valleyviews.co.uk

A warm Highland welcome awaits guests at Valleyview House Bed
& Breakfast, the new family home of Antoinette and Stephen
Robertson-Carswell. Enjoying panoramic views across the bay to
Dunnet Head and beyond, Valleyview's peaceful, country location is
only 5 minutes drive from the main ferry link to the Orkney Islands
and 25 minutes from John O'Groats. Antoinette is a locally
renowned Interior Designer and loves to use her talent to bring out
the best in their home which is constantly being upgraded.
Breakfasts at Valleyview are an experience not to be missed as
Steven, who prepares them, was previously head chef and
manager of the renowned Ulbster Arms Hotel and the only chef in
the county to hold the coveted AA rosette.

Children are very welcome at Valleyview, there's a superb
garden for them to play in and a cot or high chair are available on
request. Horses too are welcome - there are fields available for
them. Other amenities include secure parking, and drying and
laundry facilities.

🏚 historic building 📷 museum and heritage 🏛 historic site ⛰ scenic attraction 🌿 flora and fauna

convicted of being a witch.

The **Thurso Heritage Museum** is located within an old cottage in Lyn Street, and has displays and mementos relating to the town's past. It is open during the summer. At the mouth of the river are the ruins of the mock-Gothic **Thurso Castle**, built in 1878 by Sir Tollemarche Sinclair on the site of a much older castle. At Crosskirk, a few miles west of the town, are the ruins of **St Mary's Chapel**, dating from the 12th century. All that remains is the nave. At Holborn Head is the Clett Rock, a huge natural pillar, or stack, situated just offshore.

Eight miles west of the town, on the A836, is Dounreay, where Scotland's first operational nuclear reactor was built. The **Dounreay Visitor Centre** explains about nuclear power and the history of the site.

JOHN O'GROATS
13 miles N of Wick on the A99

🏠 Last House in Scotland Museum 🏰 Castle of Mey

🏠 Mary-Ann's Cottage 🏠 Northlands Viking Centre

🏛 Nybster Broch

John O' Groats is 873 miles by road from Land's End in Cornwall, and 290 miles from Kirkmaiden in Wigtownshire, Scotland's most southerly parish. It is supposed to be named after a Dutchman called Jan de Groot, who, to settle an argument about precedence within his family, built an eight sided house with eight doors, which gave onto an eight-sided table. This house has now gone, though a mound marks its site. The **Last House in Scotland Museum** contains displays and artefacts about the area.

To the west is Dunnet Head, the most northerly point on the British mainland. Between the two is the **Castle of Mey**, the late Queen Mother's Scottish home. Built in the 16th century by the 4th Earl, it is a fairy-story castle with a picturesque jumble of towers, turrets and castellations. As far as possible, the castle is still set out very much as when the Queen Mother stayed here.

Mary-Ann's Cottage in the village of Dunnet shows how successive generations of one crofting family lived and worked over 140 years. The cottage is named after its last owner, Mary-Ann Calder, whose grandfather had built the house in 1850. Mary-Ann lived in the house until 1990 when, at the age of 93 years, she entered a nursing home in Wick where she died

The **Northlands Viking Centre** in the Old School House at Auckengill, five miles south of the village, tells the story of the Vikings and Norsemen in the area, as well as recounting the life of John Nicolson, a local artist and mason. Ten minutes away are the remains of the **Nybster Broch**, built about 200BC to 200AD.

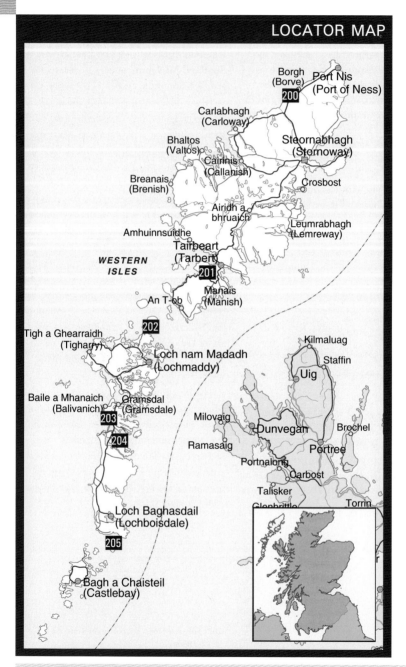

LOCATOR MAP

Borgh (Borve)
Port Nis (Port of Ness)
200

Carlabhagh (Carloway)

Bhaltos (Valtos)

Cairinis (Callanish)

Breanais (Brenish)

Steornabhagh (Stornoway)

Crosbost

Airidh a bhruaich

Leumrabhagh (Lemreway)

Amhuinnsuidhe

Tairbeart (Tarbert)
201

WESTERN ISLES

An T-ob

Manais (Manish)

Tigh a Ghearraidh (Tigharry)
202

Loch nam Madadh (Lochmaddy)

Kilmaluag

Staffin

Uig

Baile a Mhanaich (Balivanich)
Gramsdal (Gramsdale)
203

204

Milovaig

Ramasaig

Dunvegan

Brochel

Portree

Portnalong

Carbost

Talisker

Torrin

Glenbrittle

Loch Baghasdail (Lochboisdale)
205

Bagh a Chaisteil (Castlebay)

r

13 | The Western Isles

The Western Isles look like a huge kite with a long tail streaming out behind it. The body of the kite is the island of Lewis and Harris, and the tail consists mainly of the smaller islands of North Uist, Benbecula, South Uist and Barra. The whole length between Barra in the south and the Butt of Lewis in the north is about 130 miles, and they are separated from the mainland by a stretch of water called The Minch.

Stornoway, Isle of Lewis

These islands are the last bastion of true Gaeldom in Scotland, and in some places English, though spoken and understood perfectly, is still a second language. Some are also bastions of Free Presbyterianism, where the Sabbath is strictly observed, and work or leisure activities of any kind on a Sunday is frowned upon. To complicate the position further, there are some islands that are almost wholly Roman Catholic, never having been influenced by the Scottish Reformation in 1560.

The Western Isles are full of such contradictions. Gaelic culture is cherished and preserved, but there are more Norse influences here than Celtic, and many of the place names (especially in the north) have Norse origins. Up until the Treaty of Perth in 1266, the Western Isles were ruled by Norway. In that year Magnus IV surrendered all of his Scottish possessions, with the exception of Orkney and Shetland, to Alexander III of Scotland.

The weather in the Western Isles, especially in winter, can be harsh, though there are occasions where it can be astonishingly mild and sunny. Snow is rare because of the Gulf Stream, but there are between 45 and 50

ADVERTISERS AND PLACES OF INTEREST

🎞 stories and anecdotes   🦜 famous people   🎨 art and craft   🌿 entertainment and sport   🚶 walks

Vatersay

Obbe and Berneray, and Barra has a ferry connection with Eriskay. Each island in the chain has its own flavour, and all are noted for their quality of light, especially in summer.

For all their seeming isolation, the islands have a long history. The standing stones at Callanish - the second largest stone circle in Britain - are over 4000 years old, and were built for pagan ritual and to record the passing of the seasons so that crops could be sown and harvested. And there are individual standing stones, duns, brochs and old forts dotted all over the landscape.

inches of rain a year, and the winds blowing in from the Atlantic are invariably strong. The compensations, however, are enormous. The long summer evenings can be still and warm, and at midnight in the north of Lewis it is still possible to read a newspaper out of doors.

And the wildlife is astounding. Deer and otters abound, and the machair (the meadows bordering the sandy beaches) brim with flowers in summer. The seas are home to dolphins, basking sharks, whales and seals. In fact, some people claim that the waters surrounding the Western Isles are the most populated in Britain.

Of the main southern islands, Berneray, North Uist, Benbecula, South Uist and Eriskay are joined by causeways. North Uist connects to Harris by a ferry between An t-

Norse invasions began in earnest in the 8th century, and by about 850AD Norsemen ruled all of the Outer Hebrides. In 1266 the islands came into Scottish hands through the Treaty of Perth. However, this did not stop the Lords of the Isles from acting almost independently of the crown. This caused much friction between them and the Scottish kings, though the kings gradually imposed their authority. The islands eventually accepted the situation and became fully integrated into Scotland. Some historians claim, however, that the Norse language did not fully die out until the late 16th century.

🏛 historic building 🏛 museum and heritage 🏛 historic site 🌀 scenic attraction 🌿 flora and fauna

🏛 historic building 🏛 museum and heritage 🏛 historic site 🏞 scenic attraction 🌿 flora and fauna

Isle of Lewis & Harris

The main island is divided into two parts, Lewis and Harris, an ancient arrangement going back as far as the 13th century. Though joined geographically, they are usually considered to be two separate islands, and indeed the differences between them are marked. A natural boundary of mountains and high moorland runs between Loch Resort on the west and Loch Seaforth on the east, explaining the differences.

Lewis is the northern, and larger part, and up until the mid 1970s was within the county of Ross and Cromarty. Harris (and the smaller islands to the south) came under Inverness-shire. Now they form one administrative area, with the capital being Stornoway.

The underlying rock of Lewis is gneiss, one of the oldest in the world. It is largely impermeable, so does not absorb water. For this reason, the interior of the island is a large, empty peat moorland dotted with shallow lochs, while most of the settlements are on the coast. Harris is more mountainous, and has peaks reaching 2500 feet. It is also an area where the underlying rocks break through to the surface like bones, giving an essentially bleak, but nevertheless attractive, landscape. It in turn is divided into two parts, North and South Harris, with the narrow isthmus between West Loch Tarbert and East Loch Tarbert being the boundary.

Various attempts have been made over the years to encourage industry, most notably when Lord Leverhulme bought both Lewis and Harris in 1918 and tried to promote fishing. Today, the islands rely on fishing, crofting and tourism, with the weaving of Harris Tweed being an important industry on

BORGH POTTERY

Fivepenny House, Borgh, Isle of Lewis HS2 0RX
Tel: 01851 850345
e-mail: borghpottery@yahoo.co.uk
website: www.borghpottery.com

Owned and run by Alex and Sue Blair, **Borgh Pottery** was established in 1974 as Stornoway Pottery. The workshop and showroom moved to their present premises in Borve in 1978 and later became known as Borgh Pottery. Alex and Sue use a selection of their own rich and muted glazes which have a depth and quality only to be found in high-fired stoneware. For a small pottery, there is a wide range of glaze colour and finish, from gloss to matt. Their pots are all hand-thrown or hand-built using traditional techniques. This method of working allows flexibility and scope in design; it is therefore possible for Alex and Sue to accept commissions for a variety of work in stoneware or porcelain. The stoneware is ovenproof and also safe in the dishwasher. The attractive showroom at Borgh is the sole outlet for the pottery which is sold alongside other quality gifts.

An additional attraction here is the Borgh Pottery Garden which was started in 1995 and has now created a sheltered environment for birds and other wildlife. A stroll around the garden will reveal a surprising variety of plants, shrubs and interesting finds from beachcombing on the nearby Atlantic shore.

📖 stories and anecdotes 🦆 famous people 🎨 art and craft 🎭 entertainment and sport 🚶 walks

Lewis and Harris. Weaving is a cottage industry, with the weavers working at home or in sheds at the back of the house. Some will welcome you into their weaving rooms and explain the processes involved in turning wool into fine cloth.

Stornoway

🏛	Church of St Columba		
🏛	St Peter's Episcopal Church	🏛	Free Church
🏛	Museum nan Eilean	🐾	An Lanntair Arts Centre
🏛	Stornoway War Memorial	🏛	Lewis Loom Centre
🏛	St Columba's Church		

With a population of about 6000, Stornoway (from the Old Norse stjorna, meaning anchor bay) is the only town of any size in the Western Isles. It is the administrative, educational and shopping centre, and is a surprisingly cosmopolitan place, with a sizable Asian population.

The town has a fine natural harbour and an airport. On Lewis Street is **The Parish Church of St Columba**, dating from 1794, and in **St Peter's Episcopal Church** (1839) is David Livingstone's Bible and an old font from a chapel on the Flannan Isles, about 33 miles west of Lewis in the Atlantic. Its bell, which was made in 1631, was once the town bell that summoned the people to important meetings. The Gothic-style **Free Church** in Kenneth Street has the distinction of being the best attended church in all of Britain, with the Sunday evening congregation regularly exceeding 1500.

Lews Castle, now a college surrounded by public gardens, was built in the 1840s and 50s by James Matheson, a businessman who earned a fortune in the Far East trading in tea and opium. In 1843, he bought Lewis, and

began a series of improvements in what was then an isolated and inward-looking island. He built new roads, improved the housing and brought running water and gas to the town.

One of his pet projects was a plant to extract oil from the peat that blanketed the island, and in 1861 the Lewis Chemical Works began production. But problems beset the plant, and it actually blew up, putting the citizens of Stornoway into a state of fear and alarm. The venture finally folded in 1874.

The **Museum nan Eilean** in Francis Street, was opened in 1984 by the then local authority. It has artefacts and exhibits highlighting the history and archaeology of both the island of Lewis and Stornoway itself, and makes a good starting point if you want to explore the area. The **An Lanntair Arts Centre** sits across from the ferry terminal, and has contemporary and traditional exhibitions, as well as varied programmes of music and drama highlighting the Gaelic culture.

One of Stornoway's most famous sons was the 18th-century explorer and fur trader Sir Alexander Mackenzie, who gave his name to the Mackenzie River in Canada. In Francis Street, on the site of his house, is Martins Memorial, built in 1885. More than 1150 men of Lewis died in the two world wars, and the **Stornoway War Memorial** must be the most imposing in Britain. It stands on the 300-feet-high Cnoc nan Uan, and itself rises to a height of 85 feet.

The Western Isles are synonymous with Harris tweed, and at the **Lewis Loom Centre** on Bayhead you can find out about its history and how it is woven. To attain the 'orb' symbol of genuine Harris tweed, the cloth needs to be woven from virgin wool produced in Scotland, then spun, dyed and hand-woven in the Outer Hebrides.

West of Stornoway, on the Eye Peninsula, are the ruins of **St Columba's Church**, built in the 14th century on the site of a small monastic cell founded by St Catan in the 6th century. It is said that 19 MacLeod chiefs are buried here.

Around Stornoway

GREAT BERNERA
18 miles W of Stornoway off the B8059

🏠 Community Centre & Museum 🏛 Bostadh

The small island of Great Bernera measures only six miles long by three miles wide at its widest. It is connected to the mainland by the Great Bernera Bridge, opened in 1953, and the first bridge in the country made from pre-stressed concrete girders. The **Community Centre and Museum** has displays about the island, and also sells tea, coffee and cakes. On the lovely beach at **Bostadh**, an Iron Age village has been excavated, and a reconstruction of an Iron Age house built.

A cairn commemorates those men who

took part in the Bernera Riot of 1874, when crofters stood up for their right of tenure. Three of them eventually stood trial, though a later Act of Parliament gave them the rights they were fighting for.

CALLANISH
16 miles W of Stornoway on the A858

🏛 Callanish Stone Circle

Dating back at least 4000 years, the **Callanish Stone Circle** (Historic Scotland) is second only to Stonehenge in importance in Britain. It is more than just a circle of upright stones. Four great arms made up of monoliths radiate from it to the north, south, east and west, with the northern arm (which veers slightly to the east) having a double row of stones as if enclosing an approach way. And in the middle of the circle is the tallest stone of them all, measuring more than 15 feet in height.

It is a mysterious place, and has attracted many stories and myths over the years. One story tells of a race of giants who met to discuss how to defeat the new religion of Christianity that was spreading throughout the islands. This so incensed St Kieran, a Celtic monk and missionary, that he turned them all to stone. Another says that the stones were brought to Lewis by a great priest king who employed 'black men' to erect them. The men who died building the circle were buried within it.

Plus, there are the more modern, and unfortunately predictable, theories that the stones were erected by mysterious beings from outer space as a means of

Callanish Stone Circle

guiding their spacecraft, though why people with such technology should need a guidance system made of stones seems equally mysterious.

A visitors centre next to the stones tries to uncover the truth behind the stories, which may have something to do with primitive ritual and predicting the seasons for agricultural purposes.

CARLOWAY

17 miles W of Stornoway on the A858

- 🏛 Dun Carloway Broch
- 🏛 Gearrannan Blackhouse Village

The 2000-year-old **Dun Carloway Broch**, overlooking Loch Roag, is one of the best-preserved brochs in Scotland. It is more than 47 feet in diameter, and its walls are 22 feet high in places. Some of the galleries and internal stairways are still intact. The Doune Broch Centre has displays explaining what life must have been like within fortifications such as this.

One-and-a-quarter miles north of Carloway is the **Gearrannan Blackhouse Village**. It faces the Atlantic, and is a huddle of traditional thatched cottages dating from the 19th century. They have two distinctive features: there is no chimney and they housed animals as well as people. The animals made the house warmer and meant fewer buildings were needed. The smoke rising from the peat fire into the roof was also practical - it killed bugs and the smoke-enriched thatch made excellent fertiliser for the fields. These cottages were

lived in up until 1974 and were restored, complete with box beds, by the Garenin Trust between 1991 and 2001.

SHAWBOST

16 miles W of Stornoway on the A858

- 🏛 Sgoil Shiaboist Museum
- 🏛 Norse Mill & Kiln

Housed within a former church, the **Sgoil Shiaboist Museum** (Shawbost School Museum) has artefacts and objects collected by school pupils 30 years ago as part of a project that illustrates the way people used to live in Lewis. Nearby is the thatched **Norse Mill and Kiln**, a restored water mill of the type used in Lewis up until the mid 20th century.

The Shawbost Stone Circle, near the shores of the small Loch Raoinavat, only has two stones left standing. They are difficult to find, and good walking gear is recommended if you want to look for them.

BARVAS

13 miles NW of Stornoway on the A858

- 🏛 Arnol Blackhouse

At one time, most of the population of Lewis lived in small cottages known as blackhouses.

Dun Carloway Broch, Carloway

🏛 historic building   🏛 museum and heritage   🏛 historic site   🔆 scenic attraction   🌿 flora and fauna

Butt of Lewis

On the west coast of the island, at Arnol, is the **Arnol Blackhouse** (Historic Scotland), which shows what life was like in one of them. People and animals lived under the one roof, separated by thin walls, with the roof usually being of thatch and turf. They had tiny windows because of the seasonal gales and rain, and because glass was very expensive. The thick, dry stone walls (with a central core of clay and earth) kept the cottage cool in summer and warm in winter.

The Arnol house has been furnished in typical fashion, and has a clay floor. There is no fireplace, the fire being placed centrally, with no chimney. The houses got their name in the mid 19th century to distinguish them from the more modern white houses, which had mortar binding the stones. There is also an interpretation centre in a nearby cottage, which has a model of a typical blackhouse showing how they were made.

During archaeological excavations at Barvas, a 200-year-old Iron Age cemetery was uncovered. One of the finds was a beautiful iron and copper alloy bracelet, the first of its kind to be found anywhere in Scotland.

SHADER
16 miles NW of Stornoway on the A857

🏛 Steinacleit Stone Circle

The **Steinacleit Stone Circle and Standing Stones** sit on a low hill, and date from between 2000 and 3000BC. The stones are placed more in the shape of an oval than a circle, and archaeologists are unsure whether it is indeed a stone circle, a burial cairn or the remains of a settlement of some kind.

🎭 stories and anecdotes   🐦 famous people   🎨 art and craft   🎟 entertainment and sport   🚶 walks

BALLANTRUSHAL

15 miles NW of Stornoway on the B857

🏛 Clach an Trushal

The **Clach an Trushal** (Historic Scotland), at 18 feet high, is the tallest standing stone in Scotland, and is said to mark the site of an ancient battle. In the 19th century, several feet of peat were cut away from around its base, revealing the true height.

TARBERT

33 miles S of Stornoway on the A859

🏛 Amhuinnsuidhe Castle

The small village of Tarbert has a ferry connection with Uig on Skye. This is the starting point of South Harris, and an isthmus no more than half a mile wide separates East Loch Tarbert, which is an arm of the Minch, from West Loch Tarbert, which is an inlet of the Atlantic. In fact, Tairbeart in Gaelic means isthmus or place of portage, where boats were dragged across land from one stretch of water to another. **Amhuinnsuidhe Castle** was built in 1868 by the Earl of Dunsmore who owned Harris. It was the Earl's wife who introduced the weaving of Harris tweed to the island. The castle was subsequently owned by the Bulmer family, which founded the cider firm. It was here that J M Barrie wrote his play *Mary Rose*. It is now used as an upmarket conference centre.

SCALPAY

33 miles S of Stornoway

The tiny island of Scalpay, measuring three miles by two, lies off Harris's east coast. It is connected to the mainland by the £7m Scalpay Bridge, the biggest civil engineering project ever undertaken in the Western Isles. It

---

FIRSTFRUITS TEAROOM & RESTAURANT

Pier Road Cottage, Tarbert,
Isle of Harris HS3 3DG
Tel: 01859 502439

Firstfruits Tearoom & Rest is the perfect spot where you can enjoy the Harris hospitality. The tearoom has a friendly, family run atmosphere, and serves meals made from fresh local produce – all cooked to order. Choose from a variety of tea options including everything from a smaller tea with delicate sandwiches and scones to a hearty spread with nourishing savouries and delectable sweets. From May to August evening meals are available, though booking is essential, and you can also bring your own bottle at no charge.

The traditional white washed building was once a house built in the mid 1800's, inside the original wooden beams run wall to wall across the ceiling. The walls are adorned with stunning art from Ivor MacKay who has been displaying his art work here for years. Ivor is inspired by the changing moods and rugged expanse of the Island in all its seasons. The light in the Hebrides is unique and this is reflected in his work.

🏛 historic building   🏛 museum and heritage   🏛 historic site   ⌖ scenic attraction   🌿 flora and fauna

was opened in 1998 by Tony Blair, the first serving prime minister ever to visit the Western Isles. The visit is also remembered because of the biting criticism he received from one of the island's more militant inhabitants - *culiciodes impunctatus*, more commonly known as the midge. The first official crossing of the bridge was made in December 1997, when the island's oldest inhabitant, 103-year-old Kirsty Morrison, was taken across it in a vintage car.

RODEL

48 miles S of Stornoway on the A859

🏛 St Clement's Church

Rodel sits near the southern tip of Harris, and is famous for **St Clement's Church**, burial place of the MacLeods. It was built in 1500 by Alasdair Crotach (Hunchback) McLeod, who

lived in the church's tower from 1540 to his death in 1547. He is still within the church, in a magnificent tomb that shows carvings of his home at Dunvegan on Skye. By 1784, the church was in ruins, but in that year Alexander MacLeod of Berneray, a captain with the East India Company, restored it.

Other Western Isles

NORTH UIST

59 miles SW of Stornoway

🖈 Taigh Chearsabhagh   🏛 Barpa Langais

🏛 Pubull Phinn Stone Circle   🏛 Battle of Carinish

🦆 Balranald Nature Reserve

Like most of the Western Isles, North Uist is low lying, with more water than land making

ARDMAREE STORES & LOBSTER POT TEAROOM

5a Borve, Berneray, North Uist HS6 5BJ
Tel: 01876 540288
e-mail: ardmaree@yahoo.co.uk

Ardmaree Stores & Lobster Pot Tearoom share the same building in a wonderful location on Berneray Island, just 700 yards from Berneray ferry terminal and the causeway.

The Lobster Pot tearoom is a light and airy space, with the tables overlooking the sea to Harris, it is a great stopping off point before heading down to the beach or on your way back up from the beach. Subtle touches of the seashore create a clean, crisp environment where you can enjoy a relaxing meal or snack. The tearoom serves light snacks including soup, sandwiches, toasties, melts and cakes. Breakfast is available in the mornings, with sausage, egg and bacon rolls and the mighty fry-up on the menu. Local artwork is often on display in the tearoom, and is available for purchase.

Ardmaree Stores is a well stocked shop, providing grocery provisions, wines, spirits and beers. Deliveries of milk, bread, cakes and other fresh produce arrive several times a week. Local smoked salmon, other fish, meats and cheeses are available. The freezer and fridge sections add to the large range of food produce. The stores also stock ladies and gents clothes as well as outdoor wear and, in addition, there is also a DIY supplies section. For long-term visitors, newspapers can be ordered through the shop.

📖 stories and anecdotes   🦜 famous people   🖈 art and craft   ✐ entertainment and sport   𝕜 walks

up its total area of 74,884 acres. Loch Scadavay is the biggest of the lochs, and though it only has an area of eight square miles, it has a shoreline measuring 51 miles in length. It was given to the MacDonalds of Sleat in 1495 by James IV. They sold it in 1855, having cleared many of the tenants to make way for sheep. The highest point on the island, at 1127 feet, is Eaval, near the southeast corner. The island has a ferry service to An t-Obbe in Harris from Berneray, and one to Skye from Lochmaddy, the island's capital where most of the hotels and B&Bs are to be found. **Taigh Chearsabhagh**, a museum and arts centre is housed in an old inn dating from the early 18th century. Near the village is **Barpa Langais**, a Neolithic burial cairn with its burial chamber almost complete. Half a mile south east of it is the **Pubull Phinn Stone Circle**.

The stark ruins of Teampull na Trionaid (Trinity Temple) stand on the southwest shore. This was once a great place of learning in the Western Isles and some people claim that it was Scotland's first university, with scholars and students making their way here from all over the country, one being Duns Scotus (see also Duns).

It was founded in the early 13th century by one Beathag, a prioress from the priory on Iona and daughter of Somerled, Lord of the Isles. By the end of the 15th century, however, its influence began to wane, and during the Reformation it was sacked. Valuable books, manuscripts and works of art were tossed into the sea, and so much of the island's

heritage was lost. The other building on the site is Teampull MacBhiocair, (MacVicar's Temple), where the teachers were buried.

It was in this area, in 1601, that the **Battle of Carinish** took place, the last battle on British soil not to have involved firearms. A troop of MacLeods from Harris was raiding the island and took shelter in the Trinity Temple buildings when attacked by the MacDonalds. The MacDonalds ignored the status of the temple, and slaughtered every MacLeod clansman except two, who escaped.

On the island's west coast, off the A865, is the RSPB's **Balranald Nature Reserve**, where you can see waders and seabirds in various habitats.

BENBECULA
80 miles SW of Stornoway

🏛 Nunton Chapel 🏛 Borve Castle 🏛 Lionacleit

Benbecula is Beinn bheag a' bh-faodhla in Gaelic, meaning mountain of the fords. It is sandwiched between North and South Uist, with a landscape that is low and flat and dotted with shallow lochans, though Rueval, its highest peak, soars to all of 403 feet. The island marks the boundary between the

Borve Castle, Benecula

BRIDGEND COTTAGE

9 Torlum, Benbecula, Western Isles H57 5PP
Tel/Fax: 01870 603296
e-mail: amacdo5131@btinternet

Offering quality 3-star self-catering accommodation, **Bridgend Cottage** is an ideal for bird watching, walking and cycling, as well as for exploring the islands of North and South Uist. Set in a peaceful location, the cottage has 3 bedrooms, (a double, a twin and one with bunk beds), a comfortable lounge, bathroom with shower, toilet with cloakroom, and a kitchen/dining area. Outside, there's a small garden and a storage shed. The beach is just half a mile away; a local community school with swimming and other facilities is ¾ of a mile; and shops about 2½ miles.

Protestant islands to the north and the Roman Catholic islands to the south. There is no ferry terminal on the island, as it is connected to South Uist and North Uist by causeways.

The main settlement is Balivanich, or Baile na Mhanaich, meaning Monk's Town. It stands on the west coast and beside it is a small airstrip. The scant ruins of Teampall Chaluim Cille, founded by St Torranan, lie close to the village.

To the south of the village, on the B892, are the ruins of **Nunton Chapel**, supposed to have been a nunnery built in the 14th century. It was Lady Clanranald from nearby Nunton House (built from the stones of Nunton Chapel) who gave Charles Edward Stuart his disguise as a serving girl when he escaped from Benbecula to Skye in 1746.

Borve Castle, about three miles south of Balivanich, was owned by Ranald, son of John of Islay, in the 14th century. The ruins show a typical tower house of the period. Within the school at **Lionacleit**, three miles south of Balivanich, is a small museum.

SOUTH UIST

87 miles SW of Stornoway

- Our Lady of the Isles
- Loch Druidibeag Nature Reserve
- Flora MacDonald
- Kildonan Museum
- Ormiclate Castle
- SS Politician

Running down the east side of South Uist is a range of low mountains, with Beinn Mhor being the highest at 2034 feet. The west side of the island is gentler, with fine white sandy beaches. Lochboisdale, in the southeast corner, is the largest village on the island, and has a ferry connection to Mallaig, Oban and Castlebay on Barra.

The island is one of the few places in Scotland never to have fully embraced the Reformation, and is predominantly Roman Catholic. To the northwest of the island, at Rueval, is the famous statute of **Our Lady of the Isles**, overlooking Loch Bee. It was sculpted by Hew Lorimer of Edinburgh and erected in 1957. It stands 30 feet high. At the **Loch Druidibeag Nature Reserve**, which is close by, many birds such as greylag geese and

THE ORASAY INN

Lochcarnan, Isle of South Uist HS8 5PD
Tel: 01870 610298 Fax: 01870 610267
e-mail: orasayinn@btinternet.com
website: www.orasayinn.co.uk

Owned and personally managed by Isobel and Alan Graham, the **Orasay Inn** is one of the best and friendliest small hotels on the beautiful island of South Uist. It is a modern building that blends beautifully into the surrounding landscape and offers the very best in Scottish hospitality. Isobel and Alan are committed to maintaining high standards at surprisingly keen prices which means that the hotel is also one of the most popular.

There are 9 rooms available, all fully en suite and all equipped with colour TV, telephone, hair dryer, central heating and hospitality tray. The beds are extremely comfortable and the furnishings and decoration are of a high standard. Deluxe rooms have sofas and patio doors to a decked area where guests can relax on those long, lazy evenings for which the Western Isles are justly famous.

However, it's the food that makes the Orasay Inn so special. Isobel is a "Natural Cooking of Scotland" trainer and was even one of the team picked to prepare the gala dinner for the grand opening of Scotland's new parliament in 1999. Her cooking philosophy is to always use fresh, local produce and to keep the dishes simple while still displaying imagination and flair. In this she has succeeded admirably and the inn now has a reputation extending far beyond the Western Isles for its fine cuisine. A quote from the *Sunday Times* travel section reads: "Finally, don't forget to eat some seafood. The scallops in particular are enormous and one of the best ways to enjoy them is as part of a seafood platter at the Orasay Inn on

South Uist. Clean, functional and home to one of the best chefs in the Islands." Isobel's menu includes dishes based on locally caught seafood, dishes such as seared Isle of Uist scallops, baked fillet of Orasay halibut, and a gratin of seafood that includes local prawns, cockles, mussels and crab. The menu also offers chicken wrapped haggis, Hebridean venison, local lamb chops, duck and prime Scotch beef. Meals are served in the spacious dining room which commands superb views of sea and mountain. There is also a daily changing specials board where you might find such delightful surprises as deep-fried squid or red Thai curry. Co-chef Uilleam is also a qualified baker and produces wonderful fresh bread, scones and a selection of desserts.

AM POLITICIAN

3 Baile, Eriskay, Western Isles H58 5JT
Tel/Fax: 01878 720246 e-mail: stephenvc84@hotmail.com

Located on the beautiful island of Eriskay, **Am Politician** is named after the *SS Politician*, a freighter which ran aground off the island during World War II. Its cargo consisted of 15,000 bottles of whisky and the incident inspired the film *Whisky Galore*. Some of those bottles and other artefacts from the ship are on display in the bar of Am Politician which is run by Stephen Campbell, a local lad. He is also the chef and his menu offers delicious dishes of fresh local seafood, steak pies and snacks which can be enjoyed in the conservatory along with the stunning views.

mute swans, can be observed.

It was in South Uist, near Milton on Loch Kildonan, that **Flora MacDonald** was born in 1722. Her house is now completely in ruins, though the foundations can still be seen. She was no simple Gaelic lass, but the daughter of a prosperous landowning farmer who died when she was young. Her mother then married Hugh MacDonald, a member of the great MacDonald of Sleat family. She was brought up in Skye and went to school in Sleat and Edinburgh.

Kildonan Museum, north of Lochboisdale on the A865, has displays and exhibits on local history, as well as a tearoom and shop. The basis of the museum is a collection of artefacts gathered by the island priest, Father John Morrison, in the 1950s and 60s. Further north along the A865 are the ruins of **Ormiclate Castle**, built between 1701 and 1708 as a sumptuous residence for the chief of Clanranald. Alas, the chief's stay there was short lived, as it burnt down in 1715 after a rowdy Jacobite party.

Off the south coast of South Uist is the small island of Eriskay (from the Norse for Eric's Island), which is joined to South Uist by a causeway opened in 2002 and costing £9.8m. It is noted for one of the most beautiful of

Gaelic songs, the *Eriskay Love Lilt*. It was here, on July 23 1745, that Charles Edward Stuart first set foot on Scottish soil, when he stepped off a French ship to reclaim the British throne for the Stuarts. The beach where he landed is now called Prince's Beach, and legend says that his first action was to plant the sea convolvulus, which now thrives here.

It was in February 1941 that another event took place that was to make Eriskay famous. The *SS Politician* was heading towards the United States from Liverpool with a cargo of 260,000 bottles of whisky when it was wrecked off Calvey Island the Sound of Eriskay. Legend has it that as soon as the seamen were removed from the ship to safety, work began on rescuing the cargo. Eventually Customs and Excise men appeared on the island, but by this time the bottles had been spirited away into peat bogs and other hidey-holes. Only 19 people were charged with illegal possession.

Sir Compton Mackenzie used the incident as the basis for his novel *Whisky Galore*, made into a film in 1948. The wreckage can still sometimes be seen at exceptionally low tide. In the late 1980s an attempt was made to get at the rest of the cargo, but this proved unsuccessful.

The highest point on the island is Ben Scrien, at 609 feet. It is an easy climb and gives magnificent views. The island's native pony, the grey and black Eriskay pony, was at one time used to carry seaweed and peat on panniers slung across their back. In the 1950s, they nearly died out, but now are on the increase again. They are the last surviving examples of the once common Hebridean ponies that were popular all over the islands.

BARRA
105 miles S of Stornoway

🏛 Kisimul Castle 🎬 Clan Macneil

🏛 Cille-bharraidh ✒ Sir Compton Mackenzie

⚜ Our Lady of the Sea

Barra (Barr's Island) is the southernmost of the Western Isles, separated from South Uist by the Sound of Barra. To the south, is a string of tiny islands, including Sanday, Rosinish, Mingulay and Berneray.

The island's airstrip is to the north of the island, as is the fine sandy beach at Cockle Bay, a name richly deserved, as cockles are still collected there today. The main settlement is to the south at Castlebay, the terminal for the Oban ferry.

On an island in the bay itself is **Kisimul Castle** (Historic Scotland), the largest fortification in the Western Isles. Its name means the place of taxes, and it was the home of the Macneils of Barra, chiefs of Clan Macneil, who were granted the island in the 15th century, first by the Lord of the Isles and then by James VI. Others say, however, that the Macneils have been associated with the island since at least the 11th century.

The castle was originally built in about 1030, though the present building dates from the 15th century. The island on which it is built has its own fresh water wells, and this, coupled with its position, makes it almost impregnable. A story is told of how the castle was once being besieged by the Vikings, who wanted to starve it into submission. However, they soon gave up when they saw the castle guards hang bloody sides of beef from the ramparts. It was, of course, a ruse. What had been hung from the ramparts were cow hides used to make leather, smeared with dog's blood.

Isle of Barra

In 1838, the island was sold to Gordon of Cluny, who proceeded to remove the islanders from the land and ship them off to the New World. In 1937, the island was bought back by the 45th Chief of Clan Macneil, an American called Robert Lister Macneil. The 15th-century castle

Sunset over Barra

would send a servant up to the ramparts of Kisimul Castle and announce to the world: 'as the Macneil has dined, the other kings and princes of the world may now dine also.'

The ruined **Cille-bharraidh** (Church of St Barr) is located at the north end of the island, and was the burial place of the Macneils. Also buried here is **Sir Compton Mackenzie**, who wrote

had been burnt down in the late 1700s, and he set about restoring it.

The old chiefs of **Clan Macneil** had the reputation of being haughty and proud. When one Macneil Chief had finished his dinner, he

Whisky Galore (see also Eriskay). The island is predominantly Catholic, and at Heaval, a mile north east of Castlebay, is a marble statue of the Madonna and Child, called **Our Lady of the Sea**.

LOCATOR MAP

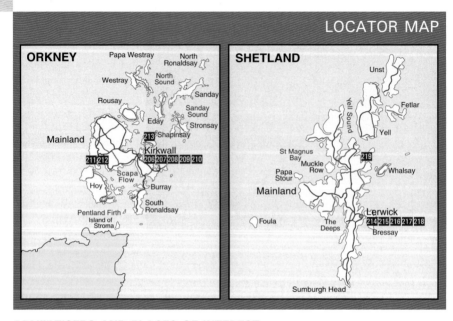

ADVERTISERS AND PLACES OF INTEREST

🏛 historic building 🏚 museum and heritage 🏛 historic site 🏞 scenic attraction 🌿 flora and fauna

14 | Orkney & Shetland

In 1469, James III married Margaret, the young daughter of Christian I of Denmark and Norway. Her father pledged Orkney and Shetland to the Scottish crown until such time as the dowry was settled in full. As he was crippled with debts, the dowry was never paid. So, in 1472, the islands became part of Scotland, creating the kingdom of Scotland as we know it today.

The Norse influences are still strong. Gaelic was never spoken here, and the place names (and many family names) all have Norse derivations. Both sets of islands are nearer Oslo than they are London, and there have even been occasional calls for the islands to be independent of Scotland.

The Brough Ness on South Ronaldsay in Orkney is no more than eight miles from the Scottish mainland, while the Shetland Islands sit much further out to sea, with the distance between Sumburgh Head and the mainland being more than 100 miles. Few people realise the distances involved, as maps of the British Isles invariably put the Shetlands in a convenient box off Scotland's northeast coast. However, fast ferries and air services put the islands within easy reach of the mainland.

In the distant past, they were at a major communications crossroads, and gained an importance that far outweighed their size.

They were on the main route from Scandinavia to Scotland, England, Ireland and the Isle of Man, and seafarers invariably stopped off there, some eventually settling. They are rich in historical sites and remains (far too many to mention them all in this guide), which show a continued occupation for thousands of years. Indeed, there are about 120 confirmed broch sites in the Shetland Islands alone. And because the landscape has never been intensely farmed or cultivated, many of these sites have remained relatively undisturbed.

The main difference between the two archipelagos can be summed up in the old saying that an Orcadian (an inhabitant of Orkney) is a crofter with a fishing boat, whereas a Shetlander is a fisherman with a croft. Orkney is therefore the more fertile of the two, though this is relative, as the landscape is nothing like the Scottish mainland farming areas, and trees are the exception rather than the rule. One thing has brought prosperity to the islands, however, and that is North Sea oil. It has transformed their economies, but at the same time has remained remarkably unobtrusive, apart from places like Sullom Voe in Shetland, the largest oil terminal and port in Europe.

DONALDSONS OF ORKNEY

38 Albert Street, Kirkwall, Orkney KW15 1HQ
Tel: -1856 872641   Fax: 01856 872995
e-mail: erikdonaldson@btconnect.com
website: www.donaldsonsoforkney.co.uk

For three generations and for more than 50 years,
Donaldsons of Orkney have been pushing the boundaries of
innovation in the meat trade with many exciting new
products, without losing sight of the traditional flavours and
recipes that founded the business. Previously known as
George Donaldson & Sons, the firm was established in 1955
by George Donaldson, the grandfather of the present
partners, Ewan and Erik.

As well as supplying traditional butcher products, they
specialise in their own cured and smoked bacon, sausages
and puddings, Orkney Smoked Beef and Smoked Hams
(Parma style). Their secret family recipe for Haggis has been
winning awards since 1983. In the 2005 Excellence in Meat
Awards, Donaldsons received the Diamond award for their Smoked Beef and in 2001 were
awarded the cup for Speciality Sausage in Scotland at the EmTec awards.

At Donaldsons they feel that by concentrating on quality and restricting themselves, they can
devote more time into getting them "just right" for customers who know a good product when
they taste it.

HILDEVAL B&B

Easthill, Kirkwall, Orkney KW15 1LY
Tel: 01856 878840
e-mail: enquiries@hildeval-orkney.co.uk
www.hildeval-orkney.co.uk

Only a short walk from Kirkwall town centre and
Orkney College,
Hildeval Bed & Breakfast occupies an elevated
position with stunning views overlooking Kirkwall
Bay towards Shapinsay and the North Isles. For owners Gerry and Shirley McGuinness, the
satisfaction of their guests is a top priority and they strive to ensure that happy memories of
Hildeval and Orkney stay with you for years to come.

All of the rooms at Hildeval have been tastefully decorated and offer a high standard of
comfort. Each of the rooms is provided with all the facilities you will need for a comfortable and
relaxing stay. These include en suite facilities; a flat screen Freeview television with inbuilt DVD
player; a selection of DVDs; wireless internet access via laptop; tea & coffee making facilities;
underfloor heating; hair dryer; ironing board and steam iron.

In the morning, you'll find a choice of fresh fruit, cereals and fruit juices, followed by a
traditional full Orkney breakfast based on fresh local produce wherever possible. For those off
exploring for the day, Gerry and Shirley can provide a packed lunch and they are happy to fill
thermos flasks or drinks bottles with a choice of tea, coffee or soft drinks. The satisfaction of their
guests is top priority and they strive to ensure that happy memories of Hildeval and Orkney stay
with their guests for years to come.

Kirkwall

🏛 St Magnus Cathedral 🦅 St Magnus

🏛 Bishop's Palace 🏛 Earl's Palace

🏛 Orkney Museum 🏛 Orkney Wireless Museum

The Orkney archipelago consists of about 70 islands, only 19 of which are inhabited. The largest island is Mainland, where the islands' capital, Kirkwall, is located. It is a small city as well as a royal burgh, as it has its own medieval cathedral, the most northerly in Britain and the most complete in Scotland.

Kirkwall has a population of about 4800, and was granted its charter as a royal burgh in 1486. It sits almost in the centre of Mainland, and divides the island into East Mainland and West Mainland. It is a lively, busy place of old stone buildings and streets paved with flagstones, with a shopping centre that serves all of the islands. The old name for the town was Kirkjuvagr, meaning the church inlet, that church not being the cathedral, but the Church of St Olaf. All that is left of the early medieval building is a doorway in St Olaf's Wynd.

St Magnus Cathedral was founded in 1137 by Saint Magnus's nephew, Rognvald Kolsson (who was later canonised), though the cathedral as you see it today dates from between the 12th and 16th centuries. It is an impressive structure of red sandstone and towers above the town. **St Magnus** was the son of Erlend, one of two earls who ruled Orkney. The King of Norway deposed the earls and appointed his own son Sigurd as Overlord. The king and his son then set out on a raiding party for Wales, taking Magnus with them. However, Magnus refused to take part in the usual rape and pillage, deciding

🎭 stories and anecdotes 🦅 famous people 🎨 art and craft 🎵 entertainment and sport 🚶 walks

LYNNFIELD HOTEL & RESTAURANT

Holm Road, St Ola, Kirkwall, Orkney KW15 1SU
Tel: 01856 872505
Fax: 01857 870038
e-mail: office@lynnfield.co.uk
website: www.lynnfield hotel.co.uk

At the **Lynnfield Hotel & Restaurant** they believe they can offer the ideal means of capturing the essence of Orkney. The hotel's quality and informality combine with Orkney's scenery, archaeology, bracing air and hospitality to create a magic that is hard to escape. Once you have visited, you may well join the thousands who catch the 'Orkney bug' and return year on year.

In the Lynnfield's restaurant diners can enjoy 4-star cuisine with dishes ased on locally sourced ingredients wherever possible. Fish comes from local boats, the beef and lamb from Orkney farms. Local vegetables are used when in season. The restaurant boasts Orkney's leading wine list with more than 70 bins and a 'Cellar Selection' that features some very special wines. The bar also stocks 60 malt whiskies, including 20 variants from neighbouring Highland Park.

The quality accommodation at Lynnfield comprises two suites, two large de luxe rooms, three superior doubles and two twin rooms. Another suite, Rammigeo, is on the ground floor, has twin beds and facilities for the less able-bodied. All rooms are equipped with a 37" television with Sky, free wi-fi, telephone and en suite bath and shower.

BELLAVISTA GUEST HOUSE

Carness Road, St Ola, Kirkwall, Orkney KW15 1UE
Tel: 01856 872306
e-mail: info@bellavistaorkney.co.uk
website: www.bellavistaorkney.co.uk

Run by mother and daughter team of Patsy and Angela Walls, **Bellavista** is a 3-star purpose-built guest house in a quiet, peaceful area of Kirkwall. It stands close to the shore and is a 15-20 minute shore-hugging walk in to the town centre. The living room enjoys excellent views of boats arriving and departing from Kirkwall Harbour and Hatston Pier. The room is equipped with TV/freeview, DVD player, coffee/tea making facilities, fridge and a selection of Orkeny books and information leaflets. Free internet access is available through using the guest computer or connecting up to wireless broadband throughout the building.

Patsy and Angela make sure that their guests have the best possible start each day with a choice of breakfast, including porridge, Orkney cheese and oatcakes, fresh fruit and home-made rhubarb jam and marmalade. Breakfast is served from 7am to 9am but if you are catching an early boat or plane, an light breakfast is available. For anyone requiring a special diet please ask when booking.

The accommodation at Bellavista comprises of a single, 2 twins, 3 doubles and a family room, all with en suite facilities and a single with private showerroom.

Other amenities include a large garden and pond, a large private off street car park and secure outbuildings for storage of bicycles and other outdoor equipment.

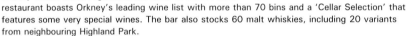

🏛 historic building 🏛 museum and heritage 🏚 historic site 🗺 scenic attraction �_____ flora and fauna

Stone Age Village, Orkney

when it was built for Bishop William the Old. The Round Tower (called the Moosie Too by locals), however, was built by Bishop Reid between 1541 and 1548. It was within the palace, in 1263, that King Haakon IV of Norway died, having just been defeated at the Battle of Largs (see also Largs). He was buried in Kirkwall Cathedral, but his body was later taken back to Bergen in Norway.

The notorious Patrick Stewart, Earl of Orkney and grandson of James V, built the adjacent **Earl's Palace** (Historic Scotland) between 1600 and 1607. At that time it was considered the finest private residence in the country and the ruins are mightily impressive. The Stewart earls were hated in the islands because they exploited the people and bled them dry. Patrick himself was arrested by James VI and executed for treason in 1615.

Within Tankerness House, built in 1574, is the **Orkney Museum**, which contains artefacts and exhibits about the island. The wooden box that contained St Magnus's bones, discovered within a pillar in the cathedral, is one of the exhibits. Tankerness House originally belonged to the cathedral, and was the home of Gilbert Foultie, the last archdeacon. It later became the property of the Baikie family, one of the islands' principal landowners. The Baikie Drawing room within the museum shows what a typical late 18th- and early 19th-century drawing room would

instead to sing psalms. The Norwegian king was displeased, and young Magnus had to flee.

After the king's death, Magnus returned to Orkney, and in 1117 arranged to meet with Haakon, the new ruler of the islands, to claim his inheritance. However, Haakon had him murdered by an axe blow to the skull. At first, it is said that Magnus was buried in a small church on Birsay, but 20 years later his remains were taken to St Olaf's Church and finally to the new cathedral when it was consecrated. Some people regarded this story as more of a legend than historical fact, but in 1919, during some restoration work, a casket containing human bones was found embedded high up in one of the cathedral's pillars. The skull had been split open with an axe. In the 18th century the remains of St Rognval were also discovered embedded in a pillar.

The ruined **Bishop's Palace** (Historic Scotland) dates mainly from the 12th century

have looked like. The **Orkney Wireless Museum** is at Kiln Corner, and has examples of wartime and domestic wireless sets used on the islands. It was founded by local man Jim MacDonald who had a lifetime's fascination with wireless and radio sets, and amassed a huge collection.

On a building in Castle Street is a plaque commemorating Kirkwall Castle, which was dismantled in 1615 and finally demolished in 1865. It had been built in the 14th century by Henry Sinclair, first Earl of Orkney. He had been given the title by Haakon of Norway in 1379, long before the islands became part of Scotland. His descendent William, the third earl, built Rosslyn Chapel in Midlothian, and his name has been linked to a pre-Columbus transatlantic crossing, the holy grail and the Knights Templar (see also Rosslyn).

Around Kirkwall

MINE HOWE
5 miles SE of Kirkwall on the A960

This deep, subterranean structure within a large mound was examined by the TV programme *Time Team* but they were unable to establish its real purpose. It was originally uncovered in 1946 and then reburied to preserve it. It consists of a chamber accessed by a stone-lined tunnel with steps. The latest thinking is that it dates from the Iron Age and had a religious significance.

LAMB HOLM
7 miles S of Kirkwall on the A961

🏯 Italian Chapel

After the sinking of the *Royal Oak* by a U-boat in 1939, a string of islands to the south of Mainland were joined by causeways called

the Churchill Barriers, to prevent submarines from slipping through again. On the 99-acre Lamb Holm, one of the islands, is the ornate **Italian Chapel**. It was built by Italian prisoners-of-war who had been captured in North Africa in 1942 and were set to work building the causeways. The chapel is remarkable considering its basis is two Nissen huts and various pieces of cast-off metal and wood. In 1960, some of the ex-POWs were invited to return to the island to restore it. Mass is still said here every day during the summer months.

KIRBUSTER
6 miles SW of Kirkwall on the A964

🏛 Kirbuster Museum

Kirbuster Museum is actually the last un-restored example of a traditional 'firehoose' in Northern Europe. Dating back to at least the 16th century, the house has a central hearth and a stone (neuk) bed, a unique artefact. Astonishingly, Kirbuster was occupied up until the 1960s. Outside, there's an 'implement shed' containing a collection of farming memorabilia, a lovely Victorian walled garden and a putting green.

MAES HOWE
8 miles W of Kirkwall off the A965

🏛 Maeshowe   🏛 Stenness Standing Stones

🏛 Watch Stone   🏛 Barnhouse Settlement

🏛 Ring of Brodgar

Maeshowe (Historic Scotland) is Britain's largest chambered cairn, and was excavated in 1861. In 1910 it was taken into state care, at which time the mound was 'rounded off' to give it the appearance we see today. When archaeologists reached the main chamber, they discovered that the Vikings had beaten them to it, as there was Norse graffiti on the walls. The name Maes Howe comes from the Old Norse and means great mound. It is a great, grassy hill, 36 feet high and 300 feet in circumference, and was built about 2700BC. A long, narrow passage leads into a central chamber with smaller side chambers, which are roofed and floored with massive slabs.

Also looked after by Historic Scotland are the four **Stenness Standing Stones**, the largest such stones in Orkney. Originally, it is thought, there were 12, and they formed a circle 104 feet in diameter. They date from about the same time as Maes Howe. The tallest stone is 16 feet tall. Not far away is an even taller stone, the **Watch Stone**, which is 18½ feet tall. To the north of the Stenness Stones, and near the shore of Harray Loch, is the **Barnhouse Settlement**, a neolithic village discovered in 1984. Agricultural activity over the years has destroyed much of it, though it is reckoned there were 15 dwellings on the site.

The **Ring of Brodgar**, also dating from about 2700BC, still has 27 of its original 67 stones. They are smaller than the Stenness Stones, and stand on a strip of land between two small lochs. Legend says that long ago a group of giants came to this spot during the night, and that one of their number started to play the fiddle. The giants began to dance in a circle, and so carried away were they that they never noticed the sun starting to rise. When the light struck them, they were turned to stone.

ORPHIR
9 miles W of Kirkwall off the A964

During early Norse rule, Orphir was one of the main Orcadian settlements. Orphir Church was built in the 11th or 12 century and dedicated to St Nicholas, some say by Haakon, who murdered St Magnus, possibly as an act of penance after a pilgrimage to Jerusalem. It was a circular church about 18 feet in diameter, with a small apse at its eastern end, and was the only such medieval church in Scotland. Nothing now remains apart from the apse and some of the east wall. An Interpretation Centre, next to the church, explains the ruins.

STROMNESS
15 miles W of Kirkwall on the A965

🏛 Stromness Museum 🎨 The Pier Arts Centre

⚓ Scapa Flow

When Sir Walter Scott visited Orkney in 1814, he complained that Stromness: 'cannot be traversed by a cart or even by a horse, for there are stairs up and down even in the principal street…'

Like Kirkwall, Stromness is basically one long winding road - simply known as the street. From this street, a great number of narrow lanes and closes branch off. This gives the town a convoluted character with steep narrow paths climbing the hillside on the north side of the street, while on the south, the houses and shops back onto the shore.

Orkney's second largest settlement, Stromness is also the home port of the vehicle ferry that plies between here and Scrabster in Caithness. Though it looks old and quaint, the town was founded in the 17th century and only received its burgh charter in 1817. The **Stromness Museum** in Alfred Street has displays on Scapa Flow, whaling, lighthouses and the Hudson's Bay Company, which had a base here and employed many Orcadians.

Housed in a complex of buildings that sit on one of the town's many piers, **The Pier**

QUERNSTONE

38 Victoria Street, Stromness, Orkney KW16 3AA
Tel/Fax: 01856 851010
e-mail: quernstoneknits@tiscali.co.uk
website: www.quernstone.co.uk

The **Quernstone** is situated in the centre of the quaint old town of Stromness, and sells an amazing range of quality gifts at affordable prices. It has been trading for over 20 years, and its windows are packed with great ideas, and you are sure to be impressed by the quality and price of the items on offer. This is the place to go if you're looking for gifts or souvenirs that are just that little bit different. Come in and browse around - there is absolutely no obligation to buy. If you are looking for locally crafted jewellery, for instance, then this is the place for you. There is also a wide range of yarns, handbags, toiletries, toys and stationery. You might prefer instead to look at the bright, well-designed soft furnishings on the upper floor, or the ceramics, glassware, lampshades and furniture. This is also the place to buy your cards, as it carries a huge stock. The shop is an Aladdin's cave of good design. You could almost spend a day here just admiring everything on offer.

On the other side of the street, is Quernstone's knitwear shop, another fascinating place that is full of colour and good design. Here the Quernstone's own knitwear designs are on show, specialising in hand-framed and hand-knitted garments in quality yarns. The range includes easy-to-wear shapes of universal appeal, from casual cropped jerseys to elegant long coats. Other knitwear brands are also stocked, including a selection of menswear, ensuring that you have a wide range to choose from. There is also a complimentary range of accessories, jewellery and gifts - in fact, something for everyone.

Arts Centre (see panel opposite) was established in 1979 to provide a showcase for an important collection of British fine art donated to 'be held in trust for Orkney' by the author, peace activist and philanthropist Margaret Gardiner (1904 - 2005). Alongside the permanent collection, the Centre curates a year-round programme of changing exhibitions and events.

Scapa Flow, between Hoy and Mainland, is one of the best natural harbours in the world. After World War I, the German fleet was brought to Scapa Flow while a decision was made about its future. However, the German officers decided the fleet's future themselves - they scuttled the ships. Most still lie at the bottom of the sea, a constant attraction for divers.

HOY

17 miles W of Kirkwall

🏞 Old Man of Hoy   🏛 Martello Tower

🏚 Dwarfie Stone

Hoy is Orkney's second largest island, and sits off the west coast of Mainland. The **Old Man of Hoy** is Great Britain's tallest and most famous sea stack. Made of sandstone, it is over 445 feet high and rises off the island's northwest coast, a constant challenge to climbers. The first successful climb was in 1966, when TV cameras were there to record it. At the southwest end of the island is a **Martello Tower**, erected between 1813 and 1815 to protect the island from the French.

The **Dwarfie Stone** is unique in the United Kingdom - a burial chamber dating

THE PIER ARTS CENTRE

28-30 Victoria Street, Stromness, Orkney KW16 3AA
Tel: 01856 850209 Fax: 01856 851462
e-mail: info@pierartscentre.com website: www.pierartscentre.com

The Pier Arts Centre in Stromness was established in 1979 to provide a home for an important collection of British fine art donated to 'be held in trust for Orkney' by the author, peace activist and philanthropist Margaret Gardiner (1904 – 2005). The permanent collection charts the development of modern art in Britain and includes key works by Barbara Hepworth, Ben Nicholson and Naum Gabo among others. The collection was one of ten in Scotland to gain Recognition as a Collection of National Significance in 2007. Alongside the permanent collection the Centre curates a year round programme of changing exhibitions and events for the education and enjoyment of the general public.

The Centre re-opened in July 2007 following a two year redevelopment of its buildings and facilities and is housed in a complex of buildings that sit on one of the many piers that characterise the historic town of Stromness. With the completion of the re-development full access to the centre's facilities has been achieved and the environmental plant and equipment is in place to provide the appropriate conditions to care for the Centre's valuable collection into the future. In addition, the Centre has a gift shop selling a wide range of art and design led products, local commissioned ranges and a selection of art related books. The original listed buildings and pier, that once housed the office and stores of the Hudson's Bay Company, have been sympathetically extended by Reiach & Hall Architects who have created a stunning new building at the harbours' edge. The quality of Reiach and Hall's work for the Centre was recognised with the Royal Incorporation of Architects in Scotland's Andrew Doolan Award for the Best building in Scotland 2007.

The Pier Arts Centre is open Monday to Saturday 10.30am -5.00pm. Admission is free. The Pier Arts Centre is a Registered Charity No SC 014815

---

from at least 3000BC cut into a great block of sandstone. Some people claim, however, that it was not a tomb, but an ancient dwelling. The most amazing thing about it is that it was hollowed out using nothing but horn tools, antlers and pieces of rock.

CLICK MILL
13 miles NW of Kirkwall on the B9057

🏠 Click Mill 🏛 Corrigall Farm Museum

Click Mill (Historic Scotland), with its turf covered roof, is the islands' last surviving example of a horizontal watermill, and got its name from the clicking sound it made

when turning. They were once common throughout Scandinavia.

At Harray, a couple of miles south of the mill, is the **Corrigall Farm Museum**, housed in a 19th-century farmhouse. Exhibits include a working barn with grain kiln and a loom.

SKARA BRAE
17 miles NW of Kirkwall on the B9056

🏠 Skaill House

In 1850, at the Bay of Skaill, a storm uncovered the remains of a village that was at least 5000 years old - older even than the pyramids. It is the oldest known prehistoric

The Old May of Hoy, Orkney

village in Europe and the remains are now looked after by Historic Scotland. They show that the people who built it from stone were sophisticated and ingenious, and that the houses were comfortable and well appointed, with beds, dressers and cupboards made of stone, as wood was hard to come by. Archaeological evidence tells us that it was built by neolithic people who farmed, hunted and fished. When it was built, it stood some distance from the sea but, due to erosion over the years, the sea is now on its doorstep.

Only 300 metres from the village is **Skaill House**, the finest mansion in Orkney. The main part of the house was originally built in 1620 for George Graham, Bishop of Orkney, though it has been extended over the years. It houses a fine collection of furniture, including Bishop Graham's bed, on which are carved the

words *GEO. GRAHAM ME FIERI FECIT* (George Graham caused me to be made).

When Skaill House was being built, 15 skeletons were uncovered to the south of the South Wing. In the 1930s, skeletons were also uncovered under the house itself. It is now thought that the house was built on the site of a Christian Pictish cemetery. It is no wonder that Skaill is said to be haunted.

BROUGH OF BIRSAY
21 miles NW of Kirkwall off the A966

🏛 Earl Stewart's Palace

📷 Kirbuster Farm Museum 🏛 Kitchener Memorial

This little island, which is connected to the mainland at low tide by a narrow causeway, has the remains of a Norse settlement and an early medieval chapel dedicated to St Peter (once the cathedral of the diocese of Orkney). After he was killed, St Magnus was possibly buried here until such time as his body could be taken to the newly-built St Magnus Cathedral in Kirkwall. When visiting the island, the times of tides must be taken into account. The tourism office at Kirkwall can advise.

The area on Mainland opposite the island is also called Birsay and here you can see the ruins of **Earl Stewart's Palace.** It was built about 1574 by Robert, Earl of Orkney, a cruel, unpopular man and father of Patrick, who was even more cruel and unpopular.

The **Kirbuster Farm Museum**, also on Mainland, occupies a 400-year-old building, which was lived in until 1961. The living rooms have been restored to show how they would have looked at that period, and the outbuildings contain interesting examples of farm implements used on Orkney over the years. There's also a Victorian garden.

Birsay to Marwick via Marwick Head

Distance: *2.8 miles (4.5 kilometres)*

Typical time: *120 mins*

Height gain: *100 metres*

Map: *Explorer 463*

Walk: *www.walkingworld.com ID:1528*

Contributor: *Colin and Joanne Simpson*

ACCESS INFORMATION:

The route as described starts from the right-angled bend on the B9056 where it overlooks Birsay Bay and finishes on the shores of Mar Wick - another bay to the south of Marwick Head. If you don't have the benefit of transport back to your start point, you can backtrack from the Kitchener Memorial and follow a path to the minor road, which can be followed back to the start.

ADDITIONAL INFORMATION:

The Kitchener Memorial, which stands on the highest cliffs was erected in memory of all those on board *HMS Hampshire* (including Lord Kitchener, minister for war), which sank off these shores in 1916.

FEATURES:

Sea, wildlife, birds, flowers, great views, moor.

DESCRIPTION:

This walk traverses the top of what are possibly the best sea cliffs on Orkney. There are excellent views north to Westray and south to Hoy and the more distant Scottish mainland - the peaks of Morven and Ben Loyal being particularly prominent. Of particular interest are the seabird colonies on the cliffs, which include puffins, guillemots and fulmars.

WALK DIRECTIONS:

1 | Start by following the track that heads straight on (approaching from the A967) between the field gate and a standing stone that forms the corner of a fence. This is the track heading due west from the corner, not the one heading north.

2 | After 300 metres and after an open area (sometimes used for parking), the track bends to the south and starts to follow the coast. From the bend in the track there are good views back over the bay to the Brough of Birsay.

3 | Continue parallel to the cliff edge and now rising gently, the path fairly indistinct at times.

4 | As you continue, the cliffs to your side become larger. After around a kilometre of gentle uphill walking, a path comes in from the left (this is the direct route to the headland from a car park) and the path becomes much more distinct, running between a fence and the cliff. There are excellent views back along the cliffs.

5 | When you reach the highest point, topped by the Kitchener Memorial, there are superb views south to the island of Hoy (with the famous Old Man of Hoy visible right of the cliffs) and beyond, to the Scottish mainland. A path continues past the memorial to rejoin the fence and then follows the fence south-westwards, before turning the headland and dropping downhill to the bay of Marwick.

6 | At the foot of the slope the path follows the water's edge to reach the road and the end of the walk. A sign facing the way back welcomes those walking in the opposite direction.

7 | As an alternative to the end to end walk (if transport cannot be arranged), you can turn back from the memorial and retrace your steps to a gate. Go through the gate and follow a path to a car park from where you can follow the road back to your start point - a total distance of 7km for the walk.

South of the island, at Marwick Head, is a squat tower - the **Kitchener Memorial**. It was erected in memory of Kitchener of Khartoum, who died when *HMS Hampshire*, on which he was travelling to Russia to discuss the progress of the war, struck a German mine near here in June 1916. Only 12 people survived the sinking of the ship.

ROUSAY
14 miles N of Kirkwall

🏚 Taversoe Tuick Chambered Cairn

🏚 Brock of Midhowe 🏛 St Magnus's Church

This island is sometimes known as the Egypt of the North, as it is crowded with archaeological sites. The **Taversoe Tuick Chambered Cairn** has two chambers, one above the other. The Blackhammer Cairn, the

Knowe of Yarso Cairn, and the Midhowe Cairn can also be seen here. The **Broch of Midhowe** has walls that still stand 13 feet high.

On Egilsay, a small island to the east, are the superb ruins of the 12th-century **St Magnus's Church**, with its round tower. It was on Egilsay in 1115 that Magnus was killed. A cairn marks the spot of his martyrdom.

WESTRAY
27 miles N of Kirkwall

🏛 Noltland Castle

The substantial ruins of **Noltland Castle** stand to the north of the island. It was built by Gilbert Balfour, who was Master of the Household to Mary Stuart and also Sheriff of Orkney. At Pierowall, the island's main settlement, are the ruins of the **Ladykirk**. To

---

ORKNEY STAINED GLASS

Monquhanny, Shapinsay, Orkney KW17 2DZ
Tel: 01856 711276
e-mail: enquiries@orkneystainedglass.com
website: www.orkneystainedglass.com

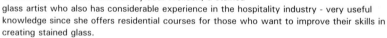

Orkney Stained Glass is sited within the ruins of a Congregational Kirk which has been refurbished to provide a modern workshop/gallery with stunning views to the north. The business is owned and run by Judi Wellden, a stained glass artist who also has considerable experience in the hospitality industry - very useful knowledge since she offers residential courses for those who want to improve their skills in creating stained glass.

Judi's own work combines traditional and modern glass techniques with contemporary design to produce a distinctive range of glass items. Her main interests are individual mosaic panels and special commissions. A programme of special exhibitions and events takes place throughout the year, as well as a series of 1 and 2-day courses. Those subscribing to the 2-day courses stay at Monquhanny, a traditional Kirk manse in a peaceful location, set within 2 acres of walled grounds and garden. The rooms are all en suite and equipped with TV, hair dryer, electric blankets and hospitality tray. Guests have the use of a cosy living room with an extensive library and music collection, and breakfasts are prepared from home-produced vegetables, eggs, herbs and Orkney produce. As one guest put it: "This must be the next best place to Narnia!"

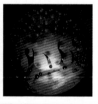

🏛 historic building 🏛 museum and heritage 🏚 historic site 🝰 scenic attraction 🌢 flora and fauna

the east of Westray is the smaller island of Papa Westray. It is connected to Westray by air, the flight (which lasts two minutes) being the shortest scheduled air flight in the world.

Lerwick

🖊 Up Helly Aa 🏛 Fort Charlotte

🏛 Shetland Museum ⚓ Arthur Anderson

Up until government reorganisation in the 1970s, Shetland was a county in its own right called Zetland, with the county buildings at Lerwick. Shetland has about 100 islands, with fewer than 20 being inhabited. As with Orkney its largest island is also called Mainland, and it is here that Lerwick is situated. It is the island's capital, and the most northerly town in Britain.

The name Lerwick comes from the Norse for muddy bay, and up until the 17th century that's all it was - a muddy bay surrounded by a handful of crude dwellings. The town was originally developed by the Dutch in the early 17th century to service their herring fleet, and from there gradually grew into a small town. It was granted its burgh charter in 1818 and has a population of about 7000. It is so far north that during June you could read a newspaper at midnight out of doors without any artificial light.

Every year, on the last Tuesday in January, the festival of **Up Helly Aa** is held. After being hauled through the streets of the town accompanied by men carrying torches and dressed as Vikings, a Viking longboat is set on fire. The ritual is thought to date back to pagan times, when the darkest days of winter were feared. It was thought that the light from celebrations of this kind attracted the light of the sun, which would then gradually return, lengthening the days. The introduction of a Viking ship, however, was a Victorian idea. Before that tar barrels were used.

Like Orkney, all the islands are rich in ancient remains. There are also many small interpretation centres and museums - too many for all of them to be mentioned in this guide.

The number of days in the year when the temperatures rise above 75 degrees are few in Shetland, but there are compensations, not least of which is the quality of light and the almost 24 hours of daylight at the height of summer. And there is less rain here than in Fort William or even North Devon.

Fort Charlotte, named after George III's wife, was built in the 1780s to protect the town from the Dutch, whom, the British government felt, had too much power in the

🎬 stories and anecdotes 🐦 famous people 🎨 art and craft ✒ entertainment and sport 🥾 walks

SHETLAND FUDGE COMPANY

96 Commercial Street, Lerwick,
Shetland ZE1 0EX
Tel/Fax: 01595 694004
e-mail: sales@shetlandfudge.com
website: www.shetlandfudge.com

The **Shetland Fudge Company** is a small family business, hand-making delicious fudge and truffles which were finalists in the Scottish Thistle Awards in 2005 and 2006, and winners of the Hospitality Assured Award in 2008. The company's creations are made in its own kitchens using the finest ingredients and local produce wherever possible. They are the only chocolatiers and fudgemakers in Shetland (and they believe in Scotland) who create by hand from their own additive-free recipes. They make in small 2-kilobatches, fresh every day.

The range of products is enormous. Amongst the tablets for example you will find a traditional Lemon Tablet with a zingy, zesty flavour; a winter-warming Lemon Ginger made with preserved stem ginger, pure lemon extract and Shetland Butter; and an Old Scatness Butter Tablet created especially for the archaeologists at the Scatness Dig. Then there are the alcoholic tablets: Rum 'n' Raisin; Irish Coffee Chocolate Truffle Fudge; Bailey's Truffle Fudge; Dooleys Liqueur Truffle Fudge and Morgans Spiced Rum and Orange. Other varieties include Mandarin Pecan Chocolate; Mint Chocolate; Raspberry Reel; and Trows Bogies which were created by the 12-year-old winner of a competition, Angie Reynolds.

The Company also offers a extensive selection of hampers, ranging from "Hair o da Dug", (a jute gift bag with 3 handmade luxury breakfast preserves), through "Thinkin o' Dee", (a willow shopping basket containing a Cotton Tea Towel, Walls Craft Bakery Oaties, Walls Craft Bakery Biscuits, Shetland Preserves, Puffin Poo and Scottish tablet), to the enormous "Blissins Blissins Blissins!" - a willow Hamper with 100% Wool Shetland Throw, two Unst Beers, one Shetland Fudge Company Iced Christmas Cake, three Preserves, two boxes of Tablet, two boxes of Fudge, three Walls bakery Oaties, three Walls Bakery Biscuits, one Reestit Mutton, one portion Shetland Smoked Mussels, and a Shetland tea towel. The hampers and all of the Company's other products are available by mail order within the UK. Orders are despatched as soon as humanly possibly, (often inhumanely possible, according to the chefs!) and on the day they are made so that your products are guaranteed to be as fresh as possible.

area due to its large herring fleet that was based here. The fort is built on a rock that dropped sheer to the shore and has a long seaward-facing side with emplacements for up to 12 guns. These looked out across Bressay Sound. The remaining four sides of the pentagon have well-preserved bastions at the corners.

Shetland Museum at Hays Dock gives an insight into the history of the islands and its people, and has some marvellous displays on archaeology. There is also an excellent photograph archive and occasional art exhibitions.

The wonderfully named Böd of Gremista is located north of the town, and was the birthplace in 1792 of **Arthur Anderson**, co-

Shetland Museum and Hays Dock

founder of the P&O line. He joined the Royal Navy, and subsequently fought in the Napoleonic wars. In 1833 he co-founded the Peninsular Steam Navigation Company, which, in 1937, became the Peninsular and Oriental

SHETLAND MUSEUM AND ARCHIVES & HAY'S DOCK CAFÉ RESTAURANT

Hay's Dock, Lerwick, Shetland, ZE1 0WP Tel: 01595 695057
e-mail: info@shetlandmuseumandarchives.org.uk/info@haysdock.co.uk
website: www.shetlandmuseumandarchives.org.uk/www.haysdock.co.uk

Every trip to Shetland should start with a visit to its Heritage Hub, the **Shetland Museum and Archives**, where you will discover Shetland's story from its geological beginnings to the present day and find out about the network of high quality heritage and cultural sites throughout the isles.

Set in a restored 19th century dock, this new building - opened in 2007 - offers a beautiful location, a wide range of facilities and a host of special events and exhibitions throughout the year. Within the building you will find two floors of displays, learning and research rooms, temporary exhibition gallery, auditorium, shop and a restored boatshed – where you can watch boats being built and restored using traditional techniques.

The displays contain a wealth of treasures, including boats suspended in mid air, world famous textiles, a model of Shetland's first known inhabitant and a trowie knowe – where mystical creatures live! The Archives house a wealth of documents from the 15th century to the present day. There is also a large collection of music and oral history material and access to a substantial photographic archive. Many people visit the Museum and Archives to eat in **Hay's Dock Café Restaurant**. Popular with both locals and visitors, this café restaurant offers superb views over Lerwick Harbour and showcases quality local produce throughout the year. Seals and other wildlife are often seen outside in Hay's Dock which you can watch while enjoying your meal. Through the day the café restaurant offers light snacks and lunches, whist in the evening there is fine dining in a relaxed atmosphere. If the weather is fine you can enjoy your meal out on the balcony. The Museum and Archives is open daily from 10am throughout the year, entry is free.

BÖD OF GREMISTA

Gremista, Lerwick, Shetland Tel: 01595 695057
e-mail: info@shetlandmuseumandarchives.org.uk
website: www.shetlandmuseumandarchives.org.uk

This 18th century fishing böd, located on the outskirts of Lerwick, was the birthplace of Arthur Anderson, co-founder of Peninsular and Oriental Stream Navigation Co. - well known today as P&O. There are displays which detail Anderson's life, including his business ventures, political career and generous local donations, as well as the history of the böd and the role it played in Shetland's booming fishing industry in the late 18th and 19th century. The Böd Of Gremista is open Wednesday to Sunday throughout the summer (May – September). Entry is free.

CROFTHOUSE MUSEUM

Boddam, Dunrossness, Shetland Tel: 01595 695057
e-mail: info@shetlandmuseumandarchives.org.uk
website: www.shetlandmuseumandarchives.org.uk

You can step back in time at the **Crofthouse Museum**. Located in a delightful setting, this typical thatched 19th century Crofthouse has been restored to how it would have looked in the 1870s. Smell the peat fire, discover the box beds and try to set the traditional Shetland mouse trap. The Crofthouse also has a lovely garden with a path which leads to a restored watermill. The Crofthouse Museum is open daily from 10am throughout the summer (May – September). Entry is free.

🏛 historic building 🏠 museum and heritage 🏛 historic site 🐾 scenic attraction 🌱 flora and fauna

SHETLAND LIGHTHOUSE HOLIDAYS

Shetland Amenity Trust, Garthspool, Lerwick, Shetland, ZE1 0NY
Tel: 01595 694688
e-mail: info@shetlandamenity.org website: www.lighthouse-holidays.com

Shetland Lighthouse Holidays offer high quality, affordable, self-catering accommodation at three of the islands' most spectacularly situated buildings, Sumburgh, Bressay and Eshaness lighthouses. Staying in the former lighthouse keepers' cottages you will discover breathtaking scenery and stunning coastal walks whatever the time of year.

They are all Stevenson lighthouses, built by ancestors of the famous author Robert Louis Stevenson, and have a fascinating history warning seafarers and housing light keepers and their families. **Sumburgh Lighthouse**, built in 1821 by Robert Louis Stevenson's Grandfather, is situated on a headland at the southern tip of the Mainland. The surrounding cliffs and shores are teeming with wildlife - Sumburgh Head is one of the best places in Britain to see puffins and whales and is also a RSPB Reserve. Also, with a number of visitor attractions and archaeological sites close by, this lighthouse is ideally placed to tour the South end of Shetland. **Bressay Lighthouse**, built in 1858, overlooks the entrance to Lerwick Harbour and is ideally placed for visiting the nature reserve at Noss and exploring the archaeology on Bressay. A short 10 minute ferry ride from Shetland's capital, Lerwick, this Lighthouse is rural while close to town. **Eshaness Lighthouse** is set amongst some of the most spectacular cliff top scenery in the UK and surrounded by fascinating geology, including the Northmavine volcano trail and the best exposure of the Great Glen Fault, and an abundance of wildlife. A true get away from it all destination. Eshaness and Bressay can accommodate up to 6 people and Sumburgh 7.

OLD SCATNESS BROCH AND IRON AGE VILLAGE

Virkie, Dunrossness   Tel: 01950 461869
e-mail: info@shetlandamenity.org website: www.oldscatness.co.uk

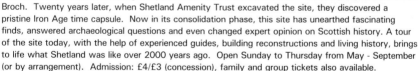

Old Scatness Broch and Iron Age Village was discovered in 1975 when Shetland's main airport, Sumburgh, expanded and works uncovered the Broch. Twenty years later, when Shetland Amenity Trust excavated the site, they discovered a pristine Iron Age time capsule. Now in its consolidation phase, this site has unearthed fascinating finds, answered archaeological questions and even changed expert opinion on Scottish history. A tour of the site today, with the help of experienced guides, building reconstructions and living history, brings to life what Shetland was like over 2000 years ago. Open Sunday to Thursday from May - September (or by arrangement). Admission: £4/£3 (concession), family and group tickets also available.

VIKING UNST

Tel: 01595 694688 e-mail: info@shetlandamenity.org
website: www.vikingshetland.com

As Shetland is at the crossroads of the North Atlantic - lying as close to Norway and Faroe as it is to mainland UK - and was part of Scandinavia until 1469, it has a strong Nordic history. Shetland's most Northerly Isle, Unst, has the highest concentration of rural longhouse sites anywhere in the world, making it the ideal place to interpret Shetland's Viking past. Shetland Amenity Trust set up the **Viking Unst** project in 2006, which now consists of a series of sites throughout the isle, including three Viking longhouse excavations and a full size replica Viking longship, with a seasonal Viking camp. There are also plans to create a reconstruction of one of the excavated longhouses. The excavation sites are open throughout the year, however the main Viking Unst activities take place throughout the summer, May - September.

Steam Navigation Company. The 18th-century building has been restored as a small museum and interpretation centre highlighting the island's maritime history.

Around Lerwick

BRESSAY
1 mile E of Lerwick

The island of Bressay sits opposite Lerwick, and shelters its harbour. The Bressay Heritage Centre, close to the ferry terminal, illustrates through displays and exhibits what life was like on the island in former times. The tiny island of Noss, off its west coast, is a nature reserve, one of the oldest on the Shetlands. Boat trips to the island are available. Bressay has some fine walks, notably on its east coast. Its highest point is Ward Hill, at 742 feet.

The ruined St Mary's Chapel is at Cullingsbrough Voe, on the island's east coast. It may date back to Viking times, and is the only cruciform church on the Shetland Islands.

MOUSA
13 miles S of Lerwick

There are about 70 confirmed broch (a round, fortified tower) sites in Shetland, and the best preserved is at Sandwick on this tiny uninhabited island off the east coast of Mainland. The Broch of Mousa (Historic Scotland) was built sometime during the Iron Age from local stone, and is over 40 feet high and 49 feet in diameter. It has lost its uppermost courses, but is still in a remarkable state of preservation, and shows the typical layout of these curious buildings, which are found nowhere else but in Scotland. The double walls slope inwards as they get higher, and embedded in them are staircases (that you

can use to climb to the top) and defensive galleries. Like other brochs, no mortar was used in its construction.

BODDAM
20 miles S of Lerwick on the A970

The Crofthouse Museum comprises a thatched house, steading and water mill, and illustrates what life was like in a 19th-century Shetland Island croft. Furnished in home-made furniture of the type used on the Shetland Islands, the cottage would have housed an extended family of children, parents and grandparents. The men would have earned their living from the sea, while the women worked the land. In the summer months the museum hosts a programme of traditional music and stories.

JARLSHOF
25 miles S of Lerwick on the A970

Lying close to Sumburgh Airport on Mainland, Jarlshof is one of the most important historical sites in Europe, and has been continuously occupied from the Bronze Age right up until the 17th century. There are Bronze Age huts, Iron Age earth houses, brochs, wheelhouses from the Dark Ages, Norse longhouses and medieval dwellings. It is managed by Historic Scotland, and there is a small museum and interpretation centre.

At Old Scatness, close to Jarlshof, is an archaeological site centred on a number of ancient brochs, wheelhouses and medieval dwellings. There is a living history area with demonstrations that reproduce ancient technologies using authentic materials. It was discovered in 1975 when a road was cut through what was thought to be a natural mound. Old walls were discovered, and work began on excavating the site in 1995.

The Ness of Burgi, a small promontory

jutting out into the sea, lies to the west of Jarlshof, and has an Iron Age fort.

FAIR ISLE
46 miles S of Lerwick

The most southerly of the Shetland Islands lies almost half way between Shetland and Orkney. It is owned by the National Trust for Scotland, and is one of the remotest inhabited islands in the country, with a population of about 65. It was originally called Fridarey, meaning island of peace, by Norse settlers. In 1558 one of the Spanish Armada vessels, the *El Gran Grifon*, was shipwrecked here. About 200 men managed to struggle ashore, and theye were looked after by the islanders as best they could. However, the sailors, hungry and exhausted, began killing of the islanders' animals for food, and they were eventually shipped off to Shetland from where they were sent home. In 1948, a Spanish delegation dedicated a cross on the island to those Spaniards who had died.

The island was once owned by George Waterston, who was the Scottish Director of the Royal Society for the Protection of Birds, and who founded a bird observatory here in 1948. The George Waterston Memorial Centre and Museum has displays about the history and wildlife of the island. The Feely Dyke, a turf wall separating common land from modern crofting land, may date from prehistoric times.

Fair Isle knitting is famous the world over, and still is a thriving craft using traditional patterns.

SCALLOWAY
6 miles W of Lerwick on the A970

Though only six miles from Lerwick, this small village sits on the Atlantic coast, while its larger neighbour sits on the coast of the North Sea.

Its name comes from the Norse Scola Voe, which means the Huts by the Bay.

Up until 1708, it was once Shetland's capital, but as Lerwick expanded so the centre of power shifted eastwards. Scalloway Castle dates from around 1600, and was built by Patrick Stewart, who was executed 15 years later in Edinburgh for treason (see also Kirkwall).

During World War II the village was a secret Norwegian base, and from here Norwegians used to be ferried across to their country in fishing boats (nicknamed "Shetland buses") to mount sabotage operations and bring back resistance fighters who were on the run from German troops. The small **Scalloway Museum** in Main Street tells the story of these men, as well as the story of Scalloway itself.

TINGWALL
6 miles NW of Lerwick on the A970

Law Ting Holm near Tingwall was where the ancient Shetland Islands parliament, or Althing, used to meet. It sits on a small promontory (which in Norse times was an island) jutting out into the Loch of Tingwall.

Just off the Scalloway to Tingwall Road is the Murder Stone, a prehistoric standing stone. It got its name from a local legend, which states that murderers were made to run between Law Ting Holm and the stone pursued by relatives of the murdered person. If the murderer made it to the stone unscathed, he wasn't executed, if he didn't, his pursuers could kill him. The Tingwall Agricultural Museum has a collection of old crofting tools.

TANGWICK
33 miles NW of Lerwick on the B9078

The Tangwick Haa Museum, based in Tangwick Haa, has displays and artefacts about the local history of the northern part of Mainland. The haa (hall) itself dates from the 17th century, and was built by the Cheyne family, the local landowners. It was restored by the Shetland Amenity Trust and opened as a museum in 1988.

WHALSAY

18 miles NE of Lerwick

This small island, no more than six miles long by two miles wide, is connected to Mainland by a ferry from Dury Voe. There are superb coastal walks and many ancient remains. The 393-feet-high Ward of Clett is its highest point, and from here a good view of the east coast of Mainland can be enjoyed. The granite Symbister House, in the island's ferry port, is the finest Georgian house in Shetland. It was built by the Bruce family, who nearly bankrupted themselves in doing so, something that did not trouble the people of the island, as the family had oppressed them for years. It now forms part of the local school. The grounds are said to be haunted by the ghost of a sailor.

FETLAR

40 miles NE of Lerwick

The small island of Fetlar is no more than seven miles long by five miles wide at its widest, and sits off the east coast of Yell, to which it is connected by ferry. The Fetlar Interpretive Centre at Beach of Houbie has displays on the island's wildlife, history and folklore, as well as genealogical archives. There is also an archive of over 3,000 photographs.

LUNNA HOUSE

Lunna, Vidlin, Shetland ZE2 8QF
Tel: 01806 577311 Fax: 01806 242850
e-mail: stay@lunnahouse.co.uk
website: www.lunnahouse.co.uk

Lunna House nestles in the north-east corner of the mainland of Shetland, on the beautiful Lunna Peninsular which is an ideal spot for rest and relaxation. Walking, beach-combing, bird, otter and seal watching and fishing are popular activities in this peaceful spot. The house is Grade II listed and, together with the surrounding area, is designated as being of outstanding historical, architectural and archaeological importance. Originating in 1663, this former Laird's mansion was used as a secret WWII SOE base for the Norwegian "Shetland Bus" Resistance movement.

The accommodation in this warm and relaxing house comprises several delightful rooms: the 'Puffin' twin bedroom, the Larsen double bedroom with 4-poster bed which has an adjoining room with twin bunk style beds making this an ideal family suite. The bedrooms have private facilities and are centrally heated and equipped with tea/coffee making facilities. There is also a large comfortable sitting room for guests.

Lunna House is located within easy reach of the ferries for Whalsay, Out Skerries, Yell and Fetlar and is about a 30 minute drive from Lerwick.

In the middle of the island are three mysterious stone circles known as Fiddler's Crus, which almost touch each other. Close by is the Haltadans, another stone circle, where 38 stones enclose two stones at its centre. The story goes that the two inner stones are a fiddler and his wife who were dancing with 38 trolls in the middle of the night. As the sun rose in the morning, its light turned them all to stone.

The island is a bird sanctuary, with the highest density of breeding waders in Britain.

YELL
30 miles N of Lerwick

The second largest island in Shetland is about 20 miles long by seven miles wide at its widest, and is connected to Mainland. Though its population is close to 1000, it still has lonely moorland and a varied coast that lend themselves to hill walking and bird watching.

The whitewashed Old Haa of Burravoe (Old Hall of Burravoe), at the island's southeast corner, is the oldest complete building on the island, and dates from 1637. It now houses a small museum and interpretation centre, and has a digital recording studio. A tapestry commemorates the crashing of a Catalina aircraft in 1941 close to Burravoe, with only three out of the crew of 10 surviving. The Lumbister RSPB Reserve sits almost in the middle of the island, between Whale Firth (said to be the smallest firth in Scotland) and the A968, the island's main road. Here you can see red-throated diver, eider, dunlin, great and Arctic skua, wheatear, curlew, merlin and snipe.

UNST
46 miles N of Lerwick

Unst is the most northerly of the Shetland Isles, and at Hermaness, where there is a nature reserve, is the most northerly point in the United Kingdom that can be reached on foot. Offshore is Muckle Flugga, with its Out Stack, ot Oosta, being the most northerly point in the United Kingdom. At the southeast corner of the island are the gaunt ruins of Muness Castle, the most northerly castle in Britain. The castle dates from 1598, and was built by Lawrence Bruce of Cultmalindie, a relative of the wayward Stewart dynasty that ruled the islands, and a man every bit as cruel and despotic as they were. He was appointed sheriff of Shetland, and when Patrick Stewart succeeded his father Robert as the Earl of Orkney, Lawrence felt so threatened that he built the castle as a place of safety. In 1608, Patrick came to Unst with 36 men to destroy it, but retreated before he had a chance to do so. In about 1627, a party of French raiders attacked and burnt the castle, and it was never rebuilt.

At Harnoldswick, in the north of the island, is Harald's Grave, an ancient burial cairn that is supposed to mark the grave of Harold the Fair of Norway. Burra Firth, on the northern coast, is one of Britain's tiniest firths, and certainly its most northern. Everything here is Britain's most northern something or other. The Post Office is Britain's most northerly post office, and Wick of Shaw is the most northerly dwelling house. The village's Methodist church is the county's most northerly church, and was built between 1990 and 1993, with a simple layout based on a traditional Norwegian design.

TOURIST INFORMATION CENTRES

ABERDEEN
23 Union Street, Aberdeen, Aberdeenshire,
Grampian AB11 5BP
Tel: 01224 288828
e-mail: aberdeen.information@visitscotland.com
website: www.aberdeen-grampian.com

ABERFELDY
The Square, Perth & Kinross, Aberfeldy,
Central Scotland PH15 2DD
Tel: 01887 820276, Fax: 01887 829495
e-mail: aberfeldytic@perthshire.co.uk
website: www.perthshire.co.uk, Phone for opening times

ABERFOYLE
Trossachs Discovery Centre, Main Street, Aberfoyle,
Central Scotland FK8 3UQ
Tel: 08707 200 604, Fax: 01877 382153
e-mail: aberfoyle@visitscotland.com
Phone for opening times

ABINGTON
Welcome Break Service Area, Junction 13, M74, Lanarkshire,
Crawford, Strathclyde ML12 6RG
Tel: 01864 502436, Fax: 01864 502765
website: www.southlanarkshire.gov.uk

ALFORD
Railway Museum, Old Station Yard, Main Street, Alford,
Aberdeenshire, Grampian AB33 8DF
Tel: 019755 62052, Seasonal opening

ALVA
Mill Trail Visitor Centre, West Stirling Street, Alva, Stirlingshire,
Central Scotland FK12 5EN
Tel: 08707 200 605, Fax: 01259 763100
e-mail: info@alva.visitscotland.com
website: www.visitscottishheartlands.org

ANSTRUTHER
Scottish Fisheries Museum, Harbourhead, Anstruther, Fife, Central
Scotland KY10 3AB
Tel: 01333 311073
e-mail: anstruther@visitfife.com, Seasonal opening

ARBROATH
Harbour Visitor Centre, Fish Market Quay, Arbroath, Angus and
Dundee, Central Scotland DD11 1PS
Tel: 01241 872 609, Alternate Tel: 0845 22 55 121
e-mail: arbroath@visitscotland.com
website: www.angusanddundee.co.uk

ARDGARTAN
Forestry Car Park, Glen Croe, by Arrochar, Dunbartonshire,
Ardgartan, Strathclyde G83 7AR
Tel: 08707 200 606, Fax: 08707 200 606
e-mail: ardgartan@visitscotland.com, Seasonal opening

AUCHTERARDER
90 High Street, Perth & Kinross, Auchterarder,
Central Scotland PH3 1BJ
Tel: 01764 663450, Fax: 01764 664235
e-mail: auchterardertic@perthshire.co.uk
website: www.perthshire.co.uk, Phone for opening times,

AVIEMORE
Grampian Road, Inverness-shire, Aviemore,
Highlands and Islands PH22 1PP
Tel: 0845 22 55 121
e-mail: info@visitscotland.com
website: www.visithighlands.com

AYR
22 Sandgate, Ayr, Ayrshire and Arran,
Strathclyde KA7 1BW
Tel: 01292 290 300
website: www.ayrshire-arran.com

BALLATER
Old Royal Station, Station Square, Ballater, Aberdeenshire,
Grampian AB35 5QB
Tel: 013397 55306

BALLOCH
Balloch Road, Dunbartonshire, Balloch,
Strathclyde G83 8LQ
Tel: 08707 200 607, Fax: 01389 751704
e-mail: balloch@visitscotland.com, Seasonal opening

BALLOCH (PARK)
National Park Gateway Centre, Balloch,
West Dunbartonshire, Central Scotland G83 8LQ
Tel: 08707 200 631, Fax: 01389 722 177
e-mail: info@lochlomond.visitscotland.com
website: www.visitscottishheartlands.com, Seasonal opening

BANCHORY
Bridge Street, Banchory, Aberdeenshire,
Grampian AB31 5SX
Tel: 01330 822000

BANFF
Collie Lodge, Banff, Aberdeenshire,
Grampian AB45 1AU
Tel: 01261 812419, Seasonal opening

BETTYHILL
Clachan Bettyhill, by Thurso, Sutherland, Bettyhill, Highlands and
Islands KW14 7SS
Tel: 01845 22 55 121
e-mail: info@visitscotland.com
website: www.visithighlands.com, Seasonal opening

BIGGAR
155 High Street, South Lanarkshire, Biggar,
Strathclyde ML12 6DL
Tel: 01899 221066, Fax: 01899 221066
website: www.seeglasgow.com, Seasonal opening

BLAIRGOWRIE
26 Wellmeadow, Perth & Kinross, Blairgowrie,
Central Scotland PH10 6AS
Tel: 01250 872960, Fax: 01250 873701
e-mail: blairgowrietic@perthshire.co.uk
website: www.perthshire.co.uk, Phone for opening times,

BO'NESS
Bo'ness and Kinneil Railway Station, Union Street, Bo'ness,
Lothian EH51 9AQ
Tel: 08707 200 608, Fax: 08707 200 608
e-mail: boness@visitscotland.com, Seasonal opening

BOWMORE
The Square, Isle of Islay, Bowmore,
Highlands and Islands PA43 7JP
Tel: 08707 200 617, Fax: 01496 810 363
e-mail: islay@visitscotland.com

BRAEMAR
The Mews, Mar Road, Braemar, Aberdeenshire, Grampian AB35
5YP
Tel: 013397 41600

BRECHIN
Pictavia Visitor Centre, Haughmuir, Brechin,
Angus and Dundee, Central Scotland DD9 6RL
Tel: 01356 623 050, Alternate Tel: 0845 22 55 121
e-mail: brechin@visitscotland.com
website: www.angusanddundee.co.uk

BRECHIN TOWN CENTRE
Brechin Town House Museum, 28 High Street, Brechin, Angus and
Dundee, Central Scotland DD9 6ER
Tel: 01356 625 536, Alternate Tel: 0845 22 55 121
e-mail: enquiries@angusanddundee.co.uk
website: www.angusanddundee.co.uk

BROADFORD
The Car Park, Broadford, Isle of Skye,
Highlands and Islands IV49 9AB
Tel: 01845 22 55 121
e-mail: info@visitscotland.com
website: www.visithighlands.com, Seasonal opening

BRODICK
The Pier, Isle of Arran, Brodick, Ayrshire and Arran, Strathclyde
KA27 8AU
Tel: 01770 303 776
website: www.ayrshire-arran.com

CALLANDER
Rob Roy and Trossachs Visitor Centre, Ancaster Square,
Callander, Stirlingshire, Central Scotland FK17 8ED
Tel: 08707 200 628, Fax: 01877 330784
e-mail: callander@visitscotland.com
Phone for opening times

CAMPBELTOWN
MacKinnon House, The Pier, Kintyre, Campbeltown, Strathclyde
PA28 6EF
Tel: 08707 200 609, Fax: 01586 553291
e-mail: campbeltown@visitscotland.com,

CARNOUSTIE
Carnoustie Library, High Street, Carnoustie,
Angus and Dundee, Central Scotland DD7 6AN
Tel: 01241 859 620, Alternate Tel: 0845 22 55 121
e-mail: enquiries@angusanddundee.co.uk
website: www.angusanddundee.co.uk

CASTLE DOUGLAS
Market Hill, Castle Douglas,
Dumfries and Galloway DG7 1AE
Tel: 01556 502611
e-mail: castledouglas@dgtb.visitscotland.com
website: www.visitdumfriesandgalloway.co.uk
Seasonal opening

CASTLEBAY
Pier Road, Isle of Barra, Castlebay, Highlands and Islands HS9
5XD
Tel: 01871 810336, Fax: 01871 810336
e-mail: castlebay@visithebrides.com
website: www.visithebrides.com, Seasonal opening

CRAIGNURE
The Pier, Isle of Mull, Craignure,
Strathclyde PA65 6AY
Tel: 08707 200 610, Fax: 01680 812497
e-mail: mull@visitscotland.com,

CRAIL
Crail Museum & Heritage Centre, 62-64 Marketgate, Crail, Fife,
Central Scotland KY10 3TL
Tel: 01333 450869
e-mail: crail@visitfife.com, Seasonal opening

CRATHIE
The Car Park, Ballater, Crathie, Aberdeenshire, Grampian AB55
4AD
Tel: 01339 742 414, Seasonal opening

CRIEFF
Town Hall, High Street, Perth & Kinross, Crieff,
Central Scotland PH7 3HU
Tel: 01764 652578, Fax: 01764 655422
e-mail: criefftic@perthshire.co.uk
website: www.perthshire.co.uk

DAVIOT WOOD
Picnic Area (A9), by Inverness, Daviot Wood,
Highlands and Islands IV2 5ER
Tel: 01845 22 55 121
e-mail: info@visitscotland.com
website: www.visithighlands.com, Seasonal opening

TOURIST INFORMATION CENTRES

DORNOCH
The Coffee Shop, The Square, Sutherland, Dornoch, Highlands and Islands IV25 3SD
Tel: 01845 22 55 121
e-mail: info@visitscotland.com
website: www.visithighlands.com

DRUMNADROCHIT
The Car Park, Inverness-shire, Drumnadrochit, Highlands and Islands IV63 6TX
Tel: 0845 22 55 121, Fax: 01506 832 222
e-mail: drumnadrochit@visitscotland.com
website: www.visithighlands.com

DRYMEN
Drymen Library, The Square, Dunbartonshire, Drymen, Strathclyde G63 0BD
Tel: 08707 200 611, Fax: 01369 660 751
e-mail: info@drymen.visitscotland.com
website: www.visitscottishheartlands.org, Seasonal opening

DUFFTOWN
2 The Square, Dufftown, Moray, Grampian AB55 4AD
Tel: 01340 820501
website: www.aberdeen-grampian.com, Seasonal opening

DUMBARTON
7 Alexandra Parade, A82 Northbound, Dunbartonshire, Milton, Strathclyde G82 2TZ
Tel: 08707 200 612, Fax: 01369 70685
e-mail: dumbarton@visitscotland.com
Phone for opening times

DUMFRIES
64 Whitesands, Dumfries, Dumfries and Galloway DG1 2RS
Tel: 01387 253862, Fax: 01378 245555
e-mail: info@dgtb.visitscotland.com
website: www.visitdumfriesandgalloway.o.uk,

DUNBAR
143a High Street, Dunbar, Lothian EH42 1ES
Tel: 0845 22 55 121, Alternate Tel: 01368 863 353
e-mail: info@visitscotland.com, Seasonal opening

DUNBLANE
Stirling Road, Dunblane, Stirlingshire, Central Scotland FK15 9EP
Tel: 08707 200 613, Fax: 08707 200 613
e-mail: info@dunblane.visitscotland.com
website: www.visitscottishheartlands.org, Seasonal opening

DUNDEE
Tourist Information & Orientation Centre, Discovery Quay, Dundee, Angus and Dundee, Central Scotland DD1 4XA
Tel: 01382 527 527
e-mail: dundee@visitscotland.com
website: www.angusanddundee.co.uk

DUNFERMLINE
1 High Street, Dunfermline, Fife, Central Scotland KY12 7DL
Tel: 01383 720 999
e-mail: dunfermline@visitfife.com

DUNKELD
The Cross, Perth & Kinross, Dunkeld, Central Scotland PH8 0AN
Tel: 01350 727688, Fax: 01350 727688
e-mail: dunkeldtic@perthshire.co.uk
website: www.perthshire.co.uk

DUNNET HEAD
Caithness, Brough, Highlands and Islands KW14 8YE
Tel: 01847 851991
e-mail: briansparks@dunnethead.com
website: www.dunnethead.com, Seasonal opening

DUNOON
7 Alexandra Parade, Dunoon, Argyll and Bute, Strathclyde PA23 8AB
Tel: 08707 200 629, Fax: 01369 706 085
e-mail: dunoon@visitscotland.com

DUNVEGAN
2 Lochside, Dunvegan, Isle of Skye, Highlands and Islands IV55 8WB
Tel: 01845 22 55 121
e-mail: info@visitscotland.com
website: www.visithighlands.com, Seasonal opening

DURNESS
Durine, by Lairg, Sutherland, Durness, Highlands and Islands IV27 4PN
Tel: 01845 22 55 121, Fax: 01506 832 222
e-mail: info@visitscotland.com
website: www.visithighlands.com, Seasonal opening

EDINBURGH
Edinburgh and Scotland Information Centre, above Waverley Shopping Centre, 3 Princes Street, Edinburgh, Lothian EH2 2QP
Tel: 0845 22 55 121
e-mail: info@visitscotland.com
website: www.edinburgh.org

EDINBURGH AIRPORT
Airport Tourist Information Desk, Edinburgh Airport, Edinburgh, Lothian EH12 9DN
Tel: 0870 040 0007, Counter inquiries only

ELGIN
17 High Street, Elgin, Moray, Grampian IV30 1EG
Tel: 01343 542 666, Alternate Tel: 01343 543 388
e-mail: Elgin@visitscotland.com

TOURIST INFORMATION CENTRES

EYEMOUTH

Auld Kirk, Market Place, Eyemouth,
Scottish Borders TD14 5HE
Tel: 01835 863170, Fax: 01750 21886
e-mail: bordersinfo@visitscotland.com
website: www.scot-borders.co.uk, Seasonal opening

FALKIRK

Lime Road, Tamfourhill, Falkirk, Stirlingshire,
Central Scotland FK1 4RS
Tel: 08707 200 614, Fax: 01324 638440
e-mail: falkirk@visitscotland.com

FORFAR

The Meffan Museum & Art Gallery, Forfar,
Angus and Dundee, Central Scotland DD8 1BB
Tel: 01307 464 123, Alternate Tel: 0845 22 55 121
e-mail: enquiries@angusanddundee.co.uk
website: www.angusanddundee.co.uk

FORRES

116 High Street, Forres, Moray, Grampian IV36 1NP
Tel: 01309 672 938
e-mail: Forres@visitscotland.com
website: www.aberdeen-grampian.com, Seasonal opening

FORT AUGUSTUS

Car Park, Inverness-shire, Fort Augustus,
Highlands and Islands PH32 4DD
Tel: 01845 22 55 121
e-mail: info@visitscotland.com
website: www.visithighlands.com, Seasonal opening

FORT WILLIAM

Cameron Centre, Cameron Square, Inverness-shire,
Fort William, Highlands and Islands PH33 6AJ
Tel: 01845 22 55 121
e-mail: info@visitscotland.com
website: www.visithighlands.com

FORTH BRIDGES

c/o Queensferry Lodge Hotel, St Margaret's Head,
North Queensferry, Fife, Central Scotland KY11 1HP
Tel: 01383 417759
e-mail: forthbridges@visitfife.com

FRASERBURGH

3 Saltoun Square, Fraserburgh, Aberdeenshire,
Grampian AB43 9DA
Tel: 01346 518315, Seasonal opening

GAIRLOCH

Achtercairn, Ross-shire, Gairloch,
Highlands and Islands IV22 2DN
Tel: 01845 22 55 121
e-mail: info@visitscotland.com
website: www.visithighlands.com, Seasonal opening

GATEHOUSE OF FLEET

Car Park, Gatehouse of Fleet,
Dumfries and Galloway DG7 2HP
Tel: 01557 814212
e-mail: gatehouseoffleettic@visitscotland.com
website: www.visitdumfriesandgalloway.co.uk, Seasonal opening

GIRVAN

Bridge Street, Girvan, Ayrshire and Arran,
Strathclyde KA26 9HH
Tel: 01465 715500, Fax: 01465 715500
e-mail: info@girvanvisitorcentre.co.uk

GLASGOW

11 George Square, Glasgow, Strathclyde G2 1DY
Tel: 0141 204 4400, Fax: 0141 221 3524
e-mail: enquiries@seeglasgow.com
website: www.seeglasgow.com

GLASGOW AIRPORT

International Arrivals, Glasgow International Airport,
Renfrewshire, Paisley, Strathclyde PA3 2ST
Tel: 0141 848 4440, Fax: 0141 849 1444
e-mail: airport@seeglasgow.com
website: www.seeglasgow.com

GRANTOWN ON SPEY

54 High Street, Inverness-shire, Grantown on Spey, Highlands and
Islands PH26 3EH
Tel: 01845 22 55 121
e-mail: info@visitscotland.com
website: www.visithighlands.com, Phone for opening times,

GRETNA GREEN

Unit 10, Gretna Gateway Outlet Village, Glasgow Road, Gretna,
Dumfries and Galloway DG16 5GG
Tel: 01461 337834
e-mail: gretna@dgtb.visitscotland.com
website: www.visitdumfriesandgalloway.co.uk, Seasonal opening

HAMILTON

Road Chef Services, M74 Northbound,
South Lanarkshire, Hamilton, Strathclyde ML3 6JW
Tel: 01698 285 590
e-mail: hamilton@seeglasgow.com
website: www.seeglasgow.com

HARESTANES

Ancrum, Jedburgh, Harestanes,
Scottish Borders TD8 6UQ
Tel: 01835 863170, Fax: 01750 21886
e-mail: bordersinfo@visitscotland.com
website: www.scot-borders.co.uk, Seasonal opening

HAWICK

Tower Mill, Hawick, Scottish Borders TD9 0AE
Tel: 01835 863170, Fax: 01750 21886
e-mail: bordersinfo@visitscotland.com
website: www.scot-borders.co.uk

TOURIST INFORMATION CENTRES

HELENSBURGH
Clock Tower, The Pier, Dunbartonshire, Helensburgh,
Strathclyde G84 7NY
Tel: 08707 200 615, Fax: 01436 672 642
e-mail: helensburgh@visitscotland.com, Seasonal opening

HUNTLY
9a The Square, Huntly, Aberdeenshire,
Grampian AB54 8BR
Tel: 01466 792255, Seasonal opening

INVERARAY
Front Street, Inveraray, Argyll and Bute,
Strathclyde PA32 8UY
Tel: 08707 200 616, Fax: 01499 302 269
e-mail: inveraray@visitscotland.com

INVERNESS
Castle Wynd, Inverness-shire, Inverness,
Highlands and Islands IV2 3BJ
Tel: 01845 22 55 121
e-mail: info@visitscotland.com
website: www.visithighlands.com

INVERURIE
Book Store, 18a High Street, Inverurie, Aberdeenshire,
Grampian AB51 3XQ
Tel: 01467 625800,

ISLAY
The Square, Main Street, Isle of Islay, Bowmore,
Strathclyde PA43 7JP
Tel: 08707 200 617, Fax: 01496 810363
e-mail: info@islay.visitscotland.com
website: www.visitscottishheartlands.org

JEDBURGH
Murray's Green, Jedburgh, Scottish Borders TD8 6BE
Tel: 01835 863170, Fax: 01750 21886
e-mail: bordersinfo@visitscotland.com
website: www.scot-borders.co.uk

JOHN O'GROATS
County Road, Caithness, John O'Groats,
Highlands and Islands KW1 4YR
Tel: 01845 22 55 121
e-mail: info@visitscotland.com
website: www.visithighlands.com, Seasonal opening

KELSO
Town House, The Square, Kelso, Scottish Borders TD5 7HF
Tel: 01835 863170
e-mail: bordersinfo@visitscotland.com
website: www.scot-borders.co.uk

KILCHOAN
Kilchoan Community Centre, Pier Road, Acharacle, Kilchoan,
Argyll and Bute, Strathclyde PH36 4LJ
Tel: 01845 22 55 121
e-mail: info@visitscotland.com
website: www.visithighlands.com, Phone for opening times

KILLIN
Breadalbane Folklore Centre, The Old Mill, Falls of Dochart,
Killin, Stirlingshire, Central Scotland FK21 8XE
Tel: 08707 200 627, Fax: 01567 820764
e-mail: killin@visitscotland.com, Seasonal opening

KINGUSSIE
Highland Folk Museum, Inverness-shire, Kingussie,
Highlands and Islands PH21 1JG
Tel: 0845 22 55 121
e-mail: info@visitscotland.com
website: www.visithighlands.com, Seasonal opening

KINROSS
Heart of Scotland Visitor Centre, Junction 6, M90,
Perth & Kinross, Kinross, Central Scotland KY13 7NQ
Tel: 01577 863680, Fax: 01577 863370
e-mail: kinrosstic@perthshire.co.uk
website: www.perthshire.co.uk

KIRKCALDY
The Merchant's House, 339 High Street, Kirkcaldy, Fife,
Central Scotland KY1 1JL
Tel: 01592 267775
e-mail: kirkcaldy@visitfife.com

KIRKCUDBRIGHT
Harbour Square, Kirkcudbright,
Dumfries and Galloway DG6 4HY
Tel: 01557 330494, Fax: 01557 332416
e-mail: kirkcudbright@dgth.visitscotland.com
website: www.visitdumfriesandgalloway.co.uk, Seasonal opening

KIRKWALL
The Travel Centre, West Castle Street, Kirkwall, Orkney,
Highlands and Islands KW15 1GU
Tel: 01856 872 856, Fax: 01856 875 056
e-mail: info@visitorkney.com
website: www.visitorkney.com

KIRRIEMUIR
Kirriemuir Gateway to the Glens Museum, The Town House,
32 High Street, Kirriemuir, Angus and Dundee,
Central Scotland DD8 4BB
Tel: 01575 575 479, Alternate Tel: 0845 22 55 121
e-mail: enquiries@angusanddundee.co.uk
website: www.angusanddundee.co.uk

TOURIST INFORMATION CENTRES

KYLE OF LOCHALSH
Car Park, Ross-shire, Kyle of Lochalsh,
Highlands and Islands IV40 8AQ
Tel: 01845 22 55 121
e-mail: info@visitscotland.com
website: www.visithighlands.com, Seasonal opening

LAIRG
Ferrycroft Countryside Centre, Sutherland, Lairg,
Highlands and Islands IV27 4AZ
Tel: 01845 22 55 121
e-mail: info@visitscotland.com
website: www.visithighlands.com, Seasonal opening

LANARK
Horsemarket, Ladyacre Road, South Lanarkshire, Lanark,
Strathclyde ML11 7LQ
Tel: 01555 661661, Fax: 01555 666143
e-mail: lanark@seeglasgow.com
website: www.seeglasgow.com

LARGS
Railway Station, Main Street, Largs, Ayrshire and Arran,
Strathclyde KA30 8AN
Tel: 01475 689 962
website: www.ayrshire-arran.com

LERWICK
Market Cross, Lerwick, Shetland,
Highlands and Islands ZE1 0LU
Tel: 08701 999 440, Fax: 01595 695 807
e-mail: info@visitshetland.com
website: www.visitshetland.com

LINLITHGOW
Burgh Halls, The Cross, Linlithgow, Lothian EH49 7RE
Tel: 01506 844 600, Alternate Tel: 01506 832 222
e-mail: info@visitscotland.com
website: www.edinburgh.org, Seasonal opening

LOCHBOISDALE
Pier Road, Isle of South Uist, Lochboisdale,
Highlands and Islands HS8 5TH
Tel: 01878 700286, Fax: 01878 700286
e-mail: lochboisdale@visithebrides.com
website: www.visithebrides.com, Seasonal opening

LOCHCARRON
Main Street, Ross-shire, Lochcarron,
Highlands and Islands IV54 8YB
Tel: 01520 722357, Fax: 01520 722324

LOCHGILPHEAD
Lochnell Street, Lochgilphead, Argyll and Bute,
Strathclyde PA30 8JN
Tel: 08707 200 618, Fax: 01546 606 254
e-mail: lochgilphead@visitscotland.com, Seasonal opening

LOCHINVER
Assynt Visitor Centre, Main Street, by Lairg, Sutherland,
Lochinver, Highlands and Islands IV27 4LX
Tel: 01845 22 55 121
e-mail: info@visitscotland.com
website: www.visithighlands.com, Seasonal opening

LOCHMADDY
Pier Road, Isle of North Uist, Lochmaddy,
Highlands and Islands HS6 5AA
Tel: 01876 500 321, Fax: 01876 500 321
e-mail: lochmaddy@visithebrides.com
website: www.visithebrides.com

MALLAIG
The Pier, Inverness-shire, Mallaig,
Highlands and Islands PH41 4SQ
Tel: 01845 22 55 121
e-mail: info@visitscotland.com
website: www.visithighlands.com

MELROSE
Abbey House, Abbey Street, Melrose, Scottish Borders TD6 9LG
Tel: 01835 863170, Fax: 01750 21886
e-mail: bordersinfo@visitscotland.com
website: www.scot-borders.co.uk

MOFFAT
Churchgate, Moffat, Dumfries and Galloway DG10 9EG
Tel: 01683 220620
e-mail: moffat@dgtb.visitscotland.com
website: www.visitdumfriesandgalloway.co.uk, Seasonal opening

MONIFIETH
Monifieth Library, High Street, Monifieth, Angus and Dundee,
Central Scotland DD5 4AE
Tel: 01382 533 819, Alternate Tel: 0845 22 55 121
e-mail: enquiries@angusanddundee.co.uk
website: www.angusanddundee.co.uk

MONTROSE
Montrose Museum, Panmure Place, Montrose, Angus and Dundee,
Central Scotland DD10 8HE
Tel: 01674 673232, Alternate Tel: 0845 22 55 121
Fax: 01674 671 810
e-mail: enquiries@angusanddundee.co.uk
website: www.angusanddundee.co.uk

NAIRN
The Library, 68 High Street, Inverness-shire, Nairn,
Highlands and Islands IV12 4AU
Tel: 01845 22 55 121
e-mail: info@visitscotland.com
website: www.visithighlands.com, Seasonal opening

TOURIST INFORMATION CENTRES

NEWTON STEWART
Dashwood Square, Newton Stewart,
Dumfries and Galloway DG8 6EQ
Tel: 01671 402431
e-mail: newtonstewart@dgtb.visitscotland.com
website: www.visitdumfriesandgalloway.co.uk, Seasonal opening

NEWTONGRANGE
Scottish Mining Museum, Newtongrange, Lothian EH26 8HB
Tel: 0845 22 55 121, Alternate Tel: 0131 663 4262
e-mail: info@visitscotland.com
website: www.edinburgh.org, Seasonal opening

NORTH BERWICK
Quality Street, North Berwick, Lothian EH39 4HJ
Tel: 0845 22 55 121, Alternate Tel: 01620 892 197
e-mail: info@visitscotland.com
website: www.edinburgh.org

NORTH KESSOCK
Picnic Site, Ross-shire, North Kessock,
Highlands and Islands IV1 1XB
Tel: 01845 22 55 121
e-mail: info@visitscotland.com
website: www.visithighlands.com, Seasonal opening

OBAN
Church Building, Argyll Square, Oban, Argyll and Bute,
Strathclyde PA34 4AN
Tel: 08707 200 630, Fax: 01631 564273
e-mail: oban@visitscotland.com

OLD CRAIGHALL
Old Craighall Service Area (A1), Musselburgh,
Lothian EH21 8RE
Tel: 0845 22 55 121, Alternate Tel: 0131 653 6172
e-mail: info@visitscotland.com
website: www.edinburgh.org, Seasonal opening

PAISLEY
9a Gilmour Street, Renfrewshire, Paisley, Strathclyde PA1 1DD
Tel: 0141 889 0711, Fax: 0141 848 1363
e-mail: paisley@seeglasgow.com
website: www.seeglasgow.com

PEEBLES
High Street, Peebles, Scottish Borders EH45 8AG
Tel: 01835 863170, Fax: 01750 21886
e-mail: bordersinfo@visitscotland.com
website: www.scot-borders.co.uk

PERTH
Lower City Mills, West Mill Street, Perth & Kinross, Perth,
Central Scotland PH1 5PQ
Tel: 01738 450600, Fax: 01738 444863
e-mail: perthtic@perthshire.co.uk
website: www.perthshire.co.uk

PERTH (INVERALMOND)
Caithness Glass, Inveralmond, Perth & Kinross, Perth,
Central Scotland PH1 3TZ
Tel: 01738 638481

PITLOCHRY
22 Atholl Road, Perth & Kinross, Pitlochry,
Central Scotland PH16 5BX
Tel: 01796 472215/472751, Fax: 01796 474046
e-mail: pitlochrytic@perthshire.co.uk
website: www.perthshire.co.uk, Phone for opening times

PORTREE
Bayfield House, Bayfield Road, Portree, Isle of Skye,
Highlands and Islands IV51 9EL
Tel: 01845 22 55 121
e-mail: info@visitscotland.com
website: www.visithighlands.com

ROTHESAY
Isle of Bute Discovery Centre, Winter Garden, Isle of Bute,
Rothesay, Argyll and Bute, Strathclyde PA20 0AT
Tel: 08707 200 619, Fax: 01700 505156
e-mail: rothesay@visitscotland.com

SELKIRK
Halliwells House, Selkirk, Scottish Borders TD7 4BL
Tel: 01835 863170, Fax: 01750 21886
e-mail: bordersinfo@visitscotland.com
website: www.scot-borders.co.uk, Seasonal opening

SPEAN BRIDGE
The Kingdom of Scotland, by Fort William, Inverness-shire,
Spean Bridge, Highlands and Islands PH34 4EP
Tel: 01845 22 55 121
e-mail: info@visitscotland.com
website: www.visithighlands.com, Seasonal opening

ST ANDREWS
70 Market Street, St Andrews, Fife,
Central Scotland KY16 9NU
Tel: 01334 472021
e-mail: standrews@visitfife.com

STIRLING (DUMBARTON ROAD)
41 Dumbarton Road, Stirling, Stirlingshire,
Central Scotland FK8 2QQ
Tel: 08707 200 620, Fax: 01786 450 039
e-mail: stirling@visitscotland.com

STIRLING (PIRNHALL)
Motorway Service Area Junction 9 M9/M80, Pirnhall, Stirling,
Stirlingshire, Central Scotland FK7 8ET
Tel: 08707 200 621, Fax: 01786 810 879
e-mail: pirnhall@visitscotland.com, Seasonal opening

TOURIST INFORMATION CENTRES

STIRLING (ROYAL BURGH)
Castle Esplanade, Stirling, Stirlingshire,
Central Scotland FK95LF
Tel: 08707 200 622, Fax: 01786 451 881

STONEHAVEN
66 Allardice Street, Stonehaven, Aberdeenshire,
Grampian AB39 2AA
Tel: 01569 762806, Seasonal opening

STORNOWAY
26 Cromwell Street, Isle of Lewis, Stornoway,
Highlands and Islands HS1 2DD
Tel: 01851 703088, Fax: 01851 705244
e-mail: stornoway@visithebrides.com
website: www.visithebrides.com

STRANRAER
28 Harbour Street, Stranraer,
Dumfries and Galloway DG9 7RA
Tel: 01776 702595, Fax: 01776 889156
e-mail: stranraer@dgtb.visitscotland.com
website: www.visitdumfriesandgalloway.o.uk,

STRATHPEFFER
Square Wheels, The Square, Ross-shire, Strathpeffer,
Highlands and Islands IV14 9DW
Tel: 01845 22 55 121
e-mail: info@visitscotland.com
website: www.visithighlands.com, Seasonal opening

STROMNESS
Ferry Terminal Building, Pier Head, Stromness, Orkney,
Highlands and Islands KW16 3AA
Tel: 01856 850 716, Fax: 01856 850 777
e-mail: stromness@visitorkney.com
website: www.visitorkney.com

STRONTIAN
Acharacle, Strontian, Argyll and Bute, Strathclyde PH36 4HZ
Tel: 01845 22 55 121
e-mail: info@visitscotland.com
website: www.visithighlands.com, Seasonal opening

TARBERT
Pier Road, Isle of Harris, Tarbert,
Highlands and Islands HS3 3DJ
Tel: 01859 502 011, Fax: 01859 502 011
e-mail: tarbert@visithebrides.com
website: www.visithebrides.com

TARBERT (LOCH FYNE)
Harbour Street, Tarbert, Argyll and Bute,
Strathclyde PA29 6UD
Tel: 08707 200 624, Fax: 01880 820 082
e-mail: tarbert@visitscotland.com, Seasonal opening

TARBET (LOCH LOMOND)
Main Street, Loch Lomond, Tarbet, Argyll and Bute,
Strathclyde G83 7DE
Tel: 08707 200 623, Fax: 01301 702 224
e-mail: tarbet@visitscotland.com, Seasonal opening

THURSO
Riverside, Caithness, Thurso, Highlands and Islands KW14 8BU
Tel: 01845 22 55 121
e-mail: info@visitscotland.com
website: www.visithighlands.com, Seasonal opening

TOBERMORY
Main Street, Isle of Mull, Tobermory, Argyll and Bute,
Strathclyde PA75 6NU
Tel: 08707 200 625, Fax: 01688 302145
e-mail: tobermory@visitscotland.com, Seasonal opening

TOMINTOUL
The Square, Tomintoul, Aberdeenshire, Grampian AB37 9ET
Tel: 01807 580285, Seasonal opening

TYNDRUM
Main Street, Tyndrum, Stirlingshire, Central Scotland FK20 8RY
Tel: 08707 200 626, Fax: 01838 400530
e-mail: tyndrum@visitscotland.com

ULLAPOOL
Argyle Street, Ross-shire, Ullapool,
Highlands and Islands IV26 2UB
Tel: 01845 22 55 121
e-mail: info@visitscotland.com
website: www.visithighlands.com, Seasonal opening

WICK
McAllan's, 66 High Street, Caithness, Wick,
Highlands and Islands KW1 4NE
Tel: 01955 602 547

INDEX OF ADVERTISERS

INDEX OF ADVERTISERS

SPECIALIST FOOD AND DRINK SHOPS

Looking for more walks?

The walks in this book have been gleaned from Britain's largest online walking guide, to be found at *www.walkingworld.com*.

The site contains over 2000 walks from all over England, Scotland and Wales so there are plenty more to choose from in this book's region as well as further afield - ideal if you are taking a short break as you can plan your walks in advance. There are walks of every length and type to suit all tastes.

Want more detail for the walks in this book? Next to every walk in this book you will see a Walk ID. You can enter this ID number on Walkingworld's 'Find a Walk' page and you will be taken straight to the details of that walk.

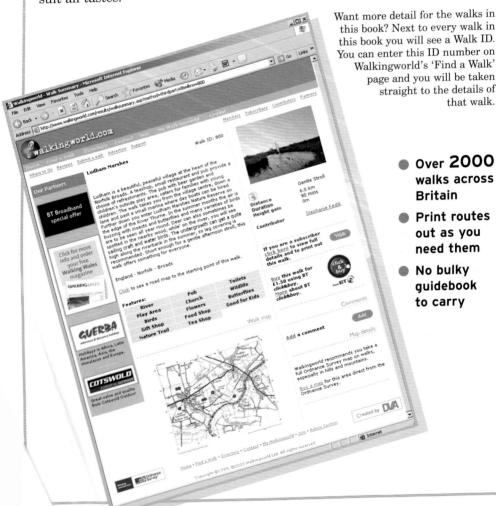

- Over **2000** walks across Britain

- **Print routes out as you need them**

- **No bulky guidebook to carry**

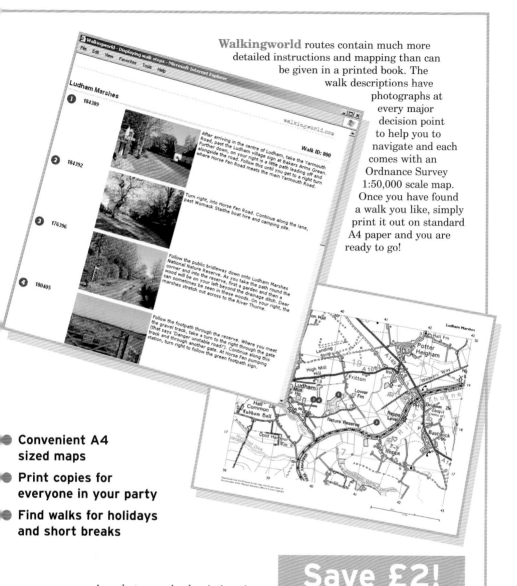

Walkingworld routes contain much more detailed instructions and mapping than can be given in a printed book. The walk descriptions have photographs at every major decision point to help you to navigate and each comes with an Ordnance Survey 1:50,000 scale map. Once you have found a walk you like, simply print it out on standard A4 paper and you are ready to go!

- **Convenient A4 sized maps**
- **Print copies for everyone in your party**
- **Find walks for holidays and short breaks**

A modest annual subscription gives you access to over 2000 walks, all in Walkingworld's easy to follow format. The database of walks is growing all the time and as a subscriber you gain access to new routes as soon as they are published.

Visit the Walkingworld website at *www.walkingworld.com*

INDEX OF WALKS

ORDER FORM

To order any of our publications just fill in the payment details below and complete the order form. For orders of less than 4 copies please add £1 per book for postage and packing. Orders over 4 copies are P & P free.

Please Complete Either:

I enclose a cheque for £ _____ made payable to Travel Publishing Ltd

Or:

CARD NO: _____ EXPIRY DATE: _____

SIGNATURE: _____

NAME: _____

ADDRESS: _____

TEL NO: _____

Please either send, telephone, fax or e-mail your order to:

Travel Publishing Ltd, Airport Business Centre, 10 Thornbury Road, Estover, Plymouth PL6 7PP
Tel: 01752 697280   Fax: 01752 697299 e-mail: info@travelpublishing.co.uk

	PRICE	QUANTITY		PRICE	QUANTITY
HIDDEN PLACES REGIONAL TITLES			**COUNTRY LIVING RURAL GUIDES**		
Cornwall	£8.99	....	East Anglia	£10.99	....
Devon	£8.99	....	Heart of England	£10.99	....
Dorset, Hants & Isle of Wight	£8.99	....	Ireland	£11.99	....
East Anglia	£8.99	....	North East of England	£10.99	....
Lake District & Cumbria	£8.99	....	North West of England	£10.99	....
Lancashire & Cheshire	£8.99	....	Scotland	£11.99	....
Northumberland & Durham	£8.99	....	South of England	£10.99	....
Peak District and Derbyshire	£8.99	....	South East of England	£10.99	....
Yorkshire	£8.99	....	Wales	£11.99	....
HIDDEN PLACES NATIONAL TITLES			West Country	£10.99	....
England	£11.99	....			
Ireland	£11.99	....			
Scotland	£11.99	....			
Wales	£11.99	....			
OTHER TITLES			**TOTAL QUANTITY**		
Off The Motorway	£11.99	....			
Garden Centres and Nurseries of Britain	£11.99	....	**TOTAL VALUE**		

READER REACTION FORM

The **Travel Publishing** *research team would like to receive readers' comments on any visitor attractions or places reviewed in the book and also recommendations for suitable entries to be included in the next edition. This will help ensure that the* **Country Living series of Rural Guides** *continues to provide its readers with useful information on the more interesting, unusual or unique features of each attraction or place ensuring that their visit to the local area is an enjoyable and stimulating experience. To provide your comments or recommendations would you please complete the forms below and overleaf as indicated and send to:*

The Research Department, Travel Publishing Ltd, Airport Business Centre, 10 Thornbury Road, Estover, Plymouth PL6 7PP

YOUR NAME:

YOUR ADDRESS:

YOUR TEL NO:

Please tick as appropriate: COMMENTS ☐   RECOMMENDATION ☐

ESTABLISHMENT:

ADDRESS:

TEL NO:

CONTACT NAME:

PLEASE COMPLETE FORM OVERLEAF

READER REACTION FORM

COMMENT OR REASON FOR RECOMMENDATION:

....

....

....

....

....

....

....

....

....

....

TOWNS, VILLAGES AND PLACES OF INTEREST